HOMILETIC

DAVID BUTTRICK

HOMILETIC

MOVES AND STRUCTURES

FORTRESS PRESS   PHILADELPHIA

Chapters 7 and 9: "Cast and Plot" appeared originally in *Pulpit Digest*, LXI (January/February 1981), pp. 53–56. Copyright © 1981 by *Pulpit Digest*. Used by permission. Chapter 10: "A Fool Farmer and the Grace of God" appeared originally in *Pulpit Digest*, LXIII (November/December 1983), pp. 57–60. Copyright © 1983 by *Pulpit Digest*. Used by permission. Chapter 21: "Trust God, Let Go. Let Go, Trust God" appeared originally in *Pulpit Digest*, LXV (January/February 1986), pp. 3–6. Copyright © 1986 by Pulpit Digest, Inc. Used by permission. P. 5: © copyright 1956 by Alan Jay Lerner and Frederick Loewe. P. 150: From H. G. Wells, *The Soul of a Bishop* (New York and London: Macmillan Co., 1917). Reprinted by permission of A. P. Watt Ltd. on behalf of The Literary Executors of the Estate of H G Wells. P. 155: From *Our Town* by Thornton Wilder. Copyright © 1938, 1957 by Thornton Wilder. Reprinted with special permission by Brandt & Brandt Literary Agents, Inc., Harper & Row, Publishers, and Penguin Books, Ltd. Pp. 261, 441: Reprinted from *Calvin: Institutes of the Christian Religion*, edited by John T. McNeill and translated by Ford Battles (Volumes XX and XXI: The Library of Christian Classics). Copyright © MCMLX W. L. Jenkins. Reprinted and used by permission of The Westminster Press, Philadelphia, PA. P. 358: From *The End of the Affair*, by Graham Greene. Copyright 1951 by Graham Greene. Copyright © renewed 1979 by Graham Greene. Reprinted by permission of Viking Penguin, Inc. P. 396: William L. O'Neill, *Coming Apart*, copyright 1971, Times Books, a Division of Random House, Inc. Biblical quotations, unless otherwise noted, are either the author's own translations or are from the Revised Standard Version of the Bible, copyright 1946, 1952, © 1971, 1973 by the Division of Christian Education of the National Council of the Churches of Christ in the U.S.A., and are used by permission.

Library of Congress Cataloging-in-Publication Data

Buttrick, David G., 1927–
  Homiletic : moves and structures.

  Includes bibliographical references and index.
  1. Preaching. I. Title.
BV4211.2.B86 1987   251   86–45208
ISBN 0–8006–0777–5

To
RACHEL MATHANA
and BENJAMIN ANDREW
and their parents
ANNE and DAVID

Contents

CONTENTS

CONTENTS

Preface to a Homiletic

Homiletics is an odd discipline. You cannot talk of sermon design without some glimmer of what sermons are made of, and you cannot comprehend the internal parts of a sermon without a grasp of sermon design—a "Homiletic Circle" of sorts. Thus, I have written a homiletic in two parts, *Moves* and *Structures,* for you to read in any order you choose. You may begin with part 1, *Moves,* a study of the components of sermons, and then go on to look at structural theory. Or, you may wish to begin with part 2, *Structures,* before studying such matters as words and images and ideas. You will have to decide.

Originally, I had planned a work that included chapters on Worship and Preaching as well as chapters on Preaching in the Social World. I have abandoned the plan since the present volume is quite enough for you to wrestle with, much less purchase. Thus, the volume you read will be limited to matters of homiletic design and procedure—the making of sermons. I do *not* discuss the delivery of sermons, the preacher's character, congregational psychology, or the setting of preaching in worship. There are already books on such matters. The present work, by contrast, is an introductory theoretical-technical homiletic.

I have attempted to do without footnotes and to bypass normal scholarly apparatus so as to keep the style fairly free and easy. Therefore, though the technical information I offer does rest on some years of research, at the risk of dogmatism I neither describe nor document studies. I have, however, provided a selected list of books for those who may wish to explore particular topics.

In any book on homiletics examples are a problem. Ideally, one could wish to draw examples from many different sources so as to display a variety of styles, but it is difficult to locate examples that do exactly what is wanted. As a result, in most cases I have written examples. Please understand that I am not holding my own style up as an ideal; your style will be much better for you.

My approach to homiletics has been described as "phenomenological." The word is cumbersome. I am by no means a schooled phenomenologist. But I am much interested in the way in which language forms in human consciousness. So in both parts I try to describe *how sermons happen in consciousness,* your consciousness as a preacher and the attendant consciousness of a congregation. My concern is prompted by a slogan for preachers from Saint Paul: "Faith comes from hearing."

To some, this work may seem unnecessarily prolix. My goal, though, is to understand what may actually take place in consciousness during the production and hearing of sermons. If my conclusions are in any way descriptively "true," then I will have designed a homiletic that will fit your "mind" and the "mind" of a congregation.

I write as a Protestant of the Reformed tradition, although I would not be willing to lay down my life for either term—"Protestant" or "Reformed." In God's strange grace I have taught fourteen years in a Presbyterian seminary, seven years in a Catholic school of theology, and I am now in a nondenominational university-based divinity school. In addition, I have served as a visiting professor with Baptists and Disciples of Christ. We live at a time when God may be dragging us (kicking and screaming) beyond our confessional identities. Therefore, I would hope these pages will be useful to priests and ministers of many traditions. Moreover, I am grateful to colleagues—professors, monks, priests, ministers, and many students—who have taught me to live gleefully beyond my own denominational heritage. Today, we must "sit loose" within our tumbledown confessional homes waiting for God to lead us further.

The homiletics I know has been learned: my father, George Buttrick, and a mentor, Paul Scherer, were influential; kind people in Fredonia, New York, put up with my preaching during parish years; and students, particularly advanced students in Pittsburgh, Saint Meinrad, Louisville, and now in Nashville, have instructed me. From someone, perhaps Schleiermacher, I have gathered the impression that a homiletician ought to be a competent theological dilettante concerned with the church's poetics. I would like to be that, though, I fear, I am somewhat less than competent.

The first chapter in each part was written while I was on the faculty of the Saint Meinrad School of Theology. I wish to thank Archabbot Timothy Sweeney, O.S.B., and President-Rector Daniel Buechlein, O.S.B., for their support. Friends, Bernard Brandon Scott and Edward Farley, were each kind enough to read one of the chapters, and I have gained from their wisdom. A fine homiletician, Lanny Cole Lawler, has read the entire manuscript and offered helpful suggestions.

Time to write has been made possible by grants. I am grateful to the Research Council of Vanderbilt University for an award which has underwritten a year of study free from teaching responsibilities. I am also indebted to the Association of Theological Schools for an additional grant. Dean H. Jackson Forstman of The Divinity School of Vanderbilt University has been unfailing in his support. Christine Scannaliato, a nifty, smart person, has pumped my manuscript pages into a computer with accuracy and remarkable patience. She has even corrected my excessively bad spelling! I am very grateful. Marshall Breeding has prepared the final manuscript, and Annette C. MacBean has expedited the entire project.

It is strange that I, who specialize in speaking, become tongue-tied, a stammerer, when telling my wife of love for her. I do love her dearly; she is a bearer of grace. Betty has spent too many hours poring over manuscript pages, frowning needed changes and, occasionally, nodding approval. So I dedicate this work first of all to Betty More Allaben Buttrick, who joins me in the subsequent dedications.

For much nonsense I beg tolerance; for anything useful, we can give God glory!

The Divinity School   D.G.B.
Vanderbilt University
Summer 1985

PART ONE
MOVES

WORDS IN
THE WORLD

1.
Naming and Narration

In the musical comedy *My Fair Lady*, Eliza Doolittle, fed up with elocution lessons, sings, "Words! Words! Words! I'm so sick of words!" Her complaint sounds familiar. At the noisy end of the twentieth century, many of us are dismayed by words. Perhaps ad agencies have gotten to us, or possibly political leaders who label a devastating missile the "peace-keeper." Whatever the cause, today words are suspect or, if not suspect, then dismissed as impotent mouthings. After all, what good is a word up against nuclear power, or a well-turned phrase when there are laser beams to deflect? So we denigrate language. Sermons are labeled "preachments," political promises "propaganda," and oratory "mere rhetoric" (as if rhetoric were ever "mere"). When some pop sage who has skimmed Marshall McLuhan pontificates that "words are dead," people nod in mute agreement. To most people words are dead indeed, particularly words known to have dripped unctuously from high-hung pulpits. Eliza Doolittle sang our song: We are sick of words.

The malaise is odd in view of our heritage. Whatever our Christian stance, we are children of Saint Paul, of Chrysostom, of Augustine, perhaps of Luther. So when Saint Paul states flat out that "faith comes from hearing" (Rom. 10:17), should we correct him by suggesting that faith comes from visual aids, and visual aids from your nearest religious publishing house? Or when Martin Luther declares, "The Word, I say, and the Word alone is bearer of God's grace," shall we refer him to a book on body language? Nothing is more peculiar than the church's loss of confidence in language. Do not Christians insist that God "spoke" and the world was; that God tossed the Word like a burning coal to scald the lips of prophets; that the Word became flesh and spoke good news; that the church is built on testimony of

5

apostles, martyrs, and saints? Yet, today, we stammer. About the only people left who do believe in the power of words are poets and revolutionaries. We, a people of the Word, are wordless.

Let us begin then with what might be termed a natural theology of language. Let us seek to rehabilitate the primal wonder that once surrounded the mystery of speaking.

NAMING A WORLD

According to experts in infant development, when babies emerge from the womb they land in a world of immediate impression. While babies' perceptual equipment is sophisticated at birth, their field of perception is limited and focused by need. Gradually infants do become aware of wider surroundings, reacting to various stimuli—taste, touch, light, sound, smell. At first a baby's world may be a bas-relief collage of undifferentiated impression. (If, as adults, we squint our eyes and try to think away all the names of things we have learned, perhaps we can imagine a baby's visual world.) Perception does develop, however, and, with perception, rudimentary conceptual "thinking," for example, ideas of similarity, presence/absence, movement, and dimension. Soon children seem to delight in surroundings; as Maurice Merleau-Ponty says, by babbling they "sing the world." Nevertheless, for many months baby's world is surroundings, not a cognitive world at all.

Then, suddenly, within the span of a scant thirty months, a miracle occurs: Children learn language. Getting a language seems to involve two different, though not unrelated, processes: hearing words, a hermeneutical task, and speaking words, a constitutive act. Like diapered Adam, every baby learns to name the world.

How do babies understand the world? Initially children respond to sounds, reacting to variations in pitch or tone or volume, as well as to a meta-language of gesture, facial expression, and so forth. Even in infancy children seem to possess subtle ability to "read between the lines" of spoken language. Soon they can distinguish different sounds and, eventually, different words—ball, Mommy, Daddy, dog, bunny. As things are named, they stand out and become entities that populate the world. Though children may hear complete sentences they distill particular code words, so that "Mary, bring me the bunny" may reduce to "——bring——bunny," and a command be grasped. Words and things come together and, ever so gradually, a world is heard.

At the same time as children hear words, they begin sounding. A developmental sequence can be traced: baby cries to cooings, to lallation (imitating one's own sounds), to echolalia (imitating the sounds of others), to eventual word formation. At twelve months, children will say only a few words but, by intonation, will give them a wide range of meaning. Normally, at a year and a half, children are on the verge of language, understanding much of what is said and using their limited vocabulary with a degree of sophistication. Most youngsters will speak in two-word systems, putting nouns together ("Mary chair" = Mary's chair), or verbs with nouns ("Mary run"), or verbs and nouns with so-called pivot words ("all-gone milk," "all-gone Daddy," etc.). Children speak a distinctive grammar that does not seem to ape adult usage, but which may derive from early modes of infant "cognition." Usually, between the ages of two and three, a linguistic explosion occurs as children assemble a working vocabulary of more than a thousand words with which to name the world. By four years of age, children have a remarkable dictionary of words, a nuanced grammar, not to mention a repertoire of language strategies for different social moments. So, in less than three years, young human beings learn to *live in language*. A miracle!

We have termed language learning a miracle and so it is. While the connection between speaking and cognition is a murky matter, ever since Lev Vygotsky some sort of correlation has been assumed. By *naming*, we *think* the world we live. For not only does language constitute the world-in-consciousness, it enables us to conceive of ourselves as selves-in-a-world. Did not Helen Keller admit that, deaf and blind, she had no "world" until a first word was grasped? Then, in spite of blindness, she was able through language to conceive the populated world in which she lived. Language thus assembles a *significant* world in consciousness. As vocabulary enlarges so, presumably, will the scope of our world-in-consciousness. No wonder Martin Heidegger called language "the house of being"! With words, we name the world.

Of course, unseen things are named in the world as well as items visually at hand. Imaginary creatures—Jabberwock or Heffalump—may be linguistic fabrications. Invisible agencies such as wind or gravity, however, may enter our world as their effects are named. Suppose that on some murmuring summer day when a child is cribbed for an afternoon nap, a window shade begins to sway in the breeze. Mother says, "Wind." "Odd," the child may muse (if that is the term), "she called it 'shade' just yesterday!" Or, again, the child may spot a leafy frond lifting and lowering outside the window. "Wind," says Mother. "Peculiar," mulls the child, "I was sure she named it 'tree' before." Gradually the notion of wind, an invisible agency known by effects, is formed in consciousness. All kinds of "unseen movers" may be brought into being by language. Perhaps the term "Holy Spirit" was originally agency naming (thus, possibly, accounting for the frequent use of the term without a definite article in the Book of Acts). Did early Christians, surprised by forceful declamation from a normally tongue-tied colleague,

7

point and say, "Holy Spirit"? In sum, language names the world into consciousness, a world both seen and unseen.

A word of caution: Do not suppose that there will be only one word for any particular thing. In different language communities, things may be named quite variously. As the scriptures note, "People . . . said that it thundered: others said, An angel spake . . ." (John 12:29, KJV). Things seen and unseen can be labeled in different ways. Suppose, for example, that Mr. John Doe has what Methodists are apt to term a heart-warming experience, some sort of religious moment. If John Doe is a devout chap, he may round his lips and in a breathy way say, "God." A psychoanalytic friend, however, may use rather different words to describe the experience, mentioning "hysteria" or perhaps muttering something about a "high level of psychosexual anxiety." Likewise, a sociological colleague may explain the event in terms of the impact of current culture religion. To push the example a stage further, suppose Mr. Doe is a sociologist with a psychoanalytic bent who happens to be a believer; he may regard his own experience as "hysteria" triggered by pop religion, yet nonetheless "God." Events, things, inner experiences—all may be variously named. Only the rigid fundamentalist or unreconstructed secularist will insist that there can be only *one* name for any given happening. As Christians we must never be dismayed by double, triple, or even quadruple naming, for multiple naming is surely the basis of evangelism. Evangelism rests on the open option that anything may be renamed gleefully into a consciousness of God.

While words name the world, they may fail to name as well. Obviously, what is not in our vocabulary may not be vivid in the conceived world. For example, Eskimos have many, many different words for snow (Eskimos have a lively interest in snow), whereas other societies have a limited snow vocabulary, extended mostly by modifiers such as slushy snow, granular snow. Thus equipped with words, Eskimos may spot kinds of snow which those from warmer climes will overlook. Or, to seize another example, city children wandering a woodland may miss much that rustics, who have been taught terms for different flowers and trees, will spy at once. Urban children's vocabulary may be limited to categorical words—tree, bird, flower—and thus they may walk the natural world with subtleties unseen. If in our age God-talk has been minimal, then, perhaps, God-consciousness may be remote at best. Perhaps the presence of God is, after all, a linguistic event, a presence in word. While the interaction between language and perception is much debated, it is likely that language acts as a grid, heightening some perceptions while screening out others. So, though language names the world, a converse may be remarked: *What is unnamed may not be for us.*

More drastically, words may misname and thus distort the world in consciousness. While we may wish to quibble with George Steiner's sweeping contention that language is a product of human egocentricity, chronic self-deception, and neighbor fear, we can scarcely deny that language can lie and misrepresent the world-in-consciousness. We do not refer to the odd fact that, again and again, words fail us. Even if we are endowed with poetic sensibility, whenever we try to wrap experience in words we end frustrated: Grammar seems to twist our lived experience out of shape—"I can't put it into words." No, here a darker motif is underscored: Words are weapons, words coerce, words lie. Do not most of us have to struggle to rename the moral world labeled in our childhood—"bad," "good," "nice," "dirty"? (Is every childhood always more law than grace?) Social attitudes are as easily deformed: Why is military spending always "strong," whereas welfare budgets are a "throwaway" on "cheats"? And, surely, recent concern over racism and sexism in language is well founded. The fact is, propaganda is a political weapon, advertising spiels can misrepresent, and bigotry is often as eloquent as sanctity. So, though words may be inadequate, and may even outlast their usefulness by inhibiting social change, mark the deeper theme: *Words can lie.*

Suspicion of language should not sour a sense of wonder. Language is miraculous indeed. We are human, distinctively human *(Homo loquens)*, because we *speak.* In the old, old story, God urged the first earthling, *'ādbām,* to name the world. The children of earthling have been busy naming the world ever since. Words do not create the world—only God creates with a Word—but language does constitute the world-in-consciousness, the significant social world in which we live. People and places, things, symbols, social roles and moral values, lands never visited, persons never met, cosmologies, psychological "models"—all these are named into consciousness and become a "world" in which people live together. Let us begin by wondering over the primal power of language: With words, we *name* the world.

TELLING A STORY

There is another kind of language, no less mysterious: It is called *story.* Storytelling also begins in childhood when someone puts verbs and nouns together in primitive story lines—"The teddy bear jumped on the bed." Ever so slowly a narrative sense forms in consciousness. Human beings hear stories and compose stories and thus develop a grasp of narrative meaning.

All through our young lives we are told stories until, much older, we are able to read stories on our own. Among the early stories we are told are family stories—for example, how Mommy met Daddy; where Grandpa and Grandma came from; about older sister being born. Later, as we move about the world, we may hear place stories: "Right over there by the gas station, Child, there used to be a hanging tree." As we grow older we may read nation stories, those hoary myths of George Washington or young Ben Franklin. Still later, perhaps in school, we will come across stories of race, of human race, and possibly even cosmic myths of how the world began. Notice that these early narratives are not unlike the assembling of Israel's story in scripture—tales of the patriarchs, place-name stories, an exodus narrative, and finally a preface added including the story of creation and the first human beings. Through the years we are told many stories by many different people; stories of our past, stories of friends, stories going on in a wider world, perhaps even stories of God. So, signal a second kind of language along with naming, a language called "story."

In addition to stories heard, human beings seem to construct their own life-story lines. Memory hands us a range of recall; episodes from our past are often called to mind by associative "triggerings" in the present. Most human beings are able to patch together a minimal chronology of their lives. Mere chronology is not narrative, however. When human beings tell themselves as a story, they do so by arranging recalled events into some sort of plot. Designing a plot is an act of interpretation and, therefore, involves a particular reading of meanings, values, causalities, and so forth. Of course, the material selected (or omitted), the significance accorded particular happenings, and the "genre" of the story may well be determined by immediate self-assessment, for example, "I am a secret unsung genius," "I am a chronic impotent," "I am a healthy all-American winner." Human beings do tell themselves (and others) life stories and, through such stories, search personal meaning.

Now all the stories we are told come together and, along with our own mnemonic story line, become in consciousness "Our Story." Stories arrange past to present (although they may be entered at different points or be rearranged in recall), and end up with us where we are. Thus stories conjoin in consciousness to tell us who we are and where we are in the world: *Stories give identity.* No wonder amnesia is such a debilitating condition. The problem for amnesiacs is not that they have forgotten their names, but that they have misplaced their stories and, as consequence, their identities. It helps little to hand an amnesiac a label—"Your name is Susan Smith"—when the real need is a recovery of narrative identity. So, incidentally, if the church has lost track of identity, titles such as "people of God" or "body of Christ" may not help; what is wanted is a rehabilitation of story. Words may name the world, but narrative consciousness tells us who we are and where in the world. Story confers identity.

A grim addendum: We can be told a wrong story, perhaps we always are.

For example, most White Americans have been told a White history, filled with White heroes: the success story of a pale-faced pioneer vision. As a result, we White Americans may not know who we are or where we are in a multiracial world. As a double result, we may mislive ourselves. No wonder one of the first things the Black-power movement of the sixties did (in addition to promoting positive modifiers for the word "black") was to campaign for a rewriting of American history texts. To grab a more intimate example: Is it possible that psychoanalytic technique involves the unraveling and reconstruction of a person's misassembled story so as to transform identity? Storytelling is much more than an innocent diversion, because stories join together to tell us who we are and where. All of us have storied identity.

PREACHING: STORY TRANSFORMED

We have put together a slapdash phenomenology of language. Language constitutes our world by *naming,* and confers identity in the world by *story.* What has talk of language got to do with preaching? Much. Preaching can rename the world "God's world" with metaphorical power, and can change identity by incorporating all our stories into "God's story." Preaching constructs in consciousness a "faith-world" related to God.

Preaching transforms identity by adding a new beginning to our stories. Writers explain that frequently the first paragraph of a novel may prefigure, and even prestructure, the whole story; that a beginning can determine the course of a story and set its style. Add a new beginning and the grasp of narrative may change. Imagine that, as a child, you were brought up as a thoroughgoing secularist (all thunder and no angels), and the stories you were told were in effect secular saga. But then one day (perhaps it was rainy and you had nothing better to do) someone sat you down and told you a whole new set of stories and, cleverly, told them as *your* stories—odd stories of Abraham and Sarah and Moses, of Paul in a basket, and of someone special named Jesus. Suddenly, quite without realizing, you acquired a prehistory, a new narrative to preface and prefigure your previously assembled story, a preface rolling out of myth into your everyday world. Like an untold adopted child suddenly told, you discovered a different identity by being given a new beginning. So, at minimum, preaching alters identity by prefacing *all* our stories and setting them in a larger story that stretches back to the dawn of God's creation.

Of course, there is more to preaching than giving a new start to our stories, a splendid Semitic past to our present. Preaching tells a story with transcendent dimension. Think again of our imagined storyteller. The odd thing about the stories was that they all had a central, if unseen character, God. The structure of the stories posed an astonishing possibility in your young secular mind: Could it be that, like Bible stories, all our stories—narratives of family, place, nation, race, not to mention personal life stories—are stories of God-with-us? More, is it conceivable that all our stories are also episodes in some larger-than-life story of God? Merely by telling stories, our fictive storyteller handed you the possibility of faith! No wonder Saint Paul insisted that "Faith comes from hearing." Our life stories, assembled from so many episodes, may be given new meaning when taken into a grand narrative of God-with-us. Even stories unfolding now may be in God's presence, and grasped by brooding about prototypical stories of God's way with others in the past. Given the power of narration, is it surprising that through most of the Christian centuries preaching has been discursive, best described as storytelling? Of course, the *way* preaching tells a story is crucial; stories of God-with-us must always be told as *our* story, and as having huge bearing on our present identity. Preaching can and does transform identity by adding a new beginning to our human stories, as well as the structural possibility of God-with-us.

In still another manner preaching transforms. Preaching conjures up an end to our stories. Notice that though our stories may assemble into a plot to tell us who we are and where in the world, they end in the here and now. Future chapters are as yet unwritten and a denouement unguessed. Yes, we can portend the future. We can imagine how the next chapter of our lives may begin, suppose the characters, the setting, and maybe fantasize a day, a month, even a few years ahead. Unfortunately, our guesses are no more than guesses, for as everyone knows our story may end abruptly, as every human story ends, with a grim ellipsis. We do not know the future. Perhaps the intrinsic excitement of life lies in its narrative mystery: We live our lives as a story wondering what is going to happen next. Life stories do unravel with narrative logic, early episodes determining later events (usually a tragic prospect!); nevertheless our plots can turn in surprising directions or conclude in quite unexpected ways. So our life stories are *being* written and are not yet concluded; they tell us who we are *here and now,* not who in God's grace we will be.

Christian preaching sketches an ending, or better The Ending, for it tells the denouement of God's story with us. Christian faith is incurably teleological. So in visioning conclusion, preaching transforms the human story and all our stories as well.

There was a family given to excesses of hospitality. Children in the family never knew whom they would find at the breakfast table, for the guest room was filled more often than not. For revenge, the kids got hold of a slightly lascivious, altogether-exciting detective story and, after tearing out the last chapter, put it out on the guest-room bedside table. Imagine red-eyed guests trudging to breakfast utterly frustrated: "How did it end?" Every now and then, some guest would come across a copy of the book in a secondhand store and would write explaining that the ending changed the whole story. What had seemed significant turned out to be a red herring, while what had appeared to be an inconsequential detail figured large in the final outcome. While Christian preaching cannot predict anyone's next episode (except to assure that it will be related to God), preaching does offer a vision of denouement that can transform our stories and, thus, our identities. For if God's story with us will end in a world reconciled—with new humanity engaged in glad, grave courtesies of love; with "the song of them that triumph and the shout of them that feast"; with the City and the Lamb and wiped-away tears—then all our stories must be revised. What may seem an unsavory, even fatal, episode in our plotted life story cannot be ultimately tragic, for see how The Story ends! What may appear to be insignificant cannot be weightless for it will be woven into wonderful denouement. Furthermore, gross tragedy, inexplicable evil such as the Holocaust, which cannot be waved aside with pat-on-the-back forgiveness, may at least become mysteriously God-full in view of The Ending. The fact is there is no forgiveness for a human history which, like the man in Kafka's *In the Penal Colony,* lives under an ever more deeply inscribed death sentence—unless somehow there is redemption for the human enterprise at the end of the God-with-us story. By adding the promise of an eschatological ending, Christian preaching counters what may appear to be necessities of plot within human history. Eschatology is, of course, a kind of poetry; imagistic enough to allow room for improvisational grace, but vivid enough to be true to life. Christian preaching dares to sing a poetry of conclusion.

Thus, Christian preaching can transform narrative identity. By locating our storied lives within a framework of beginning and end, Christian preaching poses the possibility of faith. We sense that our life stories may be related to the purposes of God that span human history; we may be living in some sort of God-with-us story. Perhaps in every episode we live with mysterious Presence-in-Absence—in a word, with grace!

BEYOND STORY:
THE SYMBOLIC-REFLECTIVE

Of course, Christian faith is more than a story connecting with our stories. The reason why Christian faith cannot be contained within the category of "story" is because, in addition to a horizontal God-with-us story line, there is a "symbolic-reflective" aspect to Christian faith formed by the *character of*

Jesus Christ and the nature of a "being-saved" community. We must never forget that Christian preaching is inescapably *Christ*ian; we speak *in* Christ *of* Christ. Though Jesus Christ comes to mind as an episode in the human story, which like any human episode may be understood within the purposes of God, nevertheless the character of Jesus Christ stands out from the story and is a "living symbol" to the Christian community. We interpret plot motifs in the light of Christ, and in him sense the form of a shaping denouement. Consider the symbolic-reflective dimension of Christian faith.

Many stories seem to be ordered by some central episode (sometimes called a turning point) which gives meaning to all that has previously happened and which appears to inaugurate strands of "plot" leading toward conclusion. We tend to read human history through such crucial events. For example, in biblical narration the exodus event, culminating with the giving of the law at Sinai, gathered stories of the patriarchs and gave them meaning, as well as imaging God's promises in terms of land. Subsequently, the emergence of the monarchy, particularly the Davidic kingship, reread stories and added monarchical imagery to final expectation. Still later, the shock of exile forced a revision of narrative and projected strange new strands of restoration into the future. Again and again in Israel's story, crucial turning-point events happened to rewrite the past and portend ever more complex patterns of plot resolution. In one way, the paradigmatic Christ-event functions similarly; the Christ-event reorders the past and prefigures God's future in a new way. The Christ-event, however, seems to be of a somewhat different nature for, in Christ, *character* interprets story to a new social reality, the being-saved community.

The odd relationship between character and plot has been the subject of much brooding since the days of Aristotle. In Aristotle character is subservient to action, to necessities of plot, except for moral distinctions, that is, good and evil characters. More recently, literary critics have tended to argue that character represents a psychological image of human beings in particular social epochs. We recognize, however, that some characters—perhaps Dostoyevsky's complex creatures or some of Faulkner's astonishing women— seem to reach beyond both plot and psychological representation; by their breadth and depth, they seem to become symbols of the human condition and even of humanity in relation to transcendence. Obviously, we may claim some such status for the figure of Jesus Christ. Though Christ does come to us as a character in human history, clearly he stands out symbolically in relation to both humanity and mysteries of transcendence. Thus, even outside of Christian community, Christ has become a living myth, at least in Western civilization.

In still another way we may study character and story. Sometimes in a story a character will emerge and become central so that story becomes the story of character. While literary critics may regard the emergence of a central character as an aesthetic liability, nevertheless central characters do form in stories and do function in a symbolic-reflective manner. Usually a central character enters story along with some new element in plot so that, thereafter, other characters in a new situation tend to relate to the central character. Perhaps we may see Jesus Christ as an emerging central character in the human story./Though Christ as a human being is a character within the human story, with Christ there is a shift in the story—namely, by resurrection the appearance of a new-order being-saved community—so that Christ stands out and becomes to us a living symbol. Christ does not destroy the human story; he liberates. Christ frees us from necessities of plot, from tugs of beginning (determinism) and ending (fatalism), from the Fall and the judgment, by disclosing in himself the presence of *Gratuitous Love.*

The character of Christ transforms the genre of the human story. In tragedy, tragic heroes and heroines gain insight into the human condition; they see patterns of determinism in past events and catch a glimpse of the common fate toward which humans stumble. Thus, "tragic revelation" is a disclosure of necessity in human affairs. Because tragic figures are brought low by structures of transcendence, for example, the petulance of Greek gods or the inflexibilities of moral law, tragedies tend to open the heavens and, indeed, to endorse structures of transcendence. Comedies, on the other hand, are social dramas in which heroes and heroines need not be slaughtered; they are flexible, they will give a little, and therefore can negotiate a happy ending via social accommodation. The only transcendence in comedy is a transcendence of social values; comedies celebrate "justification by society." So Christian faith is not tragedy or comedy. Christ discloses neither necessity nor accommodation, but rather the radical character of Gratuitous Love and a nonconformist new-life community. Thus, denouement in Christ is not social fulfillment or inevitable fate, but a wondrous reconciliation of human community and Gratuitous Love. In Christ, the genre of the Christian faith-story is *gospel.*

Joyce Carey, a British writer, was once asked how he put novels together. Obviously, novels may be scribbled from a start, with episodes added one at a time as determinism gradually overcomes choice. As obviously, novels can be designed from an ending by piecing together a sequence of causal events (with some extraneous events chucked in to maintain the illusion of freedom). But, according to Carey, wise writers will begin with the sketch of a central episode, working back to a beginning and outworking an ending. For Christian preaching, Jesus Christ and his new community is the central episode

15

God intended for the human story. Ultimately, human history is the story of Jesus Christ.

Notice *how* Christian preaching preaches: We speak of Christ *in* Christ. The point-of-view from which Christian preaching speaks is *in* Christ, that is, from within a being-saved community constituted by the Christ-event and animated by his Spirit. Every story is told from a stance, because every storyteller is located in time and space and has some particular self-understanding within human community. Obviously, preaching cannot stand in some imagined historical objectivity and, with a detached third-person perspective, tell a story of God-with-us. Nor may Christian faith speak merely from some social point-of-view such as a free-enterprise American community: Limited social hermeneutics will always make the character of Christ subservient to an ideological plot or reduce him to an ideal ideological representation. No, Christian preaching speaks from the lee side of the cross from within a community of the Spirit that is being-saved. In so doing, Christian preaching has a unique self-understanding—being-saved—that plots all human episodes into the purposes of Gratuitous Love. The hermeneutic of Christian preaching is astonishment of being-saved in the world.

In much recent literature about preaching, particularly literature that has fallen under the spell of "salvation history," the time of preaching is usually described as "in between," a time between the historical episode of Jesus Christ and a final consummation. Thus, unfortunately, the time of preaching is regarded as an interim between a once-was revelation and a not-yet denouement, essentially an entr'acte or waiting period in which we can rehearse past-tense events for the present day. Such an understanding devastates preaching as well as devaluing the history in which it speaks. As a result we no longer resonate to Paul's words, "work out your own salvation with fear and trembling, for God is at work among you." Instead, let us affirm what does define our time, namely, a being-saved community in an unfolding story related to the Living Symbol, Jesus Christ. We are not isolated selves anticipating a someday personal salvation—like poor paralyzed DeDe and GoGo awaiting a delayed Godot. We do not chatter vacuously, "killing time" until the end. No, now we live in the *momentum* of a denouement when the prose of everyday is shot through with the poetry of consummation. The hermeneutic of Christian preaching is *social* and *eschatological.* We speak in the space-time of salvation, from within a proleptic new humanity, dazzled by the presence of Gratuitous Love through the Living Symbol, Jesus Christ. With eager eyes we watch out for every new unfolding of God's salvation within the human story.

What is preaching? Christian preaching tells a story and names a name. If narrative consciousness confers identity, then preaching transforms identity, converts in the truest sense of the word, by rewriting our stories into a God-with-us story—beginning, Presence, and end. But, in view of the great disclosure of Gratuitous Love, by metaphor, preaching renames the human world as a space for new humanity related to God. What preaching may do is to build in consciousness a new "faith-world" in which we may live and love!

TOPICAL/BIBLICAL PREACHING

Of late, preaching seems to have stumbled into a trap. The "topical" preaching tradition tends to name God in the world, but has neglected narrative. The "biblical" preaching tradition can tell a biblical story, but often fails to name God-with-us in the world. Both traditions seem to have fallen victim to a cultural subjective/objective split. Let us pursue the dialectic.

The genius of topical preaching is courage to rename the world and, what is more, to name God in the world. The tragedy of topical preaching, particularly in the liberal tradition, was that it fell victim to cultural romanticism and ended up misnaming God in the world. Since before the nineteenth century and into our own day, topical preaching has tended to name God almost exclusively into religious affections. Even the so-called social gospel saw human history as the fulfilling of religious affections, temporarily blocked by evil social structures. God was primarily a felt flutter in the heart, a still, small, and decidedly inward voice. Because of residual natural theology, liberalism affirmed that God romped in dewy rose gardens, but for the most part God was truly apprehended in pious moments of religious feeling. Certainly there has been little pulpit talk of a God who tromps political rallies, or sits in at corporate board meetings, or has anything whatsoever to do with our somewhat untidy sexual bumblings (except as celebrated by German Romantics!). Mostly, the God of the pulpit has been a God in our hearts. Of course, "A.F.," after Freud, when psychologists relabeled inner dispositions, there was little left of God anywhere, except perhaps in the Bible. Of course, had the topical tradition brooded over scripture's story, it might have bumped into a God named in connection with all sorts of odd human moments, from a run-for-your-lives escape from Egypt to an inane real-estate deal by Jeremiah to a routine jail sentence for Apostle Paul to an itinerant preacher who fell victim to capital punishment outside the gates of first-century Jerusalem. Oddly enough the scriptures if asked "Where is your God?" would never reply "Here in our hearts!" So, though topical preaching dared to name God for the human world, because story was neglected it misnamed God into human subjectivity.

17

But has so-called biblical preaching done any better? Even when biblical preaching has not been cornered by rationalist exegesis and objective rationalist homiletics and has given itself to narration, biblical preaching has failed to name God in the world. Perhaps biblical preaching has been paralyzed by Barthian fears of cultural accommodations and, as a result, has recited scripture to churchly faith in a small stained-glass echo chamber. Whatever the reason, frequently biblical preaching has told a biblical story replete with oodles of biblical background, a "holy history," but has not permitted God to step out of the biblical world into human history. The God of biblical preaching has been a past-tense God of past-tense God-events whose past-tense truth ("original meaning") may be *applied* to the world, while God remains hidden within a gilt-edged book. While God once had something to do with King Ahab's ill-advised war policies, God apparently has little to do with all-American excursions in Nicaragua. (No wonder that scriptural preaching is heartily endorsed by the religious right wing.) But, bluntly, a biblical preaching that will not name God out of narrative and into the world is simply *un*biblical.

We have been polemical—deliberately so, because the issue *is* crucial. If preaching is to form and transform, somehow it must conjoin narrative and naming, and thus recover the primal power of word. Preaching is obviously more than talking about the Bible. Preaching, or at least Christian preaching, must dare to name God in conjunction with the world of lived experience. For news of God is not simply limited to the pages of scripture or the pulsings of religious inwardness; presumably God's great salvation is for the world and in the world. We must be cautious. A mighty-acts-of-God theology in which God intervenes in human causalities in some *deus ex machina* manner will not do, simply because, if nothing else, it is unintelligible. We can, however, certainly hold up human events so that they interface with God's story-line purpose and astonishing love. In so doing, we shall grasp where God's Word is working out in the world. So, for example, could we not have pointed to the burgeoning civil-rights movement of the sixties and insisted that it was instigated by the gospel? In the eighties, we may have to hold up our national policy, an increase in defense spending coupled with a decrease in welfare concern, and announce its obvious disobedience in the sight of God. God naming may be risky business because the dangers of misnaming are ever present (not to mention annoyance which such preaching may evoke in politically precommitted congregations). Nevertheless, the risk of silence is even greater: *Failure to name God with the world can only certify God's absence!* Pulpits will gain usefulness as preachers venture to name unseen patterns of grace in a fully human world.

If God naming is to be confident, however, it must be a naming in the light of story; the biblical narrative of God-with-us is normative for preaching. We can spot God's elusive presence only on the basis of precedent—previous disclosures of God that establish God's style and trace God's purpose. God-with-us has a story line and, by studying God's ways we can begin to understand who God is and where in the world God's grace is at work. If, in the past, God has been a liberator of the oppressed, not only once when the children of Israel high-tailed it out of Egypt, but again and again, then surely God's imaging grace is instrumental in movements that strive for human liberation, however ambiguous they may be. God is always related to ambiguity simply because there are *no* unambiguous human moments. Any attempt to locate God's grace on the basis of some unusual "spiritual" quality or "moral purity" in events is foolishness and can only lead to irrelevant or even demonic forms of political pietism. If the promised denouement of God's story is "Shalom," then we may suppose that God's grace will be working within causes that labor for the reconciliation of races and nations. Preachers who would risk naming God in connection with the human world must be familiar with scripture, its story line and its precedent naming. When narrative and naming come together in sermons, preaching will have unusual power and, perhaps, even the compelling ring of truth.

Preaching that dares to name God in connection with a wide range of human experience will shape in congregational consciousness a live hermeneutic for scripture. When we name God with the world, then biblical stories become meaningful. Often enough, we are told that scripture interprets life. Surely the claim is true: Christians who are immersed in scripture do find that the Bible's message casts light on life. The converse is also true, however. Our understanding of life interprets scripture. The problem for Christians is in deciding what kinds of human experience are to be lined up with biblical texts. Obviously, scripture can be tragically misread when inappropriate or even trivial analogies are drawn. Preaching instructs congregational hermeneutics, teaching congregations to interpret experience in the light of scripture and scripture in view of experience. Negative evidence is still evidence: The personalist hermeneutic of American pop piety has been formed by generations of personalist preaching. Though assuredly frightening, it is nonetheless true to say that congregational theology is largely a product of preaching. So, *how* preaching names God with the world will tend to determine how people understand scripture, its meaning, message, and application to life.

A brave, faithful preaching that risks naming God in connection with a wide range of human experience will in turn shape a congregation's grasp of scripture. If at present most American Christians suppose that God is either in churchly spheres (Bible, Eucharist, worship) or in pious hearts, we must somehow widen vision so that God may be truly God. A failure to name God in connection with the whole range of human reality will leave congregations without a repertoire of significant God-experiences with which to interpret scripture. Unguided, congregations will line up texts willy-nilly with all kinds of experience. But if the pulpit ventures to interface human experience—political movements, social patterns, as well as areas of personal life not usually signaled in sermons—with the gospel message, then preaching will build an elaborate repertoire of God-experiences with which to interpret the Bible. While scripture's story and the Living Symbol, Jesus Christ, may be normative for preaching, fearless thoughtful preaching will form a live hermeneutic for scripture in congregations.

NEW IDENTITY AND NEW WORLD

In a halting way, we have begun to rehabilitate the "house of language," to reinstate the miracle of speaking. Words beckon the world into consciousness. Words give us our storied identity.

Preachers use words. So preaching can reshape the world in consciousness and transform identity: Preaching can build a faith-world in human consciousness. If preaching speaks boldly then, perhaps, like astonished Adam, once more we may walk God's mysterious world, name it good, and see ourselves with tender wonderment as characters in God's great story of salvation.

Story and naming are the stuff of *Christ*ian preaching.

MOVES

2.
Speaking in Moves

If we are going to take a walk, we do so in steps—one step after another. If we are going to talk of anything, we do so in words, one after another. Language is inescapably linear. While we may experience life as "wholeness" with all sorts of sensations happening at the same time, when we tell our experience we do so in a series of sentences strung together one after another. Simultaneity is the nature of experience, but syntax is the rule of language.

We can attempt to break out of syntax, to jumble words and phrases, trying to express the simultaneous character of experience in an impressionistic language collage, but such jumbles may not impress at all. While a jumble of expression may imitate immediacies of experience, it will not convey experience *understood;* that is, experience interpreted in consciousness. To interpret experience we must turn to syntax. Though oral language is amazingly free and can break syntax to express both immediacy and understanding, when we speak, we will nevertheless still talk of one thing and then another and then another and so forth. Sermons involve an ordered sequence—they are not glossolalia. Sermons are a movement of language from one idea to another, each idea being shaped in a bundle of words. Thus, when we preach we speak in formed modules of language arranged in some patterned sequence. These modules of language we will call "moves."

In speaking of "moves," we are deliberately changing terminology. For years, preachers have talked of making *points* in sermons. The word "point" is peculiar; it implies a rational, at-a-distance pointing at things, some kind of objectification. Of course, for many decades preachers did seem to suppose that there were fixed truths "out there" to be talked about or pointed. Instead, we are going to speak of moves, of making moves in a *move*ment of language.

23

Sermons, no matter how intricately arranged, involve sequential talking, a series of language modules put together by some sort of logic. Just as a chain of sentences in a conversation may assemble to make meaning, so in preaching, moves (modules of language) form in consciousness to pattern an understanding. Before we can consider matters of arrangement, strategies of sermon design, and so forth, we must see what sermons are made of—namely a series of rhetorical units or moves. So we must study moves to see how they are shaped out of words and sentences and how, in turn, they form in the odd shared consciousness we call a "congregation."

Any human speaking involves sequence, even impromptu discussion between close friends. If we imagine two women, near neighbors, talking together over coffee at a kitchen table, we can conceive of their conversation. For example, they may begin by talking of their children for a few minutes, which could lead to a discussion of the school their children attend. The conversation might then broaden to view the problems of American public education, and then more difficult problems of taxation for public education. They might then turn to complain of the withholding tax taken from their own paychecks, which could prompt discussion of sexist inequalities in the pay scale for women workers. Though the entire conversation might take an hour, we can break up the movement of their talk into a sequence of moves: first they spoke of children, then of local schools, then of public education, then of taxation, and finally of prejudicial patterns in the employment of women. The separate moves trundled along, joined by associational logic to form their conversational journey. Some matters may have been discussed for nearly fifteen minutes, while other subject matters consumed relatively little time. So all human speaking involves sequence; talk of A, then B, then C, then D, and so forth. Moreover, shifts in speaking will happen by many different kinds of logic. When the two friends, talking over coffee, shifted subject matters—from a local school to public education, or from general taxation to their own personal paychecks—they did so by rather familiar forms of logic, for example, from lesser to greater, from general to particular. All human conversation, unless it is nothing more than a brief exchange of small talk, has structured sequence; it will happen in a series of moves. Moves are tied together by various "natural" logics. Sermons are similarly constructed: They will involve a series of moves—language modules—strung together in some sort of logical movement.

In general, speed of movement will be governed by the size of an audience. One-to-one conversation can travel at breakneck speed. For example, imagine hearing a conversation between two travelers meeting by chance in an airport boarding area:

"Are you going to Chicago?"

"No, I'm on my way to Traverse City, Michigan."

"There's a Cherry Festival there every summer, isn't there?"

"I don't know. I'm going to a music camp."

"You're a musician?"

"Maybe someday—I play the French horn."

"Oh, that's supposed to be difficult."

"I guess so. I'm struggling."

"Well, take some time out to go fishing. There's salmon now in Lake Michigan."

"I think I'll be too busy practicing."

If we analyze the conversation, we discover that the two travelers have covered a number of subjects in only a few sentences—Traverse City's Cherry Festival, a music camp, the difficulty of playing a French horn, salmon fishing, and practice time. Such rapid shifts in subject matter can be maintained in one-to-one conversation. But, if we were to play a recording of the conversation to an audience of two or three hundred people, the language might not register at all. Group consciousness simply cannot handle rapid shifts in subject matter. To move along from subject to subject every few sentences would "freak out" an audience; the effect would be similar to watching a movie film that has been speeded up many times the normal frames per minute. Minds will wander when pace is intense. One-to-one conversation and public address are different kinds of discourse. To form five different subject matters in group consciousness would require at least fifteen minutes of speaking time. Therefore, ministers who have the odd notion that all they have to do in a pulpit is to get up and speak naturally (and comfortably) as if in one-to-one conversation are deluded; nobody will hear what they have to say. Though a sermon may move along like a conversation from one subject matter to another, the movement of speaking is much slower. We all know how to speak one-to-one because much of our lives is spent in conversation; we converse naturally. Speaking to group consciousness, however, is quite different and, indeed, may seem to be unnatural. Public address must be learned.

The slowed-down character of public address may irritate us. We may suppose that, if we cannot cover as many different ideas in public speaking as in one-to-one discussion, preaching is doomed to be superficial, simplistic, and possibly irresponsible. No, the two kinds of speaking are different, and they accomplish quite different purposes. While public address cannot present as many ideas in a short time as can one-to-one talking, it can achieve depth and formational power impossible in the rapid linear movement of everyday conversation. In public address, bunches of sentences carry meaning that, in conversation, might be phrased in a single sentence. Within a bunch of sentences, not only can we express a meaning, but we can include images, cadences, metaphors, and syntactic patterns so that meaning may be seen and felt and formed in astonishing ways. One-to-one speaking and public address are different mediums—as different as dance from sculpture—though both modes of speaking are highly sophisticated, they do different things. Much one-to-one conversation goes in one ear and out the other, but when public language is shaped with technical proficiency, it can have awesome formational power in human consciousness. One-to-one conversational language may involve a sequence of ideas, many in a brief moment, but public address can approach the simultaneity of human experience as it mingles meaning, image, and affect in unusual ways.

There is evidence to suggest that it may take more time to form a simple meaning in communal consciousness now than in an earlier era, such as the first quarter of the twentieth century, when language was probably more stable. While in one-to-one conversation, we can say "God is a mystery" in the wink of an eye; to form the same understanding in group consciousness —oriented, imaged, explained—may take three to four minutes! A congregation of a few hundred people will not grasp ideas quickly. There is also some indication now that audience attention span is brief—not much more than four minutes to a single conceptual idea. All of which is to remark that in our present age (and for the foreseeable future), the margins within which we speak are narrower than we know. We must take nearly four minutes to form, image, and explore each idea we present, but our speaking will be limited by a congregation's inability to concentrate on any single notion for much more than four minutes. Thus, within about twenty minutes of speaking to a congregation, we can only discuss perhaps five, and certainly no more than six, different subject matters in sequence. To attempt to bypass the problem and, in a sermon, to chase down ten different ideas in twenty minutes will result in a congregation hearing little—ideas that are not formed in consciousness with care simply do not register; they are heard but not heard, and pass from consciousness in an instant. Though public address cannot present many ideas in a short time, public address can form understandings profoundly, so that they become embedded in the lives of people. We will be irritated at what will seem the intellectual limitations of public address as long as we fail to see what it *does* do, namely, *form* faith-consciousness.

The thought of having to spin out a simple idea such as "God is a mystery" for about three and one-half minutes may trouble prospective preachers. But the expanding of a single idea does not involve mere garrulousness, a repetitious, empty-worded circling of an idea. Speaking imitates the way in which consciousness grasps and understands, namely through models and images of lived experience. Therefore, if you preach "God is a mystery," you will have to decide models: Is God like a distant figure? Is God like an impenetrable mistiness unshaped but surrounding us? Does God live behind a shield of unknowing? Moreover, you will search out moments in actual lived experience when human beings do seem to sense God's Presence-in-Absence—where, when, and how does such awareness occur? You will think out theologically what it is you are attempting to convey and you will analyze cultural notions that may prevent our grasping the mystery of things. There is so much involved in any simple statement that our problem is not how to fill three or four minutes, but how to reduce, shape, and speak within such limits!

Perhaps our anxiety comes from a failure to realize that congregations will *not* do our imaging for us. If we use general categorical terms—chair, house, dog—people do not flash distinctive "pictures" in consciousness as each word is spoken. Thus, if a speaker tells an audience, "I carried my dog out for a walk this morning," the audience, or more accurately 95 percent of the audience, will picture nothing. (There are always a few people given to overactive imaging, but *only* a few.) Even if some members of the audience will image the sentence, invariably they will do so on the basis of their own experience; if they have a cocker spaniel at home, they will picture their own cocker spaniel. The bald statement, "I carried my dog out for a walk this morning," will mean little and in fact be unremembered until it is imaged, until an audience can *see* what you are speaking about. They must see the ninety-pound, sick sheepdog in your arms, see how you nearly stumble when your coat catches the swinging storm door, see you navigating the steep stairs to the yard, see how the sun is barely up in the sky (you are wearing pajama pants under your coat), and so on. Good preaching involves the imaging of ideas—the shaping of every conceptual notion by metaphor and image and syntax.

Not only must ideas be visualized, they must be presented along with structures of understanding. Ideas, at least in speaking, are *never abstract;* that is, ideas are never apart from attitudes, emotions, doubts, values, and so forth which people have toward them. Obviously, if you say, "I carried my dog out for a walk," to all-American pet lovers, the meaning will be very different from saying the same sentence to an isolated tribe that feasts on roast dogmeat daily. Not only will preaching image ideas, preaching will also represent the ways in which we interpret ideas through social attitudes, affective responses, and the like. Inasmuch as preachers live in a congregation and, indeed, share consciousness with a congregation, such representation is not impossible. We are never talking of ideas "out there," ideas that stand in pure isolation from the stuff of human consciousness. Instead, we speak ideas that are tangled up with human responses. For example, if you preach "God is a mystery" to a group of dedicated empiricists, you will handle the subject very differently than if you were speaking to a charismatic community agog over immanence. The problem in preaching is not expanding ideas, but rather constricting, shaping, and disciplining ideas. How on earth can we compress images, attitudes, concepts all together into a bundle of words not much longer than three minutes?

A sermon, any sermon, will involve a sequence of subject matters—simple meanings—arranged in some sort of structural design. Each simple meaning will be developed into a move—a language module between three and four minutes in length. To grab a perceptual analogy: just as a book is fashioned out of a sequence of shaped paragraphs each exploring a different idea, so sermons will be an assemblage of moves, each shaped by homiletic craft. In designing separate moves a preacher will be attempting to form conceptual understanding in communal consciousness. Thus, moves will be shaped in such a way as to form in consciousness, as do most human understandings—as a gestalt of modeling, imaging, affective attitudes, and concept. Though most traditional books on homiletics start by discussing the structural design of sermons, we will begin by looking at moves, discrete moves, before chasing down matters of overall design.

THINKING OUT MOVES

Designing a move is not merely an exercise in rhetorical strategy. Obviously, preachers employ exegesis, theology, tradition, cultural analysis, and so forth in presenting ideas. Nevertheless, let us not disparage rhetoric. Rightly, rhetoric is concerned with shaping moves in such a way that moves will fit human consciousness, and there contend with the social attitudes that people bring to church. Ideally, people should *not* feel that they are being talked to so much as having conceptual meaning form in consciousness as their *own* thought process. So designing moves involves theological smarts and rhetorical skill—trained rhetorical skill. Before we can discuss the technical rhetoric of moves, we must trace the way in which we think out moves for presentation.

Suppose as part of a sermon we are going to have a move that conveys the single meaning, "We are sinners." Though the meaning can be spoken in a simple sentence, somehow we must develop the idea into a module of language between three and four minutes in length. The statement itself is so bald, and in a way obvious, that elaboration may seem superfluous. Let us examine, however, all that may be involved in understanding such a statement as "We are all sinners." There is a way to think out moves that can and should become habitual for preachers.

Theological Definition

Obviously, preaching can mispreach and therefore reinforce common misunderstandings. Preachers are scarcely immune. We grow up in religious communities with pop-religious ideas swirling around us. We internalize such ideas and, frequently without further thought, accept them as givens. Thus we use terms such as "kingdom of God" or "Savior" or "sin" without trying to explore what they may be all about. And, without thinking, we pass on our tacit understandings to congregations. But if we are going to speak theological understandings we ought to be rather precise as to meaning. Of course, our problem may not be misunderstanding so much as a lack of clarity. If we are unclear as to what we are talking about we will have enormous difficulty in shaping moves. We will have to think out what on earth we do mean when we toss around a word like "sin." For example, the word "sin" is frequently defined as "missing the mark," which would seem to incorporate a model of either journey or growth—sin as a wandering off the path or sin as a failure to attain fulfillment. Thus, the phrase "missing the mark" is open to two somewhat different understandings. Still others may define sin as disobedience or lawbreaking. Here the notion seems to suggest that there are laws or commandments which are violated; the definition tends to be legal or perhaps parental. Another image of sin that has come down through Christian history is the image of contamination, as if sin is an impurity, possibly some sort of "social disease." And sin can also be understood within a relational model, as separation or alienation or estrangement. The fact is, we seem to be verging on a field of meaning in which different aspects of sin may project different kinds of metaphors and models.

Notice that we are not merely concerned with theological precision. The definition of sin with which we speak will in turn determine the images, the word-pictures we paint in presenting the idea. Homiletic thinking is always *a thinking of theology toward images*.

In order to get at meanings, we will probably have to do some homework. A simple word such as "sin" can send us to wordbooks of the Bible, to texts in theology, and so forth. Obviously we must clarify our own understandings before we speak. Most of us are quite aware of popular misunderstandings of Christian faith. Many members of a congregation hear "kingdom of God" as a reference to "somewhere after we die," a place where we will have "eternal life"—notions that are assuredly not biblical. Or consider a term such as "Savior" which, along with the word "salvation," is frequently given odd twists of meaning. While theological ambiguity is in a sense inescapable—the things of God are mysterious and profound—nevertheless, we must think out definitions, because cocksure conventional understandings are often misunderstandings. Though we will not overcome ambiguity, we do owe our congregations a degree of thoughtfulness which in turn will give focus to our speaking. Moreover, in the process of understanding, we will invariably find the images, models, and metaphors we need in order to preach.

Oppositions

As every shrewd preacher knows, congregations are not empty-headed, a collection of tabula rasa minds waiting to be scribbled with the words of God. People come to church with all kinds of "pre-understandings," misinformation, conventional wisdoms, pop theologies, and the like. Preachers must "psych out" the oppositions before they speak. Failure to recognize and, possibly, defuse oppositions will lead either to a refusal of the words we speak, or to misinterpretation of our words. Most preachers have been appalled by the way in which sermons can be heard. A minister may get up and with wondrous glee announce the free gracious mercy of God, only to have some parishioner come up after the sermon and say something like, "That's right, preacher, unless we repent, God won't forgive us!" The preacher is left reeling in confusion, wondering what on earth went wrong with the sermon. Too easily we blame listeners. Whenever such sharp misunderstandings occur they are almost always the preacher's error. We can forget to analyze and allow for convictions that are already firmly embedded in congregational minds. If we are going to preach on "We are sinners," what kinds of oppositions must we recognize?

At the outset, let us acknowledge the *resistance born of our chronic, human sinfulness.* Obviously, the idea of sin may shatter our inborn self-righteousness or threaten self-esteem. Most of us do not want to acknowledge sinfulness or, perhaps more important, do not wish to admit a *common* sinfulness. It is more comfortable to speak of sin in relation to "them"—to those sinners out there in the world. But the resistance born of our own common and chronic sinfulness is not merely a resistance to accusation; it goes deeper. We may resist the whole notion of a God who in any way may infringe upon our sovereign consciousness, no matter how good or generous such a God may be. Though there is the reality of reluctant sin—a constant opposition to the gospel—preachers must not invariably attribute failure to hear sermons to sin. Though a sinful reluctance to acknowledge God may well be a constant, it should not fan hostility in preachers because the same disinclination lives in us all. Instead, a certain tender acknowledgment of our common condition will be homiletically useful. Preachers should not be cowed by oppositions of sin, because, of course, we preach with confidence in grace, or else we would not preach at all.

A more important concern will be *Cultural Oppositions.* Cultural oppositions are usually of two kinds: oppositions that may be built into the world view, and oppositions that may be connected with *au courant* cultural attitudes. The *world view* will be a problem when theological ideas collide with twentieth-century views of cosmology, psychology, and the like. For example, the notion of a "kingdom of God" breaking into our social world may seem fairy-tale talk to congregations brought up on concepts of progressive time or of a closed universe. Likewise, the theological affirmation "God the Creator" may be difficult to preach to people schooled by "big-bang" scenarios for creation. Christian understandings that may be related to biblical mythos may be hard to convey in an age when myths have little common currency.

But, more often, problems are posed by *current social attitudes.* For example, we live at a time when psychological sciences have widespread popular appeal. Congregation members may have done course work in psychology, or may be subscribers to *Psychology Today.* At minimum, they live in the midst of a cultural "triumph of the therapeutic." Thus, people may regard the word "sin" as a leftover from some superstitious religious past. They may view "alienation" as a psychological problem and "missing the mark" as a deviation in developmental growth. At a time when people speak of "healthy self-esteem" and a "positive self-image," notions of sin will seem a detriment, something to be exorcised by psychological wisdoms lest they twist positive thinking. If a preacher does not recognize the cultural mood and, what is more, acknowledge psychological objections, preaching on "We are all sinners" may be virtually impossible. Cultural oppositions must be considered and homiletic strategies framed to address such oppositions.

Perhaps less obviously, *there are religious distortions* that must be recognized. We tend to pick up religious instruction much as we do our sexual understandings, by gossip. Everyone in a congregation is a pop theologian. Therefore, if we use terms such as "sin," which to us may seem simple enough, in congregational consciousness there may be all kinds of odd connotations. For many in a congregation, the word "sin" may mean "doing bad things," particularly bad things having to do with redeye hootch and wanton women, not to mention *very* bad things such as murder or rape which, significantly, they themselves do not do. Thus, in the congregational mind there may be "bad doers" and, of course, churchgoers who for the most part "do good." The idea of sin as an orientation of the self that affects all of life may not be generally understood. Preachers must spot religious distortions that float in congregational consciousness and, in some manner, design strategies of speaking to handle the problem.

In signaling *oppositions to the gospel,* we are not suggesting that preaching involves armed combat with congregational attitudes, as if the gospel were always antithetical to the human mind. Preaching must never tumble into surly argumentation with social attitudes. Nevertheless, we cannot ignore oppositions. What we can do is to design contrapuntal systems of language to recognize and, perhaps, defuse the power of opposition. The problem is more urgent today than in the past. We preach at a time when one cultural epoch seems to be crumbling and new forms of social understanding are forming; we preach "between the ages." In such a moment, preaching will have to disassociate the gospel from previous cultural understandings and recast faith in new thought forms. While some older homiletic texts used to insist that sermons must never acknowledge doubts, oppositions, or even misconceptions, we cannot afford such arrogance. Preaching may not stand in an imagined purity of the gospel and refuse to acknowledge the cultural mind. Preaching will have to be far more apologetic these days than during the heyday of the dialectical theology of Karl Barth, Emil Brunner, and Friedrich Gogarten. Part of our homiletic task in designing moves will be spotting oppositions and finding ways to deal with them. Inasmuch as preachers participate in the cultural mind and, at the same time, struggle with the gospel, they will experience tensions within their own consciousness. While a shrewd preacher will study the thought forms of the world-age, oppositions may well be discovered internally.

Lived Experience

We know that in preaching any idea, we will have to image. Ideas without depiction are apt to be abstract and, oddly enough, unconvincing. Therefore, if we are going to speak of "sin," we will have to find some way of picturing what it is we are talking about; we must turn to lived experience. Because the single meaning "We are all sinners" contains two key words, "we" and "all," we will have to focus on the social world in consciousness as well as on our own self-awareness. Within the social world we will notice ways in which we encounter presentments of sin—through daily papers, telecasts, novels, films, and the like, as well as our own social encounters with others in a world that has been described as "healthy, normal, and *selfish.*" Obviously, our searching of the social world will be guided by the definition of sin we have formed theologically—sin as "alienation" or "unfulfillment" or "lawbreaking" or "lovelessness" or whatever. The searching out of lived experience in the social world will probably not be too difficult.

But there is another mode of lived experience with which we must reckon, namely, our own self-awareness. Much preaching can be glib, full of homiletic strategies which congregations have heard all too often. What may make preaching profound is a willingness to search deeply the *actualities* of consciousness. For example, in actuality, how do human beings have a consciousness of "I am a sinner," if in fact they do? A preacher may tell us that "we all feel guilty," but the words may not convince. If, however, the preacher can actually describe how and when and where we feel guilty, we may be inclined to agree. So fine preachers will brood. Preachers will reach into consciousness to depict *how* we sense guiltiness. Does it show up as an eye-lowering, uneasy self-consciousness? Is it a momentary, fleeting awareness? If, for example, a cruelty slips into conversation, do we have a momentary pang; for a brief instant do we think, "Well, I ought to apologize," but then pass on? Is our awareness of wrongdoing as brief? Or, sometimes, does a sense of sin settle on us as vague regret: our lives have formed, but could have been purer, or more disciplined, somehow more gallant or meaningful —but, too late? Is there any awareness of God involved, or is the sense of sin bounced off half-articulated "oughts" that lie around on the fringes of consciousness? What *actually* happens? The question is crucial. Many preachers reach too quickly for some stock illustration to support contentions and never think down to actualities of human consciousness. Preachers who dare to probe deep levels of self-awareness, however, will be preachers whose word will have the ring of truth. Preaching does not persuade in the sense of arguing the truth of the gospel; preaching sets the gospel in lived experience, genuine experience, so that truth will be acknowledged.

Strategies

Every move has a shape, an internal design. The shape of a move is determined in an interaction of (1) theological understanding, (2) an eye for oppositions, and (3) actualities of lived experience. Gradually, as we think out a move, we will determine a strategy of presentation, a rhetorical strategy. If we are going to preach "We are all sinners," what strategies will we adopt? We could merely assert the fact as if it were a divine truth to be dumped on the human world, but such a procedure would probably be ineffective if not unkind. In order to relate a theological assertion to human understanding we will have to think out a strategy. What will we do? Will we parade signs of sin in the world—warfare, economic carelessness, prejudice—and then find similar impulses in our own lives? Or will we journey across human history and in every era spot evidence of human lovelessness? Perhaps we could set up a false contrast between "good" and "bad" people, and then discover that actually the "goods" are no better than the "bads." Because we have noticed the "triumph of the therapeutic," shall we cite experts, such as Karl Menninger, who still acknowledge the old-fashioned word "sin"? We can conceive of all kinds of approaches to presenting the notion of sin, some that seem compelling, others perhaps less compelling. In designing a move, preachers will rehearse in mind many possible strategies, as well as illustrations, examples, image systems and the like, before settling on some kind of procedure. Moves must have clear, defined internal shape, else they will not form in congregational consciousness. In selecting strategies, preachers, though sweet as saints, had better be as canny as streetfighters!

Selecting strategies, however, is different from manipulation. Preachers are not manipulators, because preaching is neither a form of brainwashing nor propaganda. We must never forget that a gospel of free grace demands that we guard the freedom of listeners. Though some preachers may suppose that all is fair if we are determining salvation, and that devious rhetoric may be justified on the basis of "It's for their own good," such a pattern of thought is alien to the gospel. When we speak of strategy we do not imply ethically ungoverned manipulation. By strategy we refer to a mode of presentation ruled by the content of the gospel on the one hand, and the patterns of our contemporary mind on the other. We are asking *how* people may best grasp Christian understandings. Moves are not haphazardly put together out of a simple topic sentence and a bale of "filler," for example, a chain of illustrations or hammering reiterations. Every move in a sermon will require a thinking through of *how* we present material, what kinds of material will be chosen, and how such material will be designed in view of theological understandings and our common cultural mind. Thinking strategy is inescapable.

Parts and Unity

In making moves we are presenting a single idea—"We are all sinners"—but doing so in a strategy that probably involves a number of parts, namely, subordinate gambits of thought. In thinking through the idea we have stumbled on different *theological* conceptions and, in all likelihood, have focused on one or more. Theological concepts have offered us models, images, and metaphors. In addition, we have considered *oppositions* which may block understanding, oppositions both cultural and religious. Further, we have searched *lived experience* for fields of consciousness that may relate to theological understandings. Finally, we may have formed some *strategy* of presentation, a strategy designed to explicate and, in some sense, convince. The problem we face can be stated: How can we get at these different concerns and still have a move which forms a single understanding in consciousness, the communal consciousness of a congregation. To complicate matters, we know we must work within limits—we must take time to understand, but not so much time that attention wanes. Let us look at a contrived example:

> We are sinners. "Sinners"—the word may sound old-fashioned, but it's true: We are all of us sinners. Oh, nowadays we avoid the term. We say we have "hang-ups," or perhaps we rattle off psychological words talking wisely of "depression," "anxiety," or a "guilt complex." But, again and again, we circle back to the old biblical word: We are sinners, all. Certainly, we can read about sin in daily papers. Big sins, murder or rape, are bold-type headlines. And, certainly, we notice sins in the lives of others. "She doesn't care about anyone else," we say, or "He's so vain." But when it comes to our own lives, how hard it is to see *our* sin. Maybe sin comes to us in a brief, flashing moment of regret when we say to ourselves, "I should go back and apologize," but then we don't and the moment is past. Or maybe, it's when at tax time we flip through our check stubs and think for an instant, "I should have given more away." Or perhaps, when we hear youngsters dream big dreams for their lives and we suddenly think, "Well, we've settled for less; we haven't been what we could have been." Then, we move away and try to forget. Listen, the world isn't divided into sinners and nonsinners: Down deep we know our lives are compromised. "We're supposed to love," says a detective-story hero. "But we all flunk," he says. Sinners—that's the biblical word, and we know it's true. We are, all of us, sinners.

The above move (written as a *single* paragraph) has an established unity: "We are all sinners." In part, the unity is established by the statement and restatement at the start and finish of the move. But the move is also made up of parts —we discuss our evasion of the word "sin," we notice sin in the world around us, and we get at a sense of sin in our own self-awareness. Thus, the move may be diagramed:

> *Statement* of Idea:
>   1. Contrapuntal: "Oh, nowadays we avoid . . ."
>   2. External Sin: "Certainly we can read . . ."
>   3. Internal Sin: "But when it comes to . . ."
> *Restatement* of Idea: "Listen, the world isn't . . ."

Remember, of course, that the move could have been designed in quite other ways with very different kinds of component parts. Almost any idea can be developed in countless ways. What does not change is a process of thinking through that underlies move construction. All human speaking involves movement; we speak of A and then B and then C and so forth. Public speaking requires the forming of separate moves, long enough to structure in consciousness but not so long as to strain attention. Thus, public speaking involves the designing of language in modules of meaning for group consciousness. The public speaking that is preaching demands that we think through moves so that theological understandings may relate to our common cultural consciousness and be true to lived experience. Preaching, like it or not, is a sophisticated form of public address. We do not merely speak, or convey information. We are forming the faith-consciousness of the church on behalf of Jesus Christ.

3.
Developing Moves

While preaching is not an art, it is artful. There is craft connected with the shaping of sermons. The odd idea that preachers whose hearts have been strangely warmed will spill out sermons, instantly compelling and exquisitely formed, is, of course, nonsense. Just as a carpenter must learn to use tools in order to make a box, so preachers must acquire basic skills to preach. Though some preachers may be unusually gifted, preachers are *not* born, they are *trained*. We learn our homiletic skills.

Designing moves is a skill we can learn. Every move in a sermon must be shaped, and each shaped differently. Though moves will be quite differently designed, there are *basic* skills which we can study. All moves have an opening "Statement" and some sort of "Closure." In between, moves have some kind of developmental pattern. So, we shall study the components of moves—openings, closings, and in between.

THE STATEMENT

Where do silences occur in speaking? Talks are made out of words and pauses; where do the pauses usually happen? Answer: pauses happen between moves. While there may be other pregnant pauses within a sermon, often for effect, generally when we shift from one developed subject to another, we pause. There is a silence almost as if we were pausing in the midst of a journey to catch our breath before we launch forth again. Studies indicate that, after a pause, audiences are alert; their attention level is high, they hear well. Such heightened attention will last for a few sentences after the pause before, gradually, attention will relax. Thus, wise speakers know that they have only a few sentences—perhaps three—in which to focus audience attention and to establish what it is they will be speaking. Therefore, the statement of a move

37

may not be delayed without good reason lest, unfocused, an audience hear but not hear. So, as a matter of craft, the first few sentences of a move are crucial and demand careful consideration.

Lately, an odd homiletic convention seems to have developed, namely, a preference for what might be described as "oblique" starts to moves, the indirect discourse of a cautious speaker. For example:

> There's an old-fashioned word. A word we are hesitant to use. You will still find the word in Bibles, or hymnbooks, or prayers we say in church. The word is almost forgotten in daily conversation. Yet, the word is crucial, the word "sin." The fact is, *we are all sinners.* . . .

In the example, we do not get to the nub of our conversation until five preliminary sentences have passed. By then, of course, attention has been relaxed. Apparently preachers suppose that oblique starts are kinder, or perhaps build suspense, or are easier for congregations to handle. Not so. Actually such starts are apt to irritate an audience. Moreover, the word "sin" enters the move in a subordinate clause which means it will enter consciousness peripherally. A congregation hearing the move will be forced to make an adjustment. The preacher began by speaking of "a word," leading the congregation to suppose some discussion of "the word" would follow. Instead, with the sixth sentence the preacher turns to focus on the subject of sin. Maybe a congregation will adjust, and maybe not. While, on occasion, a delayed start may be used to build up suspense, as a general practice the convention of the oblique start is devastating. We are given only a few sentences after a pause in which to focus consciousness and we must not waste the opportunity.

We must use *all* the sentences we are given. It will require at least three sentences, and often more, to establish initial focus in consciousness. Some older homiletic works mentioned "key sentences" and suggested that when moving into a subject matter, all that was needed was *one* clear, strong "topical sentence," after which developmental material—examples, illustrations, forms of argumentation—could occur. No, a single sentence carries little weight in group consciousness, particularly when followed by vivid developmental material. While we can switch subject matters rapidly in one-to-one conversation, with a gathered audience the process will require several sentences. In effect, a speaker is turning an audience from one focus to another, and such a turn must be made strongly. Thus, starts to moves that travel through a series of statements simply will not register in communal consciousness.

> We are all sinners. Nowadays the word isn't in style. We talk instead of psychological problems—phobias, complexes, neuroses. We aren't much into "sin." . . .

In the example there is only one "key sentence" before a contrapuntal theme is introduced. As a result, group consciousness will be confused at the outset; the move statement has not been firmly established before being countered. Probably, a congregation would simply go blank and have to catch up with the subject matter later in the move. We must realize that with group consciousness about three sentences will function with the strength of one in intimate conversation. In other words, at the start of a move when focus is crucial, we shall have to wield a block of sentences as if they were one.

> We are sinners. Sinners—the word may sound old-fashioned, but it's true. We are all of us sinners.

Preachers may feel unnatural using reiterative sentences to establish focus at the start of a move; the language will seem artificial and scarcely conversational in style. It must be remembered, though, that speaking to group consciousness is very different from one-to-one chats. If you watch an actor close at hand, gestures will seem too large and quite abnormal; but to an audience, the actor's movements will seem natural. By analogy, though a block of sentences at the start of a move will seem positively strained to a speaker, to a congregation the language may well register as a single sentence. Being natural is not the purpose of homiletics; serving our neighbors in the gospel is.

Actually, the block of sentences used to focus consciousness at the start of a move may have to be extended, if subsequent developmental material is unusually vivid. If, for example, we plan to follow the start with a highly visual illustration or with a strong contrapuntal, we will have to develop the start by exploring the subject matter more fully in order to fix focus before refocusing to any extent. When congregations drift off into wanderings of mind, it is *always* the fault of the speaker. Most often such drifting is caused by the weak starts of moves, by a failure to establish focus firmly. If we do not enter a move with strength, the entire move may fail to form in consciousness and may simply delete from the overall structure of a sermon. Human consciousness is like a camera lens. At the starts of moves, we who speak are turning the "lens" of congregational consciousness in a particular direction and establishing focus. Therefore, the opening statement of a move is all-important.

The first few sentences of a move are exceedingly difficult to prepare. For not only do the first sentences establish focus, they must accomplish a number of other things. In addition to focus, the statement of a move must show *connective logic,* the logic by which one move follows another; it must indicate the *perspective* (or "point-of-view") of the move, and it must set the "mood" of the move. Suppose, for example, that in a sermon we have two moves in sequence, one which celebrates human virtue—how neat and nice and smart we human beings can be—followed by another which admits our sin. Imagine what the conjunction of moves might be:

> . . . So we are not unkind, are we? All in all, we are decent human beings.

> Well, time to "fess up." Time to get down on our knees and admit we are sinners. "Sinners," the word is full of anguish. We are sinners all. . . .

In the example above, we see the ending of one move and the start of another. The logic of connection is dialectical—statement and counterstatement. The perspective is a down-on-our-knees confessional self-understanding, and the mood is one of reluctant anguish. So the start of a move is more than focus, although focus is absolutely crucial. The statement of a move must do many things and, therefore, requires special attention from preachers. In a very few carefully designed sentences, we must *focus* congregational consciousness, establish *logic, mood,* and *perspective.* Unless each move, at the outset, structures in consciousness, a sermon will not mean!

MOVE DEVELOPMENT

A Basic Rhetoric of Moves

Between the opening statement of a move and its closure, some idea is developed. The problem for preachers is deciding *how* to develop material. A preacher must determine what material is to be used and how the material is to be arranged. Once upon a time, ministers were trained in rhetoric. Therefore, they had at hand different rhetorical logics, strategies, tropes, and so forth. While rhetorical training could lead to insubstantial ornamentation or verbal pyrotechnics, for the most part rhetorical wisdom assisted preaching. After all, rhetoric is an ancient wisdom that undergirds all human conversation. Thus, older works on homiletics could assume rhetorical training and concentrate on matters specific to preaching. We cannot. What we can do is offer some general comments about rhetoric before providing examples of move development.

Often homiletics is based on some sort of understanding of congregation. What exactly is a "congregation"? If we assume that a congregation is made up of believers, people who share common faith, then we will tend to view preaching as an explication of common faith—faith seeking understanding. On the other hand, if congregations are regarded as representatives of the world-age, preaching may be understood as conversion and forms of development as persuasion or even argumentation—switching people from unfaith to faith. The trouble is that neither of these paradigms is appropriate and, therefore, neither gets at the true quality of homiletic language. Every congregation must be regarded as being-saved in the world; thus congregations have a peculiar double consciousness.

On a Sunday morning congregations are constituted in liturgy as "people of God" and, in fact, within the symbolic structures of liturgy understand themselves as so constituted. At the same time, we know we are "in the world" and share worldly ways of understanding. Thus, because we are "*in* but not *of* the world," preaching will have to speak to a double consciousness. Theological reality is primary, thus preaching will be explication, a "bringing into view" of our common faith. At the same time, because awareness of being-saved involves a distinguishing of Christian faith from understandings of the world-age in which we live, the language of preaching will wrestle with ideas, assumptions, social attitudes which we bring to church. If preaching does involve conversion, it is the constant conversion of Christian formation. In a worldly language, preaching shapes the faith-consciousness of the church.

In view of the peculiar character of congregations, we must try to describe a basic Christian rhetoric. Christian preaching involves a "*bringing out*" or a "bringing into view" of convictional understandings—understandings of God, of God's mysterious purposes, and of unseen wonders of grace in human lives. Christians understand God *through* symbols of revelation, therefore, Christian rhetoric "brings out" by exploring symbols. Most of the time, we live with day-to-day immediacies in consciousness, and with convictions (matters of faith) in the background. Thus, by exploring symbols, preaching will be bringing into view our often unspoken faith. Likewise, preaching will be bringing out the reality of our being-saved, which is often mediated through ritual symbols—praise, Baptism, Eucharist. "Bringing out and into view" will be accomplished by many different rhetorical means—depiction, analogy, metaphor, explanation, analysis, and credal explorations.

Thus we have deliberately bypassed the rationalistic definitions of preaching found in didactic homiletics. Preachers do not explicate teachings; they explore symbols. Faith does have content, but not a content that can be spelled out in propositional statements for instruction. So, Christian rhetoric involves a bringing out through language.

Christian rhetoric also *associates.* In preaching, we put together Christian understandings with images of lived experience. In so doing, preaching demonstrates that our Christian convictions are true to life. Preaching does not trade in formal proofs or argued syllogisms. If, in sermons, we turn to rational proofs, we will elevate reason to a position of ultimacy instead of faith-consciousness. Moreover, though rational proofs may well have a proper role in arbitrating some kinds of "truth," they cannot displace faith's appeal to lived truth. Thus, Christian preaching does not dabble in pragmatic justifications or argued tautologies; it merely interfaces Christian understandings with depictions of lived experience. In particular, preaching brings together the gospel and portrayals of being-saved new life in the world. The rhetoric of association is a language of imagery, illustration, example, testimony, and the like. In congregational consciousness, we bring out Christian meanings and associate them with fields of lived experience. In so doing, the truth of the gospel will be evident.

Of course, Christian preaching will also *disassociate.* We are being-saved-in-the-world and, therefore, possess a peculiar double consciousness—a consciousness of being-saved and a consciousness of being-in-the-world. Being-saved is aware of itself, not only in relation to Christian symbols, but as it experiences tension with worldly styles, strategies, and modes of thinking. Thus, again and again, preaching will distinguish Christian understandings from our common social attitudes—the "isms," "ologies," popular slogans, and tacit assumptions which may be fashionable. Likewise, preaching will demark Christian life styles from the conventional ethos of human communities; presumably, the ways and means of Christian love will be different. For example, if the gospel anticipates reconciled "peace on earth," it is bound to disassociate itself from forms of jingoism and superpatriotic nonsense. Preaching will speak tenderly, but, nonetheless, critically of being-in-the-world. Preaching will discriminate. Disassociation employs familiar rhetorical systems, such as dialectic, antithesis, opposition, and, at times, perhaps even a charitable giggling.

Basic Christian rhetoric, then, involves "bringing out," "associating," and "disassociating." Moves in a sermon will develop from these basic rhetorical intentions. For example, in the sample move "We are all sinners" (see p. 35), all three intentions are present: an understanding of human nature under sin, a disassociation of sin from popular psychological orientations, and an association of sin with images of social and personal lived experience. Of course, the move, following the same structural pattern, could have drawn on different types of material—quoting a particular psychiatrist, or using an illustration of someone's self-discovery of sin, or citing statistics of crime. Though types of evidence could change, the basic rhetorical intentions would still be present —bringing out, associating, and disassociating. Moves will always contain one or more of these forms of basic rhetoric.

In addition to basic rhetorical intentions, we can isolate different languages, related to particular modes of consciousness. These languages may be labeled *temporal, spatial, social,* and *personal.* As we develop moves, we can think historically, calling on memory, or we can survey the world in which we live; we can turn in on ourselves to chase down motives, fantasies, and impulses, or we can express types of social awareness. For example, if we are attempting to probe the nature of sin, we could scan pages of history, tracing human lovelessness since time began. On the other hand, we could study the world in which we live for evidence of sin, a world of wars and grinding depriva- tions. We could explore our own psyches, tracking down our split motives and our chronic self-interests. Or, we could examine our shared social preju- dices, our strident nationalisms, and the like. Human experience is appro- priated temporally (diachronic thinking), spatially (synchronic thinking), so- cially (corporate consciousness), and personally (self-awareness). Each of these orientations will produce a different language.

Books on preaching will often list different things to do when developing ideas—examples, illustrations, descriptions, explanations, appeals to author- ity, analogies, confessions, proofs, and so on. Instead, we are suggesting that all these different rhetorical strategies may be catalogued according to basic intentions—bringing out, associating, disassociating—within which there may be different orientations: spatial, temporal, personal, and social. We turn now to see how to develop moves in actual practice.

Move Designs

Between an opening statement and closure, a move is developed. Beginning with a simple sentence (e.g., "God is a mystery" or "We are all sinners"), preachers will think through theological meanings, cultural and religious oppositions, forms of lived experience, as well as optional strategies. From such initial thinking through, ideas of development will come. Modes of development will be chosen rhetorically, however, not only to fit congrega- tional consciousness, but to relate to other moves within a sermon scenario. In order to describe the process of move development, imagine that we must develop a simple sentence, "Most Christians nowadays have grown up in a church." Even with what may appear to be a self-evident statement, we will still think through the move.

There are theological issues involved in the statement, "Most Christians nowadays have grown up in a church." Obviously, the notion of church is broader than some local steeple. Rightly, church is holy, catholic, and apos- tolic. Moreover, there are issues such as church "visible" and "invisible" to reckon with. In thinking over the statement we may be dismayed. From an evangelical standpoint, the statement may bear witness to the church's failure to reach out into the world with the word of the gospel. We may sense that theologically the statement could be positive or negative: a church built on childhood familiarity might be nothing more than Kierkegaard's "Sunday Twaddle," or perhaps the statement is positive in that the grip of the gospel does shape human self-understanding so that human beings stay in community by faith. Even with what appears to be a self-evident statement, there are theological dimensions to be considered.

An analysis of actual lived experience can involve many different kinds of study. We may read up on statistical research to support the claim, and in doing so, discover that, though most Christians have grown up in church, they church-hop; they shop for churches as they shop for hamburgers in fast-food stores. We may also discover that, statistically, American Christian communities overall may well be dwindling as compared with African communities which are enlarging rapidly. Phenomenal analysis may plunge us into looking at the membership of some actual congregation, or into recall— a remembering of how it was to grow up in a church, from Sunday-morning church-pew wiggling, to Sunday-school chaos, to hymn sings in the evening, to the sweet disarray of family-night suppers.

Are there oppositions? Perhaps. The statement may be appalling to an anti-institutional Christianity. Or, the statement may simply seem to endorse a middle-class-value Christianity of a fairly thoughtless variety. In addition to reactions, the statement itself may not seem true when we view Asian, European, and African Christianity.

In thinking through this simple statement, we engage in the process of gathering all kinds of ideas, images, statistics, and theological questions. Probably, we will also read articles, look at books on the church, perhaps study surveys of church growth and the like. From a simple one-sentence statement we have gathered an astonishing amount of material that somehow must be shaped by *selection* and *organization* into a coherent move.

In preaching to a congregation in which virtually everyone present has in fact grown up in church, development of the statement will be relatively easy. All we will have to do is to put the statement together with congregational lived experience. Because the phrase "grown up" seems to imply memory, the mode of development will probably involve personal recall. For example:

> *Statement A:* Most Christians nowadays have grown up in church. Though some of us here may have been born in other cities, we share a common church background. We can hardly remember when we were not in church. Once little children, now grown adults, we've lived our lives within the church.

> *Development A:* Think back through the years. You won't recall your first day in church, the day when as a baby you were baptized—perhaps right here. But

you do remember being a kid in church. Remember wiggling during sermons, or children's day pageants, or did you run around playing tag in the fellowship hall? Think back and recall your church-school teachers. Think of the stories you were told of Moses, and Paul, and above all stories of Jesus. Later, when you were older, do you remember how proud your parents were when, finally, you stood up in church and said, "I believe," and were counted as an adult member? We do share common memories, don't we?

Closure A: We were baptized, we were instructed, we worshiped. We are church people. Most people nowadays have grown up in faith.

The system we have constructed as an example can be described as a simple system. Within the framework of the move, there is only *one* developmental system organized as a *personal, temporal* memory. Actually, such simple systems will seldom be used because congregations are rarely so unified or traditional in character, and theological understandings are normally much more complex.

Suppose, for example, that we are speaking to exactly the same congregation, but have decided that for theological reasons, we should not praise homogeneity or elevate local customs. We might wish to design a more complex move.

Statement A: Most Christians nowadays have grown up in church. Though some of us here may have been born in other cities, we share a common church background. We can hardly remember when we weren't in church.

Contrapuntal B: Of course, perhaps, we shouldn't be proud. Maybe churches in Africa which are drawing a hundred thousand converts a day are healthy. Perhaps they are more exciting than we are, and much more like the first-century Christians.

Development of Statement A: But, we are what we are. Most of us here have grown up in the church. Think back through the years. . . . etc.

Closure for Statement A: We were baptized, we were instructed, . . . etc.

In the example, we have added to the simple structure a preliminary contrapuntal section looking at Third World Christian communities and suggesting that they may be healthier than American Christian churches. Notice that in the move there are two different systems, one disassociative (B) and one associative (A), one a spatial survey of a social phenomenon and the other a personal-temporal development.

But imagine that instead of speaking to a home-grown, homogeneous congregation, we are addressing a mission church that mostly draws non-Christians into faith. Obviously, if we intend to make the same statement, "Most

Christians nowadays have grown up in church," we will have to devise a more complex system in which to develop the idea. Imagine what kind of a move we might shape:

> *Statement A:* Surprise! Know it or not, most Christians in America have grown up in church. They were born in the church, baptized as babies, and brought up in church year after year. They are old-time Christians.

> *Contrapuntal B:* How hard it is for us to imagine. Most of us stumbled newborn into our Christian faith. Here in church we learned ways of worship, heard the gospel, said our prayers for the first time. And, we're excited about our newfound faith.

> *Development C:* In a way, we're like the first Christians back in the days of the apostles. For we have been drawn out of the world into faith. To us, as to the very first Christians the gospel is new, a new good news for our lives.

> *Development of Statement A:* But look around the U.S.A., most churches were built years ago in little frontier villages. They have housed generations of Christians—founders, and children, and children's children. So most people can say truthfully, "I don't even remember when I wasn't a Christian!" Most people in churches were born to church families. They were baptized as infants, attended church school—all their lives they've lived in church.

> *Closure for Statement A:* Look, though it may be hard for us to imagine, don't forget most Christians in America are not newborn believers. Most Christians around us have grown up in the church.

The move still begins with the same sentence, "Most Christians in America have grown up in church." Even though the statement is untrue to the audience, we must still commence with the statement which we are going to establish, and with which we will close. If we were to start with the experience of our audience and then turn to look at the national norm, the move would split into two moves, each too brief to form in consciousness. No matter what the character of the congregation, the statement we intend must initiate the move. The point-of-view with which the move begins is quite different, however—"Surprise! Know it or not, . . ."

The move itself is a three-part system. After the initial statement of the move, there is a semi-contrapuntal section that recognizes the different character of the congregation—"Most of *us* stumbled newborn into Christian faith." Such a contrapuntal will be necessary simply because congregational experience casts doubt on the original statement. The first section is, however, followed by a happy identification with early Christian communities, so the audience will not feel odd or out-of-step by not being like most American churchgoers. Finally, the original statement is developed but as a spatial survey, a looking-at rather than as a personal memory. The statement is then reiterated in closure. The move is not a single development, or even a two-part system, but contains three developments: (B) We are new to faith. (C) Thus, we are like the earliest Christians. (A) But most Americans have grown up in the church.

As a rule, moves may contain *no more than three* internal developmental systems. Recent studies confirm the rule, for when humans must juggle more than three subordinate systems, consciousness tends to "freak out." Were we to add still another component part to our previous example, such as a fourth section beginning "And, do you know, most Americans are proud of their longtime Christian background. They say . . . ," then one of two results would occur; either the congregation would become restless and their minds wander, or retaining the last component, they would lose track of previous content. Though we have attempted to beat the rule in many different ways, research seems to indicate that we cannot, and that a congregation will not tolerate more than three internal developmental shifts within a single move. We can, of course, reprise previously developed ideas before closure, although such a practice has dangers, but we cannot build four or more components within a move without having a congregation reject material. The "rule of three" stands: moves may be single systems, or two-part systems, or may contain three developmental shifts, but they may not exceed three internal parts.

Contrapuntals

Because there may be oppositions or exceptions to ideas we are presenting, we have suggested that contrapuntal systems may be necessary. And, because we preach between the ages, we suppose such systems may be more necessary now than in previous eras. Contrapuntal parts to moves, however, must be handled with care. Obviously, if a contrapuntal becomes too strong we will end up with a move that splits consciousness, that preaches in two directions at the same time. After all, the move *statement* is what we are attempting to establish, not its opposition. Thus, we will keep contrapuntals under control. A contrapuntal may never exceed the time given to a development of the statement, may not have brighter imagery, or be illustrated. Basically, contrapuntal systems "let off steam" within a move and do not become major blocks of content. If a contrapuntal is crucial because oppositions are very strong, a separate contrapuntal *move* may be required. Normally, however, a contrapuntal acknowledges, but does not reinforce, an opposition. Therefore, it will occur within a move either shortly after the fixing of an initial statement or immediately prior to a strong reiterative closure. While many preachers may wish to exercise their own skepticisms, or to display their own

modern doubts, contrapuntal sections acknowledge but do not preach oppositions. They must therefore be handled with restraint.

Variety

In general, every move within a sermon scenario ought to be shaped
differently. Often we will hear a speaker who, though using vivid language
and glittering imagery, is strangely tedious. Usually the cause of our boredom
is a similarity in developmental systems—many of the ideas being presented
come to us in the same rhetorical shape. So, unless a speaker is skilled enough
to shape deliberately two different ideas in the same way so that they will
overlap in consciousness, the general rule will be *different development for
different ideas.*

Though the rule of different shapes for different moves may seem to place
a heavy burden on imagination, it does not. In the process of thinking through
a move, we will have stumbled on all sorts of material. Think of what we may
have gathered in brooding over the simple statement, "Most American Christians have grown up in the church":

> *Material about the Subject*
> Statistical studies of church membership
> Biographies of American church people
> Chapters on social sources of denominationalism
> Studies on "faith formation"
> Quotes by writers on the subject
>
> *Contrapuntal Problems*
> Third World church studies and descriptions
> Writers, e.g., Kierkegaard, who complain of "Christendom" model
> Comparison with evangelicalist groups
> Antipathy to "institutional" Christianity
>
> *Phenomenal Lived Experience*
> "Faith-journey" biographical material
> Material from fiction
> Personal recall of childhood experiences
> Images of infants baptized
> Depictions of current church life
> Illustrations
> Quotes
>
> *Theological Concerns*
> Erosion of the "evangelical" spirit
> Problem of "infant" vs. "believer" Baptism
> Problem of "visible" vs. "invisible" church
> Worldwide church-unity problems
> Definitions of "church"

This representative list could supply enough varied material for a dozen moves. Of course, a preacher will select material not only on the basis of *how* to present an idea to a particular audience, but on the basis of material in *other moves*. Moves in a whole sermon scenario must display variety, with strength designed where strength is needed. No move may be formed in isolation from other moves that will comprise a sermon. *When preachers complain that they do not have enough material on hand for the shaping of a move, it is usually an indication that the thinking-through process has not been adequately done.* Normally, the problem for preachers (that is, for *thoughtful* preachers) is the problem of reduction and selection.

Variety in development may also be ensured by keeping an eye on the kinds of rhetorical intentions involved—bringing out, associating, disassociating— as well as modes of developmental language: temporal, spatial, personal, social. Thus, for example, if many moves in a sermon feature appeals to personal recall, the sermon will inevitably be tedious no matter how interesting the content of personal memory may be. Likewise, if every move begins by making a statement and then follows with a disassociating contrapuntal system, boredom is bound to occur. Probably the most common form of repetitive development is caused by ministers who compulsively put an illustration in every move, so that moves, though different in content, sound the same because they all feature statement-illustration-closure. A mobile sequence of moves in a sermon will call for fewer illustrations, however, because a moving system will be intrinsically more exciting than types of categorical or deductive organization.

Unity

Above all, moves must be unified: They must make a single statement. Basically moves are an elaboration of an idea that can be expressed in a single clear sentence, e.g., "We are all sinners," "God is a mystery," "Most American Christians have grown up in church." A test of unity is to read a move and be sure that it can be summed up in a simple (noncompound) clear sentence. If, on rereading a move, you discover you are forced to summarize in a complex clausal sentence, the move may be pulling apart in consciousness. Still another test is to examine the opening statement and the closure to see if they are unified; if they do not match thematically, you may have constructed a split move or at least a traveling move.

What causes moves to fragment in consciousness? The causes are usually either an *alteration in focus* or a *traveling idea*. For example, it will be exceedingly difficult to hold a move together if it splits focus between a past-tense look at scripture and a present-tense viewing of our world. The same sort of split may occur if a contrapuntal system grows too large so that the move ends up with two developed ideas in dialectical tension. In both cases, a preacher may have to frame two moves. When a move splits in consciousness, the result is that we are speaking two *brief* moves, neither of which will be strong enough or long enough to form in consciousness. Thus, the whole split move may not register at all, causing a congregational lapse—a wandering of mind. With a traveling idea, the statement and closure of the move will often be quite different; the preacher has produced a sequence of ideas moving from idea A to idea C. For example, suppose we have designed a move with the following component parts:

> *Statement A:* Most Americans have grown up in church.
> *Development B:* How different from Third World churches.
> *Development C:* So perhaps we had better turn to evangelizing again.

It is almost impossible to return to our original statement—the move has traveled. The effect of such a construction is that a congregation will hear three different short ideas, none of which is developed sufficiently to form in consciousness. The rapidity of the movement of thought will almost certainly produce a blank in congregational understanding. The move has fragmented.

Preachers may discover that if they write out a sermon manuscript, it will be helpful to paragraph according to *move*. If we paragraph each section of a move's internal development, we will probably end up with a move that tends to fall apart. First sentences of paragraphs tend to be syntactically different; they break the flow of a forming idea. A sermon manuscript is above all a script for oral delivery, not an essay to be read. Therefore, rules drummed into us by grade-school grammarians do not apply. Each move in an oral sermon forms a single understanding, imaged and explored in consciousness. Though a move may take between three and four minutes to deliver, it must form as a *single* understanding in communal consciousness. Therefore, attention to unity is crucial.

CLOSURE

Every move *must have closure.* By returning to an initial statement in some manner at the close of a move, we ensure that a single understanding will form in congregational consciousness. If strong opening statements to moves are essential, so also are firm closures. When, suddenly, in the midst of a sermon, a congregation drifts off into inattention and restlessness, it is often caused by failure to close a move before initiating a new move. Let us suppose that we have two moves in sequence, one saying, "Most Christians have grown up in church," and another beginning, "How different were the first Christians." Compare the following (see pp. 44–45):

Example A:

. . . Later, when you were older, do you remember how proud your parents were when, finally, you stood up in church and said, "I believe," and were counted as an adult member?

How different were the first Christians. . . .

Example B:

. . . Later, when you were older, do you remember how proud your parents were when, finally, you stood up in church and said, "I believe," and were counted as an adult member? We do share common memories, don't we? We were baptized, we were instructed, we worshiped. We are church people. Most people, nowadays, have grown up in faith.

How different were the first Christians. . . .

In example A, there is no closure. As a result, we are still involved in remembering when a shift in focus is attempted. Congregational consciousness will be thrown into confusion and may or may not catch up with a new idea—"How different were the first Christians"—when it is presented. In example B, however, a closure has been made so that the shift to a new idea can be managed easily. As a rule, some sort of closure must be designed for every move.

Forming closure will always involve a return to the *idea* of the statement with which the move began. On occasion, the return may be accomplished by use of exactly the same sentence with which the move began. Of course, if every move in a sermon begins and ends with a similar sentence, the repetitious device may become intolerable. So, though some moves may well begin and conclude with the same sentence, others will end differently, but *always* with a return to the initiating *idea* of the move. What we may not do is to end with a different, new idea, or to end with what is a developmental part of a move. The originating statement of a move must be echoed in some fashion at the conclusion. Closure is *crucial*.

In general, the last sentence of a move ought to be simple; it should be a terse, final sentence. Compound sentences will not close. Sentences with many clauses will invariably sound as if an idea is being developed rather than stopped. For the same reason, sentences that conclude with a participle, implying a continuing action, will not work. The last sentence of a move should be a strong simple sentence, and preferably a sentence with a strong definite noun rather than sentences that begin with "It" or "This."

Sometimes the rhythmic character of a sentence will help us to achieve closure. For example, repetition in the following sentences will contribute to a sense of finality:

"Sinners—we are all of us sinners."

"We are all, all sinners."

Sometimes an entire sentence can be repeated, but only if there is some slight variation so that the first sentence in the couplet is a beat longer, as in

"We are all of us sinners. We are sinners."

A useful device is to conclude with contrasting sentences in which the first sentence is clausal and the second terse:

. . . We were baptized, we were instructed, we are long-term church people. Most of us have grown up in faith.

Rhythmic systems that work with the sounds of words can assist in closing. Like a manyfold "Amen" they can create closure with a strong sense of finality.

Some special problems ought to be mentioned. Often a move will begin with a question. Moves may never end with a question, however, because interrogative sentences "upturn" in sound, as well as imply that some sort of answer may follow. The same problem will exist with a quotation. Though it is seldom wise to begin a move with a quotation, occasionally it may be necessary. But moves may not end with a quotation because quotes tend to presume that something more will be added. The solution is to echo the quote or question as a *next-to-last* sentence. For example, suppose we have begun a move as follows:

What do we see in church? We see long-time Christians. Most of us have grown up in the church. . . .

With a question at the start, the move will have to end with a reversal of sequence, such as:

. . . What do we see in church? People who have grown up in faith.

In all the examples we have reviewed, the final sentence is brief, strong, and usually features a concrete noun.

The matter of closure is more important than we know. Moves must start strongly and end with equal strength; they must "round out" and conclude. Preachers should realize that they are in charge of focus. With language they focus congregational consciousness on some field of meaning. With closure they frame a field of meaning in consciousness so as to be able to shift focus in a different direction. Ideally, a sermon should involve a series of formed, framed ideas that move through congregational consciousness as *their* own thoughts, each module of language a designed "thought." Even quite impressionistic sermons must still be designed as a series of defined moves. While ministers may rankle—sharply defined starts and finishes will seem quite unnatural or possibly artificial—we are serving a people, not our own comfort in speaking. Fuzzy starts and finishes will produce an odd effect in the consciousness of a congregation. People will catch only occasional glimpses of meaning amid a flow of murky verbiage. They will fight to hold attention against involuntary wanderings of mind. Moves must begin and conclude with all-but-overstated strength. Internally, they must be developed with care, each differently, so as to form as natural understandings in communal consciousness.

4.
Point-of-View
in Moves

————————————————— We are now moving out of an age in which rational objectivity was the order of the day in pulpit discourse. Yet, in sermons, most preachers are third-person observers; they talk *about*. Preachers talk about the Bible page as if it were an object to be analyzed. They talk about grace as if it were some thing lying around to be looked at. Even when they represent their own religious attitudes, they objectify themselves and then discuss. But, rather clearly, twentieth-century consciousness has changed. Reality for modern men and women is much more than a world "out there"—consciousness is perspectival.

To seize an analogy, think of film making. In an earlier era, movie directors worked with a fixed-location camera and moved actors around in front of the lens. Once upon a time the procedure was considered reality, but now, when we view old films on late-night TV, they seem stilted and quite unreal. Today, directors use a camera on a moving boom so that camera angles change, lenses widen or narrow down, distances vary, imitating the way in which we actually perceive reality. Moreover, directors match the complexity of human consciousness by filming daydreams, memories, apprehensions, and the like. Thus, with different lenses and shifting camera angles, film makers give us an awesome sense of the real. While modern cinematography may have influenced our modes of perception, more likely it has followed from alterations in human consciousness. We may perceive the world quite differently today than did our grandparents. Human consciousness is not a fixity, ever the same; it alters, age to age. If eighteenth-century people regarded the world as objectively "there" before their third-person consciousness, we do not. Twentieth-century consciousness views the world from many different standpoints.

Language relates to perception. Thus, when perceptual consciousness changes, so will syntax and vocabulary. Today, we speak from varied perceptual angles, from different stances, attitudes, perspectives. Preaching that talks objectively about everything, as if from a third-person observational position, will not only seem archaic but may have an aura of unreality. The language of preaching must be perspectival to fit into congregational consciousness in a natural way. Actually, we can see the use of a perspectival language in contemporary fiction. Victorian novels like *Vanity Fair* told a story from a third-person-narrative point-of-view; they looked at life and described characters with a nailed-down, fixed-position "camera eye." In contrast, modern novels dance around in many perspectives; they may tell a story from different times and places, from different memories, using flashbacks, interior monologues, and goodness knows what else, as they imitate the peculiar simultaneous quality of human experience. The grave difficulty with a third-person observational language in preaching is that it usurps God's position and, in so doing, turns God into an "object," and God's Word into a rational truth.

With preachers, unfortunately, the third-person observational style has become a pulpit convention; we do not know how else to speak. The tip-off in many sermons is the number of objectifying phrases that are spoken: "We see that . . . ," "Let us look at . . . ," "In our text we note that . . . ," etc. In ordinary conversation we are not so pedantic. In conversation, our language is freely perspectival.

In arguing for a controlled but variable point-of-view in speaking, we are not rejecting objectivity in favor of a language of subjectivity. Pietist preaching that fills pulpits with rehearsals of feeling and odd discussions of inwardness is a theological disaster. By contrast, pulpit language must relate to a new twentieth-century consciousness that is simultaneous, perspectival, and complex. When language imitates consciousness, it can match the ways in which we actually experience life and, thus, form quite naturally in a congregational mind.

Can we get at the notion of point-of-view in speaking? Let us approach the subject with care. Oddly enough, point-of-view *devices* have been used by preachers for centuries, though seldom recognized or defined by homiletic studies. Have we not heard preachers begin some section of a sermon by saying, "Now, some of you may be thinking . . . ," and then go on to express a particular "mind," objection, or perspective? Again, preachers may represent some social attitude, as when they say, "What does the atheist believe? The atheist says. . . ." In each of these familiar gambits, preachers speak *as if* they were standing in someone else's perspective; in effect, they play a role. Likewise, preachers signal different angles of vision, e.g., "Look back through the years to little Palestine . . . ," or "Imagine how we must appear to a space traveler—specks of dust crawling on a whirling ball of earth!" Perspectives in time and space, even attitudinal perspectives, can be established and, once established, will govern style. So, initially, let us note that for centuries preachers have given voice to different perspectives; they have used point-of-view as an *occasional* rhetorical device. We find such examples in the sermons of church fathers and even in scripture.

The fallacy in our homiletic thinking has been to suppose that point-of-view is only an occasional device, a rhetorical gambit used to relieve what is otherwise third-person-objective discourse. Instead, we must understand that point-of-view is *always* in language and, therefore, must be integral to sermon design and development. We are perspectival creatures; our consciousness is oriented in time and space and aims at reality. Thus, all our speaking, whenever and wherever, will express some point-of-view. *Point-of-view determines style.* So, we must be aware of types of point-of-view and of the homiletic ground rules that govern the use of point-of-view.

CATEGORIES OF POINT-OF-VIEW

Point-of-view can best be analyzed by drawing a perceptual analogy. Study categories in the diagram.

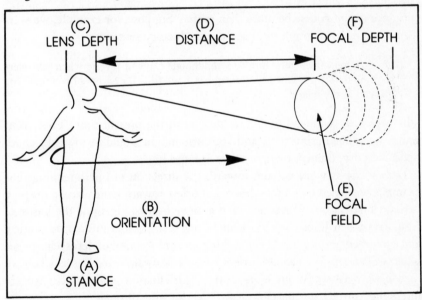

We face a number of strange terms: Stance (A), Orientation (B), Lens Depth (C), Distance (D), Focal Field (E), and Focal Depth (F). Though the terms may seem intimidating, and to have nothing to do with preaching, they govern the style of our speaking and, as we speak, they shape congregational consciousness. All speaking involves point-of-view. So, let us unpack terminology and study some examples.

Stance, Orientation, and Distance

What do we mean by *stance?* We mean the time-space from which a speaker speaks. For example,

> From the corner of an eye, glance the gnarled trunk, its layered bark, black and brown and mossy green; then, turn to look for distant light through the crisscross of pine needles. Somewhere beyond your sight, you know the branches come to a height, a point in space which some distant viewer could mark on an aerial photograph.

In reading the words, you locate yourself lying on your back beneath a pine tree. First, you glance sideways to the nearby tree trunk, then, turning, you look up through the woven pine branches toward the sky. Then, in consciousness, you think of someone else looking down from a distant position to notice the treetop and to mark its position. The stance from which you speak is lying on your back under a tree. Though your orientation in consciousness may change, your stance is fixed.

Stance can of course be more than spatial. Suppose, for example, we were to preface this paragraph with some introductory sentences:

> Do you remember your little-kid childhood? Days of reverie when you were learning to look at the world. Remember, how, from the corner of your eye, you glanced at the gnarled trunk. . . .

The prefatory sentences would locate you in the present time. Thus, your stance would be in time *now,* and your orientation would be toward a childhood memory. Stance, then, is *where* we speak.

Orientation is what we aim toward, the direction of our intending. For example, we may stand in the present but orient toward some place in the past, perhaps first-century Palestine. Or if a move begins, "Imagine the bustle of Jerusalem when Jesus entered the city," we would stand in the first century and our orientation would be a looking around the city of Jerusalem to see what we can see. We can also orient ourselves toward ourselves as when we turn inward to study our own motives. Orientation is *aim:* what we are intending toward in consciousness. We can aim through time and space toward all kinds of objects. We can also aim into our own depth, or, by conjecture, into the depth of others. We can even aim toward ideas that may be floating around in our cultural atmosphere. Orientation is simply the *direction* of our aimed consciousness.

Distance is a peculiar category that is spatial, temporal, and perhaps even emotional. Distance is actually measured in consciousness. We can speak of a starving African child as if the child were a figure on a television screen across the room, or we can describe the child as if we were cradling her in our own arms. The alternatives will each produce a quite different language. We can describe past events as if they are separated by centuries, or as immediate impressions imagined in mind. Temporal distance is a complex variable. There is also a kind of emotional distance that is created in many ways. If, for example, we use an illustration of someone's experience of God, we will bespeak a secondhand awareness of God, distanced by being someone else's reported experience. Again, for example, we can describe a scene as a series of surface impressions without any emotional involvement —a distance of alienation. With distance, the trick is to remember that distance is measured *in consciousness*. Distance is visual or temporal, attitudinal or emotional.

Focal Field, Lens Depth, and Focal Depth

Focal field can best be understood by imagining a camera lens which, widened, can take in a large scene, or, narrowed down, will pick out particular objects. So, if a move within a sermon begins "Take a look at our world . . . ," we are working with a wide lens indeed. Whereas, if we start a move by saying "Look at American policy in Central America . . . ," (an unsavory prospect!), or "See how prejudice shows up in everyday speech . . . ," these sentences would narrow focus in different ways. Focal field is not merely spatial; obviously it can be temporal—"Take a long look at human history . . . ," or "Did you see yesterday's headlines?" or "Remember your painful high-school years?" Language may even imitate alterations in the lens of a mind's eye, as, for example, when we begin a move by surveying different kinds of human behavior, and then we narrow down to discuss essential human nature. Such an alteration in focal field will show up in a changing syntax and style.

Lens depth is somewhat more difficult to describe. What we mean by lens depth is the degree of self-engagement involved in point-of-view. For example, we can look at life by merely describing the external images that play on consciousness; or, more deeply, we can look at life interpreted in some meaningful way; or we can look at life and, at the same time, express our feelings, attitudes, and "gut-level" reactions. How much of the self is engaged in a point-of-view? Compare the following brief paragraphs:

1. See the children. They reach skeletal arms for bread. Their eyes are flat, and their bellies puffed with hunger. Look, you can count their ribs.

2. Look, exhibit A, at our human lovelessness. We do not care. There are children standing at the edge of our lives, reaching bony arms for bread. They stand staring at us with big black eyes, their empty bellies bloated; staring at our unconcern, the silent watchers of our guilt.

3. O God, we feel utterly helpless. There are so many, many mouths to fill with food. You see the skeletal kids of the world reaching for bread, reaching toward us, and you choke back your outrage. Should children have to die, uncounted millions of wide-eyed children? O God, help us to be moved, help us to share, somehow.

In each of the examples, a different level of the self is expressed along with the images being depicted. In the first example, there was an immediacy of image, but little self-engagement; in the second example, a somewhat preachy intellectual grasp of imagery shaped the language; in the third example, a kind of desperate anger was expressed as a response to imagery. Lens depth is an inadequate term, but we are referring to self-involvement that reaches different depths in consciousness.

Just as there are depths of involvement, so also there are depths of perception—*focal depth*. We can speak as if we are merely recording the surface impressions of things, or we can probe more deeply into what we observe. If we are looking at other people, we can reach into their thoughts, their feelings, and even try to represent the impressions that may crowd their minds. By focal depth, we refer to how far we may be seeing *into* things and people. Compare the following paragraphs:

1. Is there anything more magic than the faith of children? You see them grave-eyed, sitting in church, as if slightly dazed by some cloudy, unseen mystery of God. You wonder what they are thinking, when, suddenly still, they seem to stare into their own thoughts.

2. There's something mysterious about the faith of children. You see them looking around themselves with big eyes as if searching for someone, perhaps searching for God. "Does God see me?"; "Is God all around at night in my room?"; "Is the empty church with the dusty light full of the spookiness of God?" No wonder children will shout/sing their little creeds: "Jesus loves me, this I know . . ."

The two paragraphs are quite different. In one, we gaze at children as alien mysteries, unable to enter their thoughts. In the second example, we have a complex language combining observation, a conjecture of a child's thoughts, and speculation as to why children may sing a song to ward off eerie awe.

In the second example, we have moved more deeply into the mind of a child; we are no longer merely observing. Focal depth refers to the degree of penetration into what we are observing.

Attitudinal Perspective

Perspective is much more than angles of perception. Point-of-view can be *attitudinal*. We are seldom dispassionate people. While we can reduce our inner involvement by deliberately speaking from scientific objectivity, such detachment is scarcely the language of preaching. Most human talking involves what might be termed "hermeneutical attitudes." Again and again, in preaching, we will be representing social attitudes through speech styles. For example, imagine that we are preaching on Jesus' words to the rich young ruler, "Go, sell everything." Can we not express a reaction to Jesus' command?

> Look, Mr. Jesus, you can't be serious! Sell everything? What do you want us to do, divest ourselves of house and car and bank account? Do we turn our children out into the street to beg for their breakfasts? Maybe your words cut to the heart of the rich young ruler, but he was a special case. Times have changed. Here in America, we take pride in a "high standard of living." If we follow you, Mr. Jesus, what happens to our economy, our advertising industry, our stock market? Sell everything? Mr. Jesus, you've got to be kidding!

Preachers can portray reactions in many ways. They can talk about our reactions, describing how we may feel. Or they can actually give voice to reactions, speak our attitudes (as in the example) for us. If we talk *about* attitudes, our language will match all the talking about language in our sermons, and, as a result, fail to grip congregational consciousness. If we actually articulate an attitude (which, usually, we share), however, we may find congregations nodding agreement; we will have spoken for them. Human social attitudes do shape style: Point-of-view can be attitudinal.

We have rehearsed categories of point-of-view, defining terms, because *all* language will embody point-of-view. Even third-person-objective language expresses a particular point-of-view; it is not neutral. Whenever we speak, then, we will be speaking some particular point-of-view, whether we are aware of it or not. *Perspectival language forms the consciousness of a congregation;* it shapes congregational point-of-view. By our speaking we form angles in congregational consciousness, perspectives, depths, attitudes. An objective, third-person point-of-view, preached throughout a sermon, will be devastating; it will distance God as an object of contemplation, distance scriptural words, and all but hamper the forming of faith. Instead, we can learn to wield point-of-view in language, thus forming and, perhaps, transforming congregational consciousness. Point-of-view is not an occasional rhetorical device, it *is* speaking. The language of preaching, as all human language, is radically perspectival.

CONTROLLING POINT-OF-VIEW

One of the problems we face in preaching is that we are speaking to a shifting contemporary consciousness. Consciousness these days can be described as volatile, easily influenced by point-of-view. In other words, congregations today seem to pick up and register point-of-view changes; they are very impressionable. Therefore, we will have to establish point-of-view at once in a move—within the first three sentences—and, in general, hold the same point-of-view throughout the move. Of course, we can change points-of-view move to move, but within *a* move we will wish to be disciplined. While there are some kinds of changes in perspective that can occur within a move, what must not happen is a nervous shifting around among different perspectives. For example, if we were trying to describe Jesus and the Canaanite woman (Matt. 15:21–28) in a single move and we shifted perspectives, talking of Jesus, then of the disciples, then of the woman, then of Jesus again, and so on, congregational consciousness would probably go blank, bewildered by having to aim in so many different directions rapidly. Perhaps, a hundred years ago, a natural tendency to third-person-objective consciousness would have kept the scene unified, but, today, each shift in focus would trigger a different perspective in consciousness. Lack of point-of-view control is a major cause of congregations that hear, but do not hear, sermons. We cannot ignore point-of-view in preaching: We can learn to control point-of-view.

Stance, Orientation, and Distance

In general, we cannot alter stance or orientation in a move. If we do so, we will usually split a move. Thus, for example, we may not imagine ourselves in first-century Jerusalem, and, then, in the same move, switch and describe the contemporary world in which we live; such a change would require a complete alteration in stance and orientation. Then/now shifts in a single move are almost always impossible. When attempted, moves split into two sections, which, because of brevity, will probably not form in consciousness. Even when stance is constant, sudden sharp turns in orientation will split moves. It is exceedingly difficult to look out at the world and then turn to look into ourselves in a single move. The change in orientation involves a radical shift in direction. Likewise, though a gradual nearing or pulling away may be managed with disciplined skill, in general it is better to establish distance at the start of a move and hold the position throughout. Sudden shifts in stance, orientation, or distance will so effect language in consciousness as to fragment moves or bewilder congregations.

Mobility and "Cue Sentences"

With most general rules, there are exceptions. At the start of a move, we can establish a *moving* stance, or *moving* orientation, with the use of a "cue sentence." We must notify congregations. For example, if we begin a move by saying, "Look around the world, and see what you see," we will be able to "travel"—our orientation could then imitate an eye surveying a scene. Likewise, our stance could be mobile if we cue our congregation with a phrase, such as "Take a trip through time; visit every age." Subsequently, we could depict different eras as if we were standing in the different times. Movement in stance or orientation or distance may be put into words, as long as we cue in congregational consciousness. If we begin a move in what is apparently a fixed stance, however, and then, without warning, attempt to travel, our congregation will probably drift off into confusion. Point-of-view is volatile and must be given cues. Of course, even if we establish movement at the start of a move, such movement must be simple and managed with care lest rapid shifts leave congregations behind. Cue sentences at the start of a move will help, and sometimes additional cue sentences ("Now step closer to our own age and drop in on the Crusades") within the move may be necessary.

Focal Field, Lens Depth, and Focal Depth

Alterations in focal field, lens depth, and focal depth can be managed with ease. Thus, we can widen or narrow focus without much difficulty, although we cannot include more than one such alteration in any single move. Likewise, we can imitate gradual movement in focal depth or lens depth, usually moving toward depth, in moves. Such movement, however, must be in a continuum. An abrupt alteration in focal depth may have to be signaled by a cue sentence—"You see other people, and you wonder, what are they feeling?" After such a cue sentence it would be possible to shift from surface description to a representation of the inner world of other people. Because moves may contain no more than three developmental sections, shifts in consciousness will have to be limited. Nevertheless, as long as stance and orientation do not change, shifts in focus, lens depth, and focal depth can be managed quite naturally.

Attitudinal Point-of-View

The handling of attitudinal point-of-view is difficult. It is almost impossible to represent (not talk *about*) two different attitudes in a single move. Certainly, we can refer to different attitudes: "Some people suppose that . . . ," and "There are others who imagine that . . ." We may not articulate an attitude, however, such as a reaction to Jesus' command to "Go sell," and then, in the same move, *voice* some alternative attitude—the shift in rhetorical style would be too complicated for a congregation to handle, even with the addition of a cue sentence. While we cannot represent more than one attitude in a single move, we can imitate a moderation in attitude—as long as we notify our congregation with a cue sentence. For example, if we include sentences such as "We grow wiser. Sometimes we soften with age," we could then modify a previously established attitude or even represent a changing attitude in process of "softening." In general, however, we should establish attitude at the beginning of a move and hold attitudinal style throughout the move.

If we intend to *voice* attitudes in a sermon, we must be cautious. We should never attempt to represent an attitude which we cannot find within ourselves or which we flatly reject. If we try to express an attitude that we do not have, our language will usually ring false. And if we speak an attitude that we despise, our hostility will almost always creep into language as sarcasm or slight ridicule. As preachers, however, we are children of a social world, a world which we internalize. We can find most human attitudes within ourselves by what might be termed "confessional exploration." For example, though ministers are people who do embrace vocational sacrifices, most ministers can articulate a language of self-interest, the mind of our age. After all, the language of self-interest has been built into all of us by advertising spiels as well as our own everyday conversations. Thus, when we articulate an attitude, we are not engaging in theatrics—playing a role. Instead, we are voicing an attitude which is *in us*, an attitude which we share with our congregation on the basis of our common humanness in a common world-mind. Though we may not be *of* the world, we are all emphatically *in* the world.

Volatile Consciousness and Point-of-View

We have said that *all* language embodies point-of-view, acknowledged or unacknowledged. So-called third-person observational language is not neutral, that is, free from perspective, but is itself a particular point-of-view. Point-of-view in language is inescapable. If, in a sermon, we never vary point-of-view, the result will be an aura of stilted unreality at best, and outright tedium at worst. Variable points-of-view characterize our everyday speaking and, therefore, ought to figure in our pulpit language. Though the matter of perspective in language may seem complicated, nevertheless, preachers cannot afford to ignore the problems—or the opportunities.

The problem with point-of-view is that language actually shapes perspectives in congregational consciousness. When we speak, without thinking we may shift around in different points-of-view. Every shift in point-of-view will act on congregational consciousness, however—whether we know it or not. Generally, we will not wish to shift around *within* moves to any great degree; instead, we will design each move in a sermon to express a single, controlled perspective. Move to move, of course, we may change perspectives as long as we establish perspective clearly.

If less than half of the language spoken in an average sermon forms in congregational consciousness, much of the attrition may be caused by an undisciplined handling of point-of-view. The problem with preaching today is that we address a volatile consciousness. Nevertheless, point-of-view in language is a gift. We can learn to *use* point-of-view. If conversion involves a change in perspective, a new way of looking at the world, then point-of-view in language can serve the cause of human transformation. By working with point-of-view, we can help human perspectives to change. With sermons designed to express different points-of-view, we can match the mind of our age and, happily, be interesting as well! So we need not run scared of perspective in language, but, learning to control point-of-view, we can preach with unusual vigor. All language is perspectival.

POINT-OF-VIEW: A DEMONSTRATION

Sermons can be designed so that *every* move expresses a different viewpoint. As a result, the strength of a sermon can be in the point-of-view shifts that form in congregational consciousness; congregations can be changed. The following sermon sketch demonstrates point-of-view in preaching.

> *Introduction:* In the chancel of a Pittsburgh church, there's a painting. The painting pictures Jesus at table with his disciples. There's Jesus in the center of the picture, dressed in white, and, around him, are disciples in stained-glass poses as if they were in church. A man came in, looked at the picture, and exclaimed: "Where are the sinners?" He said, "Didn't Jesus eat and drink with sinners?" Well, according to the New Testament, that's exactly what Jesus did, not once but repeatedly; he ate and drank with sinners. No white linen, no silver chalice, but in some boozy back room in Capernaum, Jesus, our Jesus, ate and drank with sinners.
>
> *Move 1:* Make no mistake: When the Bible says "sinners," the Bible means sinners! Unvarnished, unrepentant, dyed-in-the-wool sinners! The Bible is not talking about nice people gone astray, the good-at-heart prostitute, or the

down-deep-they're-really-religious tax collectors. No, in the Bible sinners are real sinners. Take tax collectors, for example. They were members of the Jewish Mafia, bagmen for the Roman conquerors, who gouged their own brothers and sisters for cash down. If they walked Jerusalem streets, they had hired muscle on either side. Nowadays, we'd call them Mickey Cohen, Tony Pro, or "The Godfather." As for prostitutes, they were not misguided home-town girls gone astray in the big city; they were wised-up, tight-rumped, any-trick-for-a-buck, venial people. So, who were the sinners in the Bible? As they say of pornographic films, they were totally "without socially redeeming virtues." Listen, when the Bible says "sinners," the Bible means real, honest-to-badness sinners. Jesus, our Jesus, ate and drank with sinners.

Move 1 looks at biblical meanings (from Mark 2:13–17), but does so through contemporary images and in a contemporary style. The construction of the move is obvious: Between statement and closure, the move contains two developmental sections, one referring to tax collectors and the other describing prostitutes.

Move 2: Well, times have changed, for here we are at table. We may not be the best people on earth, God knows, but by no stretch of the imagination are we the worst. And here we are at Christ's table. No, we're not going to pretend we are saints, we're not. But, on the other hand, to be honest, we are not all that bad! Yes, we lose our tempers, and we know we don't love enough, and at the end of the year, when we flip through our check stubs, we admit that we haven't given enough away to charity. But, to be truthful, we are not big-time sinners and we're not going to pretend we are just to make a Prayer of Confession sound good. There's a poem about a man draped in sackcloth, beating his breast, and crying, "O Lord, my heart is black with guile, / Of sinners I am chief." To which a guardian angel replies, "Vanity, my little man, / You're nothing of the kind." Well, there is a kind of vanity in pretend-ing we are awful sinners. We're not. We know we are not the best people on earth—no pretense—but, we're not the worst. Times have changed, for here we are at Christ's table.

Move 2 abruptly shifts point-of-view. If, in the first move, we were looking at biblical meanings, suddenly we shift to a language of contemporary self-awareness, so as to examine our common lives. The move is a simple develop-mental system circled around a brief illustration, thus, in its shape, imitating a circling around the table.

Move 3: Wait a minute. What was it Jesus said? He said, "I have not come to invite the righteous, but sinners." "I have not come for those in the right, but sinners." Well, he did. See him down in dirty Jordan water, baptized with sinners, or condemned by the Pharisees as an impure sinner, or hauled into court, judged and jailed, as a sinner; see him hung on a cross between thieves as a common crook—crucified as a sinner. All his life he lived with sinners;

eating and drinking with sinners. Have you seen those picture books for sale at Christmas, "The Life of Christ in Christian Art"? You leaf the pages and you find pictures of Jesus as a boy in the temple, Jesus preaching on the mountain, Jesus praying in a garden. You look in vain for a picture of Jesus whooping it up with sinners. Perhaps we do not want to see the picture, but we can. Stand on lower Broadway. Stare through the smoky window into the barroom where the flat-eyed men line the bar nursing their beers, and the girls with the too-loud laughter dance to the juke box, and see Jesus there with them. He lived his life and he died his death among sinners. What was it Jesus said? "I have not come for the righteous, but for sinners." He did not come for the righteous. He came for sinners.

In *move 3,* the point-of-view is quite complex. We are recalling Jesus' words while, at the same time, looking with our mind's eye at his life, at our representations of his life, and at his life as it might be lived today. The start of the move sets a mood of almost absent-minded remembering. Within the move, however, we are looking at Jesus among sinners and, thus, are positioned in consciousness as were the Pharisees in the passage. The framework, statement and closure, as well as the constant looking *at,* holds the move together.

> *Move 4:* Do you know where we are? We're on the outside looking in. We're standing outside holding on to our chill righteousness, while Jesus is inside, in the rosy room, partying with his friends, the sinners. On the outside, looking in! Like the little girl they found standing outside the banquet hall of a big hotel where they were holding a dinner for handicapped children. "I can't get in," she wailed. "There's nothing the matter with me!" So, we're holding on to our righteousness but missing a party. Our righteousness shows up in little ways, in our everyday conversation: "Well, at least I'm not . . ." "Well, at least I'm not a racist like Charlie." Or, "At least I spend some time with my kids. . . ." "At least my house isn't a pigsty." "At least I'm not . . . ," we say and distance ourselves from others—and from Jesus. For Jesus is in the bright room celebrating with his special friends, sinners. And where are we? We're on the outside looking in. Holding onto our righteousness, out in the cold, while Jesus is somewhere else.

In *move 4,* we have still another perspective change. The "looking in" was set up in the previous move by the mind's-eye "barroom" image. Here the point-of-view is a self-aware standing outside. In Mark, the passage is tricky. Jesus says, "I came not to call the righteous, but sinners." The Pharisees are self-excluded from the impromptu party precisely by their "looking at" those sinners. So, in the sermon design, we have attempted to let the same exclusion occur. In shape, the move is deliberately similar to move 2, for both moves incorporate self-awareness.

Move 5: So what can we do? Well, we can come in to Jesus as forgiven sinners. Come as forgiven sinners, there's no other way. Look, it's not a matter of salt tears and grief, of sawdust down the aisle. We cannot earn Christ's mercy by our guiltiness. All we can do is to come as we are—forgiven sinners. Past tense, forgiven. The old "at least I'm not" prides are tossed away and we line up with sinners gladly, forgiven sinners. There's a wonderful story of an evangelist who threw a party for all the riffraff in town, a wild, spilling-out-into-the-street party for sinners. There were champagne cocktails, and trays of food, and a rock band beating out "sweet Jesus" hymns. A happy party. A policeman walked by the door as a wreathy blond danced out into the street. "Every bum in town is there," sneered the policeman. "There's room for more, officer," sang the blond, "There's room for more." Well, there is, all the room in the world in the wideness of God's mercy. So, what can we do? Simple. We can join the party. We can step into Jesus Christ as forgiven sinners!

Move 5 establishes still another perspective. In the move, the preacher joins a congregation in a common predicament while, at the same time, announcing the gospel message. The illustration serves to locate us at the door of the party, looking at the festivities; so the illustration maintains the same point-of-view as the move. Of course, a conclusion will be added to the sermon, perhaps noticing the Eucharist set before us. Early Christians did associate the pericopes of "eating and drinking with sinners" with the celebration of Eucharist.

Each move in the sermon sketch features a differently established perspective, and each move is designed quite differently.

We must not think of point-of-view as an optional device. *Every* move in any sermon will have a perspective. Obviously, third-person-objective *is* a particular perspective. Because perspectival consciousness is so volatile, however, preachers will have to be aware of point-of-view, controlling the perspectives of moves with care. Varied points-of-view in a sermon will be intrinsically interesting and serviceable. By changing perspectives, we can change "minds" and reshape the faith-consciousness of the people of God.

5.
Conjoining Moves

A little girl was at work pasting pieces of paper together in a long chain. The pieces of construction paper were each a different color. It was not long before bits of paper were strewn over the floor and blobs of paste stuck to tables, chairs, and even on the edges of picture frames. "Putting things together," said the young lady, "is very, very difficult." It is! In sermons, the task of pasting moves together in some sort of logical sequence is difficult indeed. We have pictured sermons as scenarios, as moves in a sequence. Now, we must ask exactly how to put any two moves together.

Older homiletics studied "transitions," or, more precisely, transitional paragraphs, which joined ideas in a sermon. Of course, older homiletics were often forming categorical "points." About the only way to move from one categorical section to another was through some sort of transitional patchwork paragraph. For example, suppose we were preaching a topical sermon on "love," containing three categorical "points," as follows:

1. We must love in the world.
2. We must love in the church.
3. We must love in our family life.

How are we going to get from a first to a second category? Perhaps we could resort to an artificial system of numbering—"First," "Second," "Third." Though Augustine advocated enumeration, his advice is not entirely helpful. Enumeration introduces time-consciousness to sermons, and, thus, enlarges congregational restlessness. After ten minutes of "First," when a preacher announces "Second," you can almost hear the congregation groaning. Moreover, studies indicate that when sentences begin with numbers—

"First, we must love in the world"—a tension between enumeration and content is created in consciousness so that such sentences will almost always delete, becoming nonfunctional. If, however, we refuse to number (and we should), we will have to design transitional paragraphs such as the following:

> We must *love in church* where in the spirit of love we meet together. But the real test of love is not church. In families, we do not meet as strangers, but as flesh and blood, husbands, wives, mothers, fathers, children. In families, feelings can be rubbed raw. Friends, we must *love in family life.*

The paragraph is like a series of steps moving between two ideas; it travels. Because the paragraph is brief, its chance of forming in consciousness is slim. Because it travels, it cannot become a single meaning. As a result, transitional paragraphs simply fog out in congregational consciousness. People have fixed on one idea, and eventually, may catch up and orient to a new idea, but in between, during transitional paragraphs, they will probably wander off.

The real problem is categorical design. Though categorical sermons are easy for preachers to jot down, they are intrinsically tedious for congregations. In our lives, we do not think our largest thoughts categorically. Instead, we reserve categorical thinking for trivia—laundry lists, calendar appointments, cost accounting, and the like. When it comes to making sense out of life, or speaking love, or professing faith, we do not think categorically. The need for transitional paragraphs in older homiletics was itself a tip-off to the inauthenticity of the method. Most human conversation does not employ labored transitions but shifts easily, by kinds of logical association, from one idea to another. About the only time we wield transitional language is when we interrupt a flowing conversation in order to turn people toward our own agendas.

CONNECTIVE LOGIC

We regard sermons as a sequence of ideas, moves, within a movement of thought. Thus, theoretically, we should not need transitional sections at all. Joining moves in a sermon scenario will pose other kinds of problems. Essentially, our problem is *how to keep moves distinctly separate and yet logically connected.* Each move in a sermon should form as a single, strong understanding, with a firm statement to begin with, and a firm final closure. Each module of language should form in congregational consciousness as a defined meaning. We want a sermon's "bones" to show! Certainly, we do not want a smooth flow of thought in which separate understandings fuse and have no definition. Though we desire structural toughness, at the same time, we must have logical coherence; ideas must follow one another by some sort of connective logic. If the logic of a move is undefined, it may enter consciousness as a baffling non sequitur. Congregations are remarkably logical, and what they cannot associate, they may well dismiss. Therefore, as preachers, we must pay attention to connective logic and be sure that such logic forms in congregational consciousness. Moves must be separate, yet connecting logic must be well defined.

Suppose we are going to preach a sequence of moves, as follows:

> We are all sinners.
> We have been forgiven in Jesus Christ.
> We can live in a new way.

The first step in getting at the connective logic that ties the moves together into a meaning is to rephrase the moves in a colloquial language. A conversational language will display connective logic clearly.

> Be honest: We are all sinners,
> *but* we have been forgiven by Jesus Christ,
> *so* we can now live new lives.

If we think of the moves in a sermon as "topics" to be talked about, joining separate sections will be difficult. As soon as we write out the structure as if it were a conversation, however, logic becomes apparent. Of course, it will help if we brood over the theological meaning of "but" and "so." After the statement, "We are all sinners," the "but" may mean *"but remember* that Christ has forgiven us," and the "so" indicate that *"now* we are free from the past and may live in a new way." If we are going to design connections for moves, it will help to begin by spotting logic in a conversational sequence.

Of course, the kinds of logic that may connect moves can be other than conversational logic; they can be a *logic of consciousness,* that is, a logic of point-of-view. Conversations travel by association, by the logic that shows up in connectives—"but," "and," "yet," "so"—and sometimes by dialectical oppositions. But moves will also connect by a logic of consciousness, as, for example, when we move from a wide focus to a narrow focus, or when we shift from past to present to future—all perspectival shifts. The logic of these shifts may often be expressed in conversational style:

> *Look* at sin in the wide world.
> Now, *turn,* and search your own motives.
> *But hear* the gospel of Jesus Christ.

By scribbling out our moves in conversational sentences we can usually grasp the kinds of logics involved, and, sometimes, even spot point-of-view shifts.

In planning a sermon, then, we will write out move sentences in a colloquial style so that we may be more aware of the kinds of logic involved in a sequence of moves.

If we discover we are moving with *connective logic,* we will encounter the most trouble with "and" and "but." "And" and "but" are words which we use in conversation within single sentences; they put ideas together and make them one. Therefore, if two moves connect logically on the basis of "and" or "but," our problem will be one of separation. How can we keep our moves as defined, separate ideas, when logic is working to make them one?

Suppose we have two moves in sequence which can be expressed conversationally as:

> What's the use of preaching? Human nature always falls back into sin.
>
> *And,* besides, we die anyway.

Basically, the two moves are somewhat categorical; they present two different reasons for despair in preaching—because of stubborn sin *and* because of inevitable death. We can handle the conjoining of moves in two different ways. Either we can go ahead, and, with repetition, underscore the categorical nature of the moves, or we can cover up the categorical character of the moves. Notice how the two options might work.

> *Why preach?* People hear the gospel but they slide back into sin every time. . . . Human nature always seems the same. No wonder preaching is so discouraging.
>
> *Why preach?* Death mocks all our speaking. . . .

Or

> Why preach? People hear the gospel but they slide back into sin every time. . . . Human nature always seems the same. No wonder preaching is so discouraging.
>
> Of course, there's a deeper despair. Death. Death mocks all our speaking. . . .

The second system is probably better, for it creates the illusion of a movement of thought with the phrase, "there's a deeper despair."

The word "but" is deceptive. It appears to signal a sharp break in logic, *but* actually it tends to join moves. When the logic of connection is "but," often, it will be wise to insert a delaying phrase at the start of the new move. Study the following sequence.

> . . . so face facts: We are all, all of us sinners.
>
> But, in Jesus Christ we are forgiven. . . .

Notice that the end of one move will join with the beginning of the next move as a single sentence, "We are all, all of us sinners, but in Jesus Christ we are forgiven." Thus the start of the new move will not be strong. The solution is to employ an extra phrase at the start of the second move to prevent the run-on effect of the word "but." Thus,

> . . . so face facts: We are all, all of us sinners.
>
> Are you ready for the good news? We are forgiven! In Jesus Christ we are forgiven. . . .

When the logic of connection is a "but" or a "yet" conjunction, we will almost always have to insert an extra phrase to prevent the moves from flowing together in congregational consciousness.

When moves join by what we have termed a logic of consciousness, such logic must be indicated clearly. Logic of consciousness is a logic of point-of-view. We can move from a wide focus to a narrow focus, from the past to the present, from looking into the minds of others to staring into our own deep selves. Because the logic is perspectival, it is guided by a perceptual analogy. For example, suppose we have two move statements in a row that read:

> Look at sin in the world.
> Now, turn, and look into yourself.

The logic is a turning from an outward gaze to an inward viewpoint. Thus, the conjoining of the moves might be accomplished in a rather obvious way:

> . . . headlines and history books, crime statistics, and TV violence. All you have to do is scan the human world. We live in a sinful world.
>
> Now, turn right around, and stare into your own soul: We are sinners, each of us sinners. . . .

In the sermon sketch provided at the end of chapter 4, each of the moves in the sermon is formed by a point-of-view shift. The starts of each move reveal that, in some manner, the perspectival shifts are indicated. When the logic of connection is a logic of consciousness, connections can be done almost effortlessly.

As important as it is to connect moves, it is equally important to keep moves apart as separate ideas. If connective logic is not clear, moves can seem to be non sequiturs. On the other hand, moves can join in such a way as to obscure their separate status. The problem can be caused by a "slopping over" of ideas. Study the following example:

> . . . so face facts: We are all, all of us sinners. *There's got to be a way out!*
>
> Are you ready for the good news? We are forgiven. . . .

Notice that the added phrase, "There's got to be a way out," anticipates the news of forgiveness to come in the subsequent move. The phrase thus weakens the abrupt strength of the connection which, without the added phrase, would have worked nicely:

> . . . so face facts: We are all, all of us sinners.
>
> Are you ready for good news? In Jesus Christ, we are forgiven. . . .

Though the two moves may seem to come together abruptly, logic is clear and a congregation will handle the abrupt turn of thought much better than the fuzziness caused by an anticipatory phrase. Another way in which a clean shift between moves may be obscured is by reiteration. For example:

> . . . so face facts: We are all, all of us sinners.
>
> *Though we are all sinners,* there is good news. In Jesus Christ, we have been forgiven. . . .

Notice that an extra summary phrase, "Though we are all sinners," appears at the start of the new move. Because the initial clause reiterates the idea of the previous move, it will destroy the necessary break between ideas.

There is another kind of reiteration, more subtle, but equally dangerous.

> . . . so face facts: We are all, all of *us sinners.*
>
> Well, good news, Christ has forgiven *us sinners.* . . .

Even though the break between moves is sharply defined, as it should be, the echoed phrase "us sinners" will reattach the moves in consciousness. In general, the language of the start of the move should not echo phrases from the closure of a previous move.

Mobile systems of sermon construction, in which moves follow one after another in sequence, will require no transitional paragraphs. Instead, the problems will be of a different order. Each move must be formed as a separate module in consciousness with a strong statement and a strong closure. Yet, connective logic must be obvious. If a congregation cannot figure how one move follows after another, they may well drift off and fail to hear portions of a sermon. As a result, preachers will have to establish connective logic at the beginning of each new move. The best way to ensure that moves will travel along logically is to be sure that move sentences, read in order, make sense. For example, there will be no difficulty in conjoining the following moves:

> Faith comes from hearing,
> but how hard it is to hear in our noisy world;
> yet, maybe, it isn't the noise so much as our failure to preach.

But, instead, suppose the sequence were to read in a different way:

> Faith comes from hearing,
> but how hard it is to hear in our noisy world;
> so the church wields visual symbols;
> yet maybe it isn't noise, but our failure to speak.

While the first three sentences can be connected with ease to form a logical statement, now the fourth sentence no longer follows and, instead, refers back to a second sentence. When we read the four sentences printed on a page, we have no difficulty in doping out the logic of the ideas. Oral language, however, poses a problem because it forms sequentially in consciousness; congregations will *not* refer back. Thus, because the fourth idea does not follow from the third statement, a congregation hearing the ideas preached will drift off, confused by the non sequitur gap in logic. If we want moves in a sermon to come together and form a coherent understanding in congregational consciousness, we must be sure that sequential logic is *obvious*.

THE "LOGIC" OF SETS

Within a sermon, groups of moves may associate into "sets." For example, let us suppose that we have a series of five moves in a sermon, as follows:

> Be honest: We are all sinners,
> But, good news, in Jesus Christ we are forgiven,
> So, guess what, we can live in a new way.
> Well, don't you want to tell your neighbors?
> By the spreading of the gospel, God redeems the world.

If you study the sequence, you discover that the first three moves form into a set. The fourth move "Well, don't you want to tell your neighbors?" does not merely follow the third move, but rather works from the set of the first three moves. Likewise, move 5 appears to relate to move 4. Thus, we may view the entire sequence as composed of two sets of moves, as follows:

> Set 1 { Be honest: We are all sinners,
> But, good news, in Jesus Christ we are forgiven,
> So, guess what, we can live in a new way.

Set 2 $\Big\{$ Well, don't you want to tell your neighbors?
By the spread of the gospel God redeems the world.

When dealing with sets, we face two kinds of problems: We must define the set as a set, and we must join sets.

Sets may be defined in several ways, depending on the kind of logic that groups the moves. For example, suppose we have two moves which associate in a semi-categorical manner, such as:

Why preach? Human nature always stays the same. . . .
Why preach? Death mocks all our speaking. . . .

When logic is somewhat categorical, we have two choices. Either we can associate the moves by repetition at the start of each move—for example, "Why preach?"—or, better, we can use repetition prior to closure, but vary the starts. Notice the starts and finishes of the two moves:

Why preach? Human nature always stays the same. No matter how persuasive our sermons, like "crazy clay," human nature slides back into the same sins. . . . "The grass withers, the flower fades"—What's the use of preaching?

Of course, on a deeper level, why preach when death mocks all our speaking? We may lift someone's soul for an instant, but . . . Death and sin, they're always with us. "The grass withers, the flower fades." Why on earth do we bother to speak? What's the use of preaching?

We have employed an echoing refrain toward the ends of each move, a refrain which, in consciousness, will tend to bracket the moves into a set.

If the logic that connects moves into a set is a traveling logic, we will definitely work with the closure of the final move in the set. Thus, if our sequence is as follows:

Be honest: We are all sinners,
But, good news, in Jesus Christ we are forgiven,
So, guess what, now we can live in a new way,

we will build a semi-summary section into the final sentences of the last of the three moves.

. . . Yes, we're sinners, but see, we're forgiven sinners. No longer need we be trapped in sin. New lives! We've been given new lives to live.

Well, don't you want to tell your neighbors the good news? . . .

In effect, we have rehearsed the sequence of the three moves prior to closure in the third move. Thus, when the fourth move commences, it is able to work off the cumulative meaning of the set. Such summary sections must be designed subtly so that they do not stand out as pedantic rehearsals of what we have already heard. When congregations realize that they are hearing summaries, they will generally turn off the material. The regrouping of the ideas before the closure of the set is crucial, however, so that the logic that joins sets will be apparent.

When sets join, the connection will require much more force than the joining of sequential moves. Thus, the closure of a final move in a set will probably require several sentences, and the opening of a following move will have to be equally emphatic—perhaps using five sentences to establish the move statement. Preachers will wish to analyze their sermon scenarios to see if there are sets forming. Where two different sets bump together, extra strength will have to be built into the connective logic that joins the sets together.

CONJOINING MOVES: STYLE

In a previous chapter, we remarked that the starts of moves are difficult to design because they must accomplish so much: they must focus consciousness on a statement, they must display connective logic, they must indicate point-of-view, and they should establish mood. By "mood" we mean a tone, an emotional tone which will probably run through the entire move. The emotional quality of a move is a troublesome matter that requires some attention.

Many preachers today are scared to death of emotion from the pulpit. Perhaps, we fear the labored histrionics, overblown affective tirades, which, in waves of emotion, swept over pews in days gone by. As a result, many preachers pursue a cult of naturalness, and come across in casual chatter as if they were slightly laid-back talk-show hosts. Of course, the understatement of feeling is itself a form of pretense. In normal conversation we are seldom so modulated. Listen to two animated baseball fans rehearsing a game, and you will overhear emotions that are varied, and often explosive. The fact is we speak with emotion all day long, every day of our lives, as we engage in different occupations—making love, telling jokes, arguing issues, giving directions, and so forth. Therefore, ministers who subdue emotion in the name of naturalness are emphatically unnatural; they border on the bizarre. Because we rightly fear phony affect, we may end up as casual chatterers.

There is a deeper issue: the gospel. The speaking of the gospel is an *un*natural activity. Though preaching will use ordinary language, preaching the gospel in the presence of God is a fairly strange vocation. If the gospel is news of liberation, if it brings to us Jesus Christ the Savior, then it is inevitably urgent. A casual style will contradict the essential character of the gospel.

77

Moreover, casual chatter is scarcely appropriate if, indeed, we stand in the presence of the holiness of God. No wonder the prophets were urgent. No wonder apostles strained with emotion. If the gospel is life-and-death good news, then our personal lust for naturalness may be a dreadful error. Yes, we must reject all *false*, put-on emotion, but we must not turn from emotion per se.

The solution may be to realize the intimate connection between emotional tone and point-of-view. In general, point-of-view will form emotional tone. If we are representing an attitudinal point-of-view we will inevitably express feeling.

> Look, Mr. Jesus, you can't be serious! Sell everything? What do you want us to do—divest ourselves of house and car and bank account? . . .

Likewise, if we are looking at some situation with our hearts engaged, we are bound to be emotional.

> O God, we feel utterly helpless. There are so many, many mouths to fill with food. You see the skeletal kids of the world reaching for bread. . . .

Point-of-view style may also be determined by distance and focus. A long look back through time will be more dispassionate than immediate encounters with the present-day world. A wide focus on the human condition will create cumulative feeling, whereas an excursion into our own motives may set an entirely different tone. If emotion is directly related to perspective, it will be natural and will not sound artificial at all.

Emotion also relates to what is in view within a field of consciousness. Jesus Christ, strung up on a cross, bawling last words of dereliction, is not a subject for casual conversation. Or, if we want to portray God's intense love for the broken human world, we will not wish to employ a dispassionate third-person rational tone. Preachers ought to be honest with regard to their own profound feelings. While we have no desire to be pompously affected, we should not suppress genuine feeling. Instead, we can ask: What are we looking at? What is our perspective?

Probably the notion of having a pulpit style has prevented authentic emotion. For many years preachers have wanted to develop *a* style of preaching, a style of their own. Preachers would be better off, however, without *a* style. Rather, preachers should be willing to change styles, move by move, in order to serve their congregations. Meaning occurs on many levels—conceptual, imagistic, and emotional. Thus, we should be eager to shift styles according to what we have in focus and how we orient perspectivally. Notice that we cannot conjure up a style related to feeling. If we say to ourselves, "We must express anger," we will find such a style impossible to produce, and, as a result, almost always be inauthentic. Instead, we will imagine ourselves in a particular stance, oriented toward a particular object; we will put ourselves in a point-of-view and speak accordingly.

The problem in connecting moves is that mood must be established at once. Thus, mood and point-of-view will often be expressed together. Preachers will attend to the ends and beginnings of moves. If we are speaking of different things, the end of one move should have a sharply different emotional tone from the beginning of a next, new move. Compare examples:

> . . . So let's face facts: we are all, all of us sinners.

However, in Jesus Christ we have been forgiven of our sins. . . .

The beginning of the new move is not distinctively different in tone but is oddly similar to the previous conclusion. A preacher would deliberately redesign the start:

> . . . So let's face facts: we are all, all of us sinners.

Well, clap hands and do a dance. Good news, we've been forgiven. Forgiven! For . . .

The use of a prefatory phrase not only keeps the moves separate, but also establishes a different mood. When moves join on the basis of a shift in consciousness, mood is much easier to establish.

> . . . when the Bible says "sinners," the Bible means real, honest-to-badness sinners. Jesus, our Jesus, ate and drank with sinners.

Well, times have changed, for here we are at table. We may not be the best people on earth, God knows, but, by no stretch of the imagination, are we the worst. . . .

Here, the first sentence of the new move establishes the new point-of-view, and the second sentence evokes the tone of the move. In general, we must limit ourselves. The first *three* sentences in a move will embody content, connective logic, perspective, and, of course, mood.

If the sequential logic of a sermon is natural to human consciousness, shifts can be managed all but effortlessly. What is required is an awareness of problems and a modest attention to detail. Above all, we must remember *the* basic problem. Moves must form as separate meanings with strong starts and strong conclusions. At the same time, moves must display a connecting logic obvious to a congregation. Structure must be sharply defined and sequence naturally logical.

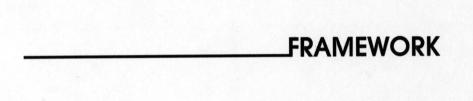

FRAMEWORK

6.
Framework—
Introductions

Some years ago, researchers polled a list of "top speakers." One of the questions asked: Which part of a speech was the most fixed—written out, and all but memorized? Answer: the introduction. The answer may surprise us because introductions sometimes seem quite improvisational, an informal sparring with an audience. Nevertheless, the answer does make sense. Introductions give focus to sermons. Introductions establish shared purpose between a speaker and an audience. Introductions command attention. So the introduction to a sermon must be designed with great care. The language of an introduction is a disciplined language.

Obviously we cannot begin writing a sermon by scribbling out an introduction and then moving on to develop the body of a sermon. We must have something to introduce—at least a somewhat expanded sermon sketch—before an introduction can be conceived. The purpose of an introduction is not to be ingratiating; it is to introduce a *particular* sermon that will follow. Thus, we will have to have a series of moves plotted and partially developed before we can think out an introduction. Though there may be preachers who, with a vague idea in mind, will produce a snappy introduction before they have formed a sermon, their products are usually a problem. Like a dud Roman candle, their sermons may flash brightly at the start and then, often, fizzle out. An introduction can be designed only after a full sermon scenario has been partially worked out.

What does an introduction do? Introductions do two things: They give *focus to consciousness* and provide some sort of *hermeneutical orientation*. All else is secondary.

FOCUS

By focus, we mean that the introduction will function like a camera lens. It will turn toward a "field of meaning" and then bring a particular subject matter into clear focus. An introduction must function to orient a congregation so that a first move may commence. To pursue a visual analogy: The introduction swings congregational consciousness toward a picture and then picks out of the picture some particular object with which to begin. Our visual analogy mentions "a picture," and then some "object" within the picture. So, in sermons, focus involves a double purpose: Locating a whole field of meaning, and isolating some particular feature within the field of meaning (usually connected with a first move). Thus, introductions may well be evocative of the entire sermon—its mood, intention, or general thematic concern. But also introductions set up a congregation so that a first move may start. If an introduction is *too* general, it may seem oddly disconnected from the first move. If the introduction is too particular, it will, subsequently, seem irrelevant to the whole sermon.

Let us imagine that we are going to preach a sermon on 1 Cor. 11:17–32, a passage which views the Lord's Supper in the midst of a bickering Corinthian church, sadly split by class divisions. The body of the sermon will be concerned with peace in a church divided, but the first move of the sermon will focus on the celebration of the Lord's Supper. Suppose, then, this introduction:

> The little church in Corinth was such a problem. As with many churches today, it was sadly divided. Factions! There were rich and poor, slave and free, bluenose and libertine—all bunched together in a bundle of conflict. Corinth was the kind of church ministers avoid, unless they've taken courses in "conflict management." For every faction got together, chose leaders, and snarled at every other faction. Corinth was a church divided.

Notice that, though the introduction does get at the sermon's general concern, we are simply not ready to begin a first move discussion of the Lord's Supper without adding some sort of mini-introduction to the Supper theme, which is always an unfortunate strategy. As the introduction stands, a sudden first-move shift to the Lord's Supper will seem an abrupt non sequitur.

So an alternative start may well be in order.

> The Lord's Supper is a sacred moment for most congregations. We gather at the Lord's table with solemnity. "This is my body," the minister announces, and we break bread together. For centuries, the table has been set as Christians gather to share one cup and receive the bread of life. So, the Lord's Supper is special, a special sacred moment in the life of a congregation.

Here, the first move will be managed with ease; we are ready to begin. But, the overall concern of the sermon, division in the church, has not been broached. As a result, when the sermon does turn toward a discussion of conflict and unity, the introduction will seem trivial or even misleading. It is even possible that the first move itself, demoted by the introduction, will delete from consciousness.

The solution to our problem is not to design a two-part introduction, one part on conflict and another part on the Supper, for such an introduction would not offer a single focus to consciousness. Somehow an introduction must evoke a general "field of meaning," and, *at the same time,* ready us for a first move. Thus, in our hypothetical example, we might end up with an introduction as follows:

> Some years ago, there was a movie about a family reunion. The family was a contentious bunch. They scrapped and split and never got along. Yet, every year, they scheduled a party, a family reunion. At a long table, they'd all sit down together. But, you couldn't help noticing the sidelong glances, the cold shoulders, the obvious slurs. Perhaps that's the way it was in Corinth. Though they gathered at one table and shared one cup together, they were at odds. Corinth was a divided church.

In our example, we have managed to put together in a unified system the general field of meaning as well as reference to the supper at Corinth, so that a first move may begin rather naturally. In addition, we have introduced both family imagery, appropriate to the church, and imagery of conflict. Thus, however clumsily, we have shaped an introduction. Of course, we must be able to move into the body of the sermon without an abrupt discontinuity—the main test of an introduction.

There is an old shibboleth about sermon design that many ministers embrace: "Tell them what you're going to do, do it, and tell them what you've done." In such a scheme an introduction lays out a ground plan for a sermon, and a conclusion rehearses "points" made. The slogan is a disaster! Introductions should *not* give away the structure of a sermon ahead of time in a pedantic fashion. If playbills in the theater were to print a synopsis of plot which we could read before a curtain rises, suspense would be destroyed; we would know what is going to happen ahead of time. Human thought is intriguing precisely because human beings think and speak differently, so that we are continually surprised by turns of mind or sudden shifts in imagination. Destruction of suspense (the possibility of the unexpected) is positively unkind. Moreover, if we tip our hand ahead of time, we invariably introduce time-consciousness, as, checking their watches, a congregation will count off promised "points." So introductions should not tell a congregation where we are going or, worse, *how* we are going to go ahead of time. Instead, introductions provide initial focus; they bring into consciousness the "scene" of the sermon before there is any moving around within the scene. A good rule for preachers as for poker players: Never tip your hand!

Introductions should not be too long inasmuch as getting into focus can be accomplished rather quickly. So, as a general guideline, introductions may run between seven and twelve sentences in length. The sentence count is not arbitrary. An introduction can scarcely function in less than seven sentences. At the same time, after more than a dozen sentences congregational impatience will usually set in. Just as too long an introduction to an after-dinner speaker can build hostility in a waiting audience, so also too long an introduction to a sermon will produce an alienating impatience. After all, introductions are merely focus and bear no weight of meaning; they can be shaped in a handful of sentences.

Lately, there has been a trend toward extended introductions. The trend seems to be prompted by a desire to relate. Many preachers are comfortable relating to a congregation without the burden of content and, therefore, will spin out friendliness instead of introducing a subject matter. Obviously, preachers need not alienate an audience with sharp confrontations at the start of a sermon. And, of course, when speaking to a strange congregation, some friendly banter may be in order (although it should be crisply demarked from the actual introduction to a sermon). Nevertheless, the ultimate subject of our sermons is the gospel and not ourselves, or our relationship with a congregation, or our being comfortable in a pulpit. Actually, it is fairly easy to establish a shared consciousness with a congregation without having to labor over interrelating. Thus, focus is the main function of an introduction and focus can normally be achieved in a few sentences.

Flipping the matter over: Introductions should not be too short. Roughly, it will take two or three sentences simply to adjust a congregation to our syntax, four to six sentences to establish focus, and a single sentence to make a firm closure for the introduction. If these objectives are necessary, then introductions cannot be managed in much less than seven or eight sentences.

Older homiletic texts seemed to suppose that the very first sentence of a sermon was crucial, a "grabber" that by sheer rhetorical force could instantly command audience attention. Evidence is to the contrary. People do not easily attend the first few sentences of a public address. Just as when we swing a camera on a scene, focus may be fuzzy before gradually clarifying, so the first two or three sentences in a sermon are seldom clearly heard—they are fuzzy. Human syntax is individual, as distinctive as a fingerprint. Therefore, congregations must adjust to the syntactical patterns of a preacher. Though ministers may conduct liturgy prior to preaching, liturgical cadences are stylized and are scarcely typical of normal speaking. Actually, whenever we begin a casual conversation with another person on the street, even someone who knows us well, at the outset, there will be a process of adjusting to our syntax. Thus, at the beginning of an introduction, the first two or three sentences cannot bear much weight. A wise preacher will keep the initial sentences of a sermon short, uncomplicated, and without much adjectival elaboration. Compare the following:

1. How wonderful that Jesus told parables—those grand stories full of profound meaning for our daily living. Did you hear the parables first in Sunday-school classrooms? Do you read parables now, over and over, in your limp, underlined Bibles? Well, Jesus didn't make up all the parables. Don't be shocked! Some of the parables are old, familiar, well-worn stories that Jesus heard and then, with genius, retold to his disciples. . . .

2. Not all the parables of Jesus are original. Some of the parables were old stories that Jesus borrowed and retold in his own way. Probably the story of the Great Feast was borrowed, for there is an old Jewish story . . .

In our first example, the texture of language is too thickly woven; we cannot grasp what is being said. The second example, though slightly redundant, will quickly orient us. The first few sentences in an introduction must be lean, simple sentences without clausal intrusions or extra adjectives. Though wordiness may seem to offer freedom for relatedness, it will destroy the start of a sermon. Likewise, opening sentences that are too dramatic ("Think of parables! Wonderful stories of Jesus!") are more apt to put off a congregation than to command attention. So, as a rule, the first two or three sentences in a sermon ought to be short and simple and without too much content weight.

The last sentence of an introduction is difficult to write: it must *stop* action. The end of the introduction and the start of a first move must be clearly separated. We do not want to fill the gap between the two with smooth-over transitional sentences. Therefore, the introduction must stop. The last words in an introduction, like a firm period at the end of a sentence, must establish a strong sense of "it's done." Not surprisingly, the longest pause in the delivery of a sermon will usually occur immediately following an introduction and before the body of a sermon begins. Thus, the last sentence of an introduction, like the closure of a move, must stop action, fix focus, and sound final. If done properly, the final sentence will

87

frame the introduction in congregational consciousness like a hung picture, so that no matter how long the pause that follows, people will be ready to start a first move.

The middle six or eight sentences of an introduction do the "double work" of focus. They establish an issue, theme, field of consciousness, mood, or whatever is required. Because the middle sentences in an introduction establish focus they should not contain much if any movement of thought. (If you can outline an introduction, you are probably in trouble!) At the outset in a sermon, congregations are not yet able to handle rapid or complex shifts in thought. Introductions will develop a single image to work from or, at most, a parallel of images. Consider the following examples:

1. Some years ago, a church was putting together a hymnbook. A committee had to decide which hymns to keep, and which to discard. The committee got into an awful fight over "Onward Christian Soldiers." Some said the hymn was well loved and had to be kept, while others claimed it was militaristic and should be dumped. Well, if we have trouble with our hymns, what will we do with the Bible? Almost every book of the Old Testament tells of battles, and the New Testament is not much better. "Put on the whole armor of God," cries Ephesians, and then goes on to talk of shield and buckler, helmet and sword. Why is it that whenever the Bible speaks of living for God it uses military metaphors? "Put on," says Ephesians. "Put on the whole armor of God." (For a sermon on Eph. 6:10–20)

2. Heard about a baby who claps hands. She loves to clap her hands over almost anything. Shove her breakfast cereal in front of her; you'll get a handclap. Sit her in a circle of toys and she'll break into applause. Her parents took her to the seashore to watch the waves roll in, and she started clapping right away. "We only worry," her parents say. "We only worry that someday she'll stop." We do, don't we? Too soon we stop appreciating life; we lose the habit of applause. Not so in the Bible. In the Bible you'll find a handclap on every page. Listen: "Everything. Everything is good!" Now there's a prodigious handclap! (For a sermon on 1 Tim. 4:1–5)

3. There is a modern painting of the crucifixion. When you look at the painting, all you see is darkness, black on black. Then, suddenly, in the center of the picture, carved in pigment, you trace the shape of a scream, a gaping mouth in the dark. The title of the painting: "Eloi, eloi, lama, sabachthani"—"My God, my God, why have you forsaken me?" The picture is true to the scriptures. It was the ninth hour and Jesus screamed, "My God, my God, why have you forsaken me!" See the shape of a scream. (For a sermon on Mark 15:33–39)

4. Have you noticed how devious children can be? How downright tricky kids are? They'll get you to promise, before you know what you're promising. "Daddy, Daddy, will you do anything we ask you?" Well, if Daddy's smart, he'll hold off until he sees what's at stake. One day two disciples, James and

John, came hustling up to Jesus: "Teacher, Teacher," they cried, "We want you to do whatever we ask you." Jesus was cautious. Then the disciples blurted out their wild desire. "Allow us to sit at your right and left when you come into glory." Did ever ambition reach so high? "Grant us to sit at your right hand in glory." (For a sermon on Mark 10:32–45)

Some features of the introductions may be signaled. Notice that in each example the first two sentences are simple, clear sentences. As for the final sentences, the second and third examples finish with terse, stopping sentences. The other two examples end with scripture citation. Because in each case the second citation of the scripture text is shortened rhythmically, a sense of ending is produced. All of the introductions combine audible and visual material. Each contains something to be seen—a hymnbook, a baby clapping, kids coming to a parent, and a somber painting. But some include dialogue—"We only worry . . . she'll stop," "Daddy, Daddy . . ."—and some an allusion to words said or sung, "Onward Christian Soldiers," "Eloi, eloi, . . ." The use of visual material is generally desirable inasmuch as it assists focus in consciousness.

Structurally, the examples are simple systems without much movement of thought. The third example is nothing more than the description of a picture and a brief comment linking the painting to scripture. The fourth example is a parallel system, an analogy, which likens avid children to the ambitious disciples. Likewise, the first example is a simple construct in which a hymnbook controversy is used to raise a question about military images in scripture. In no case is there any real movement of thought. The possible exception is in the second example in which we move from the baby image to our failure to give thanks to the Bible's continuing appreciation of life, a pattern which may be too complicated and, thus, puts the introduction into jeopardy.

Dialogue is extremely difficult to handle in sermons. When we read exchanges of dialogue on the page of a novel, we can picture the speakers, and, because dialogue is printed on different lines, we can identify who is speaking. There is evidence, however, that in oral delivery, extended exchanges of dialogue will not work, probably because point-of-view shifts are required. Thus, for example, in telling of Jesus and the disciples in our last example, we deliberately reduced the exchanges of dialogue reported in scripture. (In scripture Jesus answers "What do you want me to do?" the disciples voice their request, and then Jesus replies again.) As a rule, only one conversational exchange can be managed orally. Of course, even when dialogue is reported, it may have to be broken up so that it fits in with our own syntactical pattern. Notice that when parents speak of their clapping baby, the dialogue is broken:

" 'We only worry,' her parents say, 'We only worry that someday she'll stop.' " Lengthy sentences of dialogue should always be broken into short phrases for a congregation.

Whenever we intend to speak of scripture, and particularly when we plan to use some particular phrase from scripture, reference to scripture should appear in an introduction. If we do not include reference to the scripture we will be preaching within an introduction, then, when we do turn to scripture later, we may have to build a second mini-introduction into our sermon. In all of the examples we have provided, scripture was introduced along with a focal image. But, notice, in no case is there any labored documentation of scripture (e.g., "We read in 1 Tim. 4:4, 'Everything created by God is good.' ") or reference back to a scripture reading (e.g., "In today's gospel lesson . . ."). Such references are seldom if ever necessary and, when they do appear in an introduction, they can cause a point-of-view shift that disrupts focus. Nevertheless, if we are going to be alluding to a scriptural passage throughout a sermon, mention of the passage *must* be included in the introduction.

HERMENEUTICAL ORIENTATION

Not only do introductions focus consciousness, they orient a congregation's hermeneutical understanding. After an introduction, people should be ready to hear a sermon, and to hear in a certain *way* and with certain understandings established. Let us suppose, for example, that we are planning to preach on Jesus' water-walk to a congregation of slightly skeptical natural scientists. We realize that, to put it modestly, the miracle story will seem unbelievable, and, if we insist on historicity, our sermon will probably be dismissed. We could presumably build a lengthy apologetic for miracles into our sermon, but to do so would be to destroy the wonderful "Wow" quality of the passage. Such a problem can often be solved by a carefully designed introduction.

> Outside Rome there are rooms carved in rock—the catacombs. Early Christians hid themselves in the catacombs to escape persecution. On the rock wall, scratched in stone, is a picture of Jesus walking on the water. There's a stick-figure Jesus, a wiggly line for waves, and circles underneath to represent fish. The picture looks like a child's drawing. Nevertheless, the picture of Jesus walking on the waves spoke to early Christians of a Lord who could come to them in trouble. The picture was a picture for faith.

Notice what the introduction does: The question of historicity has been bracketed out. We are no longer speaking of historical narrative, but rather of a picture for faith. Thus, the introduction has served to orient our congregation toward what they will be hearing and, in fact, *how* they should listen. The introduction has established a hermeneutical consciousness.

In designing introductions, we will want to ask ourselves *how* we want congregations to hear our sermons. Again and again, we may wish to disrupt our audience's literalism so that they will hear different kinds of biblical rhetoric appropriately, e.g., mythic material in Genesis, or symbolic passages in the Gospel of John, or spooky end-of-the-line visions in Revelation. Hermeneutical orientation attempts to indicate *what* is being discussed and *how* to listen.

Actually any good introduction will orient hermeneutical consciousness in subtle ways. Review the four examples we have provided; in each there is some hermeneutical orientation. In the first example, we have opened up a question with regard to military imagery so that "combat models" for the Christian life cannot be heard with automatic approval. By using the image of the baby clapping in our second example, we have suggested that taking pleasure in life is innocent, thus undercutting any suspicion of pleasure at the outset. Of course, the somber "black-on-black" picture in our third example orients a congregation to hear the dark Good Friday story; they will scarcely expect a giggling sermon. In the last example, we have packaged deviousness together with the large, if uncomplicated, desires of children so that, subsequently, when we identify churchly dreams with ambitious disciples, a congregation will accept the analogy. So, all but unnoticed, hermeneutical orientation is going on in each of the introductions. Every introduction will provide hermeneutical orientation, intended or otherwise, so it may be useful for us to be aware of the process. What do introductions do? They focus consciousness and give hermeneutical orientation. What is more, they do so in a few carefully designed sentences.

SHARED CONSCIOUSNESS

Many homiletic books suggest that introductions must begin with people, with specific needs or experiences of a congregation. The theory seems to rest on the conviction that, as members of a congregation, the most important thing in the world to us *is us*—our wants, our agendas, our everyday lives. In journalism, the same position will relegate a story of a devastating earthquake to back pages while headlining the election of a local dogcatcher. The supposition is alien to the gospel which, of course, calls us beyond our own parochial interests. All things considered, an introduction ought to feature material familiar to a congregation. For example, we might not wish to speak to a church full of bucolic pig farmers by discussing art work in the Louvre, or to address slick city people with references to disc harrowing. Certainly, the posh preacher who, in speaking to a ghetto congregation, began a sermon, "The other day at our swim club . . . ," was thoughtless. The dictum that sermons must start "close to home" is not entirely useful, however. The fact is, most rural Americans get slick-covered magazines in their mailboxes and have television antennas poking up from their chimneys. To some extent, wherever we may preach, we address a general cultural mind.

A more helpful concept may be the notion of a shared consciousness. Presumably, an introduction ought to establish shared consciousness between a preacher and congregation in which some image or idea may become focal. Introductions do not have to feature things thoroughly familiar or circle around local problems; imagination can accomplish miracles. So, for example, we might not wish to begin a sermon by discussing the Widener Library in Harvard Yard (perhaps an alien image), but we certainly could begin by picturing a college campus and an ivy-clad library with stacks of books; such details can be readily imagined. If the language of an introduction is simple, and imagery vivid, we need not assume we must begin with local reference. What is important is that the style of an introduction draw preacher and congregation together into a shared consciousness getting into focus. Thus, "I and you" language will not be used and personal references will be avoided. Esoteric stuff, familiar only to a few folks, will be bypassed in favor of more common images. If we use material drawn from fiction or drama, we will avoid calling attention to documentation; obviously, "There's a stage play in which . . . ," will be better than, "Tennessee Williams was a great playwright. In one of his dramas, *The Night of the Iguana*, he . . ." Our goal is not to appeal to parochialism, but to establish a *shared* consciousness in which a sermon can unfold.

SOME PROBLEMS

Though we have outlined a general approach to introductions, we need to review certain special problems that occur. Homiletic vogues come and go. In any era, there are pulpit conventions that are positively contagious, but which need to be examined. At the risk of listing "no-nos" in negative fashion, let us review a number of conventions which are current events in the pulpit today.

Step-down Introductions

There are introductions which seem to achieve focus by a process of elimination, a kind of narrowing down to a subject matter. Imagine hearing an introduction such as the following:

> We have all heard of the apostle Paul, a brave champion of faith. After his astonishing conversion, he journeyed around the ancient world preaching the gospel. More than any other apostle, Paul spread good news on the earth. Well, one of the cities Paul visited was Corinth. Corinth was a brawling seaport filled with sleazy bars, brothels, and noisy bazaars, a difficult town in which to build a church. One of the problems which Paul encountered in Corinth had to do with the Lord's Supper. Wealthy folk came with baskets full of food while the poor, slaves, and outcasts went hungry. . . .

The preacher apparently plans to speak on 1 Corinthians 11, a passage having to do with the Lord's Supper in Corinth. The preacher arrives at focus, however, by first talking of Paul and then by describing Corinth before, finally, getting around to a discussion of Eucharist in the Corinthian church. The congregation will become irritated because at the outset they figured their preacher was going to preach on Paul. Then, abruptly, the preacher switched focus to the city of Corinth, only to shift again to the Lord's Supper —a third subject matter. The congregation will be irritated; they have been deceived twice so that when a third subject matter is ventured they will respond with diffident inattention. Step-down systems contain too many moving parts and require shifts in point-of-view. As a result, they do not focus consciousness; they fan irritation. The preacher would have been wiser to have begun with a single image relating to a diverse community at the Lord's Supper.

Tangential Intrusions

Introductions must be disciplined so as to move toward focus. Therefore, asides, wry comments, and other tangential material must be pruned away. Suppose, for example, you were to hear a preacher begin a sermon with the following words:

> Every year in Boston there's a race: The Boston Marathon. People line up, five thousand or more, and run through the city's streets. Every year, the Boston papers carry pictures of previous winners. Have you ever run a distance race? I have, and they are grueling. Well, take a look at the Bible. There's a race in the Bible. "Seeing we are surrounded by so great a cloud of witnesses, . . ."

Notice that the preacher has begun to get you focused on the image of a marathon race in order to set up a parallel with the marathon described in Hebrews, chapter 12. However, the seemingly innocent intrusion "Have you ever run a distance race?" breaks focus and requires a point-of-view adjustment. The effect is similar to getting a camera lens adjusted only to have someone nudge your arm; the camera will have to be focused all over again.

Most tangential intrusions break into introductions as either unrepressed wit on the part of the preacher or as friendly attempts to relate. Unfortunately, no matter how well meant, they disrupt focus and are apt to leave a congregation floundering. Tangential intrusions, even brief ones, cannot be tolerated.

Oblique Suspense

Lately, an odd convention, imported from film or popular fiction, has crept into sermon introductions. Imagine a sermon that starts with the following words:

> Right in the middle of a family argument, it happened. As they threw words back and forth like stones, name-calling and cutting remarks, it happened. Call it a miracle if you will, but suddenly it happened. . . .

Evidently the strategy is to set up an indeterminate scene, holding back specific information, so as to build a sense of increasing suspense. The audience does not know what "it" is, or who "they" are, or where the action is happening. Preachers who employ the device suppose that it will command attention because a congregation, driven slightly nuts by not knowing, will want to know. Unfortunately, the device, which may well work on the pages of a novel, will not work when delivered orally.

The real problem with oblique, supposedly suspenseful sermon starts is that they prevent the one thing an introduction intends to do: *focus consciousness.* Not only will such a method annoy a congregation, but, almost always, a second, explanatory introduction will have to be added to dispel the fog. And two-part introductions are seldom useful.

Personal Narrative

Introductions featuring material drawn from a preacher's personal experience seem to be a growing trend. Perhaps, the practice has been encouraged by "Tell-your-own-story" theology. Nevertheless, though personal illustrations may, on rare occasions, be used in the body of a sermon, personal experiences in an introduction are devastating. The problem is split focus. As a preacher, you are attempting at the outset of a sermon to focus congregational consciousness on an image, or an idea, or a scriptural passage, or whatever. But, by speaking of yourself, inevitably the congregation will focus on *you.* There is no way to prevent the split. Personal narratives will always introduce a *preacher,* and the intended subject matter will not form in congregational consciousness in any satisfactory fashion. Many preachers suppose that personal narrative in an introduction will display the humanness of the minister, and thus build "relationship" or "empathy" at the start of a sermon.

Perhaps. But there are other ways to relate to congregations (among them visiting people). As for the minister's humanness, it will probably be all too evident to congregations without our having to put our humanness on display. Sermons have their own special work in ministry; they speak gospel. Thus, they are not designed primarily for relating. The problem with personal material in an introduction is that it will always introduce the person rather than some focus in consciousness. Split focus at the start of a sermon is disastrous.

Humor

As we all know, after-dinner speakers will often trot out a "funny" at the start of a speech. The strategy supposes that a joke will relax an audience, and, indeed, make an audience happy to hear a speaker. Moreover, "funnies" cause us to laugh together and, thus, build up a cheerful unity. The after-dinner-speech convention has been picked up by preachers. The problem of humor slipped into introductions is twofold: (1) The humor is almost always disconnected, or at best tenuously connected with the subject matter. Therefore, after a funny, preachers will probably have to design a second introduction to refocus a congregation. Funnies are apt to be tangential intrusions. (2) While there may be passages from scripture that are hilarious (in some ways, profoundly, Christian faith *is* a laughing matter!), the gospel is ultimately serious, for it speaks of a crucified Christ to the deepest levels of human self-understanding. Humor at the start of a sermon can set a tone of down-home triviality which, predictably, people will like, but from which few sermons can recover.

The real question to ask about humor is *why;* why do we want to begin preaching with humor? Many preachers will answer the question baldly: "People really go for humor!" Indeed, they do. Yet, we do not roar with sidesplitting laughter over the deepest issues in our lives—gladness, yes, but "ha-ha," no. Probably preachers use humor at the start of sermons to say, "Look, I'm a funny, likable person," which is emphatically not an adequate motive. If a sermon requires a hermeneutical orientation of giggling joy, perhaps, laughter will be useful at the start. Otherwise, preachers may wish to avoid guffaws.

Introductions require disciplined language. The primary purpose of an introduction is to *focus* congregational consciousness *with* a hermeneutical orientation. Good introductions will be tightly designed language systems. Preachers will probably wish to write out introductions and all but memorize the words. While there can be much freedom to play around with words in the body of a sermon, introductions are too crucial for ad-libs or other impromptu elaboration. Language in an introduction must be terse, visual, and above all, focal. The trick in preparing an introduction may be to put yourself in the place of your people. Write an introduction for the sake of a congregation and not as a form of self-expression. Motto for introductions: Love your neighbors—in the pews.

7.
Framework—
Conclusions

If you leaf through a thesaurus, you will discover many synonyms for the word "Conclusion." Conclusions are "wind-ups," "stoppages," "payoffs," or "clinchers." They are also "lids," "crowns," "curtains," "tag ends," "bitter ends," not to mention exotic phrases such as "the finishing stroke" or "when the last cat is hung." Musicians will speak of "coda" and newspaper editors will scribble "30." The huge list of synonyms points to our problem: How can we describe conclusions when they have so many varied functions? Some sermons will end like a clipped sentence, while others roll on, wave after wave, until a congregation is awash with emotion. Sermons can stumble into an "altar call" to the tinkly tune of "Just as I Am," end with a brief breathy prayer, or even resort to recited doggerel. How can we say anything certain about a sermon's conclusion?

The problem is caused by different expectations, and expectations derive from various definitions of preaching. If a sermon is for conversion, then "altar calls" will be *de rigueur* so that listeners may respond with true faith. If preaching is connected with amendment of life, we can expect "go-do" conclusions. In some traditions, the conclusion to a sermon is a "school-teacher" who goes over lessons learned so that students may remember their religious ABCs—preaching is a didactic exercise. When sermons are seen as aesthetic objects, we are likely to get inspirational conclusions with all-the-stops-pulled-out emotion. In some liturgical traditions, when sermons are viewed as a preface to sacraments, conclusions are apt to be verbal mood bridges to the Eucharist. Obviously, preaching does many different things in faith-consciousness, and, therefore, discussion of conclusions will be difficult indeed. So, let us acknowledge variety and admit baldly: *Conclusions are governed by intention.* At the same time, let us pin down the obvious: *Conclusions are designed to conclude.* So much for definition.

What of shape? In general, a conclusion will not be long, perhaps no less than five sentences and possibly no more than eight. Conclusions do not introduce new ideas, but work from a series of moves that have comprised the body of a sermon. Therefore, conclusions will not develop a new, unfamiliar understanding in consciousness—discussing, illustrating, answering objections, and the like. Conclusions are simple systems of language. They will fix consciousness, fulfill an intention, and quit. If a conclusion is too brief it will not form in consciousness. If a conclusion is too long it can be as wearisome as a manyfold Amen that keeps on unfolding interminably. Though conclusions are simple and may even be somewhat improvisational, they should be sketched with care.

INTENTION

The word "Intention" is used in too many ways. Intention can be used of content—we *intend* to bring out some particular hidden meaning. Intention can refer to congregation—we *intend* toward a certain mind or cultural consciousness. Here, we are singling out another strand of meaning: Sermons intend *to do*. Preaching never talks about things in a flat, detached, nothing-is-at-stake manner. No, the language of preaching, like the language of scripture (much of which is also preaching), is performative; it is a language intending *to do*. Of course, sermons can be designed to do many things. Some sermons may merely stand back and say "Wow" to wonders of God's grace. Other sermons may be busy with ethics, poking about in how we should behave as Christians in a *"numero uno"* sort of world. Still other sermons may wrestle with mysteries of identity—who are we, and why? Every sermon will be doing something in congregational consciousness. Therefore, we must be wary of suggestions that a conclusion will have *one* invariable form or purpose. Instead, we must ask of each particular sermon, What is the language trying to do?

Sometimes we will take our cue from scripture. The intention of a scriptural passage may become our intention in preaching. If we sense that some prophetic shout is intending to bring us to our knees, our sermon may end up in an act of confession. Or, if we suppose that the Book of Revelation is dancing visions before our eyes, we may conclude a sermon with a visionary depiction. Let us review a series of examples drawn from actual preached sermons.

Suppose we have preached on the commandment to love enemies in Matthew 5. Further, suppose we have determined that the passage, addressed to Christian community, is unyielding. While the passage may not be designed to provoke repentance, it does not appear to welcome casuistry either; its character is *command*. Prior to the conclusion, the sermon has wrestled with the command, trying to evade its seeming impracticality by seeking exceptions. We have asserted, however, that the words, which speak of group enmities, call for a new-order society. Here is a conclusion:

> "You have heard it said, 'You shall love your neighbor, and hate your enemy.' But I'm telling you, Love your enemies." We've heard the words and we're still in church. Oh yes, we hedge: "Mr. Jesus, sir, does that include Black Panthers, Communists, and hippies?" We hedge, but the commandment does not change. So, what's got to change? Who's got to change? Who's got to change? God help us.

The example, which picks up phrases used previously in the sermon, fulfills intention precisely by not yielding—the command remains a command.

In preaching the doxology that concludes the eleventh chapter of Romans, we face an entirely different situation. Though the eleventh chapter features a discussion of God's mysterious purpose for Jew and Gentile, we interpret the passage as a doxological tribute to the providence of God, who plots salvation in the sweep of human events. Thus, the sermon seems to intend an act of wondering praise.

> Here we are, 1985. Can you make sense of life? Bombs in Beirut. An arms buildup in America. Such a muddle of names and dates and events. We are not much of a cast, are we?—poor players stumbling through our parts, botching our lines. Not much of a cast, but—O Lordy—what a plot! "The mighty current of God's Eternal Purpose"—in all, through all, for all. To God, dear friends, be glory through all ages, forever and ever. Amen.

Again, the conclusion draws on phrases that have scattered through the sermon, drawing them together into a doxology. So, the passage seems to want to give praise, and our conclusion does so.

In studying Heb. 12:1–4 (a lectionary selection), we notice that after an elaborate analogy between a marathon race and the Christian life, including a parallel between the race crowd and a "cloud of witnesses," the passage seems to add an odd modifying "comedown" phrase—"In your struggle you have not yet resisted to the point of shedding your blood." Thus, the final phrase leads to a peculiar conclusion:

> Well, we've been dramatic, overdramatic. Look, our race is no more than baby steps; nobody's going to crucify us. All we have to do is to serve a frightened church in a bad season. So, slip into your running shoes. On your mark, get set, and . . . There, you've said it, "Go."

Each of the examples we have provided contains concrete allusions to a congregational situation, and to some extent, each draws on previous sermonic material; nevertheless, the examples are quite different. In every case, an intention was discovered in some biblical passage and incorporated into the design of a conclusion. Thus, intentionality in scripture can guide us in forming conclusions.

Of course, the primary question may be, What does the *sermon* intend to do? Again, intentions will vary. If preaching during Holy Week, we may want nothing more than to put the image of Christ on the cross before congregational consciousness. Or, some situation in a parish may prompt us to preach, urging some sort of corporate action, for example, participation in a peace march, so that our sermon may conclude with a call to action. Sometimes, we may have no purpose other than a deepening of understanding, for example, a searching of the mystery of God-love, so that our sermon may conclude with sweet brooding thoughtfulness. Intentions vary, so we must be ever on guard lest we shape conclusions to our sermons in the same clichéd way. Each conclusion will fulfill some different intention, and each, therefore, may be different in shape, and mood, and language.

Definitions of preaching that demand all conclusions perform some particular purpose are a problem. Our sermons will, perhaps, invariably precede Eucharist, but we must not fall into the trap of providing a mood transition to Eucharist in our conclusions every Sunday. The Eucharist will manage nicely without our contriving liturgical mood. If Christ is present in the word and in the sacrament, Christ will take care of his own interrelating! Likewise, though we may speak in congregations that all but demand an altar call, we need not comply, if, in fact, some sermon or scripture does not want an altar call. After all, in Christ, we live by free graciousness and not under law, even the odd law of congregational expectation. So, if nothing else, we can conclude a sermon, stop, and then, if we must, venture a quite separate call for response. The problem: Conclusions, prompted by some fixed definition of preaching, will sound the same, and, thus, defeat their purpose. After hearing the same sorts of endings, week on week, a congregation will be cued by the familiar to grab their hymnbooks and ignore the sameness they are offered. So, initially, let us insist that conclusions will be different as they fulfill quite different intentions.

CONCLUSION

We have suggested that conclusions ought to conclude: They must end. Yet, the matter of conclusions is not so simple. Though conclusions are designed to end a sermon, presumably preachers want some sort of continuing impact or understanding. So our purpose must be rephrased: How can we end a sermon and still ensure that the effects of the gospel will continue? We wish our sermons to form in consciousness, and, at the same time, end.

Establishing Reflective Consciousness

Sermons are made from moves in sequence. Sermons travel along from move to move in some sort of plotted scenario. As a result, in hearing sermons, congregations are on a kind of journey in which first one idea, and then another, and still another will form in their consciousness. So, at conclusion, the moving *action* of a sermon stops. The consciousness that grasps traveling thought is quite different from a stopped consciousness in which ideas assemble. Thus, one of the tasks of a conclusion is to establish a stopped, reflective consciousness in a congregation. Usually, the first two sentences of a conclusion will form reflective consciousness. Listen to the starts of some conclusions:

> So what are we going to do with the words of Jesus? What are we going to do . . .

> What a "comedown"! We stood at Calvary, ready to offer our lives in some grand martyrdom, and what do we get? A long list of mundane things to do in church —bulletins to fold, the sick to visit, meetings to attend . . .

> Here we are, 1985. Do you ever get the feeling that we're losing ground? . . .

The trick here is to create a reflective consciousness without tipping off a congregation to the fact that a conclusion is taking place. Any time congregations begin to realize, "Here comes a conclusion," they are apt to reach for a hymnal or missalette, and cease listening. Thus, phrases such as "Finally" or "And in conclusion" are absolutely fatal, and should be avoided. The same sort of disaster will occur if a minister gets into the habit of beginning all conclusions in the same way, "And now as we move toward the altar . . ." Instead, look back at the examples of conclusions given during our discussion of intentionality, and see how different they are. Nevertheless, each of the examples does establish reflective consciousness.

Assembling Meanings

How can we get the moves of a sermon to assemble in consciousness, forming understanding? More, how can we ensure some lasting impact from a sermon? Older homiletics, which viewed sermons as didactic lessons to be learned, would use conclusions to rehearse points made seriatim, presuming that repetition would fix content in memory. But ordered repetition in a conclusion is unwise. A congregation will soon pick up the redundancy and, having heard it before, will simply "blank out" the whole rehearsal. Redundancy is the death of any conclusion. Yet, how else can we package meaning?

Let us speak of images and phrases. In any sermon, moves combine content with images, catch phrases, and the like, so that they form in consciousness. What we can do is to gather a few such images into a conclusion; they need not be echoed in order of original appearance, indeed should not be so arranged. Different images or phrases, drawn from different places in a sermon, may be gathered and conjoined into a meaning. Look again at a conclusion:

> Here we are, 1985. Can you *make sense of life?* Bombs in Beirut. An arms buildup in America. Such *a muddle of names and dates* and events! We're *not much of a cast,* are we?—poor players stumbling through our parts, botching our lines. Not much of a cast, but—O Lordy—*what a plot! "The mighty current of God's Eternal Purpose"*—in all, through all, for all. To God, dear friends, be *glory* through all ages, forever and ever. Amen.

Though it is difficult to see assembly without reading an entire sermon text, the italicized material is reiterative. The phrase "make sense of life" appeared in a first move, as did the phrase "a muddle of names and dates and places" (notice the slight change). The phrase, "Not much of a plot, but a whale of a cast," appeared in the sermon's introduction, but is here reversed. The quote, "The mighty current of God's Eternal Purpose," came from an illustration used in the second move of the sermon. The image of actors on a stage was drawn from the final move of the sermon, and the word "Glory" echoed in the next-to-last move doxologically. So, if we feel we must actually draw together parts of a sermon, we can do so, subtly, by weaving images and phrases into a patterned conclusion.

Of course, at other times, the movement of a sermon will "aim" at a certain conclusion. So, for example, a sermon on the Christian witness in the world may *lead to* a conclusion which will be a call to service. Such a conclusion will not echo previous material at all, but, instead, follow as a natural outcome of previous material. Often, a logical-outcome conclusion will be more connected with a last move than with other content in a sermon; thus, if the final move in a sermon is a call to charitable living in the world, a conclusion may well specify the kinds of actions—in very concrete ways—that are intended. Conclusions that follow from the sequence of a sermon will not always be a call to ethical action; they may be merely responsive. For example, a sermon may have circled around the revelation of God-love in Christ Jesus, so that a conclusion will be nothing more than an expression of deep wonderment or of love in return. In such cases, the conclusion, which is a response, will gather meaning all but automatically.

The Sense of Ending

A sense of ending is usually achieved in the final three sentences of a sermon. Closure is accomplished in many ways, but usually by some form of repetition or by a terse last sentence. In any event, the last sentence of a sermon should be short and, in general, free from adjectival or clausal elaboration. The last, brief sentence in a sermon should simply *stop*. Repetition is more difficult to describe because it may be used (and misused) in many ways. For example, the last two sentences (but no more than two) may repeat, or the third from last and last sentences may be similar, or two final sentences may be repetition with a one-word change that adds to or subtracts from the sentence length:

> See the love of God for us. The love of God!

> See the love of God. The *astonishing* love of God.

Another form of repetition can be a structural repetition that recapitulates the pattern of the entire conclusion. For example, a conclusion may have begun by vowing some brave martyrdom for Jesus, only to discover that Christ gives us unexciting earthly tasks and unlovely neighbors to love. The final sentences of such a conclusion might enact the same overall design:

> We have such big dreams for Jesus Christ! But what do we get? Neighbors to love. Nothing but neighbors to love.

Just as with the closure of a move, or the closure of an introduction, so the final two or three sentences of a sermon must produce, in congregational consciousness, a sense of ending. The sense of ending is usually achieved by syntax, rhythmics, or by the sounds of words.

SOME SPECIAL PROBLEMS

There are a number of conventional conclusions that seem to show up with frequency in the pulpit. Some conventions may be useful, if not overworked, but others are much less than successful. We will review some of these and underscore the problems involved.

Ending a Sermon with a Question

The practice seemed to snowball in the sixties, when sermons would often finish up with some sharp, confrontational "will you or won't you" question. The theory was that a congregation, stuck with an unanswered question, would leave church thinking, turning the question over in mind. Unfortunately, our evidence suggests that, when a sermon ends with a question, congregations will immediately delete the question from consciousness—many folks will not even remember that there was a question!—and go home to Sunday dinner. So, for example, if a sermon should end with "Will you or won't you bear witness to Jesus Christ?" the question will not last past being spoken; it will not be wrestled with or even remembered. How then can we get a congregation to brood over matters of choice? A better strategy is to build a picture in consciousness, for example, a depiction of someone actually witnessing for Christ. If such depiction is done with enough force and reality, congregations are confronted; listeners must reject an image of themselves that they have formed in their own consciousness.

> We can talk about God. Over coffee, when your neighbor's unloading all the troubles she's had, you can speak, you can stammer out talk of God, the God you believe. Or when you're riding to work with a friend, talking tough business or world politics, you can speak. You may feel like a fool, but you can say that tough business doesn't make sense in the gospel of love. Oh, yes, you'll be scared to death, and blush inside, and get your words all mixed up, but you'll speak. And afterward, though you may feel like an idiot, you'll know that for once, you've been what you are—a Christian.

What the system does is to engage imagination, so that people can *see* themselves bearing witness. Thus, if they reject the notion, they will have to do so by rejecting themselves in a situation. Such a strategy is much more confrontational than a posed question, which will neither be answered nor remembered.

Quotation in a Conclusion

In general, we will not wish to quote another "voice" in a conclusion. The problem has to do with point-of-view. Conclusions to sermons are usually direct-talk situations in which a preacher, with open candor, speaks to a congregation. There is a high level of eye contact, and there is a degree of intimacy evoked by directness. In the middle of a conclusion, if a preacher suddenly introduces a quote—"As John Calvin once said . . ." or "Wasn't it Saint Francis who . . ."—the preacher will turn into a ventriloquist's dummy, looking straight at the congregation but speaking someone else's words; the effect on a congregation can be unnerving. The congregation will have to break with the speaker in order to adjust to someone else's syntax and to another voice speaking. Congregations do not return to the conclusion following a quote, but drift off into disengagement. To push the matter further, the same difficulties are involved with the quoting of inspirational poetry, the quoting of scripture, or the use of illustration in a conclusion—all of which are familiar pulpit conventions. Such practices, though well worn and familiar to us all, are unwise. They intrude on the direct discourse of a conclusion and, therefore, disrupt consciousness.

Return to an Introduction

Many ministers, in concluding a sermon, will return to an image or illustration ventured in the introduction. Some homiletic texts even applaud the practice as aesthetically pleasing and "good form." For example, if the introduction to a sermon has pictured Jesus down on his knees scrubbing the feet of disciples, then, at the start of the conclusion, a minister will bring back the image of Jesus scrubbing feet, and, what is more, do so by echoing some of the same language used in the introduction. What does the device do? The practice totally *destroys* motivation; while it may provide intense satisfaction, it prevents any further response to a sermon. The custom does give strong closure to sermons, indeed, it forms a *closed circle* in consciousness, but, unfortunately, nothing else needs to be said or *done*. Admittedly, congregations will get an emotional "high" from such an ending—a sense of completion is always satisfying. (If, as a minister, you are into professional advancement, you may wish, cynically, to shape "round-out" conclusions on a regular basis.) Furthermore, the round-out conclusion will be a pleasure to preachers—nothing else in our job is ever neatly finished! Nevertheless, if we wish sermons to move and motivate, to transform lives, we will avoid conclusions that turn back and reprise introductory material. Sermon structure is not a matter of aesthetics; sermons are designed to serve God and neighbors.

Can "return conclusions" ever be useful? Yes, possibly. There is some indication that a closed-circle conclusion to a sermon will lift and frame in consciousness. Thus, for example, if we were preaching on a prophetic vision or some bright depiction from Revelation, we might deliberately employ the device. All we may be trying to do is to hang up a vision in congregational consciousness. Otherwise, round-out conclusions should be avoided like the plague; they end, but end motivation as well. Christian life is, after all, open-ended toward God's future and is emphatically active.

Rhythmic Intensification

In striving for emotional impact many ministers will repeat too much. Usually the repetition involves a series of sentences, all of which will start with the same words:

> We must go out into the world with love. We must go out into the world to love neighbors. We must go out into the world for the sake of Jesus Christ.

The problem here is that though repetition will build a sense of emotional intensity in the *preacher's* consciousness, unfortunately, it will not do much for congregations. Because the minister feels, the minister supposes that, automatically, the congregation will feel in the same way. Not so. If three or more sentences of approximately the same length, with the same beginnings, occur in sequence as a block of language, they will almost always delete from congregational consciousness. As a result, the minister will feel much, and the congregation hear nothing. While we can repeat *a* sentence at conclusion, particularly if the repetition is slightly longer or shorter, more than one repetition will almost certainly destroy the end of a sermon. Our own subjective affect is often deceptive; what we feel may not communicate at all.

Personal Testimony

While there may be times in a sermon when personal testimony will be welcome and even helpful (not often!), a conclusion is neither the time nor the place. The reason is simple. If a conclusion is designed to shape the gospel in faith-consciousness, then personal testimony will leave a congregation with a consciousness of the preacher rather than the gospel. If we refer to ourselves in a conclusion, we form awareness of *us* whether we intend to do so or not. All in all, *we* are a poor substitute for gospel. We can use the word "I" in a conclusion as long as it is used to build shared consciousness—"You and I," "You and me." Otherwise, personal reference in a conclusion will split consciousness and cause a point-of-view shift to occur as well. Could there be any exception? It is doubtful!

GENERAL GUIDELINES

Conclusions ought to be *concrete*. We ought to be able to see images, to visualize ethical actions, to all but touch words. Preachers will want to shun general, slightly abstract language such as "goals," "relationships," "duties," "feelings," and so forth. General, categorical words have no force at all; what cannot be visualized will never be done. So, if a preacher tells us that we must "love in all our relationships," we will see nothing—how can we see a "relationship"? Instead, a preacher must depict the people we should love, painting pictures of actual faces and places and opportunities.

The reason we tend to reach for vague general terms is that we sense everyone in a congregation lives in some particular situation and that congregational situations will be varied. How can we image for everyone? Therefore, we tend to grab general terms and speak of "situations" or "relationships," assuming that people will fill in with images drawn from their own particular lives. But they will not. If we provide general *images*, however, people will tend to make them specific. By general images, we mean images likely to appear in everyone's human sphere. So, a preacher may talk of sitting at a kitchen table, and congregation members may well see their own kitchen tables. Certainly, "sitting at a kitchen table" is more concrete than "situation." The trick is to reach into our own phenomenal consciousness, and to see what we see, describe what we may experience, and then to weigh images and experiences, to be sure that they are common to all. Notice, please, that we have used the word "concrete" and not "specific." If imagery is too particular it will put off a congregation. Therefore, go for concrete images and shun vague categorical labels.

Many preachers become somewhat nervous if they are told that conclusions ought to be concrete. Just how concrete can we get? Of late, direct talk from the pulpit is positively frightening to most preachers. If we get too concrete, will we not raise hackles, alienate members, or have our sermons rejected? Though there may be particular Christian traditions that are enlarging membership in America these days, for the most part, the percentage of Christians in our land is declining. It is likely that by the year A.D. 2000, Christians in the nation may be less than 30 percent of the population. Faced with a decline in congregational growth, many preachers become understandably cautious; they are uneasy over concreteness. For example, if we are preaching on a Pauline passage that refers to a division in the church in Corinth, how concrete do we get in drawing parallels? Do we speak of actual divisions, the groups and cliques in our own congregation? And what about political matters? Dare we criticize a president's defense budget directly in a sermon, thus risking an alienation of party members in the pews? At a time when Americans are easily frightened by direct truthfulness, just how candid can conclusions be?

The gospel does not grow in a climate of fear: We must be concrete. We can speak of actual divisions in a parish, or of political matters—they are there, and in the gospel they are there to be seen. We must always speak in the love of God; God-love is never timid. If we must frame a rule for conclusions, we might, at least, begin by acknowledging our own timidity: If a conclusion is so concrete that a minister is beginning to get nervous, it is probably fine!

Conclusions ought to be said in *simple language*. Preachers will wish to pare down sentences, reducing extra adjectives, preferring strong nouns and verbs in simple, often short, sentences. In conclusions, a preacher speaks directly to a congregation without artifice, posturing, or a striving for effect: Child-talk is *not* out of place. Actually, when we human beings speak of large affairs in our lives, when we speak most intimately and with more honesty than usual, we will revert to a language learned in the first few years of childhood;

we will talk simply. Such primal language will speak of perceptual reality rather than of concept, or theory, or abstract ideas. Simple language will steer clear of "church" talk, of religious phrases such as "fellowship," "witnessing," "salvation," and the like, that do not figure much in our everyday conversations—there are always childlike ways of saying the same things. So, for example, we will *not* say

> There are poor, suffering souls who toss and turn on beds of pain; they cry aloud for God's salvation . . .

but, instead, speak of

> people who are sick in the hospital. They stare out of oxygen tents or lie behind pulled curtains. They are waiting for God.

The rule for conclusions: Use direct, simple, concrete language.

What we have written may seem to go against a venerable pulpit tradition in which conclusions are designed for emotional impact or inspirational uplift. The tradition seems to be based on a Pietist assumption that feeling motivates. The assumption, unfortunately, cannot be supported; feeling may actually drain motivation. Long ago, the playwright Bertolt Brecht argued convincingly that "catharsis" is the enemy of personal and social change. While "catharsis" may purge the soul, it may spend itself in emotion, and prompt no action at all. There are many passages in scripture that intend a cool self-appraisal and a thoughtful will to change, rather than frenzies of emotion. Child-language simplicity is always better than a language self-consciously striving for effect, particularly emotional effect. "Come to my arms sweet Jesus" endings to sermons, packed with emotion, may not be terribly effective anymore. Such excursions may appear to be religious conventions tacked on to sermons; they may not convert and they may only embarrass. Let us speak simply, directly, *and* in obedience to the gospel.

We began by suggesting that conclusions do two things: they fulfill intention and they end. Thus conclusions will vary greatly according to intentional purpose and their means of establishing closure. Though conclusions ought to be prepared ahead of time, often a preacher, caught up in the intensity of preaching, will reach for a quite different language from the words planned. What our preparation does do is to provide a prior "sketch" for the shape of a conclusion. Without such preparation, many ministers will tumble into habit, ending all their sermons in much the same way, and often, with the same phrases. While, as preachers, we are seldom aware of our own habitual patterns of speech, our congregations are all too aware.

Therefore, though we will wish to give ourselves leeway to ad-lib in speaking conclusions, we ought to have sketched a conclusion ahead of time to prevent our own redundancies.

Conclusions are acts of obedience; we are doing what is intended. They are practical matters; we stop.

IMAGES

8.
Preaching—
Image and Metaphor

Preaching makes metaphor. Preachers paint word pictures and put them together; they use image, analogy, illustration, and the like. They always have. As a form of public address, preaching may be labeled "sacred rhetoric," but as calculated God-talk, preaching is clearly a *poetic* activity. While political oratory and legal argument may be designed to persuade, to sway some audience to accept a particular "true" position, preaching invokes, for it is concerned with bringing Presence to consciousness. Because sermons "bring into view" unseen reality, they will, of necessity, dabble in metaphor, image, illustration, and all kinds of depiction. After all, preaching is preoccupied with Christ who comes to us as story, and as a living symbol; thus, preaching is bound to tell stories and explore images. Inescapably, preaching is a work of metaphor.

REVELATION: HISTORY OR SYMBOL?

Many midcentury books on preaching regarded sermons as "recital." Under the aegis of biblical theology they linked preaching to the notion of salvation history, as a recounting of so-called mighty acts of God. God was presumed to be revealed in a series of big paradigmatic historical events. Of course, the idea that God is revealed in singular historical events was put forth over against previously popular convictions—God on display in nature or God disclosed to faith-piety. Thus, theology turned from celebrations of God in the natural world (which scientific description had undercut) and from explorations of religious affections (which Dr. Freud had tromped) to the realm of objective history, oddly isolated from natural setting and interpretative faith. Excited chatter about the acts of God in history—exodus, Sinai, exile, the Christ-event—began to issue from pulpits. Preachers turned a cold shoulder on speculations of God's being (Greek) and championed, instead, what was believed to be a true, biblical (Hebrew) perspective, namely God as an actor in history. Where was God revealed? Answer: in historical event *alone.*

According to proponents of salvation history, God's mighty acts have been recorded. God's past-tense revelation has been scribbled into scripture for us present-tense people. Because Christ is the culmination of God's history and cannot be superseded, "new" revelation need not be expected. While prior acts of God led to Christ and have meaning in Christ, since Christ is the crown of revelation, all subsequent disclosures of God-with-us can only be reiterations or extensions of the one, mighty Christ-event. By God's own design, however, revelation has been written into scripture, which is now God's Word to us. Notice that in a salvation-history scheme, preaching is the last link in a chain: God acts in history, God's history is recorded for us in scripture, preaching transfers scripture's testimony to the faith of the church. In salvation history, preaching is a witness to the witness to the mighty acts of God.

The historical model of revelation provokes numerous questions. Though the Bible does suggest that God is involved in human history (as well as in the realm of nature), whenever we try to explain *how* God acts, we tumble into a philosophical morass. What exactly would an act of God be? If we reject a crude notion of *deus ex machina* invasions of human freedom, which in fact the historical model did, how can we make sense out of the idea of God acting in history? We can assert that God works through human freedoms, in-directly, by some sort of unseen influence, but, then, we must explain what we may mean by "influence." The minute we start searching for modes of unseen influence, we drift toward a God who impinges on human conscious-ness. The God-who-acts theologians were horrified, however, at the mere thought of a God-to-consciousness approach; it was a dangerous subjectivity they had already condemned. As a result, when salvation-history theologians attempted to explain God's involvement in history, they either stumbled back into causal interventions, or they became unintelligible, or both!

While the Bible does refer to God acting, we must ask what distinguishes a genuine God act from other historical events. In the natural world, a psalmist may sing of cedars of Lebanon tossed about in a sudden storm, and, in holy awe, say "God." Within a different interpretive framework, however, we would describe the event as a moving low-pressure front. As a result, we are bound to wonder if revelation is in the event itself or in interpretive framework, or in an interaction of event and interpretation. The same sort of difficulty shows up in reference to historical happenings. While Israel praised God for an astonishing Red Sea deliverance, a dedicated Marxist, who may also have an eye for liberation, will read the historical event quite differently. Is there some quality to certain events that convincingly displays God's activity? If so, what? Because all events are interpreted events, could we not suppose that revelation is through interpretation rather than in event per se? Is God revealed in hermeneutics or in history? The mighty-acts-of-God theologians were at pains to sidestep certain theological positions. They rejected the notion that revelation is contained in dogmatic propositions. Likewise, they were eager to shy away from a speculative natural theology. Finally, they repudiated what they regarded as an easily compromised subjectivity which linked revelation and religious experience. As a result, they turned to objective history—the mighty acts of God. The difficulty with the position is that the notion of objective history is suspect, and the idea of a God-event is all but unintelligible. With the dialectical theologians, we may agree that revelation may not be weighed by the measure of our minds, but we must insist that revelation to be *revelation* must, at least, relate to human understandings.

We have remarked that with the rise of the historical model preaching suffered. If revelation is in past event, preaching is bound to be a recital of past history. By borrowing the idea of "word-event" we can somewhat enhance the status of preaching by arguing that preaching is a re-presentation of event, and, therefore, participates in the potency of the event as it reaches into the present day. In the historical model, preaching may be termed "Word of God" because it rehearses God-events, or because it speaks from scripture, or because God chooses to use preaching to connect a past-tense saving event to present-tense faith. Thus, though salvation-history theology tended to exalt preaching, in actuality, it reduced preaching to an end-of-the-line activity: God has acted in history; the Bible is a record of the acts of God; historical-critical research gets at original revelation through scripture; preaching preaches recovered revelation to faith.

Today, however, we must admit that *history is always history in social consciousness*. In social consciousness, events are interpreted in relation to given symbols, myths, models, rituals, and the like. The dramatic turn in contemporary theology is a *turn toward symbol*. Revelation is associated with the symbols through which we interpret life. Thus, we may begin to view God not so much as an actor in history, but as a "symbol source" or "image giver" to human social consciousness. Though there may be problems connected with such a theological shift, they are surely more manageable than those connected with the idea of a God who acts in history and is on display in self-evident God-events. To make such a shift is not a nose dive into

115

subjectivity because, after all, "objective" and "subjective" are both categories of consciousness. If we conceive of God as a Consciousness that is conscious of us, and revelation as a disclosure of God, mediated through symbols in social consciousness, we can still retain motifs that seem essential to theologies of history. The mighty acts of God may be viewed as a narrative structure in social consciousness, and Christ may be understood as a living symbol who transforms Christian social consciousness. If we begin to think of revelation in relation to the symbols, myths, and rituals that are given to social consciousness, we will take a turn toward mysteries of language and, thus, toward a renewed theology of the Word.

Preaching is a means of grace, but not merely because it provides a link connecting past-tense acts of God and present-tense faith. Preaching is a means of grace because it speaks the images, symbols, myths, and meanings which are saving and are a hermeneutic for God's self-disclosures. Of course, preaching does not neglect the past. Are not ancient myths of creation, fall, and consummation given to consciousness through preaching? And surely the narrative of God-with-us is plotted in consciousness by preaching. The Living Symbol Jesus Christ is posed before us in consciousness by preaching. Within a symbolic theological orientation, preaching is alive with the Presence of God *now*. After all, Christian symbols do testify to a God whose nature *is* self-disclosure, and to the reality of a being-saved new life in the world. Thus, preaching, as it forms faith-consciousness, is a means of God's self-disclosure and saving grace *now*. No wonder that preaching's language is a language of metaphor.

THE LANGUAGE OF ANALOGY

Preaching reaches for metaphorical language because God is a mysterious Presence-in-Absence. God is not an object in view. Therefore, preaching must resort to analogy, saying, "God is like . . ." We cannot dismiss analogy as mere projection, the fantasy stuff of an orphaned loneliness sketching its own image on the stars. No, the language of analogy is profoundly related to fields of lived experience. We can isolate types of experience out of which our God-talk arises.

Obviously, God-talk is related to *structures of human consciousness*. Consciousness is remarkably agile (if predictable). In consciousness we are free to leap about in time and space, to view ourselves and overview our deep-pool souls, to perform magic tricks of imagination. For example, we can picture ourselves standing at a pulpit preaching, and then, by a miracle of imagination, locate the pulpit on a wave-smoothed stretch of sand by a rolling sea. We can populate a congregation for our preaching by drawing together in consciousness figures from different times and places in our memory. We can even depict historical personages, such as Abraham Lincoln or Martin Luther, seated in our congregation. Then, we can step back in consciousness and be aware of ourselves doing the depicting! The amazing range of consciousness, its Chinese-box complexities and imaginative friskiness, clearly connects with patterns of God-talk. Though we are seemingly free in consciousness—in consciousness we can even view our being born and dying—nevertheless, we are also aware of limitations; we cannot be everywhere at once; we cannot stand outside of time; we do have to die. In the conjunction of "free" consciousness and actual finitude, we conjure the possibility of an infinite free consciousness, indeed, of a Consciousness that is conscious of us. The image of God as unlimited Consciousness—omnipotent, omniscient, omnipresent, and eternal—seems to arise at the moment when free human consciousness is aware of the pathos of finitude.

Of course, the trouble with God analogies that arise in connection with structures of consciousness is that they can be twisted by our own will-to-be-God. Whenever we human types want to "know like God," we end up erecting an idol. Thus, projecting our own overreaching desires, we define omnipotence as a dominating freedom to do as we please, omnipresence as liberty to be where we wish, omniscience as permission to be in on everyone's secrets, eternity as a suspended time for ourselves, and so on. So, though God analogies may be prompted by a collision between our "free" consciousness and strictures of finitude, they can turn demonic as they are twisted by our incurable will-to-be-God. (A turn of the radio dial on Sunday mornings will let you hear all kinds of demonic God-talk!)

In Christian communities, however, the image of Jesus Christ crucified will radically revise our notions of the attributes of God. Can omnipotence be an unlimited "doing as God pleases" in view of suffering love seen on the cross? Or will God's eternity be defined as a "timeless self-possession" when set beside Christ's selfless dying? The God analogies we draw must ever be modified by the display of impotent, suffering love on Calvary. While God must be conceived as an unlimited Consciousness, conscious of us, the "interior" of God's consciousness is defined by Jesus Christ.

God analogies also arise *relationally* out of our self-awareness. Because we can view ourselves and, indeed, are aware of a "me" and a "myself" in consciousness, we construct analogies of God and ourselves in relationship. We speak of the relationship between God and self, or God and community, in models drawn from the social world. Thus, we will speak of God as a Parent, or a Judge, or a Shepherd, or a Teacher, and so forth. These social images work in two directions—toward God and toward humanity. If God is Parent, we are children; if God is Ruler, we are citizens; if God is Judge, we are "on the stand." Because relational models rest on social-role analogies, they must be examined with great care. If, for example, a society is disfigured by willful male domination, the image of God the Father may well be in jeopardy. Or if the image of God as Judge is informed by an unbending law-and-order judicial system that positively relishes capital punishment, true biblical meanings may be in peril. In a way, sinful social order is a perennial problem—there are no perfect parents, teachers, judges, and so on, and there never have been. Preaching has usually coped with the problem by qualifying relational imagery with "how inadequate" or "how much more" language. In some historical eras, however, social roles may be so distorted as to render traditional images all but useless. Just because an image can be found on a page of the Bible does not guarantee its perpetual usefulness. For example, the Bible does liken God to a warrior but, in an age of military muscle-flexing and hawkish Pentagon generals, the warrior image may mispreach the gospel. The norm by which we must judge all social-role imagery is the disclosure of God-love in Jesus Christ crucified.

In addition to relational imagery, there are models that seem to emerge in connection with our *narrative consciousness*. The conjunction of faith in God and human-narrative-recall tends to generate story illustrations or examples. Stories in sermons are not included to hold interest; they show up because we associate God's grace with social history and personal human pilgrimage. Such story systems are difficult to manage: overelaborated they will tend toward allegory (which will, of course, destroy narrativity), and under-developed they can reduce the mystery of God to soap-opera banality. Many story images are drawn from social role models. Thus, we may tell a story about a parent and child, or a ruler and citizens, or a judge and a condemned prisoner. When stories are not shaped by social role models, their plots are usually theological dramas—stories of rebellion and reconciliation, stories of old life and new life, stories of wandering and welcome, and so forth. Stories must be reviewed carefully lest in structure or character they pervert the gospel of God's grace. For example, sermons at the turn of the century frequently featured stories of missionary conversion (the missionaries were always White-faced), and seemed to proclaim a gospel of America's Manifest Destiny. One New England preacher ended such a sermon story by shouting, "God has given us America!" The only way we can test narrative images is to place them beside the story of Jesus Christ the crucified. If stories are theological dramas, their structural patterns must align with the life, death, resurrection story of Jesus Christ.

The use of analogical language—metaphor, simile, image, and the like—is inevitable, and, obviously, desirable in preaching. God is a mysterious Presence-in-Absence, and may not be spoken of in a matter-of-fact "tables-and-chairs" language. Moreover, because figurative language does draw on images of lived experience it is "incarnational" and, therefore, natural to a gospel of God-with-us. Nevertheless, figurative language is potent and must be employed thoughtfully. We examine analogical language by thinking in two directions, toward social usage and toward theological intent. We must ask how an image functions socially (its value, its meaning, its emotional baggage, etc.), and then determine what theological understanding we are attempting to convey. Preaching is much too important to be top-of-the-mind, spilled-out verbiage, shaped by immediate associations of a minister's consciousness. We must consider our analogical language.

THE LANGUAGE OF DENIAL

Analogy is the language of faith. Yet analogy in and of itself is insufficient. Analogy draws the mystery of God into the human world, but in so doing it can easily domesticate God and make the gospel trivial. Because analogy is a language of "like," it can make God like us; God's love like our loves; God's sovereignty like authority in our political systems; God's kingdom like our moral spheres. The obvious danger in analogy is that it can paint our image on the face of God and scale down God's revelation to our conventional wisdoms. Thus, throughout the Christian centuries, there have been other languages used along with the language of analogy—the language of *amplification* and the dialectical language of *denial.*

The language of amplification is a language of "but how much more God . . ." In sermons we may liken God's love to worthy parental love, but, again and again, we qualify the analogy by adding, "but how much more God's love . . ." We magnify in order to establish a realm distinction between the human and the divine. At its best, the language of amplification is a kind of praise! Of course, a language that magnifies can be dangerous. If the language of amplification succumbs to our will-to-be-God, it can end up turning God into a tyrannical absolute. Or, if we magnify God casually, we can produce a God-like-us, but on a larger scale, a super-God, quite alien to the God disclosed on Calvary. A language of amplification is necessary, but it must be employed properly. We use analogy to say "God is *like,*" but magnify likeness in order to indicate a like-but-not-like dimension. We push "greatness" toward "otherness" and not toward a large-scale likeness. Rightly employed, the language of amplification will guard analogy by drawing a distinction between God's nature and our natural lives.

The other way in which analogy is qualified is by the language of denial,

119

a language designed to signal God's transcendent "otherness." As the Bible observes, God's ways are emphatically not *our* ways. In using a language of denial we are saying that all analogies fail or are inappropriate: God is Holy, God is Other. Taken to an extreme, the language of denial will drive us toward a *via negativa* silence in which mystic awe is literally speechless. (No wonder, in the midst of volubility, sermons should allow for silences!) Though our slightly romantic age may admire the profundity of silence, silent sermons chock-full of mute adoration would be less than satisfactory. Nevertheless, the language of denial will show up in sermons to prevent analogy from constructing a God-like-us, which, of course, would be no God at all.

The language of denial will function in two ways: it will qualify analogy, or it may frame analogy producing paradox. Thus, for example, we may draw on an image of parental love to preach the love of God but, then, immediately follow analogy with a demurrer: "Even our best loving is not love enough. God's love is different and we have no words to describe God's love." At other times, we will frame analogy with denial, as when a minister may say, "God's love is not like our loves." The statement is paradoxical because it conjoins analogy ("love") with denial ("not like"). Sometimes the language of denial will show up in contrasts. We may speak of God-love analogously, but then draw a sharp contrast—"Our loves are full of self-love, but God's love is utterly selfless." Basically, preaching wields a language of analogy—how else can we speak of God—but will add amplifications, modifications, and denials to analogy in order to protect the holy otherness of a Presence-in-Absence God.

What we cannot do is to leap into abstraction. There are preachers so frightened by analogy that they speak of God in a flattened out, abstract language, a denotative language devoid of human imagery. Often, the effort is prompted by a kind of religious pride that regards Christian faith as a higher religion that has outgrown immature anthropomorphisms. The result of an abstract language, however, is that God is turned into an "X to the nth" impersonal force that cannot be aligned with the notion of God-with-us in Christ Jesus. Among other things, Christian faith reads a Bible, a Bible that is crammed with the embarrassments of metaphor, analogy, and all but palpable imagery. Analogy *is* the language of faith.

How can we manage analogy? There is guidance in exploring the nature of metaphor. Metaphor has power by virtue of tension, the tension of likeness and dissimilarity. If we say of someone "He's a tiger!" we bump images from two different categories, the animal kingdom and the human world—"he" and "tiger." In the conjoining of the two dissimilar realms we create a kind of ontological mystery: Why is the being of "he" like the being of "tiger"?

Metaphors thus produce a brooding thoughtfulness as we explore an ontological mystery. Similes are less mysterious, and, of course, less potent ("He is as *cruel* as a tiger"); similes are aspectual and feature an aligning of predicates. When preaching poses analogies, such analogies work like similes and metaphors; they speak of God's attributes or of God's being. Preaching must be on guard, however, lest realm distinctions evaporate. Thus, preaching will incorporate amplifications, denials, and the language of paradox along with analogy. God is mysterious Presence-in-Absence, both immanent and transcendent. Thus, the language of preaching incorporates tension.

In managing a language of analogy we will allow our words to be ruled by the "Word become flesh," Jesus Christ. Christ is the Living Metaphor of God-with-us. The nailed-down, suffering love of Christ crucified counters our tendency to blow the attributes of God into idolatry by our own tenacious will-to-be-God. At the same time, Christ's presence as a living symbol prevents us from absorbing God's nature into images of our human nature; Christ is different. Thus, we need not fear a language of analogy. Christ as "Word become flesh" blesses a language of analogy. Yet, the nature of Jesus Christ protects every analogy: his radical humanity counters idolatry, and his mysterious divinity prevents trivial analogy. Jesus Christ, the Living Metaphor of God-with-us, watches over the language of preaching.

METAPHOR AND LIFE

We live in mysteries and we are a mystery to ourselves. Not only are there huge questions connected with being human—Why are we here on a whirling ball of earth? Why are we born and why do we die?—but there are also mysteries within the human self. In spite of our psychoanalytic wisdoms, we do not know ourselves. We may paste name tags on our souls, or trace genealogies, but we cannot answer the question of identity. We sense that, through all our days and years, we are being formed so that, at any given moment, we cannot say exactly who we are. Even our motives defy analysis: The fabric of impulse, desire, dream, and pretension is too thickly woven within us to follow separate strands. Besides, when we do look at ourselves and, indeed, into ourselves, we always catch ourselves posing! The self is a conundrum. Moreover, the human enterprise itself defies understanding. Every day, like a shaken kaleidoscope, the human world patterns differently in consciousness. We can scan headlines or peruse chapters in history, but, unfinished, the human story is uncertain. In sum, human being in the world is mysterious. We make meaning with metaphor by bumping mysteries together.

The only way we have access to our own depth is by metaphor. T. S. Eliot

121

spoke of "objective correlatives," a cumbersome term for a perennial language. He meant that whenever we try to bring out our own inner world, we are forced to point to some external image—we make metaphor. Thus, a severely depressed mental patient, who had not spoken a word for months, painted a barren, leafless tree trunk daily in art therapy. She would point at her picture and then point to herself. Finally, her cure was signaled by a lone, bright flower painted one day on the black tree. Basically, we do the same sort of thing with words when we speak of ourselves. We may grab at clichéd metaphors, saying "I'm blue," or "I'm down," or "I'm keyed up," or "I'm happy as a lark." When profoundly affected, perhaps, we will reach for poetic power and shape more original metaphors—"I feel like a lost child wandering." Eliot's contention is true; when we refer to our inner world, we are forced to point to objects, experiences, and images within an outer world. Of late, with the rise of psychoanalytic sciences, there has been some recourse to diagnostic terms—"I feel a little schizy today" or "I'm getting manic." Of course, in using such terms we are treating ourselves as symptomed illnesses, which, oddly enough, may be our intent. When we speak of ourselves without using metaphor, it is usually because we wish both to reveal and to mask our interior. So we say "I'm sad" or "I'm happy," using words which tell but do not tell much. If we genuinely wish to open our interior life to ourselves or to others, we will turn to making metaphor.

Often, we can discover social attitudes through the metaphors we may inadvertently use. If a representative of the Black community complains, "We have been shut out," the metaphor expresses a communal sense of rejection. (Spirituals are also filled with metaphors of the Black experience—"Sometimes I feel like a motherless child.") Or suppose that a political orator, champing with patriotic fervor, claims that opponents are "running down the nation." We can assume that the speaker regards detractors as either erosive ("run down" like an unkempt building) or murderous ("run down" like an accident victim), or possibly both. Rhetoricians can take a body of discourse, analyze metaphors, and, with uncanny accuracy, portray the social attitudes of a particular speaker. If, for example, a somewhat bellicose American president snarls "Make my day" during a TV interview, and, then, in commenting on the militarization of space, remarks, "The force is on our side," we can presume his social attitudes. Evidently this president allows motion-picture images to shape social policy, since both comments were drawn from cinema dialogue. Because one line is taken from a violent gun-battle movie scene, and the other line from a film on outer-space warfare, we may well suppose that the president views himself as an armed hero engaged in do-or-die battle. We express social attitudes, self-assessments, and situational understandings through the metaphors that sprinkle our speaking.

Metaphors are much more important than we know; they orient our ethical behavior. Behind our behavioral selves are systems of related metaphors, or, better, models made from congruent metaphors. Is it surprising to discover that a competitive free-enterprise society uses images drawn from competitive sports? A corporate sales force will have a "game plan" to "end run" sales resistance and "score big" against the competition. And, certainly in a mercantile society, it is not unusual to find that time is money: "I can't *spare* the time," "My time is *valuable*," "I'm *spending* too much time on the golf course," "I haven't time to *waste*." While such interlocking metaphor systems may seem innocent, they are not. If, for example, we live our lives in a time = money metaphor system we will simply not be able to imagine other "models," for example, time as love, time as freedom, time as enjoyment, and so on. Likewise, think how corporations might operate, if, instead of a competitive-game model, they were to do business within a family model, or a cooperative-builders model. Obviously, a foreign policy framed in a "cold-war" model will be quite different from a policy put together in a "global-village" model. The rather frightening fact is that social metaphor systems are not mere rhetorical ornamentation, they disclose the models that shape our minds, and set our behavioral patterns with terrifying power. We live our lives *in* metaphor.

So lived experience is neither objective event nor subjective affect. As human beings in the world we manufacture symbols which, in turn, often hold us captive. We comprehend ourselves via metaphor; we act in metaphor; we adopt social attitudes because of metaphor. Of course, metaphor making is not merely a personal proclivity, it is a social inheritance. We are born into societies that have preformed metaphorical conventions. Because most of our living is prereflective, without thinking, we will live in metaphor systems, quite unaware of their dominating power in shaping our consciousness. Preachers who wish to transform human lives will have to grasp the sheer power of metaphorical language. With metaphors, we can rename the world for faith.

PREACHING AS METAPHOR MAKING

Metaphor lives by tension. In metaphor we bring together elements from different realms, and, in their conjunction, discover new meanings. Thus, metaphor is a paradigm for preaching. In preaching, we bring out meaning from the mystery of God-with-us, and bring out the reality of being-saved-in-the-world and put them together. Preaching mediates metaphorically.

The great symbols that are given within the Hebrew-Christian tradition are, of course, metaphorical in character. The story of creation is itself a metaphor in which God, the Creator, is regarded as a maker of the world, doing creation in a matter of days, and, like a sculptor, fashioning humanity from the clay of earth. Likewise, the story of the fall is essentially metaphorical —a story of innocent humanity in the pristine garden corrupted by desire and, subsequently, burdened by shame. Through the story we read our own current events as events reiterating the primal plot of Eden. In addition to myths of origin, we have received a series of visions of God's future which also function metaphorically. The stunning images of the "Holy City" inform our social dreaming; "Someday," we sing, "there'll be a place for us," and cherish the hope. Of course, stories drawn from biblical history, the history of God with Israel, tend to become metaphor when pressed against daily headlines. Preachers may take a slice of biblical history, such as the royal consciousness of Solomon's military empire, and bring it together with national policy and, metaphorically, grasp the meaning of our contemporary history. Or preaching may reach for the story of Jesus, a story of trial, painful death, and resurrection, and, through the story, view human life, death, and destiny—our lives are cruciform and our hope is resurrection. All these procedures are the stuff of preaching and are metaphorical in character. Out of a bringing together of symbolic material and lived experience we discover meaning, meaning in the tension of a metaphorical process.

We have labeled the figure of Jesus Christ a "living symbol" to Christian consciousness, a two-way reflective image. In sermons, Jesus Christ lives metaphorically. Preachers locate the figure of Christ before the mystery of God, and, through Christ, speak of God's "interior" nature. Of course, preachers also set the figure of Christ before human nature in order to bring out the character of a true humanity. Christ appears to embody God-for-us and us-for-God. In all such overlays the figure of Christ seems to be a living metaphor for faith. In addition, the scene of the cross is used in sermons as a sweeping metaphor for the world before God. Certainly, we can pick out the social structures of our world at the cross—military force, a judicial system, organized religion, political prudence, and even democracy in action. But we can also see fallen humanity at Calvary—our fears, our guarded hostilities, our defensive guilts, our vacillating loyalties, and so forth. Thus, in sermons the image of Christ crucified functions as a panoramic metaphor, bringing out a range of human meanings. In preaching, Jesus Christ the Living Symbol juxtaposes the mystery of God-love and the mystery of the human world, and, with metaphorical energy, generates tensive meaning.

To switch our focus, the being-saved community understands itself through models and metaphors. Obviously, phrases such as "born again," "new age," "new humanity," "kingdom of God" found in the Bible, are metaphors that relate to the reality of a new-order redemptive society. The

Bible contains nearly a hundred images which seek to express the unique nature of ecclesial life—"body of Christ," "royal priesthood," "family of God," and so on. Because salvific new life is a mystery of grace it must be brought out and apprehended metaphorically. Of course, the metaphors that preaching proposes for the being-saved community relate to enacted metaphor systems such as the sacraments. The sacraments, as living models, surely bring to consciousness our identity as God's new people in the world. Think of the awesome power of Eucharist for a people, who, in the world, may live in competitive-game metaphors or time-is-money metaphors, but who, in church, gather at one table, serve one another, and receive the poured-out life of Jesus Christ. What of Baptism, which once was celebrated by stripping off clothes of old life, passing through waters, and being anointed as newborn children of God? Metaphors bring out profound life meanings, and ritual systems do so with tremendous power. In our everyday world where it is often difficult to spot Christians without a score card, living metaphors enable us to realize who we are as God's new people. We appropriate our being-saved through metaphor.

The conventional language of the pulpit, in recent years, has been an odd language indeed. Because God was presumed to have been revealed in past-tense historical events, sermons usually contained much objective referential language; we talked *about* history. On the other hand, when it came to matters of faith, we unwrapped large, quite dramatic, personal illustrations. Thus, our sermons split between an objective language which spoke of acts of God in history and a spun-out emotive language which celebrated personal faith— an odd conjunction of styles possibly prompted by a notion of objective atonement and subjective faith-response.

Categories of "objective" and "subjective" are less than useful, however. We interpret the world in consciousness metaphorically, and the self in consciousness metaphorically, and metaphor itself is an act of consciousness. Thus, in preaching, we will not wield two different languages, but, instead, speak *one* language of consciousness, a metaphorical language, as we bring out the mystery of God-with-us, and bring out the mystery of being-saved-in-the-world. Faith is formed in a nexus of image, symbol, metaphor, and ritual. Therefore, the language of preaching is essentially metaphorical.

9.
Examples and
Illustrations

Paul Scherer once observed that if the church were to die, the dagger in its heart would be the sermon. He could have been even more precise. What could kill the church is not so much sermons as sermon illustrations! With theological discernment at low ebb at present, sermons may lack substance, and, lacking substance, may overcompensate by heaping illustrations—lengthy, overblown, often mawkish illustrations. In an informal poll taken at an eastern university, students were asked their reaction to preaching. The complaint that surfaced in most of their replies was a reaction to what one student labeled "those cornball illustrations." Misuse, overuse, emotional manipulation notwithstanding, preachers have wielded examples and illustrations for centuries, ever since Jesus spoke in parables and the apostle Paul shaped analogies. In every century, there have been collections of illustrations prepared for preachers and there still are. So, though a danger, illustrations are here to stay. Our task is to learn how to use them well.

What can examples and illustrations do for us? In traditional homiletics, illustrations are regarded as analogies that can make plain the obscure; they help us to grasp murky mysteries of faith. Or illustrations are viewed as proof; they give support to statements that otherwise might be doubtful. So, in sum, examples and illustrations serve to increase understanding or bolster credence; they explain the obscure or convince the dubious. Such a view is much too simple. Think of the many, many ways in which illustrations may function. Illustrations can bridge time; in discussing the biblical world, a contemporary illustration or example can draw the past into the present or vice versa. Illustrations can build models in consciousness within which meanings can mean. Illustrations can gather huge sprawling meaning into a coherent system of comprehension. They can join concept and percept, enabling us to see what we may mean. Insofar as illustrations combine narrative, emotion, visual images, and the like, they can communicate on many levels at the same time. Or, much like metaphor, illustrations can bring together images from different realms of experience, and by their juxtaposition, break out surprising new meanings. Examples and illustrations, as they function analogously, are the native tongue of faith. They are crucial to Christian preaching.

At the outset, let us venture a working distinction between example and illustration. Though, in use, illustrations and examples may overlap, some sort of distinction must be drawn for purposes of discussion. Examples are available; they are at hand in the common consciousness of a congregation. Suppose that in preaching, a minister says:

> We all know what it's like to be sick. Remember the strange childhood illnesses we passed through—measles, chicken pox, perhaps, mumps. Remember how awful we felt. . . .

The minister is working with material that is already a part of congregational experience. The minister is merely drawing the material out of common consciousness into open recognition. However, suppose a minister says:

> Coventry Patmore tells a story of his son. The little boy was sick in bed—one of those childhood illnesses—when . . .

Here, a particular story, though it may relate to our common experience, is imported into the sermon from outside the range of congregational consciousness. In general, we may think of illustrations as imports brought into sermons by preachers. Of course, the line we have drawn between examples and illustrations can blur. If an example is so developed that it has its own story line, and seems to create its own "world," it will cease to represent common congregational awareness and become an illustration. Nevertheless, at least for purposes of discussion, let us go with the temporary distinction: Examples emerge from common congregational consciousness whereas illustrations are brought to a congregation from beyond the sphere of shared experience.

EXAMPLES

Again and again, preachers will portray lived experience in sermons. They will offer examples drawn from life. Examples function in many ways. We may single out *major* ways in which examples are used, however. Examples will be used (1) to establish the truth of statements by demonstrating that they are "true to life"; (2) to form analogies—for example, God forgives as a parent forgives; or (3) as datum for an exploration of "what's going on in our lives." Let us briefly survey cases in which examples function.

Suppose that we are trying to *establish the fact* that people, in moments of severe crisis, may turn desperately to God. To show that our contention is true to life, we may chain a series of examples, such as the following:

> You have been to the doctor for a routine examination. He says that there's a shadow on your X-ray. Maybe you'd better go in for surgery, he says, and not wait too long. You walk away from his office all scared inside. Everything you look at seems to stand out, perhaps, because you sense there may be little time. And inside your soul, the words well up, "O God."

> Or maybe your marriage, which began in a bright blush of wonder, has gradually turned sour. Now, you're throwing words back and forth like stones at each other—words, and "digs," and subtle hurts. And you suddenly realize what's going on, and, with a kind of weariness, say to yourself, "O God."

We are using examples to support a statement—people in desperation do call on God. What we are doing is imagining examples related to actual lived experiences, and drawing them together with our statement as a kind of proof: We are saying, see, our statement is true to life. Of course, if examples are used to establish reality, it is crucial that the examples be real and not merely stock notions of reality. Thus, in selecting examples, a preacher will have to check both the *types* of experience chosen and the *reality* of descriptions. Nothing is more embarrassing than a preacher who tells us how we experience, but misses the mark, so that the description does not ring true. Obviously, it is a disaster, if, after an experience has been described, the audience, on reflection, rejects the example, and thinks how bizarre the preacher is—"We *do not* experience what you say we do." Nevertheless, again and again, we will combine statement and experience to establish truth.

We also use examples when we *form analogies,* usually in connection with God-talk, but also when we are trying to grasp our own interior dramas. Suppose we are trying to speak of God's astonishing mercy:

> So God forgives us. God forgives out of astonishing mercy. Remember when you were a child and you'd done something wrong? All day long you'd been living locked up in yourself, feeling guilty, as your mother watched and waited. Finally you couldn't hold your secret inside anymore, and, sobbing, you blurted it out. Then your mother, who had guessed all along what was troubling you, gathered you in, and in a laughing teariness, told you, yes, it was wrong, but you were hers and she loved you anyway.

Here we have slapped an in-life experience up against an affirmation of God's mercy, trying to explain the experience of forgiveness. When such examples are chosen, they must be weighed with care; they must be theologically correct and must not trivialize God. Often, they will have to be followed either by a language of amplification, or a language of denial, such as:

> Look, all our human pictures fail: God is greater. God's mercy is tougher, sweeter, larger than anything we know. God *is* mercy.

In assessing examples used analogously, we must not only weigh the worth of the example against the majesty and singular grace of God, but we must examine point-of-view. Do we portray the experience of being forgiven, or do we turn the example around and describe a parent's consciousness of forgiving? Turning the example around would get at God's own motives and moods. We must be precise in what we are trying to convey.

When we reach for an example, *a slice of life as datum,* we are bringing into consciousness typical experience to study. We portray and then explore. We are probing an example so as to discover who we are.

> Have you noticed? Lately, on the TV screen, we've seen pictures of hunger. There they are, the hungry children of Ethiopia. We see them cradled, listlessly, in someone's bony lap. They can barely move. Their bellies are swollen round, their arms seem no wider than pipe cleaners. From the television screen, their black eyes stare up at us. So we walk over and switch channels, searching for sports or a half-hour sitcom. What are we doing? Perhaps we're evading ourselves. We don't want to feel guilty for what we've got. Above all, we don't want to feel responsible. Down deep, we don't want to change our lives because of them.

In the example used, we portray our own consciousness in order to study "what's going on." The example is brought before us as datum from life to be explored. Again, it is crucial that description be accurate, that is, true to life. Otherwise, we will explore a falsity and, of course, misdiscover ourselves. Examples used as data are drawn from personal consciousness, or from an awareness of the social world. The strategy is not new. In the New Testament Jesus lifted up descriptions of behavior (e.g., hypocrites praying in public), for examination. How else can we understand who we are?

Examples used in sermons may be quite brief or enlarged. Sometimes examples can be tossed off in a series of sentences:

> There are times when we all call out for God. Sometimes we speak aloud, at other times silent screams form inside us. When we've been told we're sick, and there's surgery to be done; when our marriage is on the rocks, and we can't seem to get together; when someone we love is dying, and we don't know what to say. . . .

At other times, we will develop an example so as to portray the actual shape of an experience in consciousness (e.g., the TV description given above). If an example is overdeveloped it may no longer be an expression of common congregational consciousness. Instead, an audience may regard the example as a detached experience being brought to them, in effect, as an illustration. Usually, this will occur if characters in the example appear to have a life of their own, or if the plot of an experience becomes too complex so that it is no longer common to us all. So, normally, examples will not be over-developed, but will be controlled.

Examples used in sermons will tend to be either "moments of conscious-ness" or very simple narratives. To clarify: By "moments of consciousness" we mean examples of how things may strike us, of our attitudes, of our self-awareness, of our world, and so on. By narratives, we mean brief plots of how we act or what may happen to us in our daily lives. Either type of example will require discipline. Obviously, narrative examples can so enlarge as to threaten sermons. If a story experience becomes too big, it will become a world in which we participate, and from which we may have great difficulty emerging. When a narrative example enlarges, then, like a film we sit through or a novel we read, our experience of the example may become a "thing in itself," detached from function. The example will no longer serve a purpose in the sermon. Therefore, if we use narrative experience, we will keep descrip-tion spare, stressing basic plot, and not letting the example build into a world. Likewise, examples that describe our inner attitudes or feelings or states of being must be kept under control. Overblown, they can turn into sheer feeling, and, in turn, produce heightened affect in a congregation. Many ministers suppose that if they can get a congregation to feel, they have accomplished something terribly important. Not so. Feeling per se may be nothing more than an emotional "kick"; it may not produce understanding or motivation or faith. If an example is so hyped that it overengages our feelings, it will no longer link up with understandings; it will not be analogy, or evidence of reality, or a datum to study, but will become an experience in and of itself. Examples must be controlled in order to function in sermons.

What about detail? When using examples many ministers will deliberately keep material vague, and often too vague. After all, there are many people in any congregation and everyone on hand will have different experiences—*ergo*, keep examples vague so that everyone can relate to them. If we provide too much detail, will not some members of the congregation reject the exam-ple as alien to their own experience? Thus, ministers will often speak of human experience in a general way so that everyone present may be included. Compare the following:

> When we plant things in the ground, don't we sense a living force that makes things grow? When we watch something come up out of the ground, we sense the fertility in everything.

On a fine spring day you go out to work in the yard. Perhaps you've bought a flat of marigolds to plant. You dig holes and put in green budding plants until you've dirt in your fingernails. Then, in a kind of wonder, you watch to see the yellow flowers form. There's life pushing up the flowers, life living in everything.

The second example will obviously work much better than the general vagueness of the first. Even if members of a congregation may have no experience with marigolds, or may actively dislike them, nevertheless, they can imagine the second description in their own lived experience. So, when examples are used, they should include actual concrete description, carefully designed, so that the example will be real. (On the other hand, an example of cultivating orchids might be so particular as to be beyond common consciousness!) We must include detail so that examples will relate to lived experience, but, be warned, too much detail can turn the example into a separate world and threaten its usefulness. Nevertheless, though there may be dangers in detail, vagueness will not form in consciousness at all.

How many examples may be used in a single move, and *how much* example material may be packed into a sermon overall? With regard to a sermon: We will, of course, be linking theological meaning to lived experience in *every* move. Theological meaning must always be embodied in images drawn from life. But we will not be able to have a developed example in every move, particularly examples that portray inner awareness. To do so would be to plunge an entire sermon into "subjectivity" so that the sermon might begin to sound like a modern "confessional novel," endlessly rehearsing our feelings, our attitudes, our personal impressions. We can be precise: Within a single move, we may use *only one example*, if we are either drawing an analogy or presenting datum for analysis. If we are establishing that some statement is true to life, however, we may chain two or three brief examples, but never more than three. When we do chain examples, they must be shaped in a similar, stylized manner so they may come together to form a single sense of "trueness" in consciousness.

When we gave examples to establish that people in desperation call on God —an example of a doctor's office visit and of a crumbling marriage—the examples were about the same length, and each ended in the same way with the cry "O God." If chained examples are not constructed in a similar fashion, they will tend to pull apart in consciousness and, thereby, cast doubt on statements being made. So, we may serve up *no more than three chained examples* when we are establishing the reality of statements. Otherwise, when drawing analogies or posing experiences as data for study, we will limit ourselves to only one such example, lest, by multiplying examples, we fragment moves in consciousness.

How do we find examples? By investigating our own mnemonic consciousness, that is how. We will turn into memory and call experiences to mind, searching out what actually happens in the living of life. Of course, we will be on guard lest we settle for clichés of human experience. On television, sitcoms are made of experiential clichés, and we enjoy them precisely because, though they pretend to be true to life, they are not. Sitcoms are escapist. Sermons can too easily serve up the same sort of unreality, namely, stock images of what life is like rather than actualities. When we search ourselves to locate experiential examples, we must go for what *actually* does occur. A second step must be taken, however. We must assess our own experiences to see if they are common to most people. All of us are fairly peculiar people, trying to pretend that we are not. We have singular experiences, or, more likely, common experiences that we understand in rather singular ways. The only test we have of our own experience is comparison with others. Fortunately, most ministers are listeners and also readers. In pastoral work we will hear other people speak of their experiences (if we let them come close enough to do so), and, by reading major novels, poems, and dramas, we will have access to experiences in the consciousness of our age. So, usually, we are able to sift through experiences to locate examples that are true to life—everybody's life.

ILLUSTRATIONS

Illustrations can be varied—brief quotes, described scenes, episodes involving action, pictures, stories, bits of dialogue, and the like. Furthermore, illustrations may be drawn from many sources, from the cinema screen to the pages of the Bible. Illustrations are imported; they are brought into a sermon by a preacher's own analogical imagination, and may serve different functions within discourse. Though they may come to mind readily, they must be used with care.

How can we judge illustrations? Criteria can be ticked off: (1) There must be a clear analogy between an idea in sermon content and some aspect of the illustration; (2) There ought to be a parallel between the structure of content and the shape of an illustration; (3) The illustration should be "appropriate" to the content. Let us see the criteria in action.

Suppose a minister, in preaching, wishes to say that God-with-us could have walked the earth as a VIP, an important personage, but, instead, arrived in modest birth, son of a poor peasant woman. The idea seems to be that God is unassuming. So, the preacher finds an illustration, an old "clinker," and dumps it into the sermon:

> In an art gallery, side by side, are two paintings. One painting is by the famous artist Rembrandt; it is the portrait of a great man, an important world leader. But

the other painting, by an unknown artist, is of a peasant kitchen—a rough board table, and a bunch of asparagus waiting to be cooked. Which painting do people stand and stare at? Not the portrait of the great man; no, they stand transfixed before the picture of the peasant kitchen and the picked asparagus. So God might have come to us in power, in the flesh of a famous man, but, instead, God came as . . .

Is the illustration "cornball"? Yes. But let us apply our tests to see why the illustration fails. (1) Is there a clear analogy being drawn? Yes, a peasant kitchen is lined up with Jesus' peasant birth. (2) Is there a structural similarity between content and the shape of the illustration? Yes. The argument is a two-part argument—not a significant birth, but, rather, a peasant family. In the illustration we have two pictures, a significant portrait compared to a peasant room. (3) Is the illustration appropriate to the content? Answer: *No.* Unfortunately, without realizing, the preacher has turned Jesus into a bunch of asparagus! By "appropriate" we mean that the illustration's imagery is fitting, that it has much the same moral, aesthetic, or social *value* as the idea being illustrated. The diagram shows how our tests function.

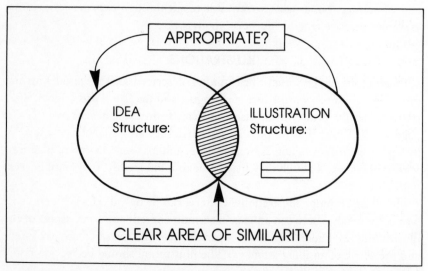

While not all illustrations will be able to match up the structure of an idea with the structural shape of the illustration, there must always be a clear analogy, an obvious point of similarity. When illustrations become impossible, or downright "cornball," it is almost always because a minister has failed to assess the value of the illustration. Illustrations must be *appropriate.* While nothing drawn from the human world can possibly match the glory of God or the mysterious wonders of grace, nevertheless, illustrations need not be trivial, mawkish, or improper. The theological notion of incarnation is surely more significant than a bunch of asparagus waiting to be boiled! Of course, had the minister stopped to think, the illustration of the two pictures might have been salvaged. The detail of the asparagus might simply have been skipped. Though the actual painting may well have contained the offending asparagus, homiletic license would surely permit exclusion. On the other hand, the homely, peasant setting of the painting is on target, so that the illustration might have served nicely if used with discipline. Though some ministers clip and file illustrative material, illustrations do not have to be used unmodified; they can and should be shaped to fit sermons.

ILLUSTRATIONS AND MOVES

Illustrations are used in moves. That is to say, illustrations are used in connection with amplified single statements of meaning. If illustrations function within moves they will be governed by the content, shape, and intention of a move, and must fit into the move's point-of-view. In this regard, let us set forth some ground rules.

Only One Illustration per Move

Only one illustration may be used in a move; we may not multiply illustrations. Though examples drawn from common experience may, at times, be multiplied (as long as they are brief examples), illustrations may not. Often ministers are tempted to string together a series of illustrations for a single idea, either as filler or as a misguided attempt to increase impact. Usually, the multiplication of illustrations is prompted by the diversity of a congregation. Because a congregation contains many different kinds of people—young and old, men and women, day laborers, professional people, technicians, artists, and the like—will not a series of illustrations, each designed to relate to a different audience, be more effective than one? Such an argument may sound right, but it is emphatically wrong. If several illustrations are used in sequence, they do not come together to illustrate a single meaning; instead, they will weaken each other and produce a confusion of meaning. Ministers seem to expect a congregation to hear different illustrations, and, in each case, to distill a point of analogy, then to put all analogies together into some kind of single analogy, and then to understand. Congregations simply will not do such mental gymnastics while hearing a sermon. Instead, multiple illustrations will always weaken analogy, and thereby make understanding even more difficult.

For example, a preacher was once trying to illustrate the notion of blood atonement. The preacher used two illustrations in tandem. First, the minister told of seeing a film in which pioneer settlers and Native Americans made peace. The chief and the pioneer leader met, and, after making a tiny incision in their wrists, let their blood flow together—a somewhat gory image. Second, the preacher told of seeing two small boys scuffling in the churchyard until they were scraped and bloody, and, of how, finally, the boys stood up and, though weary, embraced. On interview following the sermon, members of the congregation reported hearing only *one* illustration—about little boys playing "Cowboys and Indians." Oddly enough, all mention of blood and slit wrists disappeared in their recall. Why? Because when the two illustrations came together in consciousness, the congregation could not accept the notion of two children slitting wrists. As a result, they dropped the crucial detail altogether. The example demonstrates our problem. Illustrations in sequence will interact. Even if one strong illustration remains in consciousness, it will be weakened or even altered by proximity with others. There will *always* be some degree of confusion. Let us be emphatic: There may be only *one* illustration per move. Multiplying illustrations does not increase impact. Instead, two illustrations are always weaker than one, and three illustrations will be a positive disaster! What of the problem of congregational diversity? As we have mentioned before, congregational imagination is astonishing. If an illustration is vividly phrased, congregations will imagine and relate. They will relate quite readily even to somewhat unfamiliar material. So, the rule is *one illustration per move and only one.*

On-Target Illustrations

To be used, an illustration must fit the thought of the move. By "fit," we mean that an illustration must pass the criteria previously outlined. Above all, an illustration must be a clear analogy. Ministers will often have difficulty in finding an illustration that contains an exact analogy to the thought they are seeking to convey. As a result, they will often settle for "It's close." Unfortunately, "close" is never close enough. It is better to do without an illustration than to include a slightly off-target image that may distort the meaning of a move.

Suppose a preacher were preaching on the problem of theodicy, and trying to say that the Christian contention, "God is Love," is difficult to maintain in a cruel world. Here is an illustration:

> Some years ago, the old *Life* magazine featured a picture. The picture showed a pile of rubble dumped by a whirling tornado—a tragic pile of furniture, clothing, household stuff; belongings that once belonged to some family. On top of the pile was a bent church sign, reading, "God is Love."

The illustration fits. The tornado rubble is a symbol of natural evil that human beings suffer, and the bent signboard, ironically, represents Christian faith-claims. Suppose we imagine, however, that the preacher saw a somewhat different picture:

> Some years ago, a magazine featured a picture of the wreckage following a tornado. The picture showed a pile of rubble dumped by the whirling storm— a tragic pile of furniture, photographs, clothing, and household goods; belongings that once belonged to a family. On top of the pile was a sign, reading, "First Presbyterian Church"! How difficult it is to believe our Christian faith when faced with tragedy! How can we believe that God is Love in a cruel world?

While there is an indirect association going on—Church = Christian congregation = Christian conviction = God is Love—the illustration is off-target and will actually weaken meaning. So, though our second version of the illustration is stronger in style, it ends up weaker because it is slightly off-line with the structure of thought being presented. If we are Presbyterians, we may delight in imagining one of our church signs dumped on a rubbish pile; but, nevertheless, the illustration will misinform meaning and weaken the move being made.

Sometimes, by applying some imagination, an illustration can be reworked so as to fit with content. At other times, the illustration is simply inadequate. When an illustration does not quite fit, it is better to use no illustration, and to find some other way to image an idea.

Relating Strength to Strength

Illustrations must relate to the strength of moves. Actually, many preachers overillustrate sermons, pumping illustrations compulsively into every move within a sermon. As a result, minor matters may end up being strongly illustrated and, thereby, throw a sermon out of balance. While important ideas in a sermon must be strongly supported, subordinate notions need less support, and self-evident ideas may need no support other than an example. The problem will show up glaringly at times. For example, a well-known preacher came up with a sermon in the following design:

1. The church is human and divine.
2. The church is divine because it speaks God's Word.
3. The church is divine because it lives in God's Spirit.
4. But the church continually refuses God's presence.
5. Nevertheless, God is faithful to the church.

When the minister preached, there was only one illustration in the sermon —Dostoyevsky's story of the Grand Inquisitor who drove Christ away from a city—applied to the fourth move. When members of the congregation were interviewed after the sermon and asked—"What did the preacher preach about?"—to a person they reported that the sermon had fiercely accused the church. The preacher had overillustrated a negative, subordinate idea, and, as a result, had thrown the sermon out of balance. All the audience retained was the fourth section of the sermon. The example is extreme, but it demonstrates the problem. Actually, the strong ideas in the preacher's sermon were contained in sections 2, 3, and 5; sections that did need illustrative support. So, again and again, ministers will have to throw away nifty illustrations, lest, by their use, a sermon is skewed. Illustrations have enormous power: One four-sentence illustration has more potential force than twenty sentences of content. Wise preachers will seek to line up power with power, to match illustrative strength to the strength (or weakness) of particular moves. Remember, we do *not* need to illustrate everything we say.

Positive and Negative Alignments

In still another way, illustrations must relate to move content. An illustration must match the positive or negative character of the move statement. If a move is saying, "We ought to love one another," an illustration of lovelessness will not do at all. Or if we are urging a trust in God's grace, an illustration of all-American self-reliance, though prophetically perceptive, will be inappropriate. Conversely, if we are describing the selfishness in our human loving, we will not include an exemplar illustration of selfless love. A mixing of positive/negative properties will result in confusion within congregational consciousness that can often cause whole moves to be instantly forgotten. The problem for preachers is that, if preaching on love, we can always think of illustrations of lovelessness—after all, the evidence is at hand. When describing sin, Saint Paul could be quite graphic, but when it came to discussing Christian virtues, he was about as exciting as a wall-plaque sampler—love, joy, peace, and the like. Illustrations *cannot* be turned around. Many preachers suppose that they can get away with a negative illustration within a positive move, by adding some reverse English. For example:

> Look! We must forgive one another. We must forgive, because most of us have quite enough guilt without having it rubbed in. We accuse ourselves. So our real need is mercy. Forgiveness is a grace we can give one another. A little girl had been told not to play in a muddy field. But she came into her mother's kitchen, crestfallen, and covered with mud. The mother blew up and slapped the child, "What did I tell you?" she shouted, and sent the child away. *Well, it won't do! We only drive guilt deeper by our accusation. No, instead, we must forgive, and set folk free....*

Even though the example contains qualifying language, language supposedly designed to turn the illustration around; *it will not turn.* Instead, the illustration must be dumped, and a positive image introduced:

Look! We must forgive one another. We must forgive because most of us have quite enough guilt without having it rubbed in. We accuse ourselves. So our real need is mercy. Forgiveness is a grace we can give one another. A little girl had been told not to play in a muddy field. But she came into her mother's kitchen, crestfallen, and covered with mud. The mother saw her dropped-down eyes and laughed. With a towel she scrubbed the child's face clean, and kissed her: "You know you shouldn't be muddy," she said. . . .

The trouble with mixing negative and positive is that the illustration will be saying one thing and the move statement another. In our first example, though the move is pleading "We must forgive," the illustration is saying "We don't forgive." When negative and positive systems are mixed, the result will be a confusion in consciousness, and, quite possibly, a disruption in the logical continuity of a sermon. The rule is *positive with positive, negative with negative.*

Models and Images

A sermon itself will often work from a particular model. For example, if we preach on the seed/sower parable in Mark 4:3–9, our whole sermon may have to employ agricultural imagery. If we interpret Heb. 12:1–4, we are working with footrace imagery. Again and again, we will preach from passages that contain some developed image that is bound to figure in our sermons. In such cases, the illustrations we choose may have to relate to the basic model of the text, lest we end with a jarring series of mixed metaphors. The problem is not nearly as restrictive as it may seem. If we preach on the seed/sower parable, we should not suppose that every illustration used will have to be about seeds or planting. Instead, we can locate what may be described as "associated fields of imagery," such as agriculture, house plants, growth in general, few-to-many multiplications. Associated fields of imagery will not disrupt a ruling metaphor, whereas material drawn from quite alien fields (e.g., product manufacturing, business practices, governmental systems) will break up the metaphorical unity of the sermon. So we would not illustrate the Twenty-third Psalm with material referring to a Ford factory in Detroit, but would, instead, locate fields (no pun intended) that could relate to the psalm's pastoral imagery.

Sometimes, the problem will show up in a move per se, and not necessarily originate in scripture. For example, we may build a move around the idea that, when disappointed, some people run away from life. The idea we are putting forth contains an implicit image—running away. Therefore, we would not wish to choose an illustration which features images of solidly built mansions, even though it might include reference to someone who is "on the run." An illustration for the idea of "running away from life" ought

to contain images of mobility, of escape, or of hiding. If an illustration is to
fit an idea, it must match image for image and not create inadvertent static
by mixing metaphors.

Illustration Length

There are some preaching conventions that do need to be examined; the
long illustration is one. Long illustrations are apt to appear in sermons at the
ends of eras, in times of cultural breakdown. Thus, late-medieval preaching
incorporated developed, story-length illustrations, and, certainly, the late
twentieth century has witnessed the appearance of overblown, all-the-stops-
pulled-out story illustrations. Frequently, these large illustrations will show
up toward the end of sermons to provide what is often termed an emotional
"climax" (an odd sexual phrase). The practice currently seems to be bolstered
by forms of narrative theology. But the extended illustration which people
"get into" may be much less effective than we suppose. Let us compare some
examples:

> Some years ago there was an awful fire that swept a summer cottage. Sirens
> wailed and red lights whirled as fire fighters raced through the night. They were
> too late with too little. When they tried to hook up the hoses, water valves were
> stuck. Sparks from snaky wiring sputtered like firecrackers in the blaze. Sud-
> denly, there was a terrible shriek when a neighbor spotted a little child wandering
> out of the flames, her golden hair burned off, her body blistered. She stood
> wide-eyed with horror and then died. The next morning, standing in the ashes,
> two men met—a plumber and an electrician. For years they had been sworn
> enemies. In their hatred, they had not spoken to each other for nearly a decade.
> But in the ashes, they stood helpless: the electrician's wiring had caused the blaze,
> the plumber's pipes had jammed. Together, they knew an awful secret; they had
> caused a child to die, and to die horribly. Can you see them standing, facing each
> other? Silently, slowly, they reached out and shook hands. Yes, for the first time
> in years they acknowledged one another. A common bond of guilt had joined
> them together.

The illustration is being used to establish the idea that there is a kind of
unity in shared guilt. Of course, such unity is scarcely ultimate; the only
real unity is in mercy. Though the idea may be tentative, it is difficult
enough to require an illustration in order to be grasped. The overblown
illustration above poses all kinds of problems, however. The illustration is so
large, complex, and emotive that an audience will be caught up in its world
and participate emotionally in its pathos (or bathos!). As a result, the illustration has become, in and of itself, an experience. People will find it almost
impossible to disengage from the illustration and to grasp the understand-

ing, which, *supposedly*, the illustration supports. To sustain such an expansive illustration, we would have to have an enormous framework of content, lest, by sheer force, the illustration obliterate meaning. Of course, some ministers may not worry if an illustration illustrates, because they suppose that, by having a congregation "experience," they have accomplished something of significance. Nevertheless, illustrations exist to illustrate, and secondary agenda, such as "experience," will reduce the effectiveness of any illustration. We would be much better off keeping the illustration under control:

> After a terrible house fire in which a little girl was killed, two sworn enemies met in the charred ruins, a plumber and an electrician. Faulty wiring had caused the blaze and jammed pipes prevented the blaze being put out. The two men looked at each other, faced their common guilt, and, though enemies, reached out to take each other's hand. Common guilt; there is something oddly unifying in admitting our common guilt. With wide, deep eyes we can recognize each other, compassionately. We are the same broken humanity: There's a unity in guilt.

Whereas the overblown version of the illustration will detach from meaning —people may remember the illustration, but will almost certainly forget its function—the shortened version can be built into a meaning; it *will* function to illustrate. Big illustrations will usually detach from content, and, thus, defeat themselves. Illustrations limited to no more than five, or, at most, six sentences, however, will flash like metaphors in congregational consciousness, causing meaning to happen. As a rule, a disciplined illustration will function with *greater* force in the forming of meaning than an elaborate illustration: Length should not be confused with forcefulness.

SOME SPECIAL PROBLEMS

Preaching will display conventions in every age; some conventions are inherited from the past, while others may be prompted by current cultural moods. There are a number of conventions connected with the use of illustrations. Some conventions, such as the practice of quoting "authorities," we have inherited from the past; while other conventions, such as the use of personal narrative experience, seem to be more recent fads. Let us review some of these special cases.

Personal Illustrations

Personal illustrations are in vogue lately. Almost every sermon preached seems to contain personal material drawn from a preacher's own life experience. Ministers are convinced that their congregations appreciate such material, and that, all in all, personal illustrations are effective in preaching. Other benefits are said to be many: "It makes me more human," or "People can relate to me better," or "Personal illustrations are more real," and so forth. The problem with such extra agenda is that they overlook an illustration's *main purpose*, namely, to illustrate. While we hold no brief for depersonalized illustrations, we are suspicious of the current trend. A personal illustration, as we have previously suggested, will *always* split consciousness. To be blunt, there are virtually no good reasons to talk about ourselves from the pulpit.

Suppose a minister is trying to illustrate how self-consciousness can smother spontaneity. The minister may tell of a personal experience:

> The other day I was driving through Dale, Indiana. Suddenly, I caught sight of a little girl in a white dress dancing in a sunbeam. The sunbeam slanted down through the branches of a tree in her front yard. She whirled around and kicked up her heels and seemed to dance for joy. So I pulled over to the curb to watch her dance. But then she caught sight of me watching her and, hanging her head, stopped dancing. I felt as if I had killed something beautiful. Has something like that ever happened to you?

While the illustration does catch the mood of spontaneity, and does show the crippling effect of self-consciousness, it also illustrates the minister's own sensitivities. Intended or otherwise, the illustration illustrates in two directions at once. Research indicates that (1) congregations—even when prompted by "Has something like that happened to you?"—will *never* bring to mind similar experiences from their own recall, and (2) congregations will *always* remember the illustration as a disclosure of the *preacher's* character. The illustration will fix like glue on the minister who is speaking. Thus, a congregation will hear the illustration and think "Our minister is sensitive," or "Our minister is a voyeur of children," or something of the sort. The illustration will not illumine the idea intended.

So, what is the answer? Must we mask every illustration in anonymity, as was the custom years ago—"A minister was driving down a village street and saw . . ."? No, the convention is quite artificial, and is usually psyched out by a congregation. The solution may not be to throw away our experiences or to depersonalize them artificially, but rather to *offer* our experiences to a congregation, thusly:

> Have you ever watched a child at play? Perhaps a little girl in a white dress dancing in a sunbeam—a shaft of dusty light through the branches of a tree. You watch her whirl and skip and kick up her heels, all alone and joyful. But then,

suddenly, she catches sight of you watching her, and she stops. Don't you feel as if you've killed something beautiful?

What we have done is to locate the illustration in the common consciousness of a congregation so that sensitivity is *theirs,* and the sudden awareness of self-consciousness in the child happens to *them.* In congregational consciousness the illustration will have a single focus instead of a double focus, (a consciousness of the dancing girl *and* a consciousness of the preacher). There is *always* some other way of shaping an illustration so that we need not intrude on our own sermons. John the Baptist, in referring to Christ, offers a text for our preaching: "He must increase, but I must decrease" (John 3:30). Though illustrations come to mind in *our* minds, and may often be drawn from *our* own experience, we do not have to talk about ourselves in sermons no matter how exhilarating it may be. Personal illustrations *always* split focus.

Of course, we need scarcely add that often personal illustrations may border on a breach of confidence. With the rise of the pastoral-counseling movement, case histories seem to have moved into sermons: "A woman once came to me . . . ," "A man I knew had a drinking problem and . . ." Such rehearsing of pastoral services (or, conquests) are, of course, irresponsible. The notion that pastoral illustrations will create a climate of welcome so that congregation members will more easily seek out help is unlikely: Who on earth would turn to a blabbermouth with personal problems? There are ways to demonstrate our sensitivity to human need without seeming to violate personal confidences. Ministers may well use personal experiences—the little girl in the sunbeam, or a man sitting in a hospital stairway after a wife's death saying bitterly, "I guess God didn't hear us, huh?" As such material finds its way into the consciousness of a *congregation,* people will realize that a minister can understand, and may well be alert to what goes on in human hearts. We need not intrude on our own sermons, we need not blab; we can "decrease" to the glory of God. It is easy!

Quoted Material

Many ministers will pepper their sermons with citations and quotes. If we read sermons written in the first half of the present century, we will discover that most preachers quoted extensively in sermons, using brief one-liners as well as extended prose paragraphs. Probably such a practice could be justified when the language of preaching, in its lofty elegance, somewhat matched the language of prose; it is now no longer possible. Long prose quotations (of more than two sentences) do not function in sermons. What occurs in consciousness may be diagramed thusly:

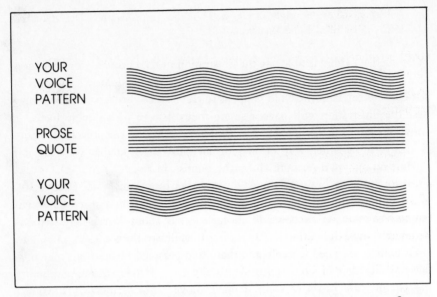

A preacher's own patterns of speech are singular, as distinctive as a finger-print. Quoted prose material will have its own syntax and cadence. Therefore, in a sermon, when we switch from our own oral patterns to the prose material, congregations will have to adjust to a different syntax—if they can. The result will be that a congregation will not hear the first quoted sentences very well (if at all), and that, when we swing back to our own speaking style, a similar blanking out may occur. In addition, we must realize that written prose language is scribbled for the eye; it is very different from an oral language. When spoken, most prose material will not sound right and, as a result, may not be heard at all. So quotations, particularly extended prose quotations, will probably not work in sermons—even quotations from scripture!

Are there any exceptions to the rule? Is there prose or poetry that can be quoted? Yes. In general, one-liners may be used as long as the language is close to colloquial. Even brief verse may be quoted, if, again, the phrasing is close to colloquial syntax. Elizabethan sonnets, or even stanzas of a hymn, however, will probably not be useful. Exchanges of dialogue may serve in sermons if they are limited in length (only *one* exchange, or one exchange and a reply). Of course, speakers in dialogue will have to be identified, and overlong phrases may have to be broken up. Thus, for example, the line, "The Bible is so disgusting; it's always talking about bodies," can be split with an identifi-cation: "The Bible is so disgusting," she said. "It's always talking about bodies." With regard to poetry, the lines

> Starch the bedroom curtains,
> Shine the silver tray,

> Put on a little make-up—
> Here comes the Judgment Day

could be quoted because they form as a series of brief, quite contemporary, phrases. However, words from Shakespeare, though lovely, may be slightly archaic, and, therefore, difficult to weave into the "speaker's syntax" of a sermon:

> Look, how the floor of heaven/Is thick inlaid with patens of bright gold:/There's not the smallest orb which thou behold'st/But in his motion like an angel sings,/Still quiring to the young-eyed cherubins: . . .

We may be able to employ brief, contemporary-language quotes in sermons, but archaic material, extended prose selections, heaped-up exchanges of dialogue, and the like will be nearly impossible.

Biblical Illustrations

Recently some scholars have argued that only scriptural illustrations should be used in preaching. The contention seems to be based on an "authority model," or on the notion that biblical illustrations will increase overall biblical literacy, or on the idea that scripture alone can rightly interpret scripture. The problem with biblical illustrations is that congregations are not well acquainted with scripture. A recent survey, which handed out a questionnaire on biblical literacy ("Name two Gospels"; "Is Paul in the Old Testament or the New?"; etc.), discovered that, though Missouri-Synod Lutherans managed to edge over 40 percent, most Christians strained to top 20 percent in score!

Most people know a scattering of stories from the Hebrew Scriptures—David versus Goliath or Moses in the bullrushes—as well as episodes from the life of Christ, perhaps those portrayed by "The Stations of the Cross." In addition, phrases from scripture may be floating around, such as, "The Lord is my Shepherd," or a few of the sayings of Jesus. Such familiar episodes and phrases can be used illustratively. What happens if we draw on unfamiliar material—"Remember the story of Naaman the Leper?" We will have to retell material, explain material, and then apply material illustratively; the process is much too involved to be useful. Moreover, if we argue that all illustrations should be drawn from scripture, we will end up creating a "closed world" in our sermons, locking God up in leather-bound Bible pages. Of course, in Black congregations, where for generations there has been a tradition of telling Bible stories, citing scriptural narrative may be possible. But for most untutored Christian congregations, the practice of using unfamiliar biblical material is impractical. We can *only* draw on a limited repertoire, a

145

repertoire in congregational consciousness, if we wish biblical illustrations to *illustrate*.

Humorous Illustrations

We can state a general rule with ease: If you are a naturally funny person, your problem will be control; if you are not a naturally funny person, do not try! A second rule might be added: Congregations should laugh only when you want them to laugh, and have a good reason for their bemusement. The problem in discussing humor in illustrations is that there are all kinds of amusements and all kinds of laughter. Look at two examples:

> There was a wealthy woman who had everything, everything but God. She had money enough, social prestige, two cars, and a poodle. But she wanted more. She longed for mystic visions, for the sweet shiver of the presence of God. So she joined a church. But, to her horror, instead of mystic visions, they gave her a Bible to read. "The Bible is so disgusting," she said. "It's always talking about bodies."

In the example, a congregation would giggle a bit after the word "poodle," and then laugh a little more loudly following the quote. The audience is, of course, laughing *at* a disdainful "spirituality." Inasmuch as the sermon will subsequently urge the congregation to slough off all false "spirrrrritual" hankerings, the laughter is designed to assist their sloughing off—they have already laughed *at* a false spirituality. But, laughter can serve in other ways:

> There was a cartoon which showed a big-city apartment full of plants. There was ivy up the walls, philodendron from the curtain rods; there were vases, jars, ashtrays full of plants—the place looked like a jungle. In the middle of the room a little lady was saying to her neighbor: "Would you believe it! It all began with one African violet!" We laugh, and laugh for joy because . . .

Here, again, laughter was deliberately built into a sermon. From a few little seeds, God brings forth a harvest—a joyful harvest by grace alone. So we want a congregation to feel joyful, to laugh out loud for the goodness of God. All we are suggesting is that laughter can be useful, and, therefore, usefully designed into sermons through illustration.

On the other hand, there are kinds of laughter that can devastate preaching. Laughter prompted by sarcasm is seldom helpful. Sarcasm is always a form of veiled hostility; it is essentially murderous. Thus, when people laugh at witty sarcasms, they will usually laugh out of shared hatreds. Such laughter in a sermon is rather clearly alien to the gospel. Perhaps even more disturbing is a laughter prompted by our own egotisms. In the pulpit, we can play to an audience and "get a laugh." When preachers justify humor in the pulpit, they will often do so by claiming "My people like it," which, of course, justifies nothing. Usually, the phrase "My people like it" can be translated more honestly "My people will like *me.*" When laughter is prompted by an underlying "My people like me because I'm funny," it will almost always escalate until sermons are rocking with laughter, and the profound currents of the gospel are diverted.

All in all, our two rules stand: (1) Congregations should laugh only when you want them to laugh, and have *good reason* for their bemusement; and (2) If you are a naturally funny person, your problem is control; if you are not a naturally funny person, do not try!

THE SHAPING OF ILLUSTRATIONS

As we have suggested, illustrations are to illustrate; that is what they do. Nothing will threaten an illustration more than an extra agendum, particularly an extra agendum not directly related to a sermon but having to do with preacher or congregation—"I want them to know I'm human," or "I want to change their political attitudes." When illustrations are expected to do more than one thing, they are weakened. So, when we design illustrations, we will be shaping them for a purpose, a *single* purpose. Illustrations must be pared down, the "point" of analogy heightened, and, as much as possible, the shape of an illustration made to match the structure of thought in a move. Many ministers today do not write out illustrations ahead of time; while they may be listed in a manuscript, they are often ad-libbed in delivery. As a result, ministers are apt to get carried away as raconteurs, overelaborating stories or slipping in tangential comments. Extraneous fat on illustrations can fog understanding, and tangential remarks destroy the coherence of illustrations. While ministers will certainly not read out illustrations, advance preparation will reduce the tendency to destroy an illustration's effectiveness through careless improvisation. There is scarcely an illustration that ever needs to exceed a half-dozen sentences in length. Compressed images are, like a narrowed stream, often much more powerful.

What about the location of illustrations? At the outset, recognize that we will not wish to illustrate every move in a sermon. While static point-making sermons were intrinsically dull and, therefore, needed much illustrative "light," sermons that travel along, move to move, are exciting and will probably need much less illustrative support. Moreover, many ideas in a sermon are somewhat obvious and will require no illumination. Do we need to illustrate the idea that "There are tragedies in everyone's life"? All we need to do is to mention a few concrete images drawn from lived experience. On the other hand, there are notions that are murky and must be shown, or ideas of such importance that they should be empowered. Crucial moves in a sermon may well be illustrated, while others can be managed quite easily in other ways. In an average sermon, less than half the moves will contain substantial illustrations. When illustrations are used, they must be *located* within moves. Generally, illustrations will be placed toward the middle of a move, sometimes a bit more toward the start, and sometimes toward the closure. What we may not do is to start a move with two or three sentences, and then immediately launch into an illustration. The illustration, in its strength, will threaten the clear, starting statement of a move. As a rule, the stronger the illustration, the *more* content will be needed prior to its inclusion. We must always have a frame of meaning well established before an illustration is used. (Illustrations must never be a substitute for content.) Likewise, if an illustration slides too far down in a move so that it appears immediately prior to closure, it may threaten the strength of the closure or even disrupt the start of a next move. There must *always* be closure. We must shape illustrations *into* moves, knitting them into content with care, yet, at the same time, protecting the strong starts and finishes of moves.

How can we keep illustrations and ideas joined together? Put another way: How can we prevent illustrations from pulling away from content so that, subsequently, an illustration will be remembered, but not the content it illustrated? There are several reasons why illustrations separate from content. We have already discussed the matter of length. If an illustration is overdeveloped so that it becomes a world and takes on a "life of its own," it will usually split from content. Thus, overdeveloped illustrations are usually self-defeating. Other problems are caused by the beginnings and ends of illustrations. The start of an illustration should flow from content without any obtrusive introduction to the illustration. Either we simply begin the illustration, "A man once . . . ," or we use a low-key syntax, "There was a . . ." What we do not need is an introduction to the illustration:

> There is a story about Albert Schweitzer. Schweitzer was a genius; a great musician, a philosopher, a biblical scholar. He dropped everything to work as a missionary doctor to lepers in Africa. Well, one day Schweitzer . . .

What such an introduction does is to insert an extra block of material *between* content and illustration, all but guaranteeing that they will separate. Still another problem at the start of an illustration is caused by the rather innocent word "I"—"I saw a movie on television the other day . . . ," "I heard a story about . . . ," "I once heard Karl Barth say . . ." The little word "I" will almost automatically creep into sermons at the starts of illustrations because, after all, it is the minister's consciousness that is bringing illustration to content—thus "I." The single "I" sentence prior to an illustration disrupts point-of-view, however, and will separate content and image. Though all but unnoticed by preachers when they preach, the "I" sentence will register in congregational consciousness and disturb the flow of thought. So, as a rule, we will wish to join illustration and content together without any "extra parts" in between. Furthermore, we will want to join the two in an unobtrusive way.

As far as the ends of illustrations are concerned, we must work off the last words of an illustration, weaving illustration and content together. Illustrations must never dangle, but must always be woven back into the flow of a sermon. Consider the following systems of language:

> . . . they gave her a Bible to read. "The Bible is so disgusting," she said, "It's always talking about bodies." Well, she's right, the Bible is always talking about bodies. "We are all one body," "We are the body of Christ," bodies! . . .

> . . . putting the fire out. The two men looked at each other, faced their common guilt, and, though enemies, reached out to take the other's hand. Common guilt: there's something oddly unifying in admitting our common guilt. With wide, deep eyes we recognize each other: we are of the same broken humanity. There's a unity in guilt.

> . . . belongings that once belonged to a family. On the top of the pile was a bent church sign, reading, "God is Love." "God is Love"—we say the words in church, but it's hard to believe in a world where tornadoes whirl, and cancers strike, and earthquakes shake whole cities into death. "God is Love?" How can we believe that God is love when bad things happen to *all* people?

What we are doing in each of the examples is initiating a thoughtful connection between content and illustration in the consciousness of a congregation, so that images and meanings blend together into one understanding. Any abrupt switch from illustration to content will tend to cause separation. By working off illustrations, however, we can knit the two modes of language together.

What about giving proper credit? Older homiletical works insisted that documentation appear in a sermon, "As John Calvin has written . . . ," "In a recent book, Karl Rahner . . ." As a result, sermons during the first half of our century were filled with name-dropping. Though responsibility is a clear issue, the rule may be rephrased: Preachers who are using someone else's material *must* ensure that congregations realize the material is *not* their own. The negative rule, "Be sure the congregation knows it is not your own," will protect integrity while avoiding endless name-dropping in a sermon. With phrases such as "Who was it who said, 'I wouldn't be caught dead without a body'?" or "A poet has sung . . . ," we signal borrowed material without needing to name names. We are not documenting, we are saying "It isn't mine" in an unobtrusive manner. Of course, we can document if we wish, but naming names can be overdone so that sermons take on a peculiar essayistic tone; footnotes do not speak well. However, we *must* differentiate our own words from the words of others.

A friend reported hearing two sermons on the same Sunday, morning and evening, in different churches. In each sermon, the preacher told a "personal experience," chuckling modestly over the ridiculous happening; unfortunately, the stories told were word for word the same! What such a catastrophe can do is to cast doubt on the gospel. People in congregations are apt to be well-read, and, if they pick out a familiar quote being passed off as the minister's own words, they will register the plagiarism. As human beings, none of us may be terribly honest, but we need not be liars! If we borrow, somehow, we must acknowledge our borrowing.

Much of the content in any sermon is made of images, examples, and illustrations, all woven together. Let us look at an example of such interweaving. Here is a move taken from a sermon on the mystery of life:

> The word "God" doesn't help much, does it? The word "God" simply doubles the mystery, for who can comprehend God? God's ways are not our ways, and God's wisdom is beyond our understanding. Can a tadpole in a swirl of Mississippi mud see the moon that draws the tide or guess the ocean to which the river flows? So we swim in time and space. We can't stand outside of life to see the hand that stirs the stars, or guess the consummations toward which our lives flow. In spite of preachers who paste together pieces of the Book of Revelation into a timetable and claim they can predict every earthquake and every human tremor, we can be less presumptuous. We do not know. How can our little minds contain the wisdom of God? H. G. Wells wrote of a bishop who asked an angel for the wisdom of God. "The angel laughed and, laying a hand on the bishop's head, said, 'Can [you] hold it? . . . Not with this little box of brains!' " Now, we Presbyterians have always suspected that bishops have boxy brains, but then so do we. Our little minds cannot hold the huge mystery of God. All we can do is to fling back our lives with Saint Paul and cry: "How uncertain are God's ways, how unknowable God's wisdom. Oh, the depth of the riches of the wisdom of God." The Christian says, "God," but to be truthful, the word "God" simply doubles the mystery.

Notice that the move contains an image system ("tadpole"), an example (preachers and the Book of Revelation), and an illustration (Wells's angel-bishop story). The illustration was difficult to manage because it involved a dialogic exchange, which, of course, had to be broken into phrases. The illustration was set up by "How can our little minds contain the wisdom of God?" and, of course, was followed by two sentences designed to work off the illustration and weave back into content. Though we gave credit to Wells for the illustration, we could as easily have said, "There is a story . . . ," which would imply a source.

Illustrations are problematical. They can be "cornball" or they may serve us well. Images, examples, and illustrations are the stuff of preaching. If illustrations are terse and well formed, they can sparkle in the texture of a sermon giving light. We may be moving into an age when sermons will no longer split between a rational denotative prose in which we declare ideas, and highly emotive illustrations in which we pump up feeling. Instead, we will speak through images, flash brief examples, and sculpt brief illustrations like metaphors to make meanings in congregational consciousness.

10.
The Image Grid

There is an amateur sculptor who has a ceramic hand in a glass case in his living room. Broken off at the wrist, the hand itself is exquisite—delicate, beautifully formed. "The best thing I ever did," the man explains immodestly. If you ask him how the rest of the statue was, he frowns. "Not so good," he admits, "but the hand, the hand is wonderful." There are similar glass-case sermon illustrations. Every once in awhile, a preacher will find the "perfect" illustration; one that fits in every way. Unfortunately, the rest of the sermon may be less than exciting. A sermon, like a poem, is a structure of words and images. One "perfect" flashing image will not make a poem. Instead, it is an interaction of images within a structure that adds up to a fine poem. What makes a good sermon is not one single illustration, but a gridwork of interacting images, examples, and illustrations. Let us look at the "Image Grid" that interacts within the structure of any fine sermon.

FORMING THE IMAGE GRID

Every sermon is a sequence of moves with each of the moves expressing a single meaning. The basic, first-stage outline for any sermon is usually not much more than a series of sentences listed on a page—seriatim ideas. It is at this point, with no more than five or six sentences on a page, that many ministers will start to gather examples, images, and illustrations. They will brainstorm ideas, skim through sermon collections, flip "illustration books," and consult their own files. Under each of the unamplified sentences they will list material they glean. Actually, such a practice is premature. If we find illustrations *before* we have formed the thought of a sermon to some degree, the illustrations can take over and either become a substitute for thinking through ideas, or, in subtle ways, distort the clear thought-structure of a

153

sermon. As a rule, then, it will always be better to develop each of the move sentences in a sermon, enlarging ideas, before searching out illustrative material.

Suppose, by way of example, we have a set of moves within a sermon as follows:

> 1. Look at nature—its awesome loveliness.
> 2. Yet, nature has a dark side.
> 3. No wonder Saint Paul says that nature must be redeemed.

With only three sentences scribbled down, we are in no position to locate images, illustrations, or examples. When ministers complain that they have a hard time gathering material for sermons, it is usually because they are trying to brainstorm before they have thought out ideas. When we try to gather material too soon, we turn brief sentences into "topic headings" which we then try to fill with images. Naturally, the procedure will be unproductive. If, however, we begin to think out each idea to see what we are saying, images will come tumbling into mind and assist our searching for further material. Let us spin out the simple sentences a little:

> 1. Take a look at the world of nature: Nature is wonderful. There is mysterious beauty in nature that can turn us into poets or artists. Even we ordinary folk can scarcely put into words what we feel as we sit by a still lake at sundown waiting for the colors to fade and the night stars to emerge. But, there is provender as well—nature is full of "gifts"—food for our tables, clothes for our backs, grapes for our goblets. It's a wonderful world.
>
> 2. But take a long second look: There's a kind of cruel freedom in nature as well, and sometimes terrible destruction. There may be grain for our table, but there's also "grain rust." And what about the black widow's bite, and the ravenous bloodletting we call "the survival of the fittest"? Lurking in every green tree are seeds of decay—the grass withers and the flower fades. Make your own list: killer tornadoes, tidal waves, poisonous weeds, dry famine. Lift Mother Nature's leafy wig and there's a death's-head underneath.
>
> 3. So, no wonder old Saint Paul looks toward a day when nature will be redeemed. Is nature also alienated from God? In the natural world is there a kind of untamed willfulness, an independence from God that God allows? Is nature as wayward as we are? Perhaps God waits for nature to "come around" and live in accordance with God's great loving purpose. Then the lion and lamb will lie down together, and a baby play in the snake's hole safely! Guess what? Nature also must be redeemed.

Notice that in doing a brief, quite tentative expansion of our basic sentence outline, we have already begun to pick up images and further ideas. In doing so we are moving toward fields of human experience that will help us to locate examples and illustrations. Imagination cannot function with an "empty page." Imagination works *with* thought. Therefore, it is in thinking out ideas that we move toward imagery.

After each of the move sentences has been elaborated so that we can begin to sense how ideas will form, we can gather material. Initially, the process does involve a kind of brainstorming—a free associating that involves dredging up out of memory half-recalled material, stuff we have seen or read or heard. We attempt to *see* what we mean by searching the world in consciousness and by remembering experience. Sometimes our free associating will send us scurrying to our bookshelves to look up a vague recollection. At other times, stuck, we may deliberately read up on an idea in theological texts so as to more firmly grasp what we may be saying. When imagination seems stymied, it is usually because we do not fully understand what we are trying to express, and is not merely an associational block. Basically, the process involves a free associating of idea and image, a seeing of what we are saying. For example, here is a list of associative material, quickly gathered for our first move:

1. *Look at the world of nature*

   Poster showing lovely forest scene with caption: "Nature is so untidy."

   Girl in Thornton Wilder's *Our Town* reciting her list of wonders—coffee, new ironed sheets, waking, sleeping: "Oh earth, you're too wonderful for anybody to realize you."

   Blind-from-birth person who sees for first time: "Too much beauty to behold!"

   Grace before meals: "Behind the snowy loaf . . ."

   Young boy seeing ecology display that shows interactions in nature: "Wow! All that's going on around us all the time!"

   Painting of a forest glade shaped like a cathedral nave.

   Scene in *The Wind in the Willows?* Numinous mystery in nature.

   Negative images: Man seeing Grand Canyon—"A place for old razor blades." Harry Stack Sullivan patient who could not relate to nature—"Gee! Ain't it cute."

   Experiences: Silence on trout stream. Sudden storm on lake.

Notice that the top-of-my-head list, quickly typed out, contains all kinds of material, some only half-recalled (e.g., Is there a scene in *The Wind in the Willows?* The reference came to mind as a vague childhood memory), and some unusable (e.g., negative illustrations could not be used in a positive statement). All the associations, however, have been scribbled down to look over; nothing has, as yet, been selected and nothing discarded. Actually, every move in a sermon plan should be brainstormed before any commitment to a particular image or illustration is made. We need to see what we have on hand for a *whole* sermon before choosing an example or illustration for any single idea. After all, we are not merely illustrating an idea, we are going to build an image/illustration framework for an entire sermon. In effect, we will gather stuff for a whole sermon and then, with an eye to structural design, select with care.

Let us look at material gathered for our subsequent two moves:

> 2. *But there's cruel freedom in nature as well*
>
> Old man who, whenever someone rhapsodized nature, would intrude with the phrase: "Remember the boll weevil!"
>
> Man in *Life* photo in midst of earthquake terror, kneeling in prayer.
>
> Church-school class asked to list in columns reasons why "Life is Good" and "Life is Bad"; second list always the longest.
>
> Ecology professor quote: "When you come right down to it, nature is cruel."
>
> Phrase: "Red tooth and claw" from somewhere?
>
> Pictures in paper of Japanese, standing, staring out to sea where tidal wave had swept away their families.
>
> 3. *No wonder nature must be redeemed*
>
> Is there a quote from dust-bowl preacher in Steinbeck's *Grapes of Wrath?*
>
> Character playing God in off-Broadway play, who, getting news of famine, says: "I gotta do somethin'!"
>
> Tribe praying for nature to be kind.
>
> Character in Charles Williams's novel who sees a vision of nature altogether beautiful—great, perfect butterflies—who shouts, "Glory, Glory!"
>
> Primitive painting—"The New Eden" that shows everything fertile and at peace.

Though a three-move set is not a sermon, let us review the three developed ideas and the lists of images, illustrations, and examples we have tentatively gathered. We must pick and choose, always keeping in mind that *not* every move must be illustrated.

At the outset, we discover that our first idea—on wonders of nature—has much support, as does the second move. Our third move, on the need for nature to be redeemed, has less material. Yet, the third move is theologically the most important, and, of course, the most difficult: We will need an illustration. The notion of nature as both fecund and handsome is fairly obvious, and we may not need to illustrate the idea at all; we can describe and image. We are already beginning to worry about matters of balance and strength.

We will also be concerned over types of illustration. For example, if we were to quote the boy in the ecology class, "Wow! All that's going on around us all the time!" then we would not be able to use the ecology professor quote in a second move—they would be much too much alike in character. Likewise, if, in a first move, we were to describe staring at a loveliness in nature, we would not wish to describe Japanese villagers staring out to sea after a catastrophe—again the reference to "staring out" in each illustration would be too similar. Of course, we will notice that in each move we could use an illustration from a literary or magazine source. The sequence of such material could give a literary cast to the sermon, which, considering the visual orientation of the sermon, might be fatal. Issues of interaction can be quite complex. If, for example, we choose to use the *Our Town* quote (after a list of pleasures and beauties), could we bring in the "boll weevil" one-liner in the next move, or would the fact that both illustrations include one-line quotes make them impossible to use in tandem? Though they interrelate nicely they may sound too much alike.

In all our lists, there were items followed by a question mark—vague recollections which would have to be looked up and checked. Unfortunately, preaching does require research. It is even possible that, as we develop our sermon structure more carefully, we will discover that a list of associative images and examples has not provided us with what we need. As a result, we may have to go back, reread, think out, and associate, in search of stronger material, or material which will balance in a better way with other images we have gathered. After all, we are not simply throwing in an illustration with every idea, helter-skelter; we are trying to form an interacting image grid for an entire sermon.

In the case of our three-move set, we may decide to handle the first move, on the beauty of nature, by combining a series of descriptive examples with the final quote from *Our Town*. In the second move, we may feel we can handle the ideas presented without any illustration, but by discussion and imagery. In our last move, we may want to develop imaginatively the image of the tribe praying for the redemption of nature. Of course, in making a selection, we will be throwing out material, some of which may be vivid, and, on the surface, seem stronger in a sermon. But we are not merely trying to gather a bunch of "impact" illustrations, we are designing a grid of *interrelating* images to serve a particular *structure* of thought. The material we discard will not be lost but will fall back into a storehouse of memory, and may well surface on some other occasion.

As we review the process of gathering and selecting material, it is well to remember that we may *not* wish to begin by illustrating a first move, and then a second, and a third, and so forth. Obviously, when we choose any one illustration, we will automatically limit our choices elsewhere. So, usually, it will be wise to select illustrative material to go along with sermon strength —where the crucial word is to be spoken. Having selected according to strength may mean that less significant material will not be illustrated at all, but will be managed in some other way. We are trying to build a structure of image, illustration, and example to coordinate with the structure of thought in a sermon, a *whole* sermon.

THE IMAGE GRID IN ACTION

In order to get at the interactional character of sermon imagery, let us examine the *body* of a sermon (without introduction or conclusion). Moves in sequence are numbered for purposes of reference:

1. "A sower went out to sow," said Jesus. You hear the story and you think to yourself, what a dumb farmer! Can you imagine any Indiana farmer stupid enough to sow seed in a thorn bush, a rock pile, or right down the center stripe of I-64? The parable is laughable; almost as silly as the Christian church sowing seed of the gospel. We may not have tossed God's Word into thorn bushes, but we've certainly preached good news in mighty odd places—from the rocky coasts of Alaska to jungle thickets of South Africa, all over the world. What's more, we still do. The other day an appeal for funds came in the mail to support a preaching mission to communist Russia—there's rocky soil! And in our own land, every evening lay preachers spout good news to the winos in Detroit's downtown, and every afternoon there's an evangelist soapboxing the gospel to push-and-shove crowds in the New York City subway system. Rock, thorn, and highway: If there's anything sillier than sowing seed in a rock pile, it's the Christian church spreading good news of the gospel. You hear the parable and you think to yourself, how dumb!

2. Of course, if anyone is a fool in the parable, the fool is God. God. For has God not commanded our speaking? Has God not told us to go to every nation, to cover the world with good news? And God doesn't seem to care whether anyone listens or not. God doesn't compile "hot prospect" lists or recommend our evangelizing only where there's cash enough to build a church—an old Presbyterian trick. God says "Preach," and the command is unconditional. So when Moses came hustling up to complain that he, Moses, was not much into public speaking, God interrupted him, saying, "Speak!" Or old Ezekiel, who reminded the Lord that, when you come right down to it, dry bones are not what you'd call a responsive congregation: God said "Preach!" There's a group of Scandinavian Christians with a wonderful custom. Whenever a minister is ordained, the candidate leaps up, strides out of the church and, at once, begins to preach to startled passers-by. Perhaps that's what God has in mind. God wants us out of our stained-glass buildings and into the world, speaking. God has commanded us to preach good news—everywhere. So, look, if there's a fool in the parable, the fool is God.

3. Well, be honest: Results are less than impressive. How few folk respond. Here we've been preaching the gospel for twenty centuries, and the world's still only about 8 percent Christian. Rock, thorn, and highway: At least the parable understands the odds. Nowadays nobody, but nobody, seems to want to hear the gospel, even in America—maybe, particularly in America. Perhaps we aren't desperate enough, hungry, hurt, or hard up enough to hear the gospel. Twentieth-century America seems rocky soil indeed. An off-Broadway play showed a couple sitting in a big-city apartment, thick pile rugs and sinky couches, when all of a sudden a Salvation Army band parades by the window blaring a Jesus song. The young man gets up, goes and slams the window, saying, "I really don't see what Jesus can do for us!" Maybe that's our problem: We don't see what Jesus can do for us. Can he fill our tanks with cheap gas, or curb our interest rates, or tell us what on earth to do with our MX missile system? Jesus doesn't seem to speak to our all-American agenda: We don't see what Jesus can do for us. Be honest! We preach the gospel, year in and year out, but results are scarcely impressive.

4. So, how easy it is to become discouraged. How easy to lose heart. When nobody's listening, who wants to speak? Perhaps that's what's happened to us "mainline" Protestant types, because nobody seems to listen, we've quit speaking. We turn evangelism over to the gray clapboard, back-street Pentecostal churches, or to Jerry Falwell wearing a Reagan button where his cross should be! Listen, we are not talking about denominational policy, about boards and agencies far away, we're talking about us right here; we've not been speaking the gospel. When was the last time you talked to anyone—even your own family—about the God you believe in? When? Some years ago a famous Protestant preacher lost his voice. The condition was diagnosed as psychological, for, as a friend explained, "He looked up one day and discovered nobody was listening!" Is that our problem? When the world seems tone-deaf to the gospel, we turn off. Instead of scattering seed, we've kept our church lawns well mowed. How easy, oh how easy it is to become discouraged, yes, to lose heart.

5. But, hold on. Hey, take a look at the end of the parable: There's going to be a harvest. Thirty, sixty, a hundred times—there's going to be a harvest. God takes our foolish leftover, throwaway seeds and turns them into triumph. There's a harvest coming: Someday every knee shall bow, and every tongue confess that Jesus Christ is Lord to the glory of God. No idle dream; it shall be. Word of the Lord, and the Lord keeps faith. A cartoon showed a big-city apartment filled with plants. There was philodendron around the curtain rods, ivy on the walls; there were buckets, pots, ashtrays all filled with plants —everywhere plants; the place looked like a jungle. In the middle of the room a little lady was explaining to her neighbor, "Would you believe it all began with one African violet!" We laugh, laugh for joy! For, God will take our foolish seeding of the gospel and turn it into miracle. There's harvest promised. Someday, the fur-capped Russian and the Detroit wino and the New York City subway crowd and the Indiana farmer will all come

together in one glad hullabaloo before God; it shall be. Hey, take a look at the end of the parable. Thirty, sixty, a hundred times over; there's going to be a harvest.

6. So guess what? Agenda for the church: Speak the gospel and trust God; Trust God and speak the gospel. What else is the church for, but to spread good news? Shall we spell it out? Your church does not exist to spruce up your morals: God may not be much interested in what we call "morality." The church does not exist to teach your children religion: Christian faith may not even be a "religion." Your church does not exist to provide you with warm Christian fellowship; you can rub human fur against human fur almost anywhere. No, the church lives to preach the gospel! And you wonder why we don't? Think back on your own life. We've all been brought up badly—always too much law and too little grace—and we live broken, patched-together lives, riddled by funny fears and guilts that, my God, we'd like to forget. But here we are now, forgiven, able to love a little once in a while. Looking back, we know it's God who's done it all—set us free to love. Well, somehow you'd think we'd want to tell someone, to spread the news of God's good grace in a world that seems so graceless. What else is the church for? There's a wonderful poster with a trite caption. The caption: "Who plants a seed trusts God"—trite. But the picture gets you: Not a picture of a farmer sowing a field, but of a grubby tenement kid poking seed into a catch of dirt on a concrete windowsill. "Who plants a seed trusts God." Image of the church in the twentieth century, trying to sow seed of the gospel in a chill, concrete world. So, agenda for the church: Trust God and speak the gospel.

In order to be able to analyze the interactions in this sermon, let us construct an image/example/illustration grid for the whole body of the sermon. What we have is as follows:

Images	*Examples*	*Illustrations*
Move 1		
"rock, thorn, highway"		
rocky coasts		
jungle thickets		
Indiana farmer	appeal for funds to	
Detroit wino	support USSR preaching	
N.Y.C. subway crowd		
Move 2		
"hot-prospect" list	Moses and God	
cash to build churches	Ezekiel and God	*ordaining*
stained-glass buildings		*minister in*
		Scandinavian sect

Move 3 "rock, thorn, highway" 8 percent Christian gas, interest rate, MX		*big-city apartment: "I really don't see what Jesus can do"*
Move 4 gray clapboard churches Jerry Falwell tone-deaf, turnoff church lawn mowing	personal evangelism question	*silent minister who loses voice*
Move 5 throwaway seeds N.T. quote thirty, sixty, a hundred fur-capped Russian Detroit wino N.Y.C. subway crowd Indiana farmer		*big-city apartment: plant growth and African violet*
Move 6 contrapuntal system: morality, religion and fellowship	appeal to experience: broken lives but able to love a little	*poster of tenement kid: "Who plants a seed trusts God"*

With a chart of all the images, examples, and illustrations from the sermon, we can begin to sense the underlying interactional grid.

The sermon (based on Mark 4:3–9, the parable of the Sower and the Harvest) works at the outset with a dominant agricultural image in referring to the church's evangelical experience. Thus, illustrations for the sermon will have to be drawn from (1) agriculture—planting, growth, harvest, and (2) preaching the good news. The dominant imagery of the passage tends to order our images, lest, inadvertently, we mix metaphors and confuse the meaning of the text. Every illustration or image in the sermon relates to the two associated fields, either agriculture or speaking/hearing the gospel. While most biblical passages do not dictate imagery, rather obviously the seed parable with its evangelical message does. Let us review the sequential pattern of the image grid.

Move 1: In the first move, we set up the two dominant image systems—

seeding and preaching the gospel. So we have on the one hand "rocky coasts" and "jungle thickets" aligned with the rock and thorn images of the text, and on the other hand "lay preachers" and an "evangelist soapboxing." The little example of the appeal for funds is also concerned with the spreading of the gospel. With these images, we introduce a refrain, a "downer" drawn from the text, "rock, thorn, highway." In addition, we stress the notion of absurdity, because, as with virtually all of Jesus' farmers, the farmer in the seed parable is an incompetent who wastes seed in foolish places.

Move 2: The second move features two biblical examples in parallel construction so that they will come together as one unit of meaning. In addition, we have the illustration of the odd ordination custom which incorporates imagery of going out into the world. The illustration puts together the idea of God's commission and the evangelical calling of the church.

Move 3: The third move picks up from the text the failure of the farmer's sowing—not much seed comes up! The move echoes the refrain introduced in the first move—"rock, thorn, and highway"—to relate the two moves. The strong illustration in the move, however, is an image of our refusal of the gospel. The gospel, represented by "a Jesus song," is shut out by a young man who symbolizes twentieth-century America. Notice that the illustration is set in a "big-city apartment," with images of indolence—the rugs and the couches.

Move 4: The fourth move is somewhat more complicated than it may seem. In move 2, we introduced an image of a minister ordained to speak, but here we have a speaking minister who goes silent. Each illustration contains a "minister," but, in sequence the minister quits preaching. The images of the gray clapboard, "shout-n'-holler" churches and of Jerry Falwell may associate somewhat with the evangelists in move 1 and with the Salvation Army group in move 2. The image of the well-mowed church lawns, an image of self-preservation, will be in tension with the command to seed.

Move 5: In the parable a few leftover seeds root and multiply by God's grace to produce an unexpected harvest. Given the farmer's absurd sowing, the parable's harvest is sudden and quite surprising. Thus, the move abruptly introduces the harvest theme. Notice that having had a "downer" refrain— "rock, thorn, highway"—we now sing out an "upper" refrain: "thirty, sixty, a hundred times." The quotation from Phil. 2:10 is introduced to invoke a sense of biblical promise. The tricky material in the move comes with an illustration and a recital, however. The somewhat amusing illustration is deliberately designed to relate to the illustration used in move 3—the "big-city apartment" where the gospel is refused. Here we have a "big-city apartment" full of plants, symbols of growth, which began with a single African violet (like a few absent-minded seeds). So, in effect, we have filled the space of rejection with a harvest and, what is more, made our congregation giggle with joy over the miracle! In addition, the move gathers in the odd, seemingly absurd preaching locations mentioned in move 1—the Russian fund-appeal people, the Detroit winos, the subway crowd, and even a symbol of foolish seeding, the Indiana farmer. Thus, by gathering images, we produce a harvest —"thirty, sixty, a hundred times" over.

Move 6: The sixth move begins with a commissioning of the church (see move 2) to "Speak the gospel and trust God." Immediately, there is a tripartite contrapuntal system to push aside our usual notions of what a church is to do and be. The appeal to personal experience that follows deliberately mentions upbringing so as to relate to growth imagery. The final illustration works with the whole sermon. While all our images have related to either agriculture or evangelical witness, throughout the sermon we have drawn in urban imagery—sowing fields may not be too compelling an idea for suburban and urban people. Here, the final illustration, with a caption that all but repeats the commission of the church to "trust God," is a picture of a city kid stuffing a single foolish seed into windowsill dirt. Since in move 5 we have seen a vision of harvest, however, foolish seeding is a sure act of trust.

If we were to take out the sequence of illustrations and images without any surrounding content, we can see that in and of themselves they all but preach a sermon! The patterned grid of images, examples, and illustrations is designed to function with the structural "argument" of the sermon. Older homiletics basically viewed illustrations as support for *particular* ideas. Often illustrations were used following blocks of content as visual proof texts for each discrete point being made. Instead, we are suggesting that images, examples, and illustrations are woven into content and provide an underlying image grid for an entire sermon; they function similarly to the clusters of images in a poem, forming in consciousness along with a meaningful structure. Just as images in a poem may recur and, in doing so, conjoin meaning, so also will images and illustrations in a sermon. No wonder we have suggested that you gather a host of images, examples, and illustrations for a whole sermon, overviewing them all in relation to sermon design, before you make your choices. Illustrations do not merely illumine discrete ideas, they interrelate in consciousness to form a whole structure of meaning.

DESIGNING INTERACTIONS FOR SERMONS

The planning of an interacting image grid may seem complex; actually, it is not. Deliberate interactions can be designed. Of course, they happen initially in our own consciousness. Ideas are always connected with visual images in a sermon so that as we think through a sequence of ideas in our own minds, images will all but automatically interrelate. The problem for us, then, is not how to interrelate concepts and, with them, images, but how to discipline a natural process so that such interrelating will happen in the consciousness of a congregation. Recalling the sermon moves we have provided, let us look at some interactional processes that are common in preaching.

Reprise

In our sermon moves, we reused images. For example, we took the images from our first move—Indiana farmer, Russian citizen, city wino, and subway crowd—and gathered them into a fifth move. Though the procedure looks easy, it is full of dangers. What occurred was that images associated with one meaning—our indiscriminate preaching of the gospel—were subsequently reused in *an entirely new context of meaning,* namely, "harvest time." The phrase, "an entirely new context of meaning," is an important clue. We must not review ideas in a sermon, or bring back previous content to discuss again; redundancy is an open invitation to a wandering of mind. Instead, images associated with one meaning can be echoed in another new context as long as there is some *structural logic* to support the reuse. In our example, the structural logic is causative in a way. God will take our inept seeding and, by grace, produce a harvest; thus, initial inept seeding will figure in a final harvest.

Though the contexts are different, as they *must* be, there is a logic prompting the reuse of images. The images actually make the logical connection happen in congregational consciousness. Normally, we would never reuse *all* images from a previous move and *never* in the same order as originally used —the reuse of images should be partial—but here we are attempting to gather in a harvest. We have, however, deliberately broken up the sequence of the original images by ending with the farmer (who began the first move). And, of course, we have had three moves between our reuse of images. We may *not* reuse images in connected moves: When images from one move are immediately reused in a following move, they will often obliterate differences in the moves or create such a strong sense of redundancy that our congregations will be bored. Images may be reused when moves logically relate, but are separated in sermon structure. Usually a few images may be echoed (from among many) and always in a somewhat different order. The device is not merely a rhetorical flourish, but serves the meaning of a sermon.

While images may be reused (possibly an image from a previous illustration), whole illustrations may *not* be reprised in a sermon. In other words, we may not make an illustration work twice in the same sermon, particularly in consecutive moves. For example, a preacher, in illustrating human compassion, told of a French woman who, when death-camp deportees were marched past her door, would reach out and give each a potato to eat, saying, "This is my body." The illustration worked fairly well to picture Christian compassion in action. In a next move, however, the preacher wanted to say that we learn compassion from acting out sharing in Eucharist. Unfortunately, he brought back his illustration and used it again, stressing the woman's sacramental words. What will happen is that the two uses of the illustration will come together to form one single story in consciousness, but, in doing so, will obliterate the different meanings being preached. The congregation, interviewed following the sermon, simply forgot the entire content of the move on sacramental rehearsal. No illustration may be used twice; we may reprise images, but not illustrations. Of course, the reuse of images must not be overworked, lest the sound of redundancy form too much in congregational consciousness.

Refrains

For years, preachers have set up rhythmic speech patterns that, thereafter, they may echo again and again. In our example, we used "rock, thorn, and highway" as a refrain, and then later set up another refrain with "thirty, sixty, a hundred times." Reusing a refrain is quite different from recalling an image. Just as in music, refrains come in at the start or the finish of a song, so refrains will tend to be used at the starts and ends of moves, but *never* in the middle of a move. For example, we can remember Martin Luther King, Jr.'s remarkable "I have a dream . . ." speech because of the refrain he used to *inaugurate* a series of sections. At the starts of moves, refrains will tend to demark categorical repetitions. At the ends of moves, however, refrains will tend to contribute to closure and to associate moves in sets, just as a refrain in a song will follow stanzas. We are concerned, however, with the use of a refrain from one move in another subsequent, but not consecutive, move. While the first use of a refrain will normally occur toward the beginning or the end of a move, an echoing of the refrain will vary somewhat. If the first use was toward the beginning of a move, the second use will probably be toward the closure, or vice versa. The reuse of the refrain will associate the ideas of one move with the ideas of another on a slightly low-key basis. Thus, in our sermon example, we echoed the phrase, " 'rock, thorn, and highway'—at least the parable understands the odds." We connected indiscriminate seeding with failure. Reuse of a previously constructed refrain can normally be done only once, and only after the initial refrain has been firmly connected with an idea. Of course, a refrain may echo in a single move as framework for the move, at start and finish. Because refrains are associated with starts and finishes, they may *not* be used in the middle of a move, lest the move split in consciousness.

Interrelating Illustrations

In the sermon provided, there are several ways in which the imagery of illustrations did interrelate. We may, however, single out two systems of interaction for particular attention: (1) the interrelating of an internal image, and (2) the interrelating of an illustration framework.

The Interrelating of an Internal Image. In our example, the procedure may be seen in the second and fourth moves. In the second move we set up an illustration of a minister being ordained to speak in the world, and in the fourth move we featured a minister going silent, losing voice in a pulpit. The interrelating was accomplished by the use of a same central image, namely, "minister." Now, when such a system is used, there must be at least one move in between the image repetition, lest a sense of redundancy occur.

Consider another example of the process. Early in a sermon, a preacher used an illustration with reference to the church's triumphalism, our desire to "make it big" in the world. The preacher told of a man who was building a new church edifice, and who

> had engineers measure the height of every building for blocks around, so that his church tower would stand taller: Said he, "The cross ought to be on top of the world!"

Later in the same sermon, the preacher was trying to say that we cannot get away with triumphalism in view of Christ's helpless death on the cross. A second illustration was used:

> A man was walking down a Boston alley when the stone cross on top of a church steeple cracked in the wind, and, whirling down, shattered at his feet—broken Jesus everywhere. And, dazed, all the man could say when interviewed was "I have seen the Lord!"

What has occurred? What has happened is that the symbol of triumphalism has been smashed to pieces, an "up-high" cross has been brought "down to earth," which is exactly what the pattern of thought in the sermon is doing. Thus, the device has served the structure of the sermon. Of course, such a reuse of image could not have been accomplished without gathering all illustrations for a sermon ahead of time and then selecting material to match the structural movement of the sermon. The device could only be used once in a sermon and should probably not be overworked in the pulpit; we should not get too tricky as preachers. On occasion, however, the device can be both helpful and powerful. Use of an image repetition in illustrations is informed by basic metaphors of "up/down," "large/small," "dark/light"—orientational metaphors that are built into all of us.

The Interrelating of Illustration Framework. In our example sermon, we had two illustrations with the same setting. See the illustrations in sequence:

> An off-Broadway play showed a couple sitting in *a big-city apartment,* thick pile rugs and sinky couches, when all of a sudden a Salvation Army band parades by blaring a Jesus song. The young man gets up, goes and slams the window, saying, "I really don't see what Jesus can do for us."

> A cartoon showed *a big-city apartment* filled with plants. There was philodendron around the curtain rods, ivy on the walls; there were buckets, pots, ashtrays, all filled with plants—everywhere plants; the place looked like a jungle. In the middle of the room a little lady was explaining to her neighbor, "Would you believe it all began with one African violet?"

Of course, the repetition of "big-city apartment" is obvious. But even without the repetition, the two illustrations would associate, because they are both descriptions with a "punch line"; they are deliberately *shaped* in a similar fashion. Here we have two illustrations with quite different central images, one of rejection and the other of fecundity, but shaped in a similar way and featuring the same setting. Used in sequence, the illustrations will act on each other, the second transforming the first—we have filled the place of rejection with a "harvest" from the parable. The device is difficult to pull off because it must be done with restraint. While two illustrations may be baldly designed in a similar shape, a repetitive feature ("big-city apartment") must be quite low-key, lest it call attention to itself too much. The device, functioning subliminally, can have unusual power. Such a device is best used when a sermon structure refers to transformation.

Obviously, when we resort to interrelating illustrations in a sermon, we are serving the structural movement of the sermon; we are helping the sermon to do what it intends. Devices of interrelating must never be homiletic "tricks" employed to show off homiletic technique. If a congregation leaves a church filled with admiration for a preacher's rhetorical skills, then a sermon has failed *utterly.* We do not preach to be liked, admired, or applauded. Sermon craft is never intended to dazzle, but always to serve. Thus, rhetorical systems that interrelate images must be used modestly, aiming at an all-but-subliminal action in consciousness. With images interacting we imitate human consciousness in order to serve faith-consciousness; we do not manipulate. While images in sermons do function poetically, sermons are emphatically *not* "artworks"; they must always be engineered to serve our neighbors (the congregation) in love. All we have done is to mention a very few such interactional methods among many that may be used. Perhaps, as a reader, you are beginning to catch sight of the image grid in action.

Some Problems

In planning a sermon, preachers will want to check the types of illustrations that are being used *throughout* the sermon. Where do illustrations come from, and what is their character? Obviously, if preaching on a sermon with agricultural imagery, illustrations drawn from literary works might pose a problem. But, even when there is no ruling metaphor to be reckoned with, we must still check the types of illustrations we use. If all illustrations in a sermon were drawn from sporting events, inadvertently we would proclaim the gospel as a "game." Or, if all illustrations were picked out of literary works, we could convey the impression that Christian faith is an exclusive "egghead" activity. Again, if all illustrations were drawn from past history, think what the impression would be. But the matter of illustration type goes further than source. We must check the shape of illustrations to be sure that as we illustrate different ideas, we do not sound the same. For example, if every illustration in a sermon were shaped as a description with a punch line we would risk a kind of tedium. Instead, we must mix up illustrations, noticing if they are visual or audible, quotes or pictures, and so on. Every illustration should relate to a particular move. Thus, if we are talking of the "Word of God," we may wish to select an illustration that contains spoken material. Or if we are preaching on an apocalyptic vision, surely we will give preference to an illustration that is, in effect, a picture. But, beyond particular moves, we will need to review an entire sermon to see what types of illustrations are being used and from where.

It may be appropriate here to raise the question of sexism. While pronouns may be a problem, illustrations, because of their power, are a double problem. For many centuries preaching has been a male activity—masculine priests and ministers in their pulpits "making points." If we review books of sermons from the past we will be appalled by role stereotypes, demeaning sexisms, and the like. Notice how often illustrations will feature male "heroes," and, conversely, how many illustrations will depict female helplessness. Worse, a survey of illustration books will display far too many illustrations in which women are rebuked, or edified, or assisted by males. And how many stock marriage homilies contain images of woman as a friendly, cocker-spaniel type who trots around with slippers and suppers for her male "hero" husband? The

evidence of sexism in sermons is downright frightening! Aware of dominations in the world and in ourselves, we who preach must examine illustrations
carefully to spot the roles that men and women play. Is it permissible to
change the sex of a character in an illustration in order to guard against a sexist
image? Why not?

In the sermon example we have provided, illustrations were reviewed either
to remove sexual identity or to assess sexual roles (because I am male my
eyesight may be dimmed by my own will-to-domination). In the second
move, after mention of Moses and Ezekiel—males quite appalled at the prospect of preaching—we might have featured a woman being ordained. The
sermon was originally written for a woman's ordination, however, and thus
the mention was scarcely necessary. Males in the sermon tend either to refuse
the gospel or to go tongue-tied, in part to compensate for the fact that a male
is preaching the sermon. There is a genuine problem with the illustration of
the cartoon lady and her line about African violets. The cartoon, which
appeared in *The New Yorker* magazine, has been anthologized at least twice
in cartoon collections, and could hardly be changed. The danger is, of course,
that the lady will be laughed at in the sermon, and may therefore seem a
ditherer. The problem is slightly eased by the fact that she is associated with
God's astonishing grace. Perhaps we could have had our tenement child in
the final move be a girl, to compensate for a possible problem with the cartoon
lady. We have rehearsed the issues in our example sermon not to demonstrate
that I am not sexist—in America we are *all* sexist by cultural conditioning
—but rather to portray a process of evaluation which must happen in the
selection of illustrations, images (which are often associated with masculine
and feminine activity), and examples. For Catholic preachers the problem is
connected with a tradition of male priesthood. But, for Protestants, there is
no less a male pulpit domination beginning with Luther, who seemed to have
viewed the sermon as a male "thrust" and faith as a female "receptivity." Our
images must be weighed with care.

In proposing the idea of an image grid, we are working with the notion
that sermons are for the forming of faith-consciousness. Older homiletics
basically regarded illustrations and examples as support for making points.
Therefore, most books on homiletics in our century have weighed illustrations in relation to single ideas. We are suggesting that sermons build a world,
a faith-world, in consciousness, made from images, metaphors, illustrations,
and examples. Therefore, we tend to regard material as adjudged in two ways
—by relating to a particular move, and by interrelating in the whole sermon
structure. What we are after is a kind of imitation of the way in which humans
grasp meaning. Meaning is never an abstract thinking, it incorporates images

of lived experience. Thus, in a sermon ideas must be imaged, and images must interact so that sermons will be natural to modes of human consciousness. Preachers are not poets, but they should have a poet's eye. More, preachers should take delight in putting words and images together as they build a world for faith.

_____LANGUAGE

11.
LANGUAGE

See different people speaking. A man points to a rock and says, "Rock." Another person is dancing, spinning in an ever-widening circle, gesturing toward a stormy sky, and singing word-sounds in a kind of chant. A woman stands at a blackboard and explains some markings: $2A\times = B \pm \sqrt{B^2-4AC}$. A poet stands staring out at a misty valley and scribbles words in a stenographic notebook. A woman in a pulpit, Bible in hand, speaks to a congregation. All these people are working with words. But what are words? More important for us, what are words in preaching?

We have noticed previously how words name the world in consciousness and, through narrative, give identity in the world. We have also probed metaphorical language as a way of getting at mysteries of God and of human beings in the world. Now we must ask a different kind of question. We must search out the odd relationship between words and consciousness. What are words in preaching?

HOMO LOQUENS

We live in language. Words are not merely stuff to thicken bulky dictionaries. No, words whirl about us; they give life significance and indeed make life possible. We are *Homo loquens.*

We *do* within language. Could we build a house, conduct business, or run governments without words? No wonder that, in the ancient myth of Babel, tower builders gave up building when their common language broke down. Without words, legislative chambers would be silent, airports stopped, courtrooms emptied, schoolrooms closed, and households reduced to a gesturing of strangers. We view space exploration as a triumph of technology, but how could we venture into the outer limits of our world without words? A high-

173

school graduation featured a banner over the podium reading, "Deeds not words" (a much admired anti-intellectualist slogan), but the distinction is false; bluntly, deeds have meaning because of words, are possible because of words, and frequently *are* words. As human beings we could not *be* without words. The reason we find a book such as *Dr. Doolittle* amusing is that it portrays talking animals. While animals do seem to signal, and gorillas may be programmed with basic vocabulary, animals rarely write poems, make puns, deliver speeches, or shout out orders in the stock market. We are *human*, precisely because we are *Homo loquens*.

We *relate* within language. While making love is a cheerful animal act, it is inconceivable apart from getting to know one another, kinds of word courtships, and living with one another in language. We love with words. We break up with words. We are angry with bristling words. We reconcile with words. While we do gesture relationships, our gestures have meaning precisely because they are associated with words and, thus, have their meaningfulness conferred by words. From a casual on-the-street greeting, to deep interchanges soul to soul, we are with one another through language. Human being, as *social* being, lives in common language.

We *think* with language. Though we tend to believe that thinking is somehow prior to speaking—"I think, therefore I speak"—in actual fact, cognition, as we know it, would be impossible without some sort of symbol system, a language. We think because we have been addressed: Learning is a linguistic enterprise. Evidently, we do not think *in* words. Nevertheless, we could not think without having language.

Oddly enough, words themselves can be enterprises. Think of puns, jokes, poems, novels—all of which are made from words; words are their substance. We speak of "playing" with words. Obviously, ritual systems, however gestural, are enacted words, that in some ways have no other raison d'être than word enactment.

Why have we recited a tribute to words? Because we live at a time when words are either regarded as optional or as limited only to some areas of life. There is the peculiar notion floating about that just as there are different senses, so there are different media and that, all things considered, one media mode is as good as another. Thus, words may be presumed to be an option because the message can be sent through mime, touch, or even by a "scent-o-gram." Not so. Gestures per se do not convey apart from meanings formed by words. Further, while "feel" may well be regarded as giving a message, some messages may be suited to feel and others not: Sensory modes are *not* interchangeable options. Furthermore, words are not limited to communication. Words, as we have seen, are almost as pervasive as the air we breathe;

we live in language. Human society is an exchange of words. Human being is a mysterious conversation. Though our age imagines that death is power and, thus, expends billions for bombs, the power of *life* is in language. No wonder the Bible is big on words: God created with a Word, and we have faith by hearing.

THE COMMUNICATION MODEL

Lately, some language theory seems to suggest that words are "things" we use. Thus, to many people, words are mere "signs," a convenient code with which people trade ideas. In basic communication theory, words are a medium of exchange. Just as a dollar bill is a convenience, a substitute for cumbersome bartering, so words are handy signs we use to transfer mental images. Words, like things, are inert until we pick them out and use them to convey thoughts which are in our minds. Thus, in a crude communication model we have a "Sender," "Words," and a "Receiver." The sender translates some particular thought into a word code for transmission. The receiver, in turn, decodes the words and, thereby, reproduces the sender's original thought. In the basic communication model, words are signals—like the "dits" and "dahs" of a Morse code—used to transmit thoughts from one person to another. Thus, behind each word is a thought, idea, or concrete reference. Communication models can be developed with great complexity to acknowledge all kinds of social, psychological, and even acoustical matters, but in essence they reduce to a sender, a receptor, and a code in between.

When applied to preaching, the model must be enlarged. Though preaching surely involves a speaker, hearers, and words, there are many other factors to be considered. The preacher's message is not an original thought, but, presumably, comes through a tradition, so that we must suppose that there is another sender who transmits to the preacher through some sort of word code. Likewise, the audience is predisposed liturgically, again through verbal messages. Preaching may involve communication on many levels in addition to words per se, such as body language, symbolic vestments, architectural placement, tonalities, and so forth. There will also be many factors involved in reception, such as the status of religion, social attitudes, pious dispositions, and the like. A communication diagram for preaching would be complicated —indeed most are—nevertheless, the underlying model is bound to involve a sender, receivers, and the transmitting of a message through signs. In the communication model, words are signs, a medium of exchange, by which understandings in consciousness are transferred.

Words are signs that stand for something else. Either words stand for things in the world—tables, chairs, trees, people—or they represent concepts in the mind. (Remember, the communication model emerged from analytic philosophy and not Ma Bell!) Thus, for the most part, "truth" in speaking tends to be associated with representational accuracy. A word is a true "sign" if there is a corresponding thing in the world—thus, heffalumps are nonsense. Or a word may be true if it represents a logically coherent idea in the mind. Because the communication model displays a preference for objective veracity, and tends to discard subjective words as fancy or as merely expressive, the model may have difficulty dealing with words such as "heffalump" or "God," which may not be readily available as reproducible ideas in mind. When words are regarded as signs, optimally they should signal with clarity. So to grasp the communication model, we must add to the basic sequence—words represent thoughts, and thoughts are based on reason or on sensory data. When we trade a thought by means of a word sign, the word should signify by referring to some actual reality.

Most books based on the communication model worry much about obstructions in the communicative process. Obstructions, sometimes labeled "static," are of many types. Basically, however, obstructions will be associated with speaker, hearer, or the word code. Thus, a speaker may not have a clear thought in mind, or may be psychologically at odds so that the word code may be in conflict with a body-language code, or the speaker may be unsure of objectives in speaking, and so on. Likewise, there can be problems in reception such as preconceptions, expectations, emotional blocks, cultural "bliks," and the like. Actually, because words are viewed as arbitrary signs, they themselves are seldom a problem except as they may be poorly enunciated, or ineptly chosen, or when there are acoustical problems that inhibit hearing. Presumably, if word signs are accurate, speakers adept, and listeners attentive, a perfect exchange of thoughts should occur.

When religious types grab the communication model to explain preaching, results can be most peculiar. Usually the communication model is extended to explain revelation. Thus, revelation is depicted in a sender-code-receptor model except that the sender is spelled with a capital "S." God communicates through word or, sometimes, through word and gesture (e.g., sacraments or historical events). Not surprisingly, the communication model has been popular with conservative Christians. If God is a Sender then the Bible may be viewed as God's word code, and preachers decode from scripture God's rational truth. Usually, the work of the Holy Spirit is associated with subjective factors which enable us to rightly decode and hear. When more liberal Christians wield the communication model they tend to stress "interpersonal" definitions of communication. In both cases, the words of a sermon are, above all, to be clear and interesting; interesting to hold attention and clear so as to transmit thoughts.

The communication model does offer helpful insight into sermon process and may well improve delivery, clarity of presentation, and effectiveness. More, the model does assist us in spotting the "bliks" and blocks that may prevent an appropriate hearing of our words. (If I say, "I'm going to buy a Christmas tree," to a tribe that performs sexual orgies under pine trees, I may well be misunderstood!) Insofar as Christian faith does involve the transmission of tradition, the communication model will be enlightening. Nevertheless, the model does present problems. Underlying the model are assumptions: (1) Words are arbitrary signs, and (2) words represent rational thoughts. If words are much *more* than an arbitrary code, the communication model tumbles down. For within the communication model words *are* devalued, they are no more than a medium of exchange. The model evolved from rationalist philosophy and, indeed, rests on rationalist assumptions with regard to reality. If the assumptions are, in fact, questionable, then the model, though useful, is to be questioned.

THE EXPRESSIVE MODEL

What are words? There are theories of language which regard words as a medium for self-expression. With words we articulate ourselves. The position is apt to lurk beneath pietist definitions of preaching. Words speak out of experience. Just as we will sob in grief or sing for joy, so the warmed heart of religious experience will be expressed in preaching. Words are linked with human subjectivity from which faith articulates.

Often the theory will appeal to the origins of language, or, at least, to a theory of origins. Language is presumed to have risen from the grunts and sighs of primitive human beings in an encounter with their all-but-magical world. Underlying language is a kind of primal wonder. Language emerges from interaction with the world. Another version of the same theory tends to locate language with internal emotions or dreams which may well have been produced by environment. Thus, language is an articulation of the primal self and connected to an affective dimension of self much as is music. When the theory of origins is applied to religious language, it is usually linked up with a notion of the numinous, the presence of the awesome and inexplicable "Holy" to primitive people. Thus, words are bound up with deep levels of religious experience.

While the theory may be developed in many ways by linking language with images in consciousness, or emotions, or will, or even the dreamy unconscious, there are two primary ways it is presented. Either language is (1) joined to some *depth of self* or (2) language is linked with *subjective intuition* that can reach into dimensions of life beyond empirical or rational realities. Not surprisingly, both positions were in vogue in the late nineteenth century and rose in reaction to a burgeoning rational scientism, in order to protect truth in the arts and religion.

When language is (1) linked with a *depth in the self*, it is usually connected either with some inaccessible level of self (affections, primal attitudes, the unconscious, and so on), or it is regarded as a medium for the expression of the *whole* self (which is more than rational thought). In religious communities, the understanding of language as self-expression is often coupled with a notion of the Holy Spirit *within* us. Presumably, God's encounter with the self occurs in the hidden depths of affect and dreaminess. Thus, in preaching, we articulate primal religious experience. Because in most religious communities there is a priority on intelligibility, the language of preaching is a *secondary* language, a compromised language, that, nevertheless, in its intonations, imagery, and the like is closely related to inward experiential revelation. Rightly, preaching speaks from faith to faith, and faith is cradled in the depths of selfhood.

When language is (2) joined to a concept of *subjective intuition*, theory takes a somewhat different shape. Here, the idea is that, while sense impression may record the objective world and reason construe meaning, there is a hidden dimension to life accessible only to inward intuition, which is a sort of "sixth sense" within the self. The sixth sense appears to be possessed by · artists and religious types, but is often undeveloped among empiricists. Thus, the theory tends toward an updated Gnosticism. The inner sense, intuition, articulates through language, particularly poetic or expressive language. When the theory is embraced by preachers, it is apt to produce a "truth through personality" definition of preaching, or a kind of guru-seer image of the ministry. Frequently we will find attention given to the "art of preaching" and to "inspired" sermon delivery, because preaching must impart inner illumination to other "inners" and must, therefore, be both artful and emotional. Above all, preaching will not be the transmission of rational truth, because, after all, rationality has only a small corner of truth in mind.

The model of language as expressive has naturally been popular, particularly in periods when romanticism has been at odds with rationalism. Within religious communities it tends to be embraced by groups who strongly affirm the presence of the Holy Spirit, by conversionist traditions, and, of course, by Pietism. Revelation is usually understood as given to experience, deep personal levels of experience. Certainly, the position in one form or another has been attractive to those who oppose what they consider to be a sterile orthodoxy or a rigid biblicism. Lately, the theory seems to be lurking in the "tell-your-own-story" school of preaching, or in the trend toward personal illustration in many pulpits.

In some ways, the model is quite compelling. Surely, faith is not a top-of-the-mind activity, but does involve the whole self in the living of life. More, though religion is neither solitary nor inward, it does engage our dreams, our feelings, and our most intimate attitudes. Certainly, if language is regarded as expressive, preaching will attend to images and cadences and other kinds of craft in order to express. It may also be alive with some degree of spontaneity which, otherwise, might be wet-blanketed by rational inhibitions. The expressive model also may recognize that preaching is not merely a talking about things or a setting forth of dogmatic ideas, but is, in some sense, an articulation of Presence. Nevertheless, the model is, in final analysis, inadequate. Language is incurably social and embodies social understandings. Likewise, preaching is inevitably concerned with historical language, a tradition that sets before us symbols of faith. Preaching as self-expression places too much burden on self and on religious affections: Our Christian faith is both *social* and *historical*.

WHAT IS LANGUAGE?

What is language? Somehow we must construct an understanding of language that goes beyond communication and self-expression, beyond rationalism and romanticism. We must build a model for language that acknowledges the mystery of words in human consciousness.

Let us begin where, in fact, we all do begin: with a *given* language. Whatever the origins of language may be, for us it is already present. We are born into a language. We emerge from the womb and wake up in the midst of an ongoing conversation, a conversation that fills the social world. We do not invent a language out of our secret selves, we inherit a language, a language-in-use. The culture into which we are born has a vocabulary, a grammar, and all sorts of speech conventions. The social language we receive names the world, establishes roles and relationships, and serves social functions—it enables us to do. When we enter the world we dive into a linguistic pool, a whirling, eddying, linguistic pool. Of course, the language we inherit is not merely a network of social signs, it is a stream of social memory as well; words can be written down. Through language we have access to human tradition in sciences, arts, and customs. In addition, words themselves have a history, and, in subtle ways, will still embody a thickness of meaning. (The word "nice" used to be a rather nasty four-letter word applied to lascivious people, but later came to mean "delicate" and even "shy" as in "She's such a nice girl," so that, now, the word can be used as delicate description of sweet morality, or as an ironic label for prissiness, or even, sarcastically, for lascivious folk.) Words are all around us as a social language gathering in time and space. We are born into language.

The language of a culture embodies what is sometimes termed a "Cultural

Formulation." Ever since Wilhelm von Humboldt, we have recognized that words shape a world view, support a value system, and even form a tacit credo —unacknowledged beliefs we may actually live by. To learn a language is not merely to memorize a list of arbitrary signs, but, rather, to put on a mind, the mind of an age. In learning language, we also learn to think about our world, our ways, and ourselves in some particular fashion. Thus, when words change we can assume that, as a culture, we may be "changing our minds." For example, a hundred years ago it was customary to speak of "body" and "soul," perhaps because the notion of a bifurcated self was common. Of late, the term "soul" seems to be sliding out of the in-use vocabulary except as the term has been rehabilitated in Black subculture as in "soul food" or "singing soul music." Instead, we have begun to use a number of words that express a holistic view of selfhood. While language is generally quite conservative and contributes to social cohesion, there are periods when, all over the world, language seems to be in flux—times such as our own. Language may alter epochally (Do we not refer to "classical," "medieval," and "Enlightenment" languages?) as cultures reformulate their understandings of the world and of the self in the world. All we are saying is that we are born into an ongoing language that shapes our understandings, our values, and even our convictions. We live in a language.

Every language is a social product. Because every language embodies a cultural formulation, languages will be oddly selective. In a language, we may see some things quite clearly, but other matters only dimly, if at all. For example, language in America of late is packed with technical terms, but is rather limited when it comes to words that express nuances in relationships or that refer to states of being. Thus, we may not have too much insight into ourselves and have difficulty in relating to others, but we are whiz-bang mechanics! All cultures will bring out some realities and all but ignore others; the world in consciousness that language constructs is always somewhat lopsided. In addition, there are taboo subjects, realms of life left unspoken by most societies. We do not usually rehearse "bedroom" conversation in a public forum. Likewise, at least in Western society, we seldom reproduce what we consider to be the rantings of the insane; their talk is "irrational" in a rational age. Some cultures will be quite intolerant of dissent. So, let us recognize that though we are born into a language, language is always skewed. The words we learn are bound to give a slanted perspective—these values but not those values, these things in the world but not those things. To learn a language is to receive social conditioning.

All social language is a "game" of rules. So for every language there is a grammar, standard usage, and, of course, many stock expressions that have become language conventions. We should not bristle at the restrictions of grammar or usage because, after all, they enable us to share a same world and to manage daily life in the world without undue strain. (Although, in times of rapid linguistic change, strains increase.) Language conventions contribute to minimal civility as well as functional simplicity. We can purchase a tank of gas, get a haircut, order groceries, and attend parties, all because we have learned conventional patterns of speech. Though language is a game of rules, however, sometimes the rules can pose problems. If we live too much within the structures of conventional language, though we will be secure and probably socially facile, we may lose track of our mysterious selves, or be locked up in a sadly one-dimensional life without political spunk or religious imagination. We may think of conventional usage and grammar as a bright, circular glade within a forest where children play games according to accepted rules, yelling stock taunts and encouragements. If a child should wander out of the bright circle and into the penumbral forest, staring if only for an instant up at some leafy nave, the child may find it difficult to speak within the bright-glade language conventions. So language rules of the game are a mixed blessing; they make social life possible but, at the same time, may restrict alien mysteries.

In addition to being born into a cultural language, most of us are to some extent subcultural creatures as well. Perhaps we have grown up in small-town Iowa, or in an urban ethnic group, or along the laid-back Mississippi Delta. In addition, we may have been born into a family-sized chunk of the Republican party or in our childhood sported Socialist party buttons. Surely now, as we live out our lives, we move through all sorts of social groupings from a workplace community, to a bowling-league klatch, to some particular church. In all human communities and subcultural groupings there will be peculiarities of language—code words, stock phrases, slogans, singular terms. As we move about we will inevitably mix up our languages. More, as subcultural groups shift status, our social language will be altered. For example, in the past three decades we have witnessed words and expressions from the black experience moving into mainstream social language. Similarly, as Third World nations expand political power, we can expect radical alterations in *lingua franca* English. While with upward escalation and social mobility subcultures may reform cultural language, some subcultures develop language as a protection against cultural absorption in order to retain a distinctive convictional or moral tradition. Thus, conservative Jewish groups will instruct children in Hebrew, retain in-group lingo, and, of course, recite traditional narratives to ensure identity. Obviously, some Christian groups will rehearse particular language conventions in order to preserve group character as well, and will often judge "outsiders" by the alien words which they may use. So social language will be altered by subcultural movement, while, at the same time, subcultural identity will be preserved by a narrowing of the linguistic rules.

In strange ways, however, language bears witness to a reality that is more than linguistic. Though we live *in* a language, our language itself indicates a "more-than-language" reality. The sense of "more than" comes to us in many ways. Perhaps, as some have argued, an infant memory of a wider perceptual field prior to language lives in us all to spook our confident speaking. But even without supposing a residual infant memory, the sense of a "more than" occurs in several ways.

1. Whenever we speak, we speak selectively; we focus and speak of one thing while excluding other things. At the blurred edges of focus there is always a "more" that is unspoken. So, if I say, "I returned a book to the university library," I am referring to a particular, singled-out action from a total field of experience in which the action occurred. The field of experience may be wider by far—the miserable search for a campus parking place, a stopping to stare at a pair of wheeling birds, a sidelong glance at a splendidly scruffy co-ed, a murmured absent-minded greeting in passing, the polished blue-china sky, a baking sunshine, and so on. Every statement we make is a speaking of an intentional focus and, therefore, bears witness to a wider unsaid world.

2. Sometimes we sense that restrictions of grammar deform actualities of experience. All human experience involves a simultaneity—perception, emotion, memory, daydream, bodily sensation—all bundled together in a remarkable "at-onceness." No grammar permits us to put the radical simultaneity of experience into words; all experience is to some extent *un*remarkable. Thus, we will say "I can't express it!" indicating some sort of disjunction between language and lived experience.

3. In acts of self-expression we are frequently surprised by the images or ideas we speak that apparently float into language from the depths or the fringes of consciousness. We are not referring to the way in which we will clarify our inchoate thinking by speaking out ideas. Rather, we are signaling discoveries in language which seem to come as a bringing out into consciousness, as if from some unseen realm. Whatever the *actual* source of ideas, we experience the coming into view of surprising ideas and imaginations as a witness to some deeper or other reality.

4. Social language itself seems to suggest a world beyond the world constructed by language. Obviously, different languages—English, French, Urdu, Bantu—seem to grid different perceptual ranges, opening some lived experiences and closing off others. Moreover, language in its changing beto-

kens processes beyond language. Thus, we sense there may well be a world beyond the world shaped by language in which we live. We are in no way suggesting that in the experiences we have described there is indication of God or some "heavenly realm" other than our own. All we are arguing is that language itself hints at a reality beyond language.

Is it any wonder, then, that we tend to view language as a veil that scrims the truth? Do vocabulary and the rules of grammar hang between human consciousness and reality, obscuring our understanding? Because we are sinners and may well wish to preserve illusions against the hard truth of God and neighbors, do we weave language as a protective falsity around our lives? Because, as sinners, we will always seek stasis and parochial securities, do we use language as a way of securing ourselves and preserving our lives? Maybe, as George Steiner suspects, language is always "After Babel." For example, if I have decided to protect my self-image by courting social approvals, I may well wish to live within the common-denominator clichés of language in order to "get along." In which case, I may even oppose those who wish to dance outside the circled glade of conventional usage—I may resent poets as dangerous threats to social solidarity. I may paper my world with conventional slogans and reject all quirky linguistic oppositions. Whole societies may function sometimes in much the same way by rejecting other languages of dissent, suspicious of any language counter to common clichés and well-worn slogans. The will to domination or the will to preservation, both primal, may multiply a language of falsity. Perhaps all language is inevitably shot through with falsity.

Nevertheless, we can only reach out into mysteries via language. How else? There is no extra sixth or seventh sense, no private pipeline intuition by which we bypass the pervasiveness of language—even faith comes from hearing and, therefore, even prayer. We are always *Homo loquens;* our glory and our finitude. We explore the "beyond our world" only by dancing the edges of language. New meanings emerge by metaphorical process, by imagination's wonderful wordplay. Through metaphor, paradox, polyvalence, and other linguistic "stretching," we bring out new meaning. Owen Barfield claims that the human race could not have conceived of gravity until two particular words gathered extra connotation and then came together to make the meaning "gravity" possible. As new words are coined and mingle with our social dictionary, we think new thoughts and reach out toward the wider reality language itself witnesses. The essential nature of language is a naming in consciousness, a bringing out and into view surrounding mysteries—the mystery of our deep-pool selves, the mystery of world, and perhaps even the mystery of a Presence-in-Absence God. So words bring presence to consciousness. Though words are emphatically human and incurably social, nevertheless, the essential character of language is to bring out and into consciousness.

The language of preaching is ultimately a language of presence, a language that brings out, a language of disclosure. Thus, the language of preaching is related to fields of consciousness where symbols form and meanings may be brought out. While preaching may be communication, it is much more a *mediation;* while it is evocation, it is also an *invocation.* The failure of the communication model is that it supposes we have fixed rational thought that we exchange by way of arbitrary signs. Therefore, the communication model will always tend to speak in the well-lit glade of clear, common meaning. On the other hand, the expressive model also tumbles into error. If communication theory demotes words into arbitrary code, the expressive model regards words as not much more than primal cries of the psyche's vocal cords. Neither position is congenial to a theology of Word. Besides, the expressive model overlooks the primacy of consciousness as well as the sociohistorical character of language. The self expressed in preaching is a self brooding over a field of consciousness, intending to bring out meaning. By overlooking the presence of symbols in consciousness, the expressive model stumbles toward narcissism. Of course, both positions—the communication model and the expressive model—though offering valid insight, straddle the objective/subjective split. Ultimately, the language of preaching is language related to consciousness, concerned with bringing out and forming in.

The language of preaching is tricky. It cannot be labeled a primary language, a language of immediacy. Though the language of preaching does dance toward the edges of language as it wields metaphor, image, analogy, and paradox, it is also designed to address children who may play in the bright glade center of language. (Notice that, in one sentence, we have appropriated concerns of both the communication and the expressive models.) Thus, the language of preaching is a "mix." Preaching is wised up with rhetorical strategy as it speaks to folk who may live in the center of language; it is poetic as it stretches ordinary conversation toward mysteries apprehended on the edges of language. Because preaching articulates a field of consciousness it will be concrete, a language of images. But the syntax of preaching may well be "peculiar" as it strives to bring out Presence through metaphorical language. The language of preaching is *a connotative language used with theological precision.*

PREACHING LANGUAGE

We began the chapter by looking at different people speaking. A man names a rock. Another man whirls sing-song in a ritual dance. A woman explains a mathematical formula. A poet scribbles a poem. But what goes on when, Bible in hand, a person preaches? Perhaps all our images merge in the complex language of preaching. We name prosaically. With the precision of a poet we put consciousness into words. Sometimes we articulate complex theological patterns. Always our language may be edging toward doxological praise. No wonder that, year in and year out, preaching is a kind of faithful excitement. No wonder!

12.
The Language
of Preaching

A famous stylist had a block. He wrote short pieces and one novella, but, all in all, his output was scant. Why was he blocked? According to a contemporary, he had a painful obsession. He spent hours searching for *the* right word. Presumably, his thesaurus was well-thumbed. While preachers should be much concerned with words, they cannot afford to be compulsive. Preaching is not literary art; it is speaking. Because preachers will put forth enough sermonic language in a lifetime to cram more than fifty thick books, they cannot allow too much fussiness over the right word in every spoken sentence. Besides, in oral delivery, careful manuscripts do change. In sermons, structure and imagery are always more important than particular words. Nevertheless, most preachers do not wish to be clichéd or wordy; and they do wish to be responsible articulators of gospel. While we will not be compulsive, fussbudgeting every word, we know that words are important, and few words are as important as the words we speak in preaching.

THE VOCABULARY OF PREACHING

Preaching speaks ordinary language, the ordinary language of human conversation. The language of preaching is not a separate holy language; sermons should not sound religious. Nor is the language of preaching "arty," designed with aesthetic concern; sermons should not sound like second-rate T. S. Eliot. Preaching rather modestly wields a basic, all-but-commonplace vocabulary. Graduates from a good theological school will have an educated vocabulary of around 12,000 words. An average member of an average congregation, however, will have a vocabulary of about 7,500 words, presuming the congregation is neither illiterate nor overly erudite.

At the outset then, there will be many words we will not sing out in our preaching—eschatology, hierophany, noetic, kairos, kerygma, soteriological, and any number of German imports ending with "-geist." Actually, a 7,500-word vocabulary will be too large for our speaking. Almost everyone has some store of "technical language" whatever their occupation. A secretary typing into a computer will know terms that may be quite unfamiliar to a hay farmer. On the other hand, the hay farmer will mutter words a secretary will blink at—haycock, windrow, ted, baling hook. Most people have a store of technical vocabulary associated with their vocations, from a plumber's "T-joint" to a nurse's "pulsimeter." If we remove technical words from our average 7,500-word vocabulary—perhaps subtracting as many as 2,000 words—we arrive at a much smaller "common" vocabulary in a congregation. Of course, in addition to technical vocabulary, most people have picked up local expressions from the geographic areas or subcultures in which they were reared. Thirty years ago, teenagers in ghetto New York City might refer to a high-school hangout as "The Dumps," whereas in northern New England the phrase "Scruff Palace" could have been used, a phrase that tumbled into the States from Canadian Maritime Provinces. Most of us may have as many as 500 such expressions whirling in our repertoire of words. So, basically, the common *shared* vocabulary of a congregation will consist of about 5,000 words. The language of preaching is basically the *common shared vocabulary* of a congregation.

To look at the matter of vocabulary in still another way, check a thesaurus. Simple words may have a host of synonyms. For example, look at a list of some of the words we can use to speak of gathering things or people:

> assembled, collected, congregate, meeting, accumulated, cumulate, massed, heaped, stacked, piled, glomerate, bunched, fascicled, fasciculated, crowded, packed, crammed, jampacked, compact, dense, close, serried, teeming, swarming, populous, thickly set, packed like sardines, thick as thieves, and so forth.

If we review the list, we can spot a range of words from colloquial expressions, "thick as thieves," to simple words, "piled, heaped, stacked, crowded, crammed," to less usual words, "congregate, accumulated, amassed," all the way to seldom-used, "fasciculated." Obviously, preaching will have a preference for the colloquial and the simple. If preachers overuse the less usual words (e.g., amassed, congregate, accumulated), perfectly fine words that are unlikely to be featured in daily conversation, their sermons will tend to have an odd essayistic tone and be difficult for congregations to grasp. The tone of erudition may flatter a preacher, but it will not assist the hearing of the gospel. So the languge of preaching should be the vocabulary of everyday conversation, a lexicon of about 5,000 words, which members of a congregation will share in common.

The somewhat limited vocabulary of preaching should not worry us much. (Remember, the vocabulary of the New Testament's *koine* Greek is not much more than 5,000 words.) A simple, concrete, often colloquial vocabulary is a language related to life. Day to day, we act, speak, and understand ourselves in a basic vocabulary—often the words we learned in the first five years of our lives. Moreover, when we speak of important moments, the profound if often troubling moments in our lives, we invariably revert to simple words. Unless we are eager to parade erudition, the limited vocabulary of preaching need not disturb us. The problem is not the size of a preaching vocabulary, but how we *use* the vocabulary. If our constructions are commonplace and our phrases clichéd, we will speak a language suited for the well-lit center of life and, thereby, translate the gospel into conventional wisdom; we will be trite. But simple words can be put together in astonishing ways. Words can combine in the magic of metaphor. Words can sing a simple beauty. Words can be packed with concrete stuff of life so that, with vividness, we can see what is spoken. The trick in preaching is to use an ordinary vocabulary in the extraordinary service of the gospel, dancing the edge of mystery, reaching into depth. With simple words we can speak close to people. With simple words we can wander into Presence. In sum, the language of preaching is given to us by our congregations. We take and use a simple vocabulary with subtlety and imagination for the sake of the gospel.

THE SOPHISTICATED, SIMPLE LANGUAGE OF PREACHING

On earlier pages we suggested that preaching, though a slowed-down discourse, could convey a kind of simultaneity of understanding. If a sermon is well spoken, we can visualize, think, feel, and, therefore, understand on many levels at once. Preaching speaks a simple vocabulary in such a way as to produce huge connotative meaning. Let us try now to comprehend the sophisticated, simple language of preaching.

Suppose we select a subject matter in order to study the ways it can be spoken. Since death is a loaded subject matter, we will speak of death. Study a first example.

> Eventually the human organism will expire. Though medical life-support systems may prolong bodily existence, eventually, by accident, cardiac arrest, or tissue deterioration, the organism will cease to function. Other human beings associated with the deceased will react to the termination of life in various ways: grief symptoms, somatic reactions, and other types of classifiable emotional trauma.

189

Obviously, such prose will *not* be the language of preaching: We have parodied a scientific language. Preachers should not sneer, complaining of "jargon" or "obfuscation"; scientists have every right to seek a language both precise and dispassionate. As with any language, including the language of preaching, human egotism may twist a good purpose into conceit. Some scientific authors may turn terminology into a precious display of erudition —as may theologians or parsons—but the purpose of scientific language, observational objectivity, is not unreasonable. It is safe to say, however, that sermon language is not a dispassionate objectivity, because faith is not aseity, faith is engaged.

So, suppose we alter our original passage by simplifying language, and by introducing at least some minimal degree of human reference.

> We all die. Though life-support systems may keep our bodies going, sooner or later, by accident or heart failure or merely growing old, we will die. People around us will suffer with us, grieve, or feel intensely.

Said aloud, the words may sound like the language of preaching, a language we do hear in many pulpits. But the paragraph is *not* in the language of preaching. All we have done is to introduce pronouns, "we" and "us" and "our," and to use a simple, nontechnical vocabulary. The language is still observational; it is still objective and without personal involvement. We have done a denotative talking about death. While the words may well sound like much preaching, actually they are inappropriate for pulpit discourse, if only because, in quantity, they would bore us to tears! When such language is used for the content of sermons, ministers will compensate by including gobs of pathos in illustrative material. In the paragraph there is some cadence created by the two triple lists, but the cadence is scarcely expressive. Though the third-person observational stance of pulpit rhetoric does produce similar paragraphs in many sermons, rightly the language of preaching is not bare statement.

Let us tinker with our paragraph in a new way.

> We die. Oh, medical science can keep us going, pump the pump of the heart, or measure the slow ooze of intravenous feeding, drop by drop by drop; we will live, but without aliveness. Sooner or later, we'll stop. An accident can end us. Or maybe there'll be a long-drawn-out lingering until we die. Those around us, they'll cry and wonder why, maybe breathe in and out with our last breathing, and finally walk away empty of us.

What we have done is *imitate*. We have tried to match cadence and the sounds of words to what we are speaking about. Thus we imitated heartbeat with "pump the pump" and matched the interminable intravenous feeding with a slowed-down syntax. Accidental death was mentioned in a terse sentence, while lingering death was spoken of in a stretched alliterative sentence. A rhymed "They'll cry and wonder why" attempted to signal affect. The final "walk away empty of us" concluded a system which began with the abrupt "We die." Though the paragraph has been overdone as an example, it does show a way of making language "come alive" through imitation. Quick things can be said quickly. Labored activity can be expressed with a labored syntax. Syntactical imitation will also employ the sounds of words, vowel-sound repetitions, and other rhetorical devices. Of course, many of the so-called tropes, such as antithesis, or anticlimax, and the like, are best understood as imitations. While many ministers are apt to overdo some devices, notably, alliteration and onomatopoetic systems, the notion of imitation is helpful. A mere striving for effect is, of course, pernicious, but imitative language can assist a congregation in grasping meaning.

Let us play now with metaphorical language.

> We all die. Starched hospitals may bustle about to keep us going, pump the heart like a bellows, or spoon-feed us intravenously, but we will live lifelessly, zombies. Sooner or later an accident will shatter us. Or, maybe we'll slowly run down like worn-out clockwork, and stop. People who love us will wail like hurt children, or wonder why, or struggle with our struggling breath, or simply walk away empty of us.

Again, the paragraph has been overdone by way of demonstration. Nonetheless, notice the bundle of metaphor and simile that has been dumped into the paragraph. Hospitals are personified as nurses, with "starch" and "bustle." The heart pumps like a "bellows." "Spoon-feed" is applied to intravenous feeding, turning patients into infants. Life is "shattered" or "runs down" like clockwork. Grievers wail "like hurt children." While only one or two developed similes may happen in a single move, residual metaphor, particularly in verbs—pump, shatter, spoon-feed, run down—can be used with some frequency.

The power of metaphorical language is awesome. With metaphor we can form attitudes, emotions, and profound understandings in congregational consciousness. Compare the following descriptions: "She moved like sea grass in the wind"; "She moved like a drum major on parade"; "She moved like a grave child taking first steps"; "She moved like a belly dancer to a drum beat." We could attempt to describe each walk without resorting to simile, by heaping up adjectives or providing actual step measurements, but such descriptions would fill pages. Instead, one brief simile can do our work almost instantly. Of course, we might heighten precision by changing the verb "moved" in some of the cases to "pranced" or "swayed" or "stepped." Visual verbs are themselves full of semi-metaphorical energy.

Ministers generally run scared of metaphorical language. They are apt to regard metaphor and simile as artificial additions to ordinary speech, as ornamentation. They fear that if they use metaphor their speech will sound affected and, therefore, call attention to language rather than content. No, metaphorical language is not abnormal, because metaphor making is native to human consciousness. Our everyday conversations are filled with metaphor and simile. Some are stock and show up all the time: "I went out quick as a bunny ...."; "Well, the joke was on me. . . ." Others may be singular and often stunning: "Didya' see him hit the homer? It went out of here like a big bird flying"; "After last night, I don't know how I crawled to work. Listen, I'm walking in a dream today." (Even vulgar metaphors are often ingenious.) If you were to wear a tape recorder so as to play back your daily conversation, you would discover that, all but unnoticed, you are using metaphorical language in almost every conversation. So metaphor is *not* inauthentic. What is artificial is attempting to preach *without* metaphorical language. The result will always be a cardboard pulpit, speaking tediums of denotation. Metaphor is your authentic language.

We can speak in still another way; we can combine concrete imagery with point-of-view. The result can be vivid.

> We die. Someday, we will all die. A doctor will smile and say, "We want to make you comfortable," but life-support machinery will be small comfort—the wheeze of a pump, the long oozing in a plastic tube. But, we'll die. Perhaps it'll be the swerving car we see too late in the corner of an eye, the screech, and then. . . . Or maybe we'll peer through the milky oxygen tent to see a white-walled room with drawn blinds, and the figures of our family like pale ghosts watching the in-and-out, in-and-out of our breathing. Can you see them walking away from your dying with wide, hurt eyes, out into the outside where everything will stand out, too real, in sudden sunshine, a huge empty secret inside themselves?

Though the paragraph is overwritten, concrete details ought to be obvious. Such language is produced by a deliberate act of visual imagination. We put ourselves in a place and, after determining an angle of vision, attempt to see what is to be seen. We are recording phenomenal detail. The problem, of course, is to do such descriptive work without an alarming number of adjectives, because adjectives clutter oral language and prevent understanding. Nevertheless, by combining phenomenal imagery with imaginative syntax and metaphorical language, sermons can form powerfully in congregational consciousness.

We have rehearsed different modes of language for a purpose. The language of preaching is never bare observational language of objective meaning. Thus, the first two examples offered should not be found in sermons. Instead, the language of preaching is a mix of image, metaphor, and imitative syntax. These kinds of language are not ornamental figures of speech we add to ordinary prose; they are the stuff of preaching. While they are made of a simple common vocabulary, they can reach into mysteries of meaning. The diction of preaching is neither commonplace nor poetic, but is the diction of an ordinary language outstretching itself. While denotative language is handy when it comes to doing business or writing instructions, the language of preaching is highly connotative. Let us define the language of preaching as *a connotative language used with theological precision.*

CHOOSING THE LANGUAGE OF PREACHING

Our excursion into language may have given the impression that ministers must be verbal artists. But no, preaching is always more *craft* than art. What is more, preaching is a *considered craft.* We never pursue effect for the sake of effect; we are always concerned with usefulness. Though we will draw on liberated imagination in bringing images into consciousness, we will weigh word choices judiciously. The norms by which we assess language can be stated: Is the language theologically apt? Does the language form in congregational consciousness? Does the language serve the statement of a particular move? Let us review our norms.

The language of preaching must be *theologically apt.* Preaching *is* doing theology. For example, let us look at the relationship between language and a particular theological understanding—the kingdom of God. Suppose that in preaching on the kingdom of God, we reach for an image of intimate, inward experience, saying, "The kingdom of God is like a lover's secret in your heart." Though the sticky phrase may be warmly received by a congregation, it will be a theological disaster. Yes, the kingdom may well be secret, but in scripture it is a social reality and never an individual possession. Though some translations of scripture do read "The kingdom of God is within you," the "you" is actually a "you-all," and Greek prepositional usage indicates that a better translation might read "The kingdom of God is *among* you." So, if we are to be theologically apt, we will have to search for an image of social reality, or, perhaps, of Presence with social reality. Likewise, were we to say, "The kingdom is greater than our greatest cities; it towers over us," again, we would court theological catastrophe. The image is much too triumphalist and, therefore, will be in tension with the strange impotency of Christ crucified. Of course, the word "kingdom" in and of itself may be a problem, for it either smacks of male domination or suggests fairy-tale fiction. Now we cannot sit down and write out requirements for an image (e.g., kingdom of God implies a rule of love which, though hidden, is, nevertheless, realized socially) and then command imagination to chase down a simile; imagination is seldom docile. Instead, by brainstorming, we will bring all sorts of images to mind. Theological understanding will help us to sift through a collection of images and to select with some precision, Homiletics is a poetics of theology. Though connotative language is often polyvalent and may seem quite wayward, it is not. We can shape connotative language with theological wisdom.

In mentioning a theological norm we are *not* urging the use of religious terminology. Though ministers may be tempted to sling religious lingo into sermons—redemption, salvation, sanctification, born again, blessing, justification, and the like—such words may no longer be terribly useful. They are good words, and they are our words, and they are convenient words in theological discussion, but because they no longer figure in daily conversational exchange, they may be alien terminology to most people in a congregation. We may try to recover the words and rehabilitate their meanings within Christian community, but words that slide out of the social vocabulary are seldom retrieved. What such words do in sermons is to drape discourse in an aura of old-time religious respectability. Thus, in some slightly anxious conservative congregations, theological terms may prove that sermons are "kosher," that is, properly religious.

We live in a rapidly changing language. Since 1955, to select an arbitrary date, more than 100,000 new words may have found their way into our dictionary. Since the start of our century we have watched a huge vocabulary slide away into social forgetfulness. In such a moment, we must find ways to seed the gospel in a new, now-forming social language. First-century preachers, the apostles, were geniuses when it came to locating metaphors for Christian understandings, some of which have become our slightly emptied religious terminology. Our task may be similar. We must search the language of human conversation and, once more, find images and metaphors to proclaim the gospel. What we cannot do is to fall back on stock theological terminology to any great degree. Instead, in our age, we must speak in a language of common image and metaphor, but do so with theological wisdom. Imagination will provide us with raw material, and theological understanding will help us to pick and choose appropriately.

We have insisted that the language of preaching is for *congregational consciousness*. The language of preaching is not primarily self-expression, a kind of art form for faith. Images that may well be meaningful to us personally may not be of much use to congregational neighbors. Ministers will draw on their own lived experience in preaching. Moreover, they will associate particular images with aspects of their own experience in what may tend to be a kind of private code. As a result, the images or metaphors we create may be hugely meaningful to us, but somewhat oblique to a congregation. Again and again, we will have to weigh our meanings within the context of social meaning. Preaching draws on two kinds of language, private meaning and public disclosure, *parole* and *langue*. If a sermon is too much a reiteration of public meanings and stock images, the gospel may be trivialized. If a sermon is too much an expression of private experience, however, the gospel may be turned into an alien eccentricity that is all but unintelligible. Ministers will necessarily draw on their own images and associations, but with a courteous love of neighbors, they will check their language for social usefulness. For example, suppose a preacher has been brought up in a blatantly cruel foster home where punishments included being locked up in a dark room without basic necessities of bed or bath or food; the minister may find a poignant image coming to mind, "Like a little child crying in a dark, locked room." On consideration, the minister may realize that most children are *not* locked away in darkness. Thus, the minister may adapt the simile—"Cry like a left-alone child"— deleting the bare, locked room. Such a distinction may seem picky, but it is not. If there are too many singular, odd images in a sermon, the gospel will be removed from common life and turned into a private pathology. We do not suggest that, frightened by our own peculiarities, we will revel in safe clichés: "Cry like a left-alone child" will be far better than the overworked "Cry like a baby." If we weave a sermon out of worn clichés, we will convey the impression that the gospel is an echo of culture's conventional wisdoms; we will be clearly understood but truly banal. No, preaching will seek a freshness of expression precisely because we explicate a *new* social reality, being-saved, but the images we choose and use must work in congregational consciousness.

Actually, the language of preaching will be functional in that it will *serve moves,* moves in a structured sermon scenario. Thus, as we use language in preparing sermons, we will be guided by our moves. Each move, as we have observed, will say a simple meaning, will embody a point-of-view, and will express some sort of mood. Thus, the language of preaching is not a language per se, but is *always* a language doing a particular move. In preparing moves, we will have considered what we mean theologically, will have turned to lived experience for actual images, and will have spotted possible obstructions to understanding. Thus, in using language to make a move, we have already located theological meaning to adjudge our words, and fields of common lived experience to weigh our private associations. Point-of-view will shape our style, as well as the move's particular function within the structure of the sermon. Thus, moves impose upon us a certain obedience which may prevent soaring "purple passages" or rhetorical showboating with words. Our language will be governed by the perspective and purpose of a move.

LANGUAGE AND PUBLIC DOMINATIONS

Though language is a social given, it is often a damaged gift. Language, we have noticed, embodies cultural convictions, values, and perspectives, some of which may be quite alien to the gospel. Language may also express social attitudes that, in the light of the gospel, are unlovely. The going metaphors that float around in common conversations may well view time as money, love as a commodity, power as admirable. And, obviously, our social language may express dominations of race or sex or wealth. So, though we must use a common vocabulary, a shared basic vocabulary, as preachers of gospel we will not wish to pass along surly prejudices or conventional wisdoms alien to the Spirit of Jesus Christ. Just because we are preaching gospel, we cannot justify using racist or sexist terms on the basis of an end/means argument, supposing that the redemption we speak will cover the "isms" of our spoken language. No, we must seek to alter language in view of the gospel.

Does language express racial bias? Yes, to a degree. The word "black," a proud word to an oppressed Black subculture, can be used in demeaning ways. Black/white language, at least in English, tends to demote "black" in favor of "white." So, in English, there are all kinds of phrases—"It's a black day," "He blackened my name," "That's blackmail!," "We blackballed him" —which incorporate a negative use of the word "black." Except for "white-wash" there are few negative uses of the word "white." Preachers, if they are White, must keep an eye out for the subtle prejudice that lives in language. Of course, more often, racism will show up in obvious ways, for example, demeaning Black dialect mimicked in a sermon illustration, or ways in which White preachers discuss the "Black problem." Unfortunately, we do live in protective subcultures. Therefore, we may, quite without realizing, pick up expressions that demean ethnic groups whether we speak of Native Americans in northern Michigan or Hispanics in Texas or Blacks in racially split cities or "White pride" rural places. The rule is simple: We must protect congregations from our own careless sinfulness and also from linguistically embedded social sins.

A special problem for Christian preachers is anti-Semitism. The problem is posed by scripture as well as by forms of Christian theology. Are the

Gospels anti-Semitic? Yes and no. The Matthean community is struggling with Jewish opposition and, therefore, bristles with anger at times. The Gospel of Luke, showing preference for Gentile Christianity, is often obtuse with regard to Jewish leadership. Though the Gospel of John may have been written and rewritten over some years, at least one layer of the Gospel reflects conflict with "The Jews." The problem of anti-Semitism is delivered by the Gospels. In spite of the corrective in Romans 11, there are pop theologies which portray Jews as "God killers" who rejected and still reject Jesus, so that some dear fool minister can get up and baldly announce that "God doesn't hear Jewish prayers." The problem of anti-Semitism is *our* problem. We must not fan anti-Semitism by Christian preaching. Instead, we must take pains to indicate the true Jewishness of Jesus; we must preach regularly and responsibly on the Hebrew scriptures; we must affirm that our Jewish brothers and sisters are chosen people and children of God in covenant. When we preach texts that seem to split Jew and Gentile we must probe for the deeper theological dispositions involved, rather than for social identities. Jesus may well have refused certain strains of thought in late Judaism—national triumphalism and exclusive salvation and ritual/legal purity—but he clearly articulates the understandings of a central Hebrew tradition, the Law and the Prophets. What is required of us as Christian preachers is *not* hostility toward Jewish provincialisms, but an awareness of our own Christian provincialism, and, therefore, unusual sensitivity to our language, lest, even inadvertently, we enlarge disgraceful anti-Semitism that, unacknowledged, lives in every Christian congregation.

The problem of sexism in language, particularly as it relates to God-talk, seems more difficult to deal with. Previously, in a discussion of sermon illustrations, we broached the problem of sexist social roles and sexist social status. Now, we must examine language. The problem, though not peculiar to English, is probably more evident in English. In languages such as French or Spanish or German there are definite and indefinite articles that express gender, for example, *"le"* and *"la."* As a result, if we live, let us say, in the French language, our whole world will be gendered. Things around us will be masculine or feminine or neuter. Because we use external things as metaphors for our "inner worlds," we will tend to draw into ourselves a rich, complex sense of gender; we are feminine *and* masculine, we are masculine *and* feminine. Unfortunately, the English language seems to have been losing gender. Years ago, when a powerful locomotive rolled into a station, people would say, "Here *she* comes!" whereas today we say, "Here *it* comes." Thus, a sense of the mystery of gender in all things has been rubbed out of our everyday English. As a result, in America, we are left with pronouns and plumbing and often pernicious role models. We also have some odd, inherited conventions, such as the use of the male generic, for example, "When a person speaks, *he* says . . . ," or the term "man" for human being. Almost all such constructions can be easily avoided without having to resort to "he and she" or "her and his" couplings. A felicitous nonsexist language can be learned, spoken, and thought, quite naturally. The more serious problem for preaching has to do with sexist God-talk, thus with images—God the King, God the Warrior, and, yes, God the Father. A first step toward a solution will be a searching for feminine imagery which is at hand in both scripture and tradition. (It is also helpful to study sermons by able women preachers who will demonstrate a natural skill in the use of feminine imagery; they should instruct male preachers.) Some of the obvious God-talk problems can be resolved neatly by simply using a different syntax. We do not need to use the construction, "When God spoke, *he* created the world," when we can say, "God spoke, and the world was created," or "The world happened when God spoke," or some other useful syntax. Though liturgical usage is a more complex problem, the word "parent" surrounded by appropriate imagery can serve sermons as satisfactorily as the word "father." Though the common usage we receive may be sexist, indeed, *is* sexist, and though we who preach *are* sexist (as well as other kinds of "ists"), in light of the gospel, we can bring our language under discipline for the sake of our congregations. The language of preaching is awesomely powerful—it names the world and shapes identity —so the language of preaching must be informed and reformed by theological obedience.

Many books on preaching set up general norms for sermonic language. Language must be "clear," they insist, or language must be "expressive." By "clear," such books seem to mean a single meaning without connotative fuzziness. By "expressive," usually they urge emotional force. Instead, we have suggested that preaching will use ordinary, common vocabulary, but *not* in order to reinforce conventional meanings. Likewise, we have offered imitative syntax, metaphor, and image, but *not* as a medium of affective self-expression. The language of preaching is peculiar; though ordinary, its use is extraordinary. For the language of preaching is a concrete language of imagery that can paint a field of consciousness and then bring out of the field meaning from mystery: The language of preaching is a language of disclosure. When we preach we are also forming congregational consciousness and not merely trading thoughts. Therefore, preachers will use words as verbal sculptors. The words of preaching are ordinary words, as ordinary and pliable as clay, but from them we shape a new world for faith.

13.
Style and Preaching

Can you imagine Jesus commissioning disciples by saying, "Go into the world and fulfill yourselves"? Not easily! The scriptures are not wild about self-fulfillment. Instead, we are advised to lop off an offending arm should it get in the way of neighbor love. Likewise, we cannot conceive of Jesus advising preachers to step into pulpits and "Develop your *own* style!" Style in preaching is not something we possess in order to express our own uniqueness; style is neighbor love in language. So we will not strive to have a style, but rather we will use styles for the preaching of the gospel and the forming of faith.

STYLE AS DOING

There is no such thing as good style per se. In preaching, language is functional; it is trying to do certain things. Thus, we cannot ask "Is the style good?" but we can ask "Is the style good at doing what wants to be done?" Actually, a minister will not have *a* style, but rather many styles as needed. In a section of James Joyce's *Ulysses*, Joyce is describing a newspaper office. Oddly enough, he writes the entire section in the style of headlines, a clipped, shouting style of banner headlines. The example may seem extreme if applied to preaching, but it does underscore an idea. In preaching, we ought to be willing to change styles to match different subject matters and different purposes. The notion of good style tends to be a literary preoccupation; orally, most of us speak in many ways. The style we use in describing a Chicago Cub baseball game (perhaps somewhat similar to the "Suffering Servant" songs in Isaiah), will be quite different from the style we speak when making love; the style we use in negotiating a business deal will be very different from the style we may instinctively employ in calming hysterical children. In every case, the style will be distinctively ours, but only because *we* are speaking. We will be speaking in many *different* ways.

The preoccupation with developing our own distinctive style in the pulpit is strangely adolescent—a preoccupation with identity. It is almost better to bypass the category of style altogether and, instead, think of how we can speak so as to match words with content, with point-of-view, and with intentional purpose. Oddly enough, as we develop linguistic range, as a byproduct we may find our style given!

Sometimes ministers suppose that style is linked to feeling. They imagine that if they can feel a certain emotion, style will automatically follow. Thus, if they can feel anger, they will be enabled to write an angry style, or if they feel calm, serene phrasing will all but effortlessly spill from their lips. But making ourselves feel particular emotions on command is not all that easy—as any capable actor knows. Feigned emotion is apt to produce nothing more than artificial language, a language that does not ring true. While styles and feelings do interrelate, feeling usually emerges from character and situation. Thus, "method" actors will adopt a role, in effect they will become a character who, in some given situation, will have feelings. But an actor does not say, "I will have such and such a feeling"; that would produce not acting but histrionics. So, in preaching, we cannot command feelings to express in style without courting inauthenticity. Instead, we can speak a point-of-view or gaze at an object in consciousness, and, usually, emotion will follow.

Imagination produces style; disciplined imagination. The phrase "disciplined imagination" may seem a contradiction, because we think of imagination as indecently frisky, untamable, or beyond our control. No, we can deliberately imagine, through the astonishing magic of consciousness. We can imagine ourselves in a particular stance without much difficulty. For example, we can imagine ourselves wandering around in crowded Jerusalem during the original Holy Week. Or, even if we are a convinced pacifist, a third-generation war protester, we are able to imagine ourselves within the consciousness of a militarist. As for objects in consciousness, our consciousness is like a screen on which we can project images as if before an inner eye. We can project a picture of Christ on the cross to contemplate. Certainly, we can readily call into consciousness depictions of the world in which we live. Things, situations, people—all these we can recall and project in consciousness. Style and imagination go arm in arm.

Another source of style is rhetorical necessity. Informed by homiletic wisdom, again and again, we will find we must do something with words. We must shape a firm start for a move, or achieve closure; we must design an illustration to match the structure of an idea; we must express a contrapuntal notion; and so forth. At such times, we use words much as a carpenter will use tools—we will pick out words and *do*. Sometimes we will think out what has to be done and then select language quite self-consciously. At other times, usually when doing familiar verbal tasks, we will speak without much thought and *do* in stock ways. Just as journalists will develop excellent style when they are doing a job of reporting, so fine pulpit style can be formed by ordinary craft doing what must be done. What is *always* devastating in a pulpit is preaching that strives for effect per se. We gain style not through self-expression, but in a kind of obedience; we put ourselves in perspectives, we visualize images to contemplate, we do the useful work of homiletics.

Style and Point-of-View

More than anything else, point-of-view determines style. In a move, we may be attempting to speak from some constant point-of-view, either from some stance in time-space or from some attitude. In effect, we are playing a role or standing in a situation. Consider the following:

> "Present our bodies"—No, we didn't come to church for such a message. Instead, give us sermons that kindle, and anthems that soar; give us lofty thoughts and lovely feelings and sweet visions of heavenly things. After all, Monday through Friday we have to put up with a world that's all too physical, with bills to pay and laundry to sort. So on Sundays, we don't need a heavy dose of "physical religion." What's more, there are many of us who feel the church has been much too concerned with "bodily things"—housing, civil rights, poverty programs. So when Father Kinsolving writes in the papers that, "The church ought to be as much concerned with the saving of the soul as the care of the body," we applaud. For down deep in all of us, there's a craving for "spiritual things." No, we say, "Give us spiritual worship!"

The question we must ask of such a paragraph is not "Does it have good style?" but "Does it represent a point-of-view?" For we cannot judge style in abstraction. Style will be the product of a person and, therefore, will have rather distinctive syntax and a particular vocabulary range; but style *does*, and the real question is always "How well does it *do?*" So we judge style according to the demands of a particular move; we judge style move by move. In the case of our example, the preacher is attempting to represent a perspective, a craving for "spiritual worship" (Rom. 12:1) along with a denigration of "bodily things." So the question we ask to judge style is "How well does the preacher articulate perspective—a point-of-view?" If, for example, in the middle of the paragraph we had a sentence reading "Some of you feel that way, don't you?" we could be critical. The intruding sentence would have disrupted the forming point-of-view. As the paragraph stands, we may want to criticize the preacher for having too many lists, triadic repetitions, for example, "lofty thoughts and lovely feelings and sweet visions of heavenly things" as well as "housing, civil rights, poverty programs." If we are contrasting ideas, we should probably avoid using similar language systems. When doing point-of-view, however, the question is "How well does the language represent?"

Style and the "Objects" of Consciousness

When we speak of an "object" in consciousness, we are bound, at the same time, to express the effect of the object on us. (Otherwise, of course, we will leap into a language of scientific or historical objectivity.) Though we will be describing an object, our syntax will be representing response. For example:

> Somehow or other, we can't seem to get the cross out of our minds. Oh, we can take down the ugly pictures of hung Jesus from the Sunday-school rooms, and try to turn Jesus into a song-and-dance *Godspell*, but then, once a year, Good Friday rolls round again, and again there's the story of the garden and the cross and the tomb. "Father," cried Jesus, "if you will, take this cup from me!" But, God didn't, and Christ walked the way to Golgotha. What was his baptism? Soldier spit. Where was his cup? Vinegar on a stick stabbed in his mouth. "Oh, the Son of man, the Son of man, must suffer many things and die." . . . Ever since childhood we've seen broken Jesus hung on a cross. "Let this cup pass," he cried, but it didn't. He was baptized by his suffering. He drank the dark cup of dying. A vision of Christ on the cross is clawed in our minds.

In the paragraph, which has been somewhat abbreviated, we are trying to portray recurring memory of the agony of Christ crucified, which, annually, comes to us through scripture readings and church art. A previous move in this sermon has portrayed easygoing "churchianity," and a subsequent move will voice a call to the church to suffer with Christ. (The first sentence of the move actually read, "Well, we could get away with it, if it weren't for the cross!") What we have done is to weave cadenced lines of scripture with visual images—"Soldier spit," "Vinegar on a stick stabbed in his mouth," "dark cup of dying," "clawed." The combination is designed to have us hear the scriptural record while, at the same time, realizing the crass agony of crucifixion. Notice, please, we are not merely dealing with a problem of joining description and affect, but also of establishing a point-of-view (the cross in our minds). The style of the paragraph, spoken aloud, will sound very different from the style of our preceding example, which represented an attitude.

Style and Content

Sometimes, our problem will be matching style to meaning. If, for example, we are going to speak of bondage to sin, we might wish to use repetition, deliberate clichés, and a degree of "flattened" language so as to evoke a sense of the dullness of sin and its dreary consequences. If, on the other hand, we intend to follow our discussion of sin by speaking of the new freedom and child gaiety we find in Christ, we would loosen up syntax and all but sing our words. Let us try to produce the different languages, a small sample of each:

> . . . Well, you can have it if you want it, but sin is dull—dull, dull, dull. Every morning you get up to stare at the same face with the same false admiration. Every day you edge out into the world to pose and pretend, to fight your neighbors. Every neighbor is in the way of your ego; every word is an opposition to your word. At night you turn on the same TV to the same programs to keep away the same thoughts. Every night you hide from your dreams and fall like stone into sleep. A little house, a little job, a little *us*. Sin is an ugly word. Sin —a desperate life.

> Free! Hey, dance if you want! Spin and kick up your heels like a kid. We're free. Free as a bird in bright blue air. Free as a wondering child. Free. Each day is new for love. You have fun listening to neighbors because you want to listen. And pleasure; you take delight in the world. Like a two-year-old, you explore lovely things. . . .

The samples, overdone, do demonstrate syntactical difference. The trick in matching style and content is not found in feeling. What you do is to picture what you are talking about. So you picture a drab, redundant egotism, if that is the way you understand sin. Then you talk out your pictures into language. In so doing, your affective self will order language. After you put down your language, you will be able to objectify your own words and, almost certainly, be able to heighten the effect you are after. For example, in our first sample (on sin), we might wish to remove the metaphor "like stone" which, however likely, may add too much color to language. Because each of the samples is the product of a second writing, we can look back and see change: repetitions were increased in the first sample, whereas parallel sentence structures were removed in the last two sentences of the second sample. Again and again, in preaching, we will be called upon to match style and content expressively. If our concern is to develop *our* style, whatever we speak will come out sounding the same. Instead, to serve a congregation, different ideas should sound differently.

Style and Move Development

Obviously, much of our work with words will be governed by what we are trying to do in any particular move. The component parts of moves can pose a problem. The move must hold together in a unity of style, but, at the same time, may demand stylistic variety as different ideas are expressed. Study two sections of a single move which we have previously printed:

> Shall we spell it out? The church does not exist to spruce up your morals, to make you nicer, neater, kinder, sweeter, day by day. God may not be much interested in what we call "morality." The church does not exist to teach your kids religion. Christian faith may not even be a religion. The church does not exist to provide you with warm fellowship. Good heavens, we can rub human fur with human fur almost anywhere!

> Think back over your own lives. We've all been brought up badly: Too much law, too little grace. And we live broken, patched-together lives, riddled by funny fears and guilts that, my God, we'd like to forget. But here we are, forgiven, able to love a little once in a while, and we know it's God who's done it all—who's set us free from ourselves for love.

The two paragraphs are component parts of the same move, but quite different in style. The first paragraph is shaped by homiletic necessity—when chaining examples, they must be shaped in the same way so that they will gather into one meaning. Thus, though the examples provided are not *exactly* the same, they are given a generally similar rhetorical shape. Of course, the inclusion of the nursery-rhyme cadence in "nicer, neater, kinder, sweeter, day by day" is a deliberate matching of style with the idea of do-good morality. The final sentence in the system with the explosive "Good heavens" intensifies and, thereby, concludes the defined system of language. In the second section, style breaks up a bit so as to match "broken, patched-together lives," and the "my God" is an evocative intrusion that both disrupts syntax and expresses a weary longing. At the same time there are unifying elements in the two sections. "Too much law" may subliminally link up with the nursery-rhyme morality, and the "f" sounds used in both systems will align. The style was determined by matching sound with meaning, and by necessities of homiletic design. The two sections are language-doing.

We are arguing that ministers should not seek a style of their own. As discrete individuals, they will have a way of speaking that is already quite distinctively their own. The real task in preaching is to take personal style and make it work for us. Our style is to represent the gospel and to serve congregational consciousness. Thus, the problem is not in getting a style together as an expression of *us,* but in continually bending our style to different purposes.

THE MEANS OF STYLE

How to get at the ways and means of oral style? In days gone by, homiletics texts would rehearse the well-known tropes, often-used figures of speech, giving examples of each—antithesis, apostrophe, chiasmus, metaphor, metonymy, oxymoron, all the way to zeugma. Rhetorical figures are helpful, however, only when we have learned to wield them *naturally* the way a carpenter handles tools. Instead, we will try to discuss general categories and, through them, try to grasp some components of style.

The Sounds of Words

Time for a "guest professor." Here is a study of words by a seventh-grade schoolgirl, Carolyn Rosner:

> Many words have meanings to me other than the ones Noah Webster thought appropriate. There is a special group that I like to use on a rainy day: gray, nymph, pearl, mourn, fern. . . . These are particularly "gloomy words." There are also words to say when happy, such as dimple, tickle, lilting, merry-go-round, and dumpling. . . .
>
> There is a sharp distinction between *rainy* words and *slow* words, which are to me expressions like imperious, polite, topaz, and canopy. These slow words are drawn out, while the rainy words just reek with gloom. . . .
>
> My favorite word is cinnamon as it seems to arch its back and hiss at one.

Young Carolyn (now in her thirties) had an ear for the sounds of words, the strange musicality of speech. So, let us notice that there will be a correlation between what we are talking about and the word sounds we choose to use. If we speak of cruelty, we will deliberately employ harsh gutteral sounds; if we sing of sweet things, we may reach for "s" and "f" sounds all but instinctively. As a result, we can look over a completed sermon and we will soon discover "sound clusters" associated with particular notions. Polysyllabic Latinate words will suddenly show up when we speak of weighty matters, whereas quick words will click with rapid-fire speed when we are describing movement. All but instinctively, we will match the sounds of words to ideas.

Some ministers may fear the sounds of words, afraid lest, in their use, sermons will somehow become arty or *arti*ficial. Not so. Ordinary speech is full of the sounds of words—"She's a sweet sensitive soul, isn't she?" "Wham —did'ya see him smack the ball!" When preachers remove such natural poetry from their speech (usually in the grip of a choking rationalism), they trudge toward tedium. Of course, the sounds of words can be overdone, particularly in the use of alliteration, and come across as contrived speech.

Two rules govern the sounds of words: Do the sounds function within a speaker's normal syntax? Do the sounds relate appropriately to a particular subject? Let us understand the two rules.

Do the sounds function within a speaker's normal syntax? If we have to leap out of ordinary speech patterns in order to incorporate some system of sounds, then the words will call attention to themselves and smack of the arty. Compare alliteration in the following examples:

> Our speech is strange. Our speech is strangled. Filled with a sense of "I should have spoken," we stand in stunned silence.

> Is there anything worse than the strange, strangulated sense of "I should have spoken"? To live on knowing that we've missed the moment when we should have spoken.

In the first example, the sounds of words are featured in a syntax that inevitably will call attention to itself. The second example, which by comparison may seem less powerful, will not stand out from patterns of speech within a move and, therefore, can contain the heaped-up "s" sounds. Another way in which the sounds of words may violate natural patterns of speaking will be with the addition of unnecessary words. Thus, naturally, we might say, "I'm desperate!" Only unnaturally would anyone remark, "I'm dreadfully desperate and in despair." If we use the sounds of words, we will not normally alter our syntax to incorporate them.

Do the sounds relate appropriately to a particular subject? Most of us do not need a treatise on poetic devices to sense the different sounds of words—they are built into our language. Murmuring "m" sounds are quite different from some assaultive "b" sounds; sibilant "s" sounds are different from "di" or "ti" sounds. If we listen to our language we will locate words that sound like what they designate. The English language is often helpful. "Smooth," with a combination of "s," "m," and double "o," sounds its meaning. "Gutteral," "grumble," "growl" associate because of their harsh sonance; even if we did not know definitions, we would readily grasp their meaning. The sounds of words will come across as artificial if they are mismatched with meaning.

Mismatching will occur in several ways. For example, if I heap up word sounds—disappointed, despair, disappear—the words combined will produce sound, but unfortunately meanings will not align; while disappoint and despair may associate, disappear is of a different field of meaning. Thus, if I were to use the sequence in speaking, the words would ring false and seem artificial. A more serious problem is created if we put together a wrong sound with a meaning, for example, gutteral sounds (like "gutteral") with a smooth description. Though such disjunctions are rare, because our language is apt, they can happen. If we use, for example, polysyllabic words to describe a person of ingenuous unaffected artlessness (which I have just done), the effect, orally, will be inappropriate.

The sounds of words will assist meaning. The sounds of words should be used with restraint, however, to achieve an all-but-subliminal effect. Study the sounds of words in a brief system we have already reviewed:

> Think back over your own lives. We've all been brought up badly: too much law, too little grace. And we live broken, patched-together lives, riddled by funny fears and guilts that, my God, we'd like to forget. But, here we are, forgiven, able to love a little once in awhile, and we know it's God who's done it all—who's set us free from ourselves for love.

We have picked the passage arbitrarily, not because it is terribly well written (it is not). But, here, in a brief passage, there is a "play" of sounds—"b," "g," "f," and "l"—and even a repetition of "sequence sounds" as in "forgiven, able to love," and "free from ourselves for love." Sound systems should not oversignal themselves. They will function, all but unnoticed, to serve the meaning we are attempting to shape.

Cadenced Language and Rhythms of Speech

All speakers speak in rhythmic systems. Some systems are familiar in sermons. We have heard preachers whose sermons sound like waves, rising and falling, rolling at us in crests of sound. Likewise, we have heard sermons that seem to mount ever more rapidly (and erotically) toward climax, before, in a hush, they ebb into silence. Of course, we have also heard sermons that proceed in measured phrasing with a terrible sameness, plodding toward conclusion. We can caricature these familiar systems of speaking, because, through the length of a sermon, they are the *same* and, thus, are characteristic of a whole discourse. Ideally, cadences that show up in sermons should vary according to *what* we are speaking. At times our speech will trip along in easy loping sounds, at other times, our sermons will be staccato; we may use great crashing rhetoric in one section of a sermon and, in the next, dance our words around in a kind of mannered gavotte. We must use the rhythms of speaking and not be trapped in them. Cadences seem to be of two sorts: rhythms caused by syntax and rhythms formed from the sounds of words.

Syntactical Rhythms. The most familiar syntactical rhythms in preaching are those caused by repetition, by doublets, and by triadic clauses. They are the most familiar and, unfortunately, the most troublesome. Let us see them in a single (dreadful) passage:

207

God calls us back. God calls us back to the faith of our founders. We must return to the moral, spiritual, and democratic values on which we were founded. Our nation is great and good, holy and happy, because we believe in God, we believe in God's Word, and we believe in doing God's will.

Repetition is used in the first two sentences. Doublets appear with "great and good, holy and happy." Triadic clauses are also obvious: "moral, spiritual, and democratic" as well as "we believe in God, we believe in God's Word, and we believe in doing God's will." The systems are familiar to us precisely because they show up, from beginning to end, in so many sermons. To some extent they are natural to public speaking. Unless disciplined, however, they can sound through an entire sermon, so that every *different* idea will be cadenced in the same way. Thus, for example, sin will sound the same as grace; Christ will sound the same as evil. When used by popular evangelists (as they are), such cadences will deliver an odd message—though the evangelist may be calling for a change of heart, the language seems to say, "Nothing will change or ever be different." So, though rhetorical rhythms will come naturally to speech, we will have to be self-critical enough to guard against overuse. Syntactical cadences can serve us well. If we use syntax to imitate ideas, our speaking will be lively indeed. Here is an example:

> Watch out! Jesus is not handing us an excuse for irresponsibility. Following him does not mean we can disown parents or cheerfully declare our children to be wards of the state. Christ's words do not lead away from the human world to a pious prayer-saying, Bible-fondling, sweet-Jesus-singing sort of faith. Christians will do business with neighbors. . . . Did Jesus retire from the world to dream great peopleless God-dreams and keep his soul well dusted? He did not. He walked the human world.

Here, we have used two spun-out sentences, each followed by short, simple-language sentences, in order to pose alternatives. The long sentence, "Christ's words do not lead away from the human world to a pious prayer-saying, bible-fondling, sweet-Jesus-singing sort of faith," stands in contrast to the directness of "Christians will do business with neighbors." Syntactical variations can work for us.

Whole moves should speak in different cadences from other moves. Remember our earlier example in which we imitated the dreary repetitions of sin, and then, in a following passage, the freedoms of grace? If every move in a sermon features too many doubled and tripled systems of language, even if there is some degree of syntactical variation, all the moves may sound the same. So, we will weed out extra doubled and tripled syntax, and, above all, never use such sentences in sequence. We will mix in short, often abrupt sentences. More, we will embrace a concept of imitation, again and again, trying to say in a way that will sound like what we are depicting, speeding up or slowing down, adding weight or reducing to simplicity, as may be necessary. The notion of imitation will assist variety in speech more than anything else.

Within sentences, rhythms are created by syllables in words, and by stresses on syllables. Compare the following rhythmed systems.

> Our ponderous, plodding ways! We wander around in circles, circling every idea, stopping to investigate or scrutinize, we wear ourselves out with wearisome fears.
>
> Click your heels and skip a little. Life's more fun than you know. Sun in the morning. Stars at night. Take delight in simple things!

In the first (and again, overdone) example, some words may be crucial. Think of the effect of substituting "heavy" for "ponderous" as well as "think and look" for "investigate and scrutinize." Conversely, imagine substituting "run around" for "skip" and "pleasant" for "fun," the extra beats added would disrupt the lightness of the language. Notice, again, the principle is one of imitation. With metered words and shaped syntax we are trying to make language sound a meaning. Many of the standard figures of speech are best understood as attempts to shape language to match ideas.

Conversational Forms

Instead of ticking off a list of figures of speech, let us look at some devices that are a part of everyone's conversational repertoire. We have discussed at length the power of metaphor and simile in preaching. We have also had a look at how images can depict the world in consciousness. But now, let us look at some occasional systems which, though rhetorical tropes, are also native to our ways of conversing.

Exclamations, Questions, and Direct Address. On a spring day walking with a friend we may interrupt ourselves with an exclamation: "What a wonderful day!" we will say. Though we have been conversing *about* things, suddenly we voice a cry of delight. Such a device will, on occasion, show up in sermons —"Oh, how great is God's mercy!" Questions will also dot our daily conversation. With a shrug we will interrupt a recital of woes. "Well, what can you do?" we will say. Rhetorical questions must be used sparingly in preaching, but they will show up. Sometimes questions will turn up at the end of a statement: "We all have troubles, don't we?" Or, sometimes, mildly phrased questions will form in among other sentences:

> God's love is a free gift. Can we earn God's love? Or purchase love with prayers? No, God loves, because God *is* love.

Sharp questions directly addressed to a congregation may not be used except at the starts of moves or within some carefully designed rhetorical framework. What about direct address? Direct address will, on rare occasions, break into conversational patterns. If in a conversation I am deploring presidential policy —spending on weapons and stinginess toward the poor—I might suddenly say, "Mr. President, you've got to change your policy!" So, sometimes, when speaking of God, a preacher may break into direct address in a kind of open prayer. Just as the device is rarely used in conversation, however, it must be sparingly ventured in preaching. Any convention overworked will tend toward triteness.

Repetition and Inversion. Repetition is frequently overdone in preaching. Usually it serves one of two functions—either it will stress for emphasis, or it will ask for a deeper consideration. Notice how repetition works in the following cases:

> We must love neighbors. Do you hear? We must love neighbors.
>
> We must love neighbors. We *must* love neighbors.
>
> We must love neighbors. "Love neighbors"—What can the command mean to us?

Repetition must be kept under control because, when everything is emphatic, nothing is important. Of course, repetitive syntax can become irritating. Occasional inversions can relieve the tedium of reiteration, as in the following sequence:

> We must love our neighbors. We must love our families. Our friends we can love. We must . . .

In general, too many repetitions of syntax should be avoided.

Synecdoche, Personification, and Apostrophe. Rhetorical terms name procedures that have emerged in ordinary conversation and, in turn, have been incorporated into public address. The three terms we have used name ordinary conversational gambits that are frequently included in sermons. Synecdoche is very common—it names a whole by one part. For example, we will say, "White House policy is unrealistic." We use "White House" to represent an entire political administration. Personification is almost as common. In an earlier example we used the phrase, "Starched hospitals may bustle . . . ," attributing personal characteristics to a building. Again, in a line such as "The tree reached toward us" we are using personification. Apostrophe is usually used in connection with synecdoche or personification, and involves address —"O America, how have you wandered from God?" These devices can be useful in preaching, as long as they relate to a natural movement of consciousness and are phrased in a conversational syntax. Most rhetorical terms are convenient labels for common habits of speech. Preachers may wish to read works on rhetoric that can offer examples of many (more than fifty) different language devices. The terms simply call attention to what in most cases we are already doing. Nevertheless, a heightened awareness of patterns of speech will enable us to be more skillful in our work with words.

COMMON PROBLEMS

If "faith comes from hearing," then we must strive to be heard. Unfortunately, congregational consciousness functions like a tape recorder. While communal consciousness can retain amazing amounts of material, like a recorder it can instantly erase. Research indicates that in a reasonably good sermon, only about 35 percent of the language will be functional; the rest will have suffered instant erasure, dropping out of consciousness almost as soon as it is spoken. While such deletions are usually the result of weak starts and finishes to moves or, possibly, a lack of point-of-view control, some erasures are caused by regrettable language patterns. So, if we are to achieve, at minimum, a 60 percent retention of language, we will have to sidestep some common pitfalls.

Some Word Problems

In general, we should avoid all sentences which begin with "this," "these," "those," and perhaps "that." As far as we have been able to determine, any "this" sentence will *instantly* delete from consciousness. In ordinary conversation, we will use "this" and "that" constructions when pointing: "I want *this* sandwich, not *that* one." In preaching, however, we are seldom pointing. Instead, the word "this" will creep into sermons as a reference to some previously spoken idea. The usage is a writer's convention: Writers, having written a paragraph on some particular idea, may begin a following paragraph, "This idea . . ." The usage works in print because we can always look back and reread. In speech the use of "this" is fatal, because we cannot look back and retrieve an idea. Sermon moves that begin with "This idea . . ." or "This situation . . ." invite wandering of mind. While there is a colloquial use of "that," as in "That's O.K.," in general we will want to remove *all* "this," "that," "these," "those" uses from our sermons. Sentences that begin with a "this" suffer instant erasure in consciousness.

The word "it," while less devastating, is also a problem. The rule can be stated simply: We can use an "it" sentence immediately following a sentence with a firm noun, but we may never have two or more "it" sentences in sequence. Not only does the word "it" depersonalize language, but in sequence "it" sentences will be an open invitation to wandering of mind. In oral language, a second "it" sentence, distanced from a noun, will usually lose its reference. The literary affectation "one," as in "One must try to see . . . ," is also a word to banish from sermons, along with all uses of the male generic, "man." In oral speaking, words such as "it," "one," "man" are oddly abstract.

Intensifiers such as "very" and "really" and "indeed" can be avoided. In writing, they have a proper function—in effect they underline words, adding emphasis. Orally they do not. About the only people who spatter conversation with "very" and "really" and "just" are slightly turned-on prepubescent teenyboppers. Otherwise, the words are seldom used in ordinary conversation. The reason can be grasped easily. In ordinary conversation when we wish to stress a word, we do so vocally: "She's a *fine* lady!" If, orally, we add "very" we actually weaken a sentence—"She's a very fine lady." "Very" adds an extra, nonvisual beat to a sentence, which, in delivery, is less emphatic than "She's a *fine* lady!" So "just," "very," "really," "actually," and the like, tend to be "junk words"; they do nothing but make language thick and less accessible to consciousness.

Delaying words or phrases at the starts of sentences are also a problem, a habit-forming problem. The delaying words are used in two ways: "Actually, we can see . . . ," or "We can see, however, that . . ." Such phrases tend to show up in academic writing—"It is clear that . . . ," "It is evident that . . ."—but are dreadful in speaking. In addition to contributing an essayistic tone to sermons, delaying words disrupt the cadences of ordinary speech, weakening every sentence in which they are used. An audience will suffer as every clear idea begins with an offbeat verbal sidestep. (Preachers probably pick up the habit from reading scholarly studies.) In speaking, delaying phrases may allow time to think out next sentences and, therefore, may soon become habitual.

Numbers seem to pose an odd problem. From research, we are inclined to argue that sentences beginning with enumeration will delete from consciousness: "First, let us . . . ," "In the third place, we can . . . ," "The idea has two components. . . ." So, though our sermon outlines may be numbered, the numbers should *not* be carted into the actual words of a sermon. Possibly, the problem is caused by our two-sided brains—who can say?—but it is detrimental to preaching. Understand that *every* sentence that splits between a number and a content will disappear from consciousness the instant it is spoken.

Though numbering systems seem to contribute clarity, in fact they destroy clarity. Advice: Do not number!

The words "thus" and "therefore" are literary conventions we almost never use in ordinary conversation. They are a language appropriate to logic or to mathematical formulas. Even if we do attempt to represent logical thinking in ordinary speech we will say "so"—"It's cold out, *so* I wore a coat." Aloud, try substituting a "thus" or "therefore" in place of "so," and sense the oddity of the result.

All these seemingly minor quibbles over language may seem pedantic; they are not. The issue is *hearing*. If certain words or phrases obstruct our hearing the gospel, then, obviously, we will excise them from our sermons. Notice that in all the examples the test we have applied is *ordinary oral usage*. Most of the matters we have discussed are word habits that have floated from the printed page into public address. Oral usage and written usage are different; we do *not* speak the way we write.

Some Syntactical Problems

As we have noted, fine preachers use rhythmic language. They strive to match cadence and meaning. There are some peculiar cadences that *prevent* hearing, however; some odd syntactical habits that will erase meaning from consciousness.

The most serious syntactical problem in preaching is caused by doublets in sentences that are trying to talk of two different things at the same time: "God wants peace and justice." Virtually *all* doublet sentences will instantly erase; they will not function in consciousness. The problem can become acute. If, in a paragraph of twelve sentences, four or five sentences contain doublets, the block of language, in its entirety, will probably dissolve, and, as a result, a congregation will lose a chunk of sermon. The effect of such sentences on an audience will be akin to what happens when we try to look in two directions at once—we see nothing! *All* doublet sentences will delete. (The only exception may be combinations that recur in everyday language, such as "ham 'n eggs.") So a simple sentence, "God wants peace and justice," will empty of meaning and not register in congregational hearing. Could a sequence of doublet sentences be used in a sermon? Only if a preacher does not care if people hear meaning, but, instead, wishes to convey a feel of complex unintelligibility. In other words, for rhythmic reasons we might include a doublet sentence or two in a move, as long as they are not essential for an assembling of meaning. Otherwise, we should avoid *all* doublet constructions.

Some preachers are fond of triple words or clauses. While an occasional triple clause—"God wants peace, and justice, and perfect obedience"—may produce a useful rhythm, in quantity such sentences can irritate a congregation. Moreover, if consecutive sentences contain triplets, both sentences will delete from consciousness; they will not be heard. The same result will happen if a single move contains too many triplets—for example, three or four sentences out of twelve. An entire move may be in jeopardy. A series of *four* clausal phrases tagged onto a sentence will convey a sense of overflowing or accumulation and, therefore, should only be used when such an effect is wanted. If too many triple and quadruple constructions sound in a single move, an audience will soon weary of what will seem to be listings.

Some cadences seem to be produced by improvisational preaching. When preachers ad-lib from too scant an outline, cadences will almost always show up. The cadences seem to be of two types: clausal repetitions and object-subject repetitions. So, if a preacher is thinking out a sermon as it is spoken, the object of one sentence is apt to become the subject of the next sentence:

> We must go down the road. The road leads to Calvary.
> Calvary, you remember, is the high hill where Christ died.
> Christ died to set us free. So we are free from . . .

If you read the passage aloud you can hear the odd "liturgical" cadence the language produces. In quantity, the language will drive a congregation slightly crazy; the congregation will simply turn off the preacher. The other common cadence produced by ad-libbers involves repetition at the ends of sentences:

> We must be willing to go down the road, down the road to Calvary. Christ died for us, died for our sins. So now we are free from guilt, free from hate, free from fears.

Such systems of language are much more common than preachers realize. Unless a minister suffers from some compulsive pathology, these cadences are normally produced by underpreparation, that is, they happen when preachers attempt to "wing it" in preaching. When the two types of cadences combine, as they will, congregations will not only refuse to hear, but will become hostile. Another result of "winging it" will be a repetition of developmental strategies of moves. Every idea in a sermon will tend to shape in the same way. Subliminally, congregations will pick up repetitions of form, and quickly lose attention. Oddly enough, our research seems to suggest that ministers who have tumbled into cadence habits are almost never aware of their problem; they may be so busy thinking next sentences that they are tone-deaf to their own recurrent patterns.

Most preachers, at one time or another, have set up sentences with similar syntax in a single paragraph. Sometimes the parallel constructions are prompted by a desire for emphasis, at other times they seem to be rhetorical gambits. Ground rules for use can be stated. Unless a preacher wants a sense of superfluity, only three repetitions of syntax will work. If the three sentences used are a perfect syntactical "match," however, the whole block of language will erase in consciousness. Thus, if we were to say in a sermon

> If Christ loves us, who can hate us. If Christ forgives us, who can blame us. If Christ chooses us, who can reject us . . .

the entire system would almost certainly delete from consciousness. The same effect will be produced by three or more questions in a row, even when language is different. What happens is that with the third use of the syntax, a sense of rhythm is produced that overpowers comprehension. Of course, the block of language will not disappear if the third sentence in the sequence is altered (or, possibly, the first sentence) by abbreviation or extension. With an abbreviation of the last sentence, a sense of established truth will be produced or, perhaps, a sense of general conclusion:

> We must love our neighbors. We must love our friends. *We must love.*

If, on the other hand, the final sentence in the system is elongated, a sense of comprehensiveness will be produced:

> We must love neighbors. We must love friends. *We must reach out to love the whole wide human world.*

Syntactical repetitions should not be overworked—one or two in a single sermon will be possible, but not more than one or two. Of course, repetitions, when they are loosened up or slightly syncopated, will probably work. Earlier we reviewed such a system:

> Shall we spell it out? The church does not exist to spruce up your morals, to make you nicer, kinder, neater, sweeter, day by day. God may not be much interested in what we call "morality." The church does not exist to teach your kids religion. Christian faith may not even be a religion. The church does not exist to provide you with warm fellowship. Good heavens, we can rub human fur with human fur almost anywhere!

Here we have three pairs of sentences where the first sentence of each pair is syntactically the same. The system may work because the second sentence in each pair is designed very differently with quite different rhythms. However, when three (or more) similar sentences are used *in sequence* without other interweaving sentences, or without end-line alteration, the system will disappear from consciousness.

Problem Expressions

What about slang phrases in sermons? All along we have argued that the vocabulary of preaching is ordinary in-use language. Surely slang phrases spackle our conversations; can they not figure in sermons? Answer: yes *and* no. If a slang phrase such as "uptight" has entered into the common *shared* vocabulary of a congregation, it can be used in preaching: "We do get uptight, don't we?" There are, however, slang words or phrases that do not yet appear to be part of common vocabulary except in defined subcultures. So, for example, the usage "He's boss" might not function terribly well. Slang, then, is a matter of judgment. The question is not do we use a particular term in everyday discourse, but rather, do our *people* regularly use the phrase? If we are undecided, we will be wise to skip the slang expression. Of course, we normally compress language in conversational usage—we need not say "do not" when normal usage says "don't," and so on. In such matters we will be guided by grammar and common usage (thus, we will not say "She don't . . ." in a sermon, though a particular congregation may so speak, but we will say "She doesn't" rather than "She does not"). In spite of Luther's famous lapses, we will not use "four-letter words" in sermons, no matter how rambunctious we may be in our daily conversations. We should not be discourteous or offensive when we are trying to speak gospel.

As we have already indicated, religious clichés are always unfortunate even though they may please a particular congregation. If we ourselves have grown up in a religious subculture that flings around religious clichés, we may have a problem clipping them out of our language. If our Christian faith is to relate to daily lived-experience, however, we cannot afford to speak a special, in-church language. Religious clichés, like any clichés, can be of many types, from the use of "fellowship" as a verb (ugh!), to echoey stock phrases, "Brothers and Sisters, we've got a greaaaaaat savior!", to religious code words such as "witness." In general, our test is ordinary conversational vocabulary. People do not often slide up to a lunch counter and say to a person on the next stool, "How good it is to fellowship with you!" Likewise, it may be less than usual to hear family members exchanging phrases such as "We've been washed in the blood" over a dining-room table. A separate in-church code of religious clichés only serves to alienate faith from life.

There are special vocabularies that seem to ring out within subcultural groups, from executive offices to hippie communes to various self-discovery groups. Within certain social spheres, word habits will tend to occur and become overused. In some human klatches "dialogue" may show up as a verb, and phrases, such as "meaningful relationships," can be invariable. In offices, we may hear all kinds of "ize" and "wise" combinations—finalize, account-wise, publicwise, and so forth. In other spheres we may listen to "decision maker," "opinion shaper," "achievement-oriented," and even "bottom-line consciousness." Again, our test must be the common *shared* vocabulary of a congregation, which fortunately has not yet given in to "dialogue" as a verb or "procedurewise" as normal usage. Though our age seems to multiply cant, vogue words need not creep into our sermons or (shudder!) our liturgies.

SOME GENERAL GUIDELINES

General guidelines are often too general to be of much use. Nevertheless, we can wave toward certain characteristics of good sermon style.

The language of preaching is *concrete*. We speak words so that people can *see* and understand. Of course by limiting the vocabulary of preaching to about 5,000 words, we have already moved toward concreteness. Any human being's basic vocabulary is apt to be a language of things and actions that can be seen. Therefore, as we have mentioned, we will steer clear of conceptual words, vague general terms such as "goals," "relationships," "situations," "desires," and the like. Instead, we will always be attempting to depict, either by the use of visual stuff (images) or by analogy. So, we will prefer a simple, vivid language in preaching. Compare:

In our homes, in daily life, we do not take time for God or prayer.

At home, around a kitchen table, or when it's tuck-in-time for bed, we don't bow our heads much, do we?

Sometimes, when homiletic texts urge "clarity," the word is misunderstood. If preachers chase clarity by turning to simple *general* words—"prayer," "life," "homes"—the words will be clear but dull. Instead, let us not worry over clarity so much as concreteness. Sermons must be imaged from beginning to end.

Above all, we must work on *verbs*. Excitement in preaching is usually created by verb *color* and *precision*. When sermons seem flat, it is often because weak verbs repeat. "Look" and "see" are perfectly good words, but they are flat and scarcely specify an action. In the living of life we do more than "look" —we peer, we scan, we peek, we stare, we study, we puzzle, we probe, we gaze, we take in, and so on. So, in a sermon having to do with the beauty of the world, if we limit ourselves to repetitions of "look," we will court tedium. "Realize" is a dull verb, particularly when repeated much; there are visual alternatives—grasp, catch on, make out, savvy, penetrate, and the like. By verb "color" we mean visual character. By verb "precision," we refer to some distinctive meaning rather than general meaning. Our verbs should be precise and full of color. Compare the following paragraphs:

> Some years ago a man attempted to revise the Bible, retaining comforting verses and omitting the rest. Among the first words he removed were these: "I have come to set a man against his father, a daughter against her mother." The words are not suitable for a Mother's Day card or appropriate for children to read. Yet, Jesus spoke those words to his disciples.

> Some years ago a man set out to edit the Bible, keeping comforting verses and scrapping the rest. Among the first words he scratched were these: "I have come to set a man against his father, a daughter against her mother." The words are scarcely fit to scribble on a Mother's Day card or to frame in the kitchen for kiddies to read. Yet, Jesus handed out such hard advice to his disciples.

In comparing the two versions, it is safe to say that "set out to," "edit," "scrapping," "scratched," "fit to scribble," "frame," and "hand out" are visual, and, therefore, more colorful than "revise," "omitting," "removed," "spoke." We find vivid verbs by imagining, seeing in mind the action we are describing. Strong verbs create strong sermons.

Orally, the weakest word we use is an *adjective*. If you could tape-record a day's conversation, you would discover that you converse in verbs and nouns and that you employ few adjectives. You will use adjectives only when you *must* use them; you will almost never use them for effect. The rule holds for preaching: unnecessary adjectives will cloy language, while an occasional necessary or "right" adjective will help. John Keats's "Ode to a Nightingale" can instruct us:

> . . . the self-same song that found a path
> Through the sad heart of Ruth, when, sick for home,
> She stood in tears amid the alien corn . . .

The adjective "alien" is astonishing. Imagine how the line would read, if, instead of "alien," we were to use the usual "tall"—all corn is "tall." Usual adjectives used in usual associations make clichés; but a perfect adjective can make language come alive. If we use adjectives, then, they must be either necessary (to define or distinguish) or well chosen. For the most part, however, we will speak without adjectives. Many preachers add too many adjectives which do little but cloy. For example, compare:

> What beauty God gives us! Sun in the morning, moon at night. Familiar faces of our friends. Thoughts to think, dreams to dream: Such wonders God gives.

> What great beauty God gives us! Red sun in the morning, silver moon in the dark night. Old familiar faces of warm friends. Huge thoughts to think, mysterious dreams to dream. Such magnificent wonders God gives.

In the second example, adjectives all but snuff out comprehension. Said aloud the words are too thickly textured; the adjectives obscure structures of meaning and, by adding extra beats, produce a language that is quite unnatural. In the first example, only one adjective is used and, perhaps, it is unnecessary. Emotional force in preaching is produced by syntax and metaphor, but seldom by adjectival elaboration. So, the rule can be stated: If you must use an adjective, find the right one, otherwise avoid adjectives in public address. Verbs and nouns are strong; adverbs have some power; but, orally, adjectives are weak words.

Preaching uses *pronouns*. We will almost never say "people have," we will say "we have." Preaching prefers a language of "we" and "our" and "us." Even when we refer to the mythic origins of humanity, we will still use "we." Instead of saying "Back in Eden, the whole human race fell into sin," we will say, "Back in Eden, *we* fell . . ." We will also use a language which draws preacher and congregation together—"you and I," "you and me." While "I" alone is *always* a dangerous word, because it can disrupt point-of-view, the word "you" is often splendid. Many preachers fear the word "you," supposing that, like a pointing finger, it can separate preacher and congregation. It can. A censorious "you" will be devastating: "*You* are sinners!" However, the word "you" functions in ordinary language in many, many ways. When we shrug our shoulders and say, "Well, what're you going to do?" the "you" functions as a code for "human being." So, "you" can often function in much the same way: "When you stand staring at a sunset, you feel . . . ," "When you get up in the morning, don't you find that . . ." For the most part preaching will sidestep general terms for human being and, instead, use "you," "we," "you and me" language.

In general, preachers should prefer *present tense* and *active voice* and simple, *short sentences*. Let us review our recommendations. The use of passive voice rather than active voice is a peculiarity that, unfortunately, seems to be increasing in pulpit language. We can see the difference:

Active: Everyone had a good time.
Passive: A good time was had by all.

Active: Shakespeare wrote a play.
Passive: A play was written by Shakespeare.

We will use passive voice when we invert sentences to break up syntactical redundancy. We will also use passive voice when we are not concerned with agency, or when we wish to imply indirect agency: "The package was delivered this morning." If passive voice is *over*used, however, it can damage sermons and give speech an odd literary quality. Passive voice adds more words to discourse and, of course, is more difficult for congregations to grasp. So we must keep passive voice to a minimum. Whenever possible, we will go for present tense rather than past tense. Because the pulpit has been working with historical-critical methods, there has been a preference for past-tense description. Almost always, however, such description can be brought into present consciousness. Compare the following:

> Jerusalem was a busy city at the time of Christ. There were wide walls around the city, and, in the center, there was the temple. The city was a honeycomb of streets and courtyards, and bazaars were filled with incessant chatter.

> Jerusalem—what a city! You sense bustle everywhere. See the walls all around, and, there, in the center of the city, the temple towering. Walk dusty alleys, honeycomb streets, discover secret courtyards, listen to the noise of bargaining in the bazaar.

Almost always, blocks of past-tense language can be avoided. The trick is to remember that past events are *present* in consciousness. A language that relates to consciousness will tend to work with present tense.

Sentence length is a problem. While we should prefer short sentences, if we use too many of them in sequence, the effect will be staccato. A series of brief subject-object sentences in a row can machine-gun congregational consciousness. On the other hand, too many long sentences or, worse, too many sentences with the same measured length will be impossible. We will aim at syntactical variety and sentence-length variety in speaking, for both characterize ordinary conversational style. When we imitate experience, we may well produce some lengthy, even complex sentences. For the most part, however, we should attempt to prepare language in various syntactical styles, but with a decided preference for short, clear sentences. Thus, if we write out sermon manuscripts (which is still probably a good idea), we will learn to write *oral*, to write for the lively patterns of our own speaking. If we do so, we will discover that most of our sentences will be short and direct.

How can ministers learn to work with words? Speaking is a craft, and, as with any craft, must be learned. We can learn to use words by using them (practice) and by hearing them used (study). Where can we find help? Obviously there are books to consult: the thesaurus, books on usage, volumes on style. Though most such books are concerned with written style, nevertheless, they may prove helpful. We will probably be aided most by poets, novelists, and dramatists. In any age, truly fine preachers have read poetry. Poets can show us how to make metaphor, how to use connotative language with rare precision, how to handle the sounds of words. More, poets will be experts on bringing out deep structures of meaning from fields of consciousness, for that is their profession. Novelists can also instruct us; they know how to make a world, and how to manage plot. As long as we do not chase down "Christ symbols" compulsively in every fictional work we read (a nasty habit!), we can gain entree into the consciousness of our age through fine novels. As for dramatists, they are special friends, for they wield oral language and, through oral language, promote ideas. You will learn more about language from poets, novelists, and dramatists than from reading chapters on sermon style penned by some professor of homiletics.

WORDS IN
THE CHURCH

14.
Preaching in Church and Out

Luther said, "The church comes into being because God's Word is spoken." Nowadays, we do not understand Luther's astonishing confidence in the Word. As far as we can see churches form and survive by management—attention to detail, successful promotion, and fiscal responsibility. Yes, ritual may build cohesion and words inspire, but business acumen plus political savvy puts a parish together and keeps it thriving. When tensions arise, a course in conflict management will come in handy; a wise preacher, we suppose, will never address issues publicly. So we have no vision of the Word at work sustaining and reforming the life of the church. Are we born too late to grasp Luther's sweeping confidence? "The church comes into being because God's Word is spoken" is a bald statement at best.

IN- AND OUT-CHURCH SPEAKING

Let us begin with an aged distinction. The church's speaking may be subdivided: There is "in-church" speaking to the faithful who have been baptized in Christ, and there is "out-church" speaking which is evangelistic and apologetic in character. While the distinction between "in" and "out," baptized and unbaptized, is found in scripture and may have sturdy theological warrant, of late it seems slightly ludicrous. In our strange, secular time, swept by what some have labeled a loss of God-consciousness (not to mention widespread biblical and theological ignorance), is there much discernible difference between ins and outs? In spite of Barthian trepidation, must not all church speaking be addressed to an outsider mentality, be both evangelistic and shrewdly apologetic? The claim is understandable, and in some ways descriptively accurate, yet it is open to debate. Ultimately, a church's identity

225

is not determined by fidelity or theological wisdom, but by Christ's election ("You did not choose me, but I chose you" [John 15:16]). On somewhat more prosaic grounds, we can observe that in-church people, whatever their convictional intensity or performance level, do have a different story. Their story includes episodes telling of who they are in relation to Christian community, and of how they got there; outside types do not. Perhaps, then, we must speak of secular ins and outs, for the common mind of our age is surely secular; but, though the *adjective* "secular" may be written across all our lives, there may be nominative distinctions that lie deeper than adjectival style. As far as preaching is concerned, the terms "in" and "out" designate place: Out-church preaching takes place in a wide world, whereas in-church preaching happens within a defined community, singularly within a liturgical context. So, though we are children of an age, and share a common mind, if nothing else, there is a valid practical distinction of place that can be drawn: We shall speak of in-church and out-church preaching.

OUT-CHURCH PREACHING

Out-church preaching is primarily the task of the laity, those who by Baptism have been ordained to a common, evangelical ministry. If the church is a chosen witness to the resurrection, a servant people with a particular task assigned, namely, preaching good news to the "end of the age," then speaking *out* is the church's calling. By sheer numerical superiority, lay people are the primary preachers of God's Word in worldly places; they speak *out*. The notion that the laity is assigned a work of preaching the gospel, though unexceptional, is seldom taken seriously. How many churches have actually designed a lay homiletic course, so as to prepare folks to give an account of themselves with apologetic smarts (instead of pushy triumphalism); or required theological study so that people will know not only whom, but what they are talking about? The message that many lay people hand out is a vapid, semi-sincere sales pitch for local parish programs: "Come to our church. We have a keen pastor, a men's bowling league, P.E.T. classes, a counseling center, the biggest Youth Club in town and, oh yes, if you like to sing, our music program with a bell choir is super—We're a full-service church." An ecclesial sales talk is scarcely what the New Testament has in mind by evangelism. Nevertheless, effective or ineffective, out-church preaching is primarily the task of the laity and, incidentally, a task for which they must be prepared.

One reason that evangelism has tumbled into neglect is the odd notion that character, "ethos," speaks louder than words; a position which American Pietism, Catholic and Protestant alike, has embraced with dangerous enthusiasm. The idea usually shows up in commonplace phrases: "Reverend, I try to *live* my faith!" Translated, the phrase implies that the last thing any sane human being would want to do is to *speak* faith, because pluralisms must be honored, and because usual images of evangelism include tent-meeting tirades, or passing out pamphlets on "Are you Saved?" in tavern doorways. Of course, if we do, in fact, lead good lives, and are exemplary characters, all the world will say is "There goes a nice person"; there will be no mention of God or Christ or theological meaning. While scripture does worry lest unseemly behavior besmirch the gospel, there are simply no texts to support the notion that good living *without testimony* is an adequate declaration of good news. When the New Testament urges the church to be witness to the resurrection, it does not have in mind a host of nice people so much as folk gripped by good news, who, like the first disciples, can hardly wait to spread it around! Being a witness to the resurrection means more than being good, if only because conventionally "good" people are often colossal bores who discredit faith. So out-church preaching of the laity does involve *speaking*.

There may be a way in which behavior does figure in evangelism. The Book of Acts is instructive. In the story of Pentecost, a huddle of Christians seized by the Spirit began to behave in very odd ways. Bystanders raised a question, asking, in effect, "Are you people smashed?"; at which point, there was occasion for Peter to leap up and preach. Again and again, whether civil disobedience (Acts 4:19), or a denouncing of the idol-making industry (Acts 19:23–27), or the liberation of a victimized girl (Acts 16:16–18), Christian behavior raised questions, which, in turn, Christians answered by giving an account of themselves—by preaching good news. Such behavior as the Book of Acts reports is, however, much more than the niceness of conventional virtue; it is out-of-step behavior, often corporate in character; it is both countercultural and communal. Of course, in America today, when you cannot tell Christians from non-Christians without labels, no questions are raised, and, consequently, there are few occasions for out-church speaking. Why would anyone bother to question a whole bunch of conventionally nice people? Oh, sometimes Christians are noticeably different, as, for example, rigorous holiness groups whose personal style may stand out; but their behavior can be typed—"They sure are *religious!*" Again, some events may be hyped by public promotion, such as Madison Square Garden evangelistic rallies, but few eyebrows are lifted, because such events also may be typed as familiar "religious" practices. The difference, then, between the Book of Acts and today would appear to be the relationship between Christian behavior and the world's ethos. When communal behavior abruptly counters set cultural values, commonplace patterns of socially approved life style, political or economic sanctities, then questions may well be asked. No wonder much early Christian preaching occurred in courtrooms!

We are not suggesting that Christians pursue the bizarre for the sake of being bizarre; there is a difference between faith's contrapuntal style and an *enfant terrible* who scandalizes for the sake of effect. Christians do not go out of their way to be offensive or define themselves by opposition alone. Obviously, Christian behavior which offends social values or threatens power structures is either an inevitable outgrowth of the gospel, or an up-against-the-wall "Here I stand" position compelled by the "powers that be"; it is either Christian doing or Christian resistance. Actually, cheerful members of the laity who say, "Reverend, I live my faith," are on target, but have trivialized or privatized "faith." (We clergy types do exactly the same thing in out-of-parish situations; we become anonymous nice people who seldom speak faith.) By contrast, New Testament living faith is usually *corporate* (check out all those plural "you"s in the early church catechism we call "The Sermon on the Mount"), and always *articulate*, giving an account of itself. Perhaps the trouble with much Christian protest in the 1960s was not its excessiveness or radical quality (New Testament faith may be both), but rather a failure to give an account of itself. Social action apart from the testimony of the gospel can become stridently self-righteous moralism. Conversely, evangelism without communal courage can be demonic, turning faith into a nasty little religious perversion. Some years ago a satiric TV show, *That Was The Week That Was*, awarded an honorary "Discreet Evangelist of the Year" title to a preacher who crisscrossed the state of Alabama holding rallies in the sixties, but who never once mentioned the subject of race! We are not arguing that social action be turned into an evangelistic ploy, for, obviously, there are causes that in themselves may be compelled by the gospel, if not by a minimal human compassion, such as feeding the hungry, clothing the naked, visiting prisoners, giving shelter (if not sanctuary) to the homeless, and so on. All we are saying is that Christian vocation is show and *tell*, that the dynamic unity of corporate social witness and evangelical testimony must not be fractured or, worse, set in either/or opposition.

Out-church preaching, then, answers questions, genuine questions, prompted by a Christian contrapuntal in the world; thus, out-church preaching is *occasional*. The form of out-church speaking will be quite different from preaching within the liturgical (read: eucharistic) community. Primarily, out-church preaching names God in the world, and only as it gives an account of itself will it refer to the narrative of God-with-us. Certainly, Christians declaiming from limp Bibles with announced texts, in a parody of sacred oratory, would be ludicrous in most, if not all, secular settings. Instead, out-church speaking will combine secular style, the style of our age, with a kind of theological impudence as it gossips the gospel. There is a wonderful story that came out of the civil-rights struggle of the sixties. A group of dedicated, but pleasantly secular, college students were operating a Freedom House in Mississippi, sustained largely by beer and peanut butter sandwiches. A handful of Christians dropped in to join the cause. "Why are *you* here?" the students' leader asked a Christian. Had the Christian replied, "We are here because we believe in human rights," the statement would have been true enough, but scarcely a declaration of the gospel—after all, who does not espouse human rights these days? Instead, with gleeful impudence, the Christian blandly announced, "We are here because Jesus Christ was raised from the dead!" Over peanut butter sandwiches and beer, subsequent give-and-take discussion ran on for hours, as the Christians in a smart secular style explained themselves. The problem for us is how to be blatantly theological while avoiding all language that can be "typed" as typical of American religiousness —no easy trick. Fortunately, there is something splendidly impudent about naming God in a thoroughly secular language!

So out-church preaching is primarily a lay vocation conducted in the human world. We need to think through tactics and design a lay homiletic. The word "homiletic" does apply to the task of the laity, for, at root, it means "conversation among people," which is exactly what out-church preaching is all about—Christians *conversing* good news.

PREACHING AND BAPTISM

Where does out-church speaking lead? To incorporation. So, naturally, out-church preaching points to Baptism. We must be cautious, however, because the purpose of evangelism is never merely the enlargement of an in-group church. We preach out of enthusiasm for God's liberating Word, or out of love for the worldly world ("God so loved the world that . . ."), or simply to give an account of ourselves when questioned; we do not preach so that the church may succeed, or that competing denominations may exceed others by topping last year's quotas. (At a time when mainline denominations appear to be shrinking, the church-growth game has become slightly desperate. Slogans have changed—from "A million more in '74" to "Lord, let us be alive in '85.") The reason why much officially promoted evangelism aborts is that the world views it as thinly disguised institutional self-interest, which, of course, it usually is. Underlying the issue is a sticky theological problem having to do with the nature of the church. Is the church, God's servant people, a witness to resurrection that speaks, calling the world into Christ's *new humanity*, to citizenship in a kingdom of God; or do we dream of a day when the whole wide world will be absorbed into *church membership*, drawn into an ecclesial "body of Christ"? Is the church a servant God employs to do a particular work; or is the church itself the end of God's saving purpose? Posed dialectically, the question can affect our understanding of Baptism, a sacrament which is already the subject of controversy. Solution to the problem is usually based on drawing a distinction between church and kingdom: the church is *not* the kingdom of God, although the church may be a proleptic sign of the kingdom, a kind of advance-guard presence of the new humanity ("Anyone in Christ is of the New Creation . . ." [2 Cor. 5:17]). So out-church speaking calls people into eucharistic community, which is a sign, however much a broken sign, of an eschatological consummation we label "new humanity." Baptism, thus, is not so much joining a church as it is incorporation in Christ's new people, of which the church is prolepsis. The issue is not picky, but is crucial if we are to rethink evangelism. If Christ himself rejected Israel's exclusivist and triumphalist understandings of kingdom, and it seems evident that he did, then, surely Christ denies triumphalist views of Christendom that still burn bright in ecclesial eyes. Where does out-church preaching lead? We must be cautious: Out-church speaking leads to incorporation by Baptism into a eucharistic community that is a sign of the new age. On the one hand, we are opposing a personal conversionist theology—redemption implies not merely new individuals, but a new *society;* and, on the other hand, we are countering any triumphalism that equates church with the end of God's saving purpose, the kingdom of God. The church may well be a travel agency for the kingdom, promoting, preparing, and even providing direction, but an excursion ticket to a travel bureau is somewhat less than exciting! Nevertheless, Baptism, as entrance into the new humanity, is the sacrament of out-church speaking.

IN-CHURCH PREACHING AND EUCHARIST

In-church preaching addresses the question of identity: "Who are we who break bread together?" So, the sacrament of in-church preaching is Eucharist.

In-church preaching will usually be done by appointed clergy, a function which should probably be guarded. (Particularly in the Catholic tradition where confusion over the proper role of the Permanent Diaconate has reached epidemic proportion.) The issue here is training, not ordination. While members of the laity may burn bright with faith, and from faith speak with urgency and rare conviction, nevertheless, quality of faith is *not* the criterion for in-church speaking; the issue, to repeat, is training. Ministers have no singular clerical "gift"; they are not ontologically altered by the laying-on of hands (in Baptism, every member has been ordained to ministry by the laying-on of hands); rather, ministers, having been called by God through the voice of the church, are trained to function in and for the church as resident interpreters or, better, theologians. In other words, clergy have been prepared to answer the question of community: "Who are we who break bread together?" In-church preaching is not so much a matter of faith kindling faith, as it is of giving faith understanding. To answer the question of identity will mean turning to the church's old, old story of God-with-us, as well as to crystallizations of the church's God naming; thus, to a whole range of theological study. Ministers are educated so that they may speak to *ecclesia,* answering the question of ecclesial identity. A minister's primary task is to respond to the query, "Who are we who break bread together in the name of Jesus Christ?"

So, Eucharist and preaching are bound together; they should not be separated. See how they interact: (1) *Eucharist shows the end of the gospel message.* When churches either ignore or only occasionally remember the Lord's Supper, they themselves must be a sign of the gospel which, unfortunately, they seldom are. Remember the wry remark that the church is always willing to trade treasure in heaven for cash down; churches are frequently sold-out. As frequently, the church is censorious, fractious, repressive, and, to quote a very young church member, "No fun at all!" As a result, we hear the good news of the gospel, but, dismayed by the church, are unconvinced. Of course, if we try to bring the life of the church in line with the gospel, we end up in law, which is antithetical to gospel. Rightly, the Lord's Supper is a living sign of the gospel in the midst of the broken body of the church, for the Lord's Supper re*members* Christ as one family, reconciled, serving one another, dependent on grace. We hear the gospel and live in the sign of the promise, the feast of the new humanity!

Now, turn our formula around: (2) *The gospel message gives meaning to Eucharist.* The gospel tells a story of God-with-us—creation, passover (unleavened bread), exodus (manna), covenant (feast), not to mention prophetic visions of consummation (messianic banquet); and of Christ's life (eating and drinking with sinners), Christ's death (the Last Supper), Christ's resurrection (Emmaus). When books on the Lord's Supper mention many meanings to the sacrament, they are noticing narrative connections that happen as story and sacrament interact. But preaching does more than tell a story; it sets Christ and community in a symbolic-reflective relationship, thus naming eucharistic Presence. Preaching gives meaning to the Lord's Supper. When preaching is neglected, then, Eucharist is left to gather meaning either from anthropology or from church, which, in the course of twenty centuries, has always led to manipulation, triumphalism, and sometimes implausible superstition. Preaching answers the question: "Who are we who break bread together in Jesus Christ?"

If in-church preaching tells a story and names a name, it will necessarily have recourse to scripture. While scripture is not the whole story of Christ and the church, it is the constitutive story, the story of the "church" in Israel transformed by Jesus Christ, and, therefore, crucial to the question of identity. Please note: We are arguing that what is essential in scripture is the story of God-with-us, and not discrete texts basking in their own inerrancy. Thus, in-church preaching need not expound texts slavishly week by week, or hold rigidly to a prescribed lectionary. The virtue of a lectionary is that it may guarantee a regular rehearsal of the story of God-with-us, and, thereby, contribute to the church's narrative self-understanding. (Ecclesial amnesia is always a problem!) Though in-church preaching may not always begin with a scriptural passage, if it would respond to the question of identity, it will necessarily recall the story that scripture *is*.

The question of identity will be answered by ethical exhortation; the gospel calls us to *be* who we *are*, namely, a living sign of God's promise to the world. In the Old Testament, the logic of ethical concern is obvious: We *are* a people in covenant with God, therefore, let us *be* holy as God is holy. The New Testament rationale is similar: In Jesus Christ we *are* reconciled with the Holy God, let us *be* reconciled and reconciling. Being (identity) and acting may be conceptually discrete, but existentially they are inseparable. We are not suggesting that scripture is jampacked with clear directives for twentieth-century action; description of a biblical ethic is notoriously difficult. What we are saying is that the preaching of gospel, as it tells a story, and as it sets us in a symbolic-reflective relationship to God-in-Christ-Jesus, is the basis for our ethical acting in the world. What makes Christian ethics Christian is not the quality of our ethical acting (there are virtuous pagans who, according to Camus, are "saints without God"), or the motive for our acting (can a "Chinese box" be said to have a motive?), but the context of community gathered in Word and Sacrament. In-church preaching is inescapably ethical: "New people of God, *be* who you *are* in the world." In-church preaching sends us *out*.

Eucharist as a sign of the new humanity cannot be locked up in church. While the sacrament is often viewed as in-house celebration, a mystery carefully restricted to those who rightly believe, in essence, the Lord's Supper is outgoing—remember, our Lord broke bread with outcasts, and fed thousands of folk his disciples were inclined to dismiss. Because Eucharist prefigures and, indeed, practices the consummation of God's promises, because it is a sign of saved new humanity (a sign most apparent *in* the world), because it celebrates God's gratuitous mercy, it does not thrive in secret. Perhaps we should picnic the Lord's Supper out in the world! Whenever Christian faith restricts itself and becomes a secret society with a guarded ritual, a modern-day "mystery cult," it betrays its own true nature: Christian faith is an open secret and its ritual, the Lord's Supper, is an open invitational event—"Closed Communion" is probably a contradiction in terms! Eucharist is a sign of hope to the world, as well as practice for Christians of their life in the world. An answer to the question "Who are we who break bread together?" can only send us scurrying out into the world, with the worldly grace of our Lord Jesus Christ.

CHRIST AND PREACHING

Do you sense that we have come full circle? Reach back in mind and recall the pattern: In-church preaching speaks to the question "Who are we who break bread?" a question that can only be answered by recourse to story (scripture) and which, answered, calls the people of God to be a new-age community in the world. So, in-church preaching prompts contrapuntal behavior which raises questions in the world—"What's going on here anyway?"—questions that can only be answered as out-church preaching speaks. Out-church preaching draws the world by faith into eucharistic community, a proleptic sign of the kingdom. What a breathless recital! Sum it up and say: the church is gathered by speaking, knows itself by speaking, and goes into the world by speaking. What was it that burly Martin Luther said? "The church comes into being because God's Word is spoken." Baptism and Eucharist work with the Word and, indeed, are inseparable from the Word. "Full circle" does describe the pattern we have drawn.

But watch out for circles! Circles can spin and go nowhere, and, sooner or later, circles can run down and stop. What keeps the church circling toward God's eschatological consummation? Christ. Jesus Christ is the Word and the Spirit by which the church has life; he is the center of our full circle. Did not the life and death and resurrection of Jesus Christ constitute the church? Is not Christ the living Word who has stirred up the ongoing conversation we call preaching? Surely Christ is the image of new humanity to which preaching calls us. He is the Lord whom preaching celebrates, and the Presence we acknowledge eucharistically. Christ is God-with-us, the secret of scripture's story, and God-with-us the hermeneutic through which we speak to the world. Sum up and say: Jesus Christ *is* the life of the church—the Word in the center of our circling words.

No wonder, then, that in-church preaching takes place in worship. In worship we hear the good news of Jesus Christ and, at the same time, pray

233

through him, praise him, offer ourselves to him, anticipate his salvation, and celebrate his Spirit with us. The New Testament speaks of "knowing Christ in a new way," which may well be to know Christ in the Spirit as we worship. Merely to know about Christ would be to know him as an objectified, remembered figure in history—"Jesus of Nazareth, born circa 4 B.C., died circa A.D. 28, a religious leader, teacher, and supposed Messiah." Instead, we hear of Jesus Christ as *our* story, while at the same time we affirm him as Living Symbol, the image of God-with-us. The language of worship is peculiar language: Our words about God-in-Christ become words *from* God-in-Christ (command) and *to* God-in-Christ (praise). We can guess why. Though we speak of God-in-Christ, we do so in the mysterious Presence of God-in-Christ. To know Christ in a "new way" is to know Christ in worship. In-church preaching *is* an act of worship.

Out-church preaching also "knows Christ in a new way"; it knows him in praxis, that is, in the present tense of speaking and acting. To *do* Jesus Christ in the world is a special way of knowing him and of celebrating his Presence, an aged notion which recent liberation theologies have affirmed. We know Christ not as an exemplar from the distant past, but *in* living obedience, *now*. No wonder that the church has supposed brave martyrs, whose lives were quite literally at stake, to have possessed a special knowledge of God-in-Christ. Conversely, what has seemed to be a dearth (or death) of Christ-consciousness today, may be attributed to the timidity of our play-it-safe, social-status, silent-minority churches. True knowledge of Christ, as Calvin observed, is not information about him, but a knowing-in-praxis of him by doing his will in the world.

New knowledge of God-in-Christ is the work of the Spirit, or so the scriptures say. The Spirit is the true "hermeneutist" of the Word, who brings to mind and interprets Jesus Christ to us. Our preaching, then, is a work of the Spirit. Who is the center of our full circle in the life of the church? Jesus Christ risen, the Word and the Spirit among us!

PART TWO
STRUCTURES

HERMENEUTICS

15.
Preaching
and Authority

In one of Arthur Miller's plays, a man stands alone on an empty stage. Once he had been a believer, but imperceptibly his faith has slipped away. "I looked up one day—and the bench was empty. No judge in sight," he recalls. Then, gazing at the audience, he adds poignantly, "And all that remained was the endless argument with oneself—this pointless litigation of existence before an empty bench."

The lines are moving, perhaps because they seem to echo the inner experience of our age. Once upon a time, the church could thunder "Thus saith the Lord!" but somehow surety has faded and now we are left with endless in-church wrangling. The glow has gone from the gilt-edged page, the glint from the shepherd's crook. The unassailable fact that faces us today is a dramatic, perhaps inevitable collapse of authority. The collapse poses a peculiar problem for preaching. If preaching is to be brave and free and fine again, we shall have to rethink the nature of authority.

AUTHORITY: POWER AND WISDOM

If you chase through dictionary definitions of "authority," you will discover that the word subdivides, having two primary meanings: Authority as *power* and authority as *wisdom*. Though many different usages may be listed drawn from different social spheres—law, religion, government—the list can be boiled down to power to command and wisdom to consult. Of course, you may bypass the dictionary if you read newspapers with care. During the uproar following an assassination attempt on an American president, the word "authority" frequently showed up on pages of newsprint. Medical authorities were called in to offer expert opinion on the extent of the president's injuries—"authority" used as wisdom. A ramrod secretary of state who

239

took charge in the emergency was accused of overstepping the bounds of his authority—"authority" used as power. Sometimes the two meanings seem to come together as when we say that the Supreme Court is a "final authority" and refer not only to judicial wisdom but to the ruling power of the court. In sum, then, two meanings cling to the word "authority," power and wisdom.

Both meanings seem to be hanging around when we speak of the "authority of scripture," or claim that the scriptures are "final authority" in matters of faith and practice. Certainly the scriptures are elevated in many Protestant churches; they stand opened on communion tables often flanked by candles. Protestants seem to believe that the scriptures have magisterial power to command belief and action. Though the Bible's words may come to us "secondhand" through sermons, liturgies, catechisms, church law, and the like, nevertheless they are presumed to be "God's Word" and, therefore, commander-in-chief of the Christian church. At the same time, when controversies arise, do we not scamper to the scriptures for adjudication? After all, we believe scripture is "wisdom from on high." So, wisdom and power, both meanings are bundled together when we speak of the "authority of scripture."

When we mention the authority of scripture we are not usually referring to specific words on specific pages so much as to the Bible's message; something we may term the "kerygma" or "good news" or the "gospel message." While we may find that particular phrases from scripture do come floating into mind (usually words impressed on memory by liturgy) and do offer guidance, actually it is the gospel message that we regard as the substance of scripture, the wisdom and power of God. So when the old formula insists that everything necessary to salvation is to be found in scripture, it is pointing to the gospel message within scripture, and not suggesting that every word or syllable is somehow packed with divine potency.

Of course, when we claim that the Bible is our "authority," we are pointing past texts, and past even the gospel in scripture, to God-for-us in Jesus Christ. Christians do seem to make parallel statements which, in sequence, lead from the "sacred page" to the "author" of scripture: "I believe in the Bible," "I mean, I believe in the message about God in the Bible," "I mean I believe in the God of the Bible." Ultimately, most Christians are not "book worshipers"; they revere God alone as their only "authority." On the other hand, many Christians seem to believe that God, revealed in Jesus Christ, has conferred authority on the scriptures; that the Bible has been designated "Word of God" by divine fiat to rule in the church.

Added to the notion of biblical authority has been some sort of safeguard on interpretation. If the Bible is viewed as God's designated authority, then the Holy Spirit, God's own Spirit, is usually regarded as the only true interpreter. There is frequent debate over who may have access to the Spirit's instruction, from the kindled heart of an individual believer to acknowledged councils of the church, from a converted preacher to the bishop of Rome, but *that* the Holy Spirit is true interpreter of God's Word has normally been affirmed. So the pattern is somewhat circular: God designates the scriptures to be "Word of God," and then God provides for the interpretation of scripture in the church by the Holy Spirit.

In sketchy form, we have attempted to represent a familiar notion of scriptural authority, a notion that seems to have broken down.

HERMENEUTICAL QUESTIONS

Of late, the whole idea of authority has been shaken; it totters. It is not the corrosive effect of scientific scripture study, the so-called historical-critical method, that has undercut authority; for while conservative Christians may have been distressed by discussions of sources, redactions, and forms, such matters could be dismissed as methodological options leaving the notion of the "Word of God" in or through scripture untroubled. No, nowadays, problems lie deeper.

Basically, the hermeneutical question is *the* question. While Rudolf Bultmann's solutions may be arguable, his genius for asking apt questions cannot be denied. Bultmann singled out difficulties posed by *history* when he wrote of "demythologizing." Quite obviously scripture is a product of history: Religious ideas expressed in scripture are all wrapped up in datable cosmologies, psychologies, and anthropologies alien to our more modern world. In the twentieth century we do not readily embrace the notion of a four-cornered flat earth topped by a sky-bowl supported on pillars except as quaint, if attractive, poetic license. Likewise, a psychology that included talk of "body and soul," of "heart" and "bowels," does not translate conveniently into modern lingo. What about biblical understandings of time, of political structure, of patriarchal family life, and of eschatology—are these all "eternal truth"? How do texts, clearly products of an earlier age and reflecting an ancient world view, articulate today? The idea that there is some sort of essential self, unaltered by the sweep of time, is no longer tenable. So, "demythologizing" *is* part of every preacher's stock in trade.

Take a text such as "You will see the Son of man sitting at the right hand of power, and coming with the clouds of heaven" (Mark 14:62). Even if scholars can get at the "mind" that scribbled the text, how do we interpret the words today? Unless we actually suppose that we will sight Jesus on a cloud from some local shopping plaza, we will have to interpret the text. In interpreting, we can locate the text within *our* reconstruction of first-century apocalyptic, but we will still be stymied when it comes to preaching the meaning of the text to American suburbanites. In preaching we tend to aim texts at kinds of contemporary consciousness. In this case, what would it be —"Someday we all must die," or "We meet the Lord in crises of faith," or "The threat of nuclear combustion approaches," or what? Again and again, in interpreting texts, we are forced to choose what fields of contemporary consciousness are appropriate targets for biblical statements and, more, what norms will guide our selection. Of course, as soon as we start talking about *choosing* norms or targets, the whole notion of biblical authority may be in jeopardy. But then, the mere fact that scripture is datable questions our affirmations of scriptural authority.

Another problem, also on Bultmann's agenda, is the problem of *interpretation.* Where is authority if the scriptures are always subject to the "pre-understandings" of interpreters, not to mention varying methods of interpretation. Take a look at how one Protestant denomination conducted debate over a proposed ordination of homosexuals. During a long period of discussion, study papers were produced, some by conservative scholars and others by scholars of less conservative mien, all dealing with the same scatter of biblical texts. Of late, most Christian communities seem to be operating with what might be termed a "judicial fair-play model"; therefore studies were evenly distributed among "conservatives" and "liberals," "pros" and "cons," with consensus anticipated. What happened was that, working with the same texts, scholars came up with rather different interpretations predictably distributed according to party lines. The example is extreme, but it does pose the problem: If interpreters can and on occasion do produce radically different readings of the same scripture, where is authority? Is authority in texts, in interpretation, in methodology, or in some sort of theological pre-understanding on the part of scholars? To have firm consensus would we not have to have agreement on theological pre-understanding and methodology? We may be exaggerating difficulties because, after all, most scholars tend to agree most of the time about most texts. Of late, however, biblical interpretation seems to be undergoing a paradigm change, so that division among interpreters may be more usual, for example, between historical-critical buffs and champions of various literary-critical approaches. Though we would certainly repudiate the idea that scripture is a Rorschach to be read by capricious subjectivity (language does somewhat order hermeneutics), nonetheless the mere *fact* of possible scholarly division does question biblical authority.

Of course, if honest, when it comes to interpretation of scripture in preaching, matters may be even more unsettled. Let fifty preachers loose with the same passage from scripture and we can safely expect at least a dozen different distillations of "God's Word." It is all very well to castigate poor preachers for (sneer!) deplorable eisegesis; frequently preachers earn the rebuke but, to be honest, meaning of texts *now* is difficult to discern. So, difficulty in interpretation plus difficulty in contemporary articulation does raise the question of authority. For the preacher, where is authority—in text, in interpretation, in imagination, in the congregation—where?

Some Christians attempt to bypass issues by an appeal to the mysterious workings of the Holy Spirit, the guarantor of "right understanding." There is no doubt that scripture does suggest that the Spirit is interpreter of Christ's words among disciples (John 16:13). "Inner testimony of the Spirit" (often understood individualistically by Protestants) is, however, a murky business indeed. Ever since Dr. Freud encouraged a degree of anxious self-analysis, how can we be certain of "inner testimonies"? Traditionally, the test of the Spirit has been the Word, or sometimes the Word interpreted by churchly consensus; but the cycle—Word interpreted by the Spirit attested by the Word—dumps us into a theological "Catch-22." If the hermeneutical question has riddled confidence in the objective truth of scripture, appeals to the Spirit do not help much, for the Spirit's testimony may also be subject to hermeneutical questioning (By what criterion do we establish that it is *The* Spirit interpreting?). If we cannot validate the Spirit by appeals to quality of feeling or churchly consensus, and we cannot, then we must judge the Spirit by the' Word, which of course plunges us back into a search for objective truth all over again. Traditional Protestantism rests on a working model of authority involving Word and Spirit, but the synthesis of Word and Spirit has collapsed, torn apart by cultural splits between reason and feeling, between so-called objective and subjective truth. No wonder we struggle in a crisis of authority! Of course, Catholics are facing many of the same problems in discussions of the role of tradition. Let us be emphatic: *We wrestle not with particular notions of "authority," but with the whole authority model per se.*

A PARABLE

On a river in northern Michigan lived a hermit; his nickname, Touchstone. He lived in a hut made of barn-boards and tar paper set in a cedar grove. As years passed, his shack sagged far to one side of perpendicular. So, one summer, visitors found he had cut a tree to size and propped up the hut. Unfortunately, the ramshackle building began to lean far in the opposite direction. Still another log was set up to straighten the shack. Then, one winter, the roof fell in. "Won't stand no more," cursed Touchstone. So he went to work and built a second hut beside the ruin, and abandoned his original home forever.

A parable of sorts!

Is our craving for authority, for some sure and unassailable truth, sin? Remember the story of Adam and Eve in the garden? When Eve backed away from eating forbidden fruit for fear of mortal threat, the snake slithered up and suggested that instead of death, she would "know like God." Notice the temptation: "To know like God." Is our lust for some fixed, final, unchanging, absolutely certain "Word of God" the old, old temptation revisited? Perhaps craving for certainty, for an infallible authority will always lead to the "death" of our life with the Living God!

Perhaps.

And perhaps it is time to build a new home.

AN ANALOGY ERROR

All along, have we been making what might be termed a disastrous "model error"? We have built a notion of authority by drawing analogy between the being of God and the nature of scripture; a dangerous misapplication of analogy. Since we label the Bible "Word of God" perhaps our odd enterprise was inevitable. Most of us recall the traditional attributes of God: God is Eternal, Immutable, Perfect in Truth, and so forth. So we have spoken of scripture in the same way: Scripture is immutable, omniscient, omnipotent, eternal, and so on. After all, we argue, how could "Word of God" not display the nature of God? As a result, many well-meaning Christians have been trapped into a ludicrous defense of the infallibility of scripture, contending against any who debunk or seem to denigrate the Bible's intrinsic authority. So if scholars dare observe that there are thousands of textual variants in manuscript editions of the Gospel of Luke, then we will insist that sometime, somewhere, there was a spotless, inerrant version (thus constructing a gap between scriptural "essence" and "existence"). Or if, contrary to the conviction that Moses penned the Pentateuch, skeptics remark that the old man seems to have written his own death account, then literalists will insist that Moses, equipped by God, was unusually prescient. Thus, the Bible has been protected and all but hermetically sealed in its own holiness so that many pious people now keep it isolated in mind away from worldly push and tumble. If scripture is the "Word of God" it must be godly—immutable, inerrant, omniscient, perfect in truth. The being of God by peculiar analogy has become for many the nature of scripture.

Long ago, the idea of "divine accommodation" was tacked onto the notion of biblical authority. The idea was a semi-incarnational analogy: God in glory condescended to limitations of finitude by taking flesh in the human world. Likewise, though God's truth is high, holy, and all but inexplicable, in scripture it comes to us in homely form. Often the idea of accommodation was used apologetically to account for rudeness of style, seeming infelicities, or evident earthiness in scripture (after all, it is difficult to believe that Holy God could enjoy risqué stories). As many scholars have suggested, the idea of accommodation does ameliorate the rigors of a too-rigorous understanding of authority. But, to be candid, the idea still works from and, in fact, to some extent *preserves* a biblical authority based on transfer of God's attributes to scripture. So, while the idea of divine accommodation may ease, it does little to resolve an original model error.

The trouble with a lofty concept of biblical authority is that it imposes a "vertical" God-in-Godself model on scripture. Thus, the Bible, forever fixed, becomes a sovereign, unassailable "wisdom from on high," that can be neither contradicted nor disobeyed with impunity. Of course, anyone with psychological acuity knows that heavy-handed authority usually breeds contempt, particularly a "fixed" authority that is bound to discourage freedom of movement. Because overt sassiness toward scripture has often earned reprisal, a subtle disdain may be encouraged instead. People keep the Bible at holy distance, politely revered but practically ignored; they move away and, as they move, the "eternal fixed truth" of scripture is absent-mindedly left behind. How can a fixed truth go along with us in the living of our lives?

CHRIST CRUCIFIED—WEAKNESS AND FOLLY

Can we reconstruct a concept of authority? Perhaps. Oddly enough, let us explore the Bible itself for guidance. Ask where in the Christian scriptures do primal meanings of authority, *power* and *wisdom,* appear? Answer: They are found together in 1 Corinthians immediately following a *debate over the question of authority* (1 Cor. 1:10–30). Apparently Christians were squabbling over truth claims of apostles: "I belong to Cephas," "I belong to Apollos," "I belong to Paul," with a few smiling smugly and saying, "I belong to Christ" (proto-Catholics aligned against competitive denominationalism?). How does Paul reply? He gestures toward the cross of Christ and says in effect, "There is the *power* and *wisdom* of God!" Read his words: "For Jews demand signs [i.e., power] and Greeks seek wisdom, but we preach Christ crucified, a stumbling block to Jews and folly to Gentiles, but to those who are called, both Jews and Greeks, Christ the power of God and the wisdom of God. For the foolishness of God is wiser than men, and the weakness of God is stronger than men" (vv. 22–23). Notice that in an argument over authority Paul does not point to the immutable sovereign being of God, but to the absurd humanity of a crucified Christ. Examine his method: (1) Paul disavows any personal authority, remarking that he has baptized no one (i.e., no one is under his sway) and that he has no eloquent wisdom to impart (vv. 16–17). Instead (2) he refers Corinthians to the *saving gospel message* they have heard, namely the "word of the cross" (vv. 18–25). Then (3) he draws analogy between the impotent foolishness of Christ crucified and the Corinthian church, a church without muscle or status or smarts, a church utterly dependent on God's call and God's saving grace through Christ Jesus (vv. 26–31). Perhaps Paul's procedure sets a proper precedent, for instead of shoring scripture's unassailable truth or pumping up a triumphal church or drawing nifty God-analogies, he leads us to Christ crucified and says in effect, "There is your authority."

Who then is authority for the church? Jesus Christ crucified is the church's sole authority—*Solus Christus!* We are not beckoned before a Christ triumphant, throned in cloudy splendor, but before a hung-up-to-die Jesus who, rated on a human scale of values, is weak and foolish. Yet, for Paul, Jesus Christ crucified is God's power and wisdom, that is, authority, perhaps because on the cross he is both Judge and Savior. Does not the cross judge the human world, a world in which authoritarian power condemned God-with-us *in the name of God*, and in which authoritarian wisdom branded God-with-us blasphemous *in the name of God?* Thus the cross judges all authority, and in particular religious authority, as *mis*-taken. Christ exercises God's authority in the church as, again and again, the gospel message places us before the cross where every human judgment is judged and, at the same time, forgiven in the largess of God's mercy. In Christ's presence, "power gospels" that promise success or promote mastery or push self-fulfillments are judged by his being-helpless; and arrogant "wisdom gospels" cocksure of right and wrong, of the saved and the damned, are judged by his being-in-the-wrong. God's authority in Christ locates us, with all our contending claims and counterclaims, before the cross as judged/forgiven people. So, instead of having a *locus* of authority, for example, Bible, experience, or tradition, we *are located* by God's authority in the presence of Christ crucified where we may know who we are—frightened, inept, unsmart, but assuredly called disciples who live by grace in God's wide mercy. Jesus Christ crucified *is* authority in the church.

But *how* are we located? We are placed before Christ crucified by the preached gospel message *recalled* as our salvation (1 Cor. 1:18, 23–24). Paul refers to a message heard, not to book or church. Though elsewhere Paul demonstrates knowledge of scripture as Scripture as well as a regard for tradition as Tradition, here, in dealing with an authority question, he hands out nothing more than a recalling of the gospel message. Paul does not, however, refer to the gospel as if it were a body of fixed objective truth; rather he calls us to *remember* the gospel message heard as *the message of salvation.* There is no appeal to subjectivity here, that is, remember the effect the gospel had on you. Instead, Paul is orienting consciousness, that is, remember, you liberated people, the gospel as the gospel of your liberation. Paul is asking the people in Corinth to remember the gospel in relation to their awareness of being-saved. The locus of authority then, if there is such, is *faith-consciousness* in which, again and again, we are brought before the cross of Christ by means of a remembered gospel message.

A mnemonic gospel message will seem utterly ridiculous to those who lust for some locus of absolute truth in a book or a magisterial office. For the speaking and remembering of the gospel is "folly," the folly of Christ crucified; but "to us who are being saved it is the power of God" (1 Cor. 1:18).

Who is located before Christ crucified? Answer: a *being-saved community*—"to us who are being saved," says Paul. We are located before Christ crucified in the communal faith-consciousness of the church. Paul does not address the Corinthians as a gaggle of individual believers, but instead appeals to their common self-understanding (church) as a hermeneutic for the gospel message (see the conjunction of v. 25 and vv. 26–27). But church qua church is not a hermeneutic for the gospel. No, rather Paul urges a particular ecclesial self-understanding appropriate to a people in the presence of Christ crucified. A church before the cross will not boast of wisdom or power, but, surprised by God's call, judged, forgiven, and given life, will be utterly dependent on God's grace alone. Where is such a church to be found? Perhaps only in the "disclosure model" of Eucharist which, rightly celebrated with the Word, does locate Christian community before the message of Christ crucified and enacts dependence on him alone. A church disclosed in Eucharist then may be hermeneutic for the gospel message. Of course, such self-understanding in the church is bound to be the work of the Spirit, the life of the Spirit with our common life. "Let [them] who boast, boast of the Lord" (v. 31).

Do you sense a building tension? We began our discussion with a definition of "authority" as power and wisdom. We acknowledged that the church may crave a locus of authority, power and wisdom, within its ongoing life. Instead, what do we get? We get a message of Jesus Christ crucified, who, by any sane standard, is foolish and impotent. To interpret Christ, we have nothing more than the Spirit with a church that is unsmart, less than distinguished, and woefully weak. So we have an analogy, but of a very different order from the "power" analogy usually drawn between the attributes of God and the character of scripture. As for *locus,* we have no fixed locus. Instead we have the faith-consciousness of a eucharistic church in which Jesus Christ crucified is recalled and interpreted by an awareness of being-saved. So we face a model tension. Just as attributes of God must be reconsidered in view of Jesus Christ crucified, weak and foolish, so if we retain the word "authority" at all, we shall have to slough off definitions of absolute power and wisdom. Of course, it may be quite possible to live as Christians without the word "authority" at all!

GIFTS OF SCRIPTURE AND TRADITION

What of scripture? Scripture is a good *gift* to the church, a gift of grace. We turn to scripture, search scripture's message, feed on scripture's words, live with scripture, and through scripture remember the message of Jesus Christ crucified as the gospel of salvation. We receive the Christian scriptures as a gift given us by the event of Jesus Christ. Clearly, early Christians struggled to comprehend the new reality of being-saved in view of the life and death and resurrection of Jesus Christ; as a result, a language was generated. The language of early Christian faith-consciousness, primarily a language of proclamation, is crystallized in the Christian scriptures. Again and again, as the church searches for identity in the world, and tries to grasp with astonishment the nature of being-saved, the church turns gratefully to scripture. The Christian scriptures are *normative* for Christian community because they contain an original remembering of the gospel within the new reality of being-saved, and thus enable us to recover and reformulate our identity in every new era. So, we receive the scriptures as a gift.

But what of the Hebrew scriptures? In what sense are Hebrew scriptures normative for the Christian being-saved community? At the outset, let us remember that Jesus was a Jew, and that the first grasp of being-saved was within a Jewish consciousness. Thus, we can scarcely comprehend the words of Christ without recourse to the tradition of Israel that shaped his world. Likewise, we cannot grasp original interpretations of Jesus Christ without turning to Hebrew scriptures. Such an argument, though surely true enough, is insufficient. We must not make Hebrew scriptures a mere tool for Christian hermeneutics. No, the Christian being-saved community emerged from and may be viewed as a true continuation of Israel and, thus, of Israel's faith-consciousness. The narrative of God-with-us constructed by the Hebrew scriptures is *our* narrative and the story in which Christ comes to us. Moreover, the great myths of creation and fall, as well as end-term prophetic visions, are ours; they interpret our being-saved in relation to Jesus Christ crucified. Century after century the church turns to scriptures, Hebrew and Christian scriptures, searching identity before the Mystery of God in Jesus Christ. So we affirm that the scriptures are a gift, a God-given provision for community.

Of course, we must underscore the word *gift;* we unwrap gifts, delight in gifts, live with gifts, and are grateful for gifts—"authority" seldom prompts gratitude.

What of tradition? Tradition is a word that is often used in two ways, of liturgical expression and of theological interpretation. There is the ongoing liturgical life of the church, a tradition of praise and of the sacraments, Baptism and Eucharist—great "signs" which bring to consciousness the often hidden reality of being-saved. The liturgical tradition, and a connected tradition of prayer and devotion by the being-saved community, brings to us the hermeneutical *context* in which the gospel message is understood. But there is also a tradition of interpretation, crystallized in creeds, confessions, ethical and theological reflection, which shapes our *pre-*understanding of the gospel message. So tradition would seem to be a twofold tradition of liturgical action and theological reflection. Tradition thus brings us vehicles of praise and a history of interpretation. Because tradition in the church is analogous to memory in the self, the church is never fully a being-saved community before God without the memory of tradition.

In every new moment then, the church turns to scripture in view of tradition and, in every new moment, preaches the gospel to a consciousness of "being-saved" in the world.

PREACHING AS MEDIATION

The ministry of preaching is usually understood in relation to authority. Preaching has been defined either in relation to Christ and scripture, or in relation to being-saved and tradition. Thus, for example, if scripture is viewed as an inerrant Word of God, sermons are apt to come tumbling down from high pulpits like tablets of stone from Sinai. If, in a Barthian scheme, scripture is understood as a God-ordained witness to the Word of God, Jesus Christ, then preaching is regarded as a witness to the witness of scripture, and a reiteration of the Word of God. On the other hand, if authority is vested in an episcopate within the being-saved community, preaching will be defined as an extension of the preaching of bishops. In Pietist communities, preaching may be viewed as an expression of the awareness of being-saved, undergirded by the authority of primal religious experience. Thus, definitions of preaching seem to be trapped in models of authority that maintain an objective and subjective split.

What is preaching if we accept Paul's strange rereading of authority? Preaching remembers Jesus Christ crucified in the midst of a being-saved community; thus preaching is the articulation of Christian faith-consciousness. Preaching searches the mystery of Jesus Christ crucified through scrip-

249

ture in the light of tradition's grasp of being-saved. Thus, at the outset, we will define preaching as mediation. Preaching gratefully turns to scripture and speaks at table, standing before Christ crucified, God-with-us, in the midst of a being-saved community. Preaching is *mediation*.

16.
The Place
of Preaching

There is an eighteenth-century painting of a preacher preaching. The preacher is leaning out of a pillared pulpit. Behind him on the chancel wall beneath vaulted darkness is a crucifix. Below, a congregation looks up—lit-circle faces in a misty nave. At the back of the church is an open door leading to the dark. There is something eerie, almost numinous, about the picture. Times have changed. Now churches are lit with recessed lights, or look out of floor-to-ceiling panes of glass. Pulpits have been scaled down to size. Still, there may be something numinous about a preacher preaching. Can we describe the locus of preaching, not in a building, but in theological structure? Ask the question: Where do preachers preach?

SPEAKING OF GOD TO PEOPLE

Described as a kind of *mediation,* preaching implies an "in-betweenness." Preachers speak of God to gatherings of human beings. Most dictionaries define preaching in a bare-bones way as "religious discourse," sometimes adding that sermons are preached to "religious communities." Presumably "religious communities" are people who, at minimum, accept some sort of God-hypothesis. So we begin with two terms: God-talk and religious people. A preacher stands "in between" performing, in speech, some sort of mediation. Preachers talk *of* God *to* people.

At the outset, speaking of God sounds either absurd or presumptuous. If God, by convention, is an unlimited Consciousness conscious of us, how can any jumble of finite brain waves presume to speak at all? To name God in the world is surely a scandal, if not downright heresy. Speech objectifies. So, to talk of God, no matter how artfully, is to objectify God in the world, to make of God some*thing* we point at with words. But, by definition, God is

251

not something we can talk about, even in the holiest terms. Theoretically, we can only stand without speaking, or at best weave a language of negativity, "God is not . . . ," which is a naming while unnaming, and an acknowledgment of transcendent "Other." The Lord's Prayer phrase, "Make holy your name," should probably be followed by choked silence. No wonder there is both absurdity and terror to the preaching office, for who can speak of God; deeper still, who *dares* speak of God?

Yet we do. Through human history there have been many kinds of "religious discourse" among religious peoples. At times, a sense of numen does seem to stir our human conversation, even if it is nothing more than a wide-open mouthed sound of awe. Do human communities encounter moments when they are conscious of a transsocial "something beyond themselves" while, at the same time, they are forced to acknowledge finitude? In such moments do human communities sense a kind of mysterious Presence-in-Absence? While Presence-in-Absence Mystery cannot be named, human beings may chatter like excited children, responding in retrospect to incursions of the Mystery. We may suppose that some sense of Presence, mysterious Presence-in-Absence, lies at the heart of human religious discourse. But what kind of language can the numinous generate? Only speculation, or excitement, or an acknowledgment of limits that eventually moves toward silence. How can we name Presence-in-Absence?

The notion that God is in some way a Presence-in-Absence to human social consciousness, an unnamable Mystery that nonetheless impinges on us, generating human chatter, puts a peculiar burden on preaching. Though preaching talks of God it does so by acknowledging a Mysterious Consciousness that is conscious of us. Thus, preaching is always a kind of embarrassment: How dare we speak of God if God is conscious of our speaking? No wonder preaching will ever tend toward stuttering silence ("Woe is me!") or doxology ("Glory, Glory, Glory!"). A talking about God might be possible, even if it leads to nothing more than negative imagery, "You are robed in swirls of mystery," but to speak of God *in* the Presence of God is more than difficult. Absence may be discussed; orphans can speak endlessly of being orphaned. But, it is precisely The Presence-in-Absence that threatens speech. So, picture yourselves as preaching, piping away at your sermons, but in the Presence. Preaching, at minimum, speaks of Mystery in the presence of The Mystery; speaks from a consciousness of Consciousness that is conscious of us.

The other term found in most definitions of preaching has to do with humanity; we preach to people. More precisely, we speak to citizens of a human world. The people to whom we speak, though possibly gathered of a Sunday morning for some religious function, are worldly human beings.

Their experience includes images of what we call "the natural world" as well as the human social world—a combined ecology in which lived experience lives. Not only do people come to church with images of lived experience dancing in consciousness, but they arrive with worldly understandings as well—"isms," "philosophies," "attitudes," and so forth. (Incidentally, so do preachers.) But, as human beings we are also aware of our limited horizons. Though we live in a world construct in consciousness, we are ever aware that the world is larger; that we live in a little glade of light beside a deep pool amid penumbral forests of unknowing: Human beings live in human mysteries. Yes, there is in all of us a world construct, what is more a world construct papered with images, slogans, pop understandings, and the like; thus, we all live in a social, shared world construct. But, part of our being human is the realization that we live in a model inadequate to reality. Like the hero in Edward Albee's *Tiny Alice*, we live in a modeled world, looking at our models while, at the same time, aware of great impinging darkness at the edge of all things. We try to read the widening stream of historical memory only to find time dropping off into mystery. We seek to make sense of the vast cosmos in which we live, and apprehend distances that outdistance mind. We turn into ourselves and discover a dark pool too deep for reaching down, where all we can do is to count the twigs and leaves that float up to our surface. We sense there is a world beyond our "world" and a self beyond our imaged "self." Thus when we show up in church we walk in with jerry-built understandings and larger than soul-sized mysteries, mysteries of human being-in-the-world. Are we ourselves each a mysterious presence-in-absence?

So, in basic structure, what do we have? We have preachers standing before the Mystery speaking to human beings who, though filled with fragments of understanding, also harbor huge mysteries. In a sense, preachers (themselves like children lost in configured mysteries) speak between the presence of human mystery and the Mystery—where else? The fact of mystery (an odd phrase) should guard against glibness, as well as restore to preaching a quality of awesome invocation. Preachers who speak as if they had a big bumper sticker, "Christ the Answer," pasted on their pulpits may not be able to address our age, an age in which the sheer complexity of things has once more moved near a hovering sense of unknowing. Properly the gospel does speak to mysteries of being in the world, so it cannot be spoken to or by persons who are too sure of their convictions. False prophets are always those who have forgotten how to tremble in the presence of the Mystery. Either preaching speaks modestly in the presence of mysteries, human and divine, or it ends up as a trivial pursuit.

ENTER REVELATION

The model of preaching we have begun with is too simple—God, the human world, and the piping voice of a preacher in between. For most religious communities the model of preaching is much more complex, because most religious communities embrace some sort of notion of revelation; they assume that God wants to be known and, what is more, wants to be spoken. Of course, revelation does not shatter mystery, because revelation is *of* Mystery, but it does change our understanding of preaching. For Christians, revelation is said to be Jesus Christ, his life and death and resurrection. Jesus Christ comes to us through sermons, lessons, and liturgies, as well as through visual stuff such as stained glass, banners, drama, and art. Christ comes to us in church and also in the world where he figures, however residually, in social mythos. Jesus Christ enters consciousness as story and as symbol, mediating God-for-humanity and humanity-for-God. Like a stained-glass figure lit from within some dark, towering church, that reflects on the faces of onlookers, Christ is said to show forth the "interior" of the Mystery of God and, by reflection, to light a mystery of human beings–toward–God. We have said that revelation makes preaching a possibility; in Christian communities, preachers speak *through* Jesus Christ.

Turn around and look at congregations. Preachers do not simply speak to a klatch of representative human beings drawn out of the human world. No, instead, preachers preach to a peculiar audience that is, in some ways, atypical of the world. Christian congregations do odd things such as sing praises, or say prayers (a most peculiar activity), or collect cash to give away (also an uncommon activity). Moreover, "Christian values" do seem to be somewhat at odds with the values of the social world. Christians seem to believe in love more than power, self-sacrifice rather than winning, reconciliation instead of competition (no wonder "Christian college" football teams are such a contradiction in terms!). Christians may be termed being-saved communities insofar as in the midst of human brokenness they may display signs of a new quality of life and have some awareness that they represent a different social reality in the world.

Preachers frequently (and sometimes self-righteously) despair over congregations, noting blatant prejudice, sexism, party spirit, discourtesy, lack of charity, will-to-domination, and the like. Nevertheless, within the humanity that huddles in church, day in and day out, there are signs, perhaps promises, of a new social order that the Bible sometimes labels "kingdom of God." When Eucharist is rightly celebrated we see a "sign" of new social reality, for we gather as God's family, serve one another, reach out in physical acts of reconciliation, and share a celebrative cup. Through Eucharist we can see something happening among us not only in the midst of our being-together but perhaps also in our individual selfhood. There are other "symbolic disclosures" such as Baptism, common worship, and involvement in social concerns that may also mediate to us the being-saved community, different from human community per se. Thus, preachers do not simply address human beings in the world, but a being-saved community in the world.

Have we begun to edge closer to an understanding of where we preach? We do not stand before the Mystery in the midst of a mysterious human world articulating some sort of gnostic wisdom from our own deep-pool depths. No. We stand before the Mystery through Jesus Christ addressing a symbolically disclosed being-saved community in a mysterious world. And what does preaching do? Preaching calls to common mind the gospel of Jesus Christ, crucified and risen, as the gospel of our liberation, our being-saved in the world. Preaching does not merely hand out Jesus Christ to the world. Without a sense of the Mystery, Jesus Christ could turn into a cardboard-cut-out Savior, either Jesus Christ "Superstar" or Jesus Christ "Idol." Without a sense of penumbral human mysteries, such as the mystery of theodicy, preaching could fan religious pride, a being-saved triumphalism that is often today hawked as Christian "self-esteem." How do we preach? We preach before the Mystery in a mysterious human world through Jesus Christ to a being-saved community.

THE PERSON WHO PREACHES

What of the preacher? What qualifies preachers to speak? Answers vary within different Christian traditions. Preachers qualify to preach because they have been granted "revelation" through some sort of religious experience, or because they have been "called" by God usually through the voice of the church, or because they have been converted and are "saved," or because they are expert in wisdoms that supposedly provide "knowledge of God," or because they have been gripped by an inner "spiritual" compulsion and cannot do otherwise. Options are many, are difficult to sort out, and may combine in particular traditions. Let us look at the person in the middle, who somehow speaks as a mediator.

Obviously preachers are human and citizens of the human world; thus preachers are worldly. As such, preachers are chock-full of understandings that have been shaped by worldly interchange, usually under the domination of "principalities and powers." Certainly there is no magic that exempts preachers from the mind of the world-age in which they live. Language embodies cultural understandings and we are all born into a language. What is more, we are reared in cultures and subcultures which are language communities. So, preachers are bound to participate in the way of the world. More, in view of the fact that Christian tradition speaks of "sinful humanity," preachers will preach as sinners among sinners. Thus, sinlessness can scarcely be a requirement for ordination. Of course, preachers need not revel in their common humanity—look at me, I am as ignorant, unlovely, and bedeviled as anyone else—for we celebrate grace, not sin. Nevertheless, at the outset, let us admit that as preachers we are human, citizens of a human world, and obviously members of what we ourselves term a "sinful humanity."

Preachers stand amid mysteries, the same mysteries as fringe the consciousness of all human creatures; we do not know. We cannot plumb the deep pool, see past the shadowy forest glade, or scan beyond the stars. There are mysteries of unknowing within the self, and mysteries of unknowing within the human world. Therefore, we should not expect preachers to possess such certainty in faith as to dispel mysteries. Mystery and finitude go hand in hand and ministers are assuredly finite. Actually some sense for the mysteries of being-in-the-world might be a criterion for ministry, for it would indicate that a potential preacher has not permitted proximate "certainties" to paper-over the penumbral mysteries in which we all live, and which are probably everpresent to the authentically religious. Though we preachers busy ourselves with symbols of revelation as our "faith seeks understanding," we do so amid resilient mysteries of being human in a human world. Let us begin by acknowledging the representative humanity of those who preach.

At the same time, please note: Preachers are members of a being-saved community and, as such, share some modest sense of being-saved-in-the-world. The odd criterion that demands a potential preacher *be* saved cannot be pushed much past life in a being-saved community without fostering sacerdotal pride. Though some ministers may have an acute sense of being-saved they have not manufactured their awareness in isolation either from shared life in Christian community or from life in the worldly world. Yes, congregations may have a right to expect some degree of maturity in faith from clergy, but perfectionist definitions of salvific attainment are always inappropriate. When it comes to being-saved, progress in grace is relative and therefore unmeasurable. So, when ordaining bodies ask candidates for ministry about their "Christian experience," they are often chasing spiritual butterflies; Christian experience as a qualification for ministry can only refer to involvement in a being-saved community and some sharing of an awareness of being-saved in the world. So, let us bear in mind that preachers are themselves members of a being-saved community in the world.

Obviously, preachers must be trained to preach. Preparation for preaching will have double focus. If preachers are to comprehend being-saved-in-the-world, they must be able to objectify worldly "wisdoms," the "isms," "philosophies," "social models," "psychologies" that people bring into church, and which in the world may be regarded as "truth" about human mysteries. But, also, ministers will have to ponder the story of the being-saved community, its changing life styles, its actions, its social self-understandings in the world. The other side to ministerial training has to do with the Mystery and with symbols of revelation, thus with philosophy, theology, and scripture. Surely preachers who speak of the Mystery through the Living Symbol, Jesus Christ, must be acquainted with Christ (scripture), with human apprehensions of the Mystery (philosophy of religion), and with the church's grasp of its symbols of revelation (historical and systematic theology). The training of preachers is not pushed merely to keep theological faculties paid (although that does seem to be a swell idea!). When religious experience alone qualifies preachers, congregations may be victimized by worldly wisdoms in disguise (dressed up as dark-suited piety), by too-glib certainties, and by misunderstandings of the Mystery disclosed in Jesus Christ. We are not campaigning for an intellectually elite ministry, or supposing that education will automatically prevent preachers from buying into all kinds of cultural claptrap— Luther was not altogether off-base when he called reason a "whore"—all we are saying is that preaching does require brooding thoughtfulness as well as special study.

What constitutes a call to the preaching office? The sign of a calling would appear to be a disposition toward God and neighbors in faith. Label it a curiosity about "the things of God" if you will, but preachers should somehow display "faith seeking understanding." The preacher is a human being who, stood before the Presence-in-Absence of Mystery, wants to know, lives to know, and who, trusting the Living Symbol Jesus Christ, wills to know through Christ. Without such a disposition preachers can turn into dreadful "house-organ voices" pushing ecclesial establishment, or, perhaps more dreadful, glib Jesus-shouters. But there is another side to the disposition. Preachers ought to care for human beings in the world who, along with the preacher, bumble about in proximate "truths," groping mysteries of being human. In this regard, however, we cannot expect preachers to be totally free from self-interest. After all, there is a certain "eros" in exploring the Mystery and in pushing into at-hand mysteries that impinge upon our common human consciousness. Nevertheless, to be called may mean to have a kind of fascination with the Mystery whose "interior" is disclosed in Jesus Christ, and a concern for neighbors that longs for the fulfillment of being-saved-in-the-world. The call to preach is, emphatically, a call to mediation.

A DOUBLE HERMENEUTIC

As mediation, preaching dabbles in what might be termed a twofold act of interpretation, a *double* hermeneutic. We are often told that preachers must be bifocal; that they should read the Bible with one eye and daily papers with the other. The shibboleth, usually attributed to Barth, is helpful for at least it sets preachers free to read newspapers without undue guilt, but otherwise is less than adequate. The bifocal hermeneutic of preaching is somewhat more complex. What do we mean by a *double* hermeneutic?

Preachers explore *the Mystery of God through Jesus Christ;* they are concerned with what is usually regarded as "revelation." Because preaching is "through Jesus Christ," preachers will turn to texts, notably to the texts of scripture. In Christian scriptures, we stumble on written recollections of apostolic preaching which, by proximity to the Christ-event, have certain primacy for us. (Early Christian literature, sometimes labeled noncanonical, can provide a significant context for the interpretation of scripture.) Yet in the New Testament, we become acquainted with Christ Jesus, storied human being and Living Symbol, and may even find ourselves drawn into a history-bridging "communion" with Christ. Of course, we cannot fully comprehend Jesus Christ without turning to the Hebrew scriptures. They give us Christ's own "world-in-consciousness" as well as the mind which interpreted Christ, a mind that already knew of God-with-us bracketed by myths of origin and visions of consummation. In interpreting scripture, we will be guided by churchly tradition; liturgies which may embody the church's earliest recitals of faith, creeds which down through the centuries have crystallized the church's grasp of revelation, and contemporary theology which in every age ponders anew the Mystery of God through Jesus Christ. In sum, to explore Jesus Christ, preachers will inevitably turn to a study of texts.

As we study Christ, we will discover that "revelation" seems to form in consciousness in somewhat different ways. Christ clearly comes to us as a character in Israel's religious story, a God-with-us story, but also as a living symbol who, standing before the Mystery, mediates the "interior" of God, that is, God's intending toward us. Certainly we read in scripture stories of Jesus, where he was born, what he said and did, and how he died. Thus, we read tales about a particular human being in a human world under God. But also in scripture we bump into odd christological titles—"Lord," "Savior," "Son of God," and the like—as well as acclamations of faith, liturgical creeds, and profound testimonies of who Christ was for an early-day being-saved Christian community. In scripture, Jesus Christ does come to us as "story" and "symbol," as human and divine. Of course, we can spot the same odd structure in Christian art. In some churches, we will see pictures of Bible stories, including episodes from the life of Christ such as the Stations of the Cross, but also images of Christ that seem to be functioning symbolically, such as a hoisted-up empty cross or an enthroned cloudy Lord, not to mention particular symbols associated with Christ—the Rock, the Lamb, the Vine, and so on. The twofold presentation of Christ, as story and symbol, is crucial. As a story within a story, Christ is interpreted by the end-term myths of the Hebrew scriptures and in turn interprets them. As Living Symbol, Christ stands between the Mystery of Presence-in-Absence and the praise of a being-saved community, opening to us the "interior" of God-love, a freedom-giving, willing-to-suffer love that still staggers the Christian imagination. So preachers will explore Jesus Christ and, in doing so, mediate the prodigious Mystery of God-love to Christian congregations.

So we will interpret Jesus Christ in the light of our *being-saved*-in-the-world. After all, Christ is good news of our salvation and not merely idle information about past-tense history. Thus, age on age, the particular shape of being-saved-in-the-world will interpret Christ in ever-new ways. While Jesus Christ may well be said to be the same "yesterday, today, and forever," our grasp of being-saved changes as in every era different dominations are named and different liberations dreamed. The texts we study are not locked up tight in a vault labeled "Original Meaning," but articulate differently as the situation of the being-saved community is reshaped. The world assembled before the cross is ever different, and patterns of being-saved-in-the-world are thus ever-changing. In short, our awareness of being-saved-in-the-world interprets revelation. Of course, if we assume that the Spirit is with the being-saved community (and we do), we are saying that the Spirit interprets revelation, an unexceptional notion that animates the Gospel of John as well as Pauline epistles.

Being-saved has a context; we are being-saved-*in-the-world*. Thus, in interpreting the gospel, ministers will bring to their study not only problems of the social world in which they live but some awareness of the resilient mysteries which befuddle us all. The notion that interpreters must check their contemporary humanness in the narthex before approaching the holy words of scripture is an odd heresy which led Dietrich Bonhoeffer, in reaction, to push for what he termed a "worldly hermeneutic." Clearly the gospel must be read by an awareness of human mysteries—mysteries of ever-present evil, of capricious suffering, of our disordered sexuality, of our capacity for madness, and so forth—which are bound to trouble any thinking person. Likewise, the gospel must be interpreted by a mind critical of the wisdoms of the age—the accepted political, social, and psychological dogmas that inform us all. Just as Jesus Christ lived in shared human unknowing ("My God, My God, why . . . ,") and dared to contend with the conventional wisdoms of his own age; so the gospel is never abstracted from the human world, but is a "Word made flesh" that tangles with our fleshly unknowings and our fleshly opinions. All we are saying is that preachers will explore revelation in the light of being-saved-in-the-*world*.

The other side of our hermeneutic work can be expressed in the axiom that *preaching interprets being-saved in view of revelation*. Christian life is a strangely hidden social reality, so preaching must show us being-saved-in-the-world and help us to grasp its reality. To get at the shape of being saved, ministers will again have recourse to texts: they will not merely poke into their own subjectivities. To distinguish the new social reality, being-saved, we will read not only in-house literature of sacramental worship, forms of spirituality, and ethical reflection, but a wider literature that will enable us to grasp the mind of our age. Without such study, clergy can too easily confuse Christian life with culturally approved virtue, and tumble into moralizing (an activity for which, unfortunately, preachers are well known). In every age, preaching must help us to recognize that we are indeed being-saved, that what the Bible terms "new humanity" is forming among us in distinction to the humanity of being-in-the-world. Drawing on revelation, preaching will teach us to acknowledge the *grace*ful shape of being-saved.

Of course, being-saved-in-the-world does imply a kind of two-way consciousness. Clearly, we are aware of ourselves busy in many different communities (labor communities, political blocs, social groupings, family, neighborhood, nation, and so on). In the several communities in which we live, particular models and metaphors will give meaning to our lives and, indeed, shape our patterns of behavior. We are, however, also aware of ourselves "in Christ," that is, within Christian community where obviously quite different images may order our lives. So preaching must interpret the odd double-mindedness of being-saved-in-the-world.

Some years ago an American dramatist complained that contemporary theater failed to depict movements of grace in everyday life; instead, when drama wanted to portray God's involvement in human affairs, it reached for extravagant fantasy stuff. The pulpit may be similarly indicted. We seem to have great difficulty breaking free from the biblical world so as to trace God's ways in contemporary experience. Somehow we must name grace by drawing together symbols of revelation with earthly images of being-saved-in-the-world. Symbols of revelation do seem to work in two directions at once; they diagnose the human enterprise and, at the same time, offer images of salvific life before God. For example, scripture offers myths, the fall and the messianic banquet, which probe rebellion and depict reconciliation. What of the cross?

Does not the cross reflect human social sinfulness and, at the same time, cast God's bright mercy upon us? Preachers, in view of revelation, will interpret the odd double mind of being-saved-in-the-world.

In interpreting being-saved, Christian preaching is bound to enter into critical debate with the proximate "truths" of the human world, the often unquestioned "dogmas" of modern society. The old dodge that preachers must not meddle in worldly affairs because the gospel is "spiritual" is pernicious. In his humanity, Jesus Christ contended with the pop theologies, political slogans, and social attitudes of his age; he was emphatically controversial. Thus, revelation in Christ does not merely address our being-saved as if it were a Sunday-morning syndrome; in distinguishing the shape of the "new humanity," preaching is bound to haggle with the truisms of "old humanity," namely, the commonplaces of our social world, and, furthermore, do so with sharp prophetic insight. Christians will only understand the reality of being-saved when it is set in contrast to styles and assumptions of being-in-the-world. In sum, the hermeneutical work of preaching is twofold: *We interpret revelation in light of being-saved, and we grasp being-saved in view of revelation.*

Notice that by employing a double hermeneutic, preaching builds for us a new faith-world. All of us drift into church with a world construct in consciousness, a world in which we actually live, work, play, and possess our souls. In our world-in-consciousness, Jesus Christ is a social memory, church founder, and legendary figure from the past. What is more, in our world the church appears as a social grouping, one among many available to us. What happens in preaching is that our world is transformed. Our human stories are put within a story of God-with-us and our social self-images are set reflectively before the Living Symbol, Jesus Christ. By preaching, our lives and, indeed, our world constructs are located in a larger world, a world in God's consciousness of us. Preaching thus builds a new faith-world in which we may live. In mediating a new world, preaching participates in the work of the Mediator, Jesus the Christ.

TRUE AND SOUND PREACHING

Toward the start of the *Institutes,* John Calvin offered a now-famous remark:

> Nearly all the wisdom we possess, that is to say, true and sound wisdom, consists of two parts: the knowledge of God and of ourselves.

The words could easily be understood as a description of preaching doing its double hermeneutical work. Preaching speaks of the Mystery of God through

Jesus Christ. Preaching interprets a being-saved community within a mysterious human world. So we might tinker with Calvin's well-chosen words:

> True and sound preaching consists of two parts: the knowledge of God and of ourselves.

Most homiletic books in our century have catalogued sermons according to "source" or "function." Thus, we read lists of types of sermons; on the one hand, "Biblical Sermons," "Theological Sermons," "Liturgical Sermons," and, on the other hand, "Life-situational," "Apologetic," or "Missionary" sermons—all the way down to "Mother's Day Sermons" and "Fund-Raising Sermons." While such lists may be helpful, they tend to split preaching between subject and object, between source and function. Of course lately the listings seem to have been compressed into a single distinction between preaching as "biblical" and (sneer!) "nonbiblical." The distinction is not terribly useful. A curled lip toward "nonbiblical" preaching is scarcely apropos. Some modes of "biblical preaching," though stuffed with scriptural citation, may be mightily irresponsible. Whereas some nonbiblical sermons may so relate being-saved to symbols of revelation as to be emphatically Christian and, thus, truly "biblical."

The point here is not to set up categories at all; instead, it is to notice "intendings" in consciousness. Though some sermons may intend toward "revelation," story and symbol, and other sermons intend toward the reality of being-saved-in-the-world, all sermons, to some extent, will engage in the double hermeneutical work of preaching. What we have been doing is trying to describe the place of preaching within a "homiletic consciousness." Homiletic consciousness is aware of mysterious Presence-in-Absence as well as penumbral human mysteries. Within homiletic consciousness, preaching intends toward Jesus Christ, story and symbol, and toward a being-saved community in the world. So homiletic consciousness takes pleasure in rewriting Calvin's finely phrased words:

> All preaching, true and sound preaching, consists of two parts: the knowledge of God and of ourselves.

17.
Preaching
as Hermeneutics

A cartoon in the newspaper showed a group of extraterrestrial archeologists studying road signs dug up on earth—a wiggly curve sign, a no-U-turn sign, a sign depicting a hamburger in a bun, a sign with a gas-pump silhouette—all lined up in a row. One of the alien archeologists is scratching his head and saying, "Well, I suppose it's a message. But what does it mean?" They were confronting a hermeneutical problem. Week after week, preachers wrestle with the same sort of problem. Before them, spread out on a page, are words from long ago and distant lands. Preachers are supposed to decipher meanings, not for an ancient age, but for *now.* So if they are reflective, preachers are forced to reckon with hermeneutical problems. Confronted with texts, with words from the past, preachers must ask not only "What do they mean?" but a deeper, more difficult question, "*How* do they mean?"

We have noticed that preachers are busy with language. Engaged in a "double hermeneutic" they read not only texts from the past, but situations in the present mostly mediated through words. In trying to get at "what's going on in the world" preachers study language—the printed headlines, the TV, weekly news magazines, social commentary, captioned pictures. Somehow preachers have to "read between the lines" and figure out meaning. When it comes to grappling with Christian symbols the problem is doubly complex; we must reckon with a span of time and different languages, not to mention quite different social "worlds." How can words once scribbled in Syrian hills to some underground religious group speak today? Let us review the shape of the hermeneutical problem, not as an abstract academic argument, but as it happens to preachers who, like it or not, must make meaning from texts.

THE PROBLEM OF HISTORY

Biblical language can be located and dated. Suppose we have in our hands a text, for example, the story of the Stilling of the Storm in Mark 4:35–41. Some scholars may tell us the text was written around A.D. 70 from somewhere in north Palestine at a time of desperate crisis. Maybe the text is a product of rewriting, if we guess an earlier "*Ur*-Mark," or perhaps it is an original composition drawing on oral tradition; we may never know. But, as preachers we are speaking in the twentieth century to some sort of Christian gathering trying to figure out not merely what the words may have meant, but what they may mean for *us* now. The question: How can words written in an earlier age to a different people have *anything* to say to us today in a twentieth-century time and place? How can words bridge time?

Perennial Truth?

We can answer the question dogmatically. We can say that the Bible is "the Word of God," contains eternal *fixed* truth, and therefore words of scripture stand true in every age; they speak *now*. While words of scripture may well speak now, surely they do not do so without interpretation. If we explore the story of the Stilling of the Storm, we may bump into some odd first-century notions. Without doubt, the storm was understood as demonic. Water was after all a home for Leviathan, was primal chaos, and was given to sudden turbulence when stirred by demons who were decidedly more than impish. If we accept the Bible's words as eternally valid, do we then announce in our sermon that sea-storms are produced by evil demons? To support such a statement we may have to dismiss most modern world views as mistaken; though today we may speak of "low-pressure cells," we are not only wrong but unfaithful, because (1) the Bible is the inerrant Word of God, (2) the Bible assumes demonic action, therefore (3) true believers will accept biblical truth and abandon all frivolous chatter about "low-pressure cells" and storms. Of course, any hermeneutic that turns preaching into tendentious argument ought to be suspect. Inerrant literalism is an extravagant position, seldom ventured by the church "fathers" or by the framers of Reformation faith. As an extravagance, the position ultimately forces preaching into a kind of heresy in which the Bible must be defended more than understood or preached.

Another version of the fixed-truth position works from a kind of "shell-game" image. Though Mark has written a text in *koine* Greek and in fact expressed a primitive world view, nevertheless *encased* in ancient language is an eternal truth that can be expressed in a different language and within a quite different world view. Matters of language and even cosmology are mere "shell"; the "kernel" of eternal truth within the shell never changes. Now the position involving words = shell/truth = kernel has been around for centuries and has even found its way into confessional statements, Catholic and Protestant alike. The position assumes (1) that content can be separated from words, and (2) that content can be translated from one time-language to another without alteration, and (3) that such content can be grasped as an objective truth apart from particular datable words. In practical sermon preparation it often boils down to an attempt to reduce texts to a single truth-statement (or topic); thus, "Word of God" = a distillation of propositional truth, the kernel within the shell. The position rests on a shaky foundation. The fact is meanings mean *in context* and, when translated from one language-in-consciousness to another are not necessarily the same. So the notion that God-with-us in Christ can command a storm (produced by demons), which made all the sense in the world within a first-century mind, may become absurdity, or even a hindrance to faith, when translated into another context. More, any attempt to state the truth separate from its original "shell" is quite impossible. Language is not an arbitrary code: To use twentieth-century language is to enter into a twentieth-century world view, for language embodies cultural assumptions. Thus, translation itself does *change* meanings. The kernel/shell model is simply not true. If we toss aside the first-century context as a "shell," we then reduce Christian faith to a series of propositional truths (in *our* language) so that it is no longer what the New Testament means by faith at all.

Of course, historical-critical method has its own set of problems. Suppose we do construct a "first-century mind" in which texts can be understood to articulate meaningfully, what exactly do we end up with? Answer: Almost nothing we can preach! When I construct a first-century Markan world in which the Stilling of the Storm means, I am doing so within a twentieth-century language-consciousness as an act of historical imagination. Thus, I end up with a mental construct in which I have something I may label "original meaning." Though as a result of my efforts I may come to understand much about the first century and even much about the Markan mind, what can I do with my original meaning? Will I not have to reduce original meaning to a kernel statement of some sort of truth or simply preach it as meaning now?—positions which, we have seen, are untenable. Of course, I can preach a sermon *about* how and what Mark understood so that my congregation will know more about the Bible, but to do so would be to alienate the word of scripture from today. A bag full of original meaning may not help much in the living of life today. When preachers talk of doing exegesis, locating original meaning, they then usually add something about "applying it today." But, applying the gospel's original meanings puts us right back into the kernel/shell game. Historical-critical method leaves us with a host of questions: Are there "objective" original meanings or is history "soft" and always the product of someone's perspectival reading? Can original meanings bridge time and, in some fashion, address our contemporary consciousness? If original meanings are located, are they not locked in a particular time and space as objects of our consciousness of the past? If they are applied, do they not change as they intend toward an entirely different world in consciousness?

A Perennial Human Experience?

For some preachers the problem of history can be obliterated by arguing not for a "fixed truth" but for a "fixed human nature" for texts to address. In other words, biblical texts are ever meaningful because they speak to a perennial human nature, or perhaps to perennial aspects of human life which, like death and taxes, never change. Look at how the assumptions may work in actual sermon production.

We read a text, such as the Stilling of the Storm, and ask for a parallel: What *in* the text lines up with my congregation's common experience? If I am speaking to a congregation locked in a dry stretch of central Kansas, a parallel in common experience may be difficult to find; my people may have little experience with nautical adventure. Kansans do know about storms, however, so the text could address our attitude toward tornadoes: Storms are, after all, an item in perennial human experience. Of course, as a preacher, I may decide that a sermon on "How to Deal with Tornadoes" may be less than compelling. Then, instead of lining up the text with a parallel in experience, I may turn to perennial structures of self. Thus, I may spot a reference in the text to "fear"—"Why are you afraid?" Jesus asks his disciples—and decide that fear is never-changing, always a part of the human psyche. I may notice that fear of demons may be somewhat different from fears detailed in *Psychology Today* but, after all, in essence, fear is fear. In my parallels, I can announce a Jesus who either reduces our fears or rescues us from storms; Jesus as either "therapist" or as *Christus ex machina*. Now, look back and notice what has happened: (1) The method of seeking a parallel has forced us to select from the text a topic to speak on, thus the text as a whole structural understanding has either been dismissed or truncated. (2) The text is aimed at either a general human predicament or at a predicament within a human self; in other words at a general *human* meaning. The text no longer functions in relation to a being-saved community in the world, but becomes a word to our general humanness. (3) The single parallel selected may turn us away from a study of the text as a symbol of revelation. Instead of searching the Mystery of God we end up with a "God" predetermined by particular human problems, a God who eases fear or a God who rescues from storms, which while pleasant to preach may not be within the "theological field" of the text. (4) The sense of mystery in the text is strangely dispelled.

Of course, the problem of parallels becomes even more acute if texts are closely linked with first-century thought-forms. If, for example, we were to preach on the Markan two-liner, "they will see the Son of man coming in clouds with great power and glory. And then he will send out the angels and gather his elect from the four winds." What do you do with such a text other than to run for cover? What is there in human experience or in some structure in the self to which the text may relate? Do we line up the text with our fantasy life, or with a vague human quality such as "anticipation," or with "someday we must die," or what? What happens in practice is that such texts are seldom preached simply because parallels are hard to find. Of course if we do line up the text with, let us say, "fear of the future," then the text's original cosmic reference and christological meaning may be obliterated entirely. While search for parallels in experience or in the inner world of self is almost habitual, there must be a "better way" so that preaching may be responsible.

A Perennial in Faith or Church?

A more sophisticated version of the perennial in human experience is the notion that there is a perennial "faith-experience" which the gospel addresses. In part, this idea comes from the thought of Bultmann. The argument seems to suggest that in every age, Christian experience involves a conversion from "inauthentic life" to "authentic life" by the gospel. Because such conversion is the nature of faith, texts are ever meaningful when interpreted with reference to the perennial *Christian* experience; first-century Christians experienced faith as a conversion and so do we. But what is the result of locating a constant in faith-experience? (1) We will tend to subjectivize texts, either ignoring social meanings or reducing them to individual experience. (2) We will tend to translate revelation of God into a revelation of the mystery of our inner *experience* of God though, oddly enough, there may be a difference. (3) We will tend to obliterate world constructs in both the first century *and* the twentieth century, for our subject matter has been reduced to an awareness of inner change. Of course, we will have to overlook an interesting question, namely, *is* "faith-experience" in two different ages the same?

Catholic and some Protestant scholars are apt to argue that the perennial bridging time is the existence, in continuum, of the church. The church as a flow of tradition does in fact bridge time. Thus, first-century texts are grasped because the church today has grown from the potential of the early Christian community, indeed is a development of the same community that once articulated the texts. Within the model we can even argue that today we may better understand a first-century text because we can see what the church has grown to be, and thus have a fuller understanding of the future reality which an earlier text was pointing toward. Of course, the argument founders if we suggest that the evolution of the church may not be unbroken self-realization but, as with all human development, can be subject to regressions, distortions, and sedimentations. Thus, for example, would we expect a triumphalist late-medieval church to read texts written by a brave, but embattled Markan-minority community correctly? If we attempt to avoid such questions by insisting that there are certain constants within the church, as, for example, a resilient fidelity, we will then tend to lock texts into "what the church has always understood them to mean," blocking new interpretations. Of course, recent voices in liberation theology have raised questions about whether a Western church fed on Christendom models of triumph can *ever* understand a gospel for the oppressed.

Is There a Perennial?

What are we to do with the huge problem of history? Can we suggest some kinds of answers? Let us venture a few possible tangents of thought.

First, let us suggest a methodological correction. Before preachers grab at parallels, they may wish to locate some theological field delineated by the text. The suggestion can be seen clearly by looking at a text such as Isa. 56:3-8. The passage has to do with exclusion of foreigners and eunuchs from the temple cult, a matter much debated in Israel, and of God's Word to the effect that the temple is to be a house of prayer for *all* people because God gathers outcasts. If a preacher goes for parallels, a sermon on our attitude toward homosexuals and unbelievers might result, a sermon which though assuredly relevant might merely skim the surface of the text or even tend toward moralism on the subject of social prejudices. If the text is set within churchly tradition it may not fare much better, for while the church seems to approve priestly eunuchs, it has not always been hospitable to nonchurch types or to practiced love between consenting eunuchs. Set within an "inauthentic-authentic life" conversion model, the text may still focus on personal attitudes as exhibited in the treatment of social outsiders. But suppose instead that we attempt to locate a field of theological meaning for the text. We might discern that underlying the specific case is a deeper issue having to do with the inclusiveness or exclusiveness of a being-saved community in view of the revelation of God. The location of a theological field may set us free to find quite different cases from those which are cited in the text, different cases which in fact may be *more* relevant to congregations in which we speak.

Second, notice that mention of a "theological field" has led us in an interesting direction, namely, toward talk of revelation of God and a being-saved community in the world. Is there any perennial that can bridge time? Answer —if we look into human nature, or human experience, or religious experience, or the shape of the church—none. Human consciousness is not a fixity; human consciousness is itself historical and, therefore, quite differently shaped in different ages. Where is there a constant that allows for change but is still a constant? Possibly the answer may be found in a *structure* of consciousness rather than in the content of consciousness. As texts were written from a structured consciousness, they must be interpreted within a similarly structured consciousness. We refer, of course, to a *preacher's* consciousness of Presence and present mysteries, within which symbols of revelation are grasped by an awareness of being-saved in community. The model we have proposed allows for change. The world in consciousness is ever-changing, mysteries of being human are variously understood, the shape of the being-saved community—not to mention images of salvation—may be different, even the ways in which we grasp symbols of revelation may alter from age to age (e.g., we no longer understand Christ's humanity/divinity within categories of "substance"). Nevertheless the *structure* of Christian consciousness is similar in every age. Thus, we may avoid having to posit either a fixed-truth gospel or a constant human experience, neither of which may be maintained against the fact of changing consciousness. If we set the Stilling of the Storm within a structured Christian consciousness, we will recognize the odd double-mindedness of being-saved in the trusting but nonetheless frightened disciples, and we will grasp revelation of Mysterious Love through the word-acts of a portrayed Jesus—"Who is this that even wind and sea obey him?" Of course, our world will be a radically different world than that of the first century—we need not rehabilitate demons. Furthermore, our understanding of God vis-à-vis the world will be different, posing quite different mysteries to address. Nevertheless, the *structure* of our double hermeneutical consciousness will be similar, and a good "place" for our interpretive art.

THE PROBLEM OF A "NEW" MEANING

Another problem facing preachers has to do with the proper scope of texts. The problem can be stated analogously. When Samuel Taylor Coleridge penned "The Ancient Mariner," he wrote out of a particular world in consciousness, and intended a particular range of meanings. In the twentieth century, with often quite different conceptual tools, for example, Freudian psychology, can Coleridge's poem mean much *more* than Coleridge knew or intended? Today we may read "The Ancient Mariner" and find meanings which, clearly, could not have been in the poet's mind when he wrote. Is meaning locked into a particular time, place, and consciousness of composition, or may it extend so as to propose new meanings which may be "valid"? Are there limits to such extended meaning? What is the proper scope of a text?

The issue is not abstract. Any preacher who is sensitive to the fact that we preach in God's consciousness of us has a fear of misinterpretation; we are responsible before God. Likewise, any preacher who senses the power of language to name the world and shape identity has a doubled fear of misinterpretation; preaching does form faith-consciousness. The question of how far the meanings of a text may extend is a preacher's question. While we may well resist the straitjacket of original meaning, most of us would not wish to turn texts into Rorschach ink blots in which we can read whatever may be tumbling about in our own psyches. The character in *Through the Looking-Glass* who announced magisterially, "When I use a word, it means just what I choose it to mean," would not, to our mind, qualify for ordination! Most preachers do want their interpretations of the world and of the scriptures to be "valid," whatever that tossed-about word may mean.

If the question of valid interpretation does not trouble us, it may be because we have confused pragmatics with truth. For many pastors, truth may tend to be defined as "whatever is therapeutically helpful" or, more crassly, as "whatever works in my parish," with the word "works" left wide open. But when we interpret revelation, we are supposedly speaking the truth about God in the presence of God, and such truth should not be weighed by "efficacy." Suppose, for example, some helter-skelter soul were to be psychologically benefited by membership in the Communist party, unified, related to others, and given purpose; would we then say that Communist ideology is true simply because it has proven efficacious? No. Yet, we are apt to judge "true interpretation" of scripture by the category of "helpfulness" to people in our parishes. "Truth" and "efficacy" are two different kinds of judgments. In speaking of God, the question we must ask of interpretation is "Is it true?" and not "Is it helpful?" Though grace may triumph efficaciously through all kinds of error (thank God!), we should not presume on grace. So, responsible preachers do worry about being true to a text. Just how much meaning is possible? What *is* the scope of a text?

Anyone who has ever penned a poem and then listened as friends (or those not so friendly) interpret the words knows that meaning may well be wider than an author may suppose. Words are obviously not lexically narrow in definition, they tend to connote; thus we speak of polyvalent meaning. Someone reading a poem you have written may come up with surprising meanings that you, as poet, did not anticipate. In some cases, you may object, perhaps on the basis of intent, saying "No way!" but at other times you may turn inward and admit that, yes, the words you wrote may well reach beyond your own awareness, that unwittingly your poem has evoked more meaning than you knew. So, when we write, we may pen a system of words that, detached from our consciousness, claims a wider range of meaning than we once intended.

To argue that writers write more than they know is only a part of our issue. Language may speak long after authors are shoveled under earth. Can texts (now quite separate from authors) tap new meanings for new and different audiences? Some years ago, a newspaper editorial parodied Lincoln's Gettysburg Address, drawing particular meaning for twentieth-century America; the editorial was even signed "A. Lincoln," in a fanciful way. Should such an editorial be scrapped outright or did it contain a proper interpretation *now?* The example parallels what goes on when we interpret biblical texts. In most cases we may not know with certainty who an author was, or even where and when a text was written; all we have at hand is a bundle of language. Biblical scholars may speak of an original meaning as they set the language in some sort of context, social or historical, but are we fenced by original meaning? If not, then is there *any* limit to interpretation? Clearly, we may read the text by drawing analogies from our own experience, analogies that enable understanding. But is there a limit to the kinds of analogy we may draw? Again, what is the scope of a text when interpreted in an entirely new context?

To sharpen the issue, return to the Stilling of the Storm. Suppose a number of different preachers, no better or worse than most of us, should interpret the text in sermons. Preacher A uses the text to say that Jesus can calm troubled souls, specifically those who are churned up by psychological fears. Another pastor, Preacher B, perhaps under the influence of Origen, allegorizes the text—disciples = Christians; boat = church; sea = life; storm = pressures of the modern world; and so on—and concludes that the Spirit of Christ is within the church so that we need never fear. Preacher C, a rigorous soul, declares that because Jesus had power to still the storm he was God, and we had better believe it! Finally, there is Preacher D who holds membership in the John Birch Society, and who (in an actual sermon!) identifies the storm with the rise of the "New Left" and pictures Jesus as a sort of early-day J. Edgar Hoover trouncing waves of radical protest while guiding true believers in a "Right" direction. Though the examples we have given are a bit silly, and most preachers would be both more subtle and more responsible, our different interpretations raise an important question: Are *all* readings of a text valid?

By what norms may we adjudge one "truer" than another if all are to some extent helpful to respective congregations? How can we toss out some interpretations while retaining others? Is original meaning our standard or are there other factors to be considered?

At the outset, we may wish to dismiss the sermon by Preacher D as a violation of the gospel as well as alien to the nature of a being-saved community: The sermon may not seem to be within *Christian* faith. What we are doing is to set a right-wing J. Edgar Hoover "Jesus" alongside the portraits of Jesus in the New Testament, and strident hatred of the "New Left" beside awareness of being-saved that includes charity. Furthermore, we may realize that our double apprehension of being-saved includes, by contrast, an awareness of "party spirit" in the world so that we suspect the sermonic hermeneutic of being slightly sub-Christian. Now, we are not dismissing the sermon on the basis of its having ideological bias for, after all, preachers as citizens of the human world share all sorts of "isms," "ologies," and other proximate understandings. No, the real issue is not bias, but the fact that the text has been placed in an entirely different structure of consciousness in which revelation through Christ has been replaced by revelation through John Birch, and the awareness of being-saved has been replaced by the self-awareness of a particular social society. Thus, we may tend to discard Preacher D's sermon as *outside* Christian hermeneutical consciousness though it may mention Jesus, disciples, God, and the like. If we suppose, however, that the other sermons in our set of examples are products of Christian hermeneutical consciousness, is there any basis for further judgments? Can we say that one preacher is closer to the mark than another and, if so, on what basis?

Sometimes a literary judgment may figure in our assessments. We might want to question Preacher B's allegory (as well as Origen's) by suggesting that Mark's dramatic narrative does not move toward allegory; narrative travels in consciousness, whereas allegory is a static form designed to explore predicates of entities. Of course, it is difficult to push such an argument too far because after all we may have to admit that Mark's dramatic narrative does not propose sermons either! Nevertheless, underlying the literary observation may be a valid concern: intention. We suppose that Mark's language is well chosen; that, for some reason, Mark has spoken in a narrative way. Does a narrative form align with our own sense of narrativity in life, or, perhaps, is it appropriate to incarnation—the *story* of God-with-us? Or has Mark chosen a narrative structure because he wishes to take listeners on a "transforming" journey of mind, moving from fear to protest to a word of Christ to a declaration of faith? Language is not only suited to subject matters, it *does* in consciousness;

biblical language is performative. So, forms of language may be chosen to *do,* and what they may do can be curtailed if framed in some other form: Making love by reciting a treatise on thermodynamics might be somewhat ludicrous! We may want to argue that to recast Mark's pericope as an allegory will frustrate the "intending" of Mark's language. If we do believe that biblical language is in some sense salvific, then intention may be more important than we know.

Of course, the question of Preacher A's interpretation, namely, a sermon in which Jesus answers psychological fears, is much more difficult. We can raise general objections such as Mark means more than "Jesus therapist," or Mark has a broader field of meaning in which "fear" is only a subordinate motif, but such observations do not get at the nub of the problem. We must turn back to the structure of Christian hermeneutical consciousness to find an answer—consciousness in which, within mysteries, the symbols of revelation are read by being-saved-in-the-world. Mark is rather clearly lining up revelation—"Who is this that even wind and sea obey him?"—with a double-minded being-saved community, called to trust rather than to fear. What Preacher A has done is aim revelation in Christ not so much toward the being-saved community as toward an individual problematic, namely, psychological fears. While Preacher A's interpretation is compassionate and probably helpful, the focus on human fear per se will tend to narrow the scope of revelation to "who is God in relation to our fears?" While we cannot, indeed should not, toss out Preacher A's interpretation as un-Christian, we can perhaps remark that it is partial and even add that such a hermeneutic week after week might delimit the gospel drastically, by turning Christian faith into nothing more than personal therapy.

What about the role of original meaning in determining the scope of a text? Obviously, we will not preach original meaning *now.* After all, original meaning of the Stilling of the Storm may have included demonology, some sort of exorcism, the idea of unruly waters of creation, plus allusions drawn from Hebrew scriptures (such as a reference to Psalm 107). While we can talk of such matters if we wish to preach *about* a text, they may not transfer easily to the twentieth-century mind. Our question is not so much what did the text mean? but what does the text prompt us to preach *now?* Though original meaning is not what we preach, surely there must be some relation between original meaning and the shape of our preaching *now.*

Our problem is to find a model that will liberate us from being fenced in by original meaning and yet, at the same time, relate us to an original meaning. Those who argue that, after all, meaning is relative to various hermeneutical "lenses" and that, in effect, one lens is as good as another, overlook the intending of a text. Yes, we can read texts through the lens of Freudian psychology, Jungian thought, Marxist political philosophy, and so forth, and, often, will gain insight in the process. Must we not suppose, however, that texts may intend *toward* a particular hermeneutical consciousness, and even intend to *do* within a particular consciousness? If such is the case, then hermeneutical lenses are not necessarily optional. No, we must seek a model that will relate contemporary interpretation to both original meaning and, somehow, original *intending*. While all models are necessarily inadequate, they can at times be suggestive.

There is a kit sold to children that contains a flashlight and a number of solid-color disks designed to fit over the lens of the light, each featuring a tiny cut-out shape. When the flashlight is projected on a wall it produces a larger image, but one determined by the design of the tiny cut-out. Let us suppose that original meaning was something that structured within first-century consciousness. The structure of the text, playing across time, will form a structure of understanding in our twentieth-century consciousness that will be different from original meaning, but which will be structured similarly. In our age we may not credit demons, or regard waters as the chaos of pre-creation, or refer automatically to Psalms for, obviously, we have a very different world view and very different notions of human nature. Nevertheless the theological field of a text may project a *shaped* theological field of understanding in our consciousness.

What of intention? In our model, the beam of light has a source, the bulb; a direction, the location of an image on a wall; and a degree of light-intensity; thus the beam of light may be said to "intend." While first-century consciousness is quite different from twentieth-century consciousness, an aiming *of* and an aiming *toward* is involved. We may, therefore, argue that, at minimum, language may aim toward a certain hermeneutical consciousness which, if nothing else, may be said to be consciousness of being-saved-in-the-world. So, though the shape of our world may change and, indeed, our notions of salvation be different, nonetheless a being-saved consciousness may be regarded as "intended." We are not suggesting that other kinds of consciousness may not read language—language is human; or that other kinds of consciousness may not by analogy understand language—a "holy hermeneutic" may not be requisite. All we are saying is that texts from scripture may intend a consciousness, the odd double-consciousness, of being-saved-in-the-world.

THE PROBLEM OF "WHAT" IS INTERPRETED

When we interpret a text, what exactly are we after? What is it that we are trying to "get at" through texts? We often speak of "reading between the lines," indicating that we are seeking something through words that may be more than literal meaning; what is this "something"? With biblical texts, the question is acute. Do we seek something we call "Word of God," or the faith of early Christians, or some kind of originating religious experience, or a revelatory historical event, or what?

To get at the question, let us imagine a text. A woman in "low spirits" has written a letter from a motel room (with, ugh, floral wallpaper) in Bucksnort, Tennessee, on V-J Day. She has written to a favorite nephew (with severe marital problems) whom she is attempting to cheer up. Suppose that, years later, we happen on the letter in some friend's musty attic. What is it that we can interpret as we read the letter?

Question: Can we reconstruct the *situation of the text?* Is some sort of historical criticism possible? If there is a date at the top of the page, we might be able by an act of historical imagination to reconstruct an era toward the conclusion of World War II when the nation celebrated victory. If there is no internal or external evidence of date, we could not—barring laboratory tests—establish a time. Of course, there are matters of vocabulary and style which might be datable in a general way; literary critics, unless dealing with an artful imitation, can on reading a text say, "It's late seventeenth century," or "It's mid-nineteenth-century Romantic." What about the setting? We can only reconstruct what is disclosed. Suppose the writer, consumed by concern for her nephew, makes no mention of Bucksnort or the motel room; we would be helpless unless we were to stumble on external evidence such as a diary left around by the writer, or biographical references from friends familiar with the writer's movements. Even if there are references in a text to things in view, they may be deceptive. Suppose the letter contains the line, "As I look at these flowers, I think of you." Some critic might suppose that the letter is written in a garden. Even if there are many references to place in the letter, they may or may not have any bearing on the interpretation of the text; they may even mislead us. If we know the letter was written on V-J Day, but contains no reference to the war's end, we may conclude that "The woman has no interest in world affairs, all she cares about is her nephew." Actually, the woman may have been vitally interested in V-J Day with a husband serving in the Pacific theater, but has set her own feelings aside in view of her nephew. Sum it up and say: We cannot reconstruct a situation without evidence and, if we do construct a situation, it may have little bearing on our interpretation of a text.

Can we get at the *psychological state of the writer?* Again, unless a writer discloses feelings we may be stymied. For example, our writer may be so concerned to cheer her nephew that she has set her own low-spirits-in-a-floral-room self aside. Possibly some analyst with a remarkable eye for style may observe that the syntax is that of a depressed person feigning cheer, and be correct; but what will we gain? If the writer's own feelings are not prominent in her field of consciousness and, therefore, a subject of discussion, psychological analysis of style might contribute little.

We have reviewed these options in some detail because they may have bearing on biblical interpretation. Some preachers may suppose that biblical texts ought to disclose a "situation" because God is revealed in events, or that biblical texts record "religious experience," largely affective, because God is known in inner experience. On the level of interpretation, these assumptions may shape the hermeneutic. If we can reconstruct a situation we will understand; or if we can describe a subjectivity we will have grasped a text. No, the Bible is remarkably disinterested in feelings and, when it comes to history, is scarcely interested in objective facts so much as meanings. So, again, what do we get at through texts?

In our example, we can describe certain "gets." We have a writer writing a letter to someone (the nephew may not be identified) trying to cheer up the someone (we may be told nothing of the nephew's marital flap). Presumably, what we can get will be (1) some index of intention—the author is writing *to* someone *for* the purpose of cheering up, and (2) some notion of the hermeneutical field out of which the writer writes—understandings of life which may be grounds for "cheer." In other words, we may be able to get at a world of meaning through the words. What we will not get is "event," "feeling," or a "propositional truth"; instead we get the language of *a hermeneutical consciousness intending*. Of course, in scripture, the consciousness we may get at through a text may be astonishingly complex and theologically sophisticated. At other times we may bump into intentional ambiguity which all but defies understanding. But, in sum, biblical language mediates a faith-consciousness shaped by impinging mysteries, relating symbols of faith and a being-saved community. The trick in interpreting is to search for what *is* given!

SOME GENERAL HERMENEUTICAL PROPOSALS

From our discussion of the problems, we can draw together guidelines for the interpretation of texts, singularly biblical texts. In future chapters we will study the interpretation of different kinds of texts; here we seek a general orientation.

1. *Biblical texts are addressed to communal consciousness.*

Virtually everything in scripture is written to a faith-community, usually in the style of communal address. Therefore, biblical texts must be set in *communal* consciousness to be understood. Even when texts are ostensibly addressed to individuals—"Theophilus" (Luke 1:3), "Philemon" (Philem. 1), "The Elect Lady" (2 John 1)—they are nonetheless addressed to individuals who share communal Christian consciousness. Thus, texts do *not* address individuals in individual self-awareness. The issue is tricky, but crucial. Because we interpret scripture individually we tend to assume that scripture speaks to individual consciousness, to an individual in existential self-awareness. Thus, our "applications" of the Bible tend to be personal in character. We read the Sermon on the Mount as an individual ethic, or Paul's discussion of sin in Romans 8 as a study in personal inward exploration. Inadvertently, we misconstrue scripture. Somehow we must learn to let texts articulate in a Christian communal consciousness. No wonder a Black hermeneutic often reads scripture more wisely than does a White all-American individualism. How can an individual Black be addressed apart from Black identity which is built into every representative member of a Black community? So, by analogy, we are arguing that biblical texts address a shared, communal faith-consciousness and *must* be so interpreted: the Bible is communal language for communities. Therefore, as interpreters we do not ask "What does the text say to *me?*" or even "What does the text say to me as representative human being?" but "What is the text saying to *our* faith-consciousness?" Most of the "you"s that show up in New Testament texts, in the letters of Paul or in the teachings of Jesus, should rightly be translated into "Southern" as "you-alls." The real problem with much therapeutic preaching today is not that it is therapeutic, for after all various therapies have helped us all, but that it turns communal language into language addressing an individual self in self-awareness.

2. *The consciousness which texts address is the "double" consciousness of being-saved in the world.*

Texts speak to double consciousness: A consciousness of being-saved that views the world, and a human worldly consciousness startled by being-saved. Thus texts addressed to double consciousness cannot properly be truncated so as to speak either to humans in human awareness or to the saved in a one-sided consciousness of being-saved. We are bifocal people and biblical language speaks to our bifocal consciousness. Therefore, it will be inappropriate to interpret the Bible through some available secular hermeneutic such as Jungian psychology or capitalist ideology. While such hermeneutics may form in our interpreting minds, they aim at interpreting human beings in the world per se and, therefore, may not open up the odd double address involved in biblical language. On the other hand, a so-called holy hermeneutic may be equally devastating, and obscure the sweet complex earthiness of many, many biblical texts.

Of course, we should recall that the same double mind has written scripture. So biblical texts may well express a double consciousness; consciousness shaped by the human world including social attitudes, proximate "truths," cosmologies, as well as the consciousness of being-saved in the world. No wonder that we bump into notions that are emphatically datable and that represent the consciousness of an earlier world (for example, demon possession and a suspicion of unruly sea waters). But, we also encounter attitudes in texts that may be in tension with being-saved, such as national triumphalism or gloating exclusivist understandings of salvation. All we have to do is look through the Book of Revelation where side by side we find soaring visions of ultimate reconciliation and rather nasty prophecies of torments in reserve. Unless hampered by overdeveloped ideas of inerrancy, our own double-mindedness can sort through texts and, with compassion born of our own brokenness, understand.

The double consciousness of being-saved in the world does enable us to read texts in a double way. For all biblical texts, though aimed at either worldly ways or the reality of being saved, imply both. If, for example, we read the stunning vision of the Holy City that rises in later chapters of Revelation, we will by reflection recognize our own world's brokenness. Or, if we study a prophetic denunciation of the world's callous disregard for neighbors, we will by reflection realize that the words are a call to neighbor love. We are suggesting that scripture, written by a double consciousness, must be read by double consciousness—a consciousness of being in the world and a consciousness of being-*saved* in the world.

3. *Speaking of God, the Bible tells stories and singles out symbols. Thus, the Bible must be interpreted within an interaction of symbol and story.*

Clearly, scripture contains narrative and, as a collection of "books," assembles into a kind of "plot," which like all good stories has a beginning and an end—myths of creation and visions of eschaton. Thus, particular biblical texts can be located in relation to the story and imply a consciousness of the story of God-with-us, the story of Presence-in-Absence and a people. Likewise, again and again, the Bible interrupts narrative to allow particular events, persons, or things to stand out symbolically. So in the Bible we find not only a moving story line but heightened symbols drawn from the story such as the law, the temple, the Red Sea crossing, and so on. The dialectic of story and symbol is seen quite clearly in Jesus Christ who comes to us as a character in God's story and yet, by resurrection, stands before us symbolically as a disclosure of God's "interior," that is, of God's intending toward us.

In interpreting scripture we suggest that both story and symbol must interrelate. Christ, *the* disclosure symbol of God, cannot be understood apart from the story of God-with-us that traverses the scriptures from beginning to end, and includes symbolic orientations such as exodus, exile, and restoration. But, likewise, the story line of scripture cannot truly be grasped except as it is read in light of the awesome disclosure of God-love through the Living Symbol of Jesus Christ. Please notice that we are not here discussing the problem of Hebrew and Christian scriptures; symbol and story are featured in both and, indeed, interlace to conjoin Hebrew and Christian scriptures. No, we are spotting types of language prompted by narrative consciousness and symbolic consciousness and saying simply that in scripture story grasps symbol and symbol opens stories. We could add that scripture as story and symbol can relate to our own lives which we tend to understand through symbols and narrations.

Perhaps we should add a word about mystery. Because stories are plots they indicate that there is a larger "whole" out of which they have been drawn; as plots they indicate that they are not the whole story. Likewise, symbols do not dispel mystery into some sort of rational statement of truth; rather they reach into and reflect mystery. Why does the Bible tell stories and brood over symbols? Precisely because the Bible is speaking of God's Presence-in-Absence amid mysteries of being in the world. Obviously, speaking of God, of a Consciousness conscious of us, will not produce denotative prose or well-lit rationalisms. By speaking in stories and symbols, the Bible reveals while, at the same time, it signals mystery. Therefore, preachers interpreting scripture should not expect to be led to propositional truth but rather to bewonderment, gratitude, and faith.

THE PROBLEM OF MISINTERPRETATION

We may now be in a position to discuss the problem of misinterpretation which is not merely possible but probable. We come to the study of texts with all kinds of baggage: methodological presuppositions, theological orientations, not to mention worldly wisdoms, cultural understandings, and that old bugaboo, sin. In recent American presidential elections, it has been obvious that right-wing politicos are reading scripture somewhat differently from left-wing types. In churches, similar convictional commitments may skew interpretations, particularly when reading controversial texts. How can we be free from personal distortions which in turn distort interpretation? Obviously, the notion of an objective "scientific" study of scripture is impossible not only because biblical language is connotative, but because any reading of texts involves some sort of pre-understanding. Is there any way to protect interpretations from *us?* While we may not lie awake nights worrying over dangers of misinterpretation, the Bible's many passages warning against "false prophets" do raise the question. What can we do to guard against misreading texts?

The problem is that as interpreters we are only *being*-saved; we approach texts "in Christ" but still with a mind formed by the human world. Of course, the texts we read may have been scribbled by the same double-mindedness. When we set texts beside texts, for example, Paul beside James, or Matthew next to Luke-Acts, we are aware of party lines, perspectival differences, unreconstructed self-interests, and so forth. Of course, when we turn into our own consciousness we may well discover that we ourselves are as perspectival, that we read scripture through all kinds of convictional lenses—such as Catholic, Protestant, evangelicalist, social-liberal, liberational. Therefore, a degree of cautious *dis*trust is not inappropriate. We should have an eye for bias in texts, yes, but also a profound wariness of our own predispositions, party lines, dogmatisms, as well as fantasies and ego-trip needs.

Of course, our double consciousness of being-saved-in-the-world can assist interpretation. Within the being-saved community, in the light of the gospel, we apprehend symbolic disclosures of a new order of life forming among us; we begin to recognize that, good heavens, we *are* being-saved. In the recognition, we sense a difference between our being-saved and the attitudes, or life styles, of our worldly ways. In other words, we begin to see what is *not* being-saved; we differentiate the "mind" of being-saved from the "mind" of our world-age. While we may not be entirely objective, we can *differentiate*. The tendency of being-saved to differentiate can discern double-mindedness in texts and in our own interpretive impulses.

We will naturally avail ourselves of all kinds of critical methods as we study texts, seeking to hear someone else's language rather than our own. Thus, we will be informed by textual criticism, historical and sociological criticism, as well as form-critical and literary-critical perspectives. We may well wish to learn "structuralist" method or to gain a phenomenological perspective which regards language as language in consciousness through a "reader-response" model. Furthermore, we will not allow party-line opinion to turn us away from *any* useful methodology. Even methods aligned with various political or psychological positions may give insight when employed by being-saved consciousness in the interpretation of texts. Ministers gripped by a fascination with Mystery through Jesus Christ will not limit their methodological options, or fail to develop new methodological skills; they want to know and, what's more, to know by honoring the freedom of the texts to speak on their *own* terms.

Can we go beyond suspicion? Perhaps. If we are only *being*-saved, please note, we are at least being-*saved*. At times, we do lift eyebrows and, astonished by grace, notice a new order of life in which we live. In such moments we gratefully delight in being-saved and, with a kind of newborn naiveté, read texts as news of our salvation. There can be a kind of clap-hands excitement, a wondering delight of mind that reads texts—like children opening unexpected gifts. Maybe there are Christian souls whose grateful delight in being-saved is chronic. For most of us, however, it may visit only after we have struggled with suspicion, have attempted a distancing of mind, have brooded over symbols of revelation, and so forth. Unfortunately, interpretation is hard, disciplined work that cannot be bypassed by magic notions of the Holy Spirit. Nevertheless, there is a reading of texts as the message of our salvation that through language yields Presence.

As interpreters, preachers have a wonderful advantage: they preach their interpretations to people. Because they hear the gospel they preach, they know that, though they may never presume on mercy, they are forgiven and, therefore, may interpret "bravely." And in preaching their interpretations are tested. We do not suggest that audience-response tests interpretation (we will not confuse "efficacy" with "truth"). Audiences may be stimulated by red-hot delivery, be aroused by sensual cadence, or merely bask in a projected friendliness. Also, according to scripture, audiences may have "itching ears" and therefore may applaud reiterations of worldly commonplace. All in all, audience feedback is a less than helpful test of interpretation. What we do suggest is that, in preaching, interpretation speaks to a being-saved community that brings to church not only the mind of an age, but also a sense of befuddling mystery. Thus, the test of interpretation may be manifold: (1) Does interpretation align the mysteries of being-in-the-world with the Mystery disclosed through symbols of revelation? (2) Does interpretation serve to define being-saved in relation to being-in-the-world and vice versa? (3) Does interpretation invoke the Presence in Mystery through Jesus Christ, story and symbol? In short, does interpretation lead to mediation?

Interpretation is fulfilled in preaching even as, oddly enough, preachers may be fulfilled in doing the awesome work of interpretation.

HOMILETICS

18.
Plots and Intentions

————————————————— Guidebooks for European travel frequently include a glossary on back pages. The glossary features words which a traveler may expect to hear frequently in a particular country. Though the glossary will list brief definitions, such definitions are usually inadequate. We do not really catch on to words until we hear them used over and over again in many different contexts. In the pages that follow, we will be using two terms, "plot" and "intention," that need definition. A glossary listing will not do the trick: We must explore meanings more deeply. Older homiletic studies spoke of sermon "outlines" and sometimes discussed the need for a clear, statable "purpose" for sermons. We are not merely replacing some old words with new words; instead, when we refer to "plot" and "intention," we are proposing quite different notions. We will explore each term in order, first "plot" and then "intention," before trying to tie the two terms together. Preaching involves the designing of "plots" for consciousness and a wielding of "intentional" language.

PLOTS

"History" and "Plots"

Let us begin by drawing a distinction between "history" and "plot," and suggest that scripture does not contain "history," but rather a series of calculated "plots." The distinction, often discussed under different terms, is well known to literary critics. By "history" we mean an event in its *fullness*—what actually takes place.

Imagine two people visiting a country carnival and walking the midway for an hour or two. There are so many impressions to record it would take a lifetime to get them all down in words. Surely, there are visual impressions from bright lights wiggling in the night, to come-on signboards, to geeks and gyrating cooch dancers, to bingo games and ring-toss chances, to grandstand performers strutting their stuff, and the like. All these images could, presumably, be described in the order in which they were seen. But a full recounting of the event would include other sensory experiences, for example, the feel of spun cotton candy, the smell of red-hots floating in the air. Then, there are the people—facial expressions, stances, actions, not to mention a chatter of words as they speak to each other. Of course, to truly record the event we would have to enter fields of consciousness, pursue fantasies, apprehensions, and trails of memory floating in minds; we would need a "history" of everyone within the thronged midway. Our list of components within the event could go on and on and on.

In telling an event, what do we do? We select and we order. We choose what to talk about, and in what sequential order. One of our walkers may decide to set up a sort of travelogue of the carnival, reciting, in order, things seen, as if taking listeners on a "walking tour" of the midway. The other might decide to select only two or three things for description, using them as symbols for the whole. Of course, interests could intrude. One walker, out of prurient interest, could dwell on the swing and sway of the cooch dancer, or find excitement in "strut-their-stuff" performers. The other, an economics major, might discuss the bingo operation, speculating on profits. Though the event itself involved a complex of impressions that happened over the span of two hours, a report of the event might be done in a matter of minutes, but quite selectively. The actual event could only be reproduced by tape recorders, television cameras, not to mention total "free" recall by all participants, but what we do is represent events by constructing "plots."

The constructing of a plot is *never* arbitrary but is formed in consciousness by an interaction of audience and the hermeneutic of a teller. Begin by understanding a rough distinction between "history" and "plot."

The Logic of Plotting

In order to get at what may be involved in shaping a "plot," we will venture toward the absurd. We will provide a "history"—that is, background information on a number of characters, and the sequence of episodes in an event. Imagine an absolutely absurd "soap-opera" story (books on homiletics should risk imagination, because otherwise, they do tend to be dull!). Here is a cast of oddball characters:

> *John* is a slightly overweight, forty-year-old chiropractor, who once aspired to become an orthopedic surgeon until he received his first-year college grades. He

was born in western Montana, where his father was a poor but honest sheep-herder. John is successful, however, and has built up a thriving practice in Sarasota, Florida. His house, on a nearby key, overlooks the Gulf of Mexico, and, to the envy of neighbors, features a three-car garage filled with Cadillac converti-bles, one of which John uses only on weekends.

Mary, John's wife, used to be a high-school cheerleader in Tulsa, Oklahoma. Her daddy was in oil. An only child, Mary still demands more than her share of attention; she feeds on praise, but, oddly enough, is frightened of sex. She still likes to dress up in her cheerleader outfit just to demonstrate that she has her girlish figure. Unfortunately, she does not. She has tried to get interested in "volunteer work," but isn't. So, when the "soaps" are not on she reads paperback "romances"—three and four a week. Sometimes she irons her gold cheerleader miniskirt for something to do.

Cerise is a "smooth looker." She jogs to keep in shape and her shape is certainly worth keeping. As a liberated woman, she operates a jackhammer for the Sarasota street department, which contributes to her chronic back problem. She once read a book about Madame Curie and decided she would go into medical research, except that she flunked high-school chemistry three times. But she has main-tained a lifelong interest in medical matters. She is twenty-four, longs for "life in the fast lane," breakdances, and collects food stamps as a hobby. She goes to John for relief from backache. Cerise was born in Bad Axe, Michigan, where her father, a ne'er-do-well mink farmer, once wanted to be a chiropractor.

Marvin is a deeply religious sociopath, who mows lawns when not surf-casting. He mows John's lawn. Marvin was born in the Okefenokee Swamp, he thinks, but has lost his birth certificate, if he ever had one. He has a little four-room apartment, each room decorated with symbols of one of the "world's great religions"—a Jewish star, the moon of Islam, a gilded crucifix, and a six-foot statue of Gautama Buddha surrounded by incense pots. His hobby is writing to the Sarasota newspaper under assumed religious names. His most recent letter, signed "Mother Teresa," was refused publication. Marvin is bitter, but still religious.

Miss Frobish is a part-time nurse and receptionist at John's chiropractic center. Though her first name is Desiree, nobody would call her anything but "Miss Frobish." She, an orphan, was reared in a convent by a small but dedicated order of gleaming Catholic sisters. When she realized that she would never become a mother superior, she left the convent and took over management of John's professional life. Her office cubicle is papered with "holy pictures." Occasionally, she meets Marvin at the library. He has invited her to inspect his "Catholic room," but, so far, she has resisted.

We have given you a list of characters because obviously any story involves the movements of motivated characters in a field of event. We might have provided episodes in an event and then developed characters. Given our list of unlikely people, here is a series of episodes to comprise "history":

1. John and Mary have a fight. Even though she has dressed in her cheerleader outfit to serve supper, she has come up with frozen fish sticks for the fifth night in a row. John storms out and drives all over town in his weekend Cadillac, even though it is only Wednesday. Mary dissolves in tears, which strikes her as somewhat romantic. At breakfast, they do not speak.

2. John has a ten o'clock appointment with Cerise; back strain again. During the treatment John notices and admires Cerise's back. He idly mentions his three Cadillacs. Even more casually, he remarks that he's considering a weekend trip to Acapulco to scan real-estate options. Their eyes meet, significantly. To Cerise, Cadillacs and Acapulco sound something like "life in the fast lane." Before you know it, they are making plans for a weekend together.

3. Miss Frobish, waiting in her cubicle, cannot help but overhear their conversation. She is aghast, but remains silent. She prays for John's immortal soul.

4. That night, a guilty John is solicitous. He takes Mary out for a fish-stick dinner. He buys her three new historical romances. He begs Mary to put on her outfit and do the cheers that made her name a byword in Tulsa. However, he also mentions, in an offhand way, that (sigh!) he must go to Atlanta on the weekend for a chiropractic convention.

5. Miss Frobish and Marvin happen to meet on the library steps. Marvin has written a letter (under the name "Muhammad, O.S.B.") which he asks Desiree Frobish to proofread. In the letter, which has to do with Truth, Beauty, and Goodness, Marvin argues that Truth is both Goodness and Beauty. Moved, Miss Frobish tells Marvin of her employer's deception, and, devoutly, they both click tongues.

6. The next day when Marvin is mowing Mary's lawn, Mary tells him that her husband has gone away to a medical meeting. She wants the lawn to look nice for his return. Overcome by his own rhetoric, Marvin blurts out The Truth!

7. Mary is appalled. John's lie has taken the romance out of reading romances. She wanders idly about her house. She puts on her uniform, but cheers choke in her throat. Finally, distraught, she turns to her closet full of tranquilizers, takes two or three bottles, and, nodding her head, snores off into death.

8. John and Cerise are on the terrace of their luxury suite in Acapulco, having decided to stay another three days. The phone rings. Miss Frobish is the bearer of sad tidings. "I suppose we should send flowers," says Cerise. Using John's credit card, they do so.

9. At the funeral, Marvin and Miss Frobish sit side by side; Marvin in a fez, Miss Frobish with her rosary. The tragedy has gotten to them. Human beings must unite to guard against untruth and immorality, they agree. Love blooms.

10. Years later, Desiree and Marvin have become famous, even wealthy, having coauthored a best-selling series on "Spirituality," now twenty-three volumes.

They are considering their own Sunday-morning TV show. They have two children: one wants to be a cheerleader and the other a chiropractor, but both are devout and practice Zen meditation daily.

We have spun out a silly story and provided biographical background of sorts, a scant production compared with the scope and complexity of some actual episodic event. By now, though, the story and characters are a "whole event" in your *field* of consciousness, ready for you to break into some sequence of retelling. Think of how many different ways we could replot the material at hand!

A. We could enter the field of event through episode 2 and have John, during his treatment of Cerise, recall, with displeasure, the fish sticks of the night before. We could skip to episode 5, involving Marvin and Miss Frobish on the library steps. We could then develop episode 7 into an interior monologue in which Mary broods over the cruel truth while recalling the catastrophic fish-stick supper—fifth in a row. Finally, we could conclude with episode 8 and end ironically with Cerise's one-liner: "I suppose we should send flowers." The effect of such a plot would be a devaluing of Mary's suicide—a mere tragic waste—while reducing all motivation to the offensive fish sticks. Notice what has been left out of the story in the process. Notice, also, that the strategy of the plot produces a mean, somewhat ironic, trivialization of event.

B. Suppose, instead, we were to tell the story as Miss Frobish's recollection. We might begin at the end: We could have Miss Frobish remember the funeral (episode 9), then recall episode 5, on the library steps, and then push back in memory to the overheard conversation in episode 3—a series of flashbacks. We might have Miss Frobish view her two children as the redemption of a tragic John and Mary. Here we have designed a story from a distant point-of-view (episode 10) as a regressive chain of memory. By restructuring the plot, we have turned the story into a dramatic moral tale of sin and redemption. Again, notice what we have excluded from the "whole field of event."

C. The story could be told from John's point-of-view in some made-up episode 11. We could have John telling his own story to a chiropractor friend in a convention barroom. A selection of episodes, perhaps 8 back to 6, would allow John to regard the tragic death of his wife as the fault of too much indiscriminate truth-telling. We might, then, imagine a monologue by John, remarking how everything has worked for the best: he has a fine, free life with Cerise; she has realized her father's dream by becoming his office nurse-receptionist; and their unblessed relationship has been moderately deepened by reading together a series of twenty-three books on spirituality. We have created a vantage point outside the original field of event in order to bring out a different, if amoral, meaning.

D. Inspired by some modern novels, we might tell the story chronologically, but through different characters' readings of what is taking place. Thus, we might

289

begin with episode 1 in Mary's understanding, switch to episode 2 through John's awareness, then turn to episode 3 in Miss Frobish's shocked mind, and so on. Some episodes might well be reduced, or skipped, or recast as memory, so that the story ends terribly with Cerise's conscious experience in episode 8. The result might be a study in different moral perspectives, or a psychological probing of different characters. As a reader, having the whole event in consciousness, you may wish to see how many other plots you can devise from our original absurd narrative. In doing so, you will discover how your own response to the story affects your composition of a plot.

Components of Plotting

Recently, there have been a number of brilliant studies of what is involved in plotting, studies that are frequently complex. We cannot explore that literature in depth. What we can do is to suggest certain factors that may be involved in *our* consciousness when proposing a plot from a story or history.

Plot and Hermeneutical Consciousness. Please notice the options presented by a story that has structured a "field of event" in consciousness. A teller may rearrange episodes in many ways. If we read the story as a story of character, motivation, and causation, we may wish to retain chronology so that 1 leads to 2 leads to 3, and so on, in a "tight" causal chain of episodes. If we adopt such a strategy, it may be because we view life as a determined causal chain. If we view events as fatally determined, we may reduce all extraneous matters—we will not reveal Marvin's four-room personal "reliquary" or Mary's fondness for historical romances—but, instead, produce a relentless cause-effect plot. If, on the other hand, we believe human beings have a degree of free choice, we may relax our story so as to include some unnecessary events, giving listeners a "feel" of free choosing. Suppose, instead, we view the human enterprise as a buffeting of random drives and impulses that, irrational, always ends tragically; we may go back and forth in plotting, even adding extra events to disclose better the desires and thoughtless impulses of our characters. Or, we may be moralists, eager (with Deuteronomic zeal) to ensure that the wicked are punished and the virtuous rewarded. Such a perspective might mean we would elaborate some episodes and virtually ignore others. Thus, Miss Frobish's earnest prayer might be spun out at length, John's prurient interest in Cerise reported in scathing detail, and so forth. Marvin, given his piety and high regard for Truth, might turn into the hero of the story. In describing different options, we are suggesting that interpreters will plot a story out of their own understanding of life, their philosophy, theology, moral values, and the like. So in a sense every plot is a confession of faith.

Genres and Repertoires. There is another side to plotting which must be mentioned. In our minds, as we plot, are "stock" genres and repertoires which are products of the social world, and are available to us. By repertoires, we mean conventional plots we have heard before: sequences as trite as "boy meets girl, boy loses girl, boy gets girl" which may underlie many romantic comedies; or "moral little people, immoral power people, triumph of little people" which may be featured in some social drama, or whatever. We have heard many stories told, and story conventions become part of our recall. By genre, we mean types of stories such as "tragedy," "comedy," "farce," "melodrama," not to mention subspecies of all sorts—including "dirty jokes," "fairy tales," "mystery stories," "science fiction"—many of which have their own kinds of conventions and styles. Genres and repertoires are at hand and available to us as we plot. Our reading of a particular history may lead us to reach for conventional forms. So the foolish story we have assembled could fit into a tragic model or a comic model or, rather clearly, be shaped into a farce. Or we could regard the story as a fit with some stock repertoire; because Marvin and Miss Frobish appear to qualify as "little people," we might adopt a "moral little people, immoral power people, triumph of little people" repertoire. Inasmuch as there may be genres of sermons, as well as sermon repertoires, the same process may occur in sermon preparation.

Point-of-View. Though we have discussed point-of-view in the first part, here we ought to mention its powerful role in plotting. When we were constructing different plots for our odd story, each of the optional plots involved point-of-view choices. In one scheme, we chose to plot the story as immediate episodes, each occurring in the consciousness of a different character. In another, we located Miss Frobish in her family years later, and told the story as a series of flashbacks. In still another option, we adopted a "third-person-omniscient" point-of-view, entering John's mind in his examining room, overhearing Miss Frobish and Marvin on the library steps, and then viewing the ironic scene in Acapulco. Each of these decisions involved choices in point-of-view. In each plot there were shifts in point-of-view—attitudinal, temporal, shifts in "distance," and so on.

Logic of Movement. Plots travel. In telling a story, a narrator moves along, episode by episode. Underlying the movement of a plot is some sort of "logic" by which parts are assembled and travel. In some cases, as we have observed, the logic of a plot may be causal, as in A causes B causes C. However, a teller may choose to stress the chanciness of human affairs, in which case events may happen in a kind of non-sequitur logic, tumbling out in a random, even haphazard fashion. In one of the plots we wove, the logic of movement was a logic of recall in which Miss Frobish worked back in her own memory. So we can tell a story in many ways, but we will do so always with some sort of logic, entering the field of the story at a particular point and moving around the narrative field with some particular logic. Ultimately, logic of movement is controlled by the way in which a teller chooses to view life—as destined, as free, as a mishmash of impulses, as psychological warfare, or whatever. Sometimes the movement of a plot may be determined by a teller's own psyche—how often is a climax/catharsis pattern read into stories out of an author's own sexuality, or a problems-without-solutions plot formed as an enactment of an author's own depressive frustrations? Sermons may well demonstrate the same enactments.

Teller-Audience Interactions. Obviously, if no one were around to hear us speak we would soon tumble into silence; stories are told to an audience, even when the audience only exists in a teller's mind. Even as I write these pages I write with some sort of audience in mind. I may rewrite trying to find ways in which I can present material to your mind. I may belabor certain matters attempting to make them clear to you, my audience. Or I may become impish, dropping in wry comments which I suppose an audience may enjoy. In plotting, the process of unfolding a story always has some audience in mind. Thus, a sequence of episodes may be designed to heighten suspense, or to form moral awareness, or whatever; telling stories is never merely a matter of self-expression. We may analyze a plot, then, as a calculated strategy in which a teller, having an audience in mind, is deliberately shaping a plot to function in audience consciousness. Obviously, a consideration of audience is very much a part of sermon plotting.

We have listed some factors, only a few, involved in the forming of a plot from a story. As a process, plotting may happen quite unconsciously and, in fact, usually does. Every day of our lives, we tell about things and, thus, do plots. Always, the process involves some whole event in consciousness that is broken into a sequence in a meaningful way. And, always, the process is governed by a hermeneutical consciousness at work. In other words, though often unconscious, plotting is an act of interpretation that happens when hermeneutical consciousness addresses some implied audience.

Plot as a General Concept

The word "plot" may be applied to all kinds of hermeneutical acts; it is not restricted to stories. If I describe a visual scene such as a still-life painting, I will do so in some sequenced language. If I report a lively debate overheard, I will enter the debate at some point and, rearranging, try to get at the subject matters under discussion. If I speak of another person's personality, my speaking will be an ordered interpretation. All speaking is structural and, therefore, may be termed "plotting."

Sermons emerge from a preacher's consciousness and are for a particular audience. Within the preacher's consciousness is some whole field of meaning which has resulted from interpretation. Because preachers are not merely expressing themselves—gushing forth—but are concerned with the forming of a congregation's faith-consciousness, they will be fairly deliberate in designing the plots (moves) of their sermons. In plotting sermons, the same factors are involved; we select and we arrange in some sequence for speaking. Sermons have a logic of movement, may draw on stock repertoires, and shape from different points-of-view. Above all, the design of a sermon is never arbitrary: The sequence chosen will be an act of interpretation dictated by a *theology*. At minimum, we may describe sermons as "plotted" scenarios for consciousness. So much, by way of a glossary, for the term "plot."

INTENTIONS

The word "intentionality" is tossed around a lot these days. The word is slippery because it is used in many disciplines and, therefore, in many different ways. We will never understand preaching, much less the language of scripture, however, without grasping the notion of intentionality.

Notice what goes on when preachers preach. The preacher possesses a two-way consciousness: The preacher is conscious of a field of meaning formed by a text (or a lived experience, or a theological idea), but a preacher is also conscious of a congregation, a collection of people in a particular time, place, and cultural moment. In each aspect of the preacher's two-way consciousness, there is a hermeneutic involved. That is to say, the preacher is interpreting a field of meaning *and* interpreting a congregation in a situation. Thus, in preaching there is a two-way intending. To put it another way, the preacher is aiming consciousness toward a particular field of meaning, but also aiming consciousness toward a particular congregational mind. But the situation is not quite so simple; in addition, the preacher may have some purpose in mind, even if it is something as vague as mediation. So we can say that in the process of preaching, the preacher is also conscious of an aiming to do. We may now be in a position to explore the term "intentional" as it may relate to sermons.

Intending Of

The title of a fine novel of life in pre–World War II Berlin, *I Am a Camera*, can help us understand the word "intending." In many ways, human consciousness is like a camera lens. We focus on a field of consciousness. We can back up, widen out, and take in much, or we can draw near, narrow down, and attend to matters in detail. With the use of "filters" we can "highlight" certain structures of meaning, leaving others in "background." In consciousness, we can even determine "composition" and choose "angles of vision." All of us, as we perceive life, can say "I am a camera."

Today, we have instant cameras so that, after snapping a picture, we can see, at once, what we are seeing. We can, perhaps, understand language as a kind of instant-camera film, for quite often we discover what it is we are seeing by speaking. The rationalist notion, lurking in the communication model, that we have preformed thought which we can put into word containers for shipment to someone else's mind, is simply not true. We discover through speaking, almost as if language were a film aimed at reality by the camera lens of consciousness—a film which enables us through speaking to "see what we are seeing."

What do we mean by an intending *of*? We mean the aim of our focused consciousness; in a sense, what we have in view. What we have in view will not only show up in language but may actually shape language to a remarkable degree. Think back to the beginning of this chapter, and recall two people walking through a carnival midway and, then later, trying to put their experience into words. The whole experience in time and space constituted a field of consciousness caught in a "wide-focus" lens. As one of the walkers speaks, however, what is *brought out* is a complex economic pattern which may underlie the carnival; a lens has "filtered" a particular structure of meaning. Now we can begin to grasp what goes on in language. Intending *of* does not merely mean to have a subject matter (e.g., the carnival scene) in a field of consciousness, but to bring out a structure of meaning. The distinction is important. When we study biblical texts, for example, we can discern a subject matter, but what is intended will be a particular structure of meaning within the subject matter, or better, *through* the subject matter. The concept of bringing out or bringing into view is crucial not only for the study of scripture but for homiletic theory. When we preach, our sermons will focus on a field of understanding, something in view, but our sermons will *intend* a structure of meaning. With the language of preaching, we will be bringing out a structure of meaning in the consciousness of a congregation, and we will do so through the design of a sermon. In the story of our errant chiropractor, we were able to bring out different structures of meaning by different plots. So, sermons may have a field, a general subject matter, but within a field *intend* a particular structure of meaning.

The distinction between "field" and "intending" is important hermeneutically. When we preach from biblical texts we are not handing out bundles of subject matter, information drawn from the field of a biblical passage. Most congregations can get along satisfactorily without having to know much about the social world of the Hittites! In preaching from texts, we will be trying to get at an *intending of* within the language of the text. In doing so, we may bring into consciousness the mysterious Presence-in-Absence of God! Why else do we preach? When we study passages from scripture, we will limn a focus, a field, a subject matter, but, then, search out an *intending of* within the language of a passage. In preaching a sermon on the passage, we will be projecting a field in congregational consciousness and *intending* a structure of understanding—perhaps, the mystery of God-with-us.

Intending Toward

Speaking presumes listeners: Language is always addressed language. During World War II, when printing presses were closed down in some Middle European nations, many writers stopped writing because they lost the reality of a presumed audience for their work. Language intends toward some other consciousness. We discover an intending *of* in our own language not by talking to ourselves so much as speaking to some sort of "other," even if the other is no more than an imaginary audience. In speaking, there is always an intending *toward*.

Preaching is a peculiar speaking of language. Preaching is language aimed at communal consciousness, the consciousness of a congregation. What exactly is the congregational consciousness which preaching intends *toward?* Most books on preaching will picture, rather romantically, individuals in a congregation with individual agonies—the grieving widow; the desperate alcoholic; the middle-aged middle executive who, though glad-handing, is eaten by an inner sense of "I'll never make it big"; the teenybopper fascinated by, yet frightened of, sexuality; an old-age person calendar-counting dying days; and so on. Congregations are comprised of individuals with individual pathos, and ministers wander among them with continual wonderment.

But, oddly enough, individuals are *not* the congregation we intend toward in preaching. We do not speak to particular human beings in particular situations so much as to a world in consciousness or, better, ways of understanding the world in consciousness. Please do not suppose that we are turning away from persons toward an abstract idea; we are not. The world

295

in consciousness happens to be where we live, and our understandings of the world in consciousness directly relate to our agonies. While it may be helpful to bring to mind particular people in situations during the preparation of sermons, actually the language of preaching is shaped for *common* consciousness.

Of course, the ways in which we understand the world in consciousness may not be all that different or personally distinctive. After all, we are children of a particular time and place, of a cultural epoch. Therefore, we share a "cultural formulation" shaped by common language and common myths, symbols, and images. Within the broad notion of a cultural mind are subcultural "attitudes," "isms," "conventions," "ologies," "perspectives," and the like. We can speak of a congregational consciousness which, in spite of differences, is communal. No wonder sociologists of religion can paste labels on congregations—"post-ghetto upward-escalating Catholic" or "Middle American middle-class Protestant"—and by labels indicate shared values, attitudes, and a range of convictions. When preaching, preachers may have in mind what might be described as an "inchoate gestalt" of congregational consciousness, a consciousness in which, naturally, the preacher participates. Though we may be intimately acquainted with individual members of a congregation, when we preach we tend to address a communal consciousness —some common way of understanding the world in consciousness.

We should not suppose that we have defined congregational consciousness with great clarity before we speak. We have deliberately used an odd, cumbersome phrase, "inchoate gestalt," to acknowledge the imprecision of our awareness. In preparing sermons, weighing language and considering strategies, we will discover the consciousness toward which we are intending. Our preaching may *bring out* structures of meaning that are hidden, unacknowledged assumptions that live in congregational consciousness. As a result, through our preaching, people may come to understand themselves, their tacit faiths and unnoticed social attitudes, the deeps of mystery within their lives. While we may have a gestalt in our field of consciousness, we *intend toward* structures of understanding within the field. In the language of preaching there will always be an *intending toward*.

Though we have been discussing preaching, we must acknowledge that in all human language there will be an intending toward. No wonder clever rhetoricians can describe the "mind" of an unknown audience simply by studying a speech. Or, again, perceptive biblical scholars will conjecture a world in consciousness being addressed by examining a scriptural passage. By spotting vocabulary, rhetorical strategies, and the like, in the Corinthian correspondence, we can construct an understanding of the world that must have been in the consciousness of the Corinthian congregation. Whenever we speak we do so with some sort of "implied audience" in mind, whether we are telling jokes or making small talk or shaping sermons. The implied audience we intend toward is never a collection of images of particular people in particular situations. No, we intend toward a consciousness, a particular understanding of the world in consciousness.

Intending to Do

Older homiletics worried over the purpose of sermons. Some homiletic texts went so far as to insist that ministers write out a single, clear sentence stating a purpose for each sermon. Unfortunately, human consciousness is never neatly focused, and sermons seldom so simple. What do we mean by intending *to do*, the performative nature of language?

Obviously, some overall definition of preaching will tend to determine how preaching is done. For example, preaching may be defined as conversion, or as an imparting of revealed truths, or as solving life's problems, or as providing inspirational uplift, or as forming faith-consciousness. These general orientations will produce different styles as well as different kinds of sermon design. If conversion is understood as a stereotyped emotional happening, sermons may be designed to travel through stages, from a weighty sense of sin, to news of Jesus, to repentance and believing. In a similar way, sermons that work from a notion of revealed truth may be heavy with scriptural citation. All we are supposing is that there will be some connection between definitions of preaching and the kinds of sermons preached.

As obviously, *what* we intend will affect sermon style and design. In preaching, we are always trying to bring out some structure of meaning within a field of consciousness. For example, we may focus on Calvary and be trying to bring out christological meaning in the cry of dereliction. As a result, our style will scarcely be jocular; instead, we will speak with somber intensity. What is more, because we are viewing a stopped scene—Christ strung up on a cross—our sermon will not be designed as an unfolding narrative. So, *what* we are intending will shape our sermons and, to a large extent, determine style.

Likewise, the consciousness we are intending *toward* will influence sermon strategy; congregations will dictate our intending *to do*. If, for example, we are preaching James's scathing critique of wealth—"Come now, you rich, weep and howl for the miseries that are coming upon you"—to a congregation that could be described as contentedly affluent, we will have to shape strategies so that our sermon will confront and, possibly, convert a particular understanding of the world in consciousness. Similarly, if we are to preach

Paul's call to freedom in Galatians to a group of uptight moral/legal folk, our strategies will have to be carefully planned. Clearly, the congregation we address will determine *how* we speak, our homiletic designs and style.

Thus, we can conceive of sermon purpose as a line of strategy drawn between an intending *of* and an intending *toward*. In sermons, we are not merely forming consciousness but, inevitably, *re*forming and *trans*forming consciousness. While preachers may well entertain some overall purpose in preaching—conversion, inspiration, explication, whatever—the actual intending *to do* of any particular sermon is a dynamic strategy worked out in between an intending *of* and an intending *toward*. Strategy will show up in the sequence of moves we design, our plotted scenario, and in the style we employ for different moves. Every sermon will involve an intending *to do*.

How does intending *to do* show up in language? How is style ordered by intentional purpose? When we speak we do so in conventional "forms." For example, if someone says to us, "Didya' hear the one about the traveling salesman and the farmer's daughter . . . ," we will brace ourselves to hear a dirty joke. (In Britain, it will usually be the bishop and the actress, a testimony to the pervasiveness of the Anglo-Catholic tradition!) Or if we receive a letter that begins, "Mr. and Mrs. Smith respectfully request your presence at . . . ," we know an invitation will be forthcoming. Or, again, suppose we hear a story beginning "Once upon a time there was a beautiful lady who sat on a bench which, when the sun shone, seemed made of gold . . . ," we will anticipate a fairy tale. All these examples are conventional language "forms," each shaped in a particular style. Their number could be multiplied because, in all our conversations, we speak in forms—a form for casual meeting on the street, a form for passing on gossip, a form for soft-selling a product, a form for saying prayers. Stock forms are helpful; they orient listeners, they determine hermeneutical consciousness, and they even predispose response.

Of course, we can be crossed up. Suppose a fairy tale which began, "Once upon a time, there was a beautiful lady who sat on a bench which, when the sun shone, seemed made of gold . . . ," continued, ". . . and her name was Tammy Schmerling, 2500 Grand Concourse, Bronx, New York"—the unhistorical language of fairy tale would be blown to bits by specific historical reference. Or imagine that we receive an invitation, reading, "Mr. and Mrs. Smith respectfully request your presence at a tea party for God," the intrusion of transcendent reference in a language designed for a social occasion might be quite alarming. Obviously, Christian preaching employs conventional forms because it addresses human beings in a human world. Christian preaching, however, seeks to bring out unconventional meaning, namely, news of

God-with-us. So, again and again, preaching will mix styles and "break" forms, producing a most peculiar diction, a diction designed to wedge a word of God in conventional language. Disruptions of style will display intending *to do* in sermons.

What about sermon design? Sermons are a sequence of plotted moves put together in a scenario by some kind of strategy. Scenarios are also ruled by convention, from familiar plots in films to well-worn conversational patterns. The reason little children will beg to hear a story over and over is that they know the plot, and are delighted when expectations are met. As adults, we are no less delighted; familiar plots reinforce our common values. Scenarios can take odd unexpected turns, however; they can be disrupted. Imagine how an audience watching *Hamlet* would react if, instead of dying, Hamlet were to stand amid the last-act carnage, dust off his hands and exclaim, "Well, there's a good job done!" An audience would be appalled. Or, again, think how we would react to a western movie if, just as hero and villain were pacing toward a "shoot-out," the hero were to drop his gun and remark, "Why are we doing this dumb shoot-out stuff?" The conversational scenarios in which we live may also be disrupted. Suppose, that, in the midst of a "nice to meetya', howareya' doing" conversational gambit, one of the chatterers were to exclaim, "Hear the Word of the Lord!" Conventional scenarios in stories, speeches, and casual conversation (and, yes, in sermons), are systems that are designed *to do*—they enable relating, they approve values, they even tend to shape behavior patterns. But, familiar plots can be disrupted by unexpected intrusions or atypical turns in event. Because God's purposes are invariably "other" than our expectations, sermon scenarios will involve a transformation of conventional plots.

We have noticed two features of language: (1) Language is performative —it is shaped in conventions of style and sequence by social custom; (2) Language can be "broken" or transformed when conventional patterns reckon with the unconventional. There are, nevertheless, conventional patterns of preaching; there is familiar "pulpit style" and there are "stock" systems of sermon design. No wonder satiric comedians have such fun spoofing sermons! Of course, even if we are not trapped in conventions of "religious speaking," because we address human beings, we are bound to employ social language conventions—familiarities of plot and style are built into our cultural mind. If we never break out of stock ways of speaking, however, the gospel will be reduced to an echo of conventional human wisdoms. Congregations may well approve; like little children who beg for a familiar story, they will be satisfied if expectations are met. But if we are trying to bring out meaning from Christian symbols and, indeed, to display the reality of being-saved-in-the-world, we will be bound to disrupt scenarios and to mix styles: Christian preaching is transformational. The language of preaching will always be odd, a language of disrupted scenarios and broken forms, as sermons seek *to do*.

Primary and Secondary Intentions

We have argued that a sermon's intending *to do* is a line of strategy drawn between what is being brought out and structures of meaning in congregational consciousness, a consciousness crammed with social scenarios and conventions of style. Sermons are shaped between *what* and *who*. So, *primary* intention will be on display in a sermon's structural design and mix of style.

Nevertheless, most sermons will incorporate what may be described as *secondary* intentions. While a basic intending *to do* will shape a sermon, there are often extra agenda that, like subplots in a drama, will figure in preaching. Secondary intentions are sometimes subordinate sections in moves or even "asides" tossed into sermons. In passages of scripture, secondary intentions are frequently labeled "redactions." For example, when Luke tells a story of the healing of a centurion's slave (Luke 7:1–10), his *primary* purpose is a contrast between two kinds of faith—faith that expects God to acknowledge "merit" ("He is worthy to have you do this for him") and a faith that merely begs grace ("Lord . . . I am not worthy . . . but say the word, and let my servant be healed"). Nevertheless, Luke's *secondary* intention may be an approval of Gentile faith and a demonstration of Jesus' concern for Gentiles. The primary purpose of the passages shows up in structural design and in the contrast that is built into dialogue; thus, the primary purpose could have been achieved without any reference to Jew and Gentile. Obviously, however, Luke has an extra agendum. Such extra agenda will almost invariably show up in our sermons. Sometimes secondary intentions can even enlarge so as to displace primary purpose, thus distorting sermon design.

Where do secondary intentions come from? We have suggested that primary intention is a line of strategy drawn between *what* is being brought out of a field of consciousness and *structures* of meaning within a congregational world in consciousness. Notice, field of consciousness and world in consciousness are wide concepts, wider than what is being brought out, and structures of meaning. Secondary intentions happen when extras in the wider field or world are picked out and articulated. So, if we were to preach on Luke 7:1–10, we might include in our sermon some comment on first-century Jew-Gentile tensions, likening them to prejudices we harbor today. The comment would probably produce either an extra superfluous move or an obvious aside in our sermon. Sometimes, secondary intention will be woven through a sermon from beginning to end. All we are doing is signaling a distinction between *primary* intending to do and secondary intendings, a distinction which may be helpful for the study of scripture and the designing of sermons.

Plot and Intention

Plots are determined by intention. Plotting is never an arbitrary art or a matter of personal whim. Instead, plots are decided by what we intend to bring out, by the world we intend toward, and, of course, by our intending to do. Plots *are* strategy. Moreover, plots of sermons are theological/homiletic strategy. When we preach, we address a world in consciousness populated by conventional styles and scenarios. Again and again, we will design sermons that break forms and disrupt expected scenarios as the meanings of the gospel collide with conventional worldly understandings. We will speak in ordinary, everyday, linguistic patterns, if for no other reason than to be intelligible. But, we will stretch language toward mysteries of God-with-us. Likewise, we will design sermon scenarios that relate to common expectations, but, again and again, turn plots toward the new, quite surprising purposes of God. All preaching is performative, an intending *to do.* The purpose of any particular sermon, however, *cannot* be stated in some clear single sentence as older homiletic texts suggested. Rather, the intending of a sermon is a line of strategy drawn between an intending *of* and an intending *toward.* Proclamation is an intentional act.

PLOT AND INTENTION IN SCRIPTURE

When preachers preach from scripture, they are engaged in a peculiar process: They replot plots and, to some extent, reintend intentional language. In order to study how plot and intention may interrelate, let us turn to a scriptural text. Is it possible that all scripture is a plotted language intending *to do*, a performative language? Let us glance at the interweaving of plot and intention in a particular biblical passage, Rom. 12:1–8:

A. [1]Therefore, I appeal to you, my family, by the mercies of God, to present your bodies as a living sacrifice, holy and acceptable to God—that is your "spiritual worship."

B. [2]Don't fit in to the way of the world now, but be transformed by new understanding, so you may demonstrate God's will—good, acceptable, and perfect. [3]By grace given me, I'm telling every one of you not to be "high-minded" in thinking of yourselves, but be "tough-minded" in thinking, according to the share of faith God has given you.

C. [4]For, just as in one body there are many parts, with no part having the same function, [5]so we, though many, are one body in Christ, and joined each to each other.

D. ⁶But, we have different gifts to use, according to the grace given us: as prophets, in prophesying; ⁷as servants, in serving; as teachers, in teaching; ⁸as preachers, in preaching; as givers, in generosity; as leaders, with leadership; as agents of compassion, with cheerfulness.

We have here a language intending *toward* and intending *to do*. A commentator has suggested that the phrase in v. 1, "spiritual worship" (variously translated), was a proud slogan of the mystery cults ("Our worship is 'spirrrr-rritual,' whereas you Christians fool around with plebian things such as bread, wine and ethics!"). If so, Paul may be addressing a congregation much drawn to "spiritual," "intelligent" worship, and eager to turn away from earthly affairs. Paul's message to them is "present your *bodies*," using terms, "holy and acceptable," associated with animal sacrifice. Then, as a shocker, he drops in the phrase, "that *is* your 'spiritual worship.'" Clearly, here is a language intending *toward* a particular understanding of the world in consciousness, and intending *to do*.

The next section (B) features two sentences in a row with parallel construction, each using an emphatic "but" *(alla)*. In such a construction, the second sentence is normally an interpretative restatement of the first sentence. "The way of the world now" is equated with a "high-minded" but spurious spirituality, and transformation involves turning to a "tough-minded," modest view of themselves as members of the body of Christ. The word "transformed" *(metamorphosis)* was a favorite term in mystery cults. So, once more, Paul deliberately undercuts his congregation by hoisting them on their own vocabulary. They are to be transformed, not into a "spiritual intelligence," but into task-accepting members of community doing the *bodily* work of Christ in the world. Again, can we not spot an intending *toward* and an intending *to do?*

In section D, after a general statement, "We are all one body," Paul lists what may seem to be rather earthly tasks in the life of the community, saying in effect, "Well, if you can teach church school, do so; if you have a bundle of cash, dole it out"—a tough-minded recital. The passage, beginning to end, is an intentional system.

What about the plot of the passage? We can summarize plot in the following sequence:

A. In view of God in Christ Jesus, offer your bodily selves—that *is* "spiritual worship."

B. Therefore, don't go along with the world's "high-minded" nonsense—a self-inflating "spirituality." But, be "tough-minded" in your self-understanding.

C. After all, we are bodily members of Christ.

D. So, if you can teach, teach; . . .

What lies behind Paul's thinking? To answer the question, we will have to chase back through Romans in order to make sense of the initial "therefore" with which the passage begins. Prior to chapter 12, Paul has marveled over God's purposes for Jew and Gentile, in the light of Christ's reconciling, sacrificial death. What does Paul have in mind by "therefore"? Paul probably intends an analogy between God's *bodily* self-giving in Christ, and the church's *bodily* service. So, beneath the language, there is an intending *of* Christ's sacrificial life and death as a model for the church, a model which, rather clearly, is in tension with the Romans' lust for "spirrrrritual" detach-ment. If we study Paul's plot, we sense that he begins with a "therefore" vision of Christ's bodily self-sacrifice and then debunks spiritual pretensions, before ending with a somewhat practical list of tasks. The plot is a strategy.

Ask an odd question: How else might Paul have plotted his strategy? He might possibly have begun with a description of the functioning of a Christian community, then described the lust for "spirrrrritual things," then called to mind Christ's sacrifice, before concluding with a call to be transformed. He did not. Instead, he has deliberately designed a "step-down" plot structure: In view of Christ, do not have "high" fantasies, but "get low," and serve in bodily ways. Because Paul is asking for a "comedown" in attitudes, he has designed a plot to match his purpose; a plot which, incidentally, may hint at a way of preaching. The passage displays an astonishing interaction of plot and intention.

When preachers preach from scripture, they replot plots and reintend intentions for a new world in consciousness. If a world intended in scripture does not appear to be alive in our age, other, often analogous, states of mind may be at hand. Though, in fact, a world-denying, self-enhancing spirituality is still with us, if it were not, we could still preach an intending *of* Christ's sacrificial death toward the consciousness of a congregation. Always, we address the strange double-mindedness of being-saved-in-the-world. Out of complex intending, we plot sermons.

19.
Structuring

Plato once went to poets to find out how they wrote their poems. He was appalled. As a group, poets were tongue-tied when it came to explaining themselves. Preachers may be as inarticulate about preaching. The process of moving from understanding to speaking seems to be a mystery. Preachers will toss around words such as "creative" or "intuitive" or "imaginative," artistic terms that are less than helpful. Though preaching may well be "creative" and may draw on a playful "imagination," preaching is *not* an art. In preaching, self-expression is disciplined by both the content of the gospel and a concern for the congregation. After all, preaching *is* mediation. Preaching lives in the middle of the Great Commandment; it loves God and neighbors. Therefore, preaching is anxious to understand Christian symbols and equally anxious over crass matters of communication. Though preachers may be as inarticulate as poets, we do need to get at what goes on in the shift from understanding to sermon; we need to specify a creative process.

We have said that preaching involves plotting. Preachers begin the process, after study, with a whole meaning in consciousness. Somehow, they must break the whole meaning into a scenario of moves for speaking. Such replotting is a process that passes through stages: (1) *forming* a basic structure; (2) *developing* the structure; and, finally, (3) putting the developed structure into a *script* for preaching. While every preacher will work in some particular way, stages in the process cannot be bypassed. No preacher is smart enough to read a passage from scripture and then, impromptu, get up and speak a *good* sermon. The process of sermon composition requires a disciplined work of mind, and is bound to be done in stages.

Busy pastors, often overloaded with parish responsibilities, crave some quick-fix way of preaching. Catholic priests, whose parishes are often ten times larger than average Protestant congregations, are particularly, and understandably, desperate. How can sermon preparation be streamlined and squeezed into a scant hour or two? Of course, in part, the demand may be an index of priorities. When preachers want some quick trip to a sermon, they are sometimes confessing their lack of commitment to preaching, or (perhaps) to thinking! They have decided priorities: Caring for people is primary, church management is necessary, and involvement in the "higher courts of the church" is required, so please pass out a fast, easy sermon-production system.

But first and foremost we are ministers of Word and Sacrament, and other parish activities derive their meaning from this, our essential calling. Bluntly, there is no short cut to sermon preparation. No human being can churn out rapid-fire creativity; the process depends on thinking, often unhurried thinking, imagination, and technical skill. Quick sermons are almost always *bad* sermons. Ultimately the issue has to do with priorities, and the question of priorities goes back to a theological understanding of ministry. Functionaries never have time; ministers of the gospel do. Moving from a whole field of meaning in consciousness to a sermon is a staged process that is bound to take time. In God's love, there is always time.

EXEGESIS AND HOMILETIC ANALYSIS

Ministers begin with study of a scripture passage or of a situation. Any public address requires the researching of a subject matter, because speaking off the top of our heads is seldom useful. So, the first step in sermon preparation is hermeneutical work, a work of understanding. To get at the process of sermon preparation, let us imagine we are preaching a passage from scripture, Matt. 2:1–12, the story of the Wisemen and Herod at the time of Jesus' birth.

We need not detail the process of study; most ministers have training in exegesis. Ministers will check a text, read a text, and study background material in Bible dictionaries, commentaries, and the like. In addition, however, we suggest that ministers take time to analyze the passage as plot, doing a semi-structural analysis. Let us see what the passage in Matthew presents:

> v. 1 Introduces, in order, the main characters to be featured: Jesus, King Herod, and Wisemen.
>
> v. 2 The Wisemen ask, "Where is he?" They have seen the star and have come to worship the new king.
>
> v. 3 Herod is distressed, perhaps threatened. Oddly enough, he asks the same question that the Wisemen asked: "Where is he?"
>
> vv. 4–6 Herod consults religious scholars, chief priests and scribes, regarding the Messiah's birthplace. Drawing on scripture, they answer, "Bethlehem."
>
> vv. 7–8 A double irony! Herod, interviewing the Wisemen, tells them that he too wishes to worship the newborn king!

vv. 9–11 The star leads the Wisemen to Jesus. They fall down and worship. Then they open up their symbolic gifts of gold, frankincense, and myrrh.

v. 12 An epilogue: The Wisemen, having come in v. 2, now return but not, of course, to King Herod.

After outlining the plot it is usually helpful to read the plot from a literary standpoint to see its design. We notice that v. 1 and v. 12 are introduction and conclusion. In between, we have a series of scenes:

A. Wisemen ask "Where?"
B. Herod's reaction
C. Information from priests and scribes
D. Herod's instructions
E. Wisemen worship and offer gifts

The passage is artfully designed to display irony. The Wisemen are searching for the Messiah in order to worship, whereas Herod is searching in order to kill. Irony occurs as Herod's actions parallel those of the Wisemen. "Where is he?" the Wisemen ask, and Herod echoes their question when consulting his religious advisors. "We are come to worship," the Wisemen announce, and again, Herod reiterates their words, ". . . that I too may come and worship him." A double irony occurs as the religious leaders of Israel serve Herod's purpose and, what is more, do so by turning to scripture! Finally, the passage features a wondrous scene when, star-led, the Wisemen bow down and offer their gifts to the child. Matthew seems to be saying that here is a proper response to the Messiah's arrival—oddly enough, by Gentiles. It does seem fairly obvious that Matthew's plot is designed to bring out an ironic contrast between Herod and the Wisemen, as well as to portray an appropriate response to Jesus Christ.

Underlying the plot is a field of theological meaning. Obviously, Matthew has written the story in light of the cross. Though Herod did not manage to kill the child, later Pilate and religious leaders did: Jesus Christ was crucified. Matthew seems to suggest that while the coming of Christ is promise for some, for others it is a terrible threat. The Messiah, who comes to usher in a new age of God, the "kingdom of heaven," is bound to threaten established power, including established religious power. Thus, Herod, "and all Jerusalem with him," is threatened. However, for those who seek liberation, who long for a new social order, who are ever on the lookout for God in the world, the coming of the Messiah is very good news indeed. The Wisemen do what the whole human world should do, they bow down in adoration and offer themselves to the Christ. We have studied the passage as a pattern of plot and intention, and we have attempted to get at a theological field of meaning that may underlie the passage.

Along the way, in our minds, another kind of process has been occurring; almost unconsciously, we have been drawing analogies with our own world of experience. When we read of the Wisemen searching for a child-king, do we not grasp their longing, sensing something more than wistful in their cry, "Where is he?" At deep levels we may be drawing lines between the biblical story and structures of longing in our own world, indeed, in our own lives. And how do we get at Herod's fierce anxiety? In a world where political upheaval is an everyday event, do we not grasp the threat of a "newborn king" to old entrenched power? And, surely, when Wisemen bow down to worship, do we not associate their praise with worship in our own community? Merely to read and understand a text means that we are, however unconsciously, drawing on analogies in our own experience.

Exegetical study of a text, as well as plot analysis, the delineation of a theological field, the drawing of analogies, all together produce in our consciousness a whole field of understanding.

THE FIELD OF UNDERSTANDING

A few years ago, a number of books were issued on biblical preaching. The books seemed to suggest that there was a direct progression from text to exegesis to sermon. The notion is not true. Preachers do not move directly from exegesis to sermon. Instead, they move from exegesis to a *field of understanding,* and then to the production of a sermon. The field of understanding is not an original meaning at all, but rather, an understanding of *contemporary* meaning with the text somewhat in background. The field of understanding structured by Matt. 2:1–12 may include the following component ideas: (1) In our world there are longings for a new order, for salvation, which we may sense in our own lives. (2) Entrenched power—social, economic, political, religious—will resist new order, seeking to destroy any new "Messiah." (3) The church tends to go along with established power. (4) Nevertheless, Christians are called to bow down and offer themselves to the "Messiah"— Christ Jesus. (5) Jesus was crucified by entrenched power. (6) But Jesus is risen, and is still both promise and threat. Notice that the movement of the text is still lurking in the structured field of understanding but that meanings are *contemporary;* they have been formed in the present tense by analogy. Somehow, the task is to break our whole field of understanding into the design for a sermon.

THE BASIC STRUCTURE

To produce a sermon, we will first need to construct a basic, stripped-down structural design. Scripture passages produce different fields of understanding, and, therefore, demand different basic designs; there are *no* stock patterns into which meaning can invariably be stuffed. There are, of course, familiar sermon repertoires, conventional patterns of sermon design at hand, conveniently filed on shelves of our minds—for example, categorical development, thesis-antithesis-synthesis, point-making didactic patterns, dramatic monologues—all of which we have heard preached from pulpits. Such stock patterns may float to the surface of our minds and present themselves as serviceable. Stock sermon "outlines" are not much help, however; they invariably distort or truncate fields of understanding. Our problem is how to break a new plot from a field of understanding prompted by Matt. 2:1-12. All speaking involves sequence, a movement from A to B to C to D, and so on. How can we break a whole field of meaning into a sequence, a scenario for preaching? Some factors may be singled out:

The Point of Entry

If we are trying to put down a basic structure for speaking, we will have to locate a beginning. We are not referring to an introduction; introductions cannot be developed until a basic structure has been determined. No, we are trying to fix on a first major "idea," or unit of meaning, in a basic sermon design. Where do we enter the field of understanding that has formed in our consciousness? Obviously, the scene at the manger has been kept by Matthew until the end of the passage, where, climactically, it stands full of wonder, adoration, and self-offering. As a result, the scene is probably not a good starting place, although, presumably, it could be done. Likewise, in replotting, we cannot easily begin with Herod's conversation with religious leaders, for the consultation depends on Herod's threatened reaction, and Herod's reaction rests on the appearance of the Wisemen. Besides, if we began with Herod's consultation, our sermon might start out with a somewhat cynical discussion of self-serving religious establishments—hardly a palatable subject for most congregations. So we may decide to begin with the Wisemen chasing their star. Now, we are not picking out a verse from a text with which to begin, for, remember, we have already pushed past original meaning to a *contemporary* field of understanding. No, in selecting the Wisemen, we are actually deciding to begin with our world's contemporary longing for a new order of things, which we may sense is both social and personal. We are choosing to begin with the sense of longing that echoes in the Wisemen's question, "Where is he?"

Picking out a point of entry is not always so obvious. Particularly when preaching non-narrative passages, the question can be quite up in the air and uncertain. In considering the question, we must look at both (1) the plot of the original passage, and (2) the kinds of contemporary experience with which we are dealing. Experiences alien to congregational consciousness may be difficult to discuss at the outset of a sermon. As for the original plot, some ideas or episodes may be subservient and, therefore, impossible starts, for example, Herod's consultation. But when we first begin to set down a sermon design in sequence, we must decide on a point of entry—not to a text, but to the field of understanding that has been formed in consciousness.

The Logic of Movement

Where do we go next? Frequently, a decision with regard to the point of entry will determine the flow of subsequent ideas. But there are other considerations. For example, if a preacher is preaching a narrative, or even a semi-narrative such as the Wisemen/Herod passage, *elements in the story* may dictate a plot. If we had begun our basic structure with Herod's threatened reaction to the arrival of Christ, we would have to turn back and discuss the Wisemen, not only to provide another option with regard to Christ, but to bring out the irony of the passage. We have begun, however, with the world's longing for a savior. Thus, to allow irony to emerge, we will inevitably have to turn and look at King Herod. What we do in forming a basic structure is to keep referring to the field of understanding where there are elements of meaning still available.

There is another side to the question of "logic of movement" that has to do with *the way we think*. Sermon scenarios must "travel" in a way that is *natural* to human consciousness. How do human beings put ideas together? How do we shift from one notion to another, naturally? We assemble ideas in many ways—by association, by extension, by contrast, by microcosm/macrocosm logic, and so forth. So, the sequence of a sermon will be influenced not only by the shape of biblical material but, crucially, by ways in which human consciousness functions. Thus, if we begin by talking of human longings for a new order, we can turn, and, by a logic of *contrast*, discuss rejection of a new order. The logic of connection—contrast—is natural to human consciousness. So, if our first basic structure sentences read:

1. "Where is he?" asked the Wisemen. They belong in our world for they sought a Savior.

then, our second sentence may follow:

2. "Where is he?" asked Herod, but he wanted to kill. Entrenched power will always be threatened by God.

One of the notions formed by the passage in our consciousness was the eyebrow-lifting idea that, when Herod called for help, the religious institution was happy to oblige. In mind, we may have greeted the idea with a rueful, if cynical, honesty: "Yes, we religious types will usually sell out for a little social status." Perhaps analogies of experience came to mind, and we recalled the Protestant churches under Hitler, or the Catholic church's endorsements of Franco in Spain, or more recent visits of the Religious Right to the White House. Obviously, the idea is subordinate to a threatened King Herod and, therefore, must follow. So we may add a third gambit:

3. Well, guess who Herod turned to? To us religious people, that's who.

In our study of the passage, we found that Matthew was probably foreshadowing the cross. In the birth narrative, we have more than a strong hint of Calvary yet to come. Of course, the minute we think of Calvary, we remember that Matthew would not have bothered to write a gospel if it were not for resurrection! As a result, we may find ourselves scribbling two more sentences, such as:

4. Well, it worked: Christ was crucified.
5. But, good news, Christ rose again, and still comes as threat and promise.

As we studied the passage, we came to realize that Matthew, when he described the manger scene, was not merely telling a story of Wisemen; he was advocating an appropriate response to Jesus Christ, namely, worship and offering. Matthew devotes three verses to a description of the scene in order to give the notion of worship full force. So, the final move in our basic structure is predetermined by the intention of the passage; Matt. 2:1–12 is, in a way, a call to worship. Our basic structure now assembled is as follows:

1. "Where is he?" asked the Wisemen. They belong in our world for they were looking for a savior.

2. "Where is he?" asked Herod, but he wanted to kill. Entrenched power will always be threatened by God.

3. Well, guess who Herod turned to? To us religious people, that's who!

4. Well, eventually Christ was crucified.

5. But he rose again and still comes to us as threat and promise.

6. So how do we respond? We worship and we offer ourselves.

If you will notice, the basic structure has been written out *as if talking to someone.* Clearly, it is not a list of topics or of abstract subject matter; its style is almost conversational. The strategy is deliberate and, indeed, crucial. While each conversational phrase may indicate a subject matter, the phrases in sequence travel along like a conversation. Earlier we observed that the movement of a basic structure ought to be "natural" to human consciousness. The use of a conversational style will enable us to assess the naturalness of our logic of movement. A topical list of subject matters will always obscure connective logic and, eventually, produce a cumbersome sermon. We are *not* making static "points," rather, we are designing a movement of thought in and for consciousness. A basic structure, put down conversationally, should move naturally.

Though we began by studying a biblical passage, the basic structure is contemporary. Because we are referring to a story, some sentences double, picking up a biblical citation and a contemporary meaning. If we were not retaining hints of biblical narrative, our sentences would be single and contemporary. But, above all, the basic structure does not split between a lengthy talking about a biblical passage and then a tedious drawing of contemporary "application." Though such sermon designs are familiar, they are, in fact, artificial. Remember, the text has *already* produced a contemporary field of understanding. We are not, therefore, breaking a text into a sermon, but rather replotting a field of understanding into a sermon—a *contemporary* sermon. Again, the use of contemporary conversational style in the basic structure will tend to ensure contemporary meaning.

How can we "test" a basic structure? The testing is quite simple: Can the basic structure be read *out loud* in sequence and make sense? By "making sense," we mean (1) Does one phrase follow another "naturally" without strain or non sequitur? (2) Are all phrases simple, noncompound sentences (except with narrative passages)? (3) When read aloud does the entire sequence seem to come together in consciousness and make a meaning? The test is easy to apply. If any of the three conditions are not met, a preacher may have to go back and try again. Getting a basic structure down may seem unimportant, but it is not. Ultimately, it is the basic structure that determines the moves in a sermon. Basic structures should be clear, have a natural, logical progression, and should come together to form a field of meaning in congregational consciousness.

We have described the forming of a basic structure as if it were a plodding, rational process. Usually, it is not. Often, a preacher will be aware of a clear, structured field of understanding in consciousness, and, as a result, will simply write out a basic structure in a matter of seconds by what may seem an act of immediate intuition. But, at other times, preachers may sketch a basic structure many times before achieving a satisfactory design. Often, the problem is caused by the fact that the field of understanding is not adequately formed, and, as a result, the text needs further study. Or, there may be a conflict between "intentions" in the language of the text and the preacher's own "intentions"; the preacher may want to do with the text what the text itself does not want to do! Or, the field of understanding may simply be theologically complex. Nevertheless, in creating a basic design, whatever its shape, the preacher is mediating a field of understanding to a congregational consciousness. The first stage in sermon development is the designing of a basic structure.

AN EXPANDED SKETCH

Obviously, a series of short sentences on a page is not a sermon. Basic structure is no more than an unfleshed design. The basic structure is very much like a sculptor's armature, a twisted-wire stick-figure on which to wind clay for a human figure. While the wire armature is crucial and will, in fact, determine the pose of the final sculpted figure (thus, sculptors will fuss and fuss to get the armature just right!), it is scarcely a finished statue. In sculpture, a second stage involves winding clay around the wire structure to form the rough shape of a figure. In producing sermons, a second stage is similar—we wind ideas around our basic sentence structure to move toward the rough shape of a sermon. We will call this second stage a sermon *sketch*.

The trick in developing a sermon sketch is to expand each single sentence in order by putting together theological understanding and lived experience. In part 1 we have discussed move development at length; we will avoid repetition. Two warnings may be in order, however. First, we are not trying to produce a finished sermon, one section at a time, from the sentences of the basic structure. Instead, we are trying to "flesh out," in a rough way, the *whole* structure. Imagine a sculptor, having built a stick-figure armature, trying to produce a perfect arm before going on to do a perfect leg! The result would be a statue quite out of proportion. No, the sculptor will wind wet clay on the armature, roughing out the *whole* figure in proportion, before going on to "finishing." So, we cannot move from basic structure to a finishing up of sermon sections one at a time. Second, at this stage, a preacher will wish to avoid any final language—just as a sculptor will keep clay moist so as to freely change, reshape, form. So a preacher will not want to let language "harden" into final phrasing, or illustrations fix before the whole sketch is overviewed. As a sample, here is a transcript of the rough notes which were a sketch for an actual sermon on the Wisemen/Herod passage, a sketch which, incidentally, had to be corrected severely:

1. Kings: "Where is he?" Searching for a savior. Belong in the twentieth century. Read the headlines: Who's going to solve energy crisis? Who will bring peace to Middle East? Who will straighten out economy—rich and poor? (*Illustra-*

tion: "Anybody straighten out mess, we'd elect God!") Maybe the way it was in first century. Wisemen came, searching: "Where is he?"

2. Move closer to home: Look in own lives. Need someone to straighten us out. Everybody in crisis: Youth, midlife, old-age crises. Complicated lives: If only we could simplify. Cash. Sex. How get back to simple life? "Where is he?" Maybe why TV cults attract. "Where?" "Shepherds had an angel, wisemen had a star, but what have I a little child to lead me . . ." "Where is he?"

3. Of course, that's what Herod said: "Where is he?" But he wanted to kill! Was threatened. Christ is personal threat. We want to run our own lives. Fear of change and intrusion on freedom. (*Illustration:* See Scherer sermon.) Who on earth wants God, anyway?

4. Who did Herod turn to? Theologians and scripture scholars, of course. Turned to church. Face it, we'd be honored. Like B. Graham in White House. Two-way trap: Herod used religion and religion charmed to be used. Church and Hitler. Perhaps because we want to get in on the power. Herod: "Let me know so I can worship." Nope, he wanted to kill.

5. Well, the little baby grew up and got killed. Not Herod and religious leaders, but Pilate and chief priests. Story of Christ's life—opposition. He came and was destroyed. (Check poem: "Did the rude beam of your stable cross you?") Not Herod; but Christ was born and destroyed.

6. But he lives! Easter. Still he comes to us. Comes as Christmas cards, or as star on tree. News of him still in the world. He is still threat and promise. Herod and Wisemen in us all. Hope for salvation but urge to kill. Longing and fear —fear of change. (*Illustration:* Different attitudes toward painting of Christ.)

7. So what to do? Only answer is worship—bow down. Give gifts—gold, frankincense, myrrh. (*Illustration:* Charles Williams's Christmas play.) Else we'd kill. Church bows down—what we do in worship: we adore and offer. Bow down everything: Pride, position, wisdom—all.

The sermon sketch we have reproduced is very rough and quite unfinished. In some sections, images and illustrations had already begun to float into mind, but few of these were apt, and almost none found their way into a final sermon. Sermon sketching is a free, unfixed process in which a preacher jots down all kinds of ideas, merely trying to flesh out the simple sentences of a basic structure.

There are many gains in doing a sketch, gains we can enumerate. First, the sketch gets our thinking out into view where, with a degree of objectivity, we can criticize and correct ourselves. Whether we are writing, or talking aloud, or taping, there ought to be some way to look at our scheme and assess it homiletically. Thus, if we were to criticize the sermon sketch we have drawn up, the following problems would be noted:

Move 2: Homiletically, is the move too much like the previous move? Both seem to have lists of problems we face. Thus, will the moves sound too much alike when preached? Reshape move 2.

Move 3: Move is underdeveloped and must be thought through. The personal analogy is all wrong. The real problem is a sociopolitical power structure maintaining a status quo. Those "in charge of the world" will be threatened by a new order.

Move 4: Mention of theologians and scripture scholars could feed congregation's anti-intellectualism. Must involve congregation itself in sellout. Avoid B. Graham reference. May need a contemporary illustration of our compliance.

Move 5: Need to develop theology here. Why is sin set on destroying God-with-us? Line from poem sounds too pretty: find some new illustrative material.

Move 6: Get rid of reference to Christmas cards and tree stars: too saccharine. Think out how, in fact, Christ still comes to human consciousness. What exactly is the nature of "threat" and "promise." Get honest, and reduce the schmaltz.

Move 7: Develop the sense of worship as the only alternative; otherwise, in sin, we will be murderous. Heighten the sense of self-offering involved. Chas. Williams's illustration looks good.

Almost all criticisms are prompted by either a concern for theological precision or a concern for congregational understanding. In other words, we have assessed the sketch in terms of its usefulness in *mediating*. What the sketch has done is to objectify our thought so as to allow criticism and, we hope, improvement.

Second, a sketch gives us some slight development of thought so that there can be a brainstorming of images and illustrations toward the production of an image grid. A preacher looking at the whole sketch may begin to sense where illustrative strength may be needed and what kinds of illustrations should be chosen. Thus, for the sermon sketch we have drawn up, some illustrations were found: Herod's speech from W. H. Auden's "For the Time Being" found its way into move 3, a quote from John Dean's *Blind Ambition* fitted move 4, and a line from *Jesus Christ Superstar* caught the love/hate ambiguity in move 6. During the week of sermon preparation we learned of a church that asked to have a Christmas pageant moved from their chancel where "it was too close to the cross"—a natural for move 5. Gradually, images and illustrations were gathered—a process which could not have been initiated without the sermon sketch. Of course, with the sketch, it is possible to locate an introduction and conclusion for the sermon, at least in a tentative way.

There is a third gain that may be mentioned. The sermon sketch gets us started on the problems of internal design in each move. In a rough way, we begin to sense the shape of each move. Just as a poet will put down words expressive of some kind of consciousness, and, then, sensing in the words a forming shape, will work to bring out and clarify the shape of a poem, so preachers, looking over a sketch, can begin to see in the ramble of thoughts different shapes for each move. We have discussed the shaping of moves previously. Here we need to notice that incipient shapes may begin to show up in a sermon sketch and, thus, offer clues for development.

FORMING A FINAL STRUCTURE

Some preachers will outline and reoutline many times before battering a sermon into some final form. What is important is that having criticized, imaged, and spotted different developmental shapes, we draw things together so as to produce a final structure. The final structure is, obviously, more than a sketch but less than a final sermon manuscript or delivered sermon.

Psychologically, something important will be happening. The sermon that began as a field of understanding in your consciousness, and was expressed by you in a bare structure and a sketch, will become detached—a thing-in-itself to be worked on. Just as a statue, which began as a drawing then became an armature on which to hang clay, is finally separated from an artist as something to be worked on and improved, so your sermon structure now takes on a kind of life of its own. You will study your forming final structure as something independent of you, now with its own internal necessities, its own implicit shape. To an extent, craft will take over!

Two processes will be involved: First, you will be working on individual parts of your structure, the separate moves, so as to clarify language, internal design, and points-of-view. Second, you will be working over the *whole* structure, making sure that moves interrelate, that logic of movement is clear and interesting, that style changes expressively, and so forth.

The final preaching script you produce—still open to some improvisational elaboration—is, in some ways, much less important than the final structure. Preachers will sometimes overwork language, honing particular phrases too much, forgetting that *meaning is structural*, that, in speaking, plot is all-important. Language may glitter, but, if deep structural meaning does not form in congregational consciousness, sermons may be nothing more than oratorical fireworks that flash but do not last. The forming of a final structure is all-important. In final structure, you are turned toward congregational neighbors in love, primarily concerned with designing a meaning *for them*. Remember, preachers are mediators, not showboats.

STRUCTURE AS PROCESS

We have rehearsed stages in a process, moving from the study of a text toward a final speaking. Every preacher will work quite differently. Some preachers will plot their sermons in some traditional A, B, C, 1, 2, 3 sort of way. Others will doodle notes on a page with arrows going in odd directions. Still others may cover sheets of paper, like a stack of artist's preliminary drawings, until they get what they are after. Some ministers will work with tape recorders or computers. Every method has dangers and gains. Clearly, we are arguing that some stages in a process are necessary: a study of text, a basic structure, a sketch, a final structure, and a script—in whatever ways these stages may be accomplished, they are *necessary*. Preaching, while not an art form, is a creative process. Therefore, as with any creative process, we must "conceive," must objectify in some manner, must allow for correction and expansion, and, finally, must draw together a finished work.

Attempts to short-circuit the process will almost always produce poor preaching, preaching that does not mediate. There is quite enough empty verbiage coming out of Madison Avenue without pulpits adding to the mass. If we try to get up and speak from nothing more than a basic structure, we may feel spontaneous but end up chattering in repetition and rhythmic cadences—a ritual of nonsense. If we go with only a sketch, all the problems inherent in an undeveloped sketch will be articulated, including dangerously "fuzzy" theology. We are not appealing to a sense of artistic pride—although perhaps it would not hurt—but, rather, we are trying to remember holy responsibilities involved in preaching. We speak of God in the presence of God. We speak to neighbors, loving our neighbors. Slapdash may be what we think we want, but not if we think deeply. If we stand before God we must be respectfully truthful. If we serve neighbors, we must care for the careful forming of their faith. Both concerns shatter the dream of quick-fix sermons: Love is a labor, particularly a love of God and neighbors.

20.
"Moments"
in Consciousness

Older homiletics accepted as "canon" a threefold process for the interpretation of texts in preaching. Homiletics would speak of reading a text (exegesis), interpreting a text (exposition), and applying a text (e.g., moral applications, spiritual applications, churchly applications). The threefold process was soon crammed into an invariable sermon design. Sermons began by talking about a text, then drew forth theological wisdom from the text, and finally ended up aiming interpretation at practical human affairs. Every sermon, in one way or another, seemed to move through the three set phases.

Through the years, the set pattern broke apart. Some homileticians took the threefold pattern and turned it into a catalogue of sermon types—textual sermons, theological sermons, and practical "life situational" sermons. Other homileticians simply pared the pattern down: Exegesis was reduced to a few comments on the biblical background of the text, interpretation became nothing more than drawing from the text a single topic or "truth" to preach on, whereas application grew large, amounting to a series of points discussed at length and often elaborately illustrated. In our day, the threefold pattern is scarcely evident. There is no way for us to go back and reclaim the threefold tradition, nor should we.

Nevertheless, perhaps our forebears were onto something that may be worth a second look. Though earlier homiletic theory was swathed in rational philosophy, there is something about the threefold pattern that deserves more than a passing nod. We will use the pattern in a new way, as a description of "locations" in consciousness which may well prompt different kinds of sermon design. Thus, we will speak of "immediacy," "reflection," and "praxis."

Think of a visitor to an art gallery. The visitor stands in front of a painting —perhaps the picture of a city street scene—and allows immediate impression to form in consciousness. Later, the visitor may sit down at some distance and think about the painting as an image in consciousness. Finally, the visitor may leave the gallery with a back-of-the-mind visual impression and, as a result, look at the urban world in a new way. We seem to be talking about phases or, perhaps, "moments" in consciousness.

PREACHING AND "MOMENTS" IN CONSCIOUSNESS

Preaching, we have said, is mediation. Preaching mediates some structured understanding in consciousness to a congregation. Therefore, preaching is speaking related to *understanding*. The language of preaching will tend to imitate phases of understanding in consciousness.

Obviously, preaching is not itself an immediate Word of God. Whenever preachers attempt to push back prior to understanding and to speak from some immediate God-awareness, they produce either arrogance or glossolalia. Bluntly, we are not given immediate, *un*mediated glimmers of God: Presence is always Presence-in-Absence. Demagoguery may suppose it speaks God's Word from some sort of God-possession; Christian preaching may not. Whenever preachers speak, supposing some inner, subconscious dalliance with God, the result is usually a freaky language deserving the apostle Paul's sharp rebuke; though dazzled by visions, he insisted it is better to utter a few words with *understanding*. We will have to admit that insofar as we explore symbols of revelation, we may open the mysterious "interior" of God to a congregation, and they, in turn, suddenly aware of Presence, may claim our words to be Word of God for them. We must be cautious, however, and even modest, in labeling our own sermons Word of God. There are enough idolatrous temptations in ministry without incautiously adding more. In sum, we do not speak from an immediacy of God.

On the other hand, we have already rejected the pulpit's chronic third-person-objective point-of-view. Preaching still speaks of the knowledge of God as if it were viewed in the past on distant tablets of stone. The problem with talking about God is that it does not easily give way to a "being with God" in faith. Instead, objective language produces a detachment from God that can only be bridged by Promethean decision or by some sort of interior conversion and realignment. Talking about God does tend to turn God into a "thing" observed, and thus border on heresy. How can we be third-person objective when we are speaking of a Consciousness that is conscious of us? What we do talk about is *fields of understanding* produced by symbols of revelation. Thus, our language is bound to relate to "moments" in a process of understanding. As we attempt to explore symbols of revelation there are phases not unlike those in the consciousness of the art-gallery visitor: there is an immediate forming of understanding; a reflecting on understanding; and a looking at the world in a new way through understanding. These phases may produce not only different languages of preaching, but even different kinds of sermon design.

IMMEDIACY

When we read a text (or situation), at first, the text itself exerts considerable influence on consciousness. We can describe the influence of the text in two ways: the language of the text prompts analogies of understanding in consciousness, and the movement of the text produces shifts in consciousness. For example, when reading the story of the Stilling of the Storm, words from the text such as "storm," "afraid," "asleep," "rebuke," and so on, are grasped because they are in our social language, and are used by us in speaking of affairs in lived experience. Thus, the words of the text work in two directions: toward the field of meaning in the text, and toward our fields of lived experience. Hearing the words, we understand. But, as the story moves along from the storm waves to the disciples' protest to Jesus' sharp question—"Why are you afraid? Have you no faith?"—to the calming of the waters to the confession of faith "Who is this?" the plot of the story forms immediate episodic movement in our consciousness. Just as the art-gallery visitor stood before a painting and allowed the painting to form an impression in consciousness, so in "immediacy" texts form us, they form our fields of consciousness.

Suppose we are going to preach a parable. Instead of having single meaning, parables produce a traveling action in consciousness. As a result, most parables may be described as a language of immediacy. So, let us choose to preach a parable, perhaps the well-known parable of the Talents. The plot is familiar. A boss goes away, entrusting property to members of his staff. When the boss returns, he asks for an accounting. Some staff members have invested and gained a return; they are praised. But one staff member, guarding his boss's trust, has buried cash in earth, because, says he, "I knew you were a hard man." The play-it-safe servant is bawled out: "You lazy no-good!" Then, the boss drops a strange one-liner: "If I were a hard man . . . you should have invested." Finally, the boss gives the man's share to other staff members. Perhaps the parable may have had reference to Sadducees and Pharisees—the Sadducees lived safely within the limits of the law, whereas the Pharisees attempted to live out the law in everything they did.

As we study the text we *understand through analogies of experience*. Certainly, in a capitalist economy, we understand investors and, in fact, may well approve of investors. In a capitalist society, we can also understand the play-it-safe staff member; to be responsible a trustee of someone else's property ought to be cautiously protective. We even can grasp the staff member's motivations: "I knew you were a hard man!" When dealing with wheeler-dealers most of us are guarded. So, we grasp the text by analogies of understanding.

In addition, *the plot of the parable as it unfolds produces, in consciousness, a series of responses.* The situation of the parable is a stock repertoire—being held accountable for a trust. We learn of the investing staff members and form some attitude toward them. We may think them risky or we may nod approval. Likewise, when we hear of the play-it-safe person, we will have some response, depending on whether we regard his behavior as "being trust-worthy" or as being "overcautious." When the boss rewards investors by giving them their trusts, their profits, and enhanced positions, we may be rather surprised! We wait to see how the boss will speak to the cautious noninvestor. "I knew you were a hard man . . ."—the staff member's speech may repel us, but we are scarcely prepared for the harsh condemnation which the boss deals out—"You lazy no-good!" Well, we think we have it straight: investing is approved and playing-it-safe is outright condemned. But, then, unexpectedly, the boss drops an odd remark: "If I were a hard man . . . you should have invested!" All of a sudden, the parable is chaos. If playing-it-safe is condemned, and if investing is a tactic for dealing with rapacious bosses, what do *we do* when relating to an utterly self-giving "Boss," whom we meet not only in the parable but at the cross? Notice the power of the parable *intending to do* in consciousness (if our somewhat singular interpretation is even halfway apt).

Sermons can be designed as systems of immediacy. What a preacher does is to imitate an immediate consciousness responding to a text. The design of the sermon will travel as a series of responses to the text in which analogies of understanding form. Thus, we may endorse with some slight anxiety the investors' strategy, drawing analogies of personal risk and self-expending in the living of life; Christians ought to risk themselves for neighbors with no holding back. Likewise, we may react to a play-it-safe religious life that tries to save its own soul by keeping unspotted from the world. No wonder the boss condemns the man; we join in a condemnation of similar tendencies in ourselves. But imagine the shock that might be built into a sermon when we discover the fear that lurks not only in playing-it-safe, but in *investing!* Suddenly, we reflect on the cross and are staggered by the unlimited self-giving love of God. Such a sermon scenario might leave a congregation up in the air, struggling to understand exactly how to respond to self-giving Love—neither by caution nor by an anxious having to produce, but how?

What happens in sermons that imitate immediacy is that passages are allowed to exert their *intentional* power on congregational consciousness through preaching. We are not sitting back and contemplating an inert, done-with passage; no, we are being altered, perhaps transformed, by the *performative movement* of the text. We do not mean to suggest that we will be bound by the actual sequence of the text itself in designing our moves. A sermon on the parable of the Talents might begin with our reaction to playing-it-safe, then turn to an endorsement of investing ourselves, before, suddenly, spotting investment as a strategy of fear, and then recognizing the generosity of God. The passage itself is rearranged, but its intentional force is still functioning. While the language of preaching is not really a language of immediacy, because, after all, ministers have studied a passage before preaching, sermons can *imitate* immediacy and, in fact, be a performative language in congregational consciousness. The mode of immediacy does permit passages to fulfill intentionality. Thus, preaching in the mode of immediacy is particularly suited to narrative passages, parables, and texts which in their moving structure seem to be designed *to do* in consciousness.

REFLECTION

A second stage in consciousness of a text (or situation) could be described as a "standing back" and "considering." Notice that we are using a metaphor of distance—"standing back"—whereas, actually, we are speaking of temporal distance. The word "consider" *(con + sidus)* may have referred originally to a fascinated study of starry constellations; again, there is hint of distant contemplation. The "moment" of reflection can be described: (1) Immediacy is past; we are no longer interacting with a text or situation. Instead, we are considering a *field of meaning* in consciousness configured by the text or situation. (2) We may be extending the field of meaning to cover (better, overlay) areas of lived experience, forming by analogy ever-wider connections. (3) We now tend to view our structured understanding in terms of an objectified model of ourselves in the world. Our description has been abstract and must be explained.

In studying the parable of the Talents, we encountered characters in a story, some who invested and one who preserved, as well as a boss described as "hard," though he was, in fact, astonishingly generous. The parable formed in consciousness and, by analogy, connected with certain contemporary life styles. In living life, we may try to earn approval by investing ourselves fully, or we may preserve ourselves in self-protective purity. Both life strategies seem to be born of fear—"I knew you were a hard man." The boss was generous, however; he took no profit and gave everything away. When we lined up the boss with a disclosure of God-in-Christ on the cross, we discovered ourselves clear beyond the parable trying to figure out an entirely new way of life, responding to prodigious God-love. The parable is no longer a text on a page. Instead, the parable has produced a structured field of contemporary consciousness for us to stand back and consider.

In the reflective mode of consciousness we consider the structure of meaning produced by a text or situation. The stuff of the text—boss and staff members—has faded into background. We contemplate a contemporary structure of meaning. *Structure* is still in consciousness; namely, two living options, two ways of viewing God (hard vs. generous), and a large unresolved question of how we should live. In reflection we will draw more and more connections between the field of meaning and lived experience. We may gaze into our own psyches, search our own anxiety before God, which can leave us bound in chains of law or drive us frantically toward self-fulfillment. We may draw wider analogies by looking at the social world in which people may well be propelled by similar fear. With the dialectic of hard Taskmaster vs. good God, we may consider theologies in which an exacting God is depicted, setting such theologies over against the disclosure of suffering love at Calvary. We might even explore law/grace controversies. Surely, we will begin to consider what a life in response to free grace could look like—a radical change for ourselves and the world! Our musings will, of course, be filled with the concrete images of lived experience. In the reflective mode of consciousness we stand back and consider a structured field of meaning, thinking *through* the field to areas of lived experience.

Above all, see what does *not* happen. We do not end up with a distilled topic or a propositional truth—stuff from which sermons are frequently shaped. Instead, we are contemplating a whole configured field of meaning. At the same time, intentionality is no longer an active force. Oh, there is still an intending *of* in the sense that there is a field of meaning under consideration. And, there is an intending *toward* because there are areas of lived experience being viewed through a structure of meaning. But the text's performative action, its intending *to do,* is done. All that remains of the text's intending *to do* is a sense that the field of meaning does challenge our usual life strategies.

Obviously, sermons can imitate reflective consciousness. While most longer parables may not lend themselves to the reflective mode, we will study our chosen example—the parable of the Talents—as a reflective system to see what might happen. The structure of a reflective sermon will relate to the structure of meaning in consciousness, although original sequence is no longer crucial, and actual references to the text less important. We are now preaching a structure of theological meaning. For example, we could conceivably design a sermon without *any* mention of the text. We could look at playing-it-safe as a religious life style adopted by those who (though cramped) always live within the law. We might, then, turn to regard those overachievers who are bent on doing the whole counsel of God—C. S. Lewis once wrote of a woman who believed in living for others and remarked that we could recognize the others by "their hunted expression"! Thus, in our sermon, we could explore the motive of fear, hidden fear of God, that can prompt life strategies. Finally, we might merely gaze at the cross, seeing there a display of self-giving Love, utterly merciful, totally generous, before ending up with the question of how we can live in response to such Love. Though unlikely, we could design a reflective sermon based on the theological structure of meaning in consciousness, *without referring to the text at all.*

We have said that the original sequence of a text is no longer crucial in reflective consciousness. While the passage unfolded in a sequential plot, it produced a somewhat static field of configured meaning, a structure of meaning. The movement of a sermon in the reflective mode of consciousness is movement around a structured field of meaning, a moving from one contemporary meaning to another. Therefore, in reflection, an original plot may be rearranged in many ways. We might, for example, begin a sermon with motivation—our hidden fear of God. We could, then, turn to look at the kinds of behavior such fear can produce (playing-it-safe or being driven to invest). Then, we could turn to the cross and there catch sight of God's prodigious Love. Finally, we could daydream new life. Another pattern, quite different, might commence at the cross before turning to behavior, then to motives, and, then to the question of new life style. While structural options are not altogether random, and a logic of movement must be determined, nevertheless, the parable's original sequence no longer governs preaching.

Sermons in the reflective mode may differ according to the fields of lived experience that we may align with structured meaning in consciousness. For example, our sermon on the parable of the Talents could be preached to a gathering of ministers, in which case behavioral options would be described in terms of ministerial life styles—a play-it-safe take-no-risks clergy vs. an eager-beaver clergy champing for professional success and the reward of still-larger parish assignments. Or, as easily, the structure of meaning could line up with corporate life styles in our driven-for-reward capitalist society. Or think how a sermon could relate to psychological self-awareness, describing, by contrast, an overscrupulous person and a person driven by fears of nonbeing. Remember, in reflection, we see *through* a structure of meaning to fields of lived experience that *can* vary.

Preaching in the reflective mode is also imitation. The preacher has already reflected on a field of meaning produced by the text. Nevertheless, in the way it forms and speaks, a sermon can imitate reflective consciousness and indeed form reflective consciousness in a congregation. Preaching in the reflective mode is particularly suited to Pauline passages, to teachings of Jesus, apocalyptic visions, allegories, wisdom literature, and some prophetic passages.

PRAXIS

A third moment in consciousness, the moment of praxis, is much more difficult to describe. Part of the difficulty has to do with the variable character of such moments. Another part of the difficulty stems from how we understand our in-action lives—terms such as "act," "will," "motive," are slippery terms indeed. At the outset, let us suggest that preaching in the mode of praxis addresses situational people who are questioning their in-action lives.

There are moments when human communities wonder what they are doing and what they *should* do. Usually, such moments occur when normal ways of deciding ourselves have broken down. Most human deciding is either prereflective on the basis of "I like" or "I want" or "This is what is usually done," or is postreflective as previous precedent decisions are merely enacted. Therefore, we do not question our in-action lives until prereflective strategies are confounded or postreflective precedents do not apply. In moments of praxis, the ambiguities of being-saved-in-the-world are intense. Too many cultural voices may contend in our consciousness and symbols of revelation may seem murky indeed.

Of course, there are moments when no in-action decision is involved, but in which identity is a question. Who are we in the particular moment in which we live and who must we be? Human life is baffling. There are mysterious reaches that outreach our minds, as well as mysterious depths within us. There are terrors of evil, wonders of grace, sudden quirky turns to human events—all of which pose questions of identity in the world. The world may offer answers to the question of identity, proximate answers, that contend in congregational consciousness. Because who we are does determine how we live, profound questions of meaning are praxis concerns.

The hermeneutical consciousness we label "praxis" is consciousness *in a situation,* oriented toward the future—What *will* we do or be?—that draws on the past in memory. After all, Christian communities *recall* Jesus Christ, story and symbol, who is said to be "Lord" of the future. Moreover, Christian communities are aware of their own peculiar past/future character; being-saved, they know they are both offspring of *old* Adam and children of the *new* age. Thus, in praxis, communities turn from a situation to search memory for some "light" in which to walk.

Let us rehearse the moment of praxis consciousness: (1) We read a situation which in a worldly hermeneutic has raised the question of our in-action lives. (2) We take the situation into a Christian hermeneutical consciousness between symbols of revelation and our awareness of being-saved in the world. (3) Within a Christian hermeneutic we search for an analogous field of meaning through which we may view our situation. Praxis consciousness is a *process*, a movement of thought. We must explore our description.

Suppose we seize on a typical situation. Imagine a particular congregation facing a practical decision. They are located at the edge of a changing neighborhood. The inner city seems to be enlarging and, beyond them, rapidly growing suburbs multiply: They are in between. More and more, their "regulars" are commuting to church from the suburbs, while new members have not yet drifted in from the enlarging inner city; they are in a bind. From a practical standpoint (read: a worldly hermeneutic), they can either stay put and die out or they can relocate and, almost certainly, prosper. What are they to do? Their prereflective strategies based on "I like" have split between "I like it here" and "I'd like it in the suburbs"; their postreflective precedents are inadequate because they have never been in such a bind before.

At this point in their crisis someone in the congregation asks, "But aren't we Christian people?" and, rather abruptly, the situation is shifted into a different kind of consciousness. Now, they must think of themselves as a being-saved community in relation to the story-symbols of God-with-us. No longer can they try to decide themselves within a simple success/failure model or even an equally simple tradition/venture model. Suddenly, their decision is set in the purposes of God and faced with the Living Symbol of Jesus Christ. Thus, as they discuss their options there will be conflict, essentially, a conflict of "models." Certainly, there will be members of the congregation still speaking from a worldly hermeneutic in terms of success/failure, and other members trying to get at what Christian symbols may have to say to their identity in the world. We are listening in on a very "hot" church meeting!

Within Christian consciousness, there may be a number of structured "fields of meaning" which may be selected to interpret their situation. Oddly enough, many of these available "fields of meaning" may have been built into memory by preaching! For example, the congregation may have heard a recent sermon on the parable of the Talents which structured a field of understanding. As a result, someone may stand up and make a little speech to the effect that they cannot play-it-safe but, on the other hand, they should not invest for reward. Instead, they must think their situation through on a new basis, namely, as a response to the free, self-giving of God. The process

327

we are describing does not necessarily produce a clear answer: this is what we will do, we are now decided, and what is more, we are confident of our decision. Most crisis situations are not easily resolved. Instead, we have stumbled on a process of thinking-in-praxis, a process which, incidentally, may guide sermon design.

We have isolated stages: (1) The reading of a situation usually by a being-in-the-world hermeneutic. (2) The taking of the situation into Christian hermeneutical consciousness where an awareness of being-saved in the world grasps symbols of revelation. Christian hermeneutical consciousness may well be critical of a natural being-in-the-world hermeneutic. (3) The locating of a theological structure of meaning through which to view a situation, normally chosen on the basis of structural similarity. While sermon design in the praxis mode will not necessarily move through the stages one by one in order, somehow it will play among these stages of thought. For example, when speaking to the congregation we have described, a preacher might begin with a worldly hermeneutic—"We are in a success/failure bind"; then turn to describe the actual situation; then draw on a structure of meaning prompted by the parable of the Talents; then speak of who we are before the God revealed in Jesus Christ. Other structural systems can be imagined with considerable variety.

Please recognize what does *not* occur. We do not move directly from situation to scripture. In other words, in the situation we have described, people would not "read" their situation and then immediately recall the parable of the Talents. Though sermons do sometimes slap scripture onto situations, the procedure is probably artificial. Worldly readings of situations will invariably lead us to wrong scriptural analogues. Instead, we move from a situation to a structured theological field of meaning which may or may not recall scripture. Thus, we do not turn from a situation to the immediacy of scriptural language without moving through reflective consciousness. And, of course, we may not think our way back to particular scripture at all.

There is another aspect of praxis preaching that needs to be mentioned: imaging. Worldly hermeneutic can pose future alternatives quite clearly. From a worldly hermeneutic we could image the dwindling down into death of a congregation, or, as easily, image a success-story congregation blooming in the suburbs. Such images are at hand and are unusually easy to conceive. Because preaching in a praxis mode does address the future, ministers must dare to envision the future. Perhaps the greatest failure of the pulpit in our century has been the failure to pose vivid images of new humanity in our world. Christian praxis may lead to decisions that may seem quite inconceivable to a worldly hermeneutic, as, for example, to stay put as a parish but to live *in an altogether new way* within an expanding inner city. A preacher preaching to the situation we have described would have to paint a picture of a different, new future and, what is more, paint the picture in vivid imaginative language.

STRUCTURING AND MOMENTS
IN CONSCIOUSNESS

We have set up descriptions of different moments in consciousness: immediacy, reflection, and praxis. In a way, the distinctions are bound to be artificial. Within a preacher's consciousness, the phases may well overlap. If preaching from scripture, the preacher has studied a passage in immediate consciousness, has reflected on the structure of meaning produced by the passage, and, probably, considered situations which have been beckoned into consciousness by the structure of meaning. Sermons a preacher produces may intermix modes of consciousness in their language and in their design. Nonetheless, sermons will probably imitate one of the stages we have described, more than others. We have already noticed that narrative passages in scripture may prompt a strategy of immediacy, whereas Pauline rhetoric may be best handled in a reflective mode.

Across the three types of consciousness we have described there have been shifts. Thus, in a language of immediacy, the text itself—its plot, its imagery, its intending—will exert great influence over sermon design. Whereas preaching in the mode of praxis will be determined by a structure of process prompted by a situation and may not draw on scripture at all. In the reflective mode we saw that sermon design will relate to the structure of a field of meaning in consciousness, but with the intending-*to-do* force of scripture left behind. All modes of preaching, of course, will be designed by a homiletical theological consciousness that is decidedly reflective.

Actually, we are not so much typing sermons—"This one is intentional," "This one is praxis"—as we are speaking of strategy. Preaching always involves some intending *to do*. We suppose that some sermons will intend to work in consciousness with immediacy; the plot of the sermon will be designed to shift in congregational consciousness with immediate force. Other sermons will intend to structure congregational consciousness, producing a reflective field of meaning. Still other sermons may be designed to move a congregation through a process of praxis from a situation at hand, to theological contemplation, to some new understanding or choosing of a future. Because we are describing different intentions we can expect that problems in sermon design will be quite different. Now, we will turn to examine sermon structuring within the modes of consciousness we have located.

STRUCTURES

21.
Preaching in the Mode of Immediacy

Much of the Bible is narrative. In Hebrew scriptures, there are myths of creation, sagas of the patriarchs, stories of exodus, kingship, exile, and restoration. In Christian scriptures, there are fewer stories, perhaps, because the symbolic character of Jesus Christ is emerging. There are, however, passion narratives, resurrection accounts, and, of course, many stories in the Book of Acts. Within the Synoptic Gospels, there are not too many authentic narratives: Pericopes in the Gospels are apt to be either settings for sayings of Jesus or structured exchanges of dialogue. Nevertheless, again and again, preachers who speak from scripture will find themselves struggling with narrative forms. So our question is, How do we preach a story?

Some preachers will try to turn biblical narrative into dramatic "autobiographical" monologues. They will play the role of a biblical character—Nicodemus or Zacchaeus or King David—speaking to twentieth-century congregations as if people could be miraculously transported to the past and allowed to listen in on the articulate consciousness of a particular biblical figure. Such sermons seem to be popular, and are often packed with instructive biblical background. Nevertheless, there may be severe difficulties with the convention. Dramatic monologues tend to turn crisp biblical narrative into psychological studies of character, so that event is dissolved into inner states or attitudes. It is no accident that the "I Nicodemus" type of sermon emerged in the nineteenth century after Browning, and has gained vogue with the rise of the psychological sciences.

The dramatic monologue almost always ends in Pietism. What is obvious about scriptural narrative is that it seldom enters the inner world of characters. There is an astonishing spareness about biblical narrative: a juxtaposing of

333

episodic events without much discussion of motivation or causality. Thus, biblical stories leave room for conjectures of grace. In dramatic monologues, psychological motivation will, generally, fill in the gaps of biblical narrative and smooth over abrupt, surprising turns of narrative, so that the mystery of God-with-us may gradually be edged out of the narrative and be replaced by psychologies of faith.

Another problem with the dramatic monologue ought to be mentioned. Basically, the method turns the preacher into a dramatic performer. Rightly, preaching is conversation with a congregation. By addressing people, preaching draws a congregation into one consciousness; it unifies. In the dramatic monologue, however, we view a performance by a persona; in effect, we attend pulpit theater. The result is not unifying. Instead, each listener is driven into personal subjectivity. Unless people get together after the sermon to discuss their individual reactions and responses, the dramatic monologue locks people in their own affective responses. Thus, though the dramatic storytelling monologue is of interest, and may be exceedingly popular, it is not necessarily preaching; it is a performance with all the attendant dangers of performance in a pulpit. While the church may well wish to welcome religious drama, or even find a place for character representation, dramatic monologues do not belong in the pulpit as a part of public worship. We ought to be wary of dramatic monologues as a way of interpreting biblical narrative.

Another popular approach to narrative forms is a retelling of biblical stories as *stories*, that is, without intrusive commentary. Storytelling, supported by "narrative theology," is very much in vogue. Just as the voice of an author has been banished from modern novels—the story itself unfolding without "Alas, dear reader" moralisms or third-person narrative commentary—so, some preachers handle biblical narrative artfully by telling a "good story." The method is bound to be popular simply because most of us enjoy good stories; edge-of-the-chair narratives are obviously more exciting than point-making sermons. The problem with the method can be analyzed. While most of us can tell stories and, in fact, spend much of our lives telling stories, few of us are skillful enough to tell a story in such a way that *theological* meaning forms. A Graham Greene or a John Updike or a Frederick Buechner can write novels in which structures of theological meaning form as part of the world of the novel, but they are unusually adept full-time writers who have perfected their craft. Of course, they also have scope; a novel may allow time for the building up of structures of meaning. Unfortunately, most preachers have only a few sermonic moments, little time for the exercise of craft, and almost no training in the highly technical business of narration. Thus, ministers may tell a swell story from the pulpit, even a swell biblical story, and yet have no theological meaning form in congregational consciousness. Story sermons are popular; most of us respond to a rattling good story. Moreover, there are gains simply because Christian congregations ought to be acquainted with their stories and, indeed, see themselves as within the larger story of God-with-us. Nevertheless, though storytelling from the pulpit may entertain, excite, and inform, it does not necessarily shape faith-consciousness. Story qua story may not be an adequate preaching.

How are we going to preach narrative passages? We can take our clue from two quite different traditions: from the conventional ways in which we tell stories to children, and from quite sophisticated patterns of Black narrative preaching. The skilled Black preacher will tell a biblical story as present-tense narrative, but move in and out of the story with analogues, explanations, and interpretations as the plot line of the story moves along. Most of us adopt a somewhat similar method when, perched on the edge of a bed, we tell good-night stories to children. As the story moves along, episode by episode, we interrupt the story line with "It's like . . ." explanations, with answers to questions from our sleepyheaded audience, with images drawn from a child's own lived experience. Such a technique comes to us naturally and does give us unusual freedom for interpretation. Certainly, the method is more attractive than telling a Bible story and then unpacking ponderous moral points or applications: "Now, what do we learn from the story? . . ." Great advantages of the method are (1) the unfolding of a crisp plot that sustains narrative excitement, and (2) freedom for the exploration of our own lives within narrative structure. In handling biblical narratives, preachers will be imitating a language of immediacy in which the movement of a plot structures consciousness and draws out what we have termed "analogies of experience." Of course, all narrative sermons will be moving toward the formation of reflective consciousness.

If reflective construction predominates, the original plot sequence may rearrange in interesting ways. If the original plot seems to be an intending *to do*, then original sequence can be an option. Decisions of structure will probably be dictated by the character of the biblical material and the kind of theological field that the preacher intends to produce. To get at such matters, we will review a number of passages that feature narrative movement and, therefore, lend themselves to a preaching in the mode of immediacy.

A SYNOPTIC PERICOPE:
LUKE 17:11–19

[11]It so happened that in going up to Jerusalem he passed through the borderland between Samaria and Galilee. [12]As he was going into a certain village, ten lepers

335

met him, men who stood afar off. [13]They raised their voices, saying, "Jesus, Master, have pity on us." [14]Catching sight of them, he said, "Go! Show yourselves to the priests." As they went, it so happened that they were healed. [15]One of them, seeing he was healed, turned back with a shout, glorifying God, [16]and fell on his face at [Jesus'] feet, giving him thanks. And he was a Samaritan. [17]Answering, Jesus said, "Weren't there ten cleansed? Where are the nine? [18]Didn't anyone come back to give God glory except this 'alien'?" [19]So, he said to him, "Get up and go! Your faith has made you whole."

Let us review exegetical matters. In v. 11, Luke has Jesus wandering through the borderland *between* Samaria and Galilee, a DMZ, which as "no man's land" was a place to dump contagious persons. What we label leprosy, namely, Hansen's disease, was probably unknown in Jesus' day. Therefore, in the Bible the word "leprosy" probably referred to some other highly contagious skin eruption. Verse 12 reports that the men "stood afar off," which was required by Levitical law. (Chapters 13 and 14 of Leviticus will be studied by preachers who plan to preach Luke's passage.) When in v. 14 we have mention of Jesus "catching sight of them," Luke probably means that Jesus saw their skin disfigurement. The imperious "Go!" in v. 14 is punctuated so as to separate it from a following explanatory clause, "Show yourselves to the priests." Presumably, a Samaritan would trundle off to Mount Gerizim, whereas Jewish lepers would journey to Jerusalem. Notice the casual use of a favorite Lukan phrase, "It so happened . . .," in reference to the healing. In vv. 15–16 we get a most unusual conjunction of terms— *doxazon* = glorifying, *euchariston* = thanking—both specific terms for worship in Luke and among early Christians. While the words could be used descriptively, more likely they are Luke's way of drawing Christian worship into the story. Incidentally, there may be theological precision involved in the verse: God is glorified and Christ is thanked. The use of "Samaritan" in v. 16 is probably symbolic; Luke probably means "Gentile." In v. 17 we have more than a touch of irony: "Weren't there ten? What happened to the nine?" Rather obviously (without speculating motives), the nine were off doing the law. In v. 19, some translations have "Your faith has healed you," but we suggest that "whole" is preferable. So much for some brief exegetical information.

One of the problems with Luke 17:11–19 is that the passage seems to suggest too many motifs. Certainly, lepers were outcasts; quite literally, they were cast out. As many scholars have noticed, the miracle stories are, in most cases, stories of liberation from social, religious, or natural oppression. There is also a Jew/Gentile theme which is underscored by Luke's aside, "And he was a Samaritan." In addition, we sense a dialectic between doing the law and returning to worship, which seems to emerge in the structure of the text. In view of the fact that prior to vv. 11–19 Luke has told the little parable of the Modest Servant, which would appear to be a call to doing the Lord's work obediently, the dialectic of law vs. worship is somewhat puzzling. What are we to make of such a mishmash of thematics? The passage is intentionally designed, but we seem to have more intentions than we can handle.

Normally, preachers will do a simple structural analysis of the text before they turn to exegetical study involving commentaries or other reference works on biblical background. We can at least grasp the story line of the passage in a sketchy fashion. Most New Testament pericopes, particularly the miracles, are framed with an introduction and a conclusion. Verse 11 is introductory—it merely locates the story, and is not part of the action. The narrative can be listed as follows:

1. Lepers: "Have pity on us!"
2. Jesus' command: "Go! Show yourselves to the priests."
3. They go and, "it so happened," are healed.
4. One of them returns, glorifying and thanking.
5. Jesus: "Where are the nine?"
6. "Your faith has made you whole."

In listing the passage, we have not included the motif of social liberation simply because it is not *structurally* featured by Luke and, therefore, may be regarded as a secondary intention. Likewise, we have skipped the Lukan phrase, "And he was a Samaritan," precisely because it appears in the passage as a rhetorical aside. Again, we may be dealing with a secondary intention that is not structurally central to the movement of the passage.

Homiletic Analysis

At this point in sermon preparation, ministers may wish to analyze each component part of the text's structure to get at theological understandings, analogues of experience, as well as a preliminary reading of roadblocks to understanding which may be within the congregational mind. Our analysis might proceed in the following manner:

1. Lepers: "Have pity on us!"

   a. *Theology:* Here we have the universal cry of a wits'-end humanity to Jesus, who is understood by Luke to be God-with-us.

   b. *Analogies of Experience:* Most of us have moments when, in desperate need, we call on God—overtly or covertly. Perhaps, when faced with a serious illness, or the dissolution of a marriage, or an impending death, or when our children are in jeopardy, we cry out to God. We may also imagine hordes of famine-ridden Africans reaching out skeletal hands: "Have pity!"

337

c. *Congregational Blocks:* None.

2. Jesus' command: "Go! Show yourselves to the priests."

   a. *Theology:* We should be shocked by the abrupt command. Jesus has flunked Pastoral Care 101: Surely, he should have said something like, "It must be difficult being a leper. . . ." Instead, we get a hard-line command, "Go!" Luke is presenting an imperious Lord Jesus Christ who, as God-with-us, has authority.

   b. *Analogies of Experience:* Analogies of experience are difficult to get at in an age as secular as ours. Again and again, however, our cries for pity do seem to be answered by commands of God. The saints tell us that when they have hustled up to God, filled with personal pathos, God has often answered with "Go!" "Love!" "Serve!"

   c. *Congregational Blocks:* Popular piety has painted a picture of caring Jesus, who, when we pray in desperate need, responds with warm support. Jesus' abrupt command may be unexpected and quite inexplicable.

3. They go and, "it so happened," are healed.

   a. *Theology:* Whenever a command of Jesus is answered by an instant doing of the command, the New Testament is probably representing what might be termed "the obedience of faith." Insofar as the command involves Levitical regulation, we may describe the lepers as "faith doing the law." In either case, here, obedience = faith.

   b. *Analogies of Experience:* As children, do we not do parental commands because we *trust* the commanders?

   c. *Congregational Blocks:* We may run into problems in understanding. Members of the congregation may think of faith as either believing certain God-ideas or as a warm-tub God-feeling inside. People resist thinking of faith as doing the words of Jesus because such a notion seems to smack of authoritarianism.

4. One of them returns, glorifying and thanking.

   a. *Theology:* We have already noticed the two words *doxazon* and *euchariston* featured in the text, both of which are Lukan words for worship. Thus, we may suppose that the verse represents Christian worship. Luther once supplied a single-sentence definition of worship: "The tenth leper turning back." Christian worship is, in essence, thanksgiving for God's saving love in Jesus Christ.

   b. *Analogies of Experience:* While basic experiences of gratitude, particularly for healing, may inform the text, specific analogies should center on *worship as gratitude*—that is, singing doxological hymns, celebrating Eucharist, and so on.

   c. *Congregational Blocks:* Blocks may be of two sorts. Some folk may think of thankfulness as an obligation, a kind of requisite etiquette toward God.

Others may have little experience in worship as thanksgiving, having grown up with either legal or didactic understandings of worship.

5. Jesus: "Where are the nine?"

a. *Theology:* We may not answer the question by guessing motivations or psychological deficiencies. Nor may we answer the question by historical reconstruction; the story makes no sense historically—Why would Jesus rebuke lepers for doing a commandment which he himself commanded? The question can only be answered within a theological structure: The nine did not return because they were doing the law.

b. *Analogies of Experience:* We have all met religious people who have reduced their lives with God to a list of "dos" and "don'ts." They seem to relate not to God but to law. Seeing such patterns in others may help us to spot the same tendencies in ourselves.

c. *Congregational Blocks:* Except for the basic illogic of the story, probably none.

6. "Your faith has made you whole."

a. *Theology:* We know that the New Testament does not embrace a faith-healing theology: Faith does not heal, God does. What is more, faith is not necessarily a requisite for healing, because God frequently seems to heal unbelievers. Instead, Luke may be referring to the "wholeness" of a Christian life which will include *both* obedience and worship. In Luke 17:11–19 we seem to have not only obedience but also worship. Together they comprise the "wholeness" of Christian faith.

b. *Analogies of Experience:* The dialectic of worship vs. social action (and its reverse, social action vs. worship) is a live issue in most churches. Obedience without worship can produce moralism, including the moralism of the social activist. On the other hand, worship without obedience can turn into a sick Pietism.

c. *Congregational Blocks:* Probably none.

What is taking place in our analysis is the forming of a structure of understanding in consciousness from which a sermon design may emerge. The analysis locates a theological field, forms contemporary meaning by analogy, and begins to spot intentional strategies with regard to a congregation. Of course, actual analogies of experience will be much more concrete as preachers explore their own lived experience as well as their particular range of social experiences. The kind of analysis we are proposing can be done with any biblical passage and, *invariably*, will assist preaching.

A Basic Structure

We have previously described homiletic design as the breaking of a whole pattern of meaning in consciousness into some sort of plotted sequence. In studying Luke 17:11–19 we have ended up with *a story* in consciousness, but not merely a story: we have put together a story with *theological structures* of meaning and with *analogies of understanding* drawn from common experience. So, we see *through* a story to theological structure, and *through* theological structure to fields of human experience. Moreover, we have spotted intentions in the passage and, in particular, one intention that was displayed in the moving plot of the story, namely, an adding of worship to the obedience of faith. To Luke worship is *doxazon* and *euchariston*. What does the passage intend *to do?* It intends to call us to worship and thus form Christian "wholeness."

Are we bound by the intending of the passage? Though Luke may be putting down legal obedience in favor of a relating to God-in-Christ through worship, are we stuck with a similar agendum? Our situation may be quite different. Back in the 1960s an odd collision of Barthian theology and social protest may have produced a kind of radical social activist moralism in churches. In the 1970s, however, the pendulum swung toward romantic Pietism, a "spirituality" of relating to God that bracketed out most social protest. If we go with Luke's intending *to do,* will we not end up, inadvertently, endorsing an agendum of the seventies? So we may wish to keep obedience and worship in balance a bit more than Luke lest, in a new context, the passage be heard as a sharp putting down of doing the gospel.

Let us look at a possible basic structure of moves for a narrative sermon on Luke 17:11–19:

1. The lepers cried "Have pity!" and we can understand.
2. How does Jesus answer? With a commandment, "Go!" Isn't that just like God?
3. Well, they went: Faith is doing the word of Jesus Christ.
4. But if faith is only obedience, it can turn into dead law.
5. One came back to worship: Christian worship gives thanks.
6. So the Christian life is both obedient faith *and* worship.

In designing a sermon plot, in general we have followed the movement of the story in Luke (which, in a reflective treatment, might not occur). We have, however, switched the sequence of the text to some degree. In the passage the lepers go, then one returns, and then Jesus asks about the other nine. Instead, we move from the lepers obeying, to the failure of nine to return, and then pick up the one worshiping leper, prior to concluding with a discussion of "wholeness." Why have we made the change in sequence? If we followed the original plot, we would have ended up with rather nervous point-of-view shifts—looking at the lepers, then looking at the one worshiper, then looking back to the lepers again. Moreover, by making a change in order we will be able to give worship climactic emphasis as well as to relate worship more easily to the theme of Christian "wholeness." There are probably other ways to plot a sermon from Luke's story and still retain intentional integrity.

Another feature of our basic structure ought to be mentioned. While some of the sentences in the basic structure refer to the story, others do not. Instead, they work from a theological structure that has been aligned with the plot line. If every move in a sermon were to begin with a first-sentence reference to the story and then a theological inference, the practice would create a redundant pattern that could drive a congregation crazy. Instead, some moves will begin with a theological understanding, for example, "4. If faith is only obedience, it can turn into dead law," and then reach back into the story. The result will be a natural interweaving of story line and theological meaning which we are seeking to achieve. Remember, we are being taught by skillful Black preaching as well as bottom-of-the-bed storytelling to children. What we have *not* done is to set up a telling of the whole story and, then, a deduction of some religious truth to apply to our lives.

A Sermon Sketch

As we know, we need more than a list of sentences to produce a sermon. While basic structure is crucial, moves must be fleshed out. So, the single sentence, "1. The lepers cried 'Have pity!' and we can understand," might be sketched as follows:

1. See ten lepers all in a row: "Jesus, Master, have pity on us!" We can understand them. Times in every life when, at wits' end, we call for help. A cancer in the tummy—"God help me." Or a marriage turning sour—"Oh, God!" Or someone we love who is going to die—"God." Not always articulate. Sometimes a silent, inner cry. But, at the end of our rope, we do reach out for help. We turn to God. Like the lepers.

The little first-move sketch is a development of thought within a narrative framework: We begin with the story and return to the story. From such a quick sketch we can almost guess the kind of move that might emerge in a final outline.

1. See the ten lepers all in a row: "Jesus, Master, have pity on us!" We can understand, can't we? There are times in everyone's life when, at wits' end, we cry out for help. When we get to a point where we know our needs are huge and our strength small, then we call for help; the word "God" shapes our lips or echoes inside our minds.

341

Example: You've been to the doctor. He mutters something about a shadow on your X-ray. "Better not wait," he says, and schedules surgery for the next day. You leave his office in a strange daze. Inside yourself, you're crying out, "God help me."

Example: Or maybe your marriage, which began in a bright blush of wonder, has slowly turned into a cold war across a kitchen table where you're tossing words at each other like stones. And, suddenly, you realize something's gone wrong: "O God!"

Example: Or someone you love is going to die. You don't know how to talk about it, even to each other. You're all tight inside, and afraid of what's coming. You begin to daydream what it'll be like walking around in an empty house: "Oh, God help me," you cry.

Look, our lives are shaped by agony. We're human and there are human tragedies that come to us all. Then, when there's nothing else to do, and, even if we don't quite believe, we find ourselves saying a kind of prayer: "God. Oh, God." Like the desperate lepers all lined in a row, bawling at the top of their lungs, "Jesus, Master, have pity." See the ten lepers calling for help.

If you look back at the brief sketch of the move, you can see that the preliminary shape of a full move is already there. Notice that the move has been developed from our homiletic analysis of the passage, for it combines theological understanding—"a universal cry of wits'-end humanity"—with analogies of experience. The move begins with a story-line reference and ends with a story-line reference, so the following move can commence with Jesus' response. If the next move were to connect on the basis of theology, without reference to the story, the final two sentences would be dropped, and be replaced by a general statement such as "There are times when everyone calls to God."

Of course, we know we cannot develop a sermon by writing finished moves one at a time; we must overview the whole structure as it expands. So a sermon sketch for Luke 17:11–19 might look something like the following:

1. Ten lepers calling, "Have pity." We can understand. Times in every life when, at wits' end, we call out for help.

   for example, Cancer in the tummy: God.
   for example, Marriage on the rocks: Oh God.
   for example, Someone dying: God help me.

   Will come to all of us. Aloud or silently, "Oh God." Like the ten lepers, "Jesus, Master, have pity."

2. What does Jesus say? Of all things, he hands out a commandment, "Go!" Just like God! Again and again, we come hustling up to God, full of our own troubles, and what do we get? A command: "Go," "Love," "Serve," "Help."

Illustration: Doctor coming home after death of own baby, full of tears. Phone rings. Emergency room calling because of auto accident: "Come." Doctor, reflecting, laughs: "O.K. God, I got your message!"

We want God to give comfort, to patch up our souls. Not always. Sometimes, God's answer is a hard command—"Go," "Do." So the lepers called to Jesus for help. What did they get? Jesus turned and said, "Go"—"Go and show yourselves to the priests." He gave a commandment.

3. Well, the lepers did as they were told. They obeyed the word of Jesus. Guess what, that's faith. Faith is obeying the word.

Contrapuntal: Oh, we think of faith as believing—maybe believing the creed printed in our bulletin. Or we think of faith as feeling, being filled full with a feeling of God in our hearts.

But, not in the Bible. In the Bible, faith has arms and legs: It does. Faith is nothing less than risking your life by doing the Word of God.

Brief examples: Saint Francis, John Calvin, Martin Luther King, Jr. They all heard word of Jesus and dared to do. They obeyed.

The lepers turned and did as Christ commanded. What is faith? Faith is doing as told: Faith is obedience.

4. Of course, if faith is no more than obedience, it can turn into a dreadful, dead law: "Doing the rules."

We've met such people. Religion, for them, is a list of commandments— "dos" and "don'ts" with the "don'ts" a longer list: Days of Obligation; prayers that have to be said at table; Bible study to be done on schedule— until God is subtly replaced by "the law."

But take a second look: The person is *us*. In all of us the sense of ought can easily take over. Then, faith turns into a weighty moralism: "I must," "I've got to."

Maybe that's what happened to the lepers. Though they were healed miraculously, they kept right on going, doing the commandment under a law of obedience. Faith, if it is only obedience, turns into stultifying law. So, the lepers, nine lepers, kept on going to Jerusalem.

5. But look! One turned back to Jesus Christ. See him down on the ground whooping it up, glorifying God, giving thanks to Jesus in a one-man nonstop cantata of praise. One leper came back to worship.

What else have we been doing here? Didn't we begin worship up on our feet giving praise? And, haven't we sung the Gloria? Soon, we will offer gifts and chant a doxology. Then, when we hear the words, "Let us give thanks to the Lord our God," we will answer, "It is right to give God thanks and praise." No wonder old Martin Luther tossed off a one-sentence definition of worship: "The tenth leper turning back!"

Illustration: Tell of puritan named "Thankful" who was famous for bellowing out *Old Hundredth.*

One leper turned back to Jesus Christ and gave thanks. He worshiped.

6. Now, do you know what Jesus meant by "whole"? "Your faith has made you whole." The Christian life is obedience, surely, but it is also worship, thankful worship. Together obedience and worship, worship and obedience, make up the Christian life.

But watch out! Worship without obedience will not do. It may look "godly," but if it doesn't do the will of God, it is nasty religious perversion.

Yet, look at obedience without worship; it can turn into moralism that will dry up our lives and destroy us.

Christian life based in gratitude for God-in-Christ. Thus, the "whole" Christian life is an alternating current of action and praise.

We have now arrived at a fairly sound sketch of a narrative sermon, without, as yet, having an introduction or conclusion or gathering all the images and illustrations we may wish. The sketch does have problems. The second move may not quite fit in with the sermon's overall intention, and may contain too strong an illustration. The third move, on the other hand, may need to be strengthened, lest it be overwhelmed by move 4. So, some revision may be necessary. In narrative systems, we need fewer illustrations because narrative movement is intrinsically exciting. The sermon sketch has two virtues: Each move has a different internal development which is *crucial* in narrative sermons, and the story line weaves in and out of the sermon so that we have avoided a clumsy split between story and interpretation. Every section of the sermon sketch draws on story, theology, and analogies of experience. The overall movement of the structure will form a reflective understanding in congregational consciousness.

General Considerations

Structural Overlays. We have argued that narrative sermons emerge from a consciousness in which a field of narrative and associations of understandings are interpreted by theological understanding. In the example we have developed, there are actually three "outlines," all going on at once. Clearly, there is narrative structure, a plot or story line that travels through the sermon sketch. But there is also a structure drawn from lived experience that could be described as (1) We cry out in desperate moments; (2) Often, God answers by handing us a commandment; (3) Faith is doing God's commands; (4) But if faith is only obedience, our lives can be destroyed; (5) So we worship thankfully; (6) Because "whole" Christian lives are made up of obedience and grateful praise.

Mere mention of "God" indicates, however, that our sermon sketch could also be expressed as a theological construct. Thus we can discern the following theological shifts: (1) Human beings in "limit situations" turn to God. (2) Sovereign God is a God of commandments. (3) The acknowledgment of God is obedient faith. (4) But God's Word is not dull law. (5) God wants a related people, *ergo* worship. (6) God's love is law and God's law is love, therefore, we respond in praise and action. Oddly enough, we could make a sermon out of each of the outlines. The power of narrative preaching, however, is in its interweaving of story, theology, and experience. Our task is not merely to tell a good story, but to tell a story that will form theological meaning for our lives.

Introduction and Conclusion. How do we design introductions and conclusions for narrative sermons? Narrative preaching is built out of story and moves toward a reflective understanding. Therefore, introductions will generally orient toward story and conclusions toward reflection.

Obviously, if we are going to tell a story, at the outset we will have to establish scene and characters. Some preachers suppose that people will hear and remember scripture readings, and that there is no need to put the story in focus again at the start of a sermon; all that is necessary is a phrase such as "In today's scripture reading . . ." Not so. Language is fleeting, particularly an oral reading of written prose language. Every narrative sermon, one way or another, will have to reinstate narrative setting so that a subsequent story may unfold. Notice that Luke begins with v. 11 which locates Jesus and v. 12 which pictures the lepers. So, an introduction for our hypothetical sermon might be phrased:

> Can you picture the scene? Jesus and ten lepers. There they are in a barren land facing each other. The lepers are lined up in raggedy clothes waving their arms. Jesus stands staring at them, catching sight of their blotched skin, taking in their rags. Lepers. Ten lepers and Jesus, facing each other in a dry land. So our story begins.

Another alternative would be to start by drawing on contemporary experience before recalling the biblical narrative.

> We've all seen beggars. Even in our own land, there are beggars—poor, broken people reaching out for help. Well, in Jesus' day, there were beggars, raggedy people, calling for help. Like the lepers. . . .

At the start of any narrative system, we shall have to refocus setting and characters so as to begin telling a story.

Conclusions are a different matter. In one sense we are done with our story and have moved into a reflective field of consciousness in which theological understandings and experience interrelate. To go back and rehearse the story again would be tedious. We do, however, have an *intention*. We discovered that the sermon is a kind of "call to worship," because worship with obedience *is* the Christian life. Thus, if we were to sketch a conclusion for our sermon, it might look something like this:

> Well, here we are—worshiping: We've been giving thanks to God all morning. Maybe we know we've been healed. God in Christ has changed our lives. Oh, yes, we know we are commanded, and soon we will go again into the world to do God's will. But now, now, it's time to whoop it up, time to give glory, and sing out praise. Here we are, the Christian church "turning back." Dear Friends, let us give thanks to the Lord our God!

Conclusions are always determined by sermon structure and by intention.

Conjoining Moves. One of the problems in narrative preaching is a natural tendency to smooth the flow of a story. *We must not.* Somehow, the structure of plot must be built strongly into congregational consciousness, so that each twist or turn in the story is defined and can do its intentional work. When we are moving with the story line, such crisp shifts can be done quite easily. In our sermon sketch, study the shift between the first and second moves, as well as the shift between the second and third move. The shifts are logical but *quite abrupt.* Shifts from story line to theology are more difficult, however. The trick is to end a move with the same orientation as the next move's start. For example, imagine what would have happened in our sermon sketch, if, in move 3, we had ended with a description of the lepers trundling off to Jerusalem. How on earth could we shift to a theological discussion of the dangers of law? In narrative preaching, preachers must give special attention to the ends and starts of moves.

Hermeneutical Consciousness. The other problem that faces us in constructing narrative sermons is how to move from story to analogies within moves. Obviously, we would become pedantic if in every move we began by talking about a past-tense story and then, with a phrase such as "Now, what does this story tell us about our lives," shifted to contemporary analogy. The solution to the problem is, again, quite simple. We do not talk about a biblical story as a past-tense event which we will describe by looking back through time. Instead, we will speak out of a consciousness that is "hearing the story *now*" and, therefore, can be aware of our contemporary lives *now.* In other words, the solution has to do with point-of-view. Above all we must avoid then/now splits in narrative sermons; happily, they can always be avoided.

346

The crucial matter in preaching stories is orientation. Though preachers have done much research in biblical background—we may know more about first-century skin diseases than we care to know—and though they may have figured out a theological meaning in detail, preachers must not yield to temptation and talk about the text and its background. Instead, we must preach *as if the congregation and ourselves were hearing the story for the first time* with immediate force. Too much description of the event will crowd out analogies of experience and theological meaning. So, instead of long sections of a sermon devoted to description of the lepers or of biblical customs with regard to leprosy, we will use the story simply as a plot to move us along in an episodic story line. After all, the gospel is *not* biblical background. Remember, one of our models for preaching biblical narrative is telling stories to children. Sleepyheaded children have a low tolerance for biblical background; they want story.

A PARABLE: MATTHEW 20:1–15

Begin by looking over a free translation of Matt. 20:1–15. In the translation, we have updated monetary values and times of day. We have also substituted a few contemporary colloquialisms for colloquial phrases in the original text.

> [1]The kingdom of heaven is like a man, a boss, who went out in the morning to hire workers for his vineyard. [2]Having bargained with the workers for $40 a day, he sent them into his vineyard. [3]Going out again at 9:00 A.M., he saw others standing around doing nothing in the village square. [4]He said to them, "You go out to my vineyard too, and I'll pay you whatever's fair." So they went. [5]Going out at noon and at 3:00 P.M., he did the same thing. [6]About 5:00 P.M., he found others standing around, and he said to them, "Why are you standing around doing nothing?" [7]They said to him, "Because no one has hired us." So, he said to them, "You too, go to my vineyard." [8]When evening came, the boss said to his foreman, "Call the workers in and pay them their wages, from the last hired to the first." [9]And those hired around five o'clock each got $40. [10]The first hired thought they would get more, but they each got $40. [11]Picking up their pay, they started grumbling at the boss, saying, [12]"Those last ones you hired worked only an hour, and you paid them what you are paying us, who've worked all day long under the hot sun!" [13]But he answered them, "Friend, I do you no wrong. Didn't you bargain with me for $40 a day? [14]Take yours and scram! Suppose I do decide to pay the last the same as you; [15]can't I do what I want with my own? Is your nose out of joint because I'm generous?"

We need not chase down much exegetical detail; essentially the parable is clear. A few comments may be helpful, however. Mention of "vineyard" in v. 1 may resonate with a number of passages in the Hebrew scriptures, for example, Jer. 12:10, Isa. 5:1–7, and others, where Israel is God's "vineyard." In v. 2, the RSV has "after agreeing" which we have chosen to translate "having bargained," because the word *symphonesas* implies agreement after usual haggling. The three different trips to employ workers are not significant —storytellers often group in threes. In the three different trips, however, there is an interesting stepping down of dialogue: With the first hired, the boss bargains a figure; with the second group, he mentions a fair wage; and with the third group, he merely dispatches them to the vineyard. While we may admire artistry, we need not attach much significance to the rhetorical device, except to notice that it establishes "hiring" and "fairness." The workers' complaint in v. 12 may slightly satirize the speech of a self-dramatizing "grievance committee." In v. 13, "Friend" may be an impatient bit of sarcasm and not an expression of goodwill at all. "Take yours and scram!" in v. 14 *is* harsh; in effect, the boss is saying, "Take what's coming to you and get out of here!" If the last verse, as a textual variant, is included, it is usually translated, "Is your eye evil because I am good?" We are dealing with an idiomatic expression in which "good" could be translated "generous." Of course, we ought to note though the boss is generous toward the five-o'clock workers, as an employer, he is not overly generous—scholars suppose that a denarius a day was minimum wage for farm workers, perhaps about $40 for twelve hours in a field today.

We have written elsewhere (see For Further Reading on "Parables") that parables have stock plots into which surreal detail is inserted to disrupt our conventional world. We also argued that parables may not be reduced to a single meaning, when, obviously, they involve the traveling action of a plot in consciousness. Both observations appear to be true of the parable of the Workers and Hours. The parable begins unexceptionally with workers being hired and bargains struck—a familiar repertoire. Suddenly, a surreal detail enters the story as *all* the workers are paid the same, including those who only put in a brief hour in the cool of evening. Our world of you-should-get-what-you-deserve justice is shattered. Actually, there is a double shock involved, for when the all-day workers complain, they are rebuked—"Take yours and scram!" Surreal is a mild word for such a disruption of our conventional world. We readers, who have identified with the daylong laborers, are shaken. We are left to puzzle out the boss's final monologue for some sort of meaning.

What is clear about the parable is that it intends *to do* in a listening consciousness. See how the parable works in our minds. The three forays in search of workers, plus mention of "fair pay," leads us to expect a just distribution of wages at the end of a day. When those hired last are paid $40, we are surprised and even impressed by the boss's kindness. But then, when the all-day workers are given the same $40, we are confounded. Automatically, we identify with the first hired as they recite their grievance; surely, they are just in their demands. The boss's words are like a slap in *our* face: "Take yours and scram!" Now we are doubly puzzled. At first, the boss's final remarks seem confusing, but finally, we muddle a meaning— there is a theology involved: (1) "Didn't *you* bargain with me for $40?" Good heavens, do we conceive our lives as a performance/merit deal with God? (2) "Can't I do what I want with my own?" See God's sovereign freedom! God is free even from *our* notions of justice. (3) "Is your nose out of joint because I'm generous?" makes sense in view of the preceding remarks. If grace is free and generous, it will be resented by anyone who lives in a bargain and calculates advantage. Of course, the boss's final speech only can "mean" within a model of *calling* which is exactly what the first part of the parable constructs.

Could the parable be preached in a reflective mode? Yes, but only with loss, for the action of the parable acted *on us*. We were drawn into an identification with the all-day workers. When everyone was paid the same, we were outraged; *our* standards of fairness were violated. More, our world, filled with notions of deserving, and presided over by a God who rewards the deserving, was shaken. Maybe only in a fallen-apart world could we begin to catch sight of a new social order, a "kingdom" based on calling rather than deserving, on free grace rather than reward. If parables are objectified and analyzed at a distance, they lose force and cannot perform radical "conversion." While we could back off and consider the parable, we should probably not: Most parables lend themselves to preaching in the mode of immediacy.

In constructing a sermon, our task is not merely interpretation—"What does the parable mean?"—but intentionality, "How can we make the parable *do?*" Somehow we must design a sermon *to do* certain things in congregational consciousness. The sermon must be so arranged that a congregation will naturally identify with all-day workers and, thus, be appalled by an apparent breach of fairness. Also, we must find a way for congregations to catch sight of a hidden bargaining with God that may underlie our religious lives. Finally, we must break open images of a free-grace world, a kingdom of heaven, in which we *do* live. We are not dealing with a content to be taught to a congregation. Rather, we are dealing with a homiletic strategy: How can we design a sermon *to do?*

Here is a sermon sketch to examine:

> *Introduction:* Henry Ford was opinionated. He had opinions about automobiles, politics, and even religion. Said Henry: "Whatever is good business, is good religion." Well, you read the parable and wonder. Here is an employer hand-

ing out the same pay for one hour's work as for twelve. Nowadays, he'd have a picket line! Any way you look it over, it's bad, bad business. But listen to Jesus: "The kingdom of God," said Jesus, "is like that!"

1. We hear the parable and all we can say is "Unfair!" Interpret the story any way you want; it still adds up to injustice. Workers work a long hot day— twelve hours out in the fields—for $40. Others show up for a quick cool hour, and they are also paid $40. Well, it's wrong—a welfare state.

   Union halls back in the thirties had a motto on their walls: "A fair dollar for a fair day's work." But, in the parable, neither the dollar nor the day's work is figured fairly: $40 for one hour, $40 for twelve. No matter how you read the parable, it's downright wrong. Unfair!

2. If the parable has something to do with religion, it's still unfair. Are we to suppose that when God checks heavenly accounts there are no differences? Some Christians have given their lives, lifelong, to God; are they to get nothing more than some "Easter-Day Irregular"? Is God going to greet Billy Graham, who has spent his life preaching the gospel, the same way as a skid-row drunk? Perhaps, God's ways are not our ways, but, at least, they ought to be fair ways! Are some rewarded for what they do, and others for what they don't do?

   (*Illustration:* Jewish story: "When I get to heaven, I'm going to grab God's beard and say, 'You God! You don't play fair' ") If boss = God, then be blunt: God's unfair.

3. So, what does God say to us? God says, "Get out! Take your religion and get out of my church!" We are shocked. Are we not God's chosen people? Have we not been faithful? We pray to God, sing God's praises, contribute to God's own church; don't we have a right to expect, at least, a nod of approval?

   Harvard Business School study of why workers work: The study concluded that people work not so much for pay as for recognition.

   We're not asking for a starry crown, or a gauzy angel gown, but for a little recognition. We ought to be God's special friends. But, instead, what do we hear? "Take your religion and go!" We're shocked.

4. Then, dimly, we do begin to understand: "Didn't I pay you what *you* bargained for?" Good heavens, all along have we been thinking of faith as a bargain? Faith as our personal contract with God?

   (*Illustration:* Maxwell Anderson's *High Tor* tells of men trapped in a swaying steam-shovel scoop who pray a bargaining prayer: "I can do a lot for you, God.") With us it's not so crass, but a bargain nonetheless. Counting up deeds with one hand and reaching for reward with the other. Doing religion in church and looking for a nod of approval. So, God gives us what we want: "Haven't I paid you what *you* bargained for?"

5. No wonder we've resented our neighbors! If we've lived in a bargain, we read the same terms of agreement on our neighbors, and then resent any free gain

they get. We've been into religious free enterprise. If we're earning our salvation, we don't want anyone else getting it free.

(*Illustration:* C. S. Lewis, *The Great Divorce:* Self-righteous man resenting a murderer's admission to heaven. Resents "bleeding charity" and demands his "rights.")

Note the calculation of the all-day workers: "We've worked all day, but *they.* . . ." A we/they calculation!

6. But, look out! In God's kingdom, it's all "bleeding charity." God's kingdom is a free-grace world in which all are called and all forgiven and all welcomed with love. Can we earn the cross of Jesus Christ? Heavens no! Can we deserve God's astonishing mercy? Never! We want to live in a world where we deserve what we get, calculated fairly. Instead, we live in free grace of God —for all.

(Check *Illustration:* Retiring missionary's speech: "I didn't do anything. I don't deserve. God is so good!") We're going to have to adjust our lives to live in the kingdom of God.

Conclusion: Tough to try to live in two worlds at once. We think we're in a world of earn-and-get dealing with a paymaster God. Well, suppose we're wrong. The real world, God's world, is free. So, look how we can live. Not calculating "rights" but giving ourselves away in love, love for love, in God's good grace.

If you review this somewhat slapdash attempt at a sermon sketch, you will notice that we have tried to design a sermon intending *to do.* Strategy can be described: (1) The sermon enters the passage at the point of the distribution of wages. Thus, the earlier hiring of workers is referred to but is not included as a part of the sermon's plot. The strategy was adopted in order to begin with identification between a congregation and the all-day workers. (2) In the second move, we drew an analogy between the economics of the text and our religious expectations (after all, the parable has to do with "kingdom of heaven"). By drawing an analogy early in the sermon, we avoid any danger of a split between talking about a text and making application of a text. (3) In the third move, we suddenly introduced the rebuke from the passage into our own churchly consciousness. The device prevents us from standing outside the text and looking at the all-day workers as a "them." We *are* them. The third move is a turning point in the sermon, for it creates an entirely new point-of-view. In the first two moves we were outraged, viewing an injustice. In moves 4 through 6, humbled by rebuke, we will be listening and trying to understand in consciousness. (4) Notice we do not try to teach the congregation from the parable. Instead, *with* the congregation we are thinking through and discovering the "rule of God." (5) The sermon sketch does not follow the exact sequence of the parable; it skips over the hiring and shuffles the order of the boss's remarks. Rearrangement has been dictated by a desire to have the sermon *do* in consciousness. Our stock fair-play world is disrupted and we are forced to ponder a whole new social order under grace. Though not all parables are as intentionally dramatic, many are. Thus, parables lend themselves to preaching in the mode of immediacy.

General Considerations

Distance and Identification. Most of us have been taught that we should not psychologize parables. We should not enter into the feelings or thoughts of characters within parables of Jesus. The advice is sound. Drama critics sometimes make a distinction between drama, such as tragedy, in which an audience is to feel with a main character and be moved ("catharsis"), and drama in which an audience is distanced so as to reflect and, perhaps, act. If we are permitted to get inside parable characters and feel with them, parables are destroyed; they lose their power to disrupt and reorient our world. More, they no longer force us to reflect and act, because distance will be dissolved into feeling. All we have to do is to read the parables in order to see that they are stark plots and offer us no entry into the affective inwardness of their characters. Parables have lean plots and sermonically must be plotted with toughness.

Nevertheless, some parables do permit alignment with characters on a temporary basis. For example, in the parable of the Unforgiving Servant (Matt. 18:23–34), we (1) *look at* a servant being forgiven a huge debt and, then, (2) look at the same servant refusing to forgive a small loan. We are not allowed to align with any character until the "other servants" show up and, irate, go to the king to complain; then we are permitted to identify. In the parable of the Workers and Hours, we do identify with the all-day workers who protest an economic injustice, although identification may be broken when they are sharply rebuked. Thereafter, we may back off and try to understand the boss's monologue. Thus, in preaching parables, in general, we will keep our distance and move toward identifications only when the parable permits. In the sermon sketch we have provided, note that at no time did we enter into the thoughts or feelings of characters in the story. Instead we looked at and, indeed, objected to injustice. So, we *identified* but did not psychologize.

The World in Parables. We have suggested that parables begin with stock representations of the world, that is, of our human world constructs—the world we may have in consciousness. We have seen, however, that surreal elements in the parables disrupt our world and force us to catch sight of some larger world impinging on us, a world presided over by the Love of God disclosed in Jesus Christ. When preaching parables, it helps to have a clear image of the stock world with which the parable may be contending. For example, in the parable of the Workers and Hours, the world is a Deutero-nomic construct in which punishments and rewards are calculated on the basis of performance by a fair-pay God. At the beginning of the sermon sketch the first two moves articulated the consciousness of such a world—a world clearly threatened by equal pay for all. At the outset, in sermons on parables, we must shape the stock world implied by the text.

But what are we to do with the world called kingdom of God? If we trace the idea of the kingdom through scripture, particularly through prophetic writings, we sense that we are dealing with a *social* symbol, the image of God's new social order. Therefore, in preaching, we must not turn the kingdom of God into a realm of inner faith. The kingdom of God, then, is neither an inwardness nor a hereafter. Actually, the kingdom is not merely a vision of an eschatological future because, though hidden, it *is* the social reality in which we live. (See the treatment of the kingdom in move 6 of our sermon sketch.) Because we live in a human, worldly world construct, we tend to view the notion of a kingdom of God as far away and fanciful, a fairy-tale kingdom devised by religious dreamers, but, actually, the kingdom is *God's* real world, and our constructs are sinful illusion.

Of course, the kingdom of God is mysterious, precisely because God is mysterious Presence-in-Absence. Preachers may not reduce kingdom para-bles to clear, quite understandable teachings. To do so would be to turn the kingdom into an adjunct of our world. On the other hand, kingdom-of-God sermons must not dwindle down into mystic silence stymied by unspeak-able mystery. We can speak of kingdom because we see ways in which the kingdom counters our world constructs and can infer the dim shape of something shattering our worlds. More, we do have the Living Symbol, Jesus Christ, who has disclosed the "interior" of God-with-us and, there-fore, the ruling Spirit of the kingdom. In preaching parables, we must imply a world countering our worlds that, though mysterious, is present in Christ Jesus.

The Location of Plot. Sermons that emerge from parables must be plotted carefully. They must move along like a story, so that, as episodes unfold, the parables intending *to do* may be fulfilled. At the same time, they must be crisply structured so that each episode (move) is defined as a separate consid-eration in consciousness. Thus, while we want movement, we must be wary of the smooth flow of storytelling; episodes must be allowed to break in on the story line without causal connections. Therefore, preachers will have to design a *very* well defined basic structure for parable sermons.

The real trick in plotting parable sermons is to locate the *action in consciousness.* The real action is no longer a narrative plot on a printed page of the Bible, but an action in our minds as we hear each episode in sequence. In the sermon sketch we have provided there is virtually no talking *about* the parable as an object of interest. Instead, each move imitates our conscious hearing of the story, our hearing and reacting, episode by episode. So, preachers will probably want to skip extensive discussions of first-century customs—how sowers sow, shepherds herd sheep, women bake bread, masters collect accounts, and so forth. Such discussions locate parables in the past, and distill an original meaning, but may not get to us at all. Instead, we are designing an action in which, happily, we share. In a way, parables are systems for "conversion," although not in the popular sense of the term. Parables are designed to convert us from life in our world to a new order of life in the midst of a mystery that the New Testament calls "the kingdom of God."

A NARRATIVE FROM HEBREW SCRIPTURE: GENESIS 22:1-19

Lately, there has been a decided turn away from preaching passages drawn from Hebrew scriptures. Except for the Black preaching tradition, the trend has been noticeable in both Catholic and Protestant communities. Ministers do seem to prefer preaching "The Gospel Lesson." Veneration of the gospel in liturgical tradition goes back to a symbolic representation, with candles and processions, of Christ's coming into the world performed in the dramatic liturgies of the Eastern church. The dramatic enactment did not intend to foster neglect of Hebrew scriptures or to urge a primary preaching of gospel lections. Nevertheless, in the past fifty years, we have seen a decided decline in sermons drawn from Hebrew scriptures. As a result, Christian congregations may be losing track of their own profound Jewishness. Therefore, we must devote special attention to preaching from Hebrew scripture and, in particular, to preaching the narratives of Hebrew scripture.

On a human level, the Hebrew scriptures may help to keep our Christian faith honest. Within the Hebrew scriptures there is wonderful earthiness, stark honesty, and a hard-nosed ethical edginess that modern-day Christians need. There is also subtlety and an eye for paradox that Christians should usefully cultivate. Most of all, the Hebrew scriptures can lead us to true understanding of Jesus, a Jew of the first century. Given our American religious heritage, which includes puritan theological straitjackets, nineteenth-century Pietisms, not to mention twentieth-century roly-poly country-western JeeeeZus songs, we need all the help we can get! Jesus is deformed when split off from continuity with the consciousness of Israel. Can we understand any of the teachings of Jesus without the precedent of Israel's religious tradition? In one sense there is nothing new in the words of Christ. When, in Matthew 5, we hear Jesus setting up contrasts—"You have heard it said . . . but, I'm telling you"—he is not setting his preaching over against the Hebrew scriptures, but, rather, offering interpretations of the tradition from *within* the tradition. While Jesus may well be at odds with movements of thought in late Judaism, as, for example, triumphant nationalism and religious exclusivism, he stands at odds from within the consciousness of true Israel. To understand the depth of Jesus' words, his continuities and discontinuities with Israel, we must explore the heritage of the Hebrew scriptures, which happen to be our scriptures as well. Of course, the problem we have is not merely in understanding Jesus' words; it is in understanding the figure of Jesus as well. All we have to do is to recall some recent film versions of "The Life of Christ" to sense our problem; with few exceptions Jesus is portrayed as a white-robed first-century mystic who floats through human affairs with a kind of distant Kahlil Gibran God-dazzle in his eyes. No, Jesus was a Jew. The parables he spoke are filled with a fondness for Jewish paradox as well as Jewish humor. He embraced creation with fine Jewish enthusiasm. He lived his life as a Jew. He died his death as a Jew. Risen, his Jewish consciousness is *not* discarded. The wonderful thing for us about the Hebrew scriptures is that, studied and preached, they give us Jesus Christ.

Can we possibly understand Christian claims about Christ apart from the Hebrew scriptures? No. If we want to grasp the salvation Christ offers, surely, we will have to understand images of the human condition—creation and fall—found in the first chapters of Genesis. Likewise, to grasp what reconciliation is all about, we will have recourse to the covenant passages, to the law of Moses, to the stinging words and soaring dreams of the prophets. We can only fully understand the import of Christ, the Living Symbol of God-with-us, with a sense of the holy otherness of God in Hebrew consciousness. The parody of Christian faith that depicts Jesus Christ as a "savior" who rescues our souls from threat of hell for heavenly places—"Oh, that will be glory for *me*"—can only be maintained by ignoring the Hebrew tradition. In the Hebrew scriptures salvation is viewed as social liberation from social bondage so that humanity may be true covenant people. The understanding that rings through the preaching of Christ and of the first-century Christians does not counter salvation images of the Hebrew scriptures but enlarges on them. If we are to preach the gospel in the twentieth century with integrity, we must

355

forego our lurking anti-Semitisms, and, once more, preach from Hebrew scriptures. Of course, for us, the problem is *how*.

In some sermons, we sense that the Hebrew scriptures are regarded as antithetical to Christ. Sometimes, such a viewpoint is supported by a notion of the Hebrew scriptures as law in a law/grace antithesis. At other times, there may be an anti-Semitic logic involved: Jesus is *our* Savior; Jesus was rejected by the Jews; Hebrew scriptures are the Jewish Bible; *ergo*, the Hebrew scriptures, though full of fine God-stuff, are, nevertheless, antithetical to Christ. Thus, we have all heard sermons that divide structurally between "Old Testament" and "New Testament," suggesting that the Old Testament offers us a God of wrath who judges under law, whereas the New Testament gives us Jesus who represents a God of love and mercy. All such sermons accomplish, other than demonstrating a preacher's ignorance of the Hebrew scriptures, is a fanning of the spark of anti-Semitism. Could such a caricature be maintained by anyone who has fed on the Psalms, or prayed with Jeremiah, or pondered Hosea, or grasped the free covenant grace offered Abraham? The preacher is so stressing the finality of Christ that the Hebrew scriptures are relegated to error. Is it any wonder, then, that sermons split into two parts?

In other sermons, the Hebrew scriptures are treated as either a partial, somewhat inadequate truth, or as a promise only fulfilled by Christ. Again, the position produces a structural design: the big last "Jesus point" at the end of a sermon. Jesus is preached as the answer, the fulfillment, or the solution to the Hebrew scripture's question, longing, or problem. While the structural design may be kinder than a split-sermon system, it still relegates the Old Testament to the status of "mere"—mere longing, or mere promise, or mere preliminary revelation. The position makes Christ implausible. Clearly, the consciousness of Christ was shaped by Hebrew scriptures; they formed his faith, his piety, his ethical concern for neighbors. Are we to assume that one side of Christ's consciousness was formed by Hebrew scriptures and some other side of Christ's consciousness by a new, supplanting God-awareness? No, for Christians, Christ brings us the Hebrew scriptures to preach.

But how? How do we preach the Hebrew scriptures in Christian liturgical contexts? Obviously we cannot preach passages from the Hebrew scriptures as if Christ were *not*. Out of a respect for the integrity of the Hebrew scriptures, we cannot preach them by blanking out Christian consciousness and pretending we are a B.C. Hebrew congregation. Such a let's-pretend posture, though it may pose as hermeneutical integrity, is ludicrous. No, instead, the Hebrew scriptures brought to us by Christ must be set within a Christian hermeneutical consciousness, that is, a consciousness in between symbols of revelation and an awareness of being-saved-in-the-world. The Hebrew scriptures were written from such a consciousness—symbols of revelation drawn from stories such as exodus, Sinai, exile, and the like addressed Israel's sense of being-saved—and, therefore, must be interpreted within such a structural consciousness.

In a proper Christian hermeneutic of the Hebrew scriptures, Christ may well interpret, illustrate, and even discriminate, but *not* annihilate. Our strategy then implies that the Hebrew scriptures will form the structure of our sermons into which Christ may enter as analogy, illumination, or as support for the Hebrew scriptures' own internal corrections. For example, if we preach Ezekiel's vision of dry bones, we will not view the passage as only an inadequate "type" of Christ's resurrection, but, rather, in Christ we will read the passage as a declaration of faith in God who again and again brings life out of death. And will not Christ enable us to grasp the God revealed in Jeremiah's walking with exiles into exile? Of course, when we do run across passages that do seem to us to be "sub-Christian" such as gleeful hand-rubbing over the fate of enemies, we will not use them as a proof of the inadequacy of the Old Testament because the Hebrew scriptures themselves provide internal balances and criticisms (e.g., Hosea), but instead allow Christ to underscore such internal correctives. (Surely, there are passages in the New Testament that may be equally embarrassing, as for example, stridencies in Matthew, Revelation's "Lake of Fire," as well as fierce hostilities expressed in 2 Peter.) No, Jesus Christ may well stand at odds with passages in the Hebrew scriptures, but he does so on the basis of his own thoroughly Jewish consciousness. In preaching from texts drawn from Hebrew scriptures, Christ, who himself was a figure in the story of God-with-Israel, reenters the structure of the story as a living symbol of revelation; Christ does not stand outside the story and relegate it to a position of inadequacy.

In the light of our preliminary discussion of the Hebrew scriptures within Christian consciousness, let us turn to study a narrative passage, Gen. 22:1–19, the familiar story of the sacrifice of Isaac. Instead of moving from structural design toward a sermon, we will study a sermon text by analyzing its parts.

A Sermon

Texts: Gen. 22:1–19 and Rev. 5:11–14

Introduction: An old German woodcut pictures the sacrifice of Isaac. There is Isaac, all trussed up, lying on a pile of brush; huge empty-circle eyes, staring. Above him stands Abraham, both hands held high, about to plunge the knife. Over to one side, in a bush, stands a white lamb, waiting. What a strange story! The story has troubled religious people for centuries, everyone from Augustine to Kafka, from Kierkegaard to Karl Barth. What can we make of the sacrifice of Isaac? Terror and grace. What can we make of the story?

1. At the outset, notice: Isaac is much more than an only child. *Isaac is hope,* hope wrapped up in human flesh. All the promises of God were riding on Isaac. Remember the story? Remember how God dropped in to tell Sarah and Abraham that their offspring would be as many as the sands of the sea, that they would give birth to nations. Well, the old folks giggled, for, according to reliable medical advice, it's mighty tough to conceive when you're pushing ninety! Then, suddenly, Isaac was born, a miracle child: God did provide! Through Isaac, there *would* be many descendants, a multitude of nations. An American playwright tells of how his Jewish parents scrimped and saved to give him everything. They bought him new clothes three times a year, bundled him off to private schools, paid for his college education. "Everything we got's wrapped up in you, boy!" his mother used to say. "Everything we got's wrapped up in you." How easy it is to focus our hopes. God gives us a land to live in and, before you know it, we're chanting, "Everything we've got is wrapped up in you, America!" Or a church to belong to: "Everything we've got is wrapped up in you, Presbyterian Church!" Listen, Isaac was more than an only child. Isaac embodied the promises of God. "Everything we got's wrapped up in you, boy." Isaac was hope, all the hope in the world.

2. So what happened? *God spoke.* "*Kill him off,*" said God, "Take your only child and kill him!" We hear the words and we're appalled. We've always talked of God as Love, spelled L-O-O-O-V-E, so the hard words shake us. "Kill him off," said God. Suddenly life is not what we thought it was—a comfortable therapist's office where on a couch called "prayer" we can spill out our souls to some caring Deity. No, instead, we're stuck with a stony place, a funeral pyre, and a knife blade flashing. Yes, God gives good gifts, but God takes away! "All our loves," cries the heroine of a British novel, "All our loves, you take away!" For every brimming child, there does seem to be a knife blade. So maybe, as the theologians say, we're going to have to "reconstruct our God-concept" to include a few of the darker shades. God may well be terribly good, but notice the adverb "terribly"! God spoke a terrible word to Abraham. As Abraham stood staring at his child Isaac, God said, "Kill him. Kill him off." God spoke.

3. Then, of all things, *Abraham obeyed.* Abraham did as he was told. He obeyed. Flat-eyed, grim, Abraham led his son up the hill, muttering "God will provide," "God will provide," with biting irony. Fanatic Abraham obeyed. To most of us, religion's rather easygoing, a "liberal persuasion," something that's even passable on campus—you can talk religion down at The University Club. Then, we flip a page in our Bibles and stumble on wild-eyed Abraham passing out the poisoned Kool-Aid in some stony Jonestown, and we're embarrassed. Down in the Southwest there's a tribe, the Penitentes. Some say they were practicing human sacrifice into the 1950s. Finally, they were investigated. "What kind of people are you to practice human sacrifice?" a prosecutor demanded. To which a tribal leader replied, "You do not take God seriously."

Well, maybe we don't. We are moderate people: We calculate our charities, confess our minimal sins, schedule a "Minute for Mission" on a weekly basis, and run for dear life from anything in excess. But, see, in Abraham, radical, blind obedience. God commanded, and Abraham was bent on doing God's will even if it meant slaughtering his only hope. So, Abraham went up the hill to kill Isaac. God spoke and Abraham obeyed.

4. Now, hear the clatter of the knife on stone. See Abraham's arms fold down to his side. For, *suddenly, Abraham caught sight of the trapped lamb:* "God *will* provide," he cried triumphantly. "God will provide!" Well, if you're Christian, you can't help thinking of Calvary, can you? Of another stone hill, and a high cross. One of the earliest pictures of the crucifixion is a Byzantine wall painting. The picture shows the stone hill and the wood-stick cross, but, instead of hung Jesus, there's a huge nailed lamb on the crossbar: Lamb of God! Look, if God will hand over an only Child as sacrifice to our rigid sins, then see, behind the hard hurt surface of life, there's not a Holy Terror, but Love: Love so amazing, so Divine, so unutterably intense it will sacrifice itself for us. Lamb on the cross, then Lamb on the Throne! So, Abraham caught sight of the trapped lamb and shouted for joy. Clatter of the knife on stone. Fold of the arm. "God will provide," cried Abraham.

5. Now, do you see what the sacrifice of Abraham is all about? *God set Abraham free for faith.* The Bible calls the story a "test" but the word is too tame. On a high stone hill, God set Abraham free, free for faith. Blind obedience was transformed into faith. Oh, how easy it is to pin all our hopes on a means of grace, and forget God, the giver. Subtly we turn God's gifts into idols. God has given us the scriptures, but see how we flank the open page with candles and frame dogma to guarantee infallibility: "Everything we've got is wrapped up in you, Bible!" Or, perhaps, God draws us into faith through a masculine church; before you know it we're protecting the pronouns and two-legged tailored vestments: "Everything we got's wrapped up in you," sung by a bass-voiced choir. Back in the sixties, a liberal Catholic journal announced gleefully, "God can get along without the Latin Mass." To which a reader replied: "Maybe God can, but we can't." Is there any idolatry like religious idolatry? No wonder God speaks and shatters our souls: "Kill it off!" God who takes away all our false loves. So, on a high hill, God called up Abraham and Isaac, and there—Amazing, *Ruthless* Grace—God set Abraham free, free for faith.

6. Well, *here we are stumbling down a stone-hill Calvary into the twentieth century.* We are free to trust God, for God will provide. Oh, we still have our Bible, our church, our liturgies, but, somehow, they are different now: the gilded sheen has rubbed off. We can love our churches, without having to hold on for dear life, particularly in an age when God may be sweeping away our denominations. And, yes, we can love the scriptures, without having to defend each sacred page, especially now when authority fights are building. We can trust the self-giving God to give us all we'll ever need: "God will provide!" There's a minister in a northern state who has papered a wall of her office:

Custom-made wallpaper repeating words line after line, all over the space. Now she can sit at her desk and read: "Trust God, Let go. Trust God, Let go." Because we trust God—Lamb on the throne—we *can* let go of all our loves: Bible, church, nation, even sexuality. We can stumble down from Calvary into a human world, sure of the grace of God.

Conclusion: Now then, here are pictures to put up in your mind. A stone hill, a pile of brush, empty-circle eyes, and a knife blade high. "Kill him off," cracks the voice of God. But, here's another picture: A wood cross on a rock hill, and a lamb nailed to the crossbar, "God will provide." Keep *both* pictures in your mind. "You God, you take away all our loves, but you give yourself!" Trust God, let go. Let go, trust God.

Discussion

The *Introduction* sets the scene and identifies characters so that an unfolding of the story line may take place. It also sets the story in tradition, Jewish (Kafka) and Christian, before raising the question, "What can *we* make of the story?" The device of a picture—the German woodcut—immediately establishes the story as a symbol to be considered rather than as historical narration.

First Move. The problem of preaching the sacrifice of Isaac is that, given biblical illiteracy, present-day Christians may not understand the significance of Isaac within the covenant promises of God. As a result, contemporary congregations may fix on the psychological pathos of the story and overlook levels of theological meaning. The problem is how to present necessary background information without becoming exegetically pedantic. The problem is solved by making background an act of memory—"Remember the story? Remember how . . ."—rather than tumbling into an objective discussion of Genesis. Furthermore, the background information is given in highly contemporary language and is followed by contemporary illustration. Then, lest "Everything we got's wrapped up in you, boy" be understood as a Jewish proclivity, two examples are added to connect the phrase with *us*. Though it is rarely necessary to build background into narrative systems, in the case of Gen. 22:1–19 it is obviously crucial.

Second Move. Suddenly, the narrative *action* takes over the sermon. But, notice, there is little description of the story. Immediately, we enter into a contemporary consciousness hearing and reacting to the story. By imitating a consciousness of the story, we can avoid then/now splits caused by first talking about the story, and then talking about our reactions. Instead, story and reaction are interwoven throughout the move. The effect, then, is to move from shock to a realization of a hard line in God, with the story in the back of our minds. Images from the story occur at the start of the move, and then in the sixth, eighth, and eleventh sentences before the move ends again with the story line.

Third Move. Now, the sermon is being moved along by the story-line episodes. Whereas the previous move featured an immediate reaction in consciousness, the third move contains a more objective awareness of the story as story, and a more objective consideration of our religious attitudes. The illustration used works off what may be a revulsion toward the whole notion of human sacrifice (which, of course, was banished in Israel), but seeks to retain the sense of serious self-sacrifice demanded of us by God. Though the move may distance us a bit more from the story, it is still an imitation of consciousness conscious of a story.

Fourth Move. Here, we begin with a slightly delayed start in order to imitate the dramatic suspense of the original story. The delay is achieved by a somewhat different point-of-view in which immediate impression precedes understanding. Now, for the first time, a specifically Christian hermeneutical consciousness enters the sermon—"Well, if you're Christian you can't help thinking of Calvary." Notice, however, that Christian consciousness enters *within* the structure of the Genesis story as an analogical consciousness. Thus, we do not disrupt the Genesis story line in order to make a Christian "point." Of course, the problem is how to form Christian analogy without tumbling into an overdrawn system of substitutionary atonement, in which, though we deserve to die for sins, Christ arrives as a sacrificial "Lamb of God" to take our place, a notion which is assuredly not in the Genesis narrative: Isaac is *not* a sin offering. Instead, we are using Christ as a disclosure symbol to bring out the intensity of God-love which *is* the depth of the Genesis story.

Fifth Move. The move begins with a radical shift in point-of-view. Suddenly, we stand back from the story and consider meaning from the standpoint of Gen. 22:1, the notion of "test." In some sermons, the test of Abraham's faith is portrayed as either quixotic cruelty on God's part or as endurance training imposed by God. Instead, we have chosen to read the story as a liberation. In the move, we echo the earlier phrase, "Everything we've got is wrapped up in you," thus bringing back into consciousness previously interpreted background. Notice the use of *Amazing Grace* as "Amazing, Ruthless Grace."

Sixth Move. A type is drawn between Abraham's high place of sacrifice and Calvary. A further analogy is formed between Abraham's radical trust and the free trust we have been granted by the cross. Though analogies are made, Christian meanings are not set against the meanings of the Genesis story but emerge *from* the story and, indeed, within the story—"God will provide!" The illustration which features a woman will interact with remarks about a masculine church in the previous move.

Conclusion. The temptation to dump Hebrew scripture for Christian meaning is usually strongest when conclusions are shaped. Instead, however, after recalling the woodcut from the introduction and the Byzantine mosaic from move 4, we urge the congregation to "Keep *both* pictures." We, then, add interpretive phrases from move 3 and move 6. What we are attempting to do is to transform the story into a symbolic field of meaning in consciousness.

PREACHING IN THE MODE OF IMMEDIACY

We may now be in a position to construct some general guidelines for preaching in the mode of immediacy. The immediate approach is most useful when interpreting passages that seem to be performative, passages that appear to be designed *to do* in consciousness. All language is for consciousness and, therefore, all language is, to some degree, performative. Some passages, however, are clearly plotted to produce an *action* in consciousness out of which meaning happens. Obviously, narrative systems, longer parables, as well as some sequentially structured stories of Jesus, may lend themselves to preaching in the mode of immediacy.

Hermeneutical Consciousness

What exactly is being imitated when we preach in the mode of immediacy? We do not talk about a story, or even tell a story, so much as imitate a consciousness hearing and reacting to a story. The preacher *shares* consciousness with a congregation and represents hermeneutical consciousness grasping a story.

Though we are imitating consciousness understanding a story episode by episode, the mode of consciousness is *immediate.* We are not standing back and reflecting on a whole story so much as hearing the story and forming immediate analogies of experience by which we understand and respond to the story as it moves along. The text and images of lived experience interact as the plot unfolds. The story line is not an object of contemplation so much as an *action* and interaction in consciousness. What the minister plots, then, is not a story, but a sequence of responses to a story as the story progresses.

Plot and Intention

In designing sermons for preaching in the mode of immediacy, ministers will study the logic of sequence, asking *why* one episode follows another. The preacher will notice surprises in sequence, dramatic turns in plot, unexpected episodes, and ask (1) *why* they were so designed and (2) *what* they do in consciousness. In other words, we will study plot as *an intending to do*.

While we may not follow the sequence of a passage episode by episode, we will be trying to design our sermons *to do* in consciousness, to fulfill intentions. Therefore, when we preach in the mode of immediacy, our sermons will have to move along as a series of sharply delineated shifts in consciousness. Even if the original story on a page of the Bible is told with considerable smoothness, our sermons must be highly structured, with each move a separately designed unit forming in consciousness. In this regard, we will seek to retain the spareness of plot which is a mark of biblical narrative and avoid excursions into the interior life of biblical characters. Biblical plots are theological constructs and not psychological studies in character.

Moving toward Reflection

A minister will have previously studied a biblical passage so that it will have formed a structured field of meaning in consciousness. When preaching in the mode of immediacy, however, the minister is going back and *imitating* the immediate unfolding of meaning prior to the formed structure. Nevertheless, the purpose of the sermon is the construction of an eventual field of meaning for reflection in congregational consciousness. Thus, through a traveling plot, the sermon will aim toward a final structured understanding in consciousness. In other words, we are not telling a story for the sake of amusement, or affect, but telling a story in such a way as to form a *new* understanding by its action in consciousness.

Preaching in the mode of immediacy can be powerful, at times almost too powerful. Its power, however, is not achieved by emotional climax or dramatic catharsis. The power of preaching with immediacy is not that it "moves" people, but that it moves in consciousness structurally.

22.
Preaching in
the Reflective Mode

When we preach in the reflective mode, what are we reflecting on? We are considering, standing back and trying to understand, but what exactly is the object of our contemplation? Bluntly, what are we talking about?

Obviously, in many sermons a passage from scripture is under consideration, some bundle of words on a Bible page. The text is an object of contemplation. In such sermons there is often a relationship between exegetical method and sermon construction. For example, if a minister is steeped in the historical-critical method, we can expect sermons to include paragraphs that discuss author, or biblical background, situation, and, sometimes, even specific wording, "We see in the text . . ." Finally, the sermon may come up with an original situational meaning which must then be applied to today. Because some biblical situation is the context of original meaning, application usually involves drawing situational parallels which may or may not be terribly convincing. Sermons which study a text usually contain many references to actual wording, quotes from the text, or large chunks of biblical information, history, or background. Under the impact of the biblical-theology movement many sermons today seem to be talking *about* passages.

Another alternative is to speak on a topic or theme which has been distilled from a passage. Such preaching seems to happen in two different ways. In one mode, some*thing* in the text is taken out to discuss, usually an idea or even a single verse that seems to contain an idea. So, when preaching on the story of Blind Bartimaeus (Mark 10:46–52), a minister may notice many different ideas in the text—the cry for help, the crowd's rebuke, Jesus' turn toward the lone beggar, or verses such as "Take heart" and "What do you want me to do for you?" and "Your faith has made you whole." Then, the minister selects one of the ideas from the passage as a topic—some*thing* is taken out of the text to preach. The method seems to treat the text as if it were a flat, fixed still-life picture containing a number of "objects," any one of which may be seized on for a sermon. The other approach to passages involves a kind of discernment. Preachers read a passage and sense that underlying the whole passage is some sort of general theme, for example, "spiritual blindness," which, once distilled from the text, may become a subject matter for preaching. While some preachers regard the theme as an eternal truth hidden in the passage, most preachers view the theme as a broad field of concern to talk about. In both cases, whether with a single idea or a general theme, preachers are forced to fabricate some sort of sermon design from their own minds.

There are problems. Both approaches, "textual" preaching and biblical "topic" preaching, have problems. When a minister talks about a text and locates a situational original meaning, problems usually show up at the point of application. A notion of situational meaning usually prompts a search for some parallel situation in our lives for the text to address. If there is no obvious situational parallel, then the text's original meaning will be allegorized or psychologized or turned into some general bon mot for living. Textual sermons frequently creak and strain at the moment of application. Though textual sermons may be fully packed with biblical information, they often struggle for "relevance." Of course, when ministers select a theme to talk on, they may be "relevant," but may often lose track of biblical understandings. Because topics have been detached, preachers are forced to build a rhetorical scheme for speaking from their own resources. They may end up speaking in a structure determined by their own psychological patterns or by rhetorical convention, for example, categorical points, question-answer sequences, thesis-antithesis-synthesis, and so on. Stock sermon designs, however, may not be appropriate to forms of biblical thought. For example, imagine trying to preach a dynamic Hebrew understanding of creation in a static point-making pattern, or to cram the mobile plot of a parable into a thesis-antithesis-synthesis pattern. Topics can too easily lead us away from profound exploration of symbols of revelation. Actually, the notion of a distilled theme is a version of the kernel/shell hermeneutic which we discussed previously.

So, our question remains: When we preach in the reflective mode, what are we reflecting on? We have argued that passages, as they are studied, form a patterned *structure of contemporary understanding* in consciousness. In a preacher's consciousness, as the moving plot of a text provokes analogies of understanding, a distinctively shaped field of meaning is formed. We are describing neither a text on a page nor a distilled theme, but rather a configured field of *contemporary* understanding. For example, if a preacher is interpreting the parable of the Pharisee and the Publican, the pattern produced in consciousness would feature two different contemporary life stances as well as a new understanding of the justifying God. The actual characters from the text may well have faded into background, and even the words of the text be distanced. What will be present in consciousness is a contemporary theological understanding produced by the structure of the text as well as contemporary images drawn from lived experience. In contradistinction to the two approaches we have described: (1) we have a structure of *contemporary* understanding, *not* some situational original meaning, and (2) we have a particular *pattern* of meaning, *not* a single idea or topic to preach. Thus, sermons in the reflective mode preach neither a text nor a topic, but, instead, they convey a patterned field of contemporary understanding in consciousness that has been produced by a passage. In an art gallery, we may stand in front of a painting and let impression form (immediacy), or later, away from the painting, we can consider the image of the painting in consciousness (reflection). When we preach in the reflective mode, the design of our sermons will relate in some way to the *pattern* of meaning in consciousness.

Much of the Bible is written in the reflective mode. Certainly, we do not get tape recordings of original events or a primal spill of oral tradition. Instead, we get plots produced by reflective consciousness, considering a remembered event or reformulating oral material. While there are passages that still work with the performative power of immediacy—parables, some narratives, some remarkably oral systems—much scripture lends itself to preaching in the reflective mode. Obviously the epistles, though probably written to be read aloud in congregations, are products of reflective consciousness. Likewise, a passage in the Hebrew scriptures such as 2 Chron. 36:11–23 is written by an author who, recalling the past, is trying to grasp theological meaning from a social catastrophe; the passage is reflective. What we must discover is *how* to design sermons in the reflective mode so that sermon structure will relate to the pattern of meaning in our consciousness.

A PAULINE PASSAGE:
2 CORINTHIANS 5:17–21

Passages from Pauline and pseudo-Pauline letters are often intimidating to present-day preachers: Some preachers never speak from the epistles. In spite of contemporary translations, ideas we stumble on in the letters do seem formidably theological. Many preachers still harbor the notion that egghead Paul came along and complicated the simple teachings of Jesus. If the letters do not come across as theologically weighty, they seem utterly alien to our contemporary world. We do not think of human history as split into time-space eons—this present age and an age to come. We cannot seem to grasp how, with Christ's death, we all are "dead to sin." When Paul talks about the "old man" and the "new man," we feel as if we are wading deep into murky mythology. As a result, if we do preach Paul we may tend to distill topics from passages. When Paul speaks of a "new creation" in 2 Corinthians 5, we trot out a sermon on new life through conversion. Or if we bump into "new creation" in Rom. 8:18–25 we distill the theme of ecology and preach on land conservation. The practice of taking ideas from Paul to preach on, while chucking the full complexity of passages, evades the depth of Christian faith. Somehow, we must find a way to get at the consciousness of Saint Paul.

Begin with an assumption: Paul's letters were *not* "difficult" for first-century congregations. To whom were the letters addressed? Answer: To congregations aptly described as "not many of you were wise according to worldly standards, not many were powerful, not many were of noble birth" (1 Cor. 1:26). We can safely guess that Paul's congregations did not glitter with Ph.D.s or card-carrying members of the elite. The folk in Corinth, no matter how streetwise, were an intellectual cut below average mainline American congregations. Though we stumble over the weight of Paul's words, we must assume that first-century people sat nodding their understanding without undue concentration. Our problem is not with an inherent difficulty in Paul's thought so much as with a hermeneutical problem posed by the passage of time. Thus, if we want to preach Paul, we will not be able to move from text to sermon on our own, or even with the aid of commentaries. We will have to prepare ourselves by reading studies in Pauline theology —not one but several (see For Further Readings).

A second caveat: Let us assume that, in general, Paul is talking about matters at hand, things that could be seen and touched and talked about in matter-of-fact ways. Many preachers read onto Paul a kind of spiritual glaze, as if his language refers to mysterious unseen realities most of the time. Not so. Again and again, study of Paul will lead us not to unseen intricacies but to earthly realities of a first-century Jew/Gentile world. Paul is addressing a concrete being-saved community in the world and is trying to help them understand themselves through Jesus Christ. Thus, unraveled, Pauline thought is remarkably preachable. Are not churches today split between the uptight and the liberated, between religious conservatives and religious liberals? And do we not struggle still with problems of racism and sexism as did the Corinthians? And, surely, we find ourselves captive, enchained in cultural myths and customs as pernicious as Paul's "principalities and powers." Though the centuries divide our mythology from Paul's mythology, a study of Pauline texts can form vivid contemporary understandings in consciousness.

An initial step in preaching Pauline material will be a reading of the text. Those who are not equipped to pore over original Greek will wish to do a comparative study of contemporary translations, noting, in particular, where translations *disagree* and where, therefore, meaning may be difficult to grasp. The passage we are examining might be translated freely as follows:

> [17]Anyone in Christ is [of] the new creation: Old things are passed away; look, they are new. [18]Everything is God's doing, who has reconciled us to Godself through Christ, and has given us the ministry of reconciliation. [19]For God was in Christ reconciling the world to Godself, not counting their sins against them, and forming among us the word of reconciliation. [20]Thus, we are ambassadors for Christ, God making appeal through us. [21]On behalf of Christ, we beg you, "Be reconciled!"

The passage is notoriously difficult to translate, difficult to interpret, and, obviously, rests on a very different world view than our own.

With Paul, as with any *non-narrative* system, we must begin by discerning the structure of the passage; first, major shifts in thought and, then, subordinate shifts. To get at structure, it may help to read the passage aloud, to sense changes in perspective, subject matter, and tense. Notice that in 2 Corinthians 5:17–21, v. 17 refers to the "in Christ" Christian community, whereas in vv. 18–19 there is talk of God's previous activity—"God *was* in Christ." Verse 19b is subordinate, explaining the means of reconciliation, namely, a cancellation of sins. In both v. 18 and v. 19, a final subordinate clause refers back to the Christian community. Verse 20 explains v. 19c with the metaphor of "ambassadors." The final verse, v. 21, appears to be direct address either to the Christian community, saying, in effect, "Be what you *are,*" or to the unconverted world. Thus, we have four major subject matters—the Christian community, the work of God in Christ, the evangelical vocation of the community, and an address, "Be reconciled!" We also have subordinate clauses which are descriptive or an explanation of means. We might outline the structure of the passage in the following way:

1. Anyone in Christ is [of] the new creation.
   a. Old things are past. Everything is new.
2. Everything is God's doing: God was in Christ reconciling the world to Godself.
   a. By means of cancelling sins.
3. God has trusted us with the message of reconciliation.
   a. That is to say, we are ambassadors for Christ.
   b. God making a pitch to the world through us.
4. Therefore, we say, "Be reconciled!"

By doing an analysis of structure, we focus attention on a *pattern* of thought in the whole passage. We do *not* attempt to pick out a single idea, such as "ambassadors for Christ," or even a general theme, such as "reconciliation." Paul's passage is an interacting system of thought and can only be understood in its structural interactions. Whenever we preach from a non-narrative passage, we will need to begin with an analysis of non-narrative plot.

Homiletic Analysis

Our next task is a homiletic analysis in which each of the shifts in Paul's language is probed. We must search underlying theology, spot possible blocks to understanding that may lurk in our contemporary minds, and gather analogies of understanding from lived experience. We will sketch the process:

1. Anyone in Christ is [of] the new creation.

   a. *Theology:* Paul's thought seems to be built on a sharp distinction between "this present age" and an "age to come," which is even now pressing upon us. The new age is a "new creation" inaugurated by Christ, the new Adam, that features a new humanity. Paul's image is *social;* he looks toward a new social order. Anyone "in Christ"—that is, in Christian community—is an advance guard of the new humanity and, thus, of the new social order.

   b. *Congregational Blocks:* We sense two serious problems, one relating to world view, the other to a matter of doubt. We have been taught too many "time lines" in grade school, so that we think of time as chronological and progressive. Paul clearly thinks of time as *kairos,* for he divides time into the present eon and an eschatologically imminent eon. Paul's understanding may be exceedingly difficult to preach. A more serious problem may be posed by the lack of evidence for a new creation. If the church is supposed to be an advance guard of the new order of things, its newness may be difficult to perceive. Too often, the church is reactionary, and, at least in America, may seem to epitomize an old order.

   c. *Analogies of Experience:* As we think of signs of the new order within the church, we tend to come up with two kinds of evidence. We can think of general Christian activity, for example, public worship, benevolence budgets, family-night suppers where social differences are somewhat overcome in a sweet chaos of "fellowship," and, of course, the eschatological "sign" of Eucharist. We also may think of individual evidence, for example, a stuffed-shirt banker who, Monday through Friday, is hard-as-nails business, but who, on Sundays, supervises the church nursery with high glee and affection—a "little sign" of the new age.

2. God was in Christ reconciling the world.

   a. *Theology:* Paul's theology of the cross is difficult. Apparently, he supposes that all humanity is united in the guilt of the cross, but that all humanity is absolved by Christ's death and resurrection. Though the crucified Christ,

God-with-us, is put to death by our common sinfulness, at the same time the crucified Christ in love dies for us and, in resurrection, restores union with us. The event of Jesus Christ produces a past tense, "God *was* in Christ," that is effective in the present.

b. *Congregational Blocks:* In addition to the sheer difficulty of understanding how one person's death may atone for the sin of all, there is a potential misunderstanding of "reconciliation." We tend to grasp reconciliation in relational models, as, for example, an estranged child being embraced by a parent. Our images are cozy. Relational models, however, may obscure the ethical edge to reconciliation. The God who has reconciled us is a righteous God. Therefore, reconciliation is more than feeling with, it involves ethically going along with God's righteousness.

c. *Analogies of Experience:* Generally, we think of one-to-one personal reconciliation models, but Paul's thought is cosmic. Thus, images of reconciliation may be difficult to locate. Maybe we can recall the case in which a foreign student was killed during hazing by a fraternity group, yet whose mother, subsequently, moved into the fraternity house as a cook, serving the group in love for the rest of her life.

3. Not counting their sins against them.

a. *Theology:* The text contains an odd bookkeeping metaphor—not tabulating sins. In other words, here we bump into a radical announcement of free grace. In Christ, God's mercy is unconditionally given—the account-book page is ripped to shreds.

b. *Congregational Blocks:* It is astonishing how unmerciful we Christians can be; we expect demands to be met before we dole out pardon. In one part of our minds, we demand repentance before mercy is granted, a demand which does not appear in 2 Corinthians 5:17–21. In another part of our minds, "law-and-order" thinking gets in the way. Some years ago, when the death penalty for a convict in a western state became a matter of debate, thousands of letters flowed in, saying, in effect, "Fry the S.O.B.!" Most of the letters appeared to have been sent by "church people." We cannot underestimate resentment of free mercy.

c. *Analogies of Experience:* How can we ever understand free mercy? We either think of childhood memories of parental forgiveness, often quite undeserved and surprising, or we think of cases we have heard that seem to demonstrate radical mercy. Unconditional mercy is, after all, fairly uncommon.

4. We are ambassadors for Christ.

a. *Theology:* Ambassadors in the first century were not similar to ambassadors in our more modern world. Primarily, ambassadors were accurate messengers. They would memorize a message correctly, including intonations, and, then, like human tape recorders, deliver the message to another monarch. Thus, the image of an ambassador connects with Paul's notion that God has entrusted a *message* of reconciliation to us. So, when Paul is speaking of ambassadors, he is not suggesting a witness through life style, he is referring to a ministry of word, the preaching of good news to the world.

b. *Congregational Blocks:* Note that models of the church in our age may be more therapeutic than vocational/evangelical. We may think of entering a church in order to join a therapeutic God-community in which we may gain healing or salvation. We seldom think of the church in instrumental ways, particularly in verbal instrumental ways.

c. *Analogies of Experience:* The analogies we locate will be governed by our theological understanding. Therefore, we must find analogies in which a word is news of reconciliation. Images should be verbal and not merely relational, that is, being kind to others and spreading a little love around.

5. Be reconciled!

a. *Theology:* The issue, here, is a matter of interpretation and, thus, theological. Does the text call the church to be what it is in Christ, namely a reconciled community of the new age; or does the verse represent the church's message to the world: "Be reconciled!"? The solution may be to let both meanings emerge in a sermon because, of course, both meanings make theological sense.

In doing a homiletic analysis of Paul's non-narrative passage, notice what has taken place. (1) By doing a homiletic analysis, the structure of the passage, along with analogies of experience, is producing in our consciousness a structured field of contemporary meaning. (2) By doing a homiletic analysis, we are already moving toward a preaching of the passage. Thus, we are avoiding a rationalist split between, first, an exegesis and, then, an application. (3) In doing our analysis, notice that we looked at theology and then turned immediately to analyze roadblocks *before* seeking analogies of experience. In non-narrative systems, we encounter ancient thought rather directly in a twentieth-century consciousness, where sharp delineations in cultural attitudes, world views, models of understanding, and so on, are sensed at once. Out of the interaction of two rather different cultural modes of thought, we are directed toward analogies of experience. Thus, we read Paul and Paul reads us and, *then,* we seek to locate fields of experience with which to comprehend the passage. For example, if we move directly from language in the passage, such as "ambassadors," to analogies of experience, we may misread the passage, for example, "ambassador" as a life style representative of a different society. Instead, by analyzing possible misunderstandings as we read, we can better focus on appropriate images in lived experience.

The Basic Plotting of Non-narrative Sermons

The result of our analysis is a field of *contemporary* understanding that includes a number of component parts. While the original sequential flow of the passage—new order, God's work in Christ, forgiveness, our ambassadorial task, and a call to reconciliation—has been disrupted, all the components are within a whole pattern of understanding within our field of consciousness. The problem now involves replotting our understanding into a basic sermon structure.

The particular passage from 2 Corinthians which we have chosen is interesting because it permits a variety of plots. For example, see what is going on in the following short paragraphs:

A. Guess what? We've been forgiven, outright forgiven! All the sins we tabulate have been torn up by God. The past no longer controls us; we have a new start. What else do you think was going on at Calvary? Even as we showed our sin by crucifying Christ, Christ showed God's mercy by absolving us: "Father forgive!" Well, it changes everything! Now, we can live together with God in a new way. Think of a new society in which we wouldn't have to run around justifying ourselves. Instead, with a kind of post mercy innocence, we could love. Is it worth talking about? You bet! Of course, that's who we are—people who talk about God's mercy. We are "ambassadors for Christ" in the world. We announce a new-start mercy, saying, "Be reconciled!"

B. Everyone here in church ought to be wearing a name tag: Your name and, underneath, a title, "Ambassador." We are Christ's ambassadors charged by God with delivering a message to the world. What's the message? "You can live in a new way, past ancient guilts and old resentments. There can be a whole new social order in the world." Why? Because we have been forgiven. In mercy, the whole world can begin again. For don't you see, at Calvary God-in-Christ forgave us all. No wonder we have a message for the world: We say, "Be reconciled!"

In paragraph A we moved from "Not counting sins," to "God was in Christ reconciling," to "Anyone in Christ is [of] the new creation," to "We are ambassadors," before concluding with "Be reconciled." In paragraph B we began with "ambassadors," moved to the notion of "new creation," turned to "Not counting sins," and then, by effect-cause logic, discussed "God was in Christ reconciling," before, finally, ending with "Be reconciled." Each of the schemes covered the whole field of meaning but each displayed a different sequence and different connective logics. When we preach in the reflective mode we are no longer bound by the original sequence of a passage. Instead, we are playing within a structured field of meaning, moving around from meaning to meaning with a logic that is usually more appropriate to our own age. In 2 Cor. 5:17–21 we are permitted much variety in sequence. Depending on where we enter the field of meaning, we can develop many different basic structures of thought. Remember, we are not talking about a text on a page with a verse-to-verse sequence; instead, we are dealing with a whole field of understanding in consciousness that can be replotted and, often, must be replotted for contemporary congregations.

In the two paragraphs we have sketched there is *no reference to the actual wording of the text,* or, at least, little mention of Paul or actual verses from the text. We have preached from a structure of understanding in consciousness, rather than *about* a text or an author. The notion that, to be biblical, preaching must make endless statements about the text—"We see in our text that . . . ," "So Saint Paul says . . . ," "The Corinthians must have heard the words . . ."—is a homiletical convention that may not be useful. Suppose we envision the problem on a scale as follows:

Talking *about*   Preaching *of*
_____**X**_____

Passages that require lengthy exegetical or historical excursuses may not lend themselves to preaching; they may not be within a "homiletic canon." Do we need to suppose that all scriptural texts intend preaching? The scriptures provide wondrous resources for the whole life of the church and not merely for the pulpit. Many passages which obviously *were* preaching may well intend to be preached, but many others are either not germane to our situation or are useful out of the pulpit—perhaps in classroom or liturgy or elsewhere. Besides, preaching is an announcement of the good news of our salvation and not a talking about biblical background, telling people all about Paul or Moses or Matthew, or even about the wording of a text.

Preaching tends to be influenced by methods of biblical interpretation. Thus, when textual criticism was *the* method, sermons discussed words of a text; when historical-critical method came to the fore, sermons featured information on biblical background and biblical situations. In both cases, methodology led to an objective talking about the Bible. But when we preach, the object of our concern is the mystery of God-in-Christ for a being-saved community. Through the Bible we explore symbols of revelation in order to proclaim the good news. Thus, the Bible itself is *not* the subject of our sermons. Even if we accept the Barthian notion of the Bible as witness to Jesus Christ, we do not preach the witness, we preach Christ. Let us suggest that "biblical preaching" is not more or less biblical according to the number of citations that show up in a sermon's words; ultimately, "biblical preaching" is a preaching of the *gospel*. When we preach in the reflective mode we need not include gobs of biblical discussion. A passage has formed a structure of contemporary understanding in consciousness and our sermons evolve from that structure in consciousness.

When designing a sermon in the reflective mode, there is always *the problem of where to begin.* Where do we enter the field of understanding? In preaching 2 Cor. 5:17–21, do we enter our field of understanding by talking of the church as "ambassador," or do we begin with news of God's mercy, or do we start out with the notion of "new creation"? Usually, we will begin with ideas that can be readily grasped, perhaps because they relate directly to our self-understanding. But we must be cautious. We are *not* saying that we begin with ideas that dovetail with our self-understanding, or that are somehow congenial to self-understanding—a happy "point of contact." No, we are trying to locate facets of the structure of meaning that address our self-understanding. Thus, in our example paragraphs, we selected "We've been forgiven" or "We ought to be wearing a name tag . . . 'Ambassadors,' " either one of which does address self-understanding. Actually, as we have noted, the idea of "ambassadors" may run counter to usual understandings of the church. Nevertheless, a role-definition word such as "ambassador" does speak to self-understanding. While we might select some other point of entry from our field of understanding, we would find entry much more difficult. For example, the idea of a "new creation," resting as it does on a two-eon theology, may be alien to contemporary thinking. Likewise, a launch into "God was in Christ reconciling" might be so formidable that a congregation would be bogged down from the start. Such difficulties might be overcome by adding a premove to the sermon, a section on estrangement in our world or a paragraph on the "old ways" of our world, which would permit entry into ideas of "reconciliation" or of a "new age." But, as a rule, we will enter our field of meaning with an idea that addresses our self-understanding, unless there appears to be good theological reasons for doing otherwise. Point of entry is never arbitrary, however—where we enter our field of meaning will usually determine how meaning subsequently unfolds.

Previously, we have mentioned that a basic structure ought to be written in *contemporary conversational language.* Using our example paragraph A, we can set up a simple sequence of move sentences.

1. Guess what? We've been forgiven.
2. What else do you think was happening on Calvary?
3. Well, reconciliation changes everything—a new social order!
4. Isn't new life worth talking about?
5. So we say, "Be reconciled!"

If we were to forego conversational language we might end up with a list of topics without any sense of connective logic.

1. God's Unconditional Forgiveness
2. The Reconciling Death of Christ
3. The New Creation
4. The Church's Evangelical Calling
5. The Christian Message of Reconciliation

Such a scheme would be impossible to put into everyday discourse without counting points or writing labored transitional paragraphs to patch together topics. When preaching from Paul it is almost always helpful to scribble out a paragraph sketch of content and then reduce the sketch to a conversational sequence of sentences in a basic structure. After all, we are preaching from a field of *contemporary* meaning and not from a text on a page of the Bible.

A word about *freedom:* In the reflective mode, within reason, we can freely add to or subtract from the field of meaning. For example, we might preface our basic structure with a move that studies our unreconciled world so that "We are forgiven" could come as very good news indeed. Or, in a discussion of the change that reconciliation in Christ can make, we could split sentence 3 in our basic structure so as to speak of both personal change and social change. Likewise, we could reduce "Be reconciled!" to a conclusion, or we could double the idea so that the phrase becomes a message to us as well as a message to the human world. We must never view the structured field of meaning in consciousness as a biblically woven straitjacket. In Catholic parishes where, with a number of Masses, brief homilies are more usual, only the *major* shifts of 2 Cor. 5:17–21 might be preached—(1) We are ambassadors, (2) telling the world news of reconciliation, (3) so that we may all live in the new way of life displayed in Eucharist. We may construct sermons freely because we are reflecting on a field of understanding in consciousness. We are not free *from* the field of consciousness, however.

To push the question of freedom: Why not revert to an older homiletic tradition that began in the seventeenth century and simply preach on a single verse from the passage? After all, each verse does seem packed with theological meaning—if not overpacked! Such preaching is obviously possible, because it is done frequently. Originally it was produced by the assumption that every verse of scripture, indeed every phrase or word, contains a pithy God-truth which may be unwrapped like a fortune cookie for all to see. The other impulse behind the custom, particularly in the seventeenth century, was that it permitted freedom to develop artful and sometimes elegant sermon designs apart from the binding restraints of a passage. Notice the temptations involved. We could preach a sermon on "Anyone in Christ is of the new creation," but without context we could end up in a conversionist/Pietist plea to become a new person inside. Or, the notion of "ambassadors" detached from the passage could turn into a sermon on representing our true homeland in a loving life style. The use of the full context, however, does permit entree to a field of understanding that relates symbols of revelation to a consciousness of being-saved in the world, which is, of course, what is going on in the Pauline letters. Preaching Paul may be difficult but, in the reflective mode, it can produce a contemporary, thoroughly exciting Word of God.

A TEACHING: MATTHEW 5:33–37

Much non-narrative preaching drawn from the Christian scriptures involves the teachings of Jesus. Jesus' teachings pose a problem for preaching because of their frequent brevity and their epigrammatic form. We shall look at a text from the Sermon on the Mount in Matthew which is brief indeed. Here is a fairly literal translation:

> [33]Again, you've heard that it was said [to people] of old, "You shall not swear yourself, but shall say your oaths before God." [34]But, I'm telling you, "Don't swear at all!" Neither by heaven, because it is God's throne; [35]Nor by earth, because it is [God's] footstool; nor by Jerusalem, because it is the city of The Great King. [36]Don't swear by your head, because you cannot make one hair white or black. [37]Let your word be 'Yes Yes, No No': Anything more is from Evil.

The passage has been subject to all kinds of extravagant interpretation from a ban on cuss words to a ban on court oaths. Some comments on the text may be in order. Verse 33, which might better be translated "You shall not swear falsely . . . ," is not a direct quote from the Hebrew scriptures, but appears to summarize a number of passages among which are Lev. 19:12 "You shall not swear by my Name falsely," and, of course, Exod. 20:7 "You shall not take the name of the Lord your God in vain," Numbers 30, and a range of other texts. In some early Christian literature, the saying of Jesus in v. 34, "Don't swear at all" (which grammatically might be translated, "Don't swear anytime at all"), appears in positive form, "Always speak the truth," which a few scholars believe may have been original. The formula, "You have heard it said . . . but I'm telling you . . . ," does not set up a sharp antithesis; rather, the formula may mean, "You have heard . . . but now I give you the true interpretation of the ancient words." The chain of three examples in v. 35 were evidently common speech *oaths* which, by avoiding the Name of God, were not regarded as binding sacred *vows;* though they sounded sacred, they were in fact deceptive. The saying in v. 37 is probably a colloquial phrase meaning "Let your 'Yes' be Yes, and your 'No' No," which is the phrasing found in some rabbinic parallels, as well as in Justin Martyr. Basically, the passage pleads truth telling in a world of falsity.

A much deeper question has to do with the teaching of Jesus per se. Without rehearsing all theological options, we can at least review some questions. Is the Sermon on the Mount a collection of individual ethic for all people to go and do? If so, "lots o' luck!"; the teachings are all but impossible in our kind of world. Is the Sermon on the Mount *praeparatio evangelica,* a preparation for the gospel, designed to bring us to our knees in helpless sin so that we will more eagerly receive news of justifying grace? Such a position turns Jesus into a manipulative evangelist who slaps us with law in order to drive us to the gospel. Is the Sermon on the Mount a radical interim ethic in view of imminent Parousia which we now accept as ideal "general principles" to be modified in the name of "Christian Realism"? The problem: "Christian Realism" always seems to lead to casuistry, and the form of the Sermon on the Mount is emphatically not casuistic. *Notice,* each of the positions we have questioned would produce a different kind of sermon structure. The reason the teachings of Jesus have to be preached reflectively is that they must be set within some sort of hermeneutical context to be interpreted at all.

So, again, what exactly are the teachings of Jesus? Some statements may be ventured: (1) The teachings call for a new society—the kingdom of God. (2) The teachings are general only as extended. They are intended for an advance-guard church, called to witness the new age *now.* (3) The teachings are not individual ethic. They presuppose a community (most are "you-all" teachings) of the Spirit engaged in worship, mutual correction, and corporate action. (4) Though we do not live in expectation of immediate Parousia, the teachings presuppose a world in which the future of God is unfolding toward the denouement of Jesus Christ. What we have done is set forth a theology within which the teachings of Jesus may be interpreted. Again, the theology we frame will clearly determine the kind of sermon structure we design. There is *no* way any preacher can move from text to sermon without recourse to theological understanding.

The passage chosen from Matthew 5 has an interesting form which may be diagrammed as follows:

Contrast of Commandments
1. "You have heard it said . . ."
   Summary statement of the law
2. "but I'm telling you . . ."
   Jesus' statement: "Don't swear at all"

Contrast of Examples
1. Examples of casuistry under law: Cases A, B, C, and Case D
2. Life in the new age: "Let your 'Yes' be Yes, and your 'No' be No"
3. An activating of contrast: "Anything more is from Evil."

Within consciousness, the intricacies of the Matthean passage will be reduced and the double contrast of the text be formed into something like a single contrast, perhaps as follows:

Past-tense Law
"You shall not swear falsely, but . . ."
Examples of duplicity under the law—A, B, C, and D
Evidence of the evil among us

Present Word of Christ
Radical word: Don't "swear by" at all!
Let your "Yes" be Yes and your "No" be No.

The field of meaning formed in consciousness is much more than rearranged verses of a text. If we have passed through homiletic analysis each component of the text will have become a theological understanding. Thus, the "You have heard it said . . ." statement will have been grasped within some sort of understanding of the law of God. Likewise, the examples of duplicity will have been interpreted within some sort of reading of human interactional sin. Jesus' command not to swear at all will be understood as a wave toward the new age, and his "Yes Yes, No No" will form as a call to the witnessing church. No wonder homiletic analysis is crucial—bare words in a text are not always much help. But in addition to theological interpretations, we will have studied congregational blocks—particularly the honest reaction "Impossible!"—and we will have searched out analogies of experience. Thus, instead of Jesus' examples we may already be hearing contemporary language: "I swear to God . . . ," "You can take my word for it," "It's the gospel truth," "Would I kid you?" and the like. In other words, by a process we have labeled "homiletic analysis," the text will have formed a field of structured *contemporary* meaning in consciousness from which a sermon may be plotted.

Here, then, is a very brief sermon sketch.

Introduction: In first-century Palestine the air was filled with oaths: "I swear by Jerusalem," "I swear by heaven." Oaths echoed wherever deals were made or products hawked. Well, oaths still echo in our world—"I swear to God," "I kid you not," "It's the gospel truth!" In the midst of the hubbub Jesus speaks. "Don't swear at all," says Jesus Christ.

1. Make no mistake, Jesus is not warning against cuss words. No. If Jesus' father hit his thumb with a hammer doing carpentry, the air in Nazareth

probably turned blue. The command is not aimed at bad language. The question with bad language is not what's said, but why. When A. Lincoln saw a slave auction and exclaimed, "Damnable!" would we reproach him? Yes, we can regret cuss words and, in particular, rue the use of "God," but when Jesus says, "Don't swear at all!" he is not nailing up a ban against bad language.

2. Jesus is looking at the world, *our* world. We live in a world of the "big lie," where words are used deceitfully. Would we need a truth-in-lending bill if there were not widespread untruth in lending? Or would the FDA curb advertising claims if claims were not frequently untrue? As for the USA calling obliteration bombing a "peace offensive," is any comment needed? In an old Li'l Abner cartoon there is a lovable character called The Shmoo. Whenever Shmoos showed up people automatically told the truth. Finally, the human race hunted down the Shmoos and destroyed them. Why? Because the whole world was falling apart—politics, business, marriages, even churches. Our world is built on falsity.

3. Well, no wonder we swear by oaths! In a world of falsity, we have to do something to underline truth. "I swear to God," we say. Or "Look, you can trust me," we plead. And no wonder that in courtrooms we administer oaths, swearing on a Bible to tell the truth. All our oath taking is an admission that most of the time truth is not our normal way of life. So by oaths we try to set up a sacred moment of truth in a world of secular, all too human, falsity. Who was it who suggested that in response to the question, "Do you swear to tell the truth, the whole truth, and nothing but the truth," we should answer in the words of the General Confession: "There is no truth in us." Fact is, our swearing is a witness to original sin.

4. So, what's the answer? A whole new world! If George Steiner is right in claiming that all language is designed for self-protection and deceiving neighbors, then it will do no good to demand truthfulness. What we need is a whole new human world to live in; a kingdom of God, perhaps. For, look, if we live before God full-time and in affection toward neighbors, truth *would* be our way of life. A character in a modern novel says it nicely, "If we live in love, we can speak true to one another." What Jesus is asking is a whole new social order built on love.

5. Meanwhile, guess what? We church types are called to be truth tellers. "Let your 'Yes' be Yes, and your 'No' be No," Jesus says to *us*. For in a "big-lie" world, we are called to show the shape of kingdom life. Will we lose cash when trading cars? Sure. Will we be branded unpatriotic? Probably. (But, in view of the cross, who calls Christ's life a success story?) We are a people chosen by Christ to show and tell what God's new world is all about. A simple meaning of what we say will be our style—no duplicity, so help us God! No playing games to deceive or protect. The name "Truthful" used to be a popular name for children. We are to live so that, in a broken world, all God's people will be named "Truthful."

Notice that, except for the first move which is included to prevent misunderstanding, the other moves have been formed by the text into a contemporary pattern of meaning. The structure then represents a reflection of the pattern of meaning formed by the passage in consciousness. To be specific: Examples A, B, C, and D from the text underlie move 2; "Anything more is from Evil" lurks beneath move 3; "Don't swear at all" is the basis for move 4; and "Let your 'Yes' be Yes, and your 'No' No" is incorporated in move 5. Though there is little talking about the first century, and even less citing of words from the text, the sermon can be understood as formed by a study of the text and as being a contemporary preaching of the passage to a being-saved community in the world.

A PROPHETIC DENUNCIATION:
AMOS 4:1–3

A translation:

¹Hear this word

> you cows of Bashan on Mount Samaria, who crush the poor, who oppress the needy, who say to their husbands, "Bring us a drink!"

²Yahweh has sworn by his Holiness:

> Look! Days are coming at you when they will haul you away on stakes; every last one of you with grappling hooks ³through the slaughtergate you'll go one after another, you'll be thrown out into Harmon

Says the Lord!

The appalling passage from Amos needs little explanation. The "Bashan cows" are wives of the social elite who lounge around in pampered luxury, their affluence earned at the expense of the poor, and who indolently demand of their "Lords and Masters"—"Give us a drinkie!" Evidently, their husbands are ruling class—court officials, landowners (5:11–12), and businessmen (8:4–6)—who could afford palaces in the capital city as well as summer houses on the slopes of Mount Samaria. The prophecy picks up the cow image and predicts that the women will be hauled away like cattle, their carcasses slung through a slaughtergate by hooks and dumped "toward Harmon" (an uncertain reading). Not surprisingly, the passage does not appear in most lectionaries.

We have deliberately picked the passage because it raises so many questions. Here, we have a fairly nasty judgment aimed at a specific group—society women—which is an unrelieved oracle of doom; the passage does not sing with dulcet gospel tones! So the passage raises the question of how we are to preach judgment from the Hebrew scriptures in a Christian context. Imagine a preacher, equipped with a situational parallel hermeneutic, preaching Amos 4:1–3 to an affluent suburban parish! What are we to do with chunks of scripture that, without any call to repentance, simply pronounce doom?

Obviously, we cannot merely transfer the passage *unaltered* to a Christian context and preach it as a Word of God for *now*. On the surface, the passage seems to propose a relentless God who metes out punishment, indeed ruthless punishment, for neglect of the poor. While an overview of human history may convince us that the passage is probably true—social neglect of the poor usually leads to violence in which oppressors, as well as those who benefit from oppression, are crushed—the problem we face in studying Amos 4 is God's involvement in such social upheavals. Does *God* bring about social retributions? Surely, the God we meet on Calvary is not a death-threat-punishment God who, like the Lord High Executioner in *The Mikado*, designs social punishments to "fit the crime." On the other hand, the usual gambit—which exempts God from involvement in social retributions by arguing that a God of love does not cause destructions but merely allows them —is not much of an answer. So we cannot preach Amos 4:1–3 *as is* as a Word of the Lord to Christian congregations.

Yet we must not set up a law vs. grace contrast and then toss out Amos 4 as an example of cruel law which has now been cancelled by the grace of our Lord Jesus Christ. Or, in a similar vein, we dare not argue that whereas the "Old Testament" proposed a God of *social* law, now in the "New Testament" we meet a God of *personal* love, so that social law is superseded. Some years ago a prominent American evangelist exempted himself from preaching on racial justice or the moral disaster of Vietnam on grounds that he was a New Testament gospeler and not an Old Testament prophet. The position cannot be defended. The Hebrew scriptures contain sweeping witness to God's intense covenant love, and, of course, the Christian scriptures display a hard edge to Jesus' preaching that can only be labeled "prophetic." Any Marcionite distinction between a Hebrew God of wrath under law and a Christian God of love in Christ Jesus is a theological caricature that must not be served up in our pulpits. When prophets spoke of God's judgment they did so remembering God's liberation of Israel, God's free covenant love, and God's good promises—a reconciled society in which love does justice. If there is a difference between the Hebrew scriptures and Christian scriptures, the difference has to do with fulfillment in Christ and not with any radical alteration in the image of God. Christians are prophetic. They are prophetic because they believe the new age has begun in Christ and, that, therefore, our social sinfulness is passé and is a stiff-necked refusal of new life together in

Christ. Not surprisingly, we find plenty of "Amos" denunciations of social neglect of the poor in Christian scriptures. If there is any alteration of the image of God in the Christian scriptures, it may best be described as a deepening of the disclosure of God. In Christ on the cross, we see the sovereignty of God as a sovereignty of Suffering Love so that notions of power are redefined by powerless Suffering Love. Moreover, in Christ we see a communion of God and humanity uniquely displayed, a communion which does not deny the Hebrew scriptures (think of Hosea or Jeremiah) but, again, informs them. So Christian scriptures do not abolish the law/judgment themes of the Hebrew scriptures, but, by showing the grace in law and the law in grace, speak in terms of grace/judgment. Note: we are not speaking of so-called cheap grace. Violations of neighbor love, such as oppression of the poor, are still violations of God's Will and, because they are inappropriate to the new age, may still result in human self-destruction. Amos is not superseded precisely because the cross is not a cop-out.

The interesting question raised by Amos 4:1–3 can be stated simply: Why did God bother to address (through Amos) the "cows of Bashan"? If doom is certain, why bother? We can venture a range of answers: (1) The text is written within the context of a broad trust in God's ultimate purpose. Though the Bashan cows may have chosen their own doom, God's purpose for the wider human world will still be fulfilled, perhaps through a saving remnant. While such an answer to the question may well be true, it does not explain why God bothers to address the victims of doom. (2) Perhaps the text only appears to be an announcement of doom. Maybe, if the Bashan cows repent, they will still be rescued from their fate. This answer turns God into a manipulative evangelist who will win souls by means of spurious threat. (3) Amos believed, as did John Calvin, that though the Bashan cows were surely doomed, nevertheless, they should turn and give God glory. Besides, death is never God's final word. Now, what makes our question urgent is the fact that the cows of Bashan were indeed destroyed; the prophet's announcement was fulfilled. Of course, we could turn our question inside out and instead of asking "Why did God address the Bashan cows?" stand back and marvel— "Look, God cares enough to converse with doomed sinners!" But in view of the unrelieved doom of the oracle, such a reversal of perspective does not seem to come off very well.

The only way we will begin to preach on the passage is to set its component parts into a theological framework. We have only three components of the text: (1) The situation: Luxurious indolence based on a victimization of the poor. (2) A predicted punishment. (3) God, through the prophet, addressing the doomed sinners. Each of these sections must be studied theologically, and

383

congregational blocks analyzed, before analogies of experience may be properly located. Briefly, we sketch the task:

1. The Situation

    a. *Theology:* We are not dealing with sin as simple lawbreaking. God's law is based on covenant love. In Christ we see what covenant love intends, namely, a communion of God and humanity. There can be no communion, however, if there is a bottom-line violation of neighbor love. *Ergo,* outright social oppression prevents covenant love from being fulfilled in communion.

    b. *Congregational Blocks:* Probably the big block in Amos 4:1–3 is an unwillingness to see the situation as sinful. Capitalist ideology and political climate may prevent people from viewing economic matters as a violation of covenant love. If we name concern for the needy as welfare statism, can we hear Amos's condemnation of wealth? Likewise, if we assume capitalism is somehow divinely inspired contra-communism, we will tend to regard poverty as self-willed—a failure of initiative and free enterprise—and luxury as deserving reward for industry. The great sin in America is being poor!

2. The Announcement of Doom

    a. *Theology:* We have noted that the theological distinction between God *causes* and God *permits* is a bit facile. Nevertheless, the Amos text does bring to mind issues of providence and human freedom. If we argue that God-love will not coerce humanity but, within limits, permits large, even terrifying freedoms, we take an initial step. In other words, we are not dealing with a God who is defined by the word "Sovereign" alone, but with a God whose name is, if anything, Sovereign Suffering Love—seen on the cross. The cross, however, also reveals human sin as a form of self-destruction. When sin destroys a neighbor, it is also self-destruction, because we have no selfhood apart from neighbors. When sin destroys Christ, it is self-destruction, because our true self is a self-for-communion with God. When the Hebrew scriptures announce punishments of God, we may be driven to ponder the self-destruction of sin within a terrifying freedom which the patience of God-love honors, indeed, honors by suffering.

    b. *Congregational Blocks:* The biggest roadblock to understanding is pop religion which pictures God as a zapper. God zaps and lives are rescued; God zaps and lives are snuffed. The popular image of God as unlimited sovereign power is clearly a block to understanding the text. A God-acts-in-history theology, in spite of virtues, may inadvertently feed such popular misconception. Somehow, through preaching, we must present a different picture of God's relating to the human world, perhaps talking less of direct interventions and more of God's forming in relationship, of images, symbols, and social language.

3. The Speaking of God

    a. *Theology:* Though the Amos text has raised a host of problems, nevertheless, God does address sinful humanity through the voice of prophets. Prophets, of course, are often morally besmirched, politically partisan, and ambiguous —What else is available? The grace hidden in the notion of God speaking to sinners can be described. God's address gives us our identity as free, responsible, moral choosers. More, God's address maintains relationship even in the midst of rebellious self-destruction. Therefore, God's address is an affirmation of covenant love.

b. *Congregational Blocks:* The big block is our Christian enthusiasm for easy "cheap grace." But, because Christ has come, our free choices are not bailed out or guaranteed a happy Jesus ending. We are not rescued from the results of social choices by cop-out grace. The idea that God holds our lives in covenant love, though we will our own self-destruction, is paradoxical but, at least, vaguely responsible. Nevertheless, the God who addresses us wills the world's redemption, including us sinners. Within the broad redemptive purpose of God, we must acknowledge both terrifying freedom and tough grace.

Though we have not detailed "Analogies of Experience," obviously, they will figure mightily in the construction of a sermon. The Amos text is embarrassingly particular as it addresses court women in Israel. Analogies of experience guided by interaction between theological understanding and cultural roadblocks will broaden the text. Perhaps the words of Amos will stretch toward an affluent America feasting on fruits of free enterprise—gourmet-food stores, imported French wines, high cholesterol sauces—while most of the human world, for example, Ethiopia in the eighties, eats dust in grinding poverty. America's steepled skyline will not prevent inevitable social retaliations. The Amos text speaking in a Christian congregation may turn around and call us to compassion. Generally, in the gospel, so-called negative texts may turn and become calls to neighbor love. Let us imagine a sermon sketch for Amos 4:1-3:

Introduction: Some years ago there was a film that pictured guests at a sumptuous party—silver trays of champagne and bowls of caviar. Then, abruptly, the film switched over to images of the starving: puffed bellies, and skeletal arms reaching out. Back and forth the images switched until all that was left was the soundtrack of the party—rising laughter and the clink of glasses— with pictures of the starving twisting toward death. Perhaps such a double picture filled the mind of Amos. Perhaps such an image can fill our minds.

1. Well, we are opulent, aren't we? We have what we like to call a high standard of living. A catalogue of gifts came in the mail featuring a sterling-silver cocktail shaker, an ivory wine rack, and, of all things, a mink-lined bottle opener. Luxury has become our way of life: Gourmet stores in our shopping malls, gold-plated faucets in our bath shops, custom-made sports cars in our parking lots. America is prosperous. We may bemoan our deficits and begrudge our taxes, but, all in all, we are rich.

2. But what about the world in which we live? There are folk on earth with a high standard of dying. While we clink our glasses and dip caviar, count the statistics. Every single second someone dies of starvation, and is swept down gutters of neglect. Every once in a while, we see images of their faces on TV, before we twist the dial to get away from them. But we know that starvation is fact. The contrast is inescapable: We are wealthy and the world, by and large, is poor, dreadfully poor.

3. The odd thing is that we feel guilty. We see the pictures and feel guilty. Oh, we can argue that "those people" are ignorant (as if ignorance were sin), that they lack initiative, or that they should try a little free enterprise, but our cant is unconvincing. Secretly, we feel responsible—perhaps because we *are* responsible! Do we need more than a high-school course in economics to know that our prosperity is related to someone else's poverty? Sin isn't simply a matter of the heart, it's scribbled across pages of every economics text. The fact is we feel guilty because, inescapably, we *are* guilty.

4. Well, in Jesus Christ, we know what we must do. We must give. It isn't a matter of dabs of compassion, a little neighbor love, all deductible. No, in Christ the skeletal hand reaching for bread is the hand of our brother or sister or mother or child. If Christ has joined the human race, God-with-us, then we are no longer neighbors but members of one family, God's family, on the face of the earth. A wonderful old woman doing soup-kitchen work in the slums of London served up food with marvelous one-liners: "Here, my Sister," she would say, "Here, Father, help yourself." Blood *is* thicker than water: The blood of Christ has made us one family. We do not give to "those starving people," we reach out to our sisters and brothers, our mothers and fathers, on earth.

5. You wonder if it's not already too late. Perhaps our neglect has already sown seeds of hate so that luxury is doomed. We export Hollywood films that show our opulence. At the same time we dribble our meager charities toward terrible starvations. Is it any wonder that world resentments rise? Our biggest export is not bread but bullets; we arm our own fate. Can we be starkly honest? Perhaps it is too late to save our nation. You read the pages of history books and flat-eyed count the civilizations that have risen to heights of prosperity only to tumble in revolution. We know that triggering the revolutions are skeletal hands that once reached for bread. The Bible has another word for social revolutions. "Judgment of God," says the Bible.

6. But listen! God is speaking to us. Though we have neglected our sisters and brothers on earth, God still speaks to us—now. God loves sinners. Said another way, God loves *us* sinners in our sinful world. We do not deal with a distant lawbook strung from the stars: We are faced toward a God who faces us in love. Oh, God-love may not bail us out from social consequence: God is just. But, though we suffer, God's own suffering love embraces us. See God-love on the cross accepting our neighbor rejection in mercy. Risen, Christ speaks: "Forgiven people, do not continue in sin; give, love, serve, share with brothers and sisters of mine." God is *now* speaking to us.

In our sermon sketch, tensions are unresolved. We have allowed Amos to warn against any happy-in-Jesus end to the sermon by retaining the prophet's accusation, announcement of doom, and implied moral demand. We have, however, introduced into the sermon the image of Suffering Love on the cross, not as a moral escape hatch but as an intensification of Love's demands. Christian faith does not say, Repent and you will be forgiven; it says, You have *been* forgiven, therefore, repent. While Amos's words were phrased as a direct address to the Bashan cows, we have shifted the sermon into shared Christian consciousness. The coming of Christ has not cancelled the prophetic word, but has relocated the prophetic word *among us*. Though we ministers may get our kicks from blazing pulpit denunciations, according to scripture the spirit of prophecy has been poured out on the *whole* community of faith.

Why have we dealt with an oracle of doom as a problem for reflective preaching? While some prophetic passages may seem to move toward preaching in the mode of immediacy, most must be interpreted within a field of theological meaning. The solution to so-called negative passages is not a counterbalancing with positive passages found in the canon. Rather, the way to handle negative passages is to reflect on them within a wide field of theological understanding; a field in which the Living Symbol Jesus Christ addresses a being-saved community in the world. Generally, prophetic passages are preached within the reflective mode.

PREACHING IN THE REFLECTIVE MODE

We may be in a position to draw out certain general observations about preaching in the reflective mode. We have looked at cases—a Pauline passage, a teaching of Jesus, and a prophetic oracle of doom. We can now piece together some broad guidelines.

Structure

In the reflective mode, sermon design is not derived directly from a passage. Instead, the design is formed from a structured field of *contemporary* meaning in consciousness that has been produced by a study of the text. Therefore, in the reflective mode sermons may not feature much direct citation of a text or even discussions of the text's situation. The main structural shape of the passage, however, may well be discernible within the sermon's design. In each of the examples we have given, the main meanings of a passage, though garbed in contemporary language, did show up in sermon sketches. Of course, there were *additional* moves which did not derive directly from a text. These additions were of two sorts: (1) additions prompted by theological interpretation, and (2) additions representing either an articulating of blocks in congregational mind or a response to such blocks. In preaching Matt. 5:33–37, we discovered we would have to add a first move to deal with the popular notion that Jesus was condemning cuss words. Or, remember, in plotting the passage from 2 Corinthians 5, we discussed the possibility of describing "new creation" both as personal and social, which would produce two moves instead of one. Such additions to basic structure will create sets within a sermon's design. In the sermon sketch on Matthew 5, the first and second moves may become a dialectical set with a "not A, but B" logic; not cuss words but a big-lie world. So, in the reflective mode of preaching, we form a sermon design that will *embody* meanings from a passage with additions (or subtractions) prompted by interpreting the passage theologically and in relation to roadblocks within contemporary cultural consciousness.

Movement

In the reflective mode, movement of a sermon design is no longer determined by the original sequential movement of a passage. Rather, movement is a moving around within the structured field of meaning in consciousness which has been produced by a study of the text. Sermons in the reflective mode are not discussions of some fixed, propositional topic; they are neither static points arranged in a row nor elaborations of a distilled truth; sermons in the reflective mode do *move*. They move because they imitate a thinking out of a *pattern* of meaning. In reflective sermons we break out a whole pattern of meaning into a thought sequence that travels as does any human thinking out with some sort of logical unfolding. We noticed in analyzing a passage from 2 Corinthians that sermon sequence could rearrange the plot of the passage in quite different ways. Original biblical sequence is not determinative; we preach from a structure of meaning in consciousness and not from a text on a page. Movement in the reflective mode will start with a point of entry and move around within a field of patterned meaning in consciousness.

Intentionality

When preaching in the mode of immediacy, the intending *to do* of a text will govern sermon construction. In the reflective mode, however, the intending *to do* of a text is not a prominent consideration. Of course, preachers will still be preoccupied with strategy; all homiletic design is a matter of considered strategy. Strategy in reflective sermons has to do with the nature of theological understandings and the problem of roadblocks within the cultural mind. For example, in sketching a sermon on Matthew 5, we deliberately introduced the idea of a whole new society *before* we turned to discuss our truth-telling lives. If we had not done so, members of a congregation would not understand themselves as representatives of a new age and, instead, would be dumped into an impractical personal ethic. Or, to select another example, in sketching a sermon on Amos 4 we introduced the idea of "perhaps, it's too late" between a move which presented Christ's demands and a move which told of God's mercy in Christ—a matter of theological strategy. Preaching in the reflective mode intends a theological field of meaning and intends toward a particular cultural consciousness. Though preaching in the reflective mode considers strategy, however, it does not design sermons that unfold in consciousness as an intending *to do* with immediate force.

Illustration/Images

In the mode of immediacy, illustrations and images are selected with an eye toward the sermon's performative intending *to do;* they must relate to each move's performative purpose and interrelate intentionally. In the reflective mode, illustrations are chosen to explicate theological meaning in relation to blocks that may be within our cultural mind. For example, in analyzing 2 Corinthians, we discovered that Paul regarded Christ's death as a reconciling of *world* to God, and we decided that any analogy chosen would have to be *social* in character. As a result, we recalled the story of a fraternity-house hazing tragedy rather than some image of one-to-one reconciliation. In reflective preaching, illustrations and images are chosen by a reflective process and are seldom immediate analogies of understanding—images that pop into mind in the reading of a text.

Reflective Consciousness

In the reflective mode, sermon language imitates a consciousness trying to think through and understand. The object of understanding is not a text on a page of the Bible, but rather is a pattern of contemporary meaning in consciousness. In reflective preaching we do not talk about a text and then turn to apply the text to our lives in a pedantic fashion. Rather, in reflection we are thinking out a contemporary meaning for our lives in the midst of life. Meanings will be both personal and social. Sermons will not, however, display a split by talking about the world "out there" and then looking at our individual one-to-one lives. Instead, when preaching in the reflective mode we will be referring to a self-in-a-world within consciousness. Thus, for example, in constructing a sketch on Amos 4, we did not talk about the world out there as being rich. Instead, we remembered seeing a catalogue of gifts, reviewed in mind our shopping malls, and spoke of "we're opulent, aren't we?" We represented the world in consciousness and ourselves in the world and, thus, avoided objective/subjective splits in our sermon design. Actually, we moved

389

toward reality: There is no such thing as a self-without-a-world or a world-without-a-self. When preaching in the reflective mode we imitate a consciousness reflecting on meaning in the world.

Preaching in the reflective mode will be much of our preaching. Most passages from scripture are themselves products of reflective consciousness. Therefore, reflective preaching from scripture will have to adapt to all kinds of biblical rhetoric. Reflective preaching is mediation; it mediates theological meaning to contemporary consciousness. Put another way, in reflection, preaching mediates symbols of revelation to a consciousness of being-saved in the world.

23.
The Reflective Mode:
Logic of Movement

In the reflective mode of preaching we discovered that sermon movement involved moving around within a field of meaning formed in consciousness by a text. Therefore, the *kind* of meaning that forms in consciousness may well determine the logic of sermon movement. When preaching in the mode of immediacy, we are usually dealing with narrative material that unfolds episode by episode with some sort of narrative logic. Non-narrative passages in scripture, however, will operate with other kinds of logic and form in consciousness quite differently. Let us look at some different types of passages.

VISUAL LOGIC: HEBREWS 12:1–4

There are passages in scripture that seem to embody *vision*. They are reflections on something viewed in consciousness. For example, in 2 Cor. 2:14–17, Paul seems to have in mind the picture of a Triumph, a great victory parade in which captives are led through the streets bearing basins of flowers, followed by ranks of soldiers, followed by a commander enthroned. He even picks up an image of street vendors (v. 17) hawking wares to the parade crowd. Behind Paul's language is a picture. Likewise, in scripture there are dreams such as Ezekiel's image of dry bones or apocalyptic visions that stand out on the pages of Revelation. The structure of such passages is formed as the eye of the mind moves around a picture. We are dealing with what might be described as visual logic.

In Heb. 12:1–4, we have a passage that appears to be built on the picture of a marathon:

> [1]So, since we have around us such a great cloud of witnesses, let us slough off any bulkiness that weighs us down, and sin which bogs us down, and let us run

with endurance the race before us; [2]looking toward Jesus, the pacesetter and finisher of faith who, for the joy before him, endured the cross, rejecting dishonor, and who is seated at the right hand of God's throne. [3]Just consider how he endured hostility from sinners, so that you will not give up or lose heart. [4]For you, in your struggle with sin, have not yet had to resist to the point of blood.

You read the passage and find yourself at the starting line of a long footrace. At first, you are aware of a crowd of previous runners, a "cloud of witnesses," and then you concern yourself with getting ready to run, throwing off excess clothing and scraping mud from your feet. In mind, as you look ahead, you recall Jesus who has run the race—"pacesetter and finisher"—and is now seated in a position of honor as befits a champion. Underlying the words of the text is the picture of an arena of watchers, among them previous runners. Jesus seems to be depicted as *the* champion whose record run is a challenge to us all. The only way to grasp the passage is to see the whole picture. The movement in the passage is the movement of a mind's eye across a visual field —first up to the stands, then down to the starting line, then to encumbrances, then to the previous runner, Jesus Christ, now highly honored. The whole picture is a model, a developed metaphor for the Christian life.

What forms in consciousness is a picture functioning metaphorically, a picture full of life meaning. Any sermon we construct will also move analogously to the mind's eye playing on a visual field. Study moves in the following sketch:

> *Introduction:* Every year in Boston there's a marathon. Thousands of runners line up to run through the city's streets. In the papers, there are pictures of previous runners. Well, in the Bible there's a marathon. A cloud of champions watching the race. Runners getting ready. Welcome to the Christian Marathon!
>
> 1. Guess what? Your Christian life is a marathon. You are running a race called "faith."
>
>> The race began when you first heard of Jesus Christ. It continued through young wiggling in church, through Sunday-school tediums, through the blush of youth-group programs, all the way to now.
>>
>> Sometimes the race seems effortless; we jog along without any trouble. But at other times, doubts assail and we bog down, wondering if God is true at all.
>>
>> William Goldman says, "Anyone can be a marathon runner, if you give your life to it!"
>
> 2. Remember Jesus. He ran the race of faith. From Baptism to the cross, see him go!
>
>> (Quote from a review of dramatic presentation of *The Gospel of Mark:* "Breathless! More like a race than a story!")

It was: Up from the Jordan, out to the wilderness, back to contend with the scribes and the Pharisees, then off to Jerusalem, up to the cross, finally flung back, shouting his triumph, "Finished," he cried.

3. Well, if we're going to race after Jesus, we're going to have to strip down. Got to shake off sins that weigh us down. Got to get lean!

We'll have to strip away all our proud illusions, the fantasies we pursue.

Cut back on possessions: the moving van that gets heavier every time we move.

Scene in *Exit the King* by Ionesco: Old king getting ready to run. "Throw everything away, lighten the load!" Rusty sword of self-defense. Crown of pride. "Lighten the load!"

4. But look! We're not alone. The stands are filled with runners from the past. A cloud of witnesses who have run the race of faith.

They don't look like much. There's Jacob who diddled his brother; and King David, the Mayor Daley of Israel; and Rahab, the whore. Not much, but they endured. They ran.

See, there are others: Saint Francis in a whirl of birds, and Martin Luther banging his beer mug on the rail as you race by, and Bonhoeffer writing not-very-good prison poetry up in the stands—they're all there.

The prize not awarded for purity, but for *fidelity*. They all stayed with the race of faith, and endured. Though God's chosen servants are not always moral (sin is chronic in us all), they are called to be faithful to the end.

Conclusion: My, but we've been dramatic, overdramatic. Our race is no big thing. No cross, no martyrdom for us. All we have to do is serve a frightened church in a bad season. So, put on your running shoes. On your mark, get set, and . . . There, you've said it!

Notice, in our sketch we put the whole picture in congregational consciousness at the start, that is, within the introduction. The moves that follow, however, depart from the sequence in the text. Our homiletic eye is moving around the picture in a different way: from starting at the starting line, to looking at Jesus in memory, to being aware of our sins, to gazing at the gathered crowd. Also, every illustration or image relates directly or indirectly to the marathon picture, a practice which must always be observed when preaching from a visual field. Even the rhythms of speech relate to racing, as, for example, in the description of Jesus' life in the second move. Above all, note that the "logic of movement" is a logic that imitates the movement of an eye over a visual field, spotting different aspects of a whole picture as it moves around. Insofar as the structure of the picture orders sermon design, we are preaching in the mode of immediacy, but, because every aspect of the picture turns us toward a consideration of our lives, the system is a product of a reflective consciousness.

AUDITORY LOGIC: ISAIAH 40:1-11

1 Comfort, comfort my people,   says your God.
2 Speak sweetly to Jerusalem,   and say to her
  that her forced labor is over,   her penalty is paid,
  that she received from Yahweh's hand   double for her sins.

3 A voice shouting:
  In the wilderness, clear   the way for Yahweh.
  In the desert, straighten   a highway for our God.
4 Let every valley be filled in,   and every mountain graded down.
  Let ridges be leveled,   and buttes become prairie.
5 For the glory of Yahweh   will be revealed.
  And all flesh   will see it together.

6. A voice shouting:
  Preach! And I answer,   What shall I preach?
  All flesh is grass,   and lasts no longer than wildflowers.
7 The grass dries up,   the flower fades,
  When the breath of Yahweh   blows on them.
8 The grass dries up,   the flower fades,
  [Surely the people is grass!]
  but the word of our God   is forever.

9 Get up on a high mountain,   Zion, announcer of good news!
  Lift your voice out loud,   Jerusalem, announcer of good news!
  Say to the cities of Judah,   Look, your God!
10 Look, Lord Yahweh is coming in power,   and his arm will rule for him.
  Look, his winnings are with him,   and his trophies beside him.
11 Like a shepherd,   he will feed his flock,
  gathering lambs in his arms,   hugging them to himself,
  and gently leading along   those who have young.

Again and again, when we read prophetic passages, we find ourselves hearing different voices and, if we are to understand a passage, identifying different speakers. In Isa. 40:1–11 we overhear voices. Notice the following shifts: vv. 1–3 feature a voice announcing an end to Jerusalem's exile; vv. 3–5 have another voice ordering a road building in the wilderness; v. 6a has still another unidentified voice commanding the prophet to speak; vv. 6b–8 contain the prophet's despairing reply; vv. 9–10a have a voice crying, "Get you up on a high mountain/Lift your voice loudly"; before the passage concludes in a stunning mixed-image system in vv. 10b–11. The passage is not so much a dialogue as it is a series of overheard voices. While we can imagine some settings, we cannot construct an overall picture to contain and explain the many different voices.

We have a passage structured by a series of sharp commands and some replies, voices without identification. If we are to preach the passage we will have to label the voices and, by an act of imagination, construct contexts for their speaking. Look again at the structure of the passage:

vv. 1–3: Apparently we are overhearing the executive voice of God announcing Jerusalem's liberation from exile. Because God speaks, liberation is sure, though it may take years to realize. God speaks and liberation *is* accomplished.

vv. 3–5: The voice that speaks is not identified. We may, however, be hearing an angelic foreman issuing orders on the basis of God's executive decision. A road is being built on which God will march to Zion in triumph, picking up Jerusalem on the way. In Advent, when Isaiah 40 is frequently preached, the road is usually described as a road from God to us—an interpretation which is bad theology. God's road goes toward a salvific future, and we go along with God.

v. 6a: Another voice, perhaps of another angelic agent, speaks to the prophet, still on the basis of God's decision. The voice commands the prophet to preach to the exiles.

vv. 6b–8: The prophet reacts, saying, in effect, "Why?" Human affairs are hopeless. Not only do bright dreams dissolve in sin, but there is inevitable death: "The grass withers." Typical preacher despair!

vv. 9–10: Either the voice from 6a or another voice interrupts the prophet's complaint with no little impatience: "You get up and (like a watchman) announce, 'Look! Your God comes with power!' "

v. 11: The message the prophet must speak contains a double image: God is like a victorious commander who will march toward Zion in triumph, and God is like a tender shepherd leading ewes and cradling lambs.

What will come together in consciousness, oddly enough, is a clamor of *contemporary* meanings voiced between God and a present-day being-saved community in a hopeless world. Let us study a possible sketch for the body of a sermon:

1. How can the church speak in a world where hopes fade? Back in the sixties we marched from Selma to Montgomery, but, now, in the eighties, the federal Human Rights Commission has been gutted. We shouted for "Peace" and put

an end to the war in Vietnam, but here we are, mining harbors in Nicaragua. Seems like every bright reform slips back into the same old sin again. A historian pronounced a verdict on the 1960s: "A hundred flowers had bloomed in vain." "The grass withers, the flower fades." Same old human story.

2. A deeper hopelessness: We die. Even if we could begin to solve our human problems, what's the use—the mortality rate still stands at 100 percent. Not only personal death, but cosmic death: Someday the whole ball of earth will dissolve with a bang or a whimper. So, with a character in modern drama, we ask: "What's the use of saving the whole world if we die?" We might put an end to war, stop prejudice, and still end up like a lonely Hamlet staring at our own death's head. "The grass withers, the flower fades." What's the use of our preaching?

3. God has a word for us. God says, "Get up. Get up and speak!" We who are church must speak to a despairing age the good news of God. God will come! The only hope of the world is a God who has dealings with earth. (*Illustration:* Telegram to a family in the midst of terrible tragedy: "God is still God.") In an age which, only a little while ago, was brooding the "Death of God," we dare announce God's presence. "God is still God."

4. And, guess what, God is merciful. That's the word we preach. Mercy for the human world. Our warfare is over, our sins are cancelled. God is Mercy. Look at the cross! Our world is there! Clanking soldiers, power politics, a frightened religious establishment, a crazy crowd crying for blood—we're there. But listen to the lone voice: "Forgive them!" Think of it: God absolves the world —our crazy-clay sin, our propensity for death. Mercy, that's the message.

5. But more, God will liberate! God's ultimate purpose will be. Mercy is not much use if still we "blunder down old bloodstained ways." But, resurrection bears witness to God's power which can raise a new world out of death. The new world, where all of us will live in sweet courtesies of love, *will be:* Tender as a mother's love, sure as a warrior's triumph. (*Illustration:* Old Arab living homeless in an exile camp who is cheered daily by the shout: "Christ is Risen!")

6. So what can *we* do? Well, perhaps a little road building. We can try to get our world ready for the triumph of God. Not the "we can save the world" nonsense of a few decades ago! *God* does the delivering. Meanwhile, we can straighten up the world, grading down and building up, anticipating God's good purpose. (*Illustration:* Road in Canada, the Queen-E-Way, remained unfinished until the queen announced a visit. Then they finished the paving, painted lines, and hung up the flowers.) Our task not salvation, but getting the world ready for the coming of God.

The sketch, whatever its drawbacks, is interesting because it does not discuss Isaiah, the background of exile, or the meaning of the eschatological term "Zion." We are not preaching *about* a text, but from a structure of contemporary understanding formed by an analysis of the text. The sermon sketch contains the movement of the passage but rearranged. Some images from the text do float into the sermon and, in fact, determine the selection of illustrative material—"A hundred flowers," the Arab in exile, the Queen-E highway, and so on. The voices from the text still echo slightly: our voice replacing the prophet, God's voice speaking at the start of move 3.

The sermon is tending toward sets. The first two moves are a set built out of the prophet's despair. Moves 3, 4, and 5 form a progressive set while move 6 stands alone echoing vv. 3–5 of the text in its imagery. What has happened is that the field of structured meaning in consciousness has been entered at a different place and then been rearranged, so the sequence of the text has been replotted completely. If we analyze the sermon sketch as a replotting of a text, we see that moves 1 and 2 work from vv. 6b–8; move 3 from vv. 9–10; move 4 from vv. 1–3; move 5 from v. 11; and move 6 from vv. 3–5. As a structure of contemporary meaning in consciousness, the passage has broken into a new sequence.

ALLEGORICAL LOGIC: JOHN 15:1–7

[1]I am the true vine, and my father is the gardener. [2]Every branch which bears no fruit, he takes off. And every one that bears fruit, he prunes clean, so it may bear more fruit. [3]Now you are clean because of the word I have spoken to you. [4]As a branch cannot bear fruit unless it stays on the vine, so you cannot unless you stay with me. [5]I am the vine, you are branches. Whoever stays with me, and I with [them], bears much fruit. Apart from me, you can do nothing. [6]Whoever does not stay with me is cast out like a dry branch, to be gathered, thrown into the fire, and burned. [7]If you stay with me, and my words with you, whatever you want to ask will happen to you.

In Hebrew and Christian scriptures, we come across passages that are developed allegories, for example, Paul's discussion of the "body of Christ" in 1 Corinthians 12, or an elaboration of the "cistern" image in Proverbs 5. The "I am" passages in the Gospel of John also appear to be allegorical systems. Because allegories are pictorial we may suppose that they will structure with visual logic as with Hebrews 12, but they do not. There is no living action in allegories; they tell no stories. If in Hebrews 12 the mind's eye roves around a picture, in allegory the mind's eye remains fixed on the same image, noticing features of the same unmoving image. In allegory, we are dealing with a static image and aspectual logic. In John 15:1–7, the author returns again and again to the same image, a vine, each time noticing some different aspectual truth. The problem in preaching allegory is tedium—how can we avoid the tedium of returning again and again to look at the same basic picture?

Basically, John 15:1–7 works with only a few allegorical aspects. John

397

observes that the relationship between Christian community and Christ is like vine to branch, that if we grow from the branch we will bear fruit, that cut from the branch our lives will wither, and that like vines we are regularly "pruned" by "the Word." As preachers, we understand the allegory in reference to the character of a contemporary Christian congregation. Thus, we ask questions of contemporary meaning: What does it mean to say that we grow from Christ? What is "bearing fruit"? and so on. We translate the passage into *contemporary description* and understand.

The problem with allegory is a homiletical problem. How can we avoid the tedium of repeated returns to the same viewed image? Look at options: (1) We can, as did John, labor the image by returning at the start of each move to the originating image—vine and branches. The risk: Tedium. (2) We can set up a separate theological structure, talking about our lives in Christ without any mention of vine and branches which, at least for urban Christians, may not be terribly compelling anyway. The risk: Loss of an informing image. There may be another option. (3) We can adopt a theological design for our sermon, talking about our contemporary life together in Christ, but allow imagery to enter our sermon through subordinate metaphor and illustration. Oddly enough, this is exactly what happens as the text forms contemporary meaning in consciousness. In consciousness, we end up with a field of contemporary descriptive understanding with vine/branch imagery faded into background. Here is a possible brief sermon sketch:

> *Introduction:* Have you noticed, in many church buildings you come across the vine and the branch? Painted on walls, carved in communion tables, set in stained glass; somewhere, there's apt to be a picture of the vine and the branch. Maybe the only way to understand the mystery of our Christian lives is to look at pictures. Christ is the branch and we are the vine.

> 1. The image is true. If honest, we'll have to admit that, cut off from Jesus Christ, we're helpless. We can't get by in the living of life with only common sense and a subscription to *Psychology Today.* We can decide to love, but may soon find love withering away in the heat of everyday life. We can determine to be charitable, but when the bills pile up and advertisements beckon, we'll soon cut percentages. Maybe Elton Trueblood was right; we are a "cut-flower civilization." Cut off from our root in Christ, our good intentions wither and die.

> 2. So, thank God we're connected to Jesus Christ. All of us. Our lives are rooted in Christ. Every Christian church has grown from the event, Jesus Christ. (*Illustration:* In an old church-history book, a picture of the "Christian Family Tree." Vines [apostles] sprouting from the cross, branching out [denominations] through the ages, spreading into our own century.) Think back through

the years. Your faith comes to you from someone, and their faith from someone, all the way back through time and space to Jesus Christ. The fact is, our own lives spring from Christ.

3. What's more, together, our lives are shaped by Christ. For, here in church, week after week, we hear the word of Christ. Sermons, church-school lessons, study circles and discussion groups—we learn of Christ. Interacting, reproving, correcting, encouraging, the word of Christ "trims" us. Sometimes harsh treatment to cause strong growth. (*Illustration:* Old woman ruthlessly cutting back rosebush, "You want beauty, don't you!") Together in church our lives are formed and reformed.

4. What's the result? Well, see what's happening through churches all over the world. We're not talking about fulfilling our own potential, no, we're pointing to charity, to brave neighbor love, to giving ourselves away. (*Illustration:* Old monk, a winetaster, has a definition of vintage: "It's vintage," he says, "When you've got so much you have to give it away!") Maybe that's what Christ has in mind for us: So much sheer love that we have to give it away. Call it bearing fruit!

The overdone sketch (with too many illustrations) will, at least, demonstrate a way of handling allegory. The moves all start as *contemporary* descriptions of our lives. The original image does show up in an introduction where it is connected with discussion of church. Thereafter, the image shows up in two ways, as metaphor ("cut off," "rooted," "grown out," "trims") and as illustration ("cut-flower civilization," "Christian Family Tree," "rosebush cutting," and "vintage"). Some allegories, for example, "I am the good shepherd," pose more complex problems because the basic image is so alien to contemporary life that shepherding illustrations would be impossible. Illustrations of child care, hospital tending, supervision, however, would probably serve in much the same fashion. All in all, allegories are difficult.

SYMBOLIC LOGIC: MARK 16:1–8

A great many passages in scripture function with what might be described as symbolic logic. Though they may purport to tell a story, in actuality they mean on a *symbolic* level. Obviously, the "signs" in John function symbolically. For example, in the Marriage Feast at Cana, all elements in the narrative are symbolic: Jesus' sharp rejoinder to his mother, the six water jugs, the obedience of the servants, the "good wine," and even the enormous quantity of "good wine." Such stories may not be preached in a here-is-what-actually-happened historical style. Instead, a congregation will have to be oriented toward the story as a mysterious system of symbols in which huge Christian meanings are hidden. Another type of symbolic story is to be found in

399

resurrection accounts. While the resurrection was surely *event*, stories of risen Christ speak to faith symbolically. Thus, resurrection material poses a particular problem for preaching.

Let us try to get at the nature of the problem. Ask what it is that the resurrection accounts do *not* give us. They do not give us actual descriptions of risen Christ and they do not give us actual descriptions of the experience of witnesses. Instead, most resurrection accounts, like 1 Cor. 15:1–20a, feature credal material and references to the corporate life and mission of the church. Perhaps we can explain what is not given by pointing to the incapacity of human language. We describe one thing in terms of another, and we get at inner states of being by means of "objective correlatives"—by metaphors. But suppose we are dealing with a unique disclosure, revelation of a quite different order; then, analogies may break down and metaphors be inadequate. We can explain, however sketchily, what we do not get; but how can we explain what we *do* get, namely, formal confessions of faiths on the one hand, and symbolic references to the life and mission of the church on the other? Are we encountering a structure in which the living reality of Christ risen *is* known; that is, between symbols of revelation and a consciousness of being-saved in community? Perhaps.

Think of the Emmaus Road narrative. Though the account moves along like a story, in v. 27 we have formula words associated with preaching, and in v. 30 we have formula words associated with Eucharist—a pattern of Word and Sacrament in the life of the church. In addition, we have credal material in v. 19 and v. 30, creeds used by early Christians. Obviously, Luke is doing much more than telling a story or, for that matter, recounting a history. The same sort of double symbolic is to be found in virtually *all* the resurrection narratives.

Look at the difficult passage in Mark 16:1–8, a passage which because of its abrupt conclusion has bothered scholars for centuries. First, let us face historical problems in the text, and do so with scathing honesty. Here is a translation:

> [1]When the Sabbath was over, Mary Magdalene and Mary the mother of James, and Salome bought spices so they could go and anoint him. [2]And very early on the first day, after the Sabbath, they came to the tomb at sunrise. [3]And they said to one another, "Who will roll the stone from the door of the tomb for us?" [4]Looking up they saw that the stone had been rolled back—it was very big! [5]Going into the tomb they saw a young man sitting on the right side dressed in a white robe and they were astonished! [6]But he said to them, "Don't be astonished. You seek Jesus, the Nazarene, who was crucified. He has risen; he is not here. Look, see the place where they put him. [7]But you go tell his disciples and Peter that he's leading the way into Galilee. There you will see him, as he told you. [8]Going out, they ran from the tomb, for they were gripped by trembling and astonishment. And they said nothing to anyone, for they were afraid.

Clearly, Mark is not interested in historical precision. As scholars have noticed, the passage is a hodgepodge of historical contradictions. Questions: *Who* came to the tomb? Compare 16:1 with 15:40 and 15:47, not to mention accounts in other Gospels. *Why* did the women come to the tomb? Presumably, Jesus had been buried with care (15:46), and, besides, given climate conditions in Palestine, decomposition of the body would have made embalming with spices quite impossible. *How* could the women forget the stone? The gravestone was large and would take more than a dozen men to move. In view of the difficulties, why would the women even set out to anoint a body? A huge question involves the odd ending to v. 8, literally, "they were afraid *for.* " All kinds of explanations have been ventured through the centuries. As history, Mark 16:1–8 is suspect. Not only does the story not mesh with other Gospel accounts, it does not dovetail with Mark's own Gospel material! Of course, such inconsistencies might not bother the Markan community; they knew Christ was risen and did not crave (as we do) historical validations.

But suppose Mark 16:1–8 is not intended to be history so much as a *symbolic story* with profound theological meaning for a congregation already quite certain of the resurrection. Read as a symbolic story, the passage makes sense, and, furthermore, makes sense to faith. Look at the levels of meaning. Verse 1 mentions anointing which (see 14:8) may well be symbolic. Verse 2 speaks of "after sunrise" which contradicts "very early on the first day" (the early watch was between 3:00 and 6:00 A.M.). Is Mark pointing to a symbolism? The day went dark with Christ's death; now, with resurrection, the sun rises! The plaintive cry, "Who will roll away the stone?" which makes little sense historically, can be understood as an admission of human helplessness in the face of death and judgment. Verse 4 is an acknowledgment of the power of God, for only God could toss aside a death stone with ease. (The use of the reverential passive supports such a reading.) The young man in v. 5 is seated (the teaching/preaching position) in honor (the right side) and, of all things, recites a credal formula: "Jesus, the Nazarene, who was crucified. He is risen; he is not here." (Compare with similar statements in Acts.) Presumably, the Markan community would have recognized the formula; in effect, saying, "Listen! He's reciting *our* creed!" Though the young man is described in apocalyptic detail as an "angel," the language of his description matches that of the young man in 14:51–52 who ran naked from the garden during Christ's arrest. Is Mark setting up a sequence in which "Christian" is stripped naked by the death of Christ but, later, robed in the white garment of new life, preaches faith in Christ's rising? The "Go tell" in v. 7 is clearly a definition of the church's evangelical mission; a reading that is supported by "he is leading the way into Galilee." In Mark, Jerusalem is the place of rejection whereas Galilee is the place for evangelical preaching, a place of mission.

Verse 8 is, of course, a difficult verse. Either we must understand the verse to mean "Afraid, they went *directly* to the disciples, speaking to no one else on the way," or we must read the verse as providing an option, that is, though the women were silent, we who now know Christ risen must speak. Certainly, as a number of scholars have noticed, the abruptness of the verse seems to leave the resurrection in the minds of a congregation as something with which they must now reckon. The entire passage, Mark 16:1–8, may be read as an evangelical-theological drama connecting resurrection with the church's life and mission. Perhaps we may read all resurrection accounts as theological documents written to Christian communities who were already quite certain of Christ risen. They knew the risen Christ as resurrection creeds were validated by the nature of their *common* life and ministry, by the reality of their being-saved in the world.

How can we preach a symbolic story? Examine a slightly amplified *basic* structure for a sermon:

1. Begin with the fact of death. Death fills our world. Armed power is the power of death. Law is enforced by threat of death. Economics often is a living at the expense of death. Death around us, yes, and death in us all.

2. We're helpless in the face of death. Death crowds us in and constricts life. Oh, we can kid ourselves with fantasies of immortality, but we do not expect to read "Immortality Columns" in the newspapers. We die: The one irreversible fact. What's more, we cannot prevent our dying. We're helpless.

3. But, hear the good news! Christ is risen! The church has been scampering down the centuries bawling out the good news: Christ is risen! We sing it in hymns, we say it in creeds, we hear it in Bible stories. Early Christian liturgical form: "Christ is risen/He is risen indeed!"

4. We are talking about the power of God! God alone can roll away the stone called death! News of Easter: Though we are filled with self-destruction, God overcomes death and the forces of death. God gives life, life in spite of death. The power of death, the threat of death, all are overthrown by a God who shouts, "Life!"

5. Well, we ought to know. We know because in our common life we are aware of the risen Christ. Christ's Word continues to speak among us. Christ's Spirit is the Spirit we share. Christ's mission is our mission. In our life together we sense, and do not doubt, that "Christ is risen; he is risen indeed!"

6. For heaven's sake, let's tell the world good news. "Go tell!" is our command, a command of the risen Christ to us. We must not tremble, afraid of opposition or ridicule or the powers of death. We are called to speak out, to sing "Jesus Christ Is Risen Today" in the streets. And we can trust the reality of risen Christ, his Spirit, to go before us, validating our words.

Our minisketch for a sermon emerged from a symbolic reading of the text, and contains some indirect allusions to the text. Such allusions will be more or less according to how we design a sermon. What is *not* done is a talking about the text in a this-is-what-took-place sort of way, describing resurrection as objective history. Such a preaching of the text in all likelihood would subvert belief and heighten cultural doubts. We might want to introduce our sermon with a reference to Axel Ender's quite unbelievable painting, "The Holy Women at the Tomb," which shows the white-robed young man perched on a rock declaiming like an orator to women who, hands on their faces, stand amazed. The use of a visual symbol in the introduction would distance a congregation from questions of historicity.

Though we have attended to resurrection accounts—most of which feature confessional statements, allusions to the church's life and mission, as well as apocalyptic imagery—we could as easily discuss the many apocalyptic passages in the Christian scriptures. Apocalyptic texts are symbolic systems which, unpacked, can speak compellingly to our own under-the-gun apocalyptic age. Though apocalyptic texts employ a repertoire of symbols drawn from Jewish intertestamental tradition, they have been transformed by Christian expectation and, therefore, may best be interpreted within a reflective mode of preaching.

LOGIC OF MOVEMENT

While much non-narrative material in scripture is structured as conversational give and take (e.g., Pauline passages) or is designed rhetorically (e.g., teachings, prophetic discourse, and so on), there are other kinds of logic of movement which we may encounter. In view of many different logics, are there summary statements which may be made?

Foreground and Background

We have argued that, as texts are understood by analogies of experience, they form *contemporary* meaning, a patterned field in consciousness. They *do.* The contemporary structure of meaning may be described as being in the foreground of consciousness. Often, however, stuff of the text may still stand structured in background, underlying contemporary meaning. For example, though a study of Hebrews 12 will produce a contemporary understanding of the Christian life, in the background we may still perceive the dim picture of a marathon race, albeit a contemporary marathon race. Or, if the allegory in John 15 has become for us a contemporary understanding of the life of the church, the image of vine and branches, though dimmed, may still be in consciousness (though, perhaps, as the image is displayed in contemporary

403

church decor). It is quite possible that less visual texts will form contemporary understandings while their actual verbiage will fade away entirely. Nevertheless, texts, or at least images from texts, may be in the background of consciousness.

The preaching convention that talks about a text and then turns to make contemporary applications is artificial simply because meaning in consciousness formed by a text is *already* contemporary. In preaching a contemporary meaning, however, we can sometimes see through current understandings to background, to images or even phrases from an originating text that, by association, may float into our sermon. In studying a text we think from text to meaning, whereas in preaching, if the text is still background, we tend to think from meaning to text. Sometimes, as with symbolic texts, the regressions in consciousness may be quite complex. For example, we may have a contemporary understanding: Christians proclaim the resurrection, under which is the symbol of a newborn white-robed Christian, under which is the "angel" of Mark 16:6. Though many texts fade with the immediacy of a formed contemporary meaning, some vivid texts do remain as background in consciousness.

Logic of Movement

Generally, the logic of sermon design will be a logic natural to the way in which contemporary human beings put meanings together. When we break a field of meaning in consciousness into a sermon sequence, we think out our moves naturally. After all we are preaching from a pattern of meaning in consciousness and not from the text on a printed page. If background is still vivid, however, the way a text moves still may be our way of thinking. Because we grasp Hebrews 12 by still seeing a picture of a marathon race, our sermon structure may well imitate an eye roving the surface of a picture. If we understand Isaiah 40 as if we were in acoustical space hearing different voices, we may well discover the voices speaking out in our sermon design as background may break into foreground. The Bible displays amazing variety in logic of movement, and sermons will do likewise. Human consciousness does not necessarily think out in neat syllogisms or with the logic of formal philosophical argument (or of rhetorical convention). Human consciousness is remarkable; it thinks out by shifting scenery in consciousness, by changing focus, by scampering around in different perspectives, by flashing images. What matters in constructing a sermon is that logic of movement be *natural* to human consciousness and, at the same time, *appropriate* to the kind of meaning that is structured in consciousness, foreground and background.

24.
Preaching and Praxis

Is there anything more disturbing than reading sermon titles? In most American cities, sermon titles are listed in the Saturday newspaper. Supposedly they grab attention and, thereby, lure churchgoers to church. As a result, sermon titles are apt to be cute or puzzling or full of questions which most people probably do not ask. Though the practice of titling sermons is a bit odd—Are sermons works of art, or forms of entertainment?—the titles do signal the fact that much American preaching is topical, a preaching that begins with human situations. The practice is not new. From early church fathers to the present day, there have been sermons which, without reference to texts from scripture or tradition, address congregations where they are, relating experience to gospel rather than gospel to experience. We will label such sermons "Preaching in the Praxis Mode."

The vogue word "praxis" may be misleading. By "praxis" we do not imply that every sermon will swirl around a problem to be solved or be prompted by some in-action decision to be made. Preaching that begins with people need not be limited to moments, when, in a bind, congregations are confronted with moral or practical decisions. At times, without any reference to action, congregations may simply want to muddle meaning from situations; they may sense a need to know who they are, or what in the world is going on around them. Thus, by "Preaching in the Praxis Mode" we mean a preaching that addresses persons *in* lived experience and, therefore, starts with a hermeneutic of lived experience. While there may well be times when we look at lived experience bothered by questions of "doing," there are other times when we view experience asking questions of "being." True Christian preaching is not only a hermeneutic of texts, but a hermeneutic of human situations.

SITUATIONS

The term "situations" is much too broad. "Situation" is a word that shows up with modifiers: people talk of the political situation or the psychological situation or the religious situation, and so forth. Is there any way for us to pare down the modifiers and isolate the kinds of situations that preaching should address?

The word "situation" can be used to describe human-being-in-the-world. We have previously observed that as human beings our lives are hedged by mysteries. Certainly there are mysteries which attend our being-in-the-world. We appear to be a transient human community, Homo sapiens, on a whirling planetary ball, in a journeying galaxy, traversing unimaginable space. No wonder we ask, "What is life?" Questions seem to cluster around mysteries that define both our dazzling humanity and our inescapable finitude. Some mysteries are connected with being-here—Why are we born? As surely, there are questions prompted by *not* being-here—Why do we die? The mystery of transient consciousness, conscious of having been born and of having to die, is inescapable and spins us into brooding speculations. Then there are mysteries of being-*here*, mysteries of a natural world so fecund yet so chancy. "Why grass is green or blood is red" are mysteries indeed! While the astonishing variety of created forms may be catalogued by scientists, or even traced in an evolutionary scheme, such descriptions do not answer the child-questions in us all, such as "Why are there cows?" (Those who have ogled running cows ask the question while giggling wildly!) Of course, there are other questions we ask about the natural world: "Why are there killer tornadoes?" or "Why must everything (including us) decompose?" In addition to questions of origin, questions of destiny, and questions of world, there are questions raised by the mystery of being-in-community. Here we bump conundrums such as "Why are we *together?*" "Why is there evil?" "What is freedom and what is law?" and so on. Sum up and say there are mysteries of being-in-the-world.

Turn now and gaze inward: There are mysteries of being-a-self. The self is a biological miracle: heartbeat, brain waves, digestive system, reproductive system, all are awesome miracles. The self is a psychological miracle as well. We live an animated conversation within ourselves: me, myself, and I. Consciousness like a Chinese box opens to mystery within mystery within mystery. The unconscious, our dreaming and our impulses, is a pool too deep and dark to plumb. Again, though descriptive sciences may analyze and label, they cannot answer the *why* questions that swirl around the self. Some years ago there was a cartoon that showed a little man surrounded by books, stacks of books, the learning of the centuries. The little man was gazing in a hand mirror. The caption: "One little thing that puzzles him!" We all live in the mystery of a self, asking, "Who am I?" There are mysteries of being-a-self that confront us.

Situations can be described in another way, not only ontologically but historically. Linguistically, the difference is indicated by the addition of the tiny word "now." Instead of asking "What is life all about?" we ask "What is life all about *now?*" and refer to our cultural moment. Again and again, the pulpit may be asked to address the social shape of the world simply because people do wonder, "What's going on in the world *now,* " and they ask the question as a religious question.

In a recent detective story, a police inspector from far India arrives in Los Angeles to solve a crime. From the airport, he is taken on a quick tour of the city. Miles of cars streaking light-lines down thruways, weather-tower skyscrapers blinking predictions, fast-food shops with roller-skating waitresses, computer printouts on floating blimps—all these images he sees. "What kind of God for such a world?" he thinks. The sheer complexity of modern life does beg the question. Political events also raise questions. The fact of nuclear weaponry nudges into mind questions of human destiny. Congregations confronted daily by TV newscasts and a spill of shocking headlines ask "What's going on?"—probing political, economic, and social affairs for meaning. Preachers may not ignore questions or suggest that, properly, they must be answered by experts—economists, political analysts, poets, and the like. Questions raised by human affairs are ultimately theological. If Hebrew scriptures are a witness, God's useful preachers have always dared speak to the question, "What in the world's going on *now?*"

The little word "now" may also be tacked on to questions of self: "What's going on in my life *now?*" Once upon a time people were informed by a pilgrim model of selfhood. They traced their pilgrimage not only from birth until death, but from sin to salvation through stages of sanctification. They were able to describe their progress, their pitfalls, their bright expectations, all within a structure of narrative meaning. Today, the mythos of self having faded, pages from *Psychology Today* are a poor substitute. People do sense that they live in a struggle of soul that is much more than a bumping-along through stages in developmental psychology. We are a people given to self-diagnosis. We have learned to label our phobic tremblings, our paranoid projections, our schizoid fantasies and honed anxieties, but, at the same time, we believe that our lives add up to something more than a bundle of symptoms on the way to oblivion. While psychological wisdoms can paste on labels, or provide useful therapies, what we demand is some soul-sized scheme of meaning for our lives—meaning that used to be wrapped in big words like "redemption" or "sanctification." The therapeutic model has been undeniably efficacious, but, even extended, it does not provide profound enough meaning for the living of our human lives. Ultimately, the question "What's going on in my life *now?*" is a question for preachers to address.

We have described situations, situations of being-in-the-world and being-in-history. Actually, questions of ontology cannot be separated from questions of history, or questions of history from ontology. For example, the cold-war arms race can be described politically, or even probed by social psychology, but to get at the arms race in depth, we will have to have some understanding of human being and social destiny. History must be read with some understanding of the human project, else it is meaningless. Likewise, in personal history, though psychology can describe symptoms and even shrewdly speculate on the origins of such symptoms, psychology cannot speak of the *meaning* of symptoms without pushing toward ontology. Historical questions do open toward ontology and ontological questions point toward historical actualities. No wonder revelation is woven out of *story* and *symbol!*

SITUATIONAL QUESTIONS

Now, let us ask how, where, and when human beings ask situational questions. Nothing is more embarrassing than a pulpit addressing questions that no one asks, or questions that are asked but are trivial. Moments when people ask situational questions would appear to be either limit moments or decision moments—moments when we are forced to consider seriously a course of action. We must try to describe these kinds of moments with some degree of precision.

What do we mean by "limit moments"? Basically, such moments are characterized by a sudden awareness of transcendent mystery and, at the same time, acknowledgment of our human finitude. We human beings are remarkable. We can be conscious of our own consciousness; we can overview ourselves in the world. Thus, as you read this page, you can be aware of yourself reading the page; in consciousness, you can stand outside of yourself and, by imagination, actually picture yourself reading. We could fill pages merely describing the kinds of perceptual tricks we are capable of in consciousness, tricks that enable us to span space and time in astonishing ways. In spite of self-transcending consciousness, however, we know that, actually, we are limited. Though we may roam the wide world on a magic carpet of consciousness, in actuality we are two-legged human beings who cannot be in many places at once. Though we may overview our lives and, in consciousness picture birth and dying, we know that we *are* bodies and that someday in the not-too-distant future we will be snuffed out—consciousness and all. At the outset let us suggest that limit moments are possible because of self-transcending consciousness and hard-rock finitude.

Limit moments occur when our world constructs are blown open. We recognize then, that the world in consciousness, the world in which we live, is inadequate, and that there is a wider, more mysterious world surrounding us. In such moments we are forced to admit a world beyond our world as well as our own finite incapacity. On the social level, we may be describing moments of huge human catastrophe, or times of political upheaval when we guess that our little systems have had their day. Two pictures vividly illustrate the categories. Some years ago a news magazine featured a picture of an earthquake happening. The photograph showed a city literally shaking, debris flying and folks tumbling for cover. In the center of the picture was a kneeling man, his head bowed in prayer and his arms flung high. The other picture, on the page of a history book, showed a curbline crowd watching a funeral cortege passing. A woman in the crowd is holding out a newspaper headline, "President Shot," and is staring flat-eyed into space. There are moments when a wider world of mystery breaks toward us, while, at the same time, we have an acute sense of our own transient finitude—our tiny lives in awesome stretches of time and space. Again and again, there will be moments of social crisis which pulpits must address.

In personal life, we recognize the same sorts of occasions. Some are moments of alarming beauty and others times of tragedy. The moment of marriage vows—"Until death do us part"—can instill in us an odd sense of lifelong covenant in the presence of death. The birth of a baby brings us a tender realization of life, miraculous life, that will outlast us. Times of psychological collapse when, riddled by anxiety, we cannot go on without help, introduce in us a terror of depths as well as a feel for finite dependency. Obviously, facing death, either of someone well-loved or of our own self, is a time of dreadful constriction. In such moments we do apprehend a world wider than we guess—perhaps a greater Consciousness that is conscious of us —and our own finitude. Of course, not every human crisis provokes such awareness. If we are thrown out of work, personal anxiety may be intense, but we may not be propelled toward ontological brooding. After all, job loss can be explained *within* our world of meaning—business fluctuations, factory relocation, a lopsided balance of trade in the world, and so on. There are all kinds of harsh traumas which, because they can be grasped within our world in consciousness, do not push us toward limits. Such situations may well be agonizing, yet do not prompt "ultimate questions." Limit moments do. Our world constructs are exposed as inadequate and a sense of finitude sweeps our souls. In such moments, we question.

One of the problems with Harry Emerson Fosdick's so-called project method was a degree of superficiality. Dr. Fosdick, a genuinely kind and generous man, designed sermons on the basis of perceived human problems and religious resources. He argued that human beings in the living of life encounter problems and crave solutions. The problems Fosdick selected, however, tended to be day-to-day problems defined *within* our worlds of meaning, for example, how to keep from losing enthusiasm, how to handle fears, how to deal with a mischievous conscience. Christian faith was regarded as a resource available to us *within our world of meaning* to assist us in the living of life. Thus, in a sense, the project method was designed to *prevent* any real shaking of our worlds of meaning. Though Fosdick was an admirable human being dedicated to being helpful, the end-of-the-line result of his method has been a "positive-thinking" pulpit on the East Coast and a "possibility-thinking" pulpit on the West Coast where mysteries of transcendence and finitude are kept at a safe distance!

What about moments of decision? How do they occur? In ongoing lived experience, most human deciding happens without undue reflection. Most of the time human beings function on the basis of "This is what I want" or "This is what is usually done"; we live prereflectively by desire or convention. Sometimes we will act postreflectively on the basis of some precedent decision. If presented with a temptation to swipe a thousand dollars, we may refuse without much reflection because, once upon a time, we resisted an impulse to grab an unguarded fifty cents from a sibling's bureau top; thus we may reenact ourselves without much moral sweat. There are moments, however, when prereflective acting is impossible because impulses and conventions are in conflict, and postreflective precedents are simply not available. In such moments human beings agonize over decisions; they ask, "What on earth am I to do?" Usually, outcomes are uncertain, but self-assessment is very much at stake. In consciousness, we may find ourselves contending with many different social voices offering altogether too much advice! What to do?

Decision moments happen not only to persons but to groups, and even to whole societies. When custom breaks down and there are no available precedents, societies may ask, "What do *we* do?" The issue of nuclear war is a case in point. In the past societies have made war-and-peace decisions on the basis of many different frames of reference such as "just war" or "national defense" or even "maintaining a balance of power." With the advent of nuclear weaponry, however, usual frames of reference are not much help. How could world obliteration ever be "just" or the eradication of millions of humans be approved as a strategy of "national defense"? Our conventional patterns of thought are no longer adequate; the situation has clearly changed. Thus, our nation appears to be torn between extremes of nuclear "freeze" and "star wars" fantasy: We do not know what to do.

In addressing moral decisions, the pulpit may be trapped in its own conventions. Why does it take the pulpit so long to catch up to the ways of the world? In the past, the pulpit has been much influenced by cultural scales of moral value, by conventional notions of virtue and sin. The pulpit has assailed, perhaps quite properly, drinking and sexual dalliance, but has seldom spoken of advertising ethics or our national-defense mentality endorsed so enthusiastically by American Legion chapters. Likewise, perhaps influenced by martyred Martin Luther King, Jr., the pulpit will rightly chide racism, but still decorously sidestep amoral free enterprise and issues of wealth and poverty. Therefore, when it comes to addressing the urgent ambiguities that people actually encounter, the pulpit tends to be a predictable, if somewhat dated, wagging finger! Somehow we must be alert to where human binds are happening.

We have signaled limit moments and decision moments. Because such moments are chronic and the questions they raise never put to rest, limit *thinking* and decision *thinking* are ever on tap in human consciousness. Even when we are not in acute crisis, the questions are still filed in consciousness as unfinished business. Again and again, the pulpit may address huge ontological mysteries, impending ethical binds, the shape of our cultural world, and so on. While most of us may well prefer to live in our proximate world with our proximate, pragmatically useful understandings, the pulpit may have as a permanent agendum the raising of more profound concerns. Preaching in the mode of praxis is a recurring possibility.

SITUATIONS AND HUMAN UNDERSTANDING

How do we read situations? We are human beings in a human social world. Initially, we grasp situations within available *social* hermeneutics. In other words, our ways of understanding, in large measure, will be culturally determined. After all, we are children of a particular time and place; we are datable people and, like it or not, we live in the mind of an age. Literary scholars will date books on the basis of cultural style, social attitudes, cosmologies, value systems, and the like, which in the course of history have been typical of particular epochs. So, if reading a nineteenth-century novel, we may remark upon notions of historical progress, objective reason, moral law, and eternal truth typical of the era. Likewise, if studying a Greek epic, we will note distinctions between forms and reality, the ideal of "polis," and a notion of human "agon," which were part of the ancient Greek cultural formulation. Our cultural mind is as datable. Whether Christian or not, we are scarcely exempt from the cultural formulation in which we live and move and have our being. Just as tadpoles in a pool cannot stand outside their puddle to view a wider ocean, in spite of our self-transcending consciousness, we swim within our epochal minds. We are late-twentieth-century people, products of Western cultural history, and we cannot be otherwise. Language, we have learned, is a social product that shapes our shared consciousness and, thus, our ways of understanding.

Modes of thought are not merely epochal. In any given era, there are "isms," "ologies," "outlooks," and "philosophies" that contend for our public minds, and preachers are not somehow above contending perspectives. Thus, it is possible to interpret our historical moment within a cold-war apocalyptic mentality as a contending between forces of evil and good, with God on the side of capitalist investors; or in a different mind schooled by detente to regard international cooperation and mutual containment as ideals. In our personal lives, we may be drawn to *potentia* thinking and suppose that self-fulfillment is our life project. Or, tutored by various therapies, we may decide we are supposed to be free from inner conflicts and possess elusive personal harmony. As for the problem of evil, different philosophies will suggest that evil is a permanent human disfigurement or a form of social immaturity or an illusion dreamed up in guilt-ridden days of yore. Within any cultural epoch there will be a multitude of perspectives available to us. We live in a world of "isms" and "ologies" and social "attitudes" which inevitably will become part of our hermeneutical equipment. We read the world through different lenses.

Of late, there are theologians who insist that we cannot interpret the world in worldly ways without tumbling into error. Only in Christ, they insist, can there be a true reading of our human nature and indeed of our human predicament. Any dabbling in social hermeneutics, they argue, will compromise Christian truth which is available only in scripture. Therefore, when we attempt to make sense out of life, we must begin with the witness to Christ in scripture rather than with worldly self-understandings. While, as we shall see, the position has some degree of validity, basically it is naive. We live in language and our thought forms are linguistically shaped. Even when we read and interpret scripture we do so from within a language. Of course, ever since von Humboldt, linguists have observed that language embodies cultural formulations. In other words, we will always interpret the gospel *along with* cultural assumptions. There is no magic Christian hermeneutic that will exempt us from citizenship in a cultural epoch and its many optional patterns of conviction. Because we are human we always interpret situations within a human hermeneutic. Indeed, it is precisely a human hermeneutic that defines situations as decisive or as limit situations.

Some solution to the problem may be found in the notion of models. We grasp the world in consciousness through various models. Obviously, it is possible for human beings to read the world as merely a human enterprise.

If, indeed, the world is nothing more than a human enterprise, then all sorts of models may be adopted—political models, economic models, psychological models, and the like. Within a lofty humanism, we may weed out attitudes and actions that seem to be less than fully human while applauding affairs that are truly human and therefore noble. Humanism's way of looking at the world is not necessarily bad because it does not include God in its model. The "virtuous pagan," for example, Socrates, may well be admirable. (We should leave condemnations of "godless humanism" to the lunatic fringe of the church!) We can argue that the humanistic model is inadequate to lived experience and, therefore, cannot interpret limit moments and decision moments appropriately; but we cannot castigate humanism for lacking seriousness or moral sensitivity. Many people function within a merely human model of the world. In fact, many of us who are Christians may so function much of the time—keeping God in mind is no easy task!

There are models of the world that are religious. At minimum, they view the human situation within a God–human beings dialectic. Religious imagination, working with analogies of consciousness, does pose a Consciousness that is conscious of us. We must be cautious, however; having a religious model is no guarantee of truth, much less righteousness. Within religious models there may be quite different understandings of God and human destiny. God by definition is infinite, a "greater than" or "other than" us. As a result, we human beings are apt to garb God in attributes woven of our own unlimited desires "to be like God." We tend to define God as unlimited power, or absolute sovereignty, or as unfettered freedom-to-do. Such definitions, unchecked by the display of impotent Suffering Love seen on the cross, will almost always turn demonic. A God of tyrannous freedom will tend to justify tyrannous freedoms; a God of unlimited potency will probably validate human power plays; a God of unchanging fixity will endorse every status quo. Let us not unequivocally cheer religious models. The virtue of a religious model is that, at least, it poses Mystery in relation to human mysteries, as well as signaling Another Will in the midst of our willful decidings. Though the religious model may construct nothing more than a baffling Kafkaesque universe, such a universe can be both more mysterious and more significant than a world defined by proximate human truths.

The fact that we *do* interpret situations humanly within religious or non-religious models raises the question of pluralism. Because we are children of an age and, therefore, have learned to view matters through many different lenses, our ways of reading situations will vary greatly in church and out. We live in a pluralistic world. The danger with recent in-church endorsements of pluralism, however, is that they may be not much more than a logic of self-preservation—any social attitudes are O.K. as long as we are groovy together in Jesus! But, unfortunately, there may be human hermeneutics—"isms," "ologies," and "attitudes"—that are antithetical to the gospel. We can suppose, then, that Christian congregations may well be in conflict, albeit loving conflict (like cheerful family scraps), over different understandings. Through argument, mutual correction, and sometimes even outright repudiation of attitudes, congregations will seek to grasp the world in light of the gospel. Today, a church much concerned with conflict management and honoring pluralism may be a church frightened of being-saved in the world; a church devoted to maintaining competitive social position by means of cultural accommodation. As human beings who live in different subcultural groups, we bring to church quite different worldly hermeneutics, but the notion that we should leave church with our understandings unruffled is absurd. If we would preach in the mode of praxis we will have to be aware of our worldly interpretations and, indeed, be able to interpret interpretations within a Christian hermeneutic.

SITUATIONS AND CHRISTIAN CONSCIOUSNESS

Christian hermeneutical consciousness functions within a religious model, but in a rather different way. Whereas the religious model sets the Mystery of God over the human world, Christian hermeneutical consciousness views the Mystery of God *through* Jesus Christ *from within* a being-saved community in the world. Inevitably, human situations are humanly understood. For example, the problem of teenage suicide comes to us already wrapped in psychological interpretation. Or the problem of nuclear weaponry enters consciousness already interpreted both by the Defense Department and by peace groups. There is simply no way to banish a human reading of human situations. Within Christian consciousness, however, situations, as well as human hermeneutics, may be revised. Let us examine the process.

Christian consciousness is double—we know we are worldly in the world, but we also know we are being-saved. However dimly, we do sense a new order of life forming among us and, sometimes, within us. Aware of new life forming, we are able to label old strategies within our worldly ways; we are able to discriminate life styles in some rudimentary fashion. No wonder that, in church discussion groups, we will frequently contrast our *own* ways of thinking; distinguishing the way *we* think in the everyday world from the way *we* are learning to think in the gospel. For example, we may notice that in our world military budgets are supported by power/defense ways of thinking, which we realize are antithetical to a gospel of deferential love. Together in Christian community, we *do* sense sharp tensions between the mind of our age and the mind of Christ Jesus. All we are saying is that as a being-saved people, we are conscious of being *in* the world but not *of* the world. We are able, in some minimal manner, to discriminate understandings in Christ from understandings common to our in-the-world humanity.

The same sorts of discriminations may happen in our self-understandings. For example, as members of a being-saved community, we may grasp our savedness as a joyful disposition to serve neighbor needs before our own. As a result, we may become acutely aware of *numero uno* thinking in the world where social expectations may demand that we be something, have something, or get somewhere. Clearly, being-saved may heighten tensions in the living of life. Preachers who suggest that being a Christian will guarantee gobs of personal peace are probably, in Luther's words, "dream preachers." While Christian life may well afford a degree of inner reconciliation—we become what we are before God—in the world tugs and tensions will usually increase. At the outset, all we are noticing is a sense of discrimination brought about by a consciousness of being-saved in the world.

A Christian hermeneutic, however, does not rest on a sense of being-saved per se, a position that could plunge us into Pietism. There is revelation. The gospel comes to us through preaching, teaching, liturgies, Confessions of Faith, and is normatively available to us in scripture. Thus, we interpret being-saved in light of revelation which is articulated in the gospel message.

As story, revelation offers narrative meaning to the human enterprise and, thus, may contend with all proximate readings of human destiny. The Christian story begins with the myths of creation and fall and moves toward a denouement which includes social reconciliation as well as communion with God. Therefore, revelation's story stands over against optimisms of social progress and huge utopian dreams which may overlook the fall. Likewise, revelation as story will judge inadequate readings of human destiny that aim toward national, racial, technological, or even ecclesial triumphalism. As story, Christian revelation addresses not only visions of human destiny but also historical questions, such as, "What's going on in the world *now?*"

Christian revelation is more than an old, old story. The figure of Jesus Christ, a Living Symbol, is central to Christian understanding. Though Jesus Christ comes to us as a character in the story of God-with-us (humanity), in resurrection Christ stands before us as the disclosure of God's "interior" Mystery (divinity). By reflection, the Living Symbol Jesus Christ is also an image of true humanity with God. Thus, the figure of Jesus Christ addresses mysteries of being-in-the-world as well as mysteries of being-together. In the light of the cross we see ourselves, our murderous falsities and our true

415

self-before-God. Before the cross, human social patterns are also on display. We must not fail to note that political processes, religious institutions, and even democracy in action ("Crucify him!") were involved in crucifixion. In *mercy,* the human social world is exposed. Before the Living Symbol Jesus Christ we see not only a fallen humanity, but also the radical character of God-love.

Our line of argument may be summed up in a series of statements: (1) Being-saved-in-the-world creates among us a sense of discrimination. As a result, in some rudimentary way, we are able to distinguish being-saved from being-in-the-world. (2) The gospel message, revelation, relates to and is ratified by the reality of being-saved. (3) Thus, in a consciousness of being-saved, the gospel will be dialectically related to proximate understandings, including "isms," "ologies," and various social "attitudes." If we are aware of being-saved as somehow different from being-in-the-world, we also sense the gospel is different from proximate worldly understandings. Therefore, we may be able to sort out the mind of our cultural epoch, appreciating and depreciating in the light of revelation, story and symbol.

We may be ready now to see how human understandings and Christian hermeneutical consciousness interrelate. For years, preachers have been eager to speak to human situations, in no small part because of genuine concern for congregations muddling along in the midst of life. There has also been an evangelical motive: the gospel must be brought to actualities of human life and human modes of understanding. Thus sermons have often been designed correlatively as human situation and Christian response. Many sermons begin with the description of a human situation as *humanly understood* and then, presto, the gospel is introduced as an answer or a solution or a cure. The procedure is dubious. If a sermon begins with human understanding of a situation then, inevitably, the gospel will be expected to satisfy the situation as it is humanly understood. For example, suppose in preaching on issues of war and peace, we describe our world situation within a model of national interest and international threat. How will the gospel fare? God will undoubtedly end up either in support of preparedness (as God seems to do in theologies of the New Right) or as a peace idealist somewhat remote from human actualities. Again, if we are dealing with a personal problem understood within psychoanalytic categories, can God relate in any way other than as a therapeutic solution, a source of psychological health? When Christian faith is brought to bear on *humanly* defined situations, then God is required to align with *our* predicaments and to satisfy *our* needs on *our* terms. The real failure of Dr. Fosdick's project method is that after situations were grasped and described, God became an available resource person to guide us in solving our problems within *our* world of meaning. No wonder that, even when well managed, "Christ is the Answer" sermons tend to be a problem! Such examples would seem to support the Barthian contention that human readings of human situations can never be preliminary to a declaration of the gospel. As we have suggested, however, there are no objective situations with detachable human interpretations. It is precisely within human understandings that events are interpreted as situations. There is no evangelical magic that will wave away our human, worldly consciousness. We may be Christian, and we may be being-saved, but we are still emphatically *in* the world.

Let us suggest that every situational sermon will have to include some critical assessment of our human understandings. We cannot begin with a humanly grasped situation and then expect God to fit into our understandings. God's ways are not our ways; and God's view of human situations is, fortunately, not ours. The reason the Book of Job ends up in a whirlwind is because it is impossible for God to respond to human wisdoms on human terms. (Of course, whirlwinds are a kind of grace; they witness a world larger than our world in consciousness as well as reminding us of frail finitude.) No, if we address situations, somewhere, somehow within our sermons there must be a contending with our assumptions, as well as a rereading of situations in the light of revelation. Again and again, the gospel seems to say, "Dear Friends, you've got it all wrong. Now we live in a *new* situation by the grace of Jesus Christ!" Though we insist that the gospel must contend with our human understandings, we imply no harsh rebuke. If "God so loved the world . . . ," then God loves the world in all its worldliness, including our proximate worldly understandings. There is something a bit smug, and even, perhaps, manipulative, about the proposal that we must set up a Christian reading of a human situation in order to provide for a proclamation of the gospel. Honesty would seem to suggest that, instead, we bring into Christian consciousness humanly understood situations—after all, what else *can* we do? Within Christian consciousness of Jesus Christ, situations will be judged in the midst of giggling mercies and some sweet affection for our fallible humanity. Within the structure of Christian consciousness, however, we will review and revise our human understandings.

Please notice: We are suggesting an alteration in sermon design. Stock sermon structures which merely align human situations with the gospel may not be useful. Thus, familiar patterns such as the "problem-solution" model or the "human quandary–Christian answer" model probably must be amended. We cannot, even structurally, set up the gospel in terms of our human understandings. Instead, somewhere in sermons we must give space to a *revision* of our understandings in the light of the gospel. Do we imply

417

that preaching will have to be more apologetic than it has been? Probably. In our age, new understandings are forming, and the gospel must relate to such understandings with dialectical vigor. We cannot endorse a prohibition against human hermeneutics prompted by some odd notion of the purity of the gospel. Human understandings *are* what we have, and, as they probe situations, they can demand profound explications of Christian faith in return. Besides, there is no certifiably pure Christian faith for us to embrace. We grasp faith through human language and, therefore, within epochal thought forms. What we do have is a *structure* of Christian hermeneutical consciousness within which we may review situations, namely a consciousness in which symbols of revelation are present to a being-saved community.

SITUATIONS AND SCRIPTURE

When we read situations, normally we do *not* turn to scripture; scripture and situations do not come together automatically in consciousness. Even if we have been steeped in scripture and have memorized a bushel-load of biblical texts, we normally do not bring to mind scripture passages when surveying situations. Thus, though many sermons begin with a situation and then, by convention, turn to an enlightening biblical passage, such sermons may be artificial; we do not *immediately* reach for scripture in the midst of human situations. Because our contention may sound all but heretical, we must examine the problem.

Ask what exactly does occur when Christian consciousness reads a situation. Suppose, for example, that some political figure advocates tax reform by urging support for a flat tax in which every citizen will pay a fixed percentage of income. At the same time, suppose our imagined political leader urges huge tax reductions for corporations as an incentive for economic growth. After all, corporate expansion presumably will produce more jobs and, therefore, more purchasers and more taxable income. Within a worldly hermeneutic, the proposals may be justified by two strands of thought: (1) Because every citizen benefits from government alike it is only fair for every citizen to pay for government alike at the same rate; and (2) corporate profits will spread so as to benefit the poor by means of "trickle-down" prosperity. Now, quite possibly, Christian consciousness will be suspicious. A Christian may doubt that corporate profit will enhance the lives of the poor. The notion that corporate self-interest will, presto, be moved with charity toward the poor may be a conventional fantasy. Moreover, on the basis of the gospel, Christian consciousness may be convinced that God has a special concern for the poor (Jesus Christ was not, after all, an affluent entrepreneur!). While a flat tax of, say, 20 percent may not dent invested wealth, it could further devastate the poverty-stricken. There are problems of distributive justice involved!

Notice what has happened. A tax proposal has been taken into Christian consciousness, a proposal that includes a hermeneutical rationale. Within Christian consciousness, the proposal and its rationale have been viewed. The myth of the fall has questioned the notion of corporate gain = benefit for the less fortunate. Moreover, a recollection of God's special concern for the poor and oppressed has been introduced, based on Christ's own solidarity with victims. Now, notice what does *not* happen—we do not immediately turn to scripture. Instead, we move from a human situation to a *theological* analysis within Christian hermeneutical consciousness.

Does Christian consciousness draw on scripture? Yes, possibly, but only *secondarily.* The sequence will almost never involve a direct shift from situation to scripture, but will involve going from situation to theological understandings and then, possibly, to particular scriptural passages. In our example, the immediate theological understanding—"God cares for the poor"—might well lead us to recall passages from the Hebrew scriptures in which God's special concern for the *anawim* is affirmed, or texts from the Christian scriptures such as "Blessed are the poor." When scriptural texts do come to mind it is often because they have been connected to theological understandings by *preaching.* What we are noticing is a reverse sequence. In preaching from scripture, we moved from text to a contemporary field of meaning in consciousness (shaped by theological understanding and analogies of experience) to a congregational situation. When preaching in the mode of praxis, the process seems to reverse. We begin with a situation, shift to a theological review of the situation in Christian consciousness, and then, possibly, to particular passages *if* they have been connected to theological understanding in consciousness and are, therefore, at hand. The sequence we have sketched may suggest a more natural way for scripture to function in our sermons when we preach in the mode of praxis.

Some writers in homiletics are firmly convinced that citation from scripture is absolutely necessary so that sermons may be buttressed by the authority of "The Word of God." But, however much ministers may crave pulpit authority, we must question the desire. Certainly, we can recall that Jesus, when asked to display authority for his words and deeds, refused. Christ's evident authority seems to have been established by the *truth* of his speaking rather than by signs or by scripture. Moreover, we may wonder if the practice of clothing sermons in scripture citation is not a using of scripture to enhance, validate, or somehow confer godly potency to *our* words. After all, though we may love the scriptures, feed on scriptures, find that we meet Christ Jesus profoundly in scriptures, why must every sermon feature scriptural citation? There is almost never an *immediate* association of situation and scripture in consciousness. If, then, such associations are fabricated inauthentically in a sermon, what is the result? The result is that scripture itself is turned into rule-book law, or a paper buttress for *our* speaking. Rightly, scripture is a gift of grace and, therefore, should not be turned into proof-text rhetorical support. Yes, there will be times when situations taken into Christian hermeneutical consciousness inevitably will recall scripture and such scripture will illumine our understanding. All we are suggesting is that there seldom will be a direct situation-to-scripture shift in consciousness through some sort of situational analogy, but rather that the sequence is more involved. We take a situation, humanly understood, into Christian consciousness where the situation is reread in the light of revelation and *then*, perhaps, we will turn to scripture. In so arguing, we suppose that we are protecting scripture—as if it needs protection—from indiscriminate alignment with situations. (At the height of the Watergate affair, a preacher grabbed by association a one-liner from Nehemiah referring to the Water Gate in Jerusalem!) When scripture is drawn into Christian consciousness by theological understanding then it may address situations appropriately. We are not suggesting that situational preaching will not use scripture; it may, but we are implying that sermons which slap scripture up against situations may be unnatural to Christian hermeneutical consciousness and, thus, encourage an artificial misuse of scripture. Motto: Let scripture be scripture.

SITUATIONS: PERSONAL AND SOCIAL

Throughout our discussion, we have distinguished social and personal situations. The distinction is not entirely useful. Personal and social are more a matter of *focus* than anything else. For the past few decades, American preaching has evinced a decided preference for the personal. Evidently, the idea has been to reach for relevance by speaking to people about what interests them most, namely, themselves. As a result the pulpit appears to be preoccupied with what might be termed a one-to-one self; either the self in one-to-one relationships or the self in a one-to-one inner dialogue. The problem with such an approach is that the pulpit may end up addressing an *abstraction;* there may be no such thing as a one-to-one self! Of course, turn-of-the-century "social gospelers" may have stumbled into the same trap. Social-gospel pulpits addressed problems in the world, an objective world "out there." Quite possibly, the world of social-gospel preaching was also an *abstraction!* Is it conceivable that, in the name of revelance, both personalist preaching and social-gospel preaching have ended up addressing abstractions in a subjective/objective split? Personalism aims at a self-without-a-world, and social-gospel preaching views a world-without-a-self, and both are obvious unrealities. In actuality, to borrow a phrase from Richard R. Niebuhr, we are all "radial" people; that is, we internalize a social world fabricated out of a jumble of language, perceptions, slogans, images, and goodness knows what else. We live in a shared world construct that has been internalized and is, therefore, always with us. In consciousness, there is always a self-in-a-social-world and a social-world-within-the-self. As we observed at outset, self and society distinctions are mostly a matter of *focus*.

The issue is theologically crucial; better, *christologically* crucial. If the pulpit addresses the gospel to no more than a one-to-one self, then Jesus Christ is *only* a personal savior. In which case, who is going to save us from "principalities and powers" in the social world? When it comes to systemic evil in the world, all we can do is long for a heavenly escape or turn and search for an extra savior—an "ism" or "ology" or political demagogue. Some years ago, around Christmas time, we received two cards in the mail on the same day. One, all pink and blue, showed cradled baby Jesus with a caption reading, "May the Christ Child come to your heart at Christmas." The other card pictured a bloated baby rocking in the dust of Bangladesh with the words "Save the Children!" underneath; the card was an appeal for funds. Our problem can be stated bluntly. If Jesus can do nothing more than to come to our hearts while in the world babies starve, then he is scarcely the savior of all. Second-century Gnostics embraced a personal savior, Jesus, but when it came to world problems they discreetly looked elsewhere. A pulpit which, in its personalism, can offer nothing more than a one-to-one savior is in danger of the same gnostic heresy. The issue is not a matter of homiletic preference; the issue is the theological status of Jesus Christ. Because the pulpit in recent American history has been consumingly personal, we have an odd result, namely, a nation filled with nice one-to-one Jesus people who will support the most appalling national policies!

Let us get at the problem in another way. Suppose you have decided that, in a triggery age, you must preach a sermon on "World Peace." So, you survey the world political situation, you remark constant warfares, you churn up some gospel norms, and end up cheering international peace efforts. Your congregation will probably buy into the gospel you preach for, after all, we Christians endorse personal peace and would be pleased to see peace extended —besides, we are all weary of warfare. As a social ideal, we believe that the world "out there" ought to be at peace. Now, ask what has *not* been addressed by your sermon. Answer: Your sermon has not spoken to the world in consciousness, a world papered with slogans such as "Never bargain from weakness" or "Winning isn't everything, it's the *only* thing" or "The best defense is a strong offense," and jammed as well with images—a top-hatted Uncle Sam saluting a flight of bombers, or medals being pinned on a Marine

Corps' dress uniform, or an Armed Forces Day Parade. We can speak to a one-to-one self or address issues in a world out there but if we never reach into the world in consciousness, preaching will be mightily ineffective. Somehow, the American pulpit must break free from its subjective/objective split.

Probe more deeply still: In the past few decades the pulpit has participated in a "triumph of the therapeutic." We have been much concerned to relate gospel to the self in psychological self-awareness. Because we live at a time when human beings do struggle with the "frozen sea" within themselves, with rigidities of the past and stark fears of the future, the pulpit has, no doubt, been genuinely helpful. Nevertheless, we must take a second look at the self-in-dialogue, the inner self, which the pulpit addresses. Years ago, George Herbert Mead asked a not-so-innocent question: He wondered where the "me" and "myself" within us come from. He concluded that in us all there is a speaking, acting agent-self, a "me," and also a self that is acted toward and spoken to, a "myself." The "myself," he remarked, is a *social* creation. The self we consider in consciousness is a self-in-a-social-world. There is no reasonable way in which we can speak to selves without acknowledging that society contributes to self-identity and that our inner struggles have social implications. Of course, the crucial conflict of faith, according to scripture, is a battle between accepting God's undeserved, freely given mercy—justification by grace; or seeking self-approval through social approval—justification by "the Powers that Be." All we are saying is that the one-to-one inner self is an odd abstraction; "myself" is a self-within-a-social-world.

The problem of self and society may be viewed in another way. Is it possible that personalist and/or social-gospel perspectives reflect cultural preoccupations? If you read the work of social analysts or cultural anthropologists, you do run across a scenario for societies which, like our own, may be passing through periods of breakdown and possible reassembly. Because there is much agreement among such analysts, we can delineate phases: (1) The beginnings of breakdown may be signaled by a number of individuals with problems or symptoms, from an increase in mental illness to a high percentage of divorces to a multiplication of drug addictions, and so on. Initially, societies respond by providing therapies—training pastoral counselors, building treatment programs, and the like. (2) A second phase may be described as a vision of social malaise followed by immediate denial. Suddenly, it occurs to people that problems are not only personal; the "system," including social institutions, may be sick. Such a vision is frightening and is almost always countered by denial, which can take the form of a nostalgic retreat to the past, to old-time economics, old-time politics, and of course to old-time religion. Societies will try to retreat to days when problems were simpler and solutions easy. (3) Finally, we may expect a time of social crisis in which, quite obviously, "old-time" solutions break down. Then, in a time of massive cultural despair, the society either holds on to itself ("But, we have *always* believed in . . .") and goes down or, with some new vision of the future, it is able to let go of cherished ways and means, and change. A new vision of the future is usually provided by an emergence of visionary speakers, many of whom may speak from pulpits.

If the rather standard description we have provided is at all true, we may sense that the pulpit has been participating in cultural phases. In the fifties, we were certainly aware of people with problems and, out of genuine compassion, we addressed the gospel to personal problems. In the sixties, we suddenly sensed systemic evil, so the church was moderately involved in civil rights, in war protest, in movements concerned with legal and economic justice. Sharp social concern, however, soon gave way to the seventies. In the late seventies, we went *right* back to old-time free enterprise, old-time States' rights, and above all, to old-time religion—"Backward, turn backward, time in your flight; Make me a Fundamentalist again for tonight"! We are cultural creatures and, therefore, we should not be surprised if pulpit preoccupations are culturally shaped.

Is there some kind of solution to the self/society impasse? Perhaps. First, let us reaffirm that distinctions between individual and social are largely distinction in *focus*. There is no self without a world-in-self and there is no world without a self-in-the-world. When we speak of the world, we will not refer to a world out there but to the world as it is constructed in congregational consciousness, which is always an envisioned and interpreted world. Likewise, when we address a self in its psychological self-awareness, we will not talk about a self grappling internal forces such as guilts, fears, hostilities, and the like. Our guilts and fears and hates are never abstract forces; they have been shaped by social intercourse and are expressed in a social world. Second, the language of preaching cannot *talk about*, it must in some fashion *represent*. So, we will not speak about an objective world, but, instead, by our language, we will represent the world in consciousness. Strangely enough, there is a huge difference between speaking of political events out there in the world and the same events as they are present in consciousness:

> El Salvador. We've heard the name but we're not quite sure where El Salvador is. A banana republic somewhere in between North and South America, down where land narrows, somewhere near the Panama Canal. On TV we see pictures of snipers fighting it out like cowboys and Indians. . . .

El Salvador may be a place in the objective world, but the El Salvador we address is located in congregational consciousness and, what is more, is an interpreted place. We must always stop to consider how the world is formed in communal consciousness. In the same way, if we want to speak of our human fears, we must stop and attempt to locate where and how in lived experience fears happen. Inevitably, we will discover that we are led into a realm of social awareness in consciousness. Though we are representing different foci in consciousness, a language that relates to fields of consciousness will move toward the overcoming of a subjective/objective split.

SITUATIONS AND SITUATIONS

What situations may preaching in the praxis mode address? Obviously, the pulpit cannot and should not attempt to survey every sort of human situation. Imagine sermon titles as varied as "Buying toys for our children," "How to live with in-laws," "Does God vote for a flat tax?" "On the preservation of sperm whales"! The list is ludicrous. Yet, in recent years, the pulpit has addressed an enormous range of human affairs from amorous teenage sexual fumblings to the lonely vigils of old age. On the other hand, if we do not admit a wide variety of human affairs, are we then restricted only to matters of ontological pith and moment? To so restrict preaching could lead to a batch of sermons filled with talk of life and death and destiny that would sound like amateur versions of cryptic T. S. Eliot! Do we only speak in moments of national crises or when some sudden tragedy shakes the congregational family? If we agree that there are legitimate occasions for situational preaching, what exactly constitutes an appropriate situation?

Obviously the gospel relates to *all* of life. There are few if any situations which cannot be informed by Christian consciousness. Furthermore, most preachers feel a sense of responsibility for a deepening of life's meaning. Human beings who settle down within proximate meanings with proximate goals can easily turn into human beings without reflective depth, surface human beings who live and die and, unfortunately, never wonder why. Surely, in every moment of our lives there can be a dimension of depth. If we plan preaching on that premise, however, we will end up with a list of topics (if we are still interested in titling sermons) to examine an incredible range of human experience. Like a Walt Whitman poem, we will so elevate the trivial that we reduce life to a series of equal intensities. Fortunately, in God's grace, we do not have to locate significance in every passing moment. How can we scale down situations for the pulpit?

Clearly, there are events that are culturally momentous. When the bomb bay sprung open on Enola Gay and atomic death slid into the world, any pulpit which did not register the trauma was probably irresponsible. If, in a parish, an entire family is wiped out by some sudden, irrational act of violence, a silent pulpit would be scandalous. Moments of congregational conflict or decision may also have to be addressed with more than prayer and pastoral care; the pulpit may have to speak. We have signaled such situations in our discussion of limit moments and decision moments. Rather obviously, such moments require interpretation in the light of the gospel.

But what else? What other situations call for homiletic attention? Are there not recurrent problems in the lives of people? What of rising social attitudes which a sensitive pastor may be aware of; should they not be addressed? Perhaps we may venture some criteria: (1) To be addressed by preaching, a situation ought to *connect* with profound ontological or historical questions. Though, theoretically, all human situations may have significance, we are referring to moments when ontological questions may be close to the surface of things, situations in which even imperceptive people may sense deeper issues at hand. Our first criterion is framed to guard the pulpit from diving into trivia in the name of practicality or helpfulness. In some situations there is a kind of transparency, so that we sense a dimension of depth. (2) To be addressed by preaching, a situation ought to relate to the store of unanswered questions which have been filed in consciousness by recurring limit moments or decision moments, crucial questions of meaning and morality. We are referring to questions which cannot be answered except by approaching Mystery and acknowledging finitude. While a question such as "Should we buy fluoride toothpaste for our children?" may well be troublesome to parents, the question may not readily bring to mind ultimate mysteries of being and deciding. (3) To be addressed by preaching, a situation ought to fit into structures of Christian consciousness. Either the situation will be one in which we sense some possible distinction in behavior between being-saved and being-in-the-world, or one in which we realize mysterious questions that beg revelation—story and symbol. Of course, our first two norms ensure that we will pick situations open to the light of revelation. Ultimate questions and transparent situations stand us before the Mystery of God in Jesus Christ.

Preaching forms congregational faith-consciousness. Therefore, most of the time in most of our preaching we will probably follow the structure of the church year. The Christian calendar is designed, year by year, to rehearse the event of Jesus Christ, God-with-us. Within liturgy, we will probably preach from scripture so that a being-saved-community may understand itself in the light of revelation, story and symbol. Christian communities need to know Jesus Christ not only as a character in the story of God-with-us, but as a risen, living symbol of God-love toward us. Of course, if we preach from scripture, we will not be ignoring human situations. True biblical preaching is never remote from life in the world. Nevertheless, there may well be occasions when preachers will turn and begin with situations. When preaching in the mode of praxis, we take real, live, human situations into Christian consciousness. There have always been pulpits, such as those that still stand in the midst of large secular universities, where situational preaching will be more usual than not. But, in every pulpit, there will be moments, situations, which command a preaching of the gospel and, therefore, a preaching in the mode of praxis.

25.
Structure in
the Mode of Praxis

Imagine yourself sitting at a desk facing a blank sheet of paper. Whirling about in your mind is an amorphous situation, some comprehension of the gospel, and a kind of gestalt image of your congregation—attitudes, faces, cultural assumptions, and the like. There you sit, pen in hand, scratching your head. Perhaps a voice calls from some nearby room, "What's the matter, you're not writing?" and all you can say is "I don't know how to start." Preaching from situations is *not* easy. Human situations spread so wide and so deep that designing sermons is difficult. How do we structure when we preach in the mode of praxis?

When we studied preaching in the mode of immediacy, we had a text before us, a text with plot and an obvious intending *to do*. We had something concrete to work with, namely, a scripture passage that disciplined our minds. Likewise, when we looked at preaching in the reflective mode, we discovered a formed structure of contemporary meaning in consciousness—a pattern in mind. Again, there was something defined to deal with in designing a sermon. But what on earth have we to guide us when we put together sermons in the mode of praxis? Our field of consciousness is overcrowded and often jumbled. There is no neatly defined "something" to guide our labors. How do we structure when we preach in the mode of praxis?

THE STUDY OF A SITUATION

At the outset, when preaching in the mode of praxis, we will have to get at a situation. While preaching in the mode of praxis may seem less restrictive, freer and easier, unfortunately, it requires enormous diligence—in a word, homework. We will have to begin by assembling information, probably more information than we will conceivably use. A process of study can be described:

Initially, we will have to *define the situation* as a situation in consciousness. We are not, after all, examining a situation that is sealed off from human attitudes or understandings. We are studying a situation which somehow has risen to prominence in communal consciousness, a consciousness in which we share. For example, let us suppose that we have decided to address the issue of homosexuality. The issue has become an issue because councils of the church are debating the question of the ordination of homosexuals and the media has picked up news of the debate. At the same time, let us imagine that a local school board has taken up the issue of whether schools should employ homosexual teachers. As a result, our congregation is mildly disturbed and the issue is being debated in public meetings, church-school classes and, of course, at parties, in offices, and other public places. In the heat of debate some church members have begun slinging scripture verses at one another like stones. So we have a situation, and, for many reasons, we may feel impelled to speak. At first, we will have to define the situation as it presents itself to consciousness. By reading articles or newspaper clippings, by recalling conversations overheard, we will attempt to lay out the situation as a situation with all its contending pros and cons. What we will be clarifying is the shape in consciousness of a humanly understood situation.

On a deeper level, we will have to isolate and analyze the *human hermeneutics involved* in the issue. While we have probably been able to spot public pros and cons, we will need to get at the underlying assumptions that may be hidden in the debate. Obviously, there are some people who are arguing that homosexuality is a free, sexual option; an orientation no better or worse than heterosexuality. In so arguing, they may be drawing on rather impressive studies which seem to indicate that homosexuality may be inborn, a disposition shaped by some collision of genes; or, if not inborn, then formed in the earliest years of life before there can be any real sense of moral choice. There are others who view homosexuality as deviance, as some sort of departure from a social or moral norm. Some of these people will insist that homosexuality is a matter of free choice and, thus, is sin. Others will suppose that homosexuals are ensnared in psychological patterns and, though unfree, are psychological deviants. Again, there may be impressive psychoanalytic material proposing that homosexuality is shaped in a rigid oedipal pattern demonically imposed by parents. Models within which problems of homosexuality are interpreted may be many. In isolating positions and assumptions we will have to study articles, research material, news magazines, and the like. But it is crucial that we get at the human hermeneutics involved in the issue. Remember, situations are never objective in a world out there, they are always *interpreted* situations. For preaching, we will have to interpret interpretations.

In addition, we must study the shape of the situation in *Christian consciousness*. As a result, we will be reaching toward our bookshelves and our files. Perhaps we will read through a survey of the church's historical attitudes toward homosexuality, attitudes which have changed through the centuries. Or, maybe, we will plow through church study materials on the issue— pronouncements, exegetical works, theological discussions, and so on. We should not study in search of some fixed answer which, of course, we will not find on any complex human issue. Remember, Christian discussions of an issue will always include human hermeneutics, cultural attitudes, perspectives drawn from different "ologies," and the like. How difficult it is on any issue to say emphatically, "The church has *always* taught . . ." So, in studying an issue, preachers will not expect to come up with something they can label "The Answer." Rather, in exploring an issue, preachers will be preparing themselves for their proper work, namely, to be resident theologians for a congregation.

In study, we will be getting hold of the shape of theological discussion. For example, the issue of homosexuality may be treated quite differently within different theological frameworks. Some Christians will argue from creation: We are created male and female and, therefore, homosexuality must be a twisting of God's purpose for creation whether voluntary or not. Others may suppose that scripture condemns homosexuality as sin and that, thus, persistent homosexuality is a continuing in sin and an unrepentant refusal of mercy available in Jesus Christ. Still others may begin by acknowledging that we are all sinners whether homosexual or heterosexual, therefore: (1) Sinlessness is scarcely requisite for preaching and teaching. (2) Degrees of sinfulness are not calculated in the sight of God. (3) As Christians we are called to "Judge not!" (4) In a being-saved community, we are reconciled sinners who encourage one another to grow in grace. (5) Being-saved communities are by nature radically inclusive. In a muddle of theological positions, a preacher must work out an issue within the structures of a Christian hermeneutical consciousness.

Our initial survey of what may be involved in getting a hold on a situation may seem intimidating and, in a way, is intimidating. Thoughtful preaching, however, is a ministerial calling and, in fact, is much more interesting than cranking a church mimeograph, scheduling endless and often mindless "important" meetings, or writing up trivia for a church newsletter. Unless we are willing to do homiletic homework we are apt to end up spouting our own uncorrected human hermeneutics from a pulpit and labeling them "Word of God"! A minister's essential work is a work of interpretation. And it *is* work. There are simply no quick sermons, at least not if we live in awe of God and with a loving respect for our neighbors in the pew. We cannot slap together sermons by scanning some *Reader's Digest* rehash article. Preaching, any form of preaching, requires research and thoughtfulness. So preaching in the mode of praxis demands the study of a situation.

A GENERAL SCHEME

When we design sermons in the mode of praxis, we begin not with a basic series of moves, but with what might be described as an overall strategy. The overall design of a situational sermon involves some arrangement of necessary components. Let us identify the necessary parts of a sermon in the mode of praxis.

1. Obviously, somewhere in our sermon, we will have to include a description of the situation as it presents itself to consciousness. While members of our congregation may already have a grasp of the situation (Would we preach on a situation that has never occurred to a congregation?), we will be bringing the situation into consciousness in some patterned fashion.

2. Somewhere, somehow, we will have to allow for a rereading of the situation by Christian consciousness. We have previously argued that we cannot slap the gospel up against humanly interpreted situations without truncating the gospel. Therefore, our sermons must include some grappling with human readings of a situation.

3. We will have to take the situation into Christian consciousness where it will be reinterpreted in light of revelation, story and symbol.

4. We will have to portray a new understanding or new course of action for congregational consciousness.

If these components are deemed necessary, they will tend to determine the overall shape of a situational sermon. Of course, they may be rearranged, or conjoined, or expressed in different ways. We are not setting up some sort of fixed sermon pattern always and invariably present in situational sermons, and always in a same set sequence. Look at a number of different schemes which are only a few of the many patterns that might be formed:

1. Christians can be in conflict over an issue,
   Because we have different worldly ideas;
   But we are to be a new people in the world,
   And, in the gospel, there is a new way.

2. Look at our situation.
   Here is how we *understand* the situation.
   But hear the gospel message.
   Now, see the situation differently.
   So we can live in a new way.

3. Here is what the gospel declares;
   But, yet, look at our human situation.
   See the result of our understandings in action.
   There can be a new way to live in the gospel.

4. We humans look at a situation and see X.
   But the gospel looks and sees Y.
   Different views produce different lives.
   Let us dare to live the gospel.

5. We face a moral dilemma.
   These are our alternatives.
   But does the gospel show a new way?
   Yes. Let us so live.

6. We are called to be a different people.
   But, see how we live in the world.
   Thus, we are in conflict.
   But hear the good news.
   We can be liberated people.

We could multiply our list of structural patterns in many ways according to the kinds of situations we may be wrestling with, and the facets of revelation we study. Notice, we have *not* begun invariably by looking at a situation, and we have *not* always included a separate section dealing with worldly interpretation. Nevertheless, each of the schemes does give room for what we have termed the necessary components of situational preaching. The schemes are not outlines with titled sections; rather, they are merely an overall shape for a sermon which will have to be worked out in relation to some particular situation. Nonetheless, when preaching in the mode of praxis, our first task may be the development of such an overall scheme.

The examples we have posed are vague. When we address a specific human situation, however, our overall scheme will take on concreteness. Suppose we are going to address the matter of homosexual ordination.

1. How did the situation arise? Church was asked to ordain a declared homosexual. Now, the issue is in the courts of the church. Newspapers have picked up the discussion. As a result, we are involved.

2. We have different views. Some say homosexuality is a sin and, therefore, ordination ought to be refused. Others say we are dealing with nothing more than a sexual preference. So we debate the issue.

3. Of course, if sinlessness is a requirement for ordination, we will have no clergy. Besides, does homosexuality interfere with a minister's true work—namely, preaching and conducting sacraments?

4. According to the gospel we are all sinners (It's not a question of degree), and we are all forgiven in the cross. We who are church are called to display God's wide, wide mercy.

5. So, we're in a bind! The world (and many of us who live in the world) is not ready to accept homosexual clergy. Thus, we must work to change the world's way of thinking in the mercy of Christ.

Whatever your opinions on the issue, note that we have set up a rough, overall scheme for a sermon. Actually, a sermon opposing the ordination of homosexuals might be produced by altering the fifth move, thusly,

5. So, we're in a bind! the world (and many of us who live in the world) is not ready to accept homosexual clergy. Yes, we may wish to work to increase the world's compassion, but, meanwhile, what do we do? We cannot risk any discredit to the gospel. Most churches have decided to refuse homosexual ordination.

In our sermon sketch, there are no headings, no labeled topics; all we have is a general design that assembles necessary components for a situational sermon. In the example, we have begun with a situation, turned to worldly viewpoints, wrestled with the viewpoints on the basis of Christian understanding, looked at the gospel of God's mercy including a grasp of the vocation of a being-saved community, and then ended with a new understanding of our situation. All necessary components of a situational sermon are included. But, again, please remember there can be variety in the overall pattern of a scheme. For example, here is a sketch for a sermon on the problem of theodicy:

1. The gospel announces that "God is Love."
2. But what then of terrible disasters?
3. Shall we say that nature is separate from God? Then, God not God.
4. Or claim tragedy is a learning experience. Then, God not good.
5. Only answer is to look at God disclosed on the cross!
6. In suffering, let us cling to God in faith, knowing that God is with us.

Notice, a presentation of the situation enters the structure *after* an announcement of the gospel. Then, alternative views are examined and criticized. There is a return to the gospel of Jesus Christ before, finally, the situation is revisioned. While all necessary components are present in the structure, they are arranged very differently. We are suggesting that a first step in designing a sermon in the mode of praxis will involve a general scheme of presentation which, in a way, is somewhat analogous to what we termed a "basic structure" when preaching from scripture. The general scheme is not in any sense a firm outline, but is rather a sketch of a *strategy* of presentation. The general scheme will involve some ordering of what we have termed the necessary components of a situational sermon.

DEVELOPMENT: SETS AND MOVES

Within the general scheme for a situational sermon there will be component parts. While sermons in the mode of immediacy may travel along from move to move in an episodic sequence, situational sermons are designed quite differently. While there will be overall movement to the sermon, within that movement we will be exploring a situation in a number of moves, or grasping revelation in a number of moves, or taking on human hermeneutical understandings in a number of moves—these groups of moves we will call "sets." Each section of the general scheme, then, will contain a set of moves, a pattern of subordinate material. Now, we must ask how we determine and design subordinate sets of moves.

The Situation

If we address a situation, the situation will have presented itself to consciousness in some particular shape. For example, if we were to preach on the issue of homosexual ordination, we would realize that the situation has entered consciousness as a debate, with contending positions drawn up in conflict. Therefore, the first set in our sermon might be designed as:

> I.
> 1. How we got the situation.
> 2. Viewpoint A
> 3. Viewpoint B

On the other hand, let us suppose we are going to preach on a situation that appears to be historically determined; we are dealing with changing attitudes in the human world. We might find ourselves designing a quite different sort of set:

> I.
> 1. Once upon a time we believed X.
> 2. Then there was a shift to Y.
> 3. Now, however, we are swinging toward Z.

Sometimes in analyzing a situation, we will find that we are dealing with nothing more than an event and a reaction. Thus, we might form a set accordingly:

I.
  1. We have witnessed a terrible tragedy.
  2. As a result, we question faith in God.

In the examples we have proposed, there is a different logic of movement within each set. The logics have been prompted by the different ways in which the situations have formed in consciousness—as alternative positions in a debate, as a progression in history, as a response to an event. There are many ways in which situations form in consciousness, for example, as a survey of sociological patterns, as a psychological uncovering, as a spectrum of political views, as a personal problem to be solved. We are arguing that the shape of a situation in consciousness can indicate the logic of a set. We have not dumped situations into a number of points or categories—"First . . . Second . . . Third." Categorical systems of development are *always* the most tedious way of understanding anything and, in general, can be avoided. But, notice also, we did not begin with a clutter of stock systems of development —for example, "thesis, antithesis, synthesis" or "Is it X? Is it Y? No, it is Z!" —and then try to cram the situation into a familiar pattern. While stock systems have developed, no doubt, from the redundancy of human situations, it is always better to start out by asking *how* a situation shapes in consciousness and then to design a subordinate set accordingly. *A set is a group of moves organized by some sort of rhetorical logic.* The rhetorical logic chosen should be appropriate to the way in which the situation has formed in consciousness.

Christian Consciousness

In the mode of praxis, we have argued that situations must be taken into a Christian consciousness of the gospel. Now, we must ask whether there are any rhetorical guidelines to assist us in designing sets of moves that may represent Christian consciousness. To get at an answer to the question, we will have to investigate the *structures* of Christian faith-consciousness within which situations may stand.

When we speak of a *narrative structure* to faith-consciousness, we are referring to an overall story of God-with-us. The story begins with myths of origin and concludes with myths of consummation, in between which is an unfolding of human events in relation to God-with-us. Clearly, the story starts with myths of origin—check the strange stories that crowd the first eleven chapters of Genesis: there are the primal myths of creation and fall as well as derivative stories, such as Cain and Abel, Noah's ark, and the amazing Tower of Babel. Faith-consciousness also harbors visions of conclusion: the dream of the peaceable kingdom portrayed by the prophets, the image of a messianic banquet, misty spires of a Holy City, the expectation of second coming. Obviously, these great mythic brackets give meaning to the unfolding story of God and God's covenant people. Within the story of God-with-us, there is another story that stands out in consciousness, namely, the story of Jesus Christ. The Jesus Christ story relates to the overall narrative of God-with-us because it is designed in much the same way. At the beginning are tales of miraculous birth and at the end are ascension and a promised second coming. In between are awesome accounts of life and death and resurrection. Usually, we will tend to turn to narrative structures within consciousness when we are confronting questions of human destiny, or even questions of "What's going on in the world *now?*"

In addition to story, there are *symbolic structures* in faith-consciousness. While symbols may enter consciousness within the story of God-with-us, they stand out and become living symbols as they disclose what we have termed the "interior" of God-toward-us—God's singular character and way of intending toward us. Symbols in consciousness seem to be reflective; that is to say, they cast light in two directions. Thus, the Living Symbol Jesus Christ lights both human nature and the mystery of God-toward-us. Symbols in faith-consciousness open to us the Mystery of God *in relation to* mysteries of the human social world. Not surprisingly, when we are confronted with situations in which we sense mysteries of human nature and society, we tend to turn to reflective symbols in consciousness. In Jesus Christ we seek light on human affairs in relation to the awesome mystery of God-with-us.

Previously, we have argued that there is an awareness of being-saved in Christian faith-consciousness. The notion of a being-saved community, a chosen people, is part of the story of God-with-us, but has been reconstituted in relation to the Living Symbol, Jesus Christ. Inescapably, we read symbol and story in the light of the reality of being-saved-in-the-world. Again, when we face questions that involve the nature of the church, or questions of Christian life in the world, we will inevitably turn to the self-understanding of the being-saved community. In so doing, however, we will locate being-saved in relation to God's purpose and intending toward us, that is, in relation to story and symbol.

We have said that situations are *taken into* Christian consciousness which, incidentally, is quite different from saying that we must *correlate* human situations and Christian faith. Furthermore, we have argued that situations humanly interpreted may not determine the shape of the gospel. So, now, we must ask exactly *how* situations are reread within Christian consciousness. Within faith-consciousness, structures of the gospel pick out structures, deep, often hidden structures within human situations. For example, suppose a war/peace situation, understood within a model of national self-interest, is taken into Christian consciousness. Narrative structures within faith-consciousness may force a rereading of the situation because, after all, national destiny is not an ultimate when set within the purposes of God. Likewise, contentions between nations, when stood before the Living Symbol of Christ crucified, may be exposed as a murderous lack of neighbor love and even as rebellion against God. In the light of being-saved we may sense that there are sharp distinctions between the new order of human community which God intends, and an old order marked by competitive national self-interests. See what is occurring: Structures in faith-consciousness are reflecting on structures in human situations, often hidden structures, so that the situation is being reread in the light of the gospel. In the process, both situation and gospel are being defined.

We are now in a position to examine our original question: Are there guidelines for the designing of sets of moves which reflect Christian consciousness? Theological ideas per se do not seem to display any fixed rhetorical shape. For example, if we examine the doctrine of creation, we will not discover a rhetorical pattern implicit within the doctrine. After all, if we view the doctrine of creation through process theology, we may produce an unfolding, one-idea-after-another pattern of discourse, whereas if we understand creation dialectically, we may find ourselves designing a sharply defined two-part rhetorical structure. Though theological ideas themselves do not imply a rhetoric, there may be rhetorical clues in the way in which faith-consciousness views situations. We have noted that when situations are stood before the Living Symbol Jesus Christ we seem to employ a two-way reflective logic: Jesus Christ discloses the Mystery of God *and* Jesus Christ casts light on profound mysteries of human being in the world, both our sinfulness and the shape of our true humanity. If narrative structures are drawn on, patterns of logic may be rather different. We may find ourselves relating myth of life—viewing human life as created, as a witness to the fall, or as called to eschatological consummation. On the other hand, an exploration of God's purpose through the story of God-with-us may lead us in the direction of a narrative rhetoric. All we are suggesting is that there may be clues to the designing of sets of moves in the way in which faith-consciousness functions. The design of a set may imitate the way in which we think through meaning.

Some examples may help us to understand:

Suppose we are dealing with an ecological situation in which we are acutely aware of the despoiling of the world. In consciousness, we may turn to narrative structures in which God's purpose in creation is related to life, the fall is connected with the barren earth, and in which eschatological consummation includes a fulfilled, fecund creation. Thus, we might end up with a set that works with a kind of narrative logic from creation to eschaton:

1. Look, God has given us a world to manage.
2. But see how we have despoiled the world.
3. Our redemption will include a redemption of the world.

Or, again, imagine that we are addressing the problem of guilt, psychologically devastating guilt. Naturally, we will turn to the cross where both our guilt and God's mercy are evident. In general, when we turn to the Living Symbol Jesus Christ, we will find ourselves working with reflective logic:

1. Look at the cross. See, there, all our guiltiness lashing out against God.
2. But, at the same time, hear the great absolution: "Father, forgive them." We have been forgiven.

Some situations may draw on many structures within faith-consciousness. For example, if we address issues of war and peace, we may stand our warring world before the cross and, at the same time, bring issues of war and peace into the narrative of God-with-us.

1. Well, when you set our world before the cross you begin to see what our warfares add up to: the destruction of our neighbor and a rebellion against God.
2. But, God is calling us to reconciliation. Look at the dream of a peaceable kingdom!

We are arguing that the sets we design to express our Christian faith are not rhetorically arbitrary. We are not dealing with a body of teaching which can be didactically set forth in a series of points. Rather, we are representing the way in which situations are interpreted within faith-consciousness. Therefore, we must see *how* we think a situation through in light of the gospel. We can ask what structures of faith-consciousness are being called forth and, therefore, what kinds of logic may be involved. Basically, the rhetoric of a set ought to imitate the ways in which faith-consciousness works with situations.

Criticism and Revisioning

A *critical contending* with the human hermeneutic is difficult to discuss. The reason we cannot describe sets of moves involved is that such contending may not happen as a separate set of moves. Often, it will happen along with a presentation of the gospel, or in the presentation of our normal human understandings, or as a single move within other sets. Inevitably the gospel will call into question our human readings of human situations. It may be important to suggest that when we criticize our worldly understandings we are not uncovering false premises or exposing faulty logic as we might in philosophical debate. Instead, we are criticizing on the basis of another understanding, namely, the gospel in faith-consciousness. Therefore, if we suggest, for example, that a worldly reading of human nature may be naive, we do so because of a more profound reading in the gospel. After all, we are preaching and not engaged in competitive debate to win points.

When it comes to *revisioning situations* we face a much more complicated matter. The kind of revisioning we do will be determined by the situation with which we are contending. If the situation is an ethical bind, we may be suggesting new courses of action. Or, if the situation is simply puzzling, we may be putting forth a new understanding. At times we may be painting a picture of social vision, for example, the image of a reconciled world. Options are determined by the kinds of situations we are struggling to understand in the gospel. Always, however, we ought to be envisioning something *new*. For example, if we are preaching on war and peace, we should not end with a series of somewhat compromised political strategies for world improvement, and if we are speaking of guilts, we would not wish to conclude with helpful psychological advice on how to ease guilt feelings. The gospel calls us to new life, not to adaptations or reiterations of old life. Clearly, the gospel should lead beyond solutions defined by our worldly hermeneutics.

Our observation leads to a peculiar rhetorical conclusion. In older homiletics we come across the idea of "balance." If, in describing a human situation, we note problems A, B, and C, then, in view of Christian faith, we should demonstrate answers to A, B, and C. In older homiletics, sets of moves were often designed to parallel each other—if we have three moves describing a problem, then we ought to have the same three moves offering a solution. The notion of "balance" in rhetorical design, however, often traps Christian faith within humanly interpreted situations. Instead, we argue that in faith-consciousness situations are seen to be different and that, therefore, situations are "*re*visioned." Thus we suggest that sets of moves in which we come to a decision, or find new meaning, or reach for a new social dream, should be designed *differently*. In other words, on theological grounds, we are rejecting the notion of homiletic balance.

We have discussed sets of moves, sets that will occur within some general scheme for a situational sermon, but these sets are not a series of subtopics under general headings, didactic points arranged in a subordinate sequence. Each set will *imitate consciousness* in some natural fashion. In describing a situation, we will be asking how the situation is shaped in consciousness. When trying to set forth the gospel we will be trying to imitate the way in which a situation is grasped in faith-consciousness. When we envision we will be guided by the shape of vision in consciousness, and not by compulsion to answer a situation "point for point." If we design sets in relation to consciousness, we will discover we are engaged in lively homiletics and not merely listing ideas or topics. We will be producing sermons that to some degree match Christian consciousness as it considers the human situational world.

A SITUATIONAL CASE

Let us imagine that we must preach during the Octave of Christian Unity and that we have been asked to address the subject of church unity. We realize that church-unity Sundays are peculiar. Like the astonishing foreign policy remark that came out of Foggy Bottom a few years ago—"We believe in international cooperation but without any loss of our national sovereignty" —most Christians do seem to believe in church unity but without yielding even a smidgen of denominational identity. So, once a year, we are nice to one another, we hold joint services or practice a pulpit exchange, and a week later we revert to type, hold onto ourselves, and hope that someday those "others" will come around to our "true" church. Nevertheless, the occasion is important and, if only a faltering step, is at least a step in a worthy direction. In addition, we can guess that the congregation for a unity service will be made up of a scattering of the faithful from a few congregations, but probably will not include local "powers" who might actually do something about church unity. The service is usually an elaborate liturgy drawn from several Christian traditions. Imagine that we have been told to address the situation of church unity and to "keep it brief."

Presumably, we will have been reading in ecumenics because it is an important area of study. Perhaps we will have read World Council material, Vatican II documents, as well as articles on the subject of church unity. In addition, we will have stumbled on anti-church-unity literature, those appalling tracts put out to warn against unseemly dalliance with "unbelievers who call themselves Christians." So, arguments pro and con may be lined up in mind. In scripture, we may have worked through the "high priestly prayer" in the Gospel of John, as well as texts in Ephesians and in Pauline letters. Possibly, we will have pored over theological works that single out "questions in dispute" for study. The situation will have been studied.

As an overall general scheme, we decide we will begin with the situation as it shapes in common consciousness, then turn to Christian consciousness, then deal with misunderstandings, before trying to urge a new mind toward ecumenics. Within the general scheme there will be sets of moves. Let us examine a brief sketch for a sermon:

Introduction: Some years ago a man quit reading the Bible. Why? "Because," said he, "It's so disillusioning when you stop!" It is. In the Bible we read wonderful words, "We are all one body," but, then, when we close the Bible and look out at the world, it *is* disillusioning.

I.   1. *Look at the church divided.* Is there "one body" anywhere? You don't have to be a theologian to wander down Main Street and count the churches: Methodist, Catholic, Baptist, Presbyterian, Lutheran, Episcopalian, and, on the side streets, Free Will Baptist, Primitive Methodist, and even, sometimes, Bible Presbyterian. If you're weary of walking, you can let your finger stroll the Yellow Pages. There are fourteen different Christian churches in our town for less than five thousand citizens. If there is "one body," it's been dismembered, and bloodied arms and legs are strewn around. C. S. Lewis said the best way to cause unfaith is to keep the mind flitting back and forth between high-sounding phrases such as "The Body of Christ" and the actual situation in churches. "One body," we say in a high-minded way, but then we start counting.

   2. To be honest, *we're not much concerned.* We don't, most of us, lie awake nights worrying over the divided church. Perhaps, we've bought into the American idea that competition is good for everyone—"free-enterprise religion." Or maybe we're too busy trying to hold on to ourselves. Most mainline Protestant churches have been shrinking. And, the Christian community in our land has been growing smaller; we're losing ground at the rate of about 15,000 Christians per day here in the U.S.A. Few religious sociologists think that Christians will be much more than a quarter of the American population by the year 2000. So our motto seems to match the famous wall graffiti: "If we don't survive, we may not do anything else." When you're fighting for survival, talk of Christian unity may not seem compelling. We are not concerned.

II. 1. Yet, *what do we believe?* We believe there is one God, only one. As the Creed proclaims: "There is one God and Father of us all." There is not a Presbyterian God and a Catholic God, not a Pat Boone God or a Bishop Lefevre God; there is one God, only one. Look, we are not advocating easy tolerance: "It doesn't matter what you believe because, after all, there's one God." No. Scientism may chase a clear mind and Marxism bow before necessities of history: There are idols. The Arabs have a story to explain why camels look so supercilious. They claim there are ten thousand names for God, but that the camel knows the right one! We Christians may tend to be as smug, for we do insist that, though there may be many idols, there is one true God—the God of Sarah and Abraham, of Isaac and Jacob, the God who is known in Jesus Christ. So, here in this church, among us, there is one God, the God known in Jesus Christ.

   2. Now brace yourself: If there is one God, then there is *only one faith in God.* Repeat: Only one faith in God. For Christians, faith is through Jesus Christ and Jesus Christ is not subdivided. Ultimately our faith does not derive from Pope John Paul II, or Martin Luther, or John Wesley,

Oral Roberts, or Jerry Falwell. No, our faith is through Jesus Christ. Trace back your own religious heritage and you'll end up with everyone else at the empty tomb of Jesus Christ. "There could not be two or three churches," shouted old John Calvin, "There could not be two or three churches, unless Christ is torn asunder!" To which he added a one-word comment: "Impossible!" Underneath, we know there is only one Christian faith because there is only one Christ.

III. 1. Well, *something in us rebels!* Something in us says, "No!" No, thank you, we'd rather not be one church. So, we parade all the stock arguments. We say we're afraid of a "Super Church." After all, we insist, if things get too big, what will happen to our individual freedoms? Besides, we are all different. We come from different economic groups, have our different friendships, we don't want to be bunched in one big heap of Christianity. We've grown up used to *our* hymns, *our* ways of worship, and we're not ready to change. Isn't there room in the world for different churches that can cater to our different needs, our different likes and dislikes? So we resist.

2. But look out! *God is working to draw us together!* Can we not hear the Word of God ringing through Christ's own words: "May they be one!" prayed Jesus Christ. Is it possible that our rebellion is actually a rebellion against the Will of God? In Europe there is a chapel for Christians from every tradition. On the chancel wall is a picture of Christ, arms wide open. And under the picture, the words: "May they be one!" So into the chapel we come—Catholics, Presbyterians, Free Will Baptists—clinging to our separate identities. Who do we meet? The God in Jesus Christ commanding us: "Be one!" Look. We may want to hold on to our separate ways, our familiar friends, our favorite hymns—our, our, our. But God has spoken: "Be one," and we dare not stand against the Will of God.

IV. 1. What are we going to do? *How can we live together?* All we can do is to work for God's Will. Guess what, no more competitive games, trying to top one another in program attendance. And no more mere tokenism— Isn't it nice we can get together once a year during the Octave of Christian Unity? Sooner or later, we are going to have to die for one another, give up our precious identity, and be one. There's a wonderful story about a strange man in Wisconsin who, one dark night, went around his village and painted over all the different church names! When they arrested him, he announced, "God told me!" Perhaps. In any case, we're going to have to work at it, because, otherwise, our rebellions will take over. We're going to have to find ways to argue together, party together, eat together as one Christian family, not just once a year, but regularly. For God has spoken in Jesus Christ. God's word to us is "Be one."

There are some odd features of our sermon sketch that may be worth attention. Let us examine the sketch in view of procedures which, previously, we have set forth.

441

The General Scheme

We have begun the sermon sketch with a presentation of the situation. Actually, we could have begun with a statement of our common faith in God and then turned to look at the situation. The choice is optional because both a realization of divisions and a realization of core common faith are in congregational consciousness.

In constructing the situation, we have set up two moves—a perception of our divisions and a recognition that ecumenicity is not, at present, a burning issue. The occasion itself, the Octave of Christian Unity, calls attention to our divisions, and the sparseness of congregation bears witness to the fact that ecumenicity is only a minority concern. Thus, the first set has been determined by the way in which the situation may be present in communal consciousness. Mention of religious free enterprise in the second move introduces one aspect of a common interpretive notion.

Notice, we are contending with common attitudes in more than one location in the sermon sketch (see I, 2; III, 1; and IV, 1). We have designed our sketch to demonstrate that necessary sections in a general scheme, such as "contending with worldly hermeneutics" or "turning to Christian consciousness," do not require any fixed sequence or pattern of construction. General schemes may display considerable variety.

Though we have not cited particular scripture in the sermon sketch, that is, we have not mentioned chapter and verse from Ephesians or the Gospel of John, scripture is very close to the surface of the sermon sketch—"One God, one faith" is a sequence from Ephesians and "Be one" is a paraphrase of the "high priestly prayer" in the Gospel of John.

Sets and Moves

We need to notice a peculiar feature of the sermon sketch. You will see that the sets join together in an overall sequence without the intrusion of transitional paragraphs. An older homiletics, working from a rather different kind of outline almost always included topic paragraphs at the beginnings of different sections. A different kind of point-making outline might well require "topic paragraphs":

    I. What is the ecumenical situation today?
      1. Churches are divided.
      2. Churches are concerned with self-preservation.

    II. Does the Gospel speak to the situation?
      1. Gospel: There is one God.
      2. Gospel: There is one faith through Christ.

III. What must be done?
    1. We must give up our separate ways.
    2. We must obey God's will.
    3. We must come together in Christ.

Such an outline would require not only transitional paragraphs at the starts of I, II, and III, but also transitional sentences to get from move to move. Topically designed outlines do tend toward categorical sets and, therefore, force on us the problem of transitions from one section, or subsection, to another. Instead, our outline is written in a conversational way (based on a general scheme) and shifts in thought are designed naturally. Sets and moves seem to follow one another without the need of extra topical paragraphs or labored transitional sentences.

Within sets, there is a logic. In section I, the logic would appear to be situation–attitude toward situation. In section II, we get a "one God *therefore* one faith" logic. In section III, we have a dialectical logic in which our desires and God's will are opposed. Thus, while the sermon sketch is probably more static than most, we have avoided the tedium of categorical outlines by a variety of logics.

Note that IV, the last move, is peculiar: It pulls in two directions. Certainly, we could reoutline sections III and IV as follows:

1. We rebel.
2. But God's will is unity.
3. Therefore, let us begin to do God's will.

On the other hand, the relationship can be expressed in outline as:

III. 1. We rebel.
    2. But God's will is unity.
IV. 1. In view of our rebellion and God's will, let us work for unity.

In other words, there is some ambiguity about IV, 1. In older homiletics, the ambiguity would not be welcomed. We have designed a sermon sketch to demonstrate that outlines can be a bit untidy and even ambiguous; they can lack balance. After all, we are *not* designing a neat pattern on a page with every section of a sermon balanced with every other section. Instead, we are trying to relate sermon structure to consciousness, which is not always as neat as we might wish.

Congregation

Normally, books on homiletics spend pages speaking about the character of a congregation, particularly when discussing situational preaching. We have not. While ministers will plan sermons as systems intending toward a particular congregational consciousness, usual discussions of congregation may not be helpful—they tend to separate minister and congregation. The idea that there is a people whose mind and ethos can be understood, so that a minister may teach, or convert, or empathize with, or whatever, is not a helpful way of thinking. Instead, we have tried to link our consciousness with congregational consciousness, our world with their world, so that preaching may speak in *a shared consciousness.* Preacher and people alike are together a being-saved community in the world. Our sermon sketch does recognize attitudes in a congregation, ways of thinking which, frequently, may prompt homiletic strategy. Remember, fine preachers often have the instincts of a streetfighter tucked in a trying-to-love-neighbors heart. It may be better, however, to locate ourselves in common consciousness *with* a congregation. Certainly, if we address the issue of ecumenicity, we know perfectly well that we clergy types are much of the problem: we are locked into denominational success/competition models, we are at home in our own liturgical traditions, and we are the ones who may be apt to chant litanies of permanence—"The Reformed Tradition!" So, rather than encouraging congregational analysis as if it were some sort of "other," we are proposing the concept of a shared consciousness.

Briefly we have discussed preaching in the mode of praxis as well as structuring in the mode of praxis. The subject is large and complicated and, to be responsible, might demand a separate volume. What we have done is nothing more than offer a preliminary sketch of problems and, perhaps, some solutions. In some Christian traditions, particularly those which follow a lectionary, situational sermons may be infrequent. In other Christian traditions, they will be more usual though they will occur within the broad sweep of an informal church year. At the outset, we argued that Christian preaching is a two-way hermeneutic, concerned on the one hand with symbols of faith and, on the other hand, with a hermeneutic of situations. Any preaching will involve both. When reading situations we turn to Christian consciousness where symbols are understood. In interpreting symbols, we will always do so in terms of our being-saved life in the world.

In five chapters, we have surveyed ways of designing sermons—in an immediate mode, a reflective mode, and in the mode of praxis. The categories, however, are scarcely rigid! We are looking at a spectrum with gradations, a series of shades of practice from immediacy to praxis. Many sermons may seem to straddle categories, to include in themselves different modes of language. Clearly, sermons in the mode of immediacy travel toward reflection, while sermons in the mode of praxis may, through reflection, turn toward scripture. Underlying the chapters you will have begun to discern a structural theory which relates designed modules of language to our common human consciousness.

THEOLOGY

26.
A Brief Theology
of Preaching

In a comic strip, a frock-coated parson is asked a question, "Why do preachers preach?" The minister scratches his head: "Hmmmmmm," he says. Then, he opens his mouth to answer but "Duhhhh" comes out. Finally, in the last panel of the comic strip, he wanders off with a giant question mark over his head. The giant question mark—"Why do preachers preach?"—hangs over all ministers.

There is no obvious social justification for preaching; people today do not sense that they have to have preaching in the same way that they must have an automobile or the services of a family physician. From a social perspective, preaching may be superfluous—unless we are eager to buy into a Durkheimian view of religion and society. Reasons for preaching can only be found in faith. So, though we may enjoy the sweet freedoms of a superfluous vocation, in faith let us struggle with the question: "Why do preachers preach?" On the basis of theological reflection we can say the following.

1. *Our preaching, commissioned by the resurrection, is a continuation of the preaching of Jesus Christ.*

According to scripture, "Jesus came preaching." He announced an imminent kingdom of God and urged people to repent and believe in the gospel. Jesus declared God's new age and called for faith, faith with courage to change. We begin by remembering a Jewish preacher, Jesus of Nazareth.

Almost immediately, Jesus constituted a symbolic community, twelve disciples, who as "fishers" were to share his declarative ministry. So, we have Jesus-Christ-in-community preaching. Arguments over which came first and, therefore, which has primacy, gospel or church, are chicken/egg disputes. They are irrelevant. God's Word, spoken, constitutes community, for God's

Word always takes flesh. What is primary is neither gospel nor church but Jesus Christ who has created both a word-community and a community-word. The community that Jesus Christ called together was not significantly religious. Jesus handed out no moral placement tests, searched no incipient spirituality, required no sense of priestly vocation; humanity seemed to be the only qualification. We must not view the disciples romantically; they were not humble—fishermen in those days were successful entrepreneurs; they were not outcasts—Levi was the only tax collector in the bunch; they were not single-minded in their response to Christ's call—the sons of Zebedee had their eyes on a main chance. Jesus Christ constituted a symbolic human community and became Jesus-Christ-in-community preaching.

The resurrection of Jesus Christ, following his cruel and unusual death, shoved the community into the world and gave the community life. Almost all resurrection accounts include a "Go tell!" commissioning of the community. The community was commissioned to continue Christ's preaching, now unquestionably validated by resurrection. The kingdom *was,* the new age *had begun,* because, though judged, condemned, and crucified, Christ had risen. Resurrection certified the truth of Christ's message and, more, established Christ, Living Symbol, as a part of the message. In essence, we have a gospel with a story line—the kingdom is come, the new age has dawned; and within the gospel, the Living Symbol, Jesus Christ, who reveals God-toward-us. Story and symbol are dimensions of *one* gospel. The community understood itself to be a witness to the resurrection, commissioned to extend the preaching of Christ in the world.

The resurrection also gave the community salvific new life. Joined to Jesus Christ, the community had passed through death, burial, and resurrection. They were judged by Christ's death (Had they not betrayed, denied, and deserted him?), but were forgiven by his risen presence with them. They were liberated from the burden of law, for Christ, condemned under the law, was risen! They were free to live as a sign of the kingdom because, with resurrection, the new age had clearly begun. Thus, the community understood itself as a *being-saved* new humanity in the world. The evident new life they shared confirmed and interpreted the gospel they preached. The resurrection of Jesus Christ was also a resurrection of Jesus-Christ-in-community; the early Christians knew that they had passed from death to life.

We continue the preaching of Jesus Christ as witnesses to the resurrection. However, the figure of Jesus Christ, Living Symbol, has not nudged to one side the message he preached, the message of the kingdom of God. The issue is crucial. Theological liberalism preached a "horizontal" gospel: Liberalism wrapped up the message of the kingdom in a bundle of social idealism.

Neo-orthodoxy, reacting to liberalism, embraced a "vertical" gospel which, to some extent, oriented "repent and believe" toward Christ alone. But, these options are not two different gospels we must choose between. The Living Symbol, Jesus Christ, does not obliterate the message of the kingdom that Jesus declared. Likewise, the message of the kingdom may not be preached without reference to the reality of Christ risen. There is one gospel that Jesus Christ declared and in which he lives! So we are a joined-to-Jesus-Christ community, given life by resurrection, which continues the preaching of Jesus in the world.

2. *In our preaching, Christ continues to speak to the church, and through the church to the world.* In this respect, preaching is grace: "I speak, yet, not I; Christ speaks through me."

Events generate language. Perhaps it would be better to say events are linguistic explosions; they generate conversations that spread through the world, through time and space. Thus, events continue as generated conversations. For example, "The War between the States" continues as phrases generated by the Civil War still function in familiar usage. Think of phrases —"Fourscore and seven years ago . . . ," "Damn Yankees," "Carpetbagger," and (scribbled on a bourbon bottle) "Rebel Yell"—but think also of symbols: from a hushed Lincoln Memorial to a Mississippi cheerleader draped in Confederate flags, singing not so sweetly of a South that "will rise again." Of course, language can die out or be modified so as to mean differently. Thus, probably (and happily) the language of the Confederacy will fade away, if, eventually, there is no sense of "Southern" identity alive. Therefore, what is astonishing about the language of the gospel is its *duration.* Though the language of the Gospel is modified, age on age, it continues. Think of sermons (at least a million a week), of religious publishing, of gospel music, of banners and stained-glass and other Christian works of art. We must assume that the gospel continues because the living reality of being-saved in the world persists, and because mysterious Presence-in-Absence still impinges on human consciousness. The gospel continues because the Living Symbol, Jesus Christ, does interpret being-saved, and still discloses the interior of the Mystery of God-with-us. Preaching is the preaching of Jesus Christ because it opens to us salvific new life and discloses the reality of God-toward-us.

Christian preaching not only reveals, it continues the work of Christ by calling, liberating, and forming a new humanity. The functions of preaching, then, continue the work of Christ who gathered a people to himself and, by death and resurrection, set them free for new life in the world. We have seen that words are not merely tokens of exchange but that they mediate reality, they bring reality into being. Christ, the mediator, brought to us God's astonishing love, and created a community for God-love. Likewise, our preaching words continue Christ's own work of revelation and redemption in the world.

The mystery of preaching is thus a mystery of grace. By the Spirit, Christ speaks through us, a broken, risen community. Note that the rationale for preaching is not institutional. We do not preach so the church may survive, or gain members, or triumph in the world. Primarily, we preach so Christ may use our words in a salvific work, revealing and redeeming. The church may well be a sign of redemption, but the church per se is not the *end* of redemption or the reason for our speaking. Preaching, therefore, is a spiritual discipline in which we offer our best words to Christ. No wonder that as preachers we are ever on guard against our own ego trips, our self-righteous moralisms, and our whoop-de-do church-boosting impulses. The burden of preaching should send us scurrying to scripture, to the study of theology, and to an earnest gleeful life of prayer. On the other hand, there is wonderful freedom for preachers in the mystery of grace: "I, yet, not I!" In Christ, the burden of preaching is light.

3. *The purpose of preaching is the purpose of God in Christ, namely the reconciliation of the world.*

In Jesus Christ we see the mysterious Love of God reaching out with spectacular modesty to the human world. "God loved the world so much," sings the Gospel of John, "that [God] gave the only Son . . . *not* to condemn the world, *but* so the world could be saved." By "saved," the scriptures envision a new social reality in communion with God; a social reality in which forgiven people are free for love and may live together as family of God. Such a vision may run counter to notions of personal salvation which rescue individuals from a deathward world for eternal life hereafter; but also counter to optimisms of human potential and social progress, because, after all, *God* must save. The notion of reconciliation also opposes any preaching which, out of lust for orthodoxy, is divisive and will not declare hope of full human *community* with God. In scripture, salvation seems to be understood in terms of the Great Commandment. Salvation is reconciliation in which we are free for love of God and neighbors. Thus, God's purpose—however, whenever, wherever—must be conceived as communion with a reconciled world. The purpose of preaching, broadly considered, is nothing less than the saving purpose of God.

Preaching is liberation. We speak to set people free. Human beings, particularly today, see themselves in bondage, and rightly so. Certainly, we are all psychologically bound by sedimentations of the past which still exert a terrifying sway over us; we enact ourselves regressively, we self-destruct over guilts, we depressively rehearse ancient rancors, we reel in dizzy *angst,* etc. Moreover, we sense we live enslaved in a world dominated by principalities and powers, systems of thought and action to which we conform in order to ensure our social acceptance. The social and psychological structures in which we live are bondage to sin and estrangement from God. Therefore, to be reconciled we will have to be set free from bondage. We will not debate which form of bondage is primary—psychological or social—such debate would be fruitless. There can be no redemption of the self without a liberation of the social world, and no redemption of the social world without release from the self's inner bondage. All we are saying is that preaching, as it shares God's saving purpose, will be a liberating word.

Preaching has a time. Preaching is a conversation generated by the event of Jesus Christ which will continue until Christ's redemptive work is done, a consummation symbolized by second coming. Though preaching has continued down through many centuries, it is nonetheless an *interim* activity. We preach between the event of Jesus Christ and the fulfillment of God's purpose in Christ. The use of the term "interim" may connote a static waiting period determined by the resiliency of sin and the fortunate patience of God. By "interim," though, we intend a time filled with the activity of God shaping salvation. The promise of God's future is already acting on our present, is exerting a plotting power over present events—denouement is unfolding even now. Thus, preaching does not hand out the offer of salvation based on past event in a *static* present time. True preaching includes a celebration of God's promise which is *now* happening among us. "Now," says Paul with remarkable enthusiasm, "Now is the day of salvation!"

4. *Preaching evokes response: The response to preaching is a response to Christ, and is, properly, faith and repentance.*

In the preaching of Jesus, the terms "repent and believe" should not be understood as a fixed sequence, two steps in a rigid *ordo salutis.* Repentance and faith are facets of the same reality. Faith in mercy is repentant, and repentance has a faith in mercy. So let us realize that faith and repentance are not steps in a pilgrimage of soul—*first* you repent and *then* you believe; rather they interface—we repent into faith and, in faith, we repent.

Moreover, let us remember that when Jesus urged people to "repent and believe," he did so in view of an impending kingdom of God, a new social reality in the world. Thus, repentance and believing may not be regarded as motions of the soul detached from new social reality, or even motions of the

453

soul in relation to Christ alone. The message of the kingdom and a call for
response belong together: We believe not merely in Jesus, but in Jesus Christ
as inaugurator of the kingdom. Therefore, faith is best understood as entrance
into a new order of life and a concomitant turning from an old order (repentance) through Jesus Christ.

Our response to the gospel is made possible by the gospel. As Saint Paul
observes: "Faith comes from hearing" (Rom. 10:17). Elsewhere, in addressing
the blither-headed Galatians, Paul remarks that the Spirit is given via "faith-
hearing" of a preached gospel. At minimum, we may say that response to the
gospel is made possible by gospel preaching. We must not separate Word and
Spirit: the Word of preaching (by the Spirit) sets us free to respond to the
Word (by the Spirit). Now, we must be cautious. We are not saying that the
way the gospel is preached will determine response, for example, conversion.
The church has leaped into all kinds of inspirational "hoke," not to mention
evangelistic manipulation, trying to effect conversion. ("As the choir sings,
'Just as I am,' raise your hands. . . . Yes, I see you, and you, and you!") If
the church has not gone in for "hoke," it frequently has designed sermons in
a conversionist pattern: First, lay on a heavy sense of guilt and, then, when
the congregation quivers in despair, hand out a carrot-on-a-stick Jesus with
mercy. Such strategies, including emotional climaxes, threats of coming
wrath, last-chance gospels, and the like, border on manipulation and are a
denial of our freedom for God. Rightly, preaching sets us free by announcing
the new era in Christ and declaring mercy. Preaching is essentially a *good*
news that liberates (see the careful contrast drawn in Rom. 1:17–18).

Preaching may also be met with what the Bible terms "hardness of heart."
No matter how winsome in style or generous in promise, preaching can be
met with fierce opposition. People may oppose the good news because they
have overinvested in "this present age," and are afraid they will lose what they
have—power, possession, or prestige. They are, of course, quite correct; they
probably will! Not surprisingly, affluent, power-structure people may have
much difficulty in even hearing the gospel. (Church growth is not likely to
occur among the "haves.") Opposition to the gospel may also come from
those who have "gotten themselves together" psychologically and, thus, fear
they may lose themselves in the new order of the gospel. Again, they are
probably quite perceptive. Psychological togetherness these days may well
mean adjustment to forms of social self-approval. The two fears—social loss
and psychological loss—are both related to "things as they are" being threatened by the new order of the gospel. The usual shibboleth that people refuse
the gospel because they are self-righteous and, therefore, will not admit their
sin and repent is too facile. The gospel may be heard as an assault on cherished

values, on life goals, on political and psychological stabilities. When Paul reaches for an explanation of why folks refuse the gospel, he snarls that "the god of this world has blinded the minds of the unbelievers," and he is no doubt quite correct.

Because preachers preach, they may become targets for a refusal of the gospel. We must be very careful, however: Preachers may deserve rebuke by being arrogant, obtuse, assertive, or self-righteous. (We preachers may not be all that lovable!) We must examine our gospel by the measure of apostolic preaching to be sure that we are preaching gospel and not merely hyperventi-lating in our pulpits in some irritating way. Nevertheless, refusal of the gospel should not surprise us. If we do preach good news of a new order in Christ Jesus it will be received gladly by some (usually those who are broken) but may be rejected by others (usually those who are "together" and have "made it big"). We should not be startled if the gospel is refused, falls on deaf ears, or even provokes angry "yuppie" oppositions.

Preaching in America during the last quarter of the twentieth century may be difficult indeed. America is powerful, affluent, and as a nation is obviously trying to hold onto itself in the world. Thus, a gospel of God's new order will scarcely be well received, particularly by established, and often quite conserv-ative, Protestant communities. In American history the rise of national power has been paralleled by the rise of a Protestant establishment. Will an estab-lished order take kindly to the disestablishing message of the gospel? Preach-ing in America may well be very difficult! Is it any wonder, then, that we have often truncated the gospel? We have preached "repent and believe" as an appeal to personal salvation, but frequently neglected to announce the "king-dom of God is at hand." Or, we may preach Christ crucified as a sufficient atonement for sin, but not mention Christ as the inauguration of God's new age. The gospel does imply a relinquishing of power, position, and even of psychological togetherness. People, American people, may well reject the gospel which does announce an end to "this present age."

When some Christians assert that the gospel requires of us a decision or perhaps, more often, a decision for Jesus, they are recognizing the confronta-tional character of the gospel. If, in fact, the gospel does call us to live in God's new social order, then it is bound to involve a world-conversion, some "let-ting go" and "deciding for," a profound alteration in our understanding of ourselves. They may also be recognizing a setting free within the gospel which may be expressed decisively. The obvious problem with the notion of a decision is that, overstated, it can undercut the conviction that we are saved by grace, and overlook the formative power of the gospel preached. When in retrospect we view our decisions of faith, we stumble on grace at every turn. We heard the gospel preached and it changed our minds. We were in the presence of a being-saved community which, to some extent, displayed the new age. The notion of decision may never be put forth at the expense of the gospel or as a denigration of the Spirit with community. What the idea of decision does is to underscore the radical revision of world that the gospel truly involves.

We have said that response to the gospel can take the shape of a response to preaching and even as a response to the preacher. For those to whom the gospel is liberation, preaching may be a Word of God, the voice of the living Christ. Those who refuse the gospel preached may sense that on some deep, terrifying level they have hardened, and have shut out the Word of God. In this regard, it may be true to say that preaching can harden opposition and drive structures of sin more deeply into resistant people. What preachers may *not* expect (but often fantasize) is widespread approval of their preaching, or even public praise. If people are grateful for a liberating word we have spoken, we may never lay claim to their approval since ultimately we affirm "the Grace of our Lord Jesus Christ." For preachers, preaching is a no-win situation. We can never greet opposition as sure evidence of sin without first examining our own thoroughly mixed motivations, our lack of love, and our strident self-aggrandizements; and we can never bask in praise as if we are anything more than mediators, the servants of grace. Though we can take no credit and, indeed, must accept our share of blame, there are compensations. Because we are preachers, we are afforded the gladness of exploring the gospel week after week and thus coming to know the Mystery of God through Jesus Christ. Gain enough!

5. *Preaching is the "Word of God" in that it participates in God's purpose, is initiated by Christ, and is supported by the Spirit with community in the world.*

When we affirm that preaching is the "Word of God" we must be careful. Obviously, a great deal of pulpit arrogance has been tossed off by preachers who, without reservation, have equated their voices with the voice of God. But, as the apostles in the Book of Acts were quick to admit, we are only human and we speak with human voices. We are frequently scared, fuzzy-headed, lazy, supercilious, and downright nonsensical. Who was it who suggested that the proper liturgical garb for preaching had to be a clown suit? We are emphatically human, and we speak human words. Preaching must be described as a human activity that draws on human understanding and employs human homiletic skills that can be learned. Thus, though we preach knee-deep in grace, we can claim no status for our words. Gratitude, wonderment, a sense of inadequacy—all are preferable to status claims, particularly status claims for the words we speak.

On the other hand, preachers should not lose track of mysteries in preaching, so that they regard sermons as human works of art or eloquence. Once more, we must modestly claim that preaching *is* "the Word of God." We may be two-legged little human beings, but we stand before the mysterious Presence-in-Absence and, through Christ, mediate understandings of God to a being-saved community in a most mysterious world. Good heavens, what a vocation! Though we are quite aware of our humanness, nevertheless, by faith we preach as if we were means of grace, which we are! We believe that through our words God reaches out, claims, converts, and saves, because we continue the preaching of Jesus Christ. So our ministerial vocation is peculiar. We are chronically bemused by our obvious inadequacy, our demonstrable humanity (we can live without the notion that we are professionals!), and, at the same time, staggered by being *chosen* to preach. Christ transfers preaching to us, and gives grace to our speaking, so that, odd as it may seem, our sermons are Word of God to human communities.

In suggesting that we preach the Word of God, we must sidestep a spiritualist position. The Spirit with our spirits does not by some God-magic hand us words to speak. Grace does not bypass humanity. The Spirit, as Luther claimed, is a matter of faith, not a self-evident experience or some sort of overwhelming God-feeling. When preachers have flat Sundays, as every preacher does, and begin boring themselves with their own sermons, it is not a sign of the Spirit's absence; the preacher merely may be underprepared (or overprepared), weary, sexually frustrated, or goodness knows what. Likewise, when words seem to tumble from our lips, spinning in wild flights of poetic wonder, it is not a sign of the Spirit's presence; we may be feeling good and, thus, be both free and fanciful. The presence of the Spirit is not self-evident but is, indeed, an article of faith—of *homiletic* faith. Wherever there is faith in Jesus Christ, the Spirit is with community and with speakers to community. While the Spirit may give homiletic gifts, courage, wisdom, and even a certain transparency of spirit to preaching, we cannot identify the Spirit with particular rhetoric or particular moments in preaching. The Spirit labors as much in our struggles as in our spontaneities. As Paul suggested, the test of the Spirit in connection with preaching is the edification and upbuilding of Christian community.

Again, if we say that preaching is or does the "Word of God," we must not argue from a fundamentalist position. The repetition of scripture, or even the careful interpretation of scripture, does not guarantee that preaching will be Word of God. To go further, reiterations of the biblical world-view or rehearsals of biblical event over against our more modern world view will not ensure that preaching is Word of God. To so argue would be to insist that by *works* of fidelity we can take charge of God's Word. No, God is free even from our fidelities! So, let us be willing to say baldly that it is possible to preach the Word of God without so much as mentioning scripture. Preachers will receive scripture as a gift of grace, and they will delight in scripture, study scripture, live with scripture so as to be grasped by the God revealed in Jesus Christ. Furthermore, preachers may indeed wish to preach from scripture as they interpret things of God to a being-saved community in the world. But we must not say that preaching from scripture is requisite for sermons to be the Word of God. An authority model descending from God to Christ to scripture to sermon could lead to a terrifying arrogance that not only contradicts gospel but destroys preaching. The little white tabs that dangle from some preachers' necks are said to symbolize the two tablets of the law (a good reason to toss them away). If scripture should become the *law* of preaching, then preaching will no longer be the Word of God.

A further caveat: We must not dally with a notion that the preacher's character is the "Word of God." Popular conviction seems to suggest that the minister's Christian personality somehow speaks through sermons so that, no matter how inept the sermon, people are drawn to God. All things considered, we should endorse loving, pious, generous ministers, but we should *not* argue that character speaks louder than words. Even when the notion is buttressed by an Aristotelian appeal to "ethos," it is still theologically impossible. What the position does is undercut preaching altogether, so that what we say is devalued in the light of who we are. The Second Helvetic Confession rightly insists that we hear the Word of God through the lips of sinful preachers because, after all, what else is there! Just as the Catholic doctrine of *ex opere* was originally framed to protect against the idea that the character of a priest could determine the efficacy of a sacrament, so as preachers (along with the Reformers) we must affirm a kind of *ex opere* of the Word. Our character does not preach. What is more, our character does not determine the gospel or the efficacy of the gospel. Admittedly, we might conceive a preacher who was such an evident "stinker" as to bring public ridicule to the gospel, but even obvious moral turpitude and scandal could not mean that the gospel would not be preached so as to convert, liberate, and save. Yes, most ministers as they preach will be preaching to themselves and, as a result, will wish to bring their broken lives into God's new age. The gospel, however, is always greater than preachers of the gospel—thank God. As text for our discussion, we recall a truly offensive Christian writer who, when asked why his character was not sweeter, replied, "My God, think what I would have been without Jesus

Christ!" The fact is, all preachers serve Christ in brokenness, trusting in grace alone. The Pietist error, in both conservative and liberal communities, has endorsed personality-cult preaching ("Truth through Personality") to the detriment of the gospel. We ourselves are never Word of God.

So, what are we thrown back on? We are flung back on a confidence in the gospel, trust in the grace of God, and prayer for the Spirit with us. Our words are human and they will not cease to be human; we will work on them just as we work at many human activities, taking pleasure in craft and drawing on intelligence. And we will do our homework like good children of God. Nevertheless, insofar as our words are instigated by Jesus Christ, serve God's salvific purpose, and are ratified by the Spirit with a being-saved-community, *they are Word of God.* We speak as we live in mysteries of grace. There is a kind of secret astonishment to preaching: We work hard, we study, we explore the Mystery of God-love and, then—with the naiveté of a trusting child, or the desperation of broken people who have to speak of wholeness, or both—we cast ourselves on grace alone. What else? We have been *chosen* to speak God's own Word. No wonder, year in, year out, preaching is terror and gladness.

FOR FURTHER READING

Part 1.
Moves

The following bibliographic sketches are designed to guide readers who may wish to pursue some of the subjects discussed. The bibliographies are limited, for they do not include foreign language titles or periodical literature, and they include only a few selected books with which I am familiar.

The bibliographies of homiletic literature follow in the bibliography for part 2: Structures.

PHENOMENOLOGY OF LANGUAGE

The approach to language in this part is influenced by a phenomenological understanding of language. A "beginner book" might be G. Gusdorf, *Speaking* (Evanston, Ill.: Northwestern Univ., 1965), perhaps followed by R. Kwant, *Phenomenology of Language* (Pittsburgh: Duquesne Univ., 1965). A more sophisticated work is J. M. Edie, *Speaking and Meaning* (Bloomington: Indiana Univ., 1976), which contains helpful bibliography. There is also a useful discussion in D. Ihde, *Sense and Significance* (Pittsburgh: Duquesne Univ., 1973). Two great names figure in phenomenology of language, Martin Heidegger and Maurice Merleau-Ponty. Three works by Heidegger are crucial for his understanding of language. They are *What Is Called Thinking?* (New York: Harper, 1968), *On the Way to Language* (New York: Harper, 1971), and *Poetry, Language, and Thought* (New York: Harper, 1971). Some of Merleau-Ponty's works that relate to language are *Consciousness and the Acquisition of Language* (Evanston, Ill.: Northwestern Univ., 1973), *The Primacy of Perception* (Evanston, Ill.: Northwestern Univ., 1964), *Signs* (Evanston, Ill.: Northwestern Univ., 1973), and *The Visible and the Invisible* (Evanston, Ill.: Northwestern Univ., 1968). Some helpful interpretive essays on Heidegger and Merleau-Ponty may be found in *Phenomenology*, ed. J. J. Kockelmans (Garden City, N.Y.: Doubleday, 1967). See also M. Foucault, *The Archeology of Knowledge and the Discourse on Language* (New York: Pantheon, 1972). Two other philosophical essays are B. Parain, *A Metaphysics of Language* (Garden City, N.Y.: Doubleday, 1971), and the important study by M. Dufrenne, *Language and Philosophy* (New York: Greenwood, 1968). I have found the rhetorical studies of Walter J. Ong to be congenial to a phenomenological approach, in particular *The*

Presence of the Word (New Haven: Yale Univ., 1967), *Why Talk?* (Corte Madera, Calif.: Chandler & Sharp, 1973), *Interfaces of the Word: Studies in the Evolution of Consciousness and Culture* (Ithaca, N.Y.: Cornell Univ., 1977), and *Orality and Literacy* (New York: Methuen, 1982).

NARRATIVE THEOLOGY

Of late, literature on narrativity and theology has multiplied. Preachers may spot hermeneutical issues in Hans W. Frei, *The Eclipse of Biblical Narrative* (New Haven: Yale Univ., 1975). Some of the essays in *Religion as Story*, ed. J. B. Wiggins (New York: Harper, 1975), will also be useful. Thereafter, in alphabetical order, notice the following: J. S. Dunne, *The Way of All the Earth* (New York: Macmillan, 1972), *Time and Myth* (Garden City, N.Y.: Doubleday, 1973), *A Search for God in Time and Memory* (Notre Dame, Ind.: Notre Dame Univ., 1977); G. Fackre, *The Christian Story* (Grand Rapids: Eerdmans, 1978); M. Goldberg, *Theology and Narrative* (Nashville: Abingdon, 1982); S. Hauerwas has studied the relationship between narrative identity and ethics in *Truthfulness and Tragedy* (Notre Dame, Ind.: Notre Dame Univ., 1977) and *A Community of Character: Toward a Constructive Christian Social Ethic* (Notre Dame, Ind.: Notre Dame Univ., 1981); J. W. McClendon, Jr., *Theology as Biography* (Nashville: Abingdon, 1974), and, with J. M. Smith, *Understanding Religious Convictions* (Notre Dame, Ind.: Notre Dame Univ., 1975); Johann Metz, *Faith in History and Society* (New York: Seabury, 1980); J. Navone, *Toward a Theology of Story* (Slough, Eng.: St. Paul, 1977), and, with T. Cooper, *Tellers of the Word* (New York: Le Jacq, 1981); R. Roth, *Story and Reality* (Grand Rapids: Eerdmans, 1973); J. Shea, *Stories of God* (Chicago: Thomas More, 1978); G. Stroup, *The Promise of Narrative Theology* (Atlanta: John Knox, 1981); Sallie [McFague] TeSelle, *Speaking in Parables* (Philadelphia: Fortress, 1975); B. Wicker, *Story-Shaped World* (Notre Dame, Ind.: Notre Dame Univ., 1975). G. Aichele, Jr., *The Limits of Story* (Philadelphia: Fortress, 1985), raises important questions. Paul Ricoeur's most recent work is *Time and Narrative* (Chicago: Univ. of Chicago, 1984). See also under "Narrative Form" in part 2: Structures. It does seem to me that, in view of a "symbolic-reflective" dimension to faith, Christianity cannot be subsumed under the rubric of "story" alone.

RECENT RHETORICAL STUDIES

Homiletics has always been in conversion with rhetoric. Although, of late, homiletics has been isolated by its attraction to biblical theology, properly it should draw on rhetorical wisdom. Ever since early Christian fathers formed a homiletic by studying Aristotle's *Rhetoric* and *Poetics,* preaching and rhetoric have interrelated. Names we read in church history are, often, as well known in rhetoric—Augustine *(De doctrina Christiana),* Boethius, the Venerable Bede, Alcuin, and others. Preachers who wish to recover rhetorical study should probably begin with classical wisdom: Edward P. J. Corbett, *Classical Rhetoric for the Modern Student* (New York: Oxford Univ., 1965) is a useful work. History can be traced in G. A. Kennedy, *Classical Rhetoric and Its Christian and Secular Tradition from Ancient to Modern Times* (Chapel Hill: Univ. of North Carolina, 1980). For an overview of contemporary approaches, see *Contemporary Theories of Rhetoric,* ed. R. Johannesen (New York: Harper, 1971), and, more recently, W. B. Horner, ed., *The Present State of Scholarship in Historical and Contemporary Rhetoric* (Columbia: Univ. of Missouri, 1983). On philosophy and rhetoric, see

I. A. Richards, *The Philosophy of Rhetoric* (New York: Oxford Univ., 1936); A. C. Baird, *Rhetoric: A Philosophical Inquiry* (New York: Ronald, 1965); E. Grassi, *Rhetoric as Philosophy* (University Park: Pennsylvania State Univ., 1980); but see also S. Ijsseling, *Rhetoric and Philosophy in Conflict* (The Hague: Martinus Nijhoff, 1976). While many studies in the field of rhetoric have bearing on homiletic theory and practice, we may single out some major rhetoricians of special import: On the thought of Richard Weaver, see R. Johannesen, R. Stricklan, and R. Eubanks, eds., *Language Is Sermonic: Richard M. Weaver on the Nature of Rhetoric* (Baton Rouge: Louisiana State Univ., 1970), with an introductory essay reviewing Weaver's many writings. On the thought of Kenneth Burke, among his many volumes, see *A Grammar of Motives* (Berkeley and Los Angeles: Univ. of California, 1969), first published in 1945, and *A Rhetoric of Motives* (Berkeley and Los Angeles: Univ. of California, 1969), first published in 1950. Also, see Burke's *The Rhetoric of Religion: Studies in Logology* (Berkeley and Los Angeles: Univ. of California, 1970). On the thought of Wayne C. Booth, see *The Rhetoric of Fiction* (Chicago: Univ. of Chicago, 1961); *Modern Dogma and the Rhetoric of Assent* (Notre Dame, Ind.: Notre Dame Univ., 1970), which also contains a survey of bibliographic resources in rhetoric; *Don't Try to Reason With Me* (Chicago: Univ. of Chicago, 1970); *A Rhetoric of Irony* (Chicago: Univ. of Chicago, 1975); and most recently, *Critical Understanding: The Powers and Limits of Pluralism* (Chicago: Univ. of Chicago, 1979). The work of Chaim Perelman is exceedingly important for homiletics: Begin with a brief work, *The Realm of Rhetoric* (Notre Dame, Ind.: Notre Dame Univ., 1982), and, then, turn to the detailed study, Ch. Perelman and L. Olbrechts-Tyteca, *The New Rhetoric: A Treatise on Argumentation* (Notre Dame, Ind.: Notre Dame Univ., 1969). See also under "Phenomenology of Language," above, for a few of the many volumes by Walter J. Ong whose work is also exceedingly important for homiletic study.

POINT-OF-VIEW

On point-of-view in literature, see Wayne C. Booth, *The Rhetoric of Fiction* (Chicago: Univ. of Chicago, 1961); a "formalist" approach in B. Uspensky, *A Poetics of Composition* (Berkeley and Los Angeles: Univ. of California, 1973); N. Friedman, *Form and Meaning in Fiction* (Athens: Univ. of Georgia, 1975); and S. S. Lanser, *The Narrative Act* (Princeton: Princeton Univ., 1981). See also J. Frank, *The Widening Gyre* (New Brunswick, N.J.: Rutgers Univ., 1963), and C. Nelson, *The Incarnate Word: Literature as Verbal Space* (Urbana: Univ. of Illinois, 1973).

In the visual arts, see important studies by E. H. Gombrich, *Art and Illusion* (Princeton: Princeton Univ., 1960), and, among many others, *The Sense of Order* (Ithaca, N.Y.: Cornell Univ., 1979). See also essays in *Daedalus: The Visual Arts Today* (Winter 1960) and in W. J. T. Mitchell, ed., *The Language of Images* (Chicago: Univ. of Chicago, 1980), with particular attention to contributions by E. H. Gombrich and W. J. T. Mitchell.

No doubt there is a significant literature in poetics and, particularly, in cinematography with which I am unfamiliar; although, see J. Monaco, *How to Read a Film* (New York: Oxford Univ., 1981). What I have done is taken categories offered in literary criticism, interpreted these categories in relation to consciousness, and, then, noticed their display in oral language. Studies I have done seem to indicate that oral language has astonishing power to orient perceptual consciousness.

METAPHORICAL LANGUAGE

The literature on figurative language is, of course, immense. On metaphor, bibliography is available in *Metaphor: An Annotated Bibliography* (Whitewater, Wis.: The Language Press, 1971), and a brief history of different conceptions of metaphor may be read in T. Hawkes, *Metaphor* (London: Methuen, 1971).

We can trace some studies. I. A. Richards, *The Philosophy of Rhetoric* (New York: Oxford Univ., 1936) is an important earlier work. Two books by Philip Wheelwright have had much impact: *The Burning Fountain* (Bloomington: Indiana Univ., 1954) and *Metaphor and Reality* (Bloomington: Indiana Univ., 1962). Max Black's philosophical analysis is in *Models and Metaphors* (Ithaca, N.Y.: Cornell Univ., 1962). E. Honig, *Dark Conceit: The Making of Allegory* (New York: Oxford Univ., 1966) contains interesting related material. Both M. B. Heser, *The Meaning of Poetic Metaphor* (The Hague: Mouton, 1967), and a suggestive work, N. Goodman, *Languages of Art: An Approach to a Theory of Symbol* (Indianapolis: Bobbs-Merrill, 1968), contain important theory. Ian G. Barbour, *Myths, Models and Paradigms* (New York: Harper, 1974) compares metaphoric thinking in religion and the sciences. Some collected essays should be noted: S. Hopper and D. Miller, *Interpretation: The Poetry of Meaning* (New York: Harcourt, 1967); A. Ortony, ed., *Metaphor and Thought* (Cambridge: Cambridge Univ., 1979); and S. Sacks, ed., *On Metaphor* (Chicago: Univ. of Chicago, 1979). A dissertation, I. Dempsey, "Metaphoric Consciousness: An Epistemology in Language Use for a Poetics" (Ph.D., University of Tulsa, 1973), is interesting. The first section of B. Wicker, *Story-Shaped World* (Notre Dame, Ind.: Notre Dame Univ., 1975) contains chapters on metaphor. For a recent, fascinating study of the social functioning of metaphor, see G. Lakoff and M. Johnson, *Metaphors We Live By* (Chicago: Univ. of Chicago, 1980). Of course, the magisterial work is by Paul Ricoeur, *The Rule of Metaphor: Multi-Disciplinary Studies of the Creation of Meaning in Language* (Toronto: Univ. of Toronto, 1977).

Theology has pondered the metaphorical character of Christian faith. Among many sources, see C. F. Woods, *Theological Explanations* (London: Nisbet, 1958); Ian T. Ramsey, *Religious Language* (New York: Macmillan, 1957), and *Models and Mystery* (London: Oxford Univ., 1964); J. Macquarrie, *God-Talk* (New York: Harper, 1967). Some recent works deserve special mention: D. Burrell, *Analogy and Philosophical Language* (New Haven: Yale Univ., 1973); D. Tracy's astonishing work, *The Analogical Imagination* (New York: Crossroad, 1981); and, of course, Sallie McFague's *Metaphorical Theology: Models of God in Religious Language* (Philadelphia: Fortress, 1982). For a study of the figurative language in scripture, see G. B. Caird, *The Language and Imagery of the Bible* (Philadelphia: Westminster, 1980), and also O. Keel, *The Symbolism of the Biblical World* (New York: Seabury, 1978).

On the matter of sermon illustrations, two often-cited works are I. Macpherson, *The Art of Illustrating Sermons* (Nashville: Abingdon, 1964), and an older work, W. E. Sangster, *The Crafter of Sermon Illustration* (Philadelphia: Westminster, 1950). More recently, see C. L. Rice, *Interpretation and Imagination* (Philadelphia: Fortress, 1970), and E. Achtemeier, *Creative Preaching* (Nashville: Abingdon, 1980) for some discussion of the subject. We do need a significant work on the use of analogy, metaphor, example, and image in preaching.

On the use of imagery, bibliography is difficult to assemble because it is multidisciplinary and usually partial. I know of few full-scale treatments of image; instead, we must search poetics, psychology, rhetoric, and perceptual philosophy. Preachers may find it useful to read the section on "Images" in J. Chiardi, *How Does a Poem Mean?* (Boston: Houghton, 1959) before examining the literature in poetics. Thereafter, some of the following may be useful: O. Barfield, *Poetic Diction: A Study in Meaning* (New York: McGraw-Hill, 1964; first published 1928); I. A. Richards, *Practical Criticism* (New York: Harcourt, 1929); W. Empson, *Seven Types of Ambiguity* (New York: Meridian, 1958); a fine study by A. MacLeish, *Poetry and Experience* (Baltimore: Penguin, 1964); E. Sewall, *The Orphic Voice* (London: Routledge, 1960), and *The Human Metaphor* (Notre Dame, Ind.: Notre Dame Univ., 1964); W. Y. Tindall, *The Literary Symbol* (Bloomington: Indiana Univ., 1955); W. H. Auden, *The Enchafed Flood* (New York: Random, 1950). See also A. Wilder, *Theopoetic* (Philadelphia: Fortress, 1976) for a theological perspective.

Literature on symbolization in psychology is, again, too large to survey. Nevertheless, two classic works must be mentioned: S. Freud, *A General Introduction to Psychoanalysis* (New York: Washington Square, 1960), the section on "Dreams," and C. G. Jung, ed., *Man and His Symbols* (New York: Dell, 1960), as well as other works by Jung himself. In addition, there is a massive two-volume study of language in psychoanalytic thought, by T. Thass-Thienemann, *The Interpretation of Language* (New York: Aronson, 1968, 1973). From a sociological perspective, see K. Boulding, *The Image* (Ann Arbor: Univ. of Michigan, 1956). See also two very significant works by H. D. Duncan, *Communication and Social Order* (New York: Oxford Univ., 1962) and *Symbols in Society* (New York: Oxford Univ., 1968). For a series of essays, see W. J. T. Mitchell, *The Language of Images* (Chicago: Univ. of Chicago, 1980).

From the standpoint of cultural anthropology, there is a sophisticated literature on symbols, a bibliography too large to review. However, readers may wish to begin with R. Firth, *Symbols, Public and Private* (Ithaca, N.Y.: Cornell Univ., 1973), which contains extensive bibliography; and then to examine V. Turner, *Dramas, Fields, and Metaphors; Symbolic Action in Human Society* (Ithaca, N.Y.: Cornell Univ., 1974). A work by D. Sperber, *Rethinking Symbolism* (New York: Cambridge Univ., 1975), will also be helpful. There are many significant figures in the field: To enter the work of C. Levi-Strauss, begin with the first essay in *The Savage Mind* (Chicago: Univ. of Chicago, 1966); for M. Douglas, begin with *Natural Symbols* (New York: Pantheon, 1982); for C. Geertz, read *The Interpretation of Cultures* (New York: Basic, 1973); for V. Turner, *The Ritual Process* (Ithaca, N.Y.: Cornell Univ., 1969). Though the literature is vast and complicated, it is of importance to homiletic theory.

In philosophy, see E. Cassier, *The Philosophy of Symbolic Forms*, 3 vols. (New Haven: Yale Univ., 1955), in particular vol. 2: *Mythical Thought.* Also see the work of S. Langer, especially, *Philosophy in a New Key* (New York: Penguin, 1942), and *Mind: An Essay on Human Feeling* (Baltimore: Johns Hopkins, 1967).

The only recent work on images in homiletics that I know of is T. Troeger, *Creating Fresh Images for Preaching* (Valley Forge, Pa.: Judson, 1982); but see also R. D. Young, *Religious Imagination: God's Gift to the Prophets* (Philadelphia: Westminster, 1979). Also consult "Recent Rhetorical Studies," above, and "On Language," and "Style," both below.

COMMUNICATION STUDIES

The field of communication seems to be split up into somewhat "positivistic" studies influenced by Noam Chomsky, "interpersonal" studies spurred by Erving Goffman and others, "media" studies somewhat swayed by Marshall McLuhan, and "semiotic" studies following Roland Barthes and others. Communication has had impact on theology; see P. Soukup, *Communication and Theology: Introduction and Review of the Literature* (London: World Assoc. for Christian Communication, 1983). The best brief introduction I have found to the fields of communication is by John Fiske, *Introduction to Communication Studies* (London: Methuen, 1982), although a basic textbook such as G. Mortenson, *Communication: The Study of Human Interaction* (New York: McGraw-Hill, 1972) may also be helpful. D. K. Berlo, *The Process of Communication* (New York: Holt, 1960) is a basic survey that has been used in several theological schools.

Some early works influential in the field are C. K. Ogden and I. A. Richards, *The Meaning of Meaning* (New York: Harcourt, 1938); A. Korzybski, *Science and Sanity* (Lakeville, Conn.: Inst. of General Semantics, 1933); and C. Morris, *Signs, Language, and Behavior* (Englewood Cliffs, N.J.: Prentice-Hall, 1946). For a semipopular survey of these early works, see B. Sondel, *The Humanity of Words* (Cleveland: World, 1958). For a remarkable tracing of the history of the communication model from classical times through nineteenth-century rhetoric, see Nancy Harper, *Human Communication Theory: The History of a Paradigm* (Rochelle Park, N.J.: Hayden, 1979). For an introduction to theoretical positions, see S. Littlejohn, *Theories of Human Communication* (Columbus, Ohio: Merrill, 1978), and the range of essays in K. Sereno and C. Mortenson, eds., *Foundations of Communication Theory* (New York: Harper, 1970). See also R. G. Smith, *Speech Communication: Theory and Models* (New York: Harper, 1970).

Other literature: C. Cherry, *On Human Communication* (Cambridge: M.I.T., 1957) is an early work often described as the "mathematical approach." For somewhat different approaches, see F. Dance, *Human Communication: Original Essays* (New York: Holt, 1967), and also P. Watzlawick, J. Beavin, and D. Jackson, *Pragmatics of Human Communication* (New York: Norton, 1967). Two titles by C. Hovland are important: *Communication and Persuasion* (New Haven: Yale Univ., 1953), and *The Order of Presentation in Persuasion* (New Haven: Yale Univ., 1957). On mass communication, see W. Schramm, *Men, Messages, and Media: A Look at Human Communications* (New York: Harper, 1973), and, with D. Roberts, *The Process and Effects of Mass Communication* (Urbana: Univ. of Illinois, 1974). For a sociological approach, see D. McQuail, ed., *Sociology of Mass Communication* (Baltimore: Penguin, 1972). On nonverbal communication, see R. Hinde, ed., *Non-Verbal Communication* (Cambridge: Cambridge Univ., 1972); M. Argyle, *The Psychology of Interpersonal Behavior* (Baltimore: Penguin, 1978), and *Bodily Communication* (London: Methuen, 1975); and the well-known book by E. Hall, *The Silent Language* (Garden City, N.Y.: Doubleday, 1973). For an excellent collection of essays, see A. G. Smith, *Communication and Culture* (New York: Holt, 1966), which broadly covers aspects of communication; and also see J. Corner and J. Hawthorne, eds., *Communication Studies* (London: Arnold, 1980).

Popular appropriation of Marshall McLuhan had impact on homiletics. McLuhan's best-known works are *The Gutenberg Galaxy: The Making of Typographic Man* (Toronto: Univ. of Toronto, 1962), and *Understanding Media: The Extensions of Man* (New York: Signet, 1964). McLuhan was a prolific writer: For bibliography and critical review, see G. E. Stearn, ed., *McLuhan: Hot and Cool* (New York: Dial, 1967).

Under the influence of Roman Jakobson and, particularly, Barthes, communication theory seems to be taking a "semiotic" turn: see R. Barthes, *Writing Degree Zero and Elements of Semiology* (Boston: Beacon, 1970). The impact of phenomenological hermeneutics is evident in J. J. Pilotta, *Interpersonal Communication: Essays in Phenomenology and Hermeneutics* (Washington, D.C.: Univ. Press of America, 1982).

A number of homileticians work from some form of the communication "model," among them are M. R. Chartier, *Preaching as Communication* (Nashville: Abingdon, 1981) with a helpful bibliography; a Catholic homiletician, G. R. Fitzgerald, *A Practical Guide to Preaching* (New York: Paulist, 1980); J. Randall Nichols, *Building the Word* (San Francisco: Harper, 1980); C. Pennington, *God Has a Communication Problem* (New York: Hawthorne, 1976); and C. W. Welsh, *Preaching in a New Key: Studies in the Psychology of Thinking and Listening* (New York: Pilgrim, 1974).

BLACK HOMILETICS

I have been influenced by the Black homiletic tradition. All things considered, it is probable that the finest preaching in America today is Black. Black preaching is scarcely monolithic, however; see J. Alfred Smith, *Preach On!* for a suggestive listing of many different "genres." Though there are some sermon collections (and even more sermons circulating on tapes)—see volumes published by Broadman, Fortress, and Judson Presses—I will limit bibliography to homiletic studies.

For background on Black homiletics, see materials collected in C. Eric Lincoln, *The Black Experience in Religion* (Garden City, N.Y.: Doubleday, 1974), and also in G. S. Wilmore and J. H. Cone, *Black Theology: A Documentary History, 1966–1979* (Maryknoll, N.Y.: Orbis, 1979), which contains an annotated bibliography. Also study C. V. Hamilton, *The Black Preacher in America* (New York: Morrow, 1972) for a sociopolitical history.

See the following (listed in chronological order): M. H. Boulware, *The Oratory of Negro Leaders 1900–1968* (Westport, Conn.: Negro Univ. Press, 1969); W. H. Pipes, *Say Amen, Brother!* (Westport, Conn.: Negro Univ. Press, 1970); B. A. Rosenberg, *The Art of the American Folk Preacher* (New York: Oxford Univ., 1970); H. H. Mitchell, *Black Preaching* (New York: Lippincott, 1970), *Black Belief* (New York: Harper, 1975), and a fine volume, *The Recovery of Preaching* (New York: Harper, 1977); J. L. Golden and R. E. Rieke, *The Rhetoric of Black America* (New York: Merrill, 1971); J. A. Johnson, Jr., *The Soul of the Black Preacher* (New York: Pilgrim, 1971) and *Proclamation Theology* (Shreveport, La.: Fourth Episcopal Dist. Press, 1977); J. E. Massey, *Responsible Pulpit* (Anderson, Ind.: Warner, 1974), as well as *The Sermon in Perspective: A Study of Communication and Charisma* (Grand Rapids: Baker, 1976), and *Designing the Sermon: Order and Movement in Preaching* (Nashville: Abingdon, 1980); A. L. Smith, ed., *Language, Communication, and Rhetoric in Black America* (New York: Harper, 1972); C. E. Boddie, *God's "Bad Boys"* (Valley Forge, Pa.: Judson, 1972); R. W. Hovda, *This Far by Faith: American Black Worship and Its African Roots* (Washington, D.C.: Liturgical Conference, 1977), a Black Catholic contribution; G. C. Taylor, *How Shall They Preach?* (Elgin, Ill.: Progressive Baptist, 1977); M. Warren, *Black Preaching: Truth and Soul* (Washington, D.C.: University Press of America, 1977), which contains extensive bibliography; H. B. Hicks, Jr., *Images of the Black Preacher* (Valley Forge, Pa.: Judson, 1977); L. L. Beale, *Toward a Black Homiletic* (New York: Vantage, 1978); A. Boesak, *The Finger of God* (Maryknoll, N.Y.: Orbis, 1982) which, though a collection of sermons, addresses Black preaching; Kelly M. Smith, a great colleague, *Social Crisis Preaching* (Macon, Ga.: Mercer Univ., 1984); and J. Alfred Smith, *Preach On!* (Nashville: Broadman, 1984).

ON LANGUAGE

Of late, we seem to have been preoccupied with language. Therefore, studies have multiplied in many fields. As a result, bibliography is all but impossible to compile. Peter Farb's *Word Play* (New York: Knopf, 1974) offers a readable, if somewhat diffuse, overview of the different areas of research. M. Leroy, *The Main Trends in Modern Linguistics* (Oxford: Blackwell, 1967) traces history, and W. G. Hardy, *Language, Thought, and Experience* (Baltimore: University Park, 1978) will help to identify "schools," as also will G. Sampson, *Schools of Linguistics* (Stanford, Calif.: Stanford Univ., 1980), who traces studies from Saussure to Jakobson. See also the lucid treatment in Max Black's *The Labyrinth of Language* (New York: Mentor, 1968). In 1916, three years after his death, Ferdinand de Saussure's *Course in General Linguistics* (New York: McGraw-Hill, 1966) was published—a "landmark" work in twentieth-century linguistic study. Since then, there are many names that stand out: Leonard Bloomfield, C. K. Ogden and I. A. Richards, Otto Jespersen, Edward Sapir, Benjamin Whorf, Stephen Ullman, Louis Hjelmslev, Vygotsky, Chomsky, and others. For some of the source material, see D. Hayden, E. Alworth, G. Tate, eds., *Classics in Linguistics* (New York: Philosophical Library, 1967). For sociolinguistics, see the influential work by E. Sapir, *Culture, Language, and Personality* (Berkeley and Los Angeles: Univ. of California, 1964) and P. P. Giglioli, ed., *Language and Social Context* (Baltimore: Penguin, 1972). For psycholinguistics, see a basic orientation in D. Slobin, *Psycholinguistics* (Glenview, Ill.: Scott, Foresman, 1971); a textbook by J. DeVito, *The Psychology of Speech and Language* (New York: Random, 1970); and essays in P. Adams, *Language in Thinking* (Baltimore: Penguin, 1972). G. L. Bruns, *Modern Poetry and the Idea of Language* (New Haven: Yale Univ., 1974) is a fascinating study of the history of changing conceptions of language in relation to poetic diction. See also G. Steiner's astonishing *After Babel* (New York: Oxford Univ., 1975), a work on translation that is broad in significance. A most important work for homiletics is O. Barfield, *Speaker's Meaning* (Middletown, Conn.: Wesleyan Univ., 1967).

Structuralism/Semiotics

It is difficult to decide where to list "structuralist" and "semiotic" studies, under "Communication Studies" or under "On Language." We will introduce the fields of study here by listing basic books and noting bibliographies.

On Structuralism. J. Culler, *Structuralist Poetics* (Ithaca, N.Y.: Cornell Univ., 1975); an anthology edited by R. and F. DeGeorge, *The Structuralists from Marx to Levi-Strauss* (Garden City, N.Y.: Doubleday, 1972); F. Jameson, *The Prison-House of Language* (Princeton: Princeton Univ., 1972), a somewhat critical presentation of "formalist" and "structuralist" positions; M. Lane, ed., *Introduction to Structuralism* (New York: Harper, 1972) with extensive bibliography; J. Piaget, *Structuralism* (New York: Basic, 1970); and R. Scholes, *Structuralism in Literature* (New Haven: Yale Univ., 1974), an excellent treatment with a helpful annotated bibliography of primary and secondary sources.

On Semiotics. T. Hawkes, *Structuralism and Semiotics* (Berkeley and Los Angeles: Univ. of California, 1977) is a very fine introduction to semiotics; J. Sturrock, ed., *Structuralism and Since* (New York: Oxford Univ., 1979) contains essays introducing major figures—Levi-Strauss, Barthes, Foucault, Lacan, and Derrida; U. Eco, *A Theory of Semiotics* (Bloomington: Indiana Univ., 1976); and R. Scholes, *Semiotics and Interpretation* (New Haven: Yale Univ., 1982).

Though Michel Foucault denies that he is a structuralist, he has written on language. Perhaps a reader might begin with his "Discourse on Language" which is appended to *The Archeology of Knowledge* (New York: Pantheon, 1972), then turn to *Language, Counter-Memory, Practice* (Ithaca, N.Y.: Cornell Univ., 1977), and then to *The Foucault Reader,* ed. P. Rabinow (New York: Pantheon, 1985).

Language in Philosophy

Prior to the emergence of phenomenological or structuralist approaches, major work in philosophy of language was from an "analytic" position. For an introduction, see W. P. Alston, *Philosophy of Language* (Englewood Cliffs, N.J.: Prentice-Hall, 1964), which offers a useful overview. From a theological stance, E. Cell, *Language, Existence, and God* (Nashville: Abingdon, 1971) gives a comprehensive survey of different positions; from the "common sense" position of G. E. Moore, the "logical positivism" of Russell and Ayer, the "language games" of Ludwig Wittgenstein, to John Wisdom and the "Oxford school" of John Austin, Antony Flew, et al. Cell's book provides an extensive guide to bibliography in several areas. For a phenomenological approach, see under "Phenomenology of Language," above.

Theology and Language

Not surprisingly, theology was challenged by "logical positivism." Some of the more important volumes in the discussion are Ian T. Ramsey, *Religious Language* (New York: Macmillan, 1957); W. Zuurdeeg, *An Analytical Philosophy of Religion* (Nashville: Abingdon, 1958); a remarkable work by J. Moreau, *Language and Religious Language* (Philadelphia: Westminster, 1961); a solid study by F. Ferre, *Language, Logic, and God* (New York: Harper, 1961); P. van Buren, *The Secular Meaning of the Gospel* (New York: Macmillan, 1963), but see also his more recent *The Edges of Language* (New York: Macmillan, 1972); a tough analytic work, W. A. Christian, *Meaning and Truth in Religion* (Princeton: Princeton Univ., 1964); a fine book by W. Hordern, *Speaking of God* (New York: Macmillan, 1964); D. High, *Language, Persons, and Belief* (New York: Oxford Univ., 1967), which develops from Wittgenstein; J. Macquarrie, *God-Talk* (New York: Harper, 1967); the important work by L. Gilkey, *Naming the Whirlwind: The Renewal of God-Language* (Indianapolis: Bobbs-Merrill, 1969); G. Ebeling, *Introduction to a Theology of Language* (Philadelphia: Fortress, 1971); L. T. Lundeen, *Risk and Rhetoric in Religion* (Philadelphia: Fortress, 1972), a Whiteheadian approach; A. Nygren, *Meaning and Method* (Philadelphia: Fortress, 1972); P. Holmer, *The Grammar of Faith* (New York: Harper, 1978); and see also the important discussion in part 2 of D. Tracy, *Blessed Rage for Order* (New York: Seabury, 1975)—think of it, a theological work with a title from Wallace Stevens! A recent important monograph is C. Raschke, *The Alchemy of the Word: Language and the End of Theology* (Missoula, Mont.: Scholars, 1979).

See also under "Recent Rhetorical Studies," and "Metaphorical Language," above, and "Style," below, as well as under "The Hermeneutical Problem" and "Narrative Form" in part 2: Structures.

STYLE

In this section we will include works on style, usage, and current American language. Though there are several bibliographies on style, see L. T. Milic, *Style and Stylistics: An Analytical Bibliography* (New York: Free Press, 1967). Some recent works include F. L. Lucas, *Style* (New York: Collier, 1962); G. Hough, *Style and Stylistics* (London: Routledge, 1969) and J. Kinneavy, *A Theory of Discourse* (Englewood Cliffs, N.Y.: Prentice-Hall, 1971). Richard A. Lanham, *Style: An Anti-Textbook* (New Haven: Yale Univ., 1974), opposes what he labels "the gospel of normative clarity" in a witty book with a useful bibliographic survey. L. T. Milic, *Stylists on Style* (New York: Scribner's, 1969) is a well-chosen anthology from the sixteenth century to the present day. W. Strunk, Jr., *The Elements of Style* (New York: Macmillan, 1959) is considered by many to be a classic. Written in the forties, R. Graves and A. Hodge, *The Reader Over Your Shoulder* (New York: Random, 1971) also can be helpful. While there are a number of guides to nonsexist language, C. Miller and K. Swift, *The Handbook of Non-Sexist Writing* (New York: Barnes, 1980) is a good guide that applies nicely to oral language.

The standard work on usage is W. Follett, *Modern American Usage,* ed. J. Barzun (New York: Hill & Wang, 1966). A "dictionary" of usage, T. M. Bernstein, *The Careful Writer* (New York: Atheneum, 1965) can be painfully "cute" at times, but may reflect trends nearer to oral usage. On slang usage, in addition to E. Partridge, *A Dictionary of Slang and Unconventional English* (New York: Macmillan, 1961), there is H. Wentworth and S. Flexner, *Dictionary of American Slang* (New York: Crowell, 1975). H. Kucera and W. N. Francis, *Computational Analysis of Present-Day American English* (Providence: Brown Univ., 1967) is a listing of in-use language according to frequency. See also E. Partridge, *A Dictionary of Cliches* (New York: Dutton, 1963) and, more recently, a wonderful book, H. Rawson, *A Dictionary of Euphemisms and Other Doubletalk* (New York: Crown, 1981). A. Herzog, *The B.S. Factor* (Baltimore: Penguin, 1974) catalogues all kinds of "cant." An old grouch, Edwin Newman, has written *Strictly Speaking: Will America be the Death of English?* (Indianapolis: Bobbs-Merrill, 1974), and other books trying valiantly to hold against a rising tide of jargon.

There have been studies of our language, among them Owen Barfield's classic *History in English Words* (Grand Rapids: Eerdmans, 1967); J. Shipley, *In Praise of English* (New York: Times Books, 1977); M. Dohan, *Our Own Words* (New York: Knopf, 1974); as well as two formidable studies by J. L. Dillard, *All-American English* (New York: Random House, 1975), and a controversial earlier work, *Black English* (New York: Random House, 1972). See also essays in L. Michaels and C. Ricks, *The State of the Language* (Berkeley and Los Angeles: Univ. of California, 1980).

Part 2.
Structures

HOMILETIC BIBLIOGRAPHIES

Recent Homiletic Thought: A Bibliography, 1935–1965, ed. W. Toohey and W. D. Thompson (Nashville: Abingdon, 1967).

Recent Homiletic Thought: An Annotated Bibliography. Vol. 2, 1966–1979, ed. A. D. Litfin and H. W. Robinson (Grand Rapids: Baker, 1983).

The journal *Homiletic* (61 W. Confederate Ave., Gettysburg, PA 17325) is published quarterly and contains critical bibliography of more recent works.

THE PROBLEM OF AUTHORITY

There are older works on authority, such as books by P. T. Forsyth and C. H. Dodd, worthy of attention. More recently, James Barr has written extensively on the problem of biblical authority; see *Fundamentalism* (Philadelphia: Westminster, 1978), *The Bible in the Modern World* (New York: Harper, 1978), *The Scope of Authority* (Philadelphia: Westminster, 1980), and *Holy Scripture* (Philadelphia: Westminster, 1983), all of which contain extensive bibliography. For a study of Reformation positions, see Robert C. Johnson, *Authority in Protestant Theology* (Philadelphia: Westminster, 1959). From a somewhat conservative position, see J. G. Rogers and D. K. McKim, *The Authority and Interpretation of the Bible* (New York: Harper, 1979) for a historical survey. See also D. H. Kelsey, *The Uses of Scripture in Recent Theology* (Philadelphia: Fortress, 1975). On the issue of inspiration, see P. J. Achtemeier, *The Inspiration of Scripture* (Philadelphia: Westminster, 1980). On the problem of unity/diversity, see James D. G. Dunn, *Unity and Diversity in the New Testament* (Philadelphia: Westminster, 1977). On the question of the canon, the famous study is by Hans von Campenhausen, *The Formation of the Christian Bible* (Philadelphia: Fortress, 1972). Recently, Edward Farley has ventured an "archeology" of the notion of authority in *Ecclesial Reflection* (Philadelphia: Fortress, 1982). Readers are advised not only to trace the argument offered in part 1, but to study with care constructive material in chapter 12.

Catholic literature on scripture and tradition multiplied in connection with Vatican

II. A sourcebook for Catholic documents on scripture is *Rome and the Study of Scripture* (St. Meinrad: Abbey, 1964). See also K. Rahner, *Inspiration in the Bible* (New York: Herder, 1961); B. Vawter, *Biblical Inspiration* (London: Hutchinson, 1972); and, more recently, John Coventry, *Christian Truth* (New York: Paulist, 1975). George H. Tavard's *Holy Writ or Holy Church* (London: Burns & Oates, 1959) is an important study. On tradition see the following: Y. Congar, *The Meaning of Tradition* (New York: Hawthorne, 1963) and *Tradition and Traditions* (London: Burns & Oates, 1966); James Mackey, *Modern Theology of Tradition* (New York: Herder, 1962); J. R. Geiselmann, *The Meaning of Tradition* (New York: Herder, 1966); and K. Rahner and J. Ratzinger, *Revelation and Tradition* (New York: Herder, 1966). See also H. Kung, *Infallible?* (Garden City, N.Y.: Doubleday, 1972). A recent important Protestant work: S. Sykes, *The Identity of Christianity* (Philadelphia: Fortress, 1984).

THE HERMENEUTICAL PROBLEM

The literature on hermeneutics is huge and highly complicated. To get into issues, readers may wish to begin with a brief history of interpretation, such as R. M. Grant and D. Tracy, *A Short History of the Interpretation of the Bible*, 2d ed. (Philadelphia: Fortress, 1984), or J. D. Wood, *The Interpretation of the Bible* (London: Duckworth, 1958). C. E. Braatan, *New Directions in Theology Today: History and Hermeneutics* (Philadelphia: Westminster, 1966) provides a first glance at some of the problems. Two nontheological works will be helpful: R. E. Palmer, *Hermeneutics* (Evanston, Ill.: Northwestern Univ., 1969) and a sharp rebuttal by E. D. Hirsch, *Validity in Interpretation* (New Haven: Yale Univ., 1967). The two gentlemen are contending over the most awesome work on hermeneutics in the century, Hans-Georg Gadamer's *Truth and Method* (New York: Seabury, 1975), and also *Philosophical Hermeneutics* (Berkeley and Los Angeles: Univ. of California, 1977). To get at the thought of R. Bultmann, readers may wish to begin with *Jesus Christ and Mythology* (New York: Scribner's, 1958), and then possibly turn to *Existence and Faith* (New York: Meridian, 1960). Bultmann's proposals were much debated, but S. Ogden, *Christ Without Myth* (New York: Harper, 1961) is a perceptive secondary source. The so-called new hermeneutic arose in the sixties, featuring the thought of Ernst Fuchs and G. Ebeling: See J. M. Robinson and John B. Cobb, Jr., *The New Hermeneutic* (New York: Harper, 1964), and especially P. J. Achtemeier, *An Introduction to the New Hermeneutic* (Philadelphia: Westminster, 1969). G. Ebeling's work is important: see *Word and Faith* (Philadelphia: Fortress, 1963) and *God and Word* (Philadelphia: Fortress, 1967). See also R. W. Funk, *Language, Hermeneutic and Word of God* (New York: Harper, 1966). W. Pannenberg's position can be read in *History and Hermeneutic, Journal for Theology and the Church*, vol. 4, ed. R. W. Funk (New York: Harper, 1967), and in *Basic Questions in Theology*, trans. G. H. Kehm (Philadelphia: Fortress, 1970). A proposal for "theological interpretation" of scripture is found in Peter Stuhlmacher, *Historical Criticism and Theological Interpretation of Scripture* (Philadelphia: Fortress, 1977). For an important Catholic position, see E. Schillebeeckx, *The Understanding of Faith* (New York: Sheed & Ward, 1974), as well as a lucid first essay in *God the Future of Man* (New York: Sheed & Ward, 1968). In recent years, the major figure in hermeneutical theology is Paul Ricoeur, who has written so extensively that we cannot list all of his works. A good entree into Ricoeur's thought is *Essays on Biblical Interpretation*, ed. L. Mudge (Philadelphia: Fortress, 1980). Particularly important for hermeneutics are *Conflict of*

Interpretations (Evanston, Ill.: Northwestern Univ., 1974); *Semeia 4: Paul Ricoeur on Biblical Hermeneutics,* ed. J. D. Crossan (Missoula, Mont.: Scholars, 1975); *Interpretation Theory* (Fort Worth: Texas Christian Univ., 1976); and, more recently, *Hermeneutics and the Social Sciences* (New York: Cambridge Univ., 1981). A helpful secondary source for Ricoeur is D. Ihde, *Hermeneutic Phenomenology* (Evanston, Ill.: Northwestern Univ., 1971). Two other thinkers must be mentioned: J. Habermas, *Knowledge and Human Interests* (Boston: Beacon, 1972), and M. Foucault, *The Archeology of Knowledge and The Discourse on Language* (New York: Pantheon, 1972). A recent work somewhat influenced by so-called canonical criticism is C. M. Wood, *The Formation of Christian Understanding* (Philadelphia: Westminster, 1981). There have been some surveys of the hermeneutical problem: A. C. Thiselton, *The Two Horizons* (Grand Rapids: Eerdmans, 1980) is a cautious, somewhat positivistic work; J. Bleicher, *Contemporary Hermeneutics* (London: Routledge, 1980) is a survey with extended treatment of Ricoeur and Habermas; J. Thompson, *Critical Hermeneutics* (New York: Cambridge Univ., 1981) discusses Ricoeur and Habermas in detail; R. J. Howard, *Three Faces of Hermeneutics* (Berkeley and Los Angeles: Univ. of California, 1982) is lucid and helpful. Meanwhile, general literary criticism has moved the hermeneutical discussion further, particularly with the work of Jacques Derrida. To get at different positions—structuralism, phenomenological criticism, deconstruction—see essays in *Structuralism and Since,* ed. J. Sturrock (New York: Oxford Univ., 1979); J. Culler, *The Pursuit of Signs* (Ithaca, N.Y.: Cornell Univ., 1981); and T. Eagleton, *Literary Theory* (Minneapolis: Univ. of Minnesota, 1983). Books by Sturrock and Eagleton will provide extensive bibliography. The discussion continues.

NARRATIVE FORM

We limit bibliography to works on the nature of narrative. A useful beginning is E. M. Forster, *Aspects of the Novel* (New York: Harcourt, 1927), followed by E. Auerbach's classic work *Mimesis* (Princeton: Princeton Univ., 1953), and Wayne Booth, *The Rhetoric of Fiction* (Chicago: Univ. of Chicago, 1961). N. Frye, *The Anatomy of Criticism* (Princeton: Princeton Univ., 1957) is concerned with genres, symbols, and archetypes. V. Propp, *The Morphology of the Folktale,* 2d ed. (Austin: Univ. of Texas, 1970) is an influential formalist work. More recent works include R. Scholes and R. Kellogg, *The Nature of Narrative* (London: Oxford Univ., 1966); R. Dietrich and R. Sundell, *The Art of Fiction* (New York: Holt, 1967); W. Berthoff et al., *The Interpretation of Narrative* (Cambridge: Harvard Univ., 1970); H. Toliver, *Animate Illusions* (Lincoln: Univ. of Nebraska, 1974); S. Chatman, *Story and Discourse* (Ithaca, N.Y.: Cornell Univ., 1978); G. Genette, *Narrative Discourse* (Ithaca, N.Y.: Cornell Univ., 1980); and S. Rimmon-Kenan, *Narrative Fiction: Contemporary Poetics* (New York: Methuen, 1983). On the problem of time in fiction, see S. Spencer, *Space, Time, and Structure in the Modern Novel* (New York: New York Univ., 1971) and P. D. Tobin, *Time and the Novel* (Princeton: Princeton Univ., 1978). For a general work on narrativity, see W. J. T. Mitchell, ed., *On Narrative* (Chicago: Univ. of Chicago, 1981). W. A. Kort, *Narrative Elements and Religious Meaning* (Philadelphia: Fortress, 1975) studies how religious meaning is formed in fictive systems. Two works by W. Iser study the designing of fictive forms in view of an "implied reader"; they are *The Implied Reader* (Baltimore: Johns Hopkins, 1975) and *The Act of Reading* (Baltimore: Johns Hopkins Univ., 1978), a book which is important for interpretation and for homiletical design; see also J. Tompkins, ed., *Reader-Response Criticism* (Baltimore: Johns Hopkins Univ., 1980). Most recently, see Paul Ricoeur, *Time and Narrative,* vol. 1 (Chicago: Univ. of Chicago, 1984). Please refer also to "Phenomenology of Language" in part 1: Moves.

There have been some recent studies in narrative preaching, among them: F. Buechner, *Telling the Truth: The Gospel as Tragedy, Comedy, and Fairy Tale* (New York: Harper, 1977); E. Steimle, M. Niedenthal, and C. Rice, *Preaching the Story* (Philadelphia: Fortress, 1980); R. A. Jensen, *Telling the Story* (Minneapolis: Augsburg, 1980); E. L. Lowry, *The Homiletical Plot: The Sermon as Narrative Art Form* (Atlanta: John Knox, 1981), and *Doing Time in the Pulpit: The Relationship Between Narrative and Preaching* (Nashville: Abingdon, 1985); and G. M. Bass, *The Song and the Story* (Lima, Ohio: C.S.S., 1984).

PREACHING FORMS OF THE
HEBREW SCRIPTURES

On the issue of the Hebrew scriptures in Christian communities, see the following: E. G. Kraeling, *The Old Testament Since the Reformation* (New York: Harper, 1955); S. Mowinckel, *The Old Testament as the Word of God* (Nashville: Abingdon, 1955); C. Westermann, ed., *Essays on Old Testament Hermeneutics* (Richmond: John Knox, 1966); J. Bright, *The Authority of the Old Testament* (Nashville: Abingdon, 1967); J. A. Sanders, *Torah and Canon* (Philadelphia: Fortress, 1972); and P. D. Hanson, *The Diversity of Scripture* (Philadelphia: Fortress, 1982). See also "The Problem of Authority," above.

On the preaching of the Hebrew scriptures, see the following: W. Cosser, *Preaching the Old Testament* (London: Epworth, 1967); H. J. Kraus, *The Threat and the Power* (Atlanta: John Knox, 1971); E. Achtemeier, *The Old Testament and the Proclamation of the Gospel* (Philadelphia: Westminster, 1973); W. C. Kaiser, Jr., *The Old Testament in Contemporary Preaching* (Grand Rapids: Baker, 1973); F. R. McCurley, Jr., *Proclaiming the Promise: Christian Preaching from the Old Testament* (Philadelphia: Fortress, 1974); Gerhard von Rad, *Biblical Interpretations in Preaching* (Nashville: Abingdon, 1977); H. G. Stuempfle, Jr., *Preaching Law and Gospel* (Philadelphia: Fortress, 1978); and a fine work by D. E. Gowan, *Reclaiming the Old Testament for the Christian Pulpit* (Atlanta: John Knox, 1980).

In preaching the Hebrew scriptures, we work with many different forms—myths, sagas, stories, types of prophetic speech, poetry, and varieties of wisdom literature. Readers may wish to study methodology in G. M. Tucker, *Form Criticism of the Old Testament* (Philadelphia: Fortress, 1971) and, on source analysis, N. Habel, *Literary Criticism of the Old Testament* (Philadelphia: Fortress, 1971). An influential Catholic work is L. A. Schokel, *The Inspired Word* (New York: Herder, 1965). For more recent literary-critical approaches, see D. Robertson, *The Old Testament and the Literary Critic* (Philadelphia: Fortress, 1977), and M. J. Buss, ed., *Encounter with the Text* (Philadelphia: Fortress, 1979). Two basic studies of Hebrew scriptural forms are K. Koch, *The Growth of the Biblical Tradition* (New York: Scribner's, 1969) and J. H. Hayes, ed., *Old Testament Form Criticism* (San Antonio: Trinity Univ., 1974); both contain extensive bibliography on particular literary types. For a report on recent research, see D. A. Knight and G. M. Tucker, eds., *The Hebrew Bible and its Modern Interpreters* (Philadelphia: Fortress, 1985).

Narratives

General Studies. See "Narrative Form," above, for works by Auerbach and Propp which have been influential. Also see A. B. Lord, *The Singer of Tales* (Cambridge: Harvard Univ., 1960). Preachers will gain great benefit from reading Robert Alter, *The Art of Biblical Narrative* (New York: Basic, 1981). Other general studies include R. C. Culley, *Semeia 3: Classical Hebrew Narrative* (Missoula, Mont.: Scholars, 1975), and *Studies in the Structure of Hebrew Narrative* (Philadelphia: Fortress, 1976); and B. O. Long, ed., *Images of Man and God: Old Testament Short Stories in Literary Focus* (Sheffield: JSOT, 1981). Also see E. M. Good, *Irony in the Old Testament* (Philadelphia: Fortress, 1965), and Z. Adar, *The Biblical Narrative* (Jerusalem: Dept. of Education and Culture of the World Zionist Org., 1959).

Studies of Particular Narratives. H. Gunkel, *The Legends of Genesis* (New York: Schocken, 1964) is a reprint of a now-famous "introduction" written by Gunkel early in the century; E. Leach, *Genesis as Myth and Other Essays* (London: Jonathan Cape, 1969); J. Fokkelman, *Narrative Art in Genesis* (Amsterdam, 1975); G. W. Coats, *Genesis* (Grand Rapids: Eerdmans, 1983), and *Rebellion in the Wilderness* (Nashville: Abingdon, 1968); J. Jackson and M. Kessler, eds., *Rhetorical Criticism: Essays in Honor of James Muilenburg* (Pittsburgh: Pickwick, 1974); C. Westermann, *The Promises to the Fathers* (Philadelphia: Fortress, 1976); D. Redford, *A Study of the Biblical Story of Joseph* (Leiden: Brill, 1970); D. Daube, *The Exodus Pattern in the Bible* (London: Faber, 1963); D. McCarthy, *Old Testament Covenant* (Richmond: John Knox, 1972); R. N. Whybray, *The Succession Narrative* (London: SCM, 1968).

Legal Forms

For preachers, a most helpful book is Walter Harrelson's *The Ten Commandments and Human Rights* (Philadelphia: Fortress, 1980). See also E. Nielsen, *The Ten Commandments in New Perspective* (London: SCM, 1968). For a survey of research, see J. J. Stamm and M. E. Andrew, *The Ten Commandments in Recent Research* (London: SCM, 1968). Some important works include: A. Alt, *Essays on Old Testament History and Religion* (Garden City, N.Y.: Doubleday, 1967); G. Mendenhall, *Law and Covenant in Israel and the Ancient Near East* (Pittsburgh: Biblical Colloquium, 1955); D. McCarthy, *Treaty and Covenant* (Rome: Pontifical Biblical Inst., 1963); D. R. Hillers, *Covenant: The History of a Biblical Idea* (Baltimore: Johns Hopkins, 1969); M. Noth, *The Laws of the Pentateuch and Other Studies* (Philadelphia: Fortress, 1967); K. Baltzer, *The Covenant Formulary* (Philadelphia: Fortress, 1971); A. Phillips, *Ancient Israel's Criminal Law* (Oxford: Blackwell, 1970). J. White, *The Legal Imagination* (Boston: Little, Brown, 1973) may provide helpful insight into the nature of legal language.

Prophetic Forms

In addition to standard works on the prophets—for example, Heschel, Linblom, Mowinckel—commentaries, and monographs, there have been volumes and articles on the forms of prophetic speech. H. Gunkel's early work appears in *Twentieth Century Theology in the Making, Vol. I: Themes of Biblical Theology*, ed. J. Pelikan (New York: Harper, 1969). Perhaps the best-known work is C. Westermann, *Basic Forms of Pro-*

phetic Speech (Philadelphia: Westminster, 1967). For other bibliography, see J. H. Hayes, ed., *Old Testament Form Criticism* (San Antonio: Trinity Univ., 1974), which contains a survey article by W. Eugene March. A general orientation by Walter Brueggemann, *The Prophetic Imagination* (Philadelphia: Fortress, 1978), will be especially helpful to preachers.

Poetic Forms

Though I confess an odd notion that psalms are for singing and not, primarily, for preaching, nevertheless, the poetry of Israel is preached. Helpful summaries of form-critical work on the psalms may be found in articles on "Hebrew Poetry" by M. Dahood, and on the "Book of Psalms" by C. Westermann, in *The Interpreter's Dictionary of the Bible: Supplementary Volume* (Nashville: Abingdon, 1976). The early form-critical study is H. Gunkel, *The Psalms: A Form-Critical Introduction* (Philadelphia: Fortress, 1967), a reprint of a work done in 1930. S. Mowinckel, a student of Gunkel, produced another major work, *The Psalms in Israel's Worship*, 2 vols. (Nashville: Abingdon, 1962). See also C. Westermann, *The Praise of God in the Psalms* (Richmond: John Knox, 1965), plus detailed commentaries by M. Dahood, L. Sabourin, and A. Weiser. Preachers may find S. Terrien, *The Psalms and Their Meaning for Today* (New York: Bobbs-Merrill, 1952) still remarkably helpful.

Wisdom Forms

Preachers will do well to study a comprehensive introduction to the wisdom tradition: James L. Crenshaw, *Old Testament Wisdom* (Atlanta: John Knox, 1981). See also G. von Rad, *Wisdom in Israel* (Nashville: Abingdon, 1972). Because most wisdom literature considers the problem of theodicy, see James L. Crenshaw, ed., *Theodicy in the Old Testament* (Philadelphia: Fortress, 1983). Preachers will want to peruse commentaries on major wisdom materials—Job, Ecclesiastes, Proverbs, and Sirach. On proverbs as a form, see W. McKane, *Proverbs: A New Approach* (Philadelphia: Westminster, 1970). On proverbial literature as a genre see A. Taylor, *The Proverb and Index to "The Proverb"* (Hatboro, Pa.: Folklore Assoc., 1962). For other form-critical studies, see the essay by J. L. Crenshaw in Hayes, *Old Testament Form Criticism* (see under "Preaching Forms of the Hebrew Scriptures," above.)

PREACHING FORMS OF THE CHRISTIAN SCRIPTURES

A number of New Testament critics have written on preaching the scriptures. Some of the better-known works since 1950 are M. S. Enslin, *Preaching from the New Testament: An Open Letter to Preachers* (Privately printed, 1952); D. G. Miller, *Fire in Thy Mouth* (Nashville: Abingdon, 1954), and *The Way of Biblical Preaching* (Nashville: Abingdon, 1957); John Knox, *The Integrity of Preaching* (Nashville: Abingdon, 1957) and see also his earlier *Criticism and Faith* (Nashville: Abingdon, 1952); C. W. F. Smith, *Biblical Authority for Modern Preaching* (Philadelphia: Westminster, 1960); C. K. Barrett, *Biblical Problems and Biblical Preaching* (Philadelphia: Fortress, 1964); L. E. Keck, *The Bible in the Pulpit: The Renewal of Biblical Preaching* (Nashville: Abingdon, 1978); W. Best, *From Text to Sermon: Responsible Use of the New Testament in Preaching* (Atlanta: John Knox, 1978); a Catholic study, J. M. Reese, *Preaching God's Burning Word* (Collegeville, Minn.: The Liturgical Press, 1975); D. Moody Smith,

Interpreting the Gospels for Preaching (Philadelphia: Fortress, 1980); R. H. Fuller, *The Use of the Bible in Preaching* (Philadelphia: Fortress, 1981); S. B. Morrow, *Speaking the Word Fearlessly: Boldness in the New Testament* (New York: Paulist, 1983); and D. Patte, *Preaching Paul* (Philadelphia: Fortress, 1984).

In preaching the Christian scriptures, preachers will be working from many different kinds of language—miracle stories, parables, controversies, resurrection stories, passion narratives, legends in Acts, and all sorts of rhetoric in the Johannine material and the epistles. Rather obviously, different forms will require different homiletic strategies. A book by Amos N. Wilder, *The Language of the Gospel: Early Christian Rhetoric* (New York: Harper, 1964) has been enormously influential and might be a fine orientation. On methodologies, Fortress Press (Philadelphia) has issued a series, Guides to Biblical Scholarship, among them: N. Perrin, *What Is Redaction Criticism?* (1969); E. V. McKnight, *What Is Form Criticism?* (1969) (see also his *Meaning in Texts* [Fortress, 1978]); W. A. Beardslee, *Literary Criticism of the New Testament* (1970); D. Patte, *What Is Structural Exegesis?* (1976) (also D. Patte and A. Patte, *Structural Exegesis from Theory to Practice* [Fortress, 1978] which is a helpful guide for ministers); N. Petersen, *Literary Criticism for New Testament Critics* (1978). See also a suggestive book by George A. Kennedy, *New Testament Interpretation Through Rhetoric Criticism* (Chapel Hill: Univ. of North Carolina, 1984). F. Kermode, *The Genesis of Secrecy* (Cambridge: Harvard Univ., 1979) is also of interest. Two recent studies may be mentioned: E. V. McNight, *The Bible and the Reader* (Philadelphia: Fortress, 1985) which surveys different literary-critical approaches, and a very helpful book for preachers, Bernard Brandon Scott, *The Word of God in Words* (Philadelphia: Fortress, 1985).

For material on the evolution of New Testament form-criticism, see W. G. Kummel, *The New Testament: The History of the Investigation of Its Problems* (Nashville: Abingdon, 1972), and essays by R. Bultmann and K. Kundsin, *Form Criticism* (New York: Willett, Clark, 1934). The early works were by Martin Debelius, *From Tradition to Gospel* (New York: Scribners, 1934) and *A Fresh Approach to the New Testament and Early Christian Literature* (New York: Scribner's, 1936); and Rudolf Bultmann, *The History of the Synoptic Tradition*, rev. ed. (New York: Harper, 1968), a work which first appeared in 1931.

We will attempt to provide some basic bibliography for kinds of New Testament rhetoric, listing various Synoptic forms before turning to Johannine and Pauline rhetoric.

Parables

For general bibliography see W. S. Kissinger, *The Parables of Jesus: A History of Interpretation and Bibliography,* ATLA Bibliography Series 4 (Metuchen, N.J.: Scarecrow, 1979), and J. D. Crossan, "A Basic Bibliography for Parables Research," *Semeia* 1 (Missoula, Mont.: Scholars Press, 1974). A useful survey of scholarship since J. Jeremias is provided by N. Perrin, *Jesus and the Language of the Kingdom* (Philadelphia: Fortress, 1976). Parable research since C. H. Dodds and Jeremias seems to have moved in two phases, early work prompted in part by the new hermeneutic and more recent literary-critical studies. In the first phase we might mention the work of A. Wilder, E. Linneman, *Jesus of the Parables* (New York: Harper, 1966), and R. Funk, *Language, Hermeneutic, and Word of God* (New York: Harper, 1966). Dan O. Via, Jr., *The Parables: Their Literary and Existential Dimension* (Philadelphia: Fortress, 1967),

479

though moving toward literary-critical categories, seems influenced by the existential-ism of the new hermeneutic. More recent work on parables includes (alphabetically arranged): J. Breech, *The Silence of Jesus* (Philadelphia: Fortress, 1983); J. D. Crossan, *In Parables* (New York: Harper, 1973), *The Dark Interval* (Niles, Ill.: Argus, 1975), *Finding is the First Act* (Philadelphia: Fortress, 1979), and *Cliffs of Fall* (New York: Seabury, 1980); R. W. Funk, *Jesus as Precursor* (Philadelphia: Fortress, 1975), and *Parables and Presence* (Philadelphia: Fortress, 1982); Bernard Brandon Scott, *Jesus, Symbol-Maker for the Kingdom* (Philadelphia: Fortress, 1981), and also his forthcoming commentary on all the parables to be published by Fortress Press; M. A. Tolbert, *Perspectives on the Parables* (Philadelphia: Fortress, 1979); and A. Wilder, *Jesus' Parables and the War of Myths* (Philadelphia: Fortress, 1982). D. Granskou, *Preaching on the Parables* (Philadelphia: Fortress, 1972) draws heavily on the work of Via. See also my article, "On Preaching a Parable: The Problem of Homiletic Method," in *Reformed Liturgy and Music*, 17, no. 1 (Winter 1983): 16–22.

Miracles

The miracle stories have posed a problem for preachers through the centuries. Miracles may originally have been witness to Jesus the miracle worker, but many of them were reshaped in Jewish-Christian controversy. In gentile communities, they were rewritten to bring out theological meaning rather than primal wonder. Thus, a literary analysis of miracles will also include an analysis of evolving tradition. E. and M. L. Keller, *Miracles in Dispute: A Continuing Debate* (Philadelphia: Fortress, 1969) provides a history of miracle interpretation. C. F. D. Moule, ed., *Miracles* (London: Mowbray, 1965), offers a number of essays. R. H. Fuller, *Interpreting the Miracles* (Philadelphia: Westminster, 1963) is a study primarily written for preachers. R. W. Funk, *Semeia 11: Early Christian Miracle Stories* (Missoula, Mont.: Scholars, 1978) contains a series of important essays. The most recent scholarly study of the miracles is Gerd Theissen, *The Miracle Stories of the Early Christian Tradition* (Philadelphia: Fortress, 1983). A work on preaching miracles is R. J. Allen, *Our Eyes Can Be Opened: Preaching the Miracle Stories of the Synoptic Gospels Today* (Washington, D.C.: University Press of America, 1983).

Controversies

The Synoptics contain a number of controversies which form by question-coun-terquestion usually followed by a saying of Jesus, for example, Controversy over Divorce, Taxes to Caesar. Though such stories were isolated by early form critics, notably Albertez, Dibelius, Bultmann, and Taylor, the only recent major work is A. J. Hultgren, *Jesus and His Adversaries* (Minneapolis: Augsburg, 1979). There is no full-scale study of the problems such stories pose for preaching, although see P. S. Gittings III, "Speak to the Dry Bones" (D. Min. diss., Pittsburgh Theological Seminary, 1978) which touches on the difficulties.

The Teachings of Jesus

There are general works on the Sermon on the Mount to help preachers, such as J. Jeremias, *The Sermon on the Mount* (Philadelphia: Fortress, 1963), and E. Thurney-sen, *The Sermon on the Mount* (Richmond: John Knox, 1964), and also technical studies, such as W. D. Davies, *The Setting of the Sermon on the Mount* (New York:

Cambridge Univ., 1966). For bibliography, see W. S. Kissinger, *The Sermon on the Mount, A History of Interpretation and Bibliography* (Metuchen, N.J.: Scarecrow, 1975). Also of help may be J. D. Derrett, *Law in the New Testament* (London: Darton, Longman, Todd, 1970). However, studies which examine form are: T. W. Manson, *The Teaching of Jesus* (New York: Cambridge Univ., 1967), a work first published in 1931; N. Perrin, *Rediscovering the Teaching of Jesus* (New York: Harper, 1967), a most important work; V. Furnish, *The Love Command in the New Testament* (Nashville: Abingdon, 1972); P. Minear, *Commands of Christ* (Nashville: Abingdon, 1972), which treats some of the "floating logia"; R. C. Tannehill, *The Sword of His Mouth* (Philadelphia: Fortress, 1975), a helpful rhetorical analysis; and J. D. Crossan, *In Fragments: The Aphorisms of Jesus* (New York: Harper, 1983) which may be important for the preacher.

Resurrection Narratives

Some general orientation will help interpretation: N. Clark, *Interpreting the Resurrection* (Philadelphia: Westminster, 1967) is a place to begin; K. Stendahl, ed., *Immortality and Resurrection* (New York: Macmillan, 1965) includes the famous essay "Immortality of the Soul or Resurrection of the Dead?" by O. Cullmann; R. Aldwinckle, *Death in the Secular City* (Grand Rapids: Eerdmans, 1974) is a thorough but somewhat cautious survey of issues; Peter Selby, *Look for the Living* (Philadelphia: Fortress, 1976) is remarkably helpful.

With regard to biblical material, a brief introduction by N. Perrin, *The Resurrection According to Matthew, Mark, and Luke* (Philadelphia: Fortress, 1977) will provide preliminary orientation. Comprehensive review of all the texts is offered in R. H. Fuller, *The Formation of the Resurrection Narratives* (New York: Macmillan, 1971); X. Leon-Dufour, *Resurrection and the Message of Easter* (New York: Holt, 1971); Pheme Perkins, *Resurrection: New Testament Witness and Contemporary Reflection* (Garden City, N.Y.: Doubleday, 1984); also R. H. Smith, *Easter Gospels* (Minneapolis: Augsburg, 1983), which may be especially helpful to preachers. In addition some monographs may be of aid: C. F. Evans, *Resurrection in the New Testament* (London: SCM, 1970) is especially good on New Testament theology; W. Marxsen, *The Resurrection of Jesus of Nazareth* (Philadelphia: Fortress, 1970) occasioned some debate; G. O'Collins, *The Resurrection of Jesus Christ* (Valley Forge, Pa.: Judson, 1973); and U. Wilckens, *Resurrection* (Atlanta: John Knox, 1978).

On preaching the resurrection, see my article "Preaching on the Resurrection," in *Religion in Life*, 45, no. 3 (Autumn 1976): 278–95. See also a suggestive study by a very fine homiletician, William L. Steele, "Preaching, Teaching, and Celebrating the Resurrection" (D.Min. diss., McCormick Theological Seminary, 1984).

Johannine Forms

In the past quarter century we have seen the publication of some awesome commentaries on the gospel by R. Brown (Doubleday) and R. Schnackenburg (Crossroads) as well as a series of one-volume commentaries since R. Bultmann (Westminster), such as those by C. K. Barrett (SPCK) and B. Lindars (Oliphant), not to mention particular studies by C. H. Dodds, R. Fortna, L. Martyn, F. F. Segovia, and others. The problem for preachers is hermeneutic: The Gospel of John is so thickly textured with allusive reference and symbolic meaning that it is exceedingly difficult to preach. A survey of contemporary scholarship may be read in R. Kysar, *The Fourth Evangelist and His Gospel* (Minneapolis: Augsburg, 1975). Two volumes which seem to me to be of special use to preachers are J. Miranda, *Being and the Messiah* (Maryknoll, N.Y.: Orbis, 1977) which is a "liberationist" interpretation, and R. A. Culpepper, *Anatomy of the Fourth Gospel: A Study in Literary Design* (Philadelphia: Fortress, 1983), which is a literary-critical study with a comprehensive bibliography. There are, of course, separate studies on the "signs" and the "I am" sayings.

Pauline Rhetoric

Daniel Patte, *Preaching Paul* (Philadelphia: Fortress, 1984) provides an excellent orientation for preachers; also see his *Paul's Faith and the Power of the Gospel* (Philadelphia: Fortress, 1983). As an introduction to Pauline thought, preachers may wish to begin with L. E. Keck, *Paul and His Letters* (Philadelphia: Fortress, 1979), or with a reading of two quite different positions, R. Scroggs, *Paul for a New Day* (Philadelphia: Fortress, 1977) and K. Stendahl, *Paul Among Jews and Gentiles* (Philadelphia: Fortress, 1976).

There are many substantial works on Pauline theology, among them: W. D. Davis, *Paul and Rabbinic Judaism* (New York: Harper, 1948; 4th ed., Philadelphia: Fortress, 1980); J. Munck, *Paul and the Salvation of Mankind* (Richmond: John Knox, 1959); H. J. Schoeps, *Paul* (Philadelphia: Westminster, 1961); D. E. H. Whiteley, *The Theology of St. Paul* (Philadelphia: Fortress, 1966); V. P. Furnish, *Theology and Ethos in Paul* (Nashville: Abingdon, 1968); E. Kasemann, *Perspectives on Paul* (Philadelphia: Fortress, 1971); H. Ridderbos, *Paul* (Grand Rapids: Eerdmans, 1975); E. P. Sanders, *Paul and Palestinian Judaism* (Philadelphia: Fortress, 1977); J. C. Beker, *Paul the Apostle* (Philadelphia: Fortress, 1980); and more recently, W. A. Meeks, *The First Urban Christians* (New Haven: Yale Univ., 1983).

There have been few studies of Pauline rhetoric, a peculiar gap considering how rhetorical Paul is. However, H. Gale, *The Use of Analogy in the Letters of Paul* (Philadelphia: Westminster, 1964); B. Rigaux, *Letters of St. Paul* (Chicago: Franciscan Herald, 1968); and W. Doty, *Letters in Primitive Christianity* (Philadelphia: Fortress, 1973) will offer some guidelines in addition to the first-cited insightful works by D. Patte.

Apocalyptic Forms

We only now are realizing how much apocalyptic material there is in the New Testament. Unfortunately, there is no study of how we can preach apocalyptic texts, which is unfortunate considering apocalyptic strands of thought in our own age. Essays in R. Funk, ed., *Journal for Theology and the Church: Apocalypticism* (New York: Herder, 1969) will provide helpful orientation. Since D. S. Russell, *The Method and Message of Jewish Apocalyptic* (Philadelphia: Westminster, 1964), there have been a number of significant studies: W. Schmithals, *The Apocalyptic Movement* (Nashville: Abingdon, 1975); P. D. Hanson, *The Dawn of Apocalyptic* (Philadelphia: Fortress, 1975); and C. Rowland, *The Open Heaven* (New York: Crossroad, 1982). See P. Hanson, ed., *Visionaries and Their Apocalypses* (Philadelphia: Fortress, 1983), and also see J. J. Collins, ed., *Semeia 14: Apocalypse: The Morphology of a Genre* (Missoula, Mont.: Scholars Press, 1979) for a collection of technical essays.

For preachers, the most helpful work may be that of Paul S. Minear beginning with

Christian Hope and the Second Coming (Philadelphia: Westminster, 1954); his commentary on Revelation, *I Saw a New Earth* (Washington, D.C.: Corpus, 1968); and his most recent works, *To Die and To Live* (New York: Seabury, 1977), and *New Testament Apocalyptic* (Nashville: Abingdon, 1981). On preaching apocalyptic, see D. T. Niles, *As Seeing the Invisible* (New York: Harper, 1961); Wm. Stringfellow, *An Ethic for Christians and Other Aliens in a Strange Land* (Waco, Tex.: Word, 1973); and J. Ellul, *Apocalypse: The Book of Revelation* (New York: Seabury, 1977). A liberation approach is offered in E. S. Fiorenza, *The Apocalypse* (Chicago: Franciscan Herald, 1976). See also F. Kermode, *The Sense of an Ending* (New York: Oxford Univ., 1981).

RECENT HOMILETIC THEORY

At midcentury, the field of homiletics was dominated by famous preachers and standard texts. The major texts were a revised edition of J. A. Broadus, *On the Preparation and Delivery of Sermons*, rev. by J. B. Weatherspoon (New York: Harper, 1944), a work first issued in 1870; A. W. Blackwood, *The Preparation of Sermons* (Nashville: Abingdon, 1956); D. G. Miller, *The Way of Biblical Preaching* (Nashville: Abingdon, 1957); H. Grady Davis, *Design for Preaching* (Philadelphia: Muhlenberg, 1958); and R. R. Caemmerer, *Preaching for the Church* (St. Louis: Concordia, 1959). Of course, the many books of Harry Emerson Fosdick were also influential, demonstrating a methodological proposal he had ventured in "What Is the Matter with Preaching?" in *Harper's* (July 1928). In Catholic theologies, the book was Thomas Liske's *Effective Preaching* (New York: Macmillan, 1962), or one of the older "manuals." The textbooks seemed to reflect a homiletic theory that derived from an odd mix of nineteenth-century Pietism, orthodox homiletic practice, and sometimes the rhetoric of Richard Whately.

In the past fifteen years, there have been many books deploring the state of the pulpit or proposing fad solutions (visual aids, dialogue sermons, "telling my story," etc.), but few substantial new proposals. There have, however, been a few. David J. Randolph, *The Renewal of Preaching* (Philadelphia: Fortress, 1969) proposed a "new homiletic" to align with the new hermeneutic. His book was exceedingly important, for it articulated a number of concerns which have been crucial to homiletic theory ever since. Randolph spoke of the "intentionality" of texts, he proposed developing homiletic designs analogous to biblical forms (e.g., story, dialogue, poetic image systems, and so on), he thoughtfully discussed hermeneutic issues, he caught sight of a rising phenomenological philosophy. The book's weakness may have been the weakness of the new hermeneutic, namely its commitment to existentialism. Nevertheless, *The Renewal of Preaching* must be regarded as one of the few important works in homiletic theory in the past two decades.

Two years later, Fred B. Craddock issued *As One Without Authority: Essays on Inductive Preaching* (Enid, Okla.: Phillips Univ., 1971), a little book that has had much impact. Craddock was also influenced by the new hermeneutic—Fuchs, Ebeling, and American scholars Wilder and Funk—and had read extensively in language studies. He rejected the rationalist-deductive methodologies of the pulpit but, at the same time, was critical of the wayward liberalism of the Fosdickian position. He proposed a homiletics of "induction" that could protect the freedom of congregations. A second volume, The Lyman Beecher Lectures for 1978, *Overhearing the Gospel* (Nashville: Abingdon, 1978), working from Kierkegaard, developed the notion of an "indirect" communication of the gospel employing an "overheard" narrative movement. A third volume, *Preaching* (Nashville: Abingdon, 1985) is a brief textbook from Craddock's understanding of homiletics. Craddock's work is always thoughtful and most important.

During the same period two books came out: Thor Hall, *The Future Shape of Preaching* (Philadelphia: Fortress, 1971), and Clyde E. Fant, *Preaching for Today* (New York: Harper, 1975). Hall appears to have been influenced by McLuhan, the ecclesiology of J. C. Hoekendijk, as well as theological approaches to hermeneutics and language. He seems to end with the preacher as a kind of facilitator for community; a person who brings together churchly self-understandings, liturgical tradition, the gospel, and contemporary existence in a free-form "word event." Fant, on the other hand, pleads for what he terms "incarnational preaching" which is neither culturally accommodative nor an uninterpreted biblicism. He appears to end up arguing for a free-form sermon to express an internalization of gospel and contemporary life by the preacher. Another volume, Milton Crum's *Manual on Preaching* (Valley Forge, Pa.: Judson), came out in 1977. Though Crum speaks of "telling the story" his basic model appears to be conversionist, a movement in the sermon from the predicament of sin to the realization of redemption with an overcoming of resistances by the gospel in between. Crum seems to assume that all scripture may be grasped as a disclosure of human sinfulness and God's grace. His model is also influenced by a therapeutic understanding of *metanoia*.

In the eighties, we have seen a turn toward narrative, which was presaged in the work of Randolph and Craddock. E. A. Steimle, M. J. Niedenthal, and C. L. Rice, *Preaching the Story* (Philadelphia: Fortress, 1980) has had considerable impact, along with a number of books on preaching as storytelling (see under "Narrative Form," above). The work of Hans Frei, *The Eclipse of Biblical Narrative* (New Haven: Yale Univ., 1974), plus a rash of books on narrative theology lie behind the movement. However, R. Lisher, "The Limits of Story," in *Interpretation* 38, no. 1 (January 1984) has raised questions. Two books by E. L. Lowry should be mentioned: *The Homiletic Plot* (Atlanta: John Knox, 1980), and *Doing Time in the Pulpit* (Nashville: Abingdon, 1985), which amplifies a conceptual framework implicit in the earlier volume. Though Lowry works from a narrative model, he actually seems to employ a "dramatic" model involving five stages from conflict to a resolution in the gospel; a kind of dramatic-homiletic *ordo salutis*. During the eighties, W. D. Thompson issued *Preaching Biblically* (Nashville: Abingdon, 1981) in which he proposed what he termed a "dyadic model" for preaching scripture. The model involves a drawing of then-now parallels between scriptural situations and contemporary life, and may reflect a rather conservative hermeneutic. My own minimal contribution to discussion appeared in two articles, "Interpretation and Preaching," in *Interpretation* 35, no. 1 (January 1981), and "On Preaching a Parable: The Problem of Homiletic Method," *Reformed Liturgy and Music* 18, no. 1 (Winter 1983).

Richard Eslinger has a book, *A New Hearing*, to be published by Abingdon, which will analyze current homiletic theory with care.

THEOLOGY OF PREACHING

At the outset, please note two books on history of doctrine which relate to theology of preaching: B. J. Cooke, *Ministry to Word and Sacraments* (Philadelphia: Fortress,

1976) and F. E. Crowe, *Theology of the Christian Word: A Study in History* (New York: Paulist, 1978).

In the Catholic tradition a number of substantial volumes were generated in connection with Vatican II. Thus, the sixties produced a literature which, unfortunately, has ebbed in the seventies and eighties. Since 1950, note the following: A. Rock, *Unless They Be Sent* (Dubuque, Iowa: Brown, 1953); J. Hofinger, *The Art of Teaching Christian Doctrine* (Notre Dame, Ind.: Notre Dame Univ., 1957); J. Danielou, *Christ and Us* (New York: Sheed & Ward, 1962); A. M. Henry, *A Mission Theology* (Notre Dame, Ind.: Fides, 1962); J. A. Jungmann, *The Good News, Yesterday and Today* (New York: Sadlier, 1962); P. Hitz, *To Preach the Gospel* (New York: Sheed & Ward, 1963); *The Word: Readings in Theology* (New York: Kenedy, 1964); J. Kahmann, *The Bible on the Preaching of the Word* (De Pere, Wis.: Norbert Abbey, 1965); D. Grasso, *Proclaiming God's Message: A Study in the Theology of Preaching* (Notre Dame, Ind.: Notre Dame Univ., 1965); O. Semmelroth, *The Preaching Word: On the Theology of Proclamation* (New York: Herder, 1965); M. Schmaus, *Preaching as a Saving Encounter* (Staten Island, N.Y.: Alba, 1966); K. Rahner, ed., *The Renewal of Preaching: Theory and Practice* (New York: Paulist, 1968). See also K. Rahner, *Hearers of the Word* (New York: Herder, 1969); H. Rahner, *A Theology of Proclamation* (New York: Herder, 1968); A. Church, *The Theology of the Word of God* (Notre Dame, Ind.: Fides, 1970); J. Burke, *Gospel Power* (New York: Alba, 1978); J. Schmeiser, ed., *Celebrating the Word* (Toronto: Anglican Book Center, 1977) contains two important Catholic essays in an ecumenical collection; N. Foley, ed., *Preaching and the Non-Ordained* (Collegeville, Minn.: Liturgical Press, 1983) contains an important essay by Schillebeeckx. See also the document produced by the Bishops' Committee on Priestly Life and Ministry, *Fulfilled in Your Hearing: The Homily in the Sunday Assembly* (Washington, D.C., 1982).

During the same period, Protestant works seem to be split between Barthian "biblical theology" and post-Bultmannian "word-event" theologies, with some occasional contributions from conservative scholars or the Anglican tradition. We do not yet have a developed theology of preaching out of the liberation tradition or one influenced by more recent phenomenological theologies. Since 1950, we can mention the following: D. G. Miller, *Fire in Thy Mouth* (Nashville: Abingdon, 1954); H. Kraemer, *The Communication of the Christian Faith* (Philadelphia: Westminster, 1956); J. Knox, *The Integrity of Preaching* (Nashville: Abingdon, 1957); Karl Barth, *The Word of God and the Word of Man* (New York: Harper & Row, 1957) and *The Preaching of the Gospel* (Philadelphia: Westminster, 1963), plus, of course, sections in many other volumes; D. T. Niles, *The Preacher's Task and the Stone of Stumbling* (New York: Harper, 1958); G. Wingren, *The Living Word: A Theological Study of Preaching and the Church* (Philadelphia: Muhlenberg, 1960); W. Luthi and E. Thurneysen, *Preaching, Confession, The Lord's Supper* (Richmond: John Knox, 1960); D. S. Cairns, *A Gospel without Myth?* (London: SCM, 1960); D. Ritschl, *A Theology of Proclamation* (Richmond: John Knox, 1960); J. E. Sellers, *The Outsider and the Word of God* (Nashville: Abingdon, 1961); E. P. Clowney, *Preaching and Biblical Theology* (Grand Rapids: Eerdmans, 1961); J. Sittler, *The Ecology of Faith* (Philadelphia: Muhlenberg, 1961); W. Pittenger, *Proclaiming Christ Today* (New York: Seabury, 1962); C. H. Thompson, *Theology of the Kerygma* (Englewood Cliffs, N.J.: Prentice-Hall, 1962); J. J. von Allmen, *Preaching and Congregation* (Richmond: John Knox, 1962); M. Philibert,

Christ's Preaching and Ours (Richmond: John Knox, 1963); J. V. L. Casserly, *Apologetics and Evangelism* (Philadelphia: Westminster, 1962); R. E. Sleeth, *Proclaiming the Word* (Nashville: Abingdon, 1964); R. Bohren, *Preaching and Community* (Richmond: John Knox, 1965); H. Ott, *Theology and Preaching* (Philadelphia: Westminster, 1965); J. Sittler, *The Anguish of Preaching* (Philadelphia: Fortress, 1966); J. I. Jones, *The Holy Spirit and Christian Preaching* (London: Epworth, 1967); T. Hall, *The Future Shape of Preaching* (Philadelphia: Fortress, 1971); G. Forell, *The Proclamation of the Gospel in a Pluralistic World* (Philadelphia: Fortress, 1973); J. Duane, *The Freedom of God: A Study of Election and Pulpit* (Grand Rapids: Eerdmans, 1973); C. E. Fant, *Bonhoeffer: Worldly Preaching* (Nashville: Nelson, 1975); R. E. C. Browne, *The Ministry of the Word* (Philadelphia: Fortress, 1976), a reprint; P. C. Marcel, *The Relevance of Preaching* (Grand Rapids: Baker, 1977); I. Pitt-Watson, *Preaching: A Kind of Folly* (Philadelphia: Westminster, 1978); R. W. Duke, *The Sermon as God's Word: Theologies for Preaching* (Nashville: Abingdon, 1980); J. L. Gonzalez and C. Gunsales-Gonzalez, *Liberation Preaching: The Pulpit and the Oppressed* (Nashville: Abingdon, 1980); D. W. C. Ford, *The Ministry of the Word* (Grand Rapids: Eerdmans, 1980); R. Lisher, *A Theology of Preaching: The Dynamics of the Gospel* (Nashville: Abingdon, 1981); N. Pittenger, *Preaching the Gospel* (Wilton, Conn.: Morehouse-Barlow, 1984). See also W. J. Carl III, *Preaching Christian Doctrine* (Philadelphia: Fortress, 1984).

Both Catholic and Protestant literature on the theology of preaching has dwindled since the sixties. We seem to be waiting for some new beginning in systematic theology.

ACKNOWLEDGMENTS

Quotations in the text are from these sources: PART 1—on p. 5, from A. J. Lerner and F. Loewe, *My Fair Lady* (New York: Coward-McCann, 1957), 146; on p. 66, from James Thompson, "Once in a Saintly Passion," in *Fine Frenzy: Enduring Themes in Poetry*, by R. Baylor and B. Stokes, 2d ed. (New York: McGraw-Hill, 1978), 164; on pp. 144–45, from Edith Lovejoy Pierce, "Main Street U.S.A.," *Wind Has No Home* (Evanston, Ill.: copyright Edith Lovejoy Pierce, 1950), 16; on p. 150, from H. G. Wells, *The Soul of a Bishop* (New York: Macmillan Co., 1917), 124; on p. 155, from Thornton Wilder, *Our Town* (New York: Coward-McCann, 1938), 124; on p. 205, from Carolyn Rosner, "Words," *The Plaid 1965* (Pittsburgh: Winchester Thurston School, 1965), 31. PART 2—on p. 239, from Arthur Miller, *After the Fall* (New York: Bantam Books, 1965), 5; on pp. 261 and 441, from John Calvin, *Institutes of the Christian Religion*, (ed. J. T. McNeill and F. L. Battles (Philadelphia: Westminster Press, 1960), 1:35 and 2:1014; on p. 314, from Christina G. Rossetti, "The Shepherds Had an Angel," in *Masterpieces of Religious Verse*, ed. J. D. Morrison (New York: Harper & Bros., 1948), 151; on pp. 325 and 440, from C. S. Lewis, *The Screwtape Letters* (New York: Macmillan Co., 1948), 135 and 16; on p. 350, from Maxwell Anderson, *High Tor* (Washington, D.C.: Anderson House, 1937), 69; on p. 351, from C. S. Lewis, *The Great Divorce* (New York: Macmillan Co., 1946), 26; on p. 392, from W. Goldman, *Marathon Man* (New York: Delacorte Press, 1974), 19; on p. 393, from E. Ionesco, *Exit the King* (New York: Grove Press, 1963), 83; on p. 396, from W. L. O'Neill, *Coming Apart* (Chicago: Quadrangle Press, 1971), 472; on p. 406, adapted from J. W. Hamilton, *Horns and Halos in Human Nature* (Westwood, N.J.: Fleming H. Revell, 1954), 57; on p. 407, from H. R. F. Keating, *Go West Inspector Ghote* (New York: Penguin Books, 1981), chap. 2.

Subject Index

The index does not include all biblical names. Words that appear often—such as God, Christ, or Consciousness—are selectively listed. Names appearing in the bibliographic essays have not been indexed.

Scripture Index